MARKS
on
GERMAN, BOHEMIAN
and
AUSTRIAN PORCELAIN

1710
to
the
PRESENT

Robert E. Röntgen

4880 Lower Valley Road, Atglen, PA 19310

Published by Schiffer Publishing Ltd.
4880 Lower Valley Road
Atglen, PA 19310
Phone: (610) 593-1777; Fax: (610) 593-2002
E-mail: Schifferbk@aol.com

Please write for a free catalog.
This book may be purchased from the publisher.
Please include $3.95 for shipping.

Try your bookstore first.

We are interested in hearing from authors
with book ideas on related subjects.

Printed in The United States of America
ISBN: 0-7643-0353-8

For

INHALT

CONTENTS

Vorwort

Marken auf Porzellan sind ein wichtiges und unentbehrliches Hilfsmittel zur Bestimmung des Herstellers und des Alters von Porzellanstücken. Die Porzellan-Manufakturen und -fabriken in Deutschland, Böhmen und Österreich waren und sind nicht nur die produktivsten in Europa, sie sind auch in vieler Beziehung miteinander verwandt, durch ihre Technik und ihren Stil, durch historische Umstände und in nicht wenigen Fällen sogar durch verwandtschaftliche Bindungen.

Über antikes europäisches Porzellan aus der Periode vor dem Beginn der Industrialisierung um 1830 gibt es eine umfassende und vielfältige Literatur. Nach der strengen deutschen Auslegung gelten nämlich nur kunstgewerbliche Gegenstände aus der vorindustriellen Zeit als Antiquitäten und damit als besonders wertvoll und begehrenswert. Die Porzellanliteratur ist im wesentlichen dieser Auffassung gefolgt und hat sich hauptsächlich mit den 120 Jahren zwischen der Erfindung des europäischen Porzellans und dem Beginn des Industriezeitalters beschäftigt.

In den USA ist die Altersgrenze für Antiquitäten fließend. Nachdem durch ein Zollgesetz bestimmt worden war, daß alle Gegenstände, die älter als hundert Jahre sind, als Antiquitäten zollfrei bleiben, übernahmen Händler und Publikum diese Definition. Mit jedem Jahr ändert sich die Grenze und heute wird auch Porzellan, das vor 1880 entstand, als antik angesehen. Das erweitert zumindest in den USA den Antiquitätenmarkt erheblich.

Doch auch jüngeres Porzellan, das weder nach der einen noch nach der anderen Definition antik ist, hat seine Sammler und Liebhaber gefunden. Ihr Problem ist, daß es nur wenig Literatur über die Porzellanmarken des 19. und 20. Jahrhunderts gibt. Zwar sind in den letzten 25 Jahren zum erstenmal einige Bücher erschienen, die sich auch mit der rapiden Entwicklung der Porzellanindustrie seit 1830 beschäftigen, aber eine umfassende Übersicht über die Porzellanmarken von 1710 bis heute fehlt noch.

Dies Buch versucht, diesen Überblick zu geben. Allerdings haben zwei Weltkriege mit ihren Umwälzungen und Zerstörungen viele Unterlagen und Quellen vernichtet, sodaß nicht für alle Marken und Porzellanhersteller vollständige Informationen zu finden sind.

Besonderer Wert wurde darauf gelegt, den Zeitraum festzustellen, in dem eine Marke benutzt wurde, da Sammler, Liebhaber und Händler verständlicherweise am Alter eines Porzellanstücks interessiert sind.

Dies Buch wäre nicht möglich gewesen ohne die verdienstvolle Arbeit der vielen Autoren von Porzellanbüchern. Allerdings war es besonders bei älteren Werken notwendig, die Angaben kritisch zu prüfen und sie in einigen Fällen zu revidieren, da sie wegen der damals beschränkten Informationsmöglichkeiten ungenau oder nicht beweisbar sind.

Preface

Marks on porcelain are an important and indispensible aid for the identification of the manufacturer and the age of a piece of porcelain. The porcelain manufacturies and factories in Germany, Bohemia and Austria were and still are not only the most productive in all of Europe, they are also related in many respects, by their technique and their style, by historical circumstances and in quite a few cases even by family bonds.

There is a comprehensive and multifarious literature about antique European porcelain manufactured before the industrial age began about 1830. According to the strict German definition, only works of arts and crafts produced in the pre-industrial era are considered antiques and therefore especially valuable and desirable. The literature about porcelain essentially followed this opinion and has concerned itself mainly with the one hundred and twenty years between the invention of the European porcelain and the beginning of industrialization.

In the United States of America the age limit is fluent. After a customs tariff had defined all objects older than one hundred years as antiques and free of duty, dealers and the public adopted this definition. With every passing year the age limit changes, and today even porcelain produced before 1880 is considered antique. This widens considerably the supply for the antiques market, at least in the U. S. A.

But also younger porcelain, not considered antique according to one of the definitions mentioned has found collectors and aficionados. Their problem is the lack of literature about the porcelain marks of the 19th and 20th century. In the last twenty-five years for the first time some books were published about the rapid development of the porcelain industry since 1830, but a comprehensive survey of porcelain marks from 1710 until today was still missing.

This book attempts to give this survey. Two World Wars with their upheavels and destructions unfortunately also have destroyed many records and sources, and it is not possible to provide complete information about every mark and every manufacturer.

Special consideration has been given to the attempt to ascertain the time period in which a mark was used. Collectors, devotees and dealers understandably are particularly interested in the age of a porcelain piece.

This book would not have been possible without the meritorious work of the many authors of porcelain books. But it was necessary, especially with older works, to examine the information they give carefully and to correct them in quite a few cases, since they were imprecise or not verifiable due to the limited sources in former times.

Der Verfasser ist sich bewußt, dass auch dies Buch schon im Augenblick des Drucks revisions- und ergänzungsbedürftig ist. Hätte er warten wollen, bis auch die letzte offene Frage beantwortet und die letzte Lücke gefüllt ist, wäre das Buch nie erschienen. Aus diesem Grund entschloß er sich, unter seine Forschungen und Recherchen einen vorläufigen Schlußstrich zu ziehen und das Ergebnis vorzulegen.

McLean, Virginia, 1980   Robert E. Röntgen

Vorwort zur Zweiten Auflage

Die politischen Ereignisse in Europa seit 1990, besonders die Auflösung der Deutschen Demokratischen Republik und ihr Beitritt zur Bundesrepublik Deutschland, machen es notwendig, dies Buch auf den neuesten Stand zu bringen. Dazu kommt, dass in den vergangenen sechzehn Jahren eine grosse Anzahl von Porzellanfabriken geschlossen worden sind.

Für mehrere bisher unidentifizierte Marken konnten die Benutzer festgestellt und einige Zeitangaben konnten spezifiziert werden. Dem Appendix sind neugefundene Marken hinzugefügt worden.

Ostseebad Kühlungsborn, Germany, September 1997   Robert E. Röntgen

Preface 2nd edition:

This author is well aware of the fact that this book too needs corrections and completions at the very moment it goes to print. But would he have waited until the last question has been answered and the last blank spot has been filled, it never would have been published. For this reason he decided to draw a preliminary line and to present the results of his research.

McLean, Virginia, 1980   Robert E. Röntgen

Preface to the Second edition

The political developments in Europa since 1990, especially the dissolution of the German Demokratic Republic (East Germany) and her joining the Federal Republic of Germany, made it necessary to update this book. In addition, a number of porcelain factories have been closed during the last sixteen years.

For some hitherto unidentified marks the owners could be found, some time periods could be specified. Newly found marks have been added to the appendix.

Ostseebad Kühlungsborn, Germany, September 1997   Robert E. Röntgen

Erläuterungen für den Benutzer

Teil I enthält die Markenabbildungen und neben jeder Marke Angaben über den Benutzer der Marke, den Fabrikationsort, den Zeitraum, in dem die Marke gebraucht wurde, und andere Angaben, die zur Identifizierung beitragen. Dieser Teil enthält auch Malermarken und Marken auf Steingut, wenn die Firma sowohl Porzellan als auch Steingut herstellte, ihr Steingut für den Laien schwer von Porzellan zu unterscheiden ist oder andere Autoren sie als Porzellanmarken aufgeführt haben. (Über den Unterschied zwischen Porzellan und Steingut siehe: Kurze Einführung in die Keramik, s. 20).

Die meisten Marken bestehen aus verschiedenen Symbolen, Motiven, Worten oder Buchstaben. In Teil I sind sie nach ihren Bestandteilen in Gruppen geordnet und fortlaufend nummeriert, wie aus folgender Liste hervorgeht.

Directions for the user of this book

Part I contains the marks and next to each mark information about the user of the mark, his location, the time period the mark was applied and other particulars helpful in identifying a mark. This part also includes some decorators' marks and marks on earthenware if the manufacturer produced porcelain as well as earthenware, his earthenware is difficult to distinguish from porcelain for a layman, or other authors have listed them as porcelain marks. (For the definition of porcelain and earthenware see: Short Introduction into Ceramics, p. 21).

Most marks are a combination of different symbols, motifs, words or letters. In Part I they are arranged in groups according to their components as shown in the list below and numbered in sequence.

Der erste Schritt sollte sein, die einzelnen Bestandteile einer Marke und die Gruppe festzustellen, in der sie enthalten sind. Beispiel

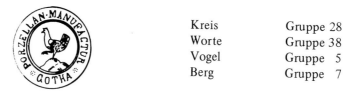

Kreis	Gruppe 28
Worte	Gruppe 38
Vogel	Gruppe 5
Berg	Gruppe 7

oder in aufsteigender Reihenfolge 5/ 7/ 28/ 38.

Die Marken sind jeweils in der niedrigsten Gruppe zu finden, das ist diejenige, die in obenstehender Gruppenliste zuerst erscheint, in diesem Fall Gruppe 5. Innerhalb der einzelnen Gruppen sind die Marken wieder in der Reihenfolge der Liste geordnet. Da die meisten Gruppen nur wenige Seiten umfassen, genügt aber üblicherweise die Feststellung der niedrigsten Gruppenzahl, um eine Marke zu finden. Diese Methode hat den zusätzlichen Vorteil, daß sie Aufmerksamkeit auf ähnlich aussehende Marken lenkt und hilft, die richtige zu finden.

Eine Zusammenstellung aller in Marken vorkommenden Symbole und Motive und ihrer Gruppen ist am Ende des Buches zu finden.

Die relative Größe der einzelnen Bestandteile hat keinen Einfluß auf die Eingruppierung einer Marke. Auf Porzellan erscheinen Marken nicht immer so klar und detailliert wie in den Abbildungen in diesem Buch. Es ist deswegen notwendig, eine Porzellanmarke genau zu analysieren.

Gelegentlich sind Unterschiede in Marken klein aber bedeutsam, weil sie auf verschiedene Benutzer hinweisen. Ein Beispiel:

R. Klemm	P. Donath	A. Hamann
Dresden	Dresden	Dresden
Nr. 1215	Nr. 1211	Nr. 1213

Gelegentlich ändert ein Hersteller seine Marke etwas, und dieser Unterschied gibt einen Hinwies auf den Zeitraum, in dem die Marke benutzt wurde, zum Beispiel:

Nr. 953   Nr. 952

Beide Marken gehörten der Aeltesten Volkstedter Porzellanfabrik in Volkstedt. Die erste Marke mit der unten offenen Krone wurde von 1915 an benutzt, die zweite mit der unten geschlossenen Krone von 1934 an. Diese Beispiele sollen unterstreichen, wie wichtig die genaue Analyse einer Marke ist.

The first step should be to analyze a mark, to identify its components and find the group they are listed in. An example:

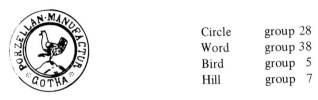

Circle	group 28
Word	group 38
Bird	group 5
Hill	group 7

or in sequence 5/ 7/ 28/ 38

The marks can always be found in the group with the lowest number, which is the group that appears first on the list of groups above, in this case group 5. Within each group the marks again are arranged in the sequence of the list of groups. Since most groups comprise only a few pages, the knowledge of the lowest group number usually is sufficient to find a mark. This method has the additional advantage that a perusal of these few pages directs attention to similar looking marks and makes it easier to distinguish the right one.

At the end of the book there is an alphabetical list of all symbols and motifs that can be found in marks in this book with the number of their group.

The relative size of the components has no influence on the classification of a mark. On porcelain the marks do not always appear as clear and detailed as in this book. It is therefore necessary to analyze a mark on porcelain very carefully. Sometimes the difference in marks are minor but significant because they point to different manufacturers. An example:

R. Klemm	P. Donath	A. Hamann
Dresden	Dresden	Dresden
No. 1215	No. 1211	No. 1213

Sometimes a manufacturer changed a mark slightly, but the difference gives a clue to the time period. Another example:

No. 953   No. 952

Both marks were used by the Oldest Volkstedt Porcelain Factory in Volkstedt. The first mark with the crown open at the bottom was used form 1915, the second with the closed crown from 1934. These examples should underline the importance of a careful analysis of a mark.

Bis in das erste Drittel des 19. Jahrhunderts wurden alle Marken mit der Hand angebracht. Dies war keine besonders herausfordernde Tätigkeit, sie wurde von Lehrlingen oder angelernten Arbeitern ausgeführt. Alte handgezeichnete Marken können von Stück zu Stück unterschiedlich sein, selbst wenn derselbe Arbeiter sie hintereinander gezeichnet hat. Besonders bei den Erzeugnissen der Manufakturen in Meißen und Wien vor etwa 1850 ist es kaum möglich, nur von der Form der handgemalten Marken her das Alter eines Porzellanstücks zu bestimmen. Genaue Jahresangaben neben einer Meißner oder Wiener Marke stützen sich auf andere Hinweise, wie Beizeichen, Formernummern, Malernummern, Form, Dekor und Malerei des bestimmten Porzellanstücks, das diese Marke trägt.

Nachdem etwa 1830 Gummistempel in Gebrauch kamen, stempelten die meisten Fabriken ihre Marke auf die Unterseite ihrer Produkte. Das geschah nicht immer sehr sorgfältig. Viele Marken sind verwischt oder verschmiert, bei anderen fehlen Teile oder feinere Details der Marke und in einigen Fällen sind sogar nur Konturen erkennbar.

1887 forderte der britische Merchandise Marks Act, daß auf allen importierten Waren der Name des Herkunftslandes angebracht sein mußte, als "Made in . . ." oder einfach nur der Landesname. Das bedeutet, dass alle Stücke, die den Namen des Herkunftslandes zeigen, seit 1887 hergestellt wurden. Auf der anderen Seite ist das Fehlen einer solchen Herkunftsbezeichnung kein Beweis dafür, dass ein Stück vor 1887 produziert wurde. Bei kleineren Artikeln erlaubten die Zollbehörden nämlich, dass der Name des Herkunftslandes aussen auf den Transportbehältern und nicht auf jedem Stück darinnen angebracht wurde.

Seit der Mitte des 20. Jahrhunderts werden zunehmend Schiebebilder für Marken benutzt. Die Marke wird mit keramischer Farbe auf eine spezielles Papier gedruckt und mit Schiebe- oder Filmlack überzogen. Nachdem das Papier angefeuchtet wird, kann der Film mit der Marke auf Porzellan übertragen werden.

Seit dem späten 19. Jahrhundert wurden zunehmend zusätzliche Bezeichnungen oder Dekor-Namen der Marke hinzugefügt, oft mit einem besonderen Stempel (ein Beispiel ist Marke Nr. 516). Mit wenigen Ausnahmen sind sie in diesem Buch nicht aufgeführt, weil sein Umfang sich sonst verdoppelt hätte.

Klammern um eine Jahreszahl bedeuten, daß für dieses Jahr die Marke zum erstenmal nachgewiesen werden konnte. Es ist möglich, daß sie aber schon einige Jahre früher in Gebrauch war. Wenn eine Jahresangabe fehlt, heißt das, daß zuverlässige Angaben noch nicht gefunden werden konnten. Die Art der Anbringung einer Marke und die Farbe sind auch angegeben - soweit sie nachweisbar sind. Die obere Zahl am Rand neben jeder Eintragung ist die laufende Nummer der Marke. Die fett gedruckte Zahl verweist auf die Seite in Teil II, auf der die Firma erwähnt ist.

Bei den Marken, in denen der Herstellungsort angegeben ist, kann der Teil II die Suche erleichtern. In diesem Teil sind die Herstellungsorte alphabetisch geordnet, und unter jedem Ort sind die Hersteller, deren Marken in Teil I erscheinen, alphabetisch aufgeführt. Die Jahreszahlen geben an, von wann bis wann die Firma bestanden hat. Fehlende Jahresangaben bedeuten, daß genaue Angaben noch nicht zu finden waren. Außerdem wird in den meisten Fällen eine kurze Übersicht über die Firmengeschichte gegeben, und es werden ihre Haupterzeugnisse erwähnt. Ein kursiv gedruckter Firmen- und Stadtname bedeutet, daß diese Firma auch unter der angegebenen Stadt zu finden ist. Außerdem wird auf die Nummern der in Teil I enthaltenen Marken der Firma verwiesen. In Teil II sind nicht alle Porzellanhersteller und -maler aufgeführt, die je existiert haben, sondern nur jene, deren Marken gefunden werden konnten.

Die Gegenüberstellung verwechslungsfähiger Marken in Teil III wiederholt der besseren Übersicht wegen auch Marken, die schon in Teil I an verschiedenen Stellen vorhanden sind. Hinzu kommen Marken ausländischer Hersteller. Die verwechslungsfähigen Marken sind so geordnet, daß in der Reihenfolge zuerst die Marken stehen, die den Originalen am ähnlichsten sind und dann die Marken folgen, die vom Original immer mehr abweichen.

Until about the end of the first third of the 19th century all marks were applied by hand. This was not a qualified job, it was done by apprentices or unskilled workers. The shape of old handdrawn marks can vary from piece to piece, even when applied by the same worker consecutively. Especially with porcelain made by the manufactories in Meissen and Vienna before about 1850 it is not possible to determine the age of a piece by the shape of the mark alone. Specific time periods mentioned next to a Meissen or Vienna mark are based on other indications, such as additional markings, moulders´ or painters´ numbers, shape, pattern or decoration of the special piece that carries the particular mark shown.

After the rubber stamp came into use about 1830, most factories stamped their marks on the bottom of their products. This was not always done very carefully and so quite a number of marks were smudged or smeared, parts or finer details of the stamps are missing and sometimes only contures are recognizable.

In 1887 the British Marchandise Marks Act demanded that on all imported foreign merchandise the name of the country of origin had to be apllied, as "Made in . . ." or just the name of the country. This means that all pieces showing the country of origin must have been made since 1887. On the other hand a missing country name is no proof that a piece was made before 1887. Since occasionally it was very difficukt to apply the name on the merchandise proper the customs authorities were satisfied wehen the country name was visible on the container and not on every piece within.

Since the middle of the 20th century increasingly slip pictures are applied. The mark is printed on a special paper with ceramic paints and covered with a so-called slip or film varnish. The printed mark and the varnish combine to a thin film. After the paper has been moistened with water, this film can be transferred onto porcelain.

If a year is set in brackets, it means that the mark was first observed for this year, but it could have been used a few years earlier. If a year is missing, it means that reliable information could not yet be obtained.

Application and color of a mark are also noted next to the mark- if verifiable. In the right margin there are two numbers next to each entry. The upper one is the consecutive number of the mark. The number in bold refers to the more detailed information about the producer in Part II.

If a mark also contains the name of a city, Part II can facilitate the search. In Part II the cities, in which porcelain was produced, are listed alphabetically. Under each city-heading the local companies, whose marks are listed in Part I, appear in alphabetical order with their legal or historical names. This alphabetical arrangement follows the German spelling. The English versions of the names are translations for better understanding. The years indicate the time period in which the company operated. Here too a missing year means that complete information could not yet been found. In most cases a short company history ist given and the main products are mentioned. A company and city name printed in italics points out that this company is also referred to under this city heading. In addition the numbers of the marks of this company in Part I are listed. Part II does not contain all porcelain manufacturers and decorators that ever existed but only those, whose marks could be found.

In Part III the compilation of marks which could be confounded with those of other producers repeat some marks from different groups in Part I for the sake of greater clarity. In addition marks of foreign companies are shown. The marks in Part III are arranged according to their similarity to the original marks, first the identical or nearly identical ones, and then those with increasing deviation from the originals.

Kurze Einführung in die Keramik

Keramik ist die allgemeine Bezeichnung für geformte und gebrannte oder getrocknete Tonwaren aller Art vom Mauerziegel bis zur Porzellanfigur. Nach ihrer Zusammensetzung und nach ihren physikalischen Eigenschaften können Tonwaren in grobkeramische und feinkeramische Erzeugnisse geteilt werden. Zur Grobkeramik gehören alle Tonwaren, deren Bruchstelle oder unglasierte Oberfläche mit dem bloßen Auge sichtbare Unregelmäßigkeiten erkennen lassen, ihr Scherben ist inhomogen. Bei der Feinkeramik erscheint die Bruchstelle oder die unglasierte Oberfläche dem bloßen Auge als glatt oder homogen.

Innerhalb der feinkeramischen Gruppe unterscheidet man wiederum zwischen porösen und dichten Stoffen. Unglasierte poröse Feinkeramik nimmt mehr als 2% ihrer Masse an Wasser auf, in einigen Fällen bis zu 18%. Bei der dichten Feinkeramik bleibt die Wasseraufnahme unter 2%.

Die Grundsubstanz aller feinkeramischen Stoffe ist Ton, ein feinkörniges Verwitterungsprodukt feldspathaltiger Gesteine wie Granit, Gneis, Quarzporphyr und Basalt. Wird der ursprünglich weiße Ton von seiner Entstehungsstätte weggeschwemmt und an anderer Stelle abgelagert, nimmt er auf seinem Wege Mineralien, Metalle und organische Stoffe auf, die ihm verschiedene Färbungen geben. Ton, der an seiner Entstehungsstätte liegengeblieben ist, hat seine weiße Farbe behalten. Er heißt Kaolin und ist der Hauptbestandteil des Porzellans.

Die porösen Erzeugnisse der Feinkeramik bestehen hauptsächlich aus farbigem Ton. Sie sind meist mit einem durch Blei- oder Zinnoxid hell gefärbten glasähnlichen Überzug versehen, der die Farbe des Tons verdecken soll und das poröse Material wasserundurchlässig macht. Hierzu gehören:

Töpferwaren	Terrakotta
Majolika	Fayence
Steingut	

Zur dichten Feinkeramik rechnet man:

Steinzeug	vitreous China
Weichporzellan	Hartporzellan

Knochenporzellan, chinesisches und japanisches Porzellan, Parian, Belleek und Lenox China gehören zum Weichporzellan. Deutsches, böhmisches und österreichisches Porzellan ist—mit sehr wenigen Ausnahmen—immer Hartporzellan.

Die drei wichtigsten Bestandteile der dichten Feinkeramik sind Ton oder Kaolin, Feldspat als Flußmittel und Quarz, um eine gleichmäßige Trocknung zu erreichen und das Verziehen zu verringern. (Beim Knochenporzellan wird der Quarz ganz oder zum Teil durch gebrannte, kalzinierte Tierknochen ersetzt.) Für Steinzeug wird meist nur hellfarbiger Ton benutzt. Bei vitreous China verwendet man eine Mischung aus Kaolin und einem besonderen farbigen Ton (ball clay), der beim Brennen cremefarben oder weiß wird.

Weichporzellan besteht aus 20–30% Kaolin, 30–50% Feldspat und 30–40% Quarz. Beim Hartporzellan ist das Verhältnis der drei Bestandteile 40–60% Kaolin, 20–30% Feldspat und 20–30% Quarz.

Short Introduction into Ceramics

Ceramics is the general term for moulded and fired or dried clay-products of all kinds, from bricks to porcelain figurines. According to their composition and their physical properties clay-products can be classified as coarse or fine ceramics. Coarse ceramics are all products whose unglazed surface or surface of fracture shows irregularities visible to the naked eye, their body is inhomogenous. Fine ceramics show a smooth or homogenous unglazed surface or surface of fracture.

Within the group of fine ceramics again porous and non-porous wares can be distinguished. Unglazed porous fine ceramics absorb more than 2% of their mass in water, in some cases up to 18%. With non-porous fine ceramics water absorption is less than 2%.

The basic ingredient of all fine ceramics is clay, a fine-grained plastic product of the decomposition of rocks containing felspar, like granite, gneiss, quartz-porphyry and basalt. If the originally white clay is washed away from the forming ground and deposited at some other location, it picks up minerals, metals and organic matter on its way, which give it different coloration. Clay that remains in its place retains the white color. Its name is kaolin and it is the main ingredient of porcelain.

Porous fine ceramics consist mainly of colored clay. They usually are coated with an opaque glaze which has been tinted by lead or tin oxides. This glaze not only covers the color of the clay but also makes the surface non-porous. Among porous fine ceramics are:

pottery	fayence
terra cotta	generally earthenware.
maiolica	

To the dense or non-porous fine ceramics belong:

stoneware	soft paste porcelain
vitreous china	hard paste porcelain.

Bone China, Chinese and Japanese porcelain, Parian, Belleek and Lenox China are soft paste porcelains. German, Bohemian and Austrian porcelain is—with very few exceptions—always hard paste porcelain.

The three important ingredients of dense or non-porous fine ceramics are clay or kaolin, felspar for vitrification and quartz to achieve a more even drying process and to prevent distortions. For stoneware usually light-colored clay is used, in vitreous china a mixture of kaolin and special clay (ball clay) that turns into a creamy or white color when fired.

Soft paste porcelain consists of 20%–30% kaolin, 30%–50% felspar and 30%–40% quartz. The mixture for hard paste porcelain is 40%–60% kaolin, 20%–30% felspar and 20%–30% quartz.

Only soft and hard paste porcelain can be considered to be true porcelain. Besides the composition the main difference between them is the temperature of the final firing. A moulded piece of porcelain first is air-dried and then in a first firing at a temperature

Zum eigentlichen Porzellan kann man nur Weich- und Hartporzellan rechnen. Der wichtigste Unterschied zwischen ihnen ist neben der Zusammensetzung die Glattbrandtemperatur. Das geformte Porzellan wird zunächst an der Luft getrocknet und anschließend in einem ersten Brand bei 800–950°C verfestigt. Anschließend kann man es mit Unterglasurfarben dekorieren, bevor es mit einer Glasur überzogen wird, die im wesentlichen verdünnte flüssige Porzellanmasse ist. Da Porzellan nach dem ersten Brand noch porös ist, saugt seine Oberfläche die Glasur auf, die sich fest mit dem Scherben verbindet.

Beim zweiten Brand scheiden sich dann Weich- und Hartporzellan. Weichporzellan wird bei Temperaturen unter 1380°C glattgebrannt, Hartporzellan bei Temperaturen über 1380°C. Bei etwa 950°C beginnen Feldspat und Quarz zu schmelzen. Bei 1100°C ist aller Feldspat geschmolzen und das Kaolin verwandelt sich in Mullit. Je höher die Temperatur, desto mehr Quarz schmilzt und die so entstehende Glasschmelze verklebt und verbindet das Mullit und den noch nicht geschmolzenen Quarz, sodaß nach Abkühlung ein hochverglaster weißer Scherben entsteht. Er besteht dann etwa zu 25% aus Mullit, zu 55–60% aus Glas und zu 15–20% aus Quarz.

Das fertige Porzellanstück kann anschließend auf der Glasur bemalt werden, und die Dekoration wird in einem dritten Brennvorgang bei 600–900°C oberflächlich eingebrannt.

Da Aufglasurfarben nicht durch eine harte Glasur geschützt sind, sind sie empfindlich gegen Kratzen und Abreiben.

Im Gegensatz zu Weichporzellan ist Hartporzellan härter als Stahl. Auch seine Beständigkeit gegen schnell wechselnde Temperaturen und gegen Schlag ist größer. Dagegen ist Weichporzellan etwas transparenter als Hartporzellan, wie Transparenz überhaupt eine Eigenschaft ist, die von allen keramischen Erzeugnissen nur Porzellan besitzt.

Ein anderes Kennzeichen ist der Klang. Poröse Stoffe haben einen kurzen dumpfen Klang, wenn sie angeschlagen werden, dichte einen schwingenden. Einfaches Porzellan gibt einen kurzen Ton, hochwertiges einen angenehmen nachhallenden Klang.

from 800°C (1470°F) to 950°C (1740°F) the ware hardens. After that it can be decorated with heat resistent underglaze colors and coated with a glaze, which is basically thinned down porcelain paste. Since porcelain is still porous after the first firing, the glaze penetrates into the surface.

The second firing separates soft and hard paste porcelain. Soft paste porcelain is fired at temperatures below 1380°C (2515°F), hard paste porcelain at temperatures above that mark. At about 950°C (1740°F) felspar and quartz begin to melt and fuse the ingredients. At 1100°C (2010°F) all felspar has melted and kaolin changes into mullit. The higher the temperature the more quartz melts and fuses together with the molten felspar, the mullit and the unmolten quartz into a white, highly vitrified body when cooled down. The fired porcelain consists of about 25% mullit, 55%–60% glass and 15%–20% quartz.

The finished porcelain piece then can be decorated overglaze and the decoration is affixed in a third firing at 600°C (1110°F) to 900°C (1650°F).

Since overglaze decorations are not protected by hard glaze, they can be scratched or rubbed off by heavy use.

In contrast to soft paste porcelain, hard paste porcelain is harder than steel. It is also more resistant to changing temperatures and mechanical impacts. Soft paste porcelain on the other hand is more translucent, but translucency generally is an attribute that among all ceramic products can only be found in porcelain.

Another characteristic sign is the sound. Porous bodies respond with a short dull sound when tapped, dense bodies with a vibrating ring. Plain porcelain emits a short, high quality porcelain a pleasant resonant ring.

Definitionen Keramischer Produkte

Biskuit, Bisque—unglasiertes Weichporzellan mit matter Oberfläche.

Basalt—schwarzes Steinzeug, auch mit Schmelzfarbendekoren.

Belleek—Weichporzellan mit geringerem Kaolin- und höherem Feldspatanteil, das meist mit einer perlmutterähnlichen Glasur überzogen ist.

Böttgersteinzeug—Steinzeug aus 88 Teilen feinstkörnigem roten Tongemenge und 12 Teilen Lehm. Von Böttger in Meißen 1708 entwickelt, aber nach der Erfindung des Porzellans vergessen. 1918 wieder entdeckt und in Meißen hauptsächlich für Figuren benutzt.

Fayence—gelblich-grau bis braunrote poröse Tonwaren mit deckenden Glasuren. Oft mit Ritz- oder Reliefdekoren, farbigen Dekoren unter einer zweiten durchsichtigen Glasur oder mit Aufglasurdekoren.

Frittenporzellan—Pseudeporzellan, das dem Glas nähersteht. Statt Kaolin oder Ton enthält es gemahlene Glasschmelze (Fritte).

Jasper Ware—unglasiertes weißes Steinzeug, das bis 1785 in der Masse gefärbt, später mit einem farbigen Überzug (Jasper dip) behautet wurde. Häufig mit weißbleibendem Reliefdekor.

Jaspisporzellan—dasselbe wie Böttgersteinzeug.

Knochenporzellan—Weichporzellan mit hoher Transparenz, bei dem der Quarz ganz oder zum größten Teil durch gebrannte Rinderknochen ersetzt ist.

Lenox—Weichporzellan mit geringerem Kaolinanteil, bei dem der Feldspat ganz oder zu einem großen Teil durch eine Fritte ersetzt ist. Ähnelt Belleek.

Majolika—creme- oder gelbfarbige poröse Tonwaren mit farbigen oder weißtrüben deckenden Glasuren oder einfachen farbigen Dekorationen unter durchsichtigen Glasuren.

Parian—unglasiertes Weichporzellan mit geringerem Kaolin- und höherem Feldspatanteil, der der Oberfläche ein marmorähnliches Aussehen gibt.

Schamotte, Chamotte—gebrannter Ton, der anderen Tonen zugesetzt wird, um feuerbeständige Kacheln und Ofen- und Kaminauskleidungen herzustellen.

Schwarzes Porzellan—siehe Basalt

Segerporzellan—Weichporzellan mit hoher Transparenz aus 25% weißbrennendem Ton, 45% Quarz und 30% Feldspat. Die niedrige Brenntemperatur von ca. 1280°C gestattet die Verwendung von mehr Dekorationsfarben als bei Hartporzellan.

Siderolith—poröse farbige Tonwaren mit Lack- oder Farbüberzügen anstelle einer Glasur (Gartenzwerge).

Steatit—keramischer Werkstoff für die Elektrotechnik aus circa 85% Speckstein und je 5–10% Ton und Feldspat.

Terrakotta—braune bis braunrote poröse Tonwaren, meist ohne Glasur aber wetterfest.

Terra sigillata—rote bis braunrote poröse Tonwaren mit glatter, dichter Oberfläche.

Vitreous China—dem Steingut verwandtes nicht transparentes Weichporzellan mit größerer Festigkeit als Steingut.

Definition of Ceramic Products

Biscuit, bisque—unglazed soft paste porcelain with dull surface.

Basalt Ware—black stoneware, also with overglaze decorations.

Belleek—soft paste porcelain with proportionally less kaolin and more felspar, often coated with a glaze looking like mother-of-pearl.

Black Porcelain—see Basalt Ware.

Bottgerstoneware—stoneware made from eighty-eight parts finely grained red clay mixture and twelve parts clay. Developed by Bottger in Meissen about 1708 but forgotten after the invention of porcelain. Rediscovered about 1918 and now used in Meissen mainly for plastic art.

Bone China—soft paste porcelain with high translucency. The quartz is completely or to a large extent substituted by calcined cattle bones.

Fayence—yellowish-gray to brown-red porous earthenware with opaque glazes. Frequently with incised or relief decorations, colored decorations under a second translucent glaze or with overglaze decorations.

Fire Clay, Chamotte—earthenware product with an addition of already fired and ground up clay, used for fireproof tiles, containers and linings of hearths and fireplaces.

Fritt Porcelain—pseudo porcelain, closer to glass. Kaolin or clay are substituted by ground glass (fritt).

Jasper Ware—unglazed white stoneware. Until 1785 tinted in the body, afterwards coated with a colored dip (Jasper dip). Frequently with reliefs, which remain white.

Jaspis Porcelain—same as Bottgerstoneware

Lenox—soft paste porcelain with less kaolin. The felspar is completely or to a large extent substituted by a fritt. Similar to Belleek.

Maiolica—cream or yellow colored porous earthenware with colored or whitish opaque glazes or simple colored decorations under translucent glazes.

Parian—unglazed soft paste porcelain with less kaolin and more felspar giving the surface an appearance similar to marble.

Seger Porcelain—soft paste porcelain with 25% clay that turns white in firing, 45% quartz and 30% felspar, highly translucent. The low firing temperature of 1280°C (2335°F) allows the use of more colors than hard paste porcelain.

Siderolith—porous colored earthenware with a varnish or enamel coating (garden gnomes).

Steatit—ceramic material for electrotechnical purposes from about 85% soapstone, 5%–10% clay and 5%–10% felspar.

Terra cotta—brown to brown-red porous earthenware, mostly without glaze but weatherproof.

Terra sigillata—red to brown-red porous earthenware with smooth and dense surface.

Vitreous China—not translucent soft paste porcelain, similar to earthenware but harder.

Explanation of Abbreviations

Erklärung der Abkürzungen

AG	joint stock company	Aktiengesellschaft
Bros.	Brothers	Gebrüder
Cie., Co., Comp.	company	Companie
Corp.	corporation	Gesellschaft
Gebr.	Brothers	Gebrüder
GMBH	limited liability company	Gesellschaft mit beschränkter Haftung
KG	limited partnership	Kommanditgesellschaft
k.k.	imperial-royal (in Austria and Bohemia until 1918)	kaiserlich-königlich (in Österreich und Böhmen bis 1918)
Nachf.	successor	Nachfolger
SAG	Soviet joint stock company in Germany	Sowjetische Aktiengesellschaft in Deutschland
VEB	People's Own Enterprise (In the German Democratic Republic for companies nationalized after 1945 or for nationally owned companies founded after 1945. After the unification of Germany all VEB were dissolved in 1990, some of them were privatized)	Volkseigener Betrieb (in der Deutschen Demokratischen Republik für nach 1945 verstaatlichte Betriebe und für staatseigene Betriebe, die nach 1945 gegründet wurden. Nach der Wiedervereinigung Deutschlands wurden 1990 alle VEB aufgelöst, einige wurden privatisiert)
VVB	Association of People's Own Enterprises	Vereinigung Volkseigener Betriebe
Wwe.	widow	Witwe

TEIL I

PART I

Marks

Marken

Porcelain and Pottery Factory Coburg Coburg (1913)–circa 1930	Porzellan- und Ton- warenfabrik Coburg Coburg (1913)–ca. 1930	1 **390**
Bros. Paris Oberkoditz (1910)–1953	Gebr. Paris Oberködiz (1910)–1953	2 **458**
Bros. Silbermann Hausen (1929)–1938 green underglaze	Gebr. Silbermann Hausen (1929)–1938 grün unterglasur	3 **416**
Bauer, Rosenthal & Co. Kronach 1897–1903	Bauer, Rosenthal & Co. Kronach 1897–1903	4 **433**
Bros. Bauscher Weiden 1906– green underglaze	Gebr. Bauscher Weiden 1906– grün unterglasur	5 **500**
Adelbert Beck Konigsee (1913)–	Adelbert Beck Königsee (1913)–	6 **430**
VEB Art and Decorative Porcelain Work Volkstedt circa 1951–circa 1957 blue	VEB Kunst- und Zier- porzellanwerk Volkstedt ca. 1951–ca. 1957 blau	7 **494**
Schwarzenberg Porcelain Factory Schwarzenberg 1908–1931	Schwarzenberger Por- zellanfabrik Schwarzenberg 1908–1931	8 **477**

C. M. Hutschenreuther
Hohenberg
(1925)–circa 1941
export mark, registe-
red in U.S.A. by
Graham & Zenger, New York
City

C. M. Hutschenreuther
Hohenberg
(1925)–ca. 1941
Exportmarke, regi-
striert in den USA
durch Graham & Zenger
in New York

9
419
455

Wilhelm Simon
Hildburghausen
(1875)–1910

Wilhelm Simon
Hildburghausen
(1875)–1910

10
417

Porcelain Factory Waldsassen
Waldsassen
(1966)-1993
also in combination
with: 100 Jahre

Porzellanfabrik Waldsassen
Waldsassen
(1966)-1993
auch in Verbindung
mit: 100 Jahre

11
498

Greiner, Gullich and
Sternkopf
Lucka
(1896)–

Greiner, Gullich und
Sternkopf
Lucka
(1896)–

12
441

Rothemund, Hager & Co.
Altenkunstadt
1919–1933
green underglaze

Rothemund, Hager & Co.
Altenkunstadt
1919–1933
grün unterglasur

13
372

Stiglbauer & Merz
Nuremberg
(1885)–1905

Stiglbauer & Merz
Nürnberg
(1885)–1905

14
457

Britannia Porcelainworks
Meierhofen
(1898)–circa 1925

Britannia Porcelainworks
Meierhöfen
(1898)–ca. 1925

15
445

Adolf Laufer Turn-Teplitz 1918–1938	Adolf Laufer Turn-Teplitz 1918–1938	16 **490**
C. H. Tuppack Tiefenfurth (1931)–1935 blue	C. H. Tuppack Tiefenfurth (1931)–1935 blau	17 **488**
H. Schomburg & Sons Berlin (1880)–1913	H. Schomburg & Söhne Berlin (1880)–1913	18 **382**
Oscar Schlegelmilch Langewiesen (1904)–	Oscar Schlegelmilch Langewiesen (1904)–	19 **436**
Porcelain Factory Victoria Altrohlau 1891–1918 blue overglaze or underglaze	Porzellanfabrik Victoria Altrohlau 1891–1918 blau aufglasur oder unterglasur	20 **374**
Porcelain Factory Victoria Altrohlau 1888–1901 blue or black over- glaze, blue under- glaze	Porzellanfabrik Victoria Altrohlau 1888–1901 blau oder schwarz aufglasur, blau unter- glasur	21 **374**
Porcelain Factory Victoria Altrohlau 1891–1918 blue overglaze or underglaze	Porzellanfabrik Victoria Altrohlau 1891–1918 blau aufglasur oder unterglasur	22 **374**
A. Riedeler Konigsee after 1892–circa 1950	A. Riedeler Königsee nach 1892–ca. 1950	23 **430**

Simon & Halbig
Grafenhain
(1875)–circa 1930
blue or black

Simon & Halbig
Gräfenhain
(1875)–ca. 1930   24
blau oder schwarz   **410**

Rudolph Heinz & Co.
Neuhaus
1885–circa 1921

Rudolph Heinz & Co.
Neuhaus   25
1885–ca. 1921   **452**

A. Lamm
Dresden
1910–
decorator's mark
overglaze

A. Lamm
Dresden
1910–
Malermarke   26
aufglasur   **395**

Jean Beck
Munich
(1900)–1915
overglaze
decorator's mark

Jean Beck
München
(1900)–1915
aufglasur   27
Malermarke   **450**

Porcelain Factory Mengersreuth
Mengersreuth
(1908)–1913

Porzellanfabrik Mengersreuth
Mengersreuth   28
(1908)–1913   **448**

Villeroy & Boch
Mettlach
circa 1874–circa 1918
on earthenware

Villeroy & Boch
Mettlach
ca. 1874–ca. 1918   29
auf Steingut   **449**

Villeroy & Boch
Mettlach
since 1874 to present
stamp on earthenware

Villeroy & Boch
Mettlach
seit 1874 bis heute   30
Stempel auf Steingut   **449**

Villeroy & Boch
Mettlach
since 1874 to present
stamp on earthenware
also with "Dresden" or
"Schramberg" or "Waller-
fangen" or "Septfontaine"
instead of "Mettlach" for
the Villeroy & Boch fac-
tories in those cities

Villeroy & Boch
Mettlach
seit 1874 bis heute
Stempel auf Steingut
auch mit "Dresden" oder
"Schramberg" oder "Wallerfangen" oder "Septfontaine"
anstelle von "Mettlach" für
die Villeroy & Boch Fa-   31
briken in diesen Städten   **449**

Villeroy & Boch Mettlach (1876)–present on earthenware	Villeroy & Boch Mettlach (1876)–heute auf Steingut	32 **449**
Carl Hubbe Haldensleben (1913)–circa 1920 on earthenware and porcelain	Carl Hubbe Haldensleben (1913)–ca. 1920 auf Steingut und Por- zellan	33 **414**
August Schmidt Ilmenau circa 1930 decorator's mark overglaze	August Schmidt Ilmenau ca. 1930 Malermarke aufglasur	34 **422**
Wagner & Apel Lippelsdorf 20th century	Wagner & Apel Lippelsdorf 20. Jahrhundert	35 **440**
K. Steinmann Tiefenfurth (1896)–circa 1918	K. Steinmann Tiefenfurth (1896)–ca. 1918	36 **488**
Smidt & Duensing Bremen (1894)–circa 1921 decorator's mark overglaze	Smidt & Duensing Bremen (1894)–ca. 1921 Malermarke aufglasur	37 **386**
VEB Porcelainwork Kahla Kahla (1957)– for products of the factory's training school	VEB Porzellanwerk Kahla Kahla (1957)– für Erzeugnisse der Betriebsberufsschule	38 **424**
Fasold & Stauch Bock-Wallendorf (1927)–circa 1945	Fasold & Stauch Bock-Wallendorf (1927)–ca. 1945	39 **384**
Epiag Elbogen circa 1920–1945 green	Epiag Elbogen ca. 1920–1945 grün	40 **399**

R. & E. Haidinger Elbogen circa 1815–1873 impressed	R. & E. Haidinger Elbogen ca. 1815–1873 eingeprägt	41 **399**
R. & E. Haidinger Elbogen 1833–1860 impressed	R. & E. Haidinger Elbogen 1833–1860 eingeprägt	42 **399**
R. & E. Haidinger Elbogen circa 1815–1873 blue underglaze	R. & E. Haidinger Elbogen ca. 1815–1873 blau unterglasur	43 **399**
R. & E. Haidinger Elbogen circa 1815–1873 blue underglaze	R. & E. Haidinger Elbogen ca. 1815–1873 blau unterglasur	44 **399**
R. & E. Haidinger Elbogen circa 1815–1873 blue underglaze	R. & E. Haidinger Elbogen ca. 1815–1873 blau unterglasur	45 **399**
Springer & Co. Elbogen (1915)–1918 blue or green under- glaze	Springer & Co. Elbogen (1915)–1918 blau oder grün unter- glasur	46 **399**
Springer & Co. Elbogen (1915)–1918 green or blue under- glaze	Springer & Co. Elbogen (1915)–1918 grün oder blau unter- glasur	47 **399**
Epiag Elbogen circa 1920–circa 1945 green underglaze	Epiag Elbogen ca. 1920–ca. 1945 grün unterglasur	48 **399**
Epiag Elbogen 1939–1945 green	Epiag Elbogen 1939–1945 grün	49 **399**

	Epiag	Epiag	
	Elbogen	Elbogen	
	(1941)—1945	(1941)—1945	
	green underglaze	grün unterglasur	
	also in combination	auch in Verbindung	50
	with: ASMANIT	mit: ASMANIT	**399**
	Matthes & Ebel	Matthes & Ebel	
	Mabendorf	Mäbendorf	51
	(1928)—1929	(1928)—1929	**442**
	Oepiag	Oepiag	
	Elbogen	Elbogen	
	1918—1920	1918—1920	
	green or blue under-	grün oder blau unter-	52
	glaze	glasur	**399**
	Oepiag	Oepiag	
	Elbogen	Elbogen	
	1918—1920	1918—1920	53
	green underglaze	grün unterglasur	**399**
	Springer & Co.	Springer & Co.	
	Elbogen	Elbogen	
	(1910)—1918	(1910)—1918	54
	green underglaze	grün unterglasur	**399**
	Springer & Co.	Springer & Co.	
	Elbogen	Elbogen	
	(1891)—1918	(1891)—1918	
	blue or green under-	blau oder grün unter-	55
	glaze or impressed	glasur oder eingeprägt	**399**
	Oepiag	Oepiag	
	Elbogen	Elbogen	
	1918—1920	1918—1920	56
	blue or green underglaze	blau oder grün unterglasur	**399**
	Springer & Co.	Springer & Co.	
	Elbogen	Elbogen	
	(1911)—1918	(1911)—1918	57
	green underglaze	grün unterglasur	**399**

J. S. Maier & Co. Poschetzau 1939–1945 the same mark with "Czechoslovakia" instead of "Germany" was used 1919–1939	J. S. Maier & Co. Poschetzau 1939–1945 die gleiche Marke mit "Czechoslovakia" anstelle von "Germany" wurde von 1919–1939 benutzt **58** **463**
Conta & Boehme Possneck (1878)–circa 1937 impressed	Conta & Boehme Pößneck (1878)–ca. 1937 eingeprägt **59** **463**
Wachtersbach Earthenware Factory Schlierbach 1903–1904 on earthenware	Wächtersbacher Steingut- fabrik Schlierbach 1903–1904 auf Steingut **60** **473**
F. & S. Rosenthal Schauberg circa 1930–circa 1938	F. & S. Rosenthal Schauberg **61** ca. 1930–ca. 1938 **471**
United Porcelain Factories Meierhofen 1925–1939	Vereinigte Porzellanfabriken Meierhöfen **62** 1925–1939 **445**
VEB Porcelain Decora- ting Shop Kaltenlengsfeld 1946– decorating mark overglaze	VEB Porzellan-Kunst- malerei Kaltenlengsfeld 1946– Malereimarke **63** aufglasur **425**
United Porcelain Factories Meierhofen 1925–1939	Vereinigte Porzellanfabriken Meierhöfen **64** 1925–1939 **445**
Bros. Benedikt Meierhofen circa 1883–1925	Gebr. Benedikt Meierhöfen **65** ca. 1883–1925 **445**

Baehr & Proeschild Ohrdruf (1919)–before 1945	Baehr & Proeschild Ohrdruf (1919)–vor 1945	66 **459**
Baehr & Proeschild Ohrdruf after 1900–circa 1919	Baehr & Proeschild Ohrdruf nach 1900–ca. 1919	67 **459**

A. Riedeler
Konigsee
    –circa 1950
	A. Riedeler
	Königsee
	    –ca. 1950
		68
		430

VEB Wallendorf Porcelain Factory Wallendorf 1959-circa 1990	VEB Wallendorfer Porzellanfabrik Wallendorf 1959- ca. 1990	69 **499**
VEB Schaubach Art Wallendorf 1958-1959	VEB Schaubach-Kunst Wallendorf 1958-1959	70 **499**
Porcelain Factory Porcelain Factory Moschendorf Hof - Moschendorf after 1871–circa 1945 impressed on dolls heads	Porzellanfabrik Moschen- Porzellanfabrik Moschendorf Hof - Moschendorf nach 1871–ca. 1945 eingeprägt auf Puppenköpfen	71 **419**
Bros. Benedikt Meierhofen after 1882–1925	Gebr. Benedikt Meierhöfen nach 1882–1925	72 **445**
Bros. Deyhle Schwabisch-Gmund circa 1941	Gebr. Deyhle Schwäbisch-Gmünd ca. 1941	73 **476**
Landgravial Porcelain Manufactory Kassel 1766–1788 blue underglaze	Landgräfliche Por- zellanmanufaktur Kassel 1766–1788 blau unterglasur	74 **426**

Langravial Porcelain Manufactory Kassel 1766–1788 blue underglaze	Landgräfliche Porzellanmanufaktur Kassel 1766–1788 blau unterglasur	75 **426**
Landgravial Porcelain Manufactory Kassel 1766–1788 blue underglaze	Landgräfliche Porzellanmanufaktur Kassel 1766–1788 blau unterglasur	76 **426**
Landgravial Porcelain Manufactory Kassel 1766–1788 blue underglaze	Landgräfliche Porzellanmanufaktur Kassel 1766–1788 blau unterglasur	77 **426**
Landgravial Porcelain Manufactory Kassel 1766–1788 purple overglaze	Landgräfliche Porzellanmanufaktur Kassel 1766–1788 purpur aufglasur	78 **426**
Landgravial Porcelain Manufactory Kassel 1766–1788 blue underglaze	Landgräfliche Porzellanmanufaktur Kassel 1766–1788 blau unterglasur	79 **426**
Joseph Adam Hannong Frankenthal 1759–1762 blue underglaze	Joseph Adam Hannong Frankenthal 1759–1762 blau unterglasur	80 **402**
Paul Anton Hannong Frankenthal 1755–1759 blue underglaze	Paul Anton Hannong Frankenthal 1755–1759 blau unterglasur	81 **402**
State's Porcelain Manufactory Nymphenburg Nymphenburg (1921)–present blue underglaze for reproductions of Frankenthal porcelain, always with year and contemporary Nymphenburg shield mark	Staatliche Porzellan-Manufaktur Nymphenburg Nymphenburg (1921)–heute blau unterglasur für Reproduktionen von Frankenthal Porzellan, immer mit Jahreszahl und zeitgenössischer Nymphenburg-Marke	82 **457**

	Porcelain Factory Waldsassen Waldsassen (1969)-1993	Porzellanfabrik Waldsassen Waldsassen (1996)-1993	83 **498**
	L. Hutschenreuther Selb (1956)—	L. Hutschenreuther Selb (1956)—	84 **479**
	Swaine & Co. Huttensteinach (1887)–circa 1920	Swaine & Co. Hüttensteinach (1887)–ca. 1920	85 **420**
	Rhenania Porcelain Factory Duisdorf 1935– also in combination with: Duisdorf-Bonn	Rhenania Porzellan- fabrik Duisdorf 1935– auch in Verbindung mit: Duisdorf-Bonn	 86 **397**
	West German Porcelain Factory Duisdorf 1904–1935	Westdeutsche Porzellan- fabrik Duisdorf 1904–1935	 87 **397**
	W. Einwaldt Berlin 1868– decorator's mark overglaze	W. Einwaldt Berlin 1868– Malermarke aufglasur	 88
	Hutschenreuther AG Selb (1975)—	Hutschenreuther AG Selb (1975)—	89 **479**
	C. Schumann Arzberg -1996 various colors also in combination with: Germany Echt Kobalt	C. Schumann Arzberg -1996 verschiedene Farben auch in Verbindung mit: Germany Echt Kobalt	 90 **377**

C. Schumann
Arzberg
(1932)-1996
green or black/red/gold
also in combination with:
Dresden
Royal Bavaria
Dresdner Art
Germany

C. Schumann
Arzberg
(1932)-1996
grün oder schwarz/rot/gold
auch in Verbindung mit:
Dresden
Royal Bavaria
Dresdner Art — 91
Germany — **377**

C. Schumann
Arzberg
20th century-1996
green or blue
underglaze

C. Schumann
Arzberg
20. Jhdt.-1996
grün oder blau — 92
unterglasur — **377**

Porcelain Factory Tettau
Tettau
(1916)—
blue or green under-
glaze, green overglaze
also in combination
with: Royal Bayreuth
       Belmont

Porzellanfabrik Tettau
Tettau
(1916)—
blau oder grün unter-
glasur, grün aufglasur
auch in Verbindung
mit: Royal Bayreuth — 93
      Belmont — **487**

Porcelain Factory Tettau
Tettau
1902—
blue or green under-
glaze, other colors
overglaze

Porzellanfabrik Tettau
Tettau
1902—
blau oder grün unter-
glasur, andere Farben — 94
aufglasur — **487**

Porcelain Factory Tettau
Tettau
after 1902—
green or blue under-
glaze, blue or grey
or gold overglaze

Porzellanfabrik Tettau
Tettau
nach 1902—
grün oder blau unter-
glasur, blau oder grau — 95
oder gold aufglasur — **487**

Royally privileged
Porcelain Factory Tettau
Tettau
1968—present
green underglaze

Königl. priv. Porzellan-
fabrik Tettau
Tettau
1968—heute — 96
grün unterglasur — **487**

Sontag & Sons
Tettau
(1887)—1902
green or blue under-
glaze

Sontag & Söhne
Tettau
(1887)—1902
grün oder blau unter- — 97
glasur — **487**

Royally privileged Porcelain Factory Tettau Tettau after 1957–	Königl. priv. Porzellanfabrik Tettau Tettau nach 1957–	98	**487**
Royally privileged Porcelain Factory Tettau Tettau after 1957–	Königl. priv. Porzellanfabrik Tettau Tettau nach 1957–	99	**487**
Royally privileged Porcelain Factory Tettau Tettau after 1957– blue or green	Königl. priv. Porzellanfabrik Tettau Tettau nach 1957– blau oder grün	100	**487**
Royally privileged Porcelain Factory Tettau Tettau (1968)–present blue or green	Königl. priv. Porzellanfabrik Tettau Tettau (1968)–heute blau oder grün	101	**487**
Royally privileged Porcelain Factory Tettau Tettau 1968–present green underglaze, gold/ blue/red overglaze	Königl. priv. Porzellanfabrik Tettau Tettau 1968–heute grün unterglasur, gold/ blau/rot aufglasur	102	**487**
Winter & Co. Elbogen 1880–1891	Winter & Co. Elbogen 1880–1891	103	**400**
Rhenish Porcelain Manufactory Oberkassel 1882–circa 1905	Rheinische Porzellanmanufaktur Oberkassel 1882–ca. 1905	104	**458**
unidentified probably Bohemia before 1918 red overglaze	nicht identifiziert wahrscheinlich Böhmen vor 1918 rot aufglasur	105	

L. Hutschenreuther	L. Hutschenreuther	
Selb	Selb	
−1945	−1945	106
green underglaze	grün unterglasur	**479**

Josef Rieber & Co. AG	Josef Rieber & Co. AG	
Mitterteich	Mitterteich	107
(1964)−	(1964)−	**449**

Josef Rieber & Co.	Josef Rieber & Co.	
Selb	Selb	108
circa 1918−1923	ca. 1918−1923	**480**

Porcelain Factory Bavaria	Porzellanfabrik Bavaria	
Ullersricht	Ullersricht	
(1929)−circa 1932	(1929)−ca. 1932	
also in combination	auch in Verbindung	
with: Bavaria Ivory	mit: Bavaria Ivory	109
Bavaria Elfenbein	Bavaria Elfenbein	**491**

Porcelain Factory Bavaria	Porzellanfabrik Bavaria	
Ullersricht	Ullersricht	110
(1927)−circa 1932	(1927)−ca. 1932	**491**

Porcelain Factory Schlottenhof	Porzellanfabrik Schlottenhof	
Schlottenhof	Schlottenhof	111
circa 1932−circa 1941	ca. 1932−ca. 1941	**474**

Porcelain Factory Bavaria	Porzellanfabrik Bavaria	
Ullersricht	Ullersricht	112
1919−circa 1932	1919−ca. 1932	**491**

Otto Kunz	Otto Kunz	
Neuhofen	Neuhofen	113
1947−present	1947−heute	**453**

Bawo & Dotter	Bawo & Dotter	
Fischern/New York City	Fischern/New York	114
1884–circa 1914	1884–ca. 1914	**401**
red overglaze	rot aufglasur	**454**

L. Hutschenreuther	L. Hutschenreuther	
Selb	Selb	
1920–1938	1920–1938	
mark of the art depart-	Marke der Kunstabtei-	
ment in Selb	lung in Selb	115
overglaze	aufglasur	**394**

L. Hutschenreuther	L. Hutschenreuther	
Selb	Selb	
1920–1967	1920–1967	116
green underglaze	grün unterglasur	**479**

L. Hutschenreuther	L. Hutschenreuther	
Selb	Selb	
1955–1969	1955–1969	
mark of the art depart-	Marke der Kunstabtei-	
ment in Selb	lung in Selb	117
green overglaze	grün aufglasur	**479**

Hutschenreuther AG	Hutschenreuther AG	
Selb	Selb	
1969–present	1969–heute	118
green underglaze	grün unterglasur	**479**

Hutschenreuther AG	Hutschenreuther AG	
Selb	Selb	119
(1974)–present	(1974)–heute	**479**

Bohemia	Bohemia	
Neurohlau	Neurohlau	120
1931–1945	1931–1945	**453**

Joseph Adam Hannong	Joseph Adam Hannong	
Frankenthal	Frankenthal	
1759–1762	1759–1762	121
blue underglaze	blau unterglasur	**402**

Joseph Adam Hannong	Joseph Adam Hannong	
Frankenthal	Frankenthal	
1759–1762	1759–1762	122
blue underglaze	blau unterglasur	**402**

Paul Anton Hannong Frankenthal 1755–1759 blue underglaze	Paul Anton Hannong Frankenthal 1755–1759 blau unterglasur	123 **402**
Sontag & Birkner Tettau 1866–1887 gold overglaze	Sontag & Birkner Tettau 1866–1887 gold aufglasur	124 **487**
W. Jager Eisenberg after 1900–1960	W. Jäger Eisenberg nach 1900–1960	125 **398**
Bohemia Neurohlau (1921)–1945	Bohemia Neurohlau (1921)–1945	126 **453**
Bohemia Neurohlau (1922)–1945	Bohemia Neurohlau (1922)–1945	127 **453**
Bohemia Neurohlau (1928)–1945	Bohemia Neurohlau (1928)–1945	128 **453**
Richard Kampf Grunlas 1918–1939	Richard Kämpf Grünlas 1918–1939	129 **413**
Keramag Ratingen (1949)–	Keramag Ratingen (1949)–	130 **464**
Ceramics Factory Marktschwaben circa 1929–1937	Keramische Fabrik Marktschwaben ca. 1929–1937	131 **445**

	First Steinbach Porcelain Factory Steinbach 1923–1938	Erste Steinbacher Porzellanfabrik Steinbach 1923–1938	132 **484**
	Earthenware Works Breslau Breslau (1937)–1945	Steingutwerke Breslau Breslau (1937)–1945	133 **386**
	Ducal Brunswick and Royal Porcelain Manufactory Furstenberg circa 1753–1813 impressed or incised	Herzoglich Braunschweigische und Königliche Porzellanmanufaktur Fürstenberg ca. 1753–1813 eingeprägt oder eingeritzt	134 **405**
	Count Frankenberg's Porcelain Factory Tillowitz (1887)–1938	Gräflich Frankenberg' sche Porzellanfabrik Tillowitz (1887)–1938	135 **488**
	Richard Muller & Co. Colln-Meissen (1885)– on earthenware	Richard Müller & Co. Cölln-Meissen (1885)– auf Tonwaren	136 **390**
	Hannover Porcelain Factory Lamspringe (1928)–1934	Hannoversche Porzellanfabrik Lamspringe (1928)–1934	137 **435**
	Julius Dressler Biela after 1900–circa 1945	Julius Dressler Biela nach 1900–ca. 1945	138 **383**
	Zeh, Scherzer & Co. Rehau (1882)-circa 1991	Zeh, Scherzer & Co. Rehau (1882)-ca. 1991	139 **466**

| | Zeh, Scherzer & Co.
Rehau
(1919)-circa 1991 | Zeh, Scherzer & Co.
Rehau
(1919)-ca. 1991 | 140
466 |

Zeh, Scherzer & Co.
Rehau
(1919)-circa 1991

Zeh, Scherzer & Co.
Rehau
(1919)-ca. 1991

140
466

Zeh, Scherzer & Co.
Rehau
(1894)-circa 1919

Zeh, Scherzer & Co.
Rehau
(1894)-ca.1919

141
466

Hertel, Jacob & Co.
Rehau
after 1922-circa 1969
green

Hertel, Jacob & Co.
Rehau
nach 1922-ca. 1969
grün

142
466

Hertel, Jacob & Co.
Rehau
circa 1945−1949
green

Hertel, Jacob & Co.
Rehau
ca. 1945−1949
grün

143
466

Hertel, Jacob & Co.
Rehau
1967-1969
green

Hertel, Jacob & Co.
Rehau
1967-1969
grün

144
466

Melitta Works
Rehau/Minden
(1969)-circa 1975

Melitta Werke
Rehau/Minden
(1969)-ca. 1975

145
466

Porcelain Factory Schonwald
Schonwald
circa 1898−1927

Porzellanfabrik Schönwald
Schönwald
ca. 1898−1927

146
475

Bros. Meinhold
Schweinsburg
(1899)−1910

Gebr. Meinhold
Schweinsburg
(1899)−1910

147
478

A. Lamm
Dresden
(1887)−
decorator's mark
overglaze

A. Lamm
Dresden
(1887)−
Malermarke
aufglasur

148
395

Ferdinand Vasold Liezen (1935)–	Ferdinand Vasold Liezen (1935)–	149 **439**
Steinberger & Co. Kriegern circa 1919–1945	Steinberger & Co. Kriegern ca. 1919–1945	150 **433**
Emanuel Steinberger Vienna 1950–before 1978	Emanuel Steinberger Wien 1950–vor 1978	151 **502**
Schwarzburg Workshops Unterweissbach 1908–circa 1938 impressed	Schwarzburger Werkstätten Unterweißbach 1908–ca. 1938 eingeprägt	152 **492**
Schwarzburg Workshops Unterweissbach 1908–circa 1938 impressed	Schwarzburger Werkstätten Unterweißbach 1908–ca. 1938 eingeprägt	153 **492**
Kampfe & List Neuhaus after 1831–circa 1900	Kämpfe & List Neuhaus nach 1831–ca. 1900	154 **452**
Hertwig & Co. Katzhütte (1914)-circa 1958	Hertwig & Co. Katzhütte (1914)- ca. 1958	155 **426**
Hertwig & Co. Katzhütte (1914)-circa 1958	Hertwig & Co. Katzhütte (1914)-ca. 1958	156 **426**
Hertwig & Co. Katzhütte (1914)-circa 1958	Hertwig & Co. Katzhütte (1914)-circa 1958	157 **426**

Hertwig & Co. Katzhütte circa 1941-circa 1958	Hertwig & Co. Katzhütte circa 1941- circa 1958	158 **426**
Hertwig & Co. Katzhütte circa 1941-circa 1958	Hertwig & Co. Katzhütte ca. 1941-ca. 1958	159 **426**
Albin Eichhorn Goritzmuhle 1891–	Albin Eichhorn Göritzmühle 1891–	160 **408**
Berthold Eck Unterneubrunn (1876)–1895	Berthold Eck Unterneubrunn (1876)–1895	161 **492**
H. Reinl Hirschen (1912)–circa 1945	H. Reinl Hirschen (1912)–ca. 1945	162 **417**
J. Milota Klentsch 1889–	J. Milota Klentsch 1889–	163 **428**
Ducal Real Porcelain Factory Ludwigsburg 1770–1775 blue underglaze	Herzoglich Aechte Porcelain Fabrique Ludwigsburg 1770–1775 blau unterglasur	164 **441**
Royal Porcelain Manufactory Ludwigsburg 1806–1816 red or gold overglaze	Königliche Porzellan Manufaktur Ludwigsburg 1806–1816 rot oder gold aufglasur	165 **441**
Wurttemberg Porcelain Manufactory Schorndorf 1904–1939	Württembergische Porzellanmanufaktur Schorndorf 1904–1939	166 **475**

Porcelain Manufactory Ludwigsburg Ludwigsburg 1948–present blue underglaze	Porzellanmanufaktur Ludwigsburg Ludwigsburg 1948–heute blau unterglasur	167 **441**	
Ducal Real Porcelain Factory Ludwigsburg 1780–1805 blue underglaze	Herzoglich Aechte Porcelain Fabrique Ludwigsburg 1780–1805 blau unterglasur	168 **441**	
Ducal Real Porcelain Factory Ludwigsburg circa 1780–1805 blue underglaze	Herzoglich Aechte Porcelain Fabrique Ludwigsburg ca. 1780–1805 blau unterglasur	169 **441**	
Dressel, Kister & Cie. Passau (1902)–1904 blue underglaze	Dressel, Kister & Cie. Passau (1902)–1904 blau unterglasur	170 **460**	
Wurttemberg Porcelain Manufactory Schorndorf 1918–1939 blue underglaze	Württembergische Porzellanmanufaktur Schorndorf 1918–1939 blau unterglasur	171 **475**	
Wilhelm Kunstner Pfullingen after 1923– decorator's mark overglaze	Wilhelm Künstner Pfullingen nach 1923– Malermarke aufglasur	172 **461**	
Franziska Hirsch Dresden (1901)–circa 1930 decorator's mark overglaze	Franziska Hirsch Dresden (1901)–ca. 1930 Malermarke aufglasur	173 **395**	
Thomas & Co. Sophienthal after 1928– green	Thomas & Co. Sophienthal nach 1928– grün	174 **482**	

Ducal Real Porcelain Factory Ludwigsburg 1770–1780 blue underglaze	Herzoglich Aechte Porcelain Fabrique Ludwigsburg 1770–1780 blau unterglasur	175 **441**
Count Thun & Weber and Chr. Nonne Klosterle 1794–1805 blue underglaze	Graf Thun & Weber und Chr. Nonne Klösterle 1794–1805 blau unterglasur	176 **428**
Count Thun & Weber and Chr. Nonne Klosterle 1794–1805 blue underglaze	Graf Thun & Weber und Chr. Nonne Klösterle 1794–1805 blau unterglasur	177 **428**
Count Thun & Weber and Chr. Nonne Klosterle 1794–1805 blue underglaze or different colors overglaze	Graf Thun & Weber und Chr. Nonne Klösterle 1794–1805 blau unterglasur oder verschiedene Farben aufglasur	178 **428**
Count Thun & Weber and Chr. Nonne Klosterle 1794–1805 blue underglaze or different colors overglaze	Graf Thun & Weber und Chr. Nonne Klösterle 1794–1805 blau unterglasur oder verschiedene Farben aufglasur	179 **428**
Count Thun & Weber and Chr. Nonne Klosterle 1794–1805 blue underglaze or different colors overglaze	Graf Thun & Weber und Chr. Nonne Klösterle 1794–1805 blau unterglasur oder verschiedene Farben aufglasur	180 **428**
Count Thun & Weber and Chr. Nonne Klosterle 1794–1805 black or red overglaze	Graf Thun & Weber und Chr. Nonne Klösterle 1794–1805 schwarz oder rot aufglasur	181 **428**

Bros. Horn	Gebr. Horn	
Hornberg	Hornberg	
(1886)–circa 1905	(1886)–ca. 1905	182
on colored earthenware	auf farbigem Steingut	**420**

Bros. Horn	Gebr. Horn	
Hornberg	Hornberg	
(1886)–circa 1905	(1886)–ca. 1905	
on whiteglazed	auf weißglasiertem	183
earthenware	Steingut	**420**

Villeroy & Boch	Villeroy & Boch	
Mettlach	Mettlach	
circa 1845–circa 1869	ca. 1845–ca. 1869	184
relief on earthenware	Relief auf Steingut	**449**

Margravial Fine Porce-	Markgräfliche Feine	
lain Factory	Porcelain Fabrique	
Ansbach-Bruckberg	Ansbach-Bruckberg	
1757–1791	1757–1791	
blue underglaze	blau unterglasur	185
court mark	Hofmarke	**375**

Margravial Fine Porce-	Markgräfliche Feine	
lain Factory	Porcelain Fabrique	
Ansbach-Bruckberg	Ansbach-Bruckberg	
1757–1791	1757–1791	
blue underglaze	blau unterglasur	186
court mark	Hofmarke	**375**

Margravial Fine Porce-	Markgräfliche Feine	
lain Factory	Porcelain Fabrique	
Ansbach-Bruckberg	Ansbach-Bruckberg	
1757–1791	1757–1791	
blue underglaze	blau unterglasur	187
court mark	Hofmarke	**375**

Bawo & Dotter	Bawo & Dotter	
Fischern and New York City	Fischern und New York	188
1884–1914	1884–1914	**401**
decorator's mark	Malermarke	**454**

Berlin Porcelain	Berliner Porzellan-	
Manufactory	manufaktur	
Teltow	Teltow	189
1904–circa 1911	1904–ca. 1911	**486**

J. Poppauer
Franz
(1884)–1885

J. Poppauer
Franz
(1884)–1885

190
403

Wermer & Riessberger
Franz
(1885)–

Wermer & Riessberger
Franz
(1885)–

191
403

unidentified
blue overglaze
on porcelain of the
Royal Porcelain Manu-
factory Berlin in
addition to the scepter mark,
probably mark of U. S.
distributor

nicht identifiziert
blau aufglasur
auf Porzellan der
Königlichen Porzellan
Manufaktur Berlin neben der
Szeptermarke,
wahrscheinlich Marke
eines US-Händlers

192

C. H. Tuppack
Tiefenfurth
circa 1919–1935

C. H. Tuppack
Tiefenfurth
ca. 1919–1935

193
488

J. von Schwarz
Nuremberg
(1878)–

J. von Schwarz
Nürnberg
(1878)–

194
457

F. S. Oest Widow & Co.
Berlin
(1887)–after 1900
on earthenware

F. S. Oest Wwe. & Co.
Berlin
(1887)–nach 1900
auf Steingut

195
382

Royal Porcelain
Manufactory
Berlin
1849–1870
blue underglaze

Königliche Porzellan
Manufaktur
Berlin
1849–1870
blau unterglasur

196
380

Royal Porcelain Manufactory Berlin 1847–1849 blue underglaze	Königliche Porzellan Manufaktur Berlin 1847–1849 blau unterglasur	197 **380**
Royal Porcelain Manufactory Berlin 1847–1849 blue underglaze	Königliche Porzellan Manufaktur Berlin 1847–1849 blau unterglasur	198 **380**
F. A. Schumann Berlin 1851–1869 blue underglaze	F. A. Schumann Berlin 1851–1869 blau unterglasur	199 **383**
F. A. Schumann Berlin 1835–1851 blue underglaze	F. A. Schumann Berlin 1835–1851 blau unterglasur	200 **383**
A. Rappsilber Konigszelt (1880)–circa 1912	A. Rappsilber Königszelt (1880)–ca. 1912	201 **430**
C. Tielsch & Co. Altwasser (1875)–circa 1935 blue or green underglaze	C. Tielsch & Co. Altwasser (1875)–ca. 1935 blau oder grün unterglasur	202 **374**
F. A. Schumann Berlin 1835–1851 blue underglaze	F. A. Schumann Berlin 1835–1851 blau unterglasur	203 **383**
Haas & Czjzek Schlaggenwald (1916)–1918 green or blue underglaze	Haas & Czjzek Schlaggenwald (1916)–1918 grün oder blau unterglasur	204 **472**
Joseph Schachtel Charlottenbrunn (1887)–circa 1919	Joseph Schachtel Charlottenbrunn (1887)–ca. 1919	205 **389**

Royal Porcelain Manufactory Berlin 1844–1847 blue underglaze	Königliche Porzellan Manufaktur Berlin 1844–1847 blau unterglasur	206 **380**
Royal Porcelain Manufactory Berlin circa 1823–1832 red-brown overglaze decorating mark	Königliche Porzellan Manufaktur Berlin ca. 1823–1832 rotbraun aufglasur Malereimarke	207 **380**
Moritz Zdekauer Altrohlau 1884–1909 green underglaze or overglaze	Moritz Zdekauer Altrohlau 1884–1909 grün unterglasur oder aufglasur	208 **373**
K. Steinmann Tiefenfurth (1887)–circa 1938 blue or green	K. Steinmann Tiefenfurth (1887)–ca. 1938 blau oder grün	209 **488**
Porcelain Factory Konigszelt Konigszelt after 1912–circa 1928	Porzellanfabrik Königszelt Königszelt nach 1912–ca. 1928	210 **430**
Reichenstein Porcelain Manufactory Reichenstein after 1835–	Reichensteiner Porzellan- manufaktur Reichenstein nach 1835–	211 **466**
F. A. Schumann Berlin circa 1851–1869 blue underglaze	F. A. Schumann Berlin ca. 1851–1869 blau unterglasur	212 **383**
Striegau Porcelain Factory Stanowitz after 1873–circa 1927	Striegauer Porzellanfabrik Stanowitz nach 1873–ca. 1927	213 **484**
Amphora Works Turn 1903–1918	Amphora Werke Turn 1903–1918	214 **489**

Porcelain Factory Weiden	Porzellanfabrik Weiden	
Bros. Bauscher	Gebr. Bauscher	
Weiden	Weiden	215
1909–	1909–	**500**
H. A. Kruse	H. A. Kruse	
Bremen	Bremen	
(1883)–	(1883)–	
decorator's mark	Malermarke	216
overglaze	aufglasur	**386**
Fischer & Mieg	Fischer & Mieg	
Pirkenhammer	Pirkenhammer	217
(1887)–1918	(1887)–1918	**461**
Oepiag	Oepiag	
Pirkenhammer	Pirkenhammer	218
1918–1920	1918–1920	**461**
P. Giesel	P. Giesel	
Breslau	Breslau	
(1887)–circa 1915	(1887)–circa 1915	219
on earthenware	auf Steingut	**386**
Bros. Bordolo	Gebr. Bordolo	
Grunstadt	Grünstadt	
(1896)–	(1896)–	220
on earthenware	auf Steingut	**413**
Glasser & Greiner	Glasser & Greiner	
Schmiedefeld	Schmiedefeld	221
(1886)–circa 1913	(1886)–ca. 1913	**474**
Erdmann Schlegelmilch	Erdmann Schlegelmilch	
Suhl	Suhl	
–circa 1938	–ca. 1938	222
green	grün	**485**
C. Tielsch & Co.	C. Tielsch & Co.	
Altwasser	Altwasser	
probably 1845–1870	wahrscheinlich 1845–1870	223
blue or green underglaze	blau oder grün unterglasur	**374**

Carl Scheidig Grafenthal circa 1935–1972 red overglaze	Carl Scheidig Gräfenthal ca. 1935–1972 rot aufglasur	224 **411**	
Altrohlau Porcelain Factories Altrohlau circa 1909–1945 green underglaze	Altrohlauer Porzellan- fabriken Altrohlau ca. 1909–1945 grün unterglasur	225 **373**	
Altrohlau Porcelain Factories Altrohlau circa 1918–1939 green underglaze	Altrohlauer Porzellan- fabriken Altrohlau ca. 1918–1939 grün unterglasur	226 **373**	
Altrohlau Porcelain Factories Altrohlau (1941)–1945 green underglaze	Altrohlauer Porzellan- fabriken Altrohlau (1941)–1945 grün unterglasur	227 **373**	
H. Baensch Lettin (1887)–circa 1930	H. Baensch Lettin (1887)–ca. 1930	228 **438**	
Buckau Porcelain Manufactory Magdeburg-Buckau circa 1850– blue underglaze	Buckauer Porzellan- manufaktur Magdeburg-Buckau ca. 1850– blau unterglasur	229 **442**	
Haager, Hoerth & Co. Zell on Harmersbach 1897–circa 1907 on earthenware	Haager, Hoerth & Co. Zell am Harmersbach 1897–ca. 1907 auf Steingut	230 **506**	
Georg Schmider Zell on Harmersbach (1898)– on earthenware	George Schmider Zell am Harmersbach (1898)– auf Steingut	231 **506**	
Georg Schmider Zell on Harmersbach 1913– on earthenware	Georg Schmider Zell am Harmersbach 1913– auf Steingut	232 **506**	

Ceramic Works Offstein and Worms Offstein (1921)– also in combination with: Offstein Worms	Keramische Werke Offstein und Worms Offstein (1921)– auch in Verbindung mit: Offstein Worms	233 **459**
Greiner & Herda Oberkotzau 1898–1943 green or red overglaze	Greiner & Herda Oberkotzau 1898–1943 grün oder rot aufglasur	234 **458**
Haager, Hoerth & Co. Zell on Harmersbach circa 1873–circa 1898	Haager, Hoerth & Co. Zell am Harmersbach ca. 1873–circa 1898	235 **506**
New York and Rudolstadt Pottery and Nathan Straus & Sons Rudolstadt/New York City 1904–after 1924	New York and Rudolstadt Pottery und Nathan Straus & Sons Rudolstadt/New York 1904–nach 1924	236 **469** **456**
New York & Rudolstadt Pottery and Nathan Straus & Sons Rudolstadt/New York City (1906)–after 1924	New York & Rudolstadt Pottery und Nathan Straus & Sons Rudolstadt/New York (1906)–nach 1924	237 **469** **456**
Adolf Persch Hegewald 1902–1918	Adolf Persch Hegewald 1902–1918	238 **416**
Carl Scheidig Grafenthal 1906–1935	Carl Scheidig Gräfenthal 1906–1935	239 **411**
Woldemar Adler Berchtesgaden 1957–circa 1965 decorator's mark overglaze	Woldemar Adler Berchtesgaden 1957–ca. 1965 Malermarke aufglasur	240 **380**

C. M. Hutschenreuther	C. M. Hutschenreuther	
Arzberg	Arzberg	
1948–	1948–	241
green underglaze	grün unterglasur	377
Krautheim & Adelberg	Krautheim & Adelberg	
Selb	Selb	
1912–1922	1912–1922	242
green underglaze	grün unterglasur	479
Arno Stauch	Arno Stauch	
Tettau	Tettau	
circa 1922–	ca. 1922–	
decorator's mark	Malermarke	243
overglaze	aufglasur	487
J. Rupp - Kuhn	J. Rupp - Kuhn	
Fraulautern	Fraulautern	
(1894)–	(1894)–	244
on earthenware	auf Steingut	403
J. Rupp - Kuhn	J. Rupp - Kuhn	
Fraulautern	Fraulautern	
1896–1906	1896–1906	245
on earthenware	auf Steingut	403
P. Rauschert	P. Rauschert	246
Schmiedeberg	Schmiedeberg	
1932–1945	1932–1945	474
Sontag & Sons	Sontag & Söhne	
Geiersthal	Geiersthal	
after 1900–1919	nach 1900–1919	
decorator's mark	Malermarke	247
mostly in gold overglaze	meist in gold aufglasur	406
Jacobi, Adler & Co.	Jacobi, Adler & Co.	
Neuleiningen	Neuleiningen	
(1887)–circa 1930	(1887)–ca. 1930	248
on earthenware	auf Steingut	453
Engineer Fritsch & Weidermann	Ing. Fritsch & Weidermann	
Altrohlau	Altrohlau	
1921–1939	1921–1939	
from 1939–1945	von 1939–1945 die	
the same mark with	gleiche Marke mit	
"Germany" instead of	"Germany" anstelle von	249
"Czechoslovakia"	"Czechoslovakia"	374

60

Margravial Fine Porcelain Factory Ansbach-Bruckberg 1757–1791 blue underglaze court mark	Markgräfliche Feine Porcelain Fabrique Ansbach-Bruckberg 1757–1791 blau unterglasur Hofmarke	250	**375**
Margravial Fine Porcelain Factory Ansbach-Bruckberg 1757–1791 blue underglaze court mark	Markgräfliche Feine Porcelain Fabrique Ansbach-Bruckberg 1757–1791 blau unterglasur Hofmarke	251	**375**
Reichenstein Porcelain Manufactory Reichenstein (1887)– blue	Reichensteiner Porzellanmanufaktur Reichenstein (1887)– blau	252	**466**
C. Tielsch & Co. Altwasser (1875)–circa 1934 blue underglaze	C. Tielsch & Co. Altwasser (1875)–ca. 1934 blau unterglasur	253	**374**
C. Tielsch & Co. Altwasser (1875)–circa 1934 blue underglaze	C. Tielsch & Co. Altwasser (1875)–ca. 1934 blau unterglasur	254	**374**
C. Tielsch & Co. Altwasser (1875)–circa 1934 blue underglaze	C. Tielsch & Co. Altwasser (1875)–ca. 1934 blau unterglasur	255	**374**
P. Giesel Breslau (1896)–circa 1915 on earthenware	P. Giesel Breslau (1896)–ca. 1915 auf Steingut	256	**386**
G. Greiner & Co. Schauberg circa 1871–1927	G. Greiner & Co. Schauberg ca. 1871–1927	257	**471**
F. A. Schumann Berlin 1851–1869 blue underglaze	F. A. Schumann Berlin 1851–1869 blau unterglasur	258	**383**

A. Heckmann Annaburg 1874–before 1924 on earthenware	A. Heckmann Annaburg 1874–vor 1924 auf Steingut	259 **375**
C. Tielsch & Co. Altwasser (1909)–circa 1934 blue or green underglaze also in combination with: Silesia Germany	C. Tielsch & Co. Altwasser (1909)–ca. 1934 blau oder grün unterglasur auch in Verbindung mit: Silesia Germany	260 **374**
C. Tielsch & Co. Altwasser (1909)–circa 1934 blue or green underglaze	C. Tielsch & Co. Altwasser (1909)–ca. 1934 blau oder grün unterglasur	261 **374**
C. Tielsch & Co. Altwasser 1934–1945 blue or green underglaze	C. Tielsch & Co. Altwasser 1934–1945 blau oder grün unterglasur	262 **374**
Moritz Zdekauer Altrohlau 1884–1909 green underglaze or green or black overglaze	Moritz Zdekauer Altrohlau 1884–1909 grün unterglasur oder grün oder schwarz aufglasur	263 **373**
Moritz Zdekauer Altrohlau 1884–1909 green underglaze	Moritz Zdekauer Altrohlau 1884–1909 grün unterglasur	264 **373**
Drechsel & Strobel Marktleuthen (1900)–circa 1903	Drechsel & Strobel Marktleuthen (1900)–ca. 1903	265 **444**
Porcelain Factory Kolmar Kolmar 1897–circa 1944	Porzellanfabrik Kolmar Kolmar 1897–ca. 1944	266 **432**
Jaeger & Co. Marktredwitz –1979 green underglaze	Jaeger & Co. Marktredwitz –1979 grün unterglasur	267 **444**

Jaeger & Co. Marktredwitz after 1949-1979 black/red/gold overglaze	Jaeger & Co. Marktredwitz nach 1949-1979 schwarz/rot/gold aufglasur	268 **444**
R. M. Krause Schweidnitz circa 1929 decorator's mark overglaze	R. M. Krause Schweidnitz ca. 1929 Malermarke aufglasur	269 **478**
Brambach Porcelain Factory Brambach after 1904—circa 1915	Brambacher Porzellanfabrik Brambach nach 1904—ca. 1915	270 **386**
Johann Seltmann Vohenstrauss after 1901—	Johann Seltmann Vohenstrauß nach 1901—	271 **494**
Clayware Factory Schwandorf Schwandorf (1891)—	Tonwarenfabrik Schwandorf Schwandorf (1891)—	272 **477**
Austrian Ceramic Wilhelmsburg 1946—circa 1960	Österreichische Keramik Wilhelmsburg 1946—ca. 1960	273 **504**
Ditmar - Urbach Znaim after 1920—1945	Ditmar - Urbach Znaim nach 1920—1945	274 **508**
Clayware Factory Schwandorf Schwandorf —circa 1945	Tonwarenfabrik Schwandorf Schwandorf —ca. 1945	275 **477**

Zwickau Porcelain Factory Zwickau 1927–1933	Zwickauer Porzellan-fabrik Zwickau 1927–1933

276
508

New Porcelain Factory Tettau Tettau 1904–1935 green underglaze or gold overglaze	Neue Porzellanfabrik Tettau Tettau 1904–1935 grün unterglasur oder gold aufglasur

277
487

A. Severin & Co. Bunde 1929– decorator's mark overglaze	A. Severin & Co. Bünde 1929– Malermarke aufglasur

278
388

A. Severin & Co. Bunde 1929– decorator's mark overglaze	A. Severin & Co. Bünde 1929– Malermarke aufglasur

279
388

Karl Steubler Zwickau circa 1920–circa 1953 decorator's mark overglaze	Karl Steubler Zwickau ca. 1920–ca. 1953 Malermarke aufglasur

280
508

Bros. Mehner Eulau circa 1930 decorator's mark overglaze	Gebr. Mehner Eulau ca. 1930 Malermarke aufglasur

281
401

L. J. Schulz and Uhlenhorst Studio Hamburg (1959)– decorator's mark overglaze	L. J. Schulz und Uhlenhorst Studio Hamburg (1959)– Malermarke aufglasur

282
416

Ilmenau Porcelain Factory Ilmenau circa 1938–circa 1947	Ilmenauer Porzellan-fabrik Ilmenau ca. 1938–ca. 1947

283
421

Ilmenau Porcelain Factory and VEB Porcelainwork Count von Henneberg Ilmenau (1934)–circa 1969	Ilmenauer Porzellan-fabrik und VEB Porzellanwerk Graf von Henneberg Ilmenau (1934)–ca. 1969	284	**421**
Ilmenau Porcelain Factory and VEB Porcelainwork Count von Henneberg Ilmenau 1934–1973	Ilmenauer Porzellan-fabrik und VEB Porzellanwerk Graf von Henneberg Ilmenau 1934–1973	285	**421**
VEB Porcelainwork Count von Henneberg Ilmenau (1949)–1973	VEB Porzellanwerk Graf von Henneberg Ilmenau (1949)–1973	286	**421**
Ilmenau Porcelain Factory Ilmenau 1929–circa 1938 green underglaze	Ilmenauer Porzellan-fabrik Ilmenau 1929–ca. 1938 grün unterglasur	287	**421**
Fischer, Naumann & Co. Ilmenau (1887)–circa 1937 on earthenware	Fischer, Naumann & Co. Ilmenau (1887)–ca. 1937 auf Steingut	288	**422**
F. E. Henneberg & Co. Gotha after 1834–1881	F. E. Henneberg & Co. Gotha nach 1834–1881	289	**409**
F. E. Henneberg & Co. Gotha –circa 1881	F. E. Henneberg & Co. Gotha –ca. 1881	290	**409**
VEB Henneberg Porcelain Ilmenau 1973-1990	VEB Henneberg Porzellan Ilmenau 1973-1990	291	**421**

VEB Henneberg Porcelain
Ilmenau
1973-1990

VEB Henneberg Porzellan
Ilmenau 292
1973-1990 **421**

VEB Henneberg Porcelain
Ilmenau
1977- 200th anniversary mark

VEB Henneberg Porzellan
Ilmenau 293
1977 - Marke zur 200 Jahrfeier **421**

Volkstedt Porcelain
Factory Richard Eckert & Co.
Volkstedt
1895–1918

Volkstedter Porzellan-
fabrik Richard Eckert & Co.
Volkstedt 294
1895–1918 **497**

Schumann & Klett
Ilmenau
after 1872–circa 1927
decorator's mark
overglaze

Schumann & Klett
Ilmenau
nach 1872–ca. 1927
Malermarke 295
aufglasur **422**

J. J. Scharvogel
Munich
1898–circa 1913
impressed

J. J. Scharvogel
München
1898–ca. 1913 296
eingeprägt **451**

Ilmenau Porcelain Factory
Ilmenau
circa 1820–1871

Ilmenauer Porzellanfabrik
Ilmenau 297
ca. 1820–1871 **421**

Ilmenau Porcelain Factory
Ilmenau
circa 1820–1871

Ilmenauer Porzellanfabrik
Ilmenau 298
ca. 1820–1871 **421**

unidentified
Bohemia
red overglaze
probably mark of
U. S. importer

nicht identifiziert
Böhmen
rot aufglasur
wahrscheinlich Marke 299
eines US-Importeurs

Erdmann Schlegelmilch
Suhl
circa 1896–circa 1938
brown

Erdmann Schlegelmilch
Suhl
ca. 1896–ca. 1938 300
braun **485**

Erdmann Schlegelmilch Suhl (1886)–circa 1938 green	Erdmann Schlegelmilch Suhl (1886)–ca. 1938 grün	301 **485**
Erdmann Schlegelmilch Suhl (1896)–circa 1938	Erdmann Schlegelmilch Suhl (1896)–ca. 1938	302 **485**
Meissen Stove and Porcelain Factory Meissen after 1872–circa 1930	Meißner Ofen- und Porzellanfabrik Meißen nach 1872–ca. 1930	303 **447**
Silesian Porcelain Factory P. Donath Tiefenfurth (1910)–1916	Schlesische Porzellanfabrik P. Donath Tiefenfurth (1910)–1916	304 **488**
Graef & Krippner and Heinrich & Co. Selb after 1906–circa 1940	Graef & Krippner und Heinrich & Co. Selb nach 1906–ca. 1940	305 **479**
Hagenburger-Schwalb Hettenheidelheim (1939)–	Hagenburger-Schwalb Hettenheidelheim (1939)–	306 **417**
Porcelain Factory Spechtsbrunn Spechtsbrunn (1930)–circa 1954	Porzellanfabrik Spechtsbrunn Spechtsbrunn (1930)–ca. 1954	307 **483**
Elster Porcelainworks Muhlhausen 1922–1924	Elster Porzellanwerke Mühlhausen 1922–1924	308 **450**
Thomas & Co. Sophienthal 1928–1931	Thomas & Co. Sophienthal 1928–1931	309 **482**
Worms Terra Sigillata Manufactory Worms 1948–present on fine earthenware	Wormser Terra Sigillata Manufaktur Worms 1948–heute auf Feinsteingut	310 **506**

C. F. Boseck & Co. Haida (1892)–after 1934 decorator's mark overglaze	C. F. Boseck & Co. Haida (1892)–nach 1934 Malermarke aufglasur	311 **414**	
Rudolf Ditmar Znaim (1881)–circa 1919	Rudolf Ditmar Znaim (1881)–ca. 1919	312 **508**	
Rudolf Ditmar's Heirs Znaim (1920)–circa 1938	Rudolf Ditmars Erben Znaim (1920)–ca. 1938	313 **508**	
Richard Lichtenstern & Co. Wilhelmsburg circa 1920–circa 1938 on earthenware	Richard Lichtenstern & Co. Wilhelmsburg ca. 1920–ca. 1938 auf Steingut	314 **504**	
Bros. Urbach Turn - Teplitz 1882–1919	Gebr. Urbach Turn - Teplitz 1882–1919	315 **490**	
Ditmar - Urbach Znaim after 1920–circa 1945	Ditmar - Urbach Znaim nach 1920–ca. 1945	316 **490**	
Reinhold Schlegelmilch Tillowitz after 1869–circa 1938	Reinhold Schlegelmilch Tillowitz nach 1869–ca. 1938	317 **488**	
Wachtersbach Earthen- ware Factory Schlierbach 1908–1910 on earthenware	Wächtersbacher Stein- gutfabrik Schlierbach 1908–1910 auf Steingut	318 **473**	
unidentified possibly Klosterle 19th century	nicht identifiziert möglicherweise Klösterle 19. Jahrhundert	319 **428**	
Bros. Hofmann Erkersreuth after 1900–circa 1936	Gebr. Hofmann Erkersreuth nach 1900–ca. 1936	320 **401**	
Kranichfeld Porcelain Manufactory Kranichfeld 1903–	Kranichfelder Porzellan- manufaktur Kranichfeld 1903–	321 **433**	

Kranichfeld Porcelain Manufactory Kranichfeld 1903—	Kranichfelder Porzellan- manufaktur Kranichfeld 1903—	322 **433**
Lorenz Reichel Schirnding 1902—1909	Lorenz Reichel Schirnding 1902—1909	323 **472**
Bauer, Rosenthal & Co. Kronach (1898)—circa 1903 green underglaze	Bauer, Rosenthal & Co. Kronach (1898)—ca. 1903 grün unterglasur	324 **433**
Bauer, Rosenthal & Co. and Ph. Rosenthal & Co. Kronach 1898—after 1903 green underglaze	Bauer, Rosenthal & Co. und Ph. Rosenthal & Co. Kronach 1898—nach 1903 grün unterglasur	325 **433**
Ph. Rosenthal & Co. Kronach (1903)— green underglaze	Ph. Rosenthal & Co. Kronach (1903)— grün unterglasur	326 **433**
Bros. Schoenau, Swaine & Co. Huttensteinach after 1920—circa 1954	Gebr. Schoenau, Swaine & Co. Hüttensteinach nach 1920—ca. 1954	327 **420**
Franz Junkersdorf Dresden 1909— decorator's mark overglaze	Franz Junkersdorf Dresden 1909— Malermarke aufglasur	328 **395**
Sontag & Sons Tettau (1895)—1902	Sontag & Söhne Tettau (1895)—1902	329 **487**
Adolph Hamann Dresden (1903)— decorator's mark overglaze	Adolph Hamann Dresden (1903)— Malermarke aufglasur	330 **394**
Franz Schamschula Konstadt circa 1930 decorator's mark overglaze	Franz Schamschula Konstadt ca. 1930 Malermarke aufglasur	331 **432**

Karlsbad Porcelain Factory Fischern 1900–1910	Karlsbader Porzellan- fabrik Fischern 1900–1910	332 **402**
Porcelain Manufactory Burgau Burgau-Goschwitz (1901)–1929	Porzellanmanufaktur Burgau Burgau-Göschwitz (1901)–1929	333 **388**
P. Giesel Breslau (1898)–1908 on earthenware	P. Giesel Breslau (1898)–1908 auf Steingut	334 **386**
Hugo Lonitz and Hugo Lonitz & Co. Haldensleben (1875)–1904	Hugo Lonitz und Hugo Lonitz & Co. Haldensleben (1875)–1904	335 **415**
E. Scharf Saalfeld after 1907–before 1945 decorator's mark overglaze	E. Scharf Saalfeld nach 1907–vor 1945 Malermarke aufglasur	336 **469**
J. Hering & Son Koppelsdorf after 1908–1945	J. Hering & Sohn Köppelsdorf nach 1908–1945	337 **431**
Saxonian Porcelain Factory Carl Thieme Potschappel (1876)–1888	Sächsische Porzellanfabrik Carl Thieme Potschappel (1876)–1888	338 **463**
J. Hering & Son Koppelsdorf after 1908–1945	J. Hering & Sohn Köppelsdorf nach 1908–1945	339 **431**
Slama & Co. Vienna 1959–	Slama & Co. Wien 1959–	340 **502**

BUTTERFLY

Geo. Borgfeldt & Co.	Geo. Borgfeldt & Co.	
New York City	New York	
1913–	1913–	341
importer's mark	Importeurmarke	**454**
Vienna Art Ceramic	Wierner Kunstkeramik	
Vienna	Wien	342
after 1906–	nach 1906–	**503**
Vienna Art Ceramic	Wiener Kunstkeramik	
Vienna	Wien	343
1898–1906	1898–1906	**503**
Saxonian Porcelain	Sächsische Porzellanfabrik	
Factory Carl Thieme	Carl Thieme	
Potschappel	Potschappel	
(1903)–	(1903)–	
blue underglaze or	blau unterglasur	344
overglaze	oder aufglasur	**463**
The Mosanic Pottery	The Mosanic Pottery	345
Mitterteich	Mitterteich	
(1905)–circa 1918	(1905)–ca. 1918	**450**
W. Goebel	W. Goebel	
Rodental	Rödental	
1950–1955	1950–1955	
black or blue or green	schwarz oder blau oder	346
or brown underglaze	grün oder braun unterglasur	**467**
W. Goebel	W. Goebel	
Rodental	Rödental	
1954–circa 1956	1954–ca. 1956	347
blue	blau	**467**
W. Goebel	W. Goebel	
Rodental	Rödental	
1957	1957	348
blue or black underglaze	blau oder schwarz unterglasur	**467**
W. Goebel	W. Goebel	
Rodental	Rödental	
1957	1957	349
blue or black underglaze	blau oder schwarz unterglasur	**467**
W. Goebel	W. Goebel	
Rodental	Rödental	
1958	1958	350
blue or black underglaze	blau oder schwarz unterglasur	**467**

W. Goebel	W. Goeble	
Rodental	Rödental	
1960–1972	1960–1972	351
blue or black underglaze	blau oder schwarz unterglasur	**467**

W. Goebel	W. Goebel	
Rodental	Rödental	
1972–present	1972–heute	352
blue underglaze	blau unterglasur	**467**

Haas & Czjzek	Haas & Czjzek	
Schlaggenwald	Schlaggenwald	
(1901)–	(1901)–	353
green underglaze	grün unterglasur	**472**

Black Forest Earthenware	Schwarzwälder Stein-	
Factory	gutfabrik	
Hornberg	Hornberg	
(1908)–	(1908)–	354
on earthenware	auf Steingut	**420**

Black Forest Earthenware	Schwarzwälder Stein-	
Factory	gutfabrik	
Hornberg	Hornberg	
(1906)–	(1906)–	355
on earthenware	auf Steingut	**420**

Black Forest Earthenware	Schwarzwälder Stein-	
Factory	gutfabrik	
Hornberg	Hornberg	
(1906)–	(1906)–	356
on earthenware	auf Steingut	**420**

Woldemar Adler	Woldemar Adler	
Berchtesgaden	Berchtesgaden	
1919–circa 1957	1919–ca. 1957	
decorator's mark	Malermarke	357
overglaze	aufglasur	**380**

Josef Sommer	Josef Sommer	
Garmisch-Partenkirchen	Garmisch-Partenkirchen	
1933–	1933–	
decorator's mark	Malermarke	358
overglaze	aufglasur	**406**

Porcelain Factory	Porzellanfabrik	
"Valkyrie"	"Walküre"	
Bayreuth	Bayreuth	359
(1928)-1948	(1928)-1948	**379**

Kronach Porcelain Factory Stockhardt & Schmidt-Eckert Kronach 1912–	Kronacher Porzellanfabrik Stockhardt & Schmict-Eckert Kronach 1912–	360 **434**
Menzl & Co. Aich 1918–1922 impressed or blue or green underglaze	Menzl & Co. Aich 1918–1922 eingeprägt oder blau oder grün unterglasur	361 **371**
Reinhold Schlegelmilch Tillowitz (1927)–circa 1938 green underglaze	Reinhold Schlegelmilch Tillowitz (1927)–ca. 1938 grün unterglasur	362 **488**
Fasold & Stauch Bock-Wallendorf 1953–1961 underglaze	Fasold & Stauch Bock-Wallendorf 1953–1961 unterglasur	363 **384**
Royal Porcelain Kups 1972– black	Royal Porzellan Küps 1972– schwarz	364 **434**
Adolf Schippel Eichwald 1894–	Adolf Schippel Eichwald 1894–	365 **397**
Eduard Bantz Kiel (1895)–	Eduard Bantz Kiel (1895)–	366 **427**
Haas & Czjzek Chodau 1918–1939	Haas & Czjzek Chodau 1918–1939	367 **389**
Porcelain Factory Schonwald Schonwald 1953–1972 green underglaze also in combination with: Fairwood (1957–1972)	Porzellanfabrik Schönwald Schönwald 1953–1972 grün unterglasur auch in Verbindung mit: Fairwood (1957–1972)	368 **475**

Porcelain Factory Schonwald Schonwald (1911)–circa 1927 green underglaze	Porzellanfabrik Schönwald Schönwald (1911)–ca. 1927 grün unterglasur	369 **475**
Porcelain Factory Schonwald Schonwald (1927)–	Porzellanfabrik Schönwald Schönwald (1927)–	370 **475**
Porcelain Factory Schonwald and E. & A. Muller Schonwald (1927)–	Porzellanfabrik Schönwald und E. & A. Müller Schönwald (1927)–	371 **475**
Porcelain Factory Schonwald and E. & A. Muller Schonwald circa 1930–circa 1945 green underglaze	Porzellanfabrik Schönwald und E. & A. Müller Schönwald ca. 1930–ca. 1945 grün unterglasur	372 **475**
Porcelain Factory Schonwald Schonwald circa 1925–circa 1927 green underglaze	Porzellanfabrik Schönwald Schönwald ca. 1925–ca. 1927 grün unterglasur	373 **475**
Haas & Czjzek Schlaggenwald 1918–1939 green underglaze	Haas & Czjzek Schlaggenwald 1918–1939 grün unterglasur	374 **472**
Haas & Czjzek Schlaggenwald after 1918–circa 1945 green	Haas & Czjzek Schlaggenwald nach 1918–ca. 1945 grün	375 **472**
VEB Thuringian Porce- lainworks Branch Konigsee Konigsee 1945–circa 1962	VEB Thüringer Porzel- lanwerke Betrieb Königsee Königsee 1945–ca. 1962	376 **430**
Christian Carstens Grafenroda (1927)–circa 1945	Christian Carstens Gräfenroda (1927)–ca. 1945	377 **410**

VEB Grafenroda Ceramic Grafenroda after 1945 on earthenware	VEB Gräfenroda Keramik Gräfenroda nach 1945 auf Steingut	378 **410**
Porcelain Factory Schonwald Schonwald (1968)—present green underglaze	Porzellanfabrik Schönwald Schönwald (1968)—heute grün unterglasur	379 **475**
J. S. Maier & Comp. Poschetzau circa 1939—1945	J. S. Maier & Comp. Poschetzau ca. 1939—1945	380 **463**
Porcelain Factory Schonwald Schonwald 1972—present green underglaze	Porzellanfabrik Schönwald Schönwald 1972—heute grün unterglasur	381 **475**
Porcelain Factory Schonwald Schonwald 1972—present green underglaze	Porzellanfabrik Schönwald Schönwald 1972—heute grün unterglasur	382 **475**
Wilhelm Diebener Gotha (1954)—circa 1964 on earthenware	Wilhelm Diebener Gotha (1954)—ca. 1964 auf Steingut	383 **409**
Haas & Czjzek Chodau circa 1939—1945	Haas & Czjzek Chodau circa 1939—1945	384 **389**
Kampfe & List Neuhaus on Rennweg (1887)—circa 1900	Kämpfe & List Neuhaus am Rennweg (1887)—ca. 1900	385 **452**
J. Schnabel & Son Dessendorf circa 1900—circa 1931	J. Schnabel & Sohn Dessendorf ca. 1900—ca. 1931	386 **393**

Johann Glatz	Johann Glatz	
Villingen	Villingen	387
(1883)–1924	(1883)–1924	**494**
Egon Stein	Egon Stein	
Tellnitz	Tellnitz	388
1902–1940	1902–1940	**486**
VEB Thuringian Porce-	VEB Thüringer Porzel-	
lainworks	lanwerke	
Gehren	Gehren	389
1947–1969	1947–1969	**406**
Villeroy & Boch	Villeroy & Boch	
Schramberg	Schramberg	390
(1895)–1912	(1895)–1912	**476**
VEB Thuringian Porce-	VEB Thüringer Porzel-	
lainworks	lanwerke	
Gehren	Gehren	
(1951)–circa 1958	(1951)–ca. 1958	
green underglaze or	grün unterglasur oder	391
overglaze	aufglasur	**406**
Otto Herrmann Spindler	Otto Herrmann Spindler	
Frauenwald	Frauenwald	392
after 1898–	nach 1898–	**403**
Krister Porcelain	Krister Porzellan-	
Manufactory	manufaktur	
Waldenburg	Waldenburg	393
(1902)–1913	(1902)–1913	**497**
Haas & Czjzek	Haas & Czjzek	
Chodau	Chodau	394
1905–	1905–	**389**
Arno Apel	Arno Apel	
Ebersdorf	Ebersdorf	
1954–1957	1954–1957	395
gold overglaze	gold aufglasur	**397**

Donath & Co.
Dresden
1872–1916
decorator's mark
gold overglaze, used to
cover original manu-
facturers mark, usually
accompanied by one of
Donath's marks

Donath & Co.
Dresden
1872–1916
Malermarke
gold aufglasur, benutzt,
um die Herstellermarke
zu verdecken, gewöhnlich
zusammen mit einer
Donath-Marke

396
394

Grossbaum & Sons
Dresden
1892–1914
decorator's mark
gold overglaze, used to
cover original manu-
facturers mark, usually
accompanied by one of
Grossbaum's marks

Grossbaum & Söhne
Dresden
1892–1914
Malermarke
gold aufglasur, benutzt,
um die Herstellermarke
zu verdecken, gewöhnlich
zusammen mit einer
Grossbaum-Marke

397
394

Franziska Hirsch
Dresden
1894–1930
decorator's mark
gold overglaze, used to
cover original manu-
facturer's mark, usually
accompanied by one of
the Hirsch marks

Franziska Hirsch
Dresden
1894–1930
Malermarke
gold aufglasur, benutzt,
um die Herstellermarke
zu verdecken, gewöhnlich
zusammen mit einer
Hirsch-Marke

398
395

Helena Wolfsohn
Dresden
circa 1880–1945
decorator's mark
gold overglaze, used to
cover original manu-
facturer's mark, usually
accompanied by one of
Wolfsohn's marks

Helena Wolfsohn
Dresden
ca. 1880–1945
Malermarke
gold aufglasur, benutzt,
um die Herstellermarke
zu verdecken, gewöhnlich
zusammen mit einer
Wolfsohn-Marke

399
396

Saxonian Porcelain
Factory Carl Thieme
Potschappel
circa 1888–circa 1901
decorator's mark
gold overglaze, used to
cover original manu-
facturer's mark, usually
accompanied by one of
Thieme's marks

Sächsische Porzellan-
fabrik Carl Thieme
Potschappel
ca. 1888–ca. 1901
Malermarke
gold aufglasur, benutzt,
um die Herstellermarke
zu verdecken, gewöhnlich
zusammen mit einer
Thieme-Marke

400
463

Richard Wehsener
Dresden
decorator´s mark
gold overglaze, used to
cover original manu-
facturers mark

Richard Wehsener
Dresden
Malermarke
gold aufglasur, benutzt
um die Herstellermarke 401
zu verdecken **396**

Royal Porcelain Manufactory
Meissen
circa 1717–circa 1724
blue underglaze

Königliche Porzellan Manufaktur
Meißen
ca. 1717–ca. 1724 402
blau unterglasur **446**

Jaeger & Co.
Marktredwitz
1912-before 1979
on hotel porcelain
green underglaze

Jaeger & Co.
Marktredwitz
1912-vor 1979
auf Hotelporzellan 403
grün unterglasur **444**

Jaeger & Co.
Marktredwitz
(1911)-circa 1917
green underglaze
mark for U.S. importer
possibly Geo. Borgfelt
in New York City

Jaeger & Co.
Marktredwitz
(1911)-ca. 1917
grün unterglasur
Marke für US-Importeur
möglicherweise Geo. 404
Borgfelt in New York **444**

Jaeger & Co.
Marktredwitz
(1902)-before 1979
green underglaze

Jaeger & Co.
Marktredwitz
(1902)-before 1979 405
grün unterglasur **444**

Jaeger, Thomas & Co.
Marktredwitz
1898–1902
green underglaze

Jaeger, Thomas & Co.
Marktredwitz
1898–1902 406
grün unterglasur **444**

Ernst March Sons
Berlin
(1899)–1904
on earthen- and stone-
ware

Ernst March Söhne
Berlin
(1899)–1904
auf Steingut und 407
Steinzeug **382**

Dr. Norbert Baratta
Vienna/Poltar
circa 1920–circa 1930

Dr. Norbert Baratta
Wien/Poltar 408
ca. 1920–ca. 1930 **501**

Dr. Norbert Baratta Vienna/Poltar circa 1920–circa 1930	Dr. Norbert Baratta Wien/Poltar ca. 1920–ca. 1930	409 **501**
Porcelain Factory Waldsassen Waldsassen (1920)-before 1993	Porzellanfabrik Waldsassen Waldsassen (1920)-vor 1993	410 **498**
Porcelain Factory Waldsassen Waldsassen (1920)-before 1993	Porzellanfabrik Waldsassen Waldsassen (1920)-vor 1993	411 **498**
Moritz Zdekauer Altrohlau circa 1884–1909	Moritz Zdekauer Altrohlau ca. 1884–1909	412 **373**
C. Tielsch & Co. Altwasser (1895)–circa 1918 blue underglaze or red overglaze	C. Tielsch & Co. Altwasser (1895)–ca. 1918 blau unterglasur oder rot aufglasur	413 **374**
Joseph Schachtel Charlottenbrunn (1896)–circa 1919	Joseph Schachtel Charlottenbrunn (1896)–ca. 1919	414 **389**
Oespag Wilhelmsburg 1959–present	Oespag Wilhelmsburg 1959–heute	415 **504**
Rosenthal Selb 1908–1953 blue or green underglaze or red overglaze also in combination with: Bahnhof Selb	Rosenthal Selb 1908–1953 blau oder grün unter- glasur oder rot aufglasur auch in Verbindung mit: Bahnhof Selb	416 **480**
Rosenthal Selb (1933)–	Rosenthal Selb (1933)–	417 **480**

Rosenthal	Rosenthal	
Selb	Selb	
1969–present	1969–heute	418
green underglaze	grün unterglasur	**480**

Richard S. Rosler	Richard S. Rösler	
Schauberg	Schauberg	419
1948–present	1948–heute	**471**

Alfred Stellmacher	Alfred Stellmacher	
Turn-Teplitz	Turn-Teplitz	420
after 1859–1897	nach 1859–1897	**490**

Ernst Wahliss	Ernst Wahliss	
Turn-Teplitz	Turn-Teplitz	421
(1894)–circa 1921	(1894)–ca. 1921	**491**

Reinhold Bosdorf	Reinhold Bosdorf	
Teplitz-Schonau	Teplitz-Schönau	
circa 1930	ca. 1930	
decorator's mark	Malermarke	422
overglaze	aufglasur	**486**

unidentified	nicht identifiziert	423
gold overglaze	gold aufglasur	

Porcelain Factory	Porzellanfabrik	
Freiwaldau Bing AG	Freiwaldau Bing AG	
Freiwaldau	Freiwaldau	424
1923–circa 1929	1923–ca. 1929	**405**

Porcelain Factory Mitterteich	Porzellanfabrik Mitterteich	
Mitterteich	Mitterteich	425
1923-circa 1931	1923-ca. 1931	**450**

Porcelain Factory Mitterteich	Porzellanfabrik Mitterteich	
Mitterteich	Mitterteich	426
(1931)–circa 1945	(1931)–ca. 1945	**450**

Porcelain Factory Mitterteich Mitterteich 1931-	Porzellanfabrik Mitterteich Mitterteich 1931-	427	**427**
Porcelain Factory Mitterteich Mitterteich after 1918— gold and blue overglaze or blue underglaze	Porzellanfabrik Mitterteich Mitterteich nach 1918— gold und blau aufglasur oder blau unterglasur	428	**450**
Max Roesler Rodach (1894)— with "Rodach" or "Darmstadt" for the Roesler factories in those cities	Max Roesler Rodach (1894)— mit "Rodach" oder "Darmstadt" für die Roesler-Fabriken in diesen Städten	429	**467**
Retsch & Co. Wunsiedel (1919)—	Retsch & Co. Wunsiedel (1919)—	430	**506**
Saxonian Porcelain Factory Carl Thieme Potschappel (1913)—	Sächsische Porzellan- fabrik Carl Thieme Potschappel (1913)—	431	**463**
Grandducal Maiolica Manufactory Karlsruhe 1904—1927	Großherzogliche Majolika Manufaktur Karlsruhe 1904—1927	432	**426**
Oscar Schlegelmilch Langewiesen after 1892—	Oscar Schlegelmilch Langewiesen nach 1892—	433	**436**
Porcelain Factory Merkelsgrun Merkelsgrun 1918—1939	Porzellanfabrik Merkelsgrün Merkelsgrün 1918—1939	434	**448**
Retsch & Co. Wunsiedel 1950—	Retsch & Co. Wunsiedel 1950—	435	**506**

Porcelain Factory Schirnding Schirnding 1948–1974 underglaze	Porzellanfabrik Schirnding Schirnding 1948–1974 unterglasur	436	**472**
Porcelain Factory Merkelsgrun Merkelsgrun 1912–1918 green underglaze	Porzellanfabrik Merkelsgrün Merkelsgrün 1912–1918 grün unterglasur	437	**448**
Porcelain Factory Schirnding Schirnding 1974–present underglaze	Porzellanfabrik Schirnding Schirnding 1974–heute unterglasur	438	**472**
Gareis, Kuhnl & Cie. Waldsassen after 1899–circa 1969	Gareis, Kühnl & Cie. Waldsassen nach 1899–ca. 1969	439	**498**
Porcelain Factory Merkelsgrun Merkelsgrun 1912–1918	Porzellanfabrik Merkelsgrün Merkelsgrün 1912–1918	440	**448**
R. & E. Haidinger Elbogen circa 1850–1873	R. & E. Haidinger Elbogen ca. 1850–1873	441	**400**
Plastographic Company Vienna/Ladowitz (1899)–	Plastographische Gesellschaft Wien/Ladowitz (1899)–	442	**502**
Porcelain Factory Lower Rhine Rees (1955)–before 1964	Porzellanfabrik Niederrhein Rees (1955)–vor 1964	443	**465**
Sauer & Roloff Haldensleben (1908)–	Sauer & Roloff Haldensleben (1908)–	444	**415**

Porcelain Factory Gunthersfeld Gehren (1930)–1945	Porzellanfabrik Günthersfeld Gehren (1930)–1945	445 **406**
Krautzberger, Mayer & Purkert Wistritz after 1911–circa 1945	Krautzberger, Mayer & Purkert Wistritz nach 1911–ca. 1945	446 **506**
Earthenware Factory Grunstadt Grunstadt 20th century	Steingutfabrik Grünstadt Grünstadt 20. Jahrhundert	447 **413**
Hermann Voigt Schaala (1880)–1938	Hermann Voigt Schaala (1880)–1938	448 **470**
Hermann Voigt Schaala (1880)–1938	Hermann Voigt Schaala (1880)–1938	449 **470**
Dux Porcelain Manufactory Dux (1918)–1945	Duxer Porzellanmanufaktur Dux (1918)–1945	450 **397**
Duchcov Porcelain Dux (1947)–present	Duchcovsky Porcelan Dux (1947)–heute	451 **397**
Duchcov Porcelain Dux (1953)–present	Duchcovsky Porcelan Dux (1953)–heute	452 **397**
Dux Porcelain Manufactory Dux after 1912–	Duxer Porzellanmanufaktur Dux nach 1912–	453 **397**
Dux Porcelain Manufactory Dux after 1912–	Duxer Porzellanmanufaktur Dux nach 1912–	454 **397**

Gotthelf Greiner Grossbreitenbach 1782–1788 blue underglaze	Gotthelf Greiner Großbreitenbach 1782–1788 blau unterglasur	455 **412**
Gotthelf Greiner Ilmenau 1786–1792 blue underglaze	Gotthelf Greiner Ilmenau 1786–1792 blau unterglasur	456 457 **421**
Gotthelf Greiner and G. Greiner's Sons Limbach 1787–circa 1850	Gotthelf Greiner und G. Greiners Söhne Limbach 1787–ca. 1850	458 **439**
Gotthelf Greiner Limbach circa 1787–circa 1797 purple or green or gold or black overglaze	Gotthelf Greiner Limbach ca. 1787–ca. 1797 purpur oder grün oder gold oder schwarz aufglasur	459 **439**
Gotthelf Greiner Limbach circa 1787–circa 1797 blue underglaze	Gotthelf Greiner Limbach ca. 1787–ca. 1797 blau unterglasur	460 **439**
Gotthelf Greiner and G. Greiner's Sons Limbach 1787–circa 1850 blue underglaze, purple or green or gold or black overglaze	Gotthelf Greiner und G. Greiners Söhne Limbach 1787–ca. 1850 blau unterglasur, purpur oder grün oder gold oder schwarz aufglasur	461 **439**
Gotthelf Greiner and G. Greiner's Sons Limbach 1787–circa 1850 blue underglaze, purple or green or gold or black overglaze	Gotthelf Greiner und G. Greiners Söhne Limbach 1787–ca. 1850 blau unterglasur, purpur oder grün oder gold oder schwarz aufglasur	462 **439**
same as 462	wie 462	463 **439**
same as 462	wie 462	464 **439**

Gotthelf Greiner and
G. Greiner's Sons
Limbach
1787–circa 1850
blue underglaze, purple
or green or gold or
black overglaze

Gotthelf Greiner und
G. Greiners Söhne
Limbach
1787–ca. 1850
blau unterglasur, purpur
oder grün oder gold oder   465
schwarz aufglasur   **439**

Family Greiner
Kloster Veilsdorf
1797–circa 1822
blue underglaze

Familie Greiner
Kloster Veilsdorf
1797–ca. 1822   466
blau unterglasur   **429**

Family Greiner
Kloster Veilsdorf
1797–circa 1822
blue underglaze

Familie Greiner
Kloster Veilsdorf
1797–ca. 1822   467
blau unterglasur   **429**

Family Greiner   Familie Greiner   468
Kloster Veilsdorf   Kloster Veilsdorf   469
1797–circa 1853   1797–ca. 1853   470
blue underglaze   blau unterglasur   **429**

G. Greiner's Sons
Grossbreitenbach
circa 1820
blue underglaze

G. Greiners Söhne
Großbreitenbach
ca. 1820   471
blau unterglasur   **412**

H. Buhl & Sons
Grossbreitenbach
after 1887–

H. Bühl & Söhne
Großbreitenbach   472
nach 1887–   **412**

Annaburg Earthenware
Factory
Annaburg
before 1924–1945
on earthenware

Annaburger Steingut-
fabrik
Annaburg
vor 1924–1945   473
auf Steingut   **375**

Porcelain Factory Limbach
Limbach
(1887)–circa 1919
blue

Porzellanfabrik Limbach
Limbach
(1887)–ca. 1919   474
blau   **439**

Gotthelf Greiner and
G. Greiner's Sons
Limbach
1787–circa 1850
blue underglaze, purple
or green or gold or
black overglaze

Gotthelf Greiner und
G. Greiners Söhne
Limbach
1787–ca. 1850
blau unterglasur, purpur
oder grün oder gold oder   475
schwarz aufglasur   **439**

Porcelain Factory Limbach
Limbach
after 1887–circa 1919
blue or green

Porzellanfabrik Limbach
Limbach
nach 1887–ca. 1919   476
blau oder grün   **439**

Porcelain Factory Limbach
Limbach
after 1887–circa 1919
blue or green

Porzellanfabrik Limbach
Limbach
nach 1887–ca. 1919   477
blau oder grün   **439**

Porcelain Factory Limbach
Limbach
(1919)–1944
blue or green

Porzellanfabrik Limbach
Limbach
(1919)–1944   478
blau oder grün   **439**

Porcelain Factory Limbach
Limbach
(1919)–1944
blue or green

Porzellanfabrik Limbach
Limbach
(1919)–1944   479
blau oder grün   **439**

VEB Porcelainwork Freienorla
Freienorla
circa 1946–circa 1958
Christian Nonne
Volkstedt
1800-1830
overglaze blob to the right to
cover crossed forks

VEB Porzellanwerk Freienorla
Freienorla   480
ca. 1946–ca. 1958   **404**
Christian Nonne
Volkstedt
1800-1830
aufglasur Übermalung rechts   481
verdeckt gekreuzte Gabeln   **494**

Ley & Weidermann
Haldensleben
after 1882–
on earthenware

Ley & Weidermann
Haldensleben
nach 1882–   482
auf Steingut   **415**

H. Buhl & Sons Grossbreitenbach (1896)–1932	H. Bühl & Söhne Großbreitenbach (1896)–1932	483	**412**
Rudolf Kammer Volkstedt 1953–1972	Rudolf Kämmer Volkstedt 1953–1972	484	**496**
Brux Porcelain Manufactory Brux 1924–1939	Brüxer Porzellanmanufaktur Brüx 1924–1939	485	**387**
Anton Heller Turn-Teplitz (1889)–circa 1920	Anton Heller Turn-Teplitz (1889)–ca. 1920	486	**490**
United Porcelainworks and VEB Special Porcelain Eisenberg 1960-1972	Vereinigte Porzellanwerke und VEB Spezialporzellan Eisenberg 1960-1972	487	**398**
Sebastian Schmidt Schmiedefeld (1892)– and Eberhard Suhr Rudolstadt (1906)–	Sebastian Schmidt Schmiedefeld (1892)– und Eberhard Suhr Rudolstadt (1906)–	488	**474**
VEB Porcelainworks Konigsee and Garsitz Konigsee (1964)–1968	VEB Porzellanwerke Königsee und Garsitz Königsee (1964)–1968	489	**430**
Paul Rauschert Steinwiesen 1971–present black/red	Paul Rauschert Steinwiesen 1971–heute schwarz/rot	490	**485**
C. G. Schierholz & Son and Von Schierholz Porcelain Manufactory Plaue (1907)–1927 green or blue underglaze	C. G. Schierholz & Sohn und Von Schierholzsche Porzellanmanufaktur Plaue (1907)–1927 grün oder blau unterglasur	491	**462**

Von Schierholz Porcelain Manufactory Plaue anniversary mark 1967	Von Schierholzsche Porzellanmanufaktur Plaue Jubiläumsmarke 1967	492 **462**
Von Schierholz Porcelain Manufactory Plaue 1907-1972 blue or green underglaze	Von Schierholzsche Porzellanmanufaktur Plaue 1907-1972 blau oder grün unterglasur	493 **462**
Von Schierholz Porcelain Manufactory 1912-1972 blue or green underglaze	Von Schierholzsche Porzellanmanufaktur 1912-1972 blau oder grün unterglasur	494 **462**
Von Schierholz Porcelain Manufactory Plaue 1951–1972 green or blue underglaze	Von Schierholzsche Porzellanmanufaktur Plaue 1051–1972 grün oder blau unterglasur	495 **462**
C. G. Schierholz & Son and Von Schierholz Porcelain Manufactory Plaue (1907)–1927 green or blue underglaze	C. G. Schierholz & Sohn und Von Schierholzsche Porzellanmanufaktur Plaue (1907)–1927 grün or blau unterglasur	496 **462**
Heinrich & Co. Selb 1907–1911 blue or green underglaze	Heinrich & Co. Selb 1907–1911 blau oder grün unterglasur	497 **479**
Paepke & Schafer Haida circa 1930 decorator's mark overglaze	Paepke & Schäfer Haida ca. 1930 Malermarke aufglasur	498 **414**

Julius Dressler
Biela
(1900)–circa 1945

Julius Dressler
Biela
(1900)–ca. 1945

499

383

Sauer & Roloff
Haldensleben
(1908)–

Sauer & Roloff
Haldensleben
(1908)–

500

415

Alboth & Kaiser
Staffelstein
1927–circa 1953

Alboth & Kaiser
Staffelstein
1927–ca. 1953

501

484

Porcelain Factory Kahla
Kahla
(1938)–1945

Porzellanfabrik Kahla
Kahla
(1938)–1945

502

423

Carl Knoll
Fischern
(1916)–1918
green underglaze

Carl Knoll
Fischern
(1916)–1918
grün unterglasur

503

402

Carl Knoll
Fischern
(1916)–1918
green underglaze

Carl Knoll
Fischern
(1916)–1918
grün unterglasur

504

402

Porcelain Factory Waldsassen
Waldsassen
1966 anniversary mark
green underglaze

Porzellanfabrik Waldsassen
Waldsassen
1966 Jubiläumsmarke
grün unterglasur

505

498

Wachtersbach Earthenware
Factory
Schlierbach
1903–1921
mark of art department
different colors

Wächtersbacher Steingut-
fabrik
Schlierbach
1903–1921
Marke der Kunstabteilung
verschiedene Farben

506

473

Zeh, Scherzer & Co.
Rehau
(1882)–circa 1929

Zeh, Scherzer & Co.
Rehau
(1882)–ca. 1929

507

466

J. F. Lenz
Zell on Harmersbach
circa 1830
on earthenware

J. F. Lenz
Zell am Harmersbach
ca. 1830
auf Steingut

508

507

Erdmann Schlegelmilch
Suhl
circa 1900

Erdmann Schlegelmilch
Suhl
ca. 1900

509

485

Wachtersbach Earthenware
Factory
Schlierbach
1860–1865
black

Wächtersbacher Steingut-
fabrik
Schlierbach
1860–1865
schwarz

510

473

Royal Porcelain Manufactory
Ludwigsburg
1810–1816
gold overglaze.

Königliche Porzellan Manufaktur
Ludwigsburg
1810–1816
gold aufglasur

511

441

VEB Porcelainwork Lettin
Lettin
(1954)-1990

VEB Porzellanwerk Lettin
Lettin
(1954)-1990

512

438

Reinhold Schlegelmilch
Tillowitz/Suhl
(1904)–
green underglaze

Reinhold Schlegelmilch
Tillowitz/Suhl
(1904)–
grün unterglasur

513

489

unidentified
imitation of mark no.
513
red overglaze
possibly American after
1945

nicht identifiziert
Nachahmung der Marke
513
rot aufglasur
möglicherweise amerika-
nisch nach 1945

514

Reinhold Schlegelmilch
Tillowitz/Suhl
after 1904–circa 1938
green/red

Reinhold Schlegelmilch
Tillowitz/Suhl
nach 1904–ca. 1938
grün/rot

515

489

"Cottonplant"	Reinhold Schlegelmilch Tillowitz/Suhl after 1904—circa 1938 mark for U. S. importer	Reinhold Schlegelmilch Tillowitz/Suhl nach 1904—ca. 1938 516 Marke für US-Importeur **489**
	Reinhold Schlegelmilch Tillowitz/Suhl after 1904—circa 1938 mark for export to U. S. A.	Reinhold Schlegelmilch Tillowitz/Suhl nach 1904—ca. 1938 517 Marke für Export nach den USA **489**
	Reinhold Schlegelmilch Tillowitz 1919—1921 green/red/gold	Reinhold Schlegelmilch Tillowitz 1919—1921 518 grün/rot/gold **489**
	Reinhold Schlegelmilch Tillowitz after 1904—circa 1938	Reinhold Schlegelmilch Tillowitz 519 nach 1904—ca. 1938 **489**
	Reinhold Schlegelmilch Tillowitz (1904)—circa 1938 green	Reinhold Schlegelmilch Tillowitz (1904)—ca. 1938 520 grün **489**
rdmann Reinhold	Erdmann & Reinhold Schlegelmilch Suhl/Tillowitz 1911 anniversary mark	Erdmann & Reinhold Schlegelmilch Suhl/Tillowitz 1911 521 Jubiläumsmarke **485**
Suhl.	Reinhold Schlegelmilch Tillowitz/Suhl (1904)—1932 green	Reinhold Schlegelmilch Tillowitz/Suhl (1904)—1932 522 grün **489**
TILLOWITZ Silesia	Reinhold Schlegelmilch Tillowitz after 1904—circa 1938 green	Reinhold Schlegelmilch Tillowitz nach 1904—ca. 1938 523 grün **489**
	VEB Porcelainwork "Weimar Porzellan" Blankenhain (1975)-1990	VEB Porzellanwerk "Weimar Porzellan" Blankenhain 524 (1975)-1990 **384**

C. & E. Carstens and
VEB Porcelainwork
"Weimar Porcelain"
Blankenhain
(1933)-circa 1975

C. & E. Carstens und
VEB Porzellanwerk
"Weimar-Porzellan"
Blankenhain
(1933)-ca. 1975

525
384

Stadtilm Porcelain
Factory
Stadtilm
(1961)–1972

Stadtilmer Porzellan-
fabrik
Stadtilm
(1961)–1972

526
483

Porcelain Factory Tirschenreuth
Tirschenreuth
after 1903–
green underglaze

Porzellanfabrik Tirschenreuth
Tirschenreuth
nach 1903–
grün unterglasur

527
489

Porcelain Factory Kalk
Eisenberg
after 1945–1972
green underglaze

Porzellanfabrik Kalk
Eisenberg
nach 1945–1972
grün unterglasur

528
398

Bros. Heubach
Lichte
(1894)–

Gebr. Heubach
Lichte
(1894)–

529
438

Hadrich & Son
Reichenbach
after 1903–circa 1950
decorator's mark
overglaze

Hädrich & Sohn
Reichenbach
nach 1903–ca. 1950
Malermarke
aufglasur

530
466

Oscar Gustav Schade
Dresden
(1894)–
decorator's mark
overglaze

Oscar Gustav Schade
Dresden
(1894)–
Malermarke
aufglasur

531
395

Unger & Schilde and
VEB Porcelainwork Gera-
Roschutz
Roschutz
(1906)-1953

Unger & Schilde und
VEB Porzellanwerk Gera-
Roschütz
Roschütz
(1906)-1953

532
468

Beyer & Bock Volkstedt (1927)–1960 blue overglaze or underglaze	Beyer & Bock Volkstedt (1927)–1960 blau aufglasur oder unterglasur	**533** **496**
Porcelain Factory Moschendorf Hof-Moschendorf (1904)–1938 green	Porzellanfabrik Moschendorf Hof-Moschendorf (1904)–1938 grün	**534** **419**
Porcelain Manufactory Pressig Pressig (1953)–	Porzellanmanufaktur Pressig Pressig (1953)–	**535** **464**
C. & E. Carstens Reichenbach –1948 green	C. & E. Carstens Reichenbach –1948 grün	**536** **466**
Reichenbacher Porcelain Factory and VEB Porcelainwork Reichenbach (1949)-1969 green	Reichenbacher Porzellanfabrik und VEB Porcelainwork Reichenbach (1949)-1969 grün	**537** **466**
VEB Porcelainwork Reichenbach Reichenbach 1969-1900 similar to no. 537 except for VEB instead of crown on top of wreath green	VEB Porzellanwerk Reichenbach Reichenbach 1969-1900 ähnlich wie Nr. 537 aber mit VEB anstelle der Krone über dem Kranz grün	**538** **466**
Bros. Winterling Roslau 1906–	Gebr. Winterling Röslau 1906–	**539** **468**
Heinrich Winterling Marktleuthen 1903–1945 green underglaze	Heinrich Winterling Marktleuthen 1903–1945 grün unterglasur	**540** **444**

Porcelain-Union
Klosterle
1921–1927
with "T" instead of "K"
for factory in Turn-Teplitz

Porzellan-Union
Klösterle
1921–1927
mit "T" anstelle von "K"   541
für Fabrik in Turn-Teplitz   **428**

Geo. Borgfeldt Co.
New York City
        –circa 1978
importer's mark

Geo. Borgfeldt Co.
New York
        –ca. 1978   542
Importeurmarke   **454**

unidentified
gold overglaze

nicht identifiziert   543
gold aufglasur

Josef Rieber & Co.
Mitterteich
after 1923–

Josef Rieber & Co.
Mitterteich   544
nach 1923–   **449**

C. & E. Carstens
Sorau
1918–circa 1945

C. & E. Carstens
Sorau   545
1918–ca. 1945   **482**

Dressel, Kister & Cie.
Passau
circa 1907–1922

Dressel, Kister & Cie.
Passau   546
ca. 1907–1922   **460**

VEB Porcelainwork Weisswasser
Weisswasser
(1957)-1990

VEB Porzellanwerk Weißwasser
Weißwasser   547
(1957)-1990   **500**

Georg Schmider
Zell on Harmersbach
(1898)–after 1910
on earthenware

Georg Schmider
Zell am Harmersbach
(1898)–nach 1910   548
auf Steingut   **507**

Georg Schmider Zell on Harmersbach presently on earthenware	Georg Schmider Zell am Harmersbach heute auf Steingut	549 **507**
J. Kratzer & Sons Haindorf after 1880–1945	J. Kratzer & Söhne Haindorf nach 1880–1945	550 **414**
Porcelain Factory Weisswasser Weisswasser circa 1919–1945	Porzellanfabrik Weißwasser Weißwasser ca. 1919–1945	551 **500**
Matthes & Ebel and Max Josef Heim Mabendorf (1928)–1937	Matthes & Ebel und Max Josef Heim Mäbendorf (1928)–1937	552 **442**
Epiag Altrohlau 1920–1945 green underglaze	Epiag Altrohlau 1920–1945 grün unterglasur	553 **374**
Oepiag Altrohlau 1918–1920 green underglaze	Oepiag Altrohlau 1918–1920 grün unterglasur	554 **374**
Epiag Altrohlau 1920–1939 green underglaze	Epiag Altrohlau 1920–1939 grün unterglasur	555 **374**
Epiag Altrohlau 1928–1939 green	Epiag Altrohlau 1928–1939 grün	556 **374**
Epiag Altrohlau 1939–1945 green	Epiag Altrohlau 1939–1945 grün	557 **374**

Oscar & Edgar Gutherz	Oscar & Edgar Gutherz		
Altrohlau	Altrohlau		
1899–1918	1899–1918	558	
green	grün	**374**	

unidentified	nicht identifiziert	
probably Bohemia	wahrscheinlich Böhmen	
before 1918	vor 1918	559
red overglaze	rot aufglasur	

Georg Schmider	Georg Schmider	
Zell on Harmersbach	Zell am Harmersbach	
presently	heute	560
on earthenware	auf Steingut	**507**

Oscar Schaller & Co.	Oscar Schaller & Co.	
Successor	Nachf.	
Schwarzenbach	Schwarzenbach	561
after 1918–	nach 1918–	**477**

Strobel & Wilken	Strobel & Wilken	
New York City	New York	
circa 1900–1914	ca. 1900–1914	
gold overglaze	gold aufglasur	
on Bohemian porcelain	auf böhmischem Porzellan	562
made for Strobel & Wilken	für Strobel & Wilken hergestellt	**456**

Paepke & Schafer	Paepke & Schäfer	
Haida	Haida	
circa 1930	ca. 1930	
decorator's mark	Malermarke	563
overglaze	aufglasur	**414**

VEB Porcelainwork Reichenbach	VEB Porzellanwerk Reichenbach	
Reichenbach	Reichenbach	564
1969-1990	1969-1990	**466**

August Schweig	August Schweig	
Weisswasser	Weißwasser	565
1895–circa 1940	1895–ca. 1940	**500**

Rosenthal	Rosenthal	
Selb	Selb	566
(1956)–	(1956)–	**480**

VEB Porcelainwork Triptis	VEB Porzellanwerk Triptis	
Triptis	Triptis	567
(1949)–circa 1959	(1949)–ca. 1959	**489**

Riessner, Stellmacher and Kessel Turn-Teplitz 1892–1905	Riessner, Stellmacher und Kessel Turn-Teplitz 1892–1905	568	**489**
Bros. Redlhammer Gablonz (1894)–	Gebr. Redlhammer Gablonz (1894)–	569	**406**
Eichhorn & Bandorf Elgersburg (1895)–1905	Eichhorn & Bandorf Elgersburg (1895)–1905	570	**400**
Sontag & Sons Geiersthal (1898)–1908 decorator's mark overglaze	Sontag & Söhne Geiersthal (1898)–1908 Malermarke aufglasur	571	**406**
J. von Schwarz Nuremberg (1901)–	J. von Schwarz Nürnberg (1901)–	572	**457**
Oldest Volkstedt Porcelain Factory Volkstedt 1894– blue	Aelteste Volkstedter Porzellanfabrik Volkstedt 1894– blau	573	**494**
Porcelain Factory Jokes Jokes 1914–1945	Porzellanfabrik Jokes Jokes 1914–1945	574	**423**
Porcelain Factory Muhlbach Bruchmuhlbach 1951–circa 1970	Porzellanfabrik Mühlbach Bruchmühlbach 1951–ca. 1970	575	**386**
Porcelain Factory Bavaria Ullersricht (1926)–circa 1932	Porzellanfabrik Bavaria Ullersricht (1926)–ca. 1932	576	**491**

Upper Franconian Porcelain Factory Kups after 1900–1919	Oberfränkische Porzellanfabrik Küps nach 1900–1919	577 **434**
Bros. Heubach Lichte after 1882–	Gebr. Heubach Lichte nach 1882–	578 **438**
Bros. Heubach Lichte (1882)–	Gebr. Heubach Lichte (1882)–	579 **438**
Bros. Heubach Lichte (1882)–	Gebr. Heubach Lichte (1882)–	580 **438**
Bros. Heubach Lichte after 1882–	Gebr. Heubach Lichte nach 1882–	581 **438**
Ernst Heubach Koppelsdorf —circa 1919 on dolls heads	Ernst Heubach Köppelsdorf —ca. 1919 auf Puppenköpfen	582 **432**
VEB Porcelainwork Lichte Lichte 1954-circa 1972	VEB Porzellanwerk Lichte Lichte 1954-ca. 1972	583 **438**
unidentified blue overglaze	nicht identifiziert blau aufglasur	584

Porcelain Factory Lettin Lettin circa 1930–before 1945	Porzellanfabrik Lettin Lettin ca. 1930–vor 1945	585 **438**
Oldest Volkstedt Porcelain Factory Volkstedt 1895– blue	Aelteste Volkstedter Porzellanfabrik Volkstedt 1895– blau	586 **494**
C. H. Tuppack Tiefenfurth 1922–1935	C. H. Tuppack Tiefenfurth 1922–1935	587 **488**
Morgenroth & Co. Gotha (1887)–1918	Morgenroth & Co. Gotha (1887)–1918	588 **410**
Bros. Stauch Rudolstadt after 1900–1934	Gebr. Stauch Rudolstadt nach 1900–1934	589 **469**
Carl Spitz Brux (1909)–circa 1945	Carl Spitz Brüx (1909)–ca. 1945	590 **387**
Carl Spitz Brux (1909)–1918	Carl Spitz Brüx (1909)–1918	591 **387**
Lindner Porcelain Factory Kups 1948–present blue underglaze or overglaze	Lindner Porzellanfabrik Küps 1948–heute blau unterglasur oder aufglasur	592 **434**
Porcelainwork Auma Auma 1955–1972	Porzellanwerk Auma Auma 1955–1972	593 **377**

Porcelain Factory Lettin Lettin circa 1930−circa 1945	Porzellanfabrik Lettin Lettin ca. 1930−ca. 1945	594 **438**
Porcelain Factory Mengersreuth Mengersreuth circa 1915−circa 1930	Porzellanfabrik Mengersreuth Mengersreuth ca. 1915−ca. 1930	595 **448**
H. Schomburg & Sons Grossdubrau (1919)−1929	H. Schomburg & Söhne Großdubrau (1919)−1929	596 **413**
VEB Porcelainwork Lichte and VEB Decorative Por- celainworks Lichte Lichte (1958)-1990 blue	VEB Porzellanwerk Lichte und VEB Zierporzellan- werke Lichte Lichte (1958)-1990 blau	597 **438**
Bros. Heubach Lichte after 1909−circa 1945	Gebr. Heubach Lichte nach 1909−ca. 1945	598 **438**
F. & W. Goebel Rodental/Oeslau 1871−1890	F. & W. Goebel Rödental/Oeslau 1871−1890	599 **467**
F. & W. Goebel and W. Goebel Rodental/Oeslau circa 1890−1900	F. & W. Goebel und W. Goebel Rödental/Oeslau ca. 1890−1900	600 **467**
W. Goebel Rodental/Oeslau circa 1900 impressed on dolls heads	W. Goebel Rödental/Oeslau ca. 1900 eingeprägt auf Puppenköpfen	601 **467**
W. Goebel Rodental/Oeslau circa 1900 impressed on dolls heads	W. Goebel Rödental/Oeslau ca. 1900 eingeprägt auf Puppenköpfen	602 **467**
Royal Porcelain Manufactory Nymphenburg probably around 1850	Königliche Porzellan Manufaktur Nymphenburg wahrscheinlich um 1850	603 **457**

Cuno & Otto Dressel	Cuno & Otto Dressel	
Sonneberg	Sonneberg	
after 1873–circa 1943	nach 1873–ca. 1943	
impressed or stamped	eingeprägt oder gestem-	604
on dolls heads	pelt auf Puppenköpfen	**482**

Vienna Porcelain Factory	Wiener Porzellanfabrik	
Augarten	Augarten	
Vienna	Wien	
1923–	1923–	
blue	blau	
also in combination	auch in Verbindung	605
with: Augarten	mit: Augarten	**503**

Royal Porcelain Manufactory	Königliche Porzellan Manufaktur	
Nymphenburg	Nymphenburg	
1850–1862	1850–1862	606
impressed	eingeprägt	**457**

Krautheim & Adelberg	Krautheim & Adelberg	
Selb	Selb	
1884–1912	1884–1912	
decorating mark	Malereimarke	607
brown overglaze	braun aufglasur	**479**

Josef Strnact	Josef Strnact	
Greising	Greising	
circa 1930	ca. 1930	
decorator's mark	Malermarke	608
overglaze	aufglasur	**412**

Rhenish Porcelain Factory	Rheinische Porzellanfabrik	
Mannheim	Mannheim	609
(1899)–1933	(1899)–1933	**443**

Kuchler & Co.	Küchler & Co.	
Ilmenau	Ilmenau	610
after 1900–	nach 1900–	**422**

Philip Aigner	Philip Aigner	
Vienna	Wien	611
circa 1900	ca. 1900	**501**

Josef Bock	Josef Böck	
Vienna	Wien	
after 1893–circa 1933	nach 1893–ca. 1933	612
decorator's mark	Malermarke	**503**

Erika Lutz	Erika Lutz	
Halle-Saale	Halle-Saale	
after 1960–	nach 1960–	
decorator's mark	Malermarke	613
overglaze	aufglasur	**415**

Bloch & Co.	Bloch & Co.	
Eichwald	Eichwald	
circa 1916–circa 1940	ca. 1916–ca. 1940	614
blue	blau	**397**

Meissen Stove and Porcelain	Meißner Ofen- und	
Factory C. Teichert	Porzellanfabrik C. Teichert	
Meissen, 1882-1929	Meißen, 1882-1929	
Bloch & Co.	Bloch & Co.	615
Eichwald, 1886-1940	Eichwald, 1886-1940	**397**

Meissen Stove and Porce-	Meißner Ofen- und	
lain Factory C. Teichert	Porzellanfabrik C. Teichert	
Meissen, 1882-1929	Meißen, 1882-1929	
Bloch & Co.	Bloch & Co.	616
Eichwald, 1886-1940	Eichwald, 1886-1940	**447**

Bloch & Co.	Bloch & Co.	
Eichwald	Eichwald	
circa 1886–ca. 1940	ca. 1886–ca. 1940	617
blue underglaze	blau unterglasur	**397**

Porcelain Factory Arnstadt	Porzellanfabrik Arnstadt	
Arnstadt	Arnstadt	618
after 1905–1938	nach 1905–1938	**376**

Kerafina	Kerafina	
Marktredwitz	Marktredwitz	619
(1954)–	(1954)–	**444**

M. Sterner	M. Sterner	
Mannheim	Mannheim	620
(1896)–1907	(1896)–1907	**443**

Schoenau & Hoffmeister Burggrub 1909–1952	Schoenau & Hoffmeister Burggrub 1909–1952	621 **388**
Schoenau & Hoffmeister Burggrub 1909–1952	Schoenau & Hoffmeister Burggrub 1909–1952	622 **388**
Stern Porcelain Manu- factory E. Leber & Son Tiefenfurt circa 1920–circa 1933	Stern Porzellanmanu- faktur E. Leber & Sohn Tiefenfurt ca. 1920–ca. 1933	623 **488**
Armand Marseille Koppelsdorf circa 1925–circa 1933 on dolls heads	Armand Marseille Köppelsdorf ca. 1925–ca. 1933 auf Puppenköpfen	624 **432**
Armand Marseille Koppelsdorf circa 1925–circa 1933 on dolls heads	Armand Marseille Köppelsdorf ca. 1925–ca. 1933 auf Puppenköpfen	625 **432**
Carl Krister Waldenburg 1885–1903	Carl Krister Waldenburg 1885–1903	626 **497**
Ilmenau Porcelain Factory Ilmenau (1905)–circa 1938 blue or green	Ilmenauer Porzellanfabrik Ilmenau (1905)–ca. 1938 blau oder grün	627 **421**
Ilmenau Porcelain Factory Ilmenau (1903)–circa 1938 blue or green	Ilmenauer Porzellanfabrik Ilmenau (1903)–ca. 1938 blau oder grün	628 629 **421**
Simon & Halbig Grafenhain after 1895 on dolls heads for Kammer & Reinhardt	Simon & Halbig Gräfenhain nach 1895 auf Puppenköpfen für Kämmer & Reinhardt	630 **410**

HALBIG

K ✡ R

Simon & Halbig	Simon & Halbig
Grafenhain	Gräfenhain
after 1895	nach 1895
on dolls heads for	auf Puppenköpfen für 631
Kammer & Reinhardt	Kämmer & Reinhardt **410**

Porcelain Factory Freienorla	Porzellanfabrik Freienorla
Freienorla	Freienorla 632
1924–circa 1933	1924–ca. 1933 **404**

R. Merkelbach	R. Merkelbach
Hohr-Grenzhausen	Höhr-Grenzhausen 633
(1895)–	(1895)– **419**

Fritz Bensinger	Fritz Bensinger
Mannheim	Mannheim
circa 1930	ca. 1930
decorator's mark	Malermarke 634
overglaze	aufglasur **443**

Max Oscar Arnold	Max Oscar Arnold
Neustadt	Neustadt
after 1888–1929	nach 1888–1929 635
on dolls heads	auf Puppenköpfen **453**

Max Oscar Arnold	Max Oscar Arnold
Neustadt	Neustadt
1915–1929	1915–1929
on dolls heads for	auf Puppenköpfen für
Welsch & Co. in	Welsch & Co. in
Sonneberg	Sonneberg 636
	453

Prince-Electoral Porce-	Churfürstliche Por-
lain Manufactory	zellain Manufaktur 637
Nymphenburg	Nymphenburg 638
circa 1763–1767	ca. 1763–1767 639
blue underglaze	blau unterglasur **457**

Engers GmbH	Engers GmbH
Neuwied	Neuwied
presently	heute 640
on tiles	auf Fliesen **454**

Heinrich Baensch Lettin after 1900–circa 1930	Heinrich Baensch Lettin nach 1900–ca. 1930	641 **438**
VEB Porcelainwork Lichte Lichte (1966)-1990 blue	VEB Porzellanwerk Lichte Lichte (1966)-1990 blau	642 **438**
A. Fischer Ilmenau 1907–1952	A. Fischer Ilmenau 1907–1952	643 **422**
Silesian Porcelain Factory P. Donath Tiefenfurth (1896)-1916	Schlesische Porzellan- fabrik P. Donath Tiefenfurth (1896)-1916	644 **488**
VEB Decorative Porce- lainwork Lichte Lichte (1966)-1990 blue	VEB Zierporzellanwerk Lichte Lichte (1966)-1990 blau	645 **438**
E. & A. Muller Schwarza-Saale after 1890–circa 1945	E. & A. Müller Schwarza-Saale nach 1890–ca. 1945	646 **477**
Adolph Hamann Dresden 1866–after 1949 decorator's mark blue overglaze	Adolph Hamann Dresden 1866–nach 1949 Malermarke blau aufglasur	647 **394**
Karl Eduard Hamann Dresden 1891–1892 decorator's mark blue overglaze	Karl Eduard Hamann Dresden 1891–1892 Malermarke blau aufglasur	648 **394**
Richard Klemm Dresden (1893)–1916 decorator's mark blue overglaze	Richard Klemm Dresden (1893)–1916 Malermarke blau aufglasur	649 **395**
Engers GmbH Neuwied presently on tiles	Engers GmbH Neuwied heute auf Fliesen	650 **454**

Kerafina
Marktredwitz
1950–1958
different colors overglaze

Kerafina
Marktredwitz
1950–1958   651
verschiedene Farben aufglasur   **444**

VEB Porcelainwork Lettin
Lettin
circa 1956-1990

VEB Porzellanwerk Lettin
Lettin   652
ca. 1956-1990   **438**

attributed to
Amphora
Riessner & Kessel
Turn-Teplitz
1905–1910

zugeschrieben
Amphora
Riessner & Kessel
Turn-Teplitz   653
1905–1910   **489**

Bloch & Co.
Eichwald
(1913)–1940
blue or green underglaze

Bloch & Co.
Eichwald
(1913)–1940   654
blau oder grün unterglasur   **397**

Prince Friedrich
Christian of Saxony
Altshausen
(1955)–

Prinz Friedrich
Christian zu Sachsen
Altshausen   655
(1955)–   **374**

unidentified
decorator's mark
gold overglaze, used to
cover original manu-
facturers mark

nicht identifiziert
Malermarke
gold aufglasur, benutzt
um Herstellermarke   656
zu verdecken

Oscar Schlegelmilch
Langewiesen
after 1900–

Oscar Schlegelmilch
Langewiesen   657
nach 1900–   **436**

Hans Richter
Berlin
circa 1881–1907
decorator's mark
overglaze

Hans Richter
Berlin
ca. 1881–1907
Malermarke   658
aufglasur   **382**

Wessel Work
Bonn
(1961)–

Wessel-Werk
Bonn   659
(1961)–   **385**

Wessel Work
Bonn
1961–

Wessel-Werk
Bonn   660
1961–   **385**

Porcelain Manufactory Konstanz Constance (1929)–1935	Porzellanmanufaktur Konstanz Konstanz (1929)–1935	661 **433**
August Roloff Munster 1927–1929 decorator's mark overglaze	August Roloff Münster 1927–1929 Malermarke aufglasur	662 **451**
P. H. Leonard New York City circa 1890–circa 1908 importer's mark on Bohemian porcelain	P. H. Leonard New York ca. 1890–ca. 1908 Importeurmarke auf böhmischem Porzellan	663 **455**
P. H. Leonard New York City 1890–circa 1908 importer's mark on Bohemian porcelain	P. H. Leonard New York 1890–ca. 1908 Importeurmarke auf böhmischem Porzellan	664 **455**
Prince Friedrich Christian of Saxony Altshausen (1950)–	Prinz Friedrich Christian zu Sachsen Altshausen (1950)–	665 **374**
Margravial Porcelain Administration Baden-Baden 1778 blue underglaze	Markgräfliche Porzellanregie Baden-Baden 1778 blau unterglasur	666 **378**
same as 666	wie 666	667 **378**
same as 666	wie 666	668 **378**
same as 666	wie 666	669 **378**
same as 666	wie 666	670 **378**
same as 666	wie 666	671 **378**

	same as 666	wie 666	672 **378**
	same as 666	wie 666	673 **378**
	same as 666	wie 666	674 **378**
	Vienna Porcelain Factory Augarten Vienna 1923– blue underglaze also in combination with: Augarten	Wiener Porzellanfabrik Augarten Wien 1923– blau unterglasur auch in Verbindung mit: Augarten	675 **503**
	Vienna Porcelain Factory Augarten Vienna 1923– blue underglaze	Wiener Porzellanfabrik Augarten Wien 1923– blau unterglasur	676 **503**
WIEN	same as 676	wie 676	677 **503**
Wien	same as 676	wie 676	678 **503**
Wahliss.	Ernst Wahliss Turn-Teplitz (1903)–circa 1921	Ernst Wahliss Turn-Teplitz (1903)–ca. 1921	679 **491**
	Royal Porcelain Manufactory Nymphenburg 1890–1895 blue underglaze	Königliche Porzellan Manufaktur Nymphenburg 1890–1895 blau unterglasur	680 **457**
Nymphenburg	Royal Porcelain Manufactory and State's Porcelain Manufactory Nymphenburg (1895)– green underglaze or impressed	Königliche Porzellan Manufaktur und Staatliche Porzellan Manufaktur Nymphenburg (1895)– grün unterglasur oder eingeprägt	681 **457**

Prince Friedrich Christian of Saxony Altshausen (1950)–	Prinz Friedrich Christian zu Sachsen Altshausen (1950)–	682	**374**

New Porcelain Factory Tettau and Gerold & Co. and New Porcelain Company Tettau 1948-present also with "NP-Tettau" above mark

Neue Porzellanfabrik Tettau und Gerold & Co. und Neue Porzellangesellschaft Tettau 1948-heute auch mit "NP-Tettau" über der Marke — 683 **487**

Wachtersbach Earthenware Factory Schlierbach 1914– black or blue or green

Wächtersbacher Steingutfabrik Schlierbach 1914– schwarz oder blau oder grün — 684 **473**

Wachtersbach Earthenware Factory Schlierbach 1932–present black or blue

Wächtersbacher Steingutfabrik Schlierbach 1932–heute schwarz oder blau — 685 **473**

Wachtersbach Earthenware Factory Schlierbach 1929–1930 different colors mark of art department

Wächtersbacher Steingutfabrik Schlierbach 1929–1930 verschiedene Farben Marke der Kunstabteilung — 686 **473**

Karl Schaaff Zell on Harmersbach after 1874–1907 on earthenware

Karl Schaaff Zell am Harmersbach nach 1874–1907 auf Steingut — 687 **507**

Geyer & Koerbitz Eisenberg 1882–1904 on earthenware

Geyer & Koerbitz Eisenberg 1882–1904 auf Steingut — 688 **398**

C. M. Hutschenreuther Hohenberg (1893)–circa 1923 decorating mark

C. M. Hutschenreuther Hohenberg (1893)–ca. 1923 Malereimarke — 689 **419**

A. Fischer Ilmenau after 1907–1952	A. Fischer Ilmenau nach 1907–1952	690 **422**
C. Schumann Arzberg after 1900–	C. Schumann Arzberg nach 1900–	691 **377**
Schumann & Schreider Schwarzenhammer after 1905–	Schumann & Schreider Schwarzenhammer nach 1905–	692 **478**
Berlin Porcelain Manufactory Teltow 1904–circa 1911	Berliner Porzellanmanu- faktur Teltow 1904–ca. 1911	693 **486**
C. M. Hutschenreuther Hohenberg 1914–1938	C. M. Hutschenreuther Hohenberg 1914–1938	694 **419**
C. M. Hutschenreuther Hohenberg 1939–1945	C. M. Hutschenreuther Hohenberg 1939–1945	695 **419**
C. M. Hutschenreuther Hohenberg circa 1946–circa 1949 green	C. M. Hutschenreuther Hohenberg ca. 1946–ca. 1949 grün	696 **419**
C. M. Hutschenreuther Hohenberg 1950–1963 green underglaze or overglaze	C. M. Hutschenreuther Hohenberg 1950–1963 grün unterglasur oder aufglasur	697 **419**

C. M. Hutschenreuther Hohenberg 1964–1969	C. M. Hutschenreuther Hohenberg 1964–1969	698	**419**
C. M. Hutschenreuther Hohenberg/Dresden 1918–1945 mark of the Art Department in Dresden	C. M. Hutschenreuther Hohenberg/Dresden 1918–1945 Marke der Dresdner Kunstabteilung	699	**394**
C. M. Hutschenreuther Hohenberg/Dresden 1918–1945 mark of the Art Department in Dresden	C. M. Hutschenreuther Hohenberg/Dresden 1918–1945 Marke der Dresdner Kunstabteilung	700	**394**
C. M. Hutschenreuther Hohenberg/Dresden 1918–1945 mark of Art Department in Dresden	C. M. Hutschenreuther Hohenberg/Dresden 1918–1945 Marke der Dresdner Kunstabteilung	701	**394**
Porcelain Factory Tirschenreuth Tirschenreuth 1969–present green underglaze	Porzellanfabrik Tirschenreuth Tirschenreuth 1969–heute grün unterglasur	702	**489**
Porcelain Manufactory Union Kleindembach (1917)–1927	Porzellanmanufaktur Union Kleindembach (1917)–1927	703	**427**
Porcelain Factory Kahla Kahla 1931-1945 green or blue	Porzellanfabrik Kahla Kahla 1931-1945 grün oder blau	704	**423**
Porcelain Factory Muhlbach Bruchmuhlbach after 1951–circa 1970	Porzellanfabrik Mühlbach Bruchmühlbach nach 1951–ca. 1970	705	**386**

F. A. Mehlem Bonn 1888–circa 1920 on earthenware	F. A. Mehlem Bonn 1888–ca. 1920 auf Steingut	706 385

F. A. Mehlem
Bonn
1888–circa 1920
on earthenware

F. A. Mehlem
Bonn
1888–ca. 1920
auf Steingut

706
385

F. A. Mehlem
Bonn
(1895)–circa 1920
also in combination
with: Royal Bonn
      Pompadour

F. A. Mehlem
Bonn
(1895)–ca. 1920
auch in Verbindung
mit: Royal Bonn
      Pompadour

707
385

F. A. Mehlem
Bonn
(1888)–circa 1920
blue or brown
on earthenware

F. A. Mehlem
Bonn
(1888)–ca. 1920
blau oder braun
auf Steingut

708
385

F. A. Mehlem
Bonn
(1890)–circa 1920
on earthenware

F. A. Mehlem
Bonn
(1890)–ca. 1920
auf Steingut

709
385

Galluba & Hofmann
Ilmenau
(1905)–circa 1927

Galluba & Hofmann
Ilmenau
(1905)–ca. 1927

710
422

Heber & Co.
Neustadt
1900–1922

Heber & Co.
Neustadt
1900–1922

711
453

Lorenz & Trabe
Selb
before 1925–
decorator's mark
overglaze

Lorenz & Trabe
Selb
vor 1925–
Malermarke
aufglasur

712
480

Julius Lange
Kahla
(1910)–circa 1940
decorator's mark
overglaze

Julius Lange
Kahla
(1910)–ca. 1940
Malermarke
aufglasur

713
424

Lorenz & Trabe
Selb
before 1925–
decorator's mark
overglaze

Lorenz & Trabe
Selb
vor 1925–
Malermarke
aufglasur

714
480

A. Fischer
Ilmenau
after 1907–1952

A. Fischer
Ilmenau   715
nach 1907–1952   **422**

Fischer & Co.
Oeslau
1950–circa 1975

Fischer & Co.
Oeslau   716
1950–ca. 1975   **459**

Pfeiffer & Lowenstein
Schlackenwerth
(1916)–circa 1941

Pfeiffer & Löwenstein
Schlackenwerth   717
(1916)–ca. 1941   **472**

Unger & Schilde
Roschutz
after 1900–1953

Unger & Schilde
Roschütz   718
nach 1900–1953   **468**

E. & A. Muller
Schwarza-Saale
(1895)–

E. & A. Müller
Schwarza-Saale   719
(1895)–   **477**

August Frank
Kahla
1894–1965
decorator's mark
overglaze

August Frank
Kahla
1894–1965
Malermarke   720
aufglasur   **423**

Kahla Porcelain Manufactory
Kahla
1964–1972

Kahlaer Porzellanmanufaktur
Kahla   721
1964–1972   **423**

Beyer & Bock
Volkstedt
(1905)–circa 1931
impressed or green under-
glaze or overglaze
also in combination
with: Auguste Victoria
    Prussia
    Royal Rudolstadt
also without crown

Beyer & Bock
Volkstedt
(1905)–ca. 1931
eingeprägt oder grün
unter- oder aufglasur
auch in Verbindung
mit: Auguste Victoria
    Prussia
    Royal Rudolstadt   722
auch ohne Krone   **496**

B. Bloch
Eichwald
(1915)–circa 1920
blue or green underglaze

B. Bloch
Eichwald
(1915)–ca. 1920   723
blau oder grün unterglasur   **397**

Anton Lang	Anton Lang		
Budau	Budau		
1860–1880	1860–1880		724
impressed	eingeprägt		**387**
C. M. Hutschenreuther	C. M. Hutschenreuther		
Hohenberg	Hohenberg		725
(1904)–	(1904)–		**419**
J. Engler	J. Engler		
Linz	Linz		
after 1883–	nach 1883–		
decorator's mark	Malermarke		726
overglaze	aufglasur		**440**
R. M. Krause	R. M. Krause		
Schweidnitz	Schweidnitz		
1882–circa 1929	1882–ca. 1929		
decorator's mark	Malermarke		727
overglaze	aufglasur		**478**
Porcelain Factory Arzberg	Porzellanfabrik Arzberg		
Arzberg	Arzberg		
1927–	1927–		728
green underglaze	grün unterglasur		**376**
Porcelain Factory Schonwald	Porzellanfabrik Schönwald		
Schonwald	Schönwald		729
1911–1927	1911–1927		**475**
Porcelain Factory Plankenhammer	Porzellanfabrik Plankenhammer		
Plankenhammer	Plankenhammer		730
1910–circa 1920	1910–ca. 1920		**462**
Porcelain Factory Tirschenreuth	Porzellanfabrik Tirschenreuth		
Tirschenreuth	Tirschenreuth		
(1903)–	(1903)–		731
green underglaze	grün unterglasur		**489**
Porcelain Factory	Porzellanfabrik		
Retsch & Co.	Retsch & Co.		
Wunsiedel	Wunsiedel		732
(1953)–	(1953)–		**506**

Siegmund Paul Meyer	Siegmund Paul Meyer	
Bayreuth	Bayreuth	
1899—1947	1899—1947	733
green underglaze	grün unterglasur	**379**
Count Thun's Porcelain	Gräflich Thun'sche	
Factory	Porzellanfabrik	
Klosterle	Klösterle	
1895—circa 1945	1895—ca. 1945	734
green underglaze	grün unterglasur	**428**
Wachtersbach Earthenware	Wächtersbacher Steingut-	
Factory	fabrik	
Schlierbach	Schlierbach	
1921—1928	1921—1928	
different colors overglaze	verschiedene Farben aufglasur	735
mark of art department	Marke der Kunstabteilung	**473**
Georg Schmider	Georg Schmider	
Zell on Harmersbach	Zell am Harmersbach	736
about 1924 on porcelain	um 1924 auf Porzellan	**507**
Bauer & Lehmann	Bauer & Lehmann	
Kahla	Kahla	737
circa 1935—1964	ca. 1935—1964	**423**
C. M. Hutschenreuther	C. M. Hutschenreuther	
Hohenberg	Hohenberg	738
1914—	1914—	**419**
C. M. Hutschenreuther	C. M. Hutschenreuther	
Hohenberg	Hohenberg	
1914—	1914—	739
green or black	grün oder schwarz	**419**
C. M. Hutschenreuther	C. M. Hutschenreuther	
Hohenberg	Hohenberg	
1914—	1914—	740
green or black	grün oder schwarz	**419**
unidentified	nicht identifiziert	741
gold overglaze	gold aufglasur	

Edmund Kruger	Edmund Krüger		
Blankenhain	Blankenhain	742	
after 1900–1937	nach 1900–1937	**384**	

Edmund Kruger	Edmund Krüger		
Blankenhain	Blankenhain	743	
after 1900–1937	nach 1900–1937	**384**	

Ebeling & Reuss	Ebeling & Reuss		
Devon/Philadelphia	Devon/Philadelphia		
1955–present	1955–heute	744	
importer's mark	Importeurmarke	**393**	

Ebeling & Reuss	Ebeling & Reuss		
Devon/Philadelphia	Devon/Philadelphia		
1955–present	1955–heute	745	
importer's mark	Importeurmarke	**393**	

Ernst Wahliss	Ernst Wahliss		
Turn-Teplitz	Turn-Teplitz	746	
(1899)–circa 1918	(1899)–ca. 1918	**491**	

Jakob Ferdinand Lenz	Jakob Ferdinand Lenz		
Zell on Harmersbach	Zell am Harmersbach		
(1880)-1909	(1880)-1909	747	
on earthenware	auf Steingut	**507**	

Bros. Martin	Gebr. Martin		
Lubau	Lubau	748	
after 1900–circa 1918	nach 1900–ca. 1918	**440**	

Marchian Earthenware	Märkische Steingut-		
Factory	fabrik		
Vordamm	Vordamm	749	
(1900)–circa 1945	(1900)–ca. 1945		
on earthenware and porcelain	auf Steingut und Porzellan	**497**	

Hermann Ohme	Hermann Ohme		
Niedersalzbrunn	Niedersalzbrunn	750	
1908–circa 1930	1908–ca. 1930	**456**	

Royal Porcelain Kups 1972–present	Royal Porzellan Küps 1972–heute	751 **435**
VEB Porcelain Decorating Shop Kahla 1972-circa 1974 decorator´s mark overglaze	VEB Porzellanmalerei Kahla 1972- ca. 1974 Malermarke aufglasur	752 **423**
Porcelain Factory Schirnding Schirnding circa 1909–circa 1925	Porzellanfabrik Schirnding Schirnding ca. 1909–ca. 1925	753 **472**
Porcelain Factory Schirnding Schirnding 1925–1936	Porzellanfabrik Schirnding Schirnding 1925–1936	754 **472**
Porcelain Factory Tirschenreuth Tirschenreuth 1969–present green underglaze	Porzellanfabrik Tirschenreuth Tirschenreuth 1969–heute grün unterglasur	755 **489**
Porcelain Factory AValkyrie@ Bayreuth 1948-1987 green underglaze	Porzellanfabrik Walküre Bayreuth 1948-1987 grün unterglasur	756 **379**
Zeh, Scherzer & Co. Rehau (1899)–circa 1909	Zeh, Scherzer & Co. Rehau (1899)–ca. 1909	757 758 **466**
Alexandra Porcelainworks Turn-Teplitz circa 1900–circa 1921	Alexandra Porzellanwerke Turn-Teplitz ca. 1900–ca. 1921	759 **491**
Bohemia Neurohlau (1937)–1945	Bohemia Neurohlau (1937)–1945	760 761 **453**

Saxonian Porcelain Factory Carl Thieme Potschappel (1905)–	Sächsische Porzellan-fabrik Carl Thieme Potschappel (1905)–	762 **463**
Thomas & Co. Sophienthal (1929)–	Thomas & Co. Sophienthal (1929)–	763 **482**
Thomas & Co. Sophienthal circa 1948–present green underglaze or overglaze	Thomas & Co. Sophienthal 1948–heute grün unterglasur oder aufglasur	764 **482**
Thomas & Co. Sophienthal 1948–present green underglaze or overglaze	Thomas & Co. Sophienthal 1948–heute grün unterglasur oder aufglasur	765 **482**
Porcelain Factory Victoria Altrohlau (1904)–circa 1945	Porzellanfabrik Victoria Altrohlau (1904)–ca. 1945	766 **374**
Bros. Lichtenstern Wilhelmsburg 1890–1910 on earthenware	Gebr. Lichtenstern Wilhelmsburg 1890–1910 auf Steingut	767 **504**
Wilhelm Jager Eisenberg (1911)–circa 1945	Wilhelm Jäger Eisenberg (1911)–ca. 1945	768 **398**
Carl Spitz Brux after 1918–circa 1945	Carl Spitz Brüx nach 1918–ca. 1945	769 **387**
Prince Friedrich Christian of Saxony Altshausen (1950)–	Prinz Friedrich Christian zu Sachsen Altshausen (1950)–	770 **374**

Heinrich & Co.	Heinrich & Co.	
Selb	Selb	
1905–1907	1905–1907	771
blue or green underglaze	blau oder grün unterglasur	**479**

Porcelain Factory Gunthersfeld	Porzellanfabrik Günthersfeld	
Gehren	Gehren	772
after 1902–circa 1945	nach 1902–ca. 1945	**406**

Porcelain Factory Kalk	Porzellanfabrik Kalk	
Eisenberg	Eisenberg	773
after 1900–	nach 1900–	**398**

Porcelain Factory Kalk	Porzellanfabrik Kalk	
Eisenberg	Eisenberg	774
after 1900–	nach 1900–	**398**

D. von Eisenhart	D. von Eisenhart	
Schriesheim	Schriesheim	
1945–before 1959	1945–vor 1959	
decorator's mark	Malermarke	775
overglaze	aufglasur	**476**

Carl Schneider's Heirs	Carl Schneider's Erben	
Grafenthal	Gräfenthal	776
circa 1965–circa 1972	ca. 1965–ca. 1972	**411**

Charles Ahrenfeldt & Son	Charles Ahrenfeldt & Son	
New York City/Altrohlau	New York/Altrohlau	
1886–1910	1886–1910	777
importer's mark	Importeurmarke	**454**

Charles Ahrenfeldt & Son	Charles Ahrenfeldt & Sohn	
New York City/Altrohlau	New York/Altrohlau	
1886–1910	1886–1910	778
importer's mark	Importeurmarke	**454**

Haas & Czjzek	Haas & Czjzek	
Schlaggenwald	Schlaggenwald	779
(1922)–1939	(1922)–1939	**472**

119

Rosenthal China Corporation
New York City
1925–circa 1941

Rosenthal China Corporation
New York
1925–ca. 1941

780
455

Konitz Porcelain Factory
Konitz
after 1909–circa 1945

Könitzer Porzellanfabrik
Könitz
nach 1909–ca. 1945

781
431

Fischer & Mieg and
Oepiag and Epiag
Pirkenhammer
(1910)–1945
green underglaze or
red overglaze

Fischer & Mieg und
Oepiag und Epiag
Pirkenhammer
(1910)–1945
grün unterglasur oder
rot aufglasur

782
461

Oepiag
Pirkenhammer
1918–1920

Oepiag
Pirkenhammer
1918–1920

783
461

Fischer & Mieg
Pirkenhammer
(1916)–1918
blue or green underglaze
or overglaze

Fischer & Mieg
Pirkenhammer
(1916)–1918
blau oder grün unter-
oder aufglasur

784
461

Epiag
Pirkenhammer
1939–1945
green underglaze

Epiag
Pirkenhammer
1939–1945
grün unterglasur

785
461

Paul Muller
Selb
1890–1917

Paul Müller
Selb
1890–1917

786
480

Porcelain Factory Fraureuth
Fraureuth
(1919)–circa 1935

Porzellanfabrik Fraureuth
Fraureuth
(1919)–ca. 1935

787
403

Wachtersbach Earthenware Factory Schlierbach 1861–1873 blue or black on earthenware	Wächtersbacher Steingutfabrik Schlierbach 1861–1873 blau oder schwarz auf Steingut	788 **473**
Oscar Schaller & Co. Successor Windischeschenbach (1977)–present	Oscar Schaller & Co. Nachf. Windischeschenbach (1977)–heute	789 **505**
Heinrich Baensch Lettin circa 1900–circa 1930	Heinrich Baensch Lettin ca. 1900–ca. 1930	790 **438**
Rosenthal Selb (1922)–	Rosenthal Selb (1922)–	791 **480**
Schaubach Art Wallendorf 1926–1952	Schaubach-Kunst Wallendorf 1926–1952	792 **498**
VEB Schaubach Art Wallendorf 1953–1958	VEB Schaubach-Kunst Wallendorf 1953–1958	793 **498**
Drechsel & Strobel Marktleuthen (1895)–circa 1903	Drechsel & Strobel Marktleuthen (1895)–ca. 1903	794 **444**
A. Porzelius Unterweissbach probably 1880–1890	A. Porzelius Unterweißbach wahrscheinlich 1880–1890	795 **492**

Robert Hanke Ladowitz after 1900–circa 1918 red overglaze	Robert Hanke Ladowitz nach 1900–ca. 1918 rot aufglasur	796 **435**
Saxonian Porcelain Factory Carl Thieme Potschappel (1913)–	Sächsische Porzellan- fabrik Carl Thieme Potschappel (1913)–	797 **463**
Heinz Schaubach and VEB Porcelain Factory Unterweissbach Unterweissbach 1940–1962	Heinz Schaubach und VEB Porzellanfabrik Unterweißbach Unterweißbach 1940–1962	798 **492**
Muller & Co. Volkstedt after 1907–1949	Müller & Co. Volkstedt nach 1907–1949	799 **496**
Muller & Co. variation of no. 799 with incomplete letter "M"	Müller & Co. Variation der Nr. 799 mit unvollständigem Buchstaben "M"	800 **496**
Volkstedt Porcelain Manufactory Seedorf 1950–circa 1960 blue underglaze	Volkstedter Porzellan- manufaktur Seedorf 1950–ca. 1960 blau unterglasur	801 **478**
Oscar Schaller Schwarzenbach (1909)–circa 1918 blue or impressed	Oscar Schaller Schwarzenbach (1909)–ca. 1918 blau oder eingeprägt	802 **477**
Wagner & Apel Lippelsdorf circa 1945–1972	Wagner & Apel Lippelsdorf ca. 1945–1972	803 **440**
Alboth & Kaiser Staffelstein 1922–1953	Alboth & Kaiser Staffelstein 1922–1953	804 **484**

August Roloff	August Roloff	
Munster	Münster	
after 1919–	nach 1919–	
decorator's mark	Malermarke	805
overglaze	aufglasur	**451**
Dussel & Co.	Düssel & Co.	
Rehau	Rehau	
after 1945–circa 1976	nach 1945–ca. 1976	
decorator's mark	Malermarke	806
gold overglaze	gold aufglasur	**466**
Epiag	Epiag	
Pirkenhammer	Pirkenhammer	
1918–1939	1918–1939	
green underglaze	grün unterglasur	
also in combination	auch in Verbindung	807
with: Dresden	mit: Dresden	**461**
Otto Hadrich's Widow	Otto Hädrichs Witwe	
Reichenbach	Reichenbach	
after 1886–circa 1950	nach 1886–ca. 1950	
decorator's mark	Malermarke	808
overglaze	aufglasur	**466**
VEB Porcelain Factory Unter-	VEB Porzellanfabrik Unter-	
weissbach	weißbach	
Unterweissbach	Unterweißbach	
(1956)–circa 1962	(1956)–ca. 1962	809
see also no. 798	siehe auch Nr. 798	**492**
J. D. Kestner	J. D. Kestner	
Ohrdruf	Ohrdruf	
1895–before 1930	1895–vor 1930	810
red overglaze	rot aufglasur	**459**
Josef Kuba	Josef Kuba	
Karlsbad	Karlsbad	
1900–1945	1900–1945	811
blue overglaze	blau aufglasur	**426**

Josef Kuba Wiesau 1947–present overglaze	Josef Kuba Wiesau 1947–heute aufglasur	81? **50·**
L. Wessel Bonn (1887)–1907	L. Wessel Bonn (1887)–1907	813 **38!**
L. Wessel Bonn (1893)–	L. Wessel Bonn (1893)–	814 **385**
L. Wessel Bonn (1892)–1902	L. Wessel Bonn (1892)–1902	815 **385**
Josef Kuba Karlsbad 1900–1945 blue overglaze	Josef Kuba Karlsbad 1900–1945 blau aufglasur	816 **426**
Porcelain Manufactory "Bavaria" Waldershof after 1916–1977	Porzellanmanufaktur "Bavaria" Waldershof nach 1916–1977	817 **498**
Franz Neukirchner Porcelain Manufactory Marktredwitz 1916–1977	Franz Neukirchner Por- zellanmanufaktur Marktredwitz 1916–1977	818 **445**
Leni Parbus Oberkotzau after 1904– decorator's mark overglaze	Leni Parbus Oberkotzau nach 1904– Malermarke aufglasur	819 **459**

New York and Rudolstadt Pottery Rudolstadt/New York City after 1900–circa 1918	New York and Rudolstadt Pottery Rudolstadt/New York nach 1900–ca. 1918	820 **469**
Oscar Schaller & Co. Successor Windischeschenbach 1950–	Oscar Schaller & Co. Nachf. Windischeschenbach 1950–	821 **505**
VEB Porcelain Factory Unterweissbach Unterweissbach 1959-1990	VEB Porzellanfabrik Unterweißbach Unterweißbach 1959-1990	822 **492**
Porcelain Factory Waldsassen Waldsassen (1931)–circa 1950 also in combination with: Germany US Zone	Porzellanfabrik Waldsassen Waldsassen (1931)–ca. 1950 auch in Verbindung mit: Germany US Zone	823 **498**
Fischer, Bruce & Co. Philadelphia 1933–1940; 1949–present importer's mark	Fischer, Bruce & Co. Philadelphia 1933–1940; 1949–heute Importeurmarke	824 **461**
Porcelain Factory Waldsassen Waldsassen (1971)-1993	Porzellanfabrik Waldsassen Waldsassen (1971)-1993	825 **498**
Porcelain Factory Merkelsgrun Merkelsgrun (1903)–circa 1912	Porzellanfabrik Merkelsgrün Merkelsgrün (1903)–ca. 1912	826 **448**
Bawo & Dotter Fischern/New York City 1884–1914 decorator's and importer's mark	Bawo & Dotter Fischern/New York 1884–1914 Maler- und Importeur- marke	827 **401** **454**

L. Wessel
Bonn
(1892)–

L. Wessel
Bonn   828
(1892)–   **385**

L. Hutschenreuther
Selb
1920–1928

L. Hutschenreuther
Selb   829
1920–1928   **479**

C. M. Hutschenreuther
Hohenberg
1946–
export mark

C. M. Hutschenreuther
Hohenberg
1946–   830
Exportmarke   **419**

Erdmann Schlegelmilch
Suhl
about 1900
green

Erdmann Schlegelmilch
Suhl
um 1900   831
grün   **485**

Zeh, Scherzer & Co.
Rehau
after 1945-1991

Zeh, Scherzer & Co.
Rehau   832
nach 1945-1991   **466**

Porcelain Factory Moschendorf
Hof-Moschendorf
(1898)–circa 1938
green

Porzellanfabrik Moschendorf
Hof-Moschendorf
(1898)–ca. 1938   833
grün   **419**

Georg von Hoffmann
Ludwigsburg
1948–before 1978
decorator's mark
overglaze

Georg von Hoffmann
Ludwigsburg
1948–vor 1978
Malermarke   834
aufglasur   **442**

unidentified
Munich
decorator's mark
overglaze

nicht identifiziert
München
Malermarke   835
aufglasur

C. M. Hutschenreuther
Hohenberg
(1889)–

C. M. Hutschenreuther
Hohenberg   836
(1889)–   **419**

C. M. Hutschenreuther Hohenberg (1890)–	C. M. Hutschenreuther Hohenberg (1890)–	837 **419**
Porcelain Factory Konigszelt Konigszelt (1913)–circa 1928	Porzellanfabrik Königszelt Königszelt (1913)–ca. 1928	838 **430**
unidentified attributed to a factory in Giesshubel but questionable	nicht identifiziert einer Fabrik in Gieß- hübel zugeschrieben, aber fraglich	839
Heinrich & Co. Selb 1947–present mark of art department in Seethal	Heinrich & Co. Selb 1947–heute Marke der Kunstabtei- lung in Seethal	840 **479**
Schlaggenwald Porcelain Industry, Schlaggenwald 1919-circa 1928	Schlaggenwalder Porzellan- industrie, Schlaggenwald 1919-ca. 1928	841
Sommer & Matschak Schlaggenwald 1904–circa 1945	Sommer & Matschak Schlaggenwald 1904–ca. 1945	842 **472**
Friedrich Kaestner Oberhohndorf (1928)–circa 1972 green underglaze	Friedrich Kaestner Oberhohndorf (1928)–ca. 1972 grün unterglasur	843 **457**
Josef Kuba Wiesau 1947– overglaze	Josef Kuba Wiesau 1947– aufglasur	844 **504**
Rosenthal Selb 20th century blue underglaze also in combination with: Delft	Rosenthal Selb 20. Jahrhundert blau unterglasur auch in Verbindung mit: Delft	845 **480**

Porcelain Manufactory Gloria Bayreuth 1947–present blue overglaze	Porzellanmanufaktur Gloria Bayreuth 1947–heute blau aufglasur	846 **379**
Porcelain Factory Cortendorf Coburg-Cortendorf (1956)–1973	Porzellanfabrik Cortendorf Coburg-Cortendorf (1956)–1973	847 **390**
Porcelain Factory Christian Seltmann Weiden 1911-1914 green underglaze	Porzellanfabrik Christian Seltmann Weiden 1911-1914 grün unterglasur	848 **500**
Robert Hanke Ladowitz circa 1882–1914 red overglaze	Robert Hanke Ladowitz ca. 1882–1914 rot aufglasur	849 **435**
VEB Thuringian Porcelainworks Konigsee (1960)-1962	VEB Thüringer Porzellanwerke Königsee (1960)-1962	850 **430**
Eduard Bay Ransbach (1970)–present	Eduard Bay Ransbach (1970)–heute	851 **464**
Eduard Bay Ransbach (1970)–present	Eduard Bay Ransbach (1970)–heute	852 853 **464**
Porcelain Factory Bernhardshutte Oberklingensporn 1924–circa 1930	Porzellanfabrik Bernhardshütte Oberklingensporn 1924–ca. 1930	854 **458**
Oldest Volkstedt Porcelain Factory Volkstedt after 1915–	Aelteste Volkstedter Porzellanfabrik Volkstedt nach 1915–	855 **494**

Carl Alberti	Carl Alberti	
Uhlstadt	Uhlstädt	856
−1954	−1954	**491**
Eduard Stiassny	Eduard Stiassny	
Maffersdorf	Maffersdorf	857
after 1919−	nach 1919−	**442**
Furstenberg Porcelain	Fürstenberger Porzellan-	
Manufactory	manufaktur	
Furstenberg	Fürstenberg	
1897−1939	1897−1939	858
overglaze, export mark	aufglasur, Exportmarke	**405**
Josef Rieber & Co.	Josef Rieber & Co.	859
Mitterteich	Mitterteich	860
1923−	1923−	**449**
Fr. Pfeffer Porcelain	Fr. Pfeffer Porzellan-	
Factory	fabrik	
Gotha	Gotha	861
after 1900−circa 1945	nach 1900−ca. 1945	**409**
Pfeiffer & Lowenstein	Pfeiffer & Löwenstein	862
Schlackenwerth	Schlackenwerth	863
(1914)−1918	(1914)−1918	**472**
Porcelain Factory	Porzellanfabrik	
Reichmannsdorf Carl	Reichmannsdorf Carl	
Scheidig	Scheidig	
Reichmannsdorf	Reichmannsdorf	864
after 1901−1945	nach 1901−1945	**467**
Rudolf Heinz & Co.	Rudolf Heinz & Co.	
Neuhaus on Rennweg	Neuhaus am Rennweg	865
circa 1936−circa 1961	ca. 1936−ca. 1961	**452**
Porcelain Factory	Porzellanfabrik	
Christian Seltmann	Christian Seltmann	
Weiden	Weiden	
1914-1948	1914-1948	866
green underglaze	grün unterglasur	**500**

Winterling Windischeschenbach presently green underglaze	Winterling Windischeschenbach heute grün unterglasur	867 **505**
Ernst Lindner Kups 1948–	Ernst Lindner Küps 1948–	868 **434**
Fritz Worm Munich (1951)– decorator's mark overglaze	Fritz Worm München (1951)– Malermarke aufglasur	869 **451**
Bohemia Neurohlau (1928)–1945	Bohemia Neurohlau (1928)–1945	870 **453**
H. Buhl & Sons Grossbreitenbach (1921)–1932	H. Bühl & Söhne Großbreitenbach (1921)–1932	871 **412**
C. M. Hutschenreuther Arzberg circa 1918–circa 1945 green underglaze	C. M. Hutschenreuther Arzberg ca. 1918–ca. 1945 grün unterglasur	872 **377**
Porcelain Factory Friesland Varel (1971)–present	Porzellanfabrik Friesland Varel (1971)–heute	873 **493**
Hermann Ohme Niedersalzbrunn after 1882–circa 1930	Hermann Ohme Niedersalzbrunn nach 1882–ca. 1930	874 **456**
Bros. Mayer Wiesau 1947– decorator's mark overglaze	Gebr. Mayer Wiesau 1947– Malermarke aufglasur	875 **504**

Prince-Electoral Privileged Porcelain Factory Hochst 1756—1776 blue underglaze	Churfürstlich Privilegierte Porcelain Fabrique Höchst 1756—1776 blau unterglasur	876 877 878 **418**
same as 876		879 880 881 **418**
Fasold & Stauch Bock-Wallendorf circa 1903-circa 1972 blue	Fasold & Stauch Bock-Wallendorf ca. 1903-ca. 1972 blau	882 **384**
C. C. Puhlmann & Son Darmstadt (1970)—circa 1977	C. C. Puhlmann & Sohn Darmstadt (1970)—ca. 1977	883 **392**
unidentified gold overglaze on earthenware	nicht identifiziert gold aufglasur auf Steingut	884
Rosenthal Selb (1961)—	Rosenthal Selb (1961)—	885 **480**
Porcelain Factory Kahla Kahla (1931)-circa 1945 green export mark	Porzellanfabrik Kahla Kahla (1931)- ca. 1945 grün Exportmarke	886 **423**
unidentified green overglaze	nicht identifiziert grün aufglasur	887
Orben, Knabe & Co. Geschwenda circa 1909—1939	Orben, Knabe & Co. Geschwenda ca. 1909—1939	888 **407**
Bros. Metzler & Ortloff Ilmenau —1972	Gebr. Metzler & Ortloff Ilmenau —1972	889 **422**

	English	German	
	Porcelain Factory Fraureuth Fraureuth (1898)–1935 blue or green underglaze also in combination with: Fraureuth	Porzellanfabrik Fraureuth Fraureuth (1898)–1935 blau oder grün unterglasur auch in Verbindung mit: Fraureuth	890 **403**
	Dressel, Kister & Co. Passau 1905–1922 blue underglaze	Dressel, Kister & Co. Passau 1905–1922 blau unterglasur	891 **460**
	Beyer & Bock Volkstedt after 1931–circa 1945	Beyer & Bock Volkstedt nach 1931–ca. 1945	892 **496**
	Porcelain Factory Fraureuth Fraureuth (1928)–circa 1935	Porzellanfabrik Fraureuth Fraureuth (1928)–ca. 1935	893 **403**
	Porcelain Factory Fraureuth Fraureuth (1898)–circa 1928	Porzellanfabrik Fraureuth Fraureuth (1898)–ca. 1928	894 **403**
	Bros. Bordolo Grunstadt (1887)– on earthenware	Gebr. Bordolo Grünstadt (1887)– auf Steingut	895 **413**
	Oscar Schaller & Co. and Oscar Schaller & Co. Successor Schwarzenbach (1915)– blue underglaze or overglaze	Oscar Schaller & Co. und Oscar Schaller & Co. Nachf. Schwarzenbach (1915)– blau unterglasur oder aufglasur	896 **477**
	Groschl & Spethmann Turn-Teplitz after 1899–	Gröschl & Spethmann Turn-Teplitz nach 1899–	897 **490**
	Rothemund, Hager & Co. Altenkunstadt 1919–1933	Rothemund, Hager & Co. Altenkunstadt 1919–1933	898 **372**

Carl Knoll Fischern circa 1900– impressed or green or blue	Carl Knoll Fischern ca. 1900– eingeprägt oder grün oder blau	**899** **402**
Geo. Borgfeldt Corporation New York City 1936–circa 1976 importer's mark	Geo. Borgfeldt Corporation New York 1936–ca. 1976 Importeurmarke	**900** **454**
Porcelain Factory Moschendorf Hof-Moschendorf circa 1900–1938	Porzellanfabrik Moschendorf Hof-Moschendorf ca. 1900–1938	**901** **419**
Hochst Porcelain Manufactory Hochst 1947–1964 blue underglaze	Höchster Porzellanmanufaktur Höchst 1947–1964 blau unterglasur	**902** **418**
VEB Porcelainwork Kahla Kahla (1956)– green	VEB Porzellanwerk Kahla Kahla (1956)– grün	**903** **423**
VEB Porcelainwork Kahla Kahla (1957)-1964 green	VEB Porzellanwerk Kahla Kahla (1957)-1964 grün	**904** **423**
VEB United Porcelainworks Kahla-Konitz and VEB Porcelain Combine Kahla Kahla 1964-1990	VEB Vereinigte Porzellanwerke Kahla Könitz and VEB Porzellankombinat Kahla Kahla 1964-1990	**905** **423**
Zeh, Scherzer & Co. Rehau after 1945-1991 green underglaze	Zeh, Scherzer & Co. Rehau after 1945-1991 grün unterglasur	**906** **466**

133

J. Brauers	J. Brauers	
Gohfeld	Gohfeld	907
(1950)–	(1950)–	**409**
Schafer & Vater	Schäfer & Vater	
Rudolstadt	Rudolstadt	908
(1896)–circa 1962	(1896)–ca. 1962	**469**
New York and Rudolstadt	New York and Rudolstadt	
Pottery	Pottery	
Rudolstadt	Rudolstadt	909
1882–circa 1918	1882–ca. 1918	**469**
New York & Rudolstadt	New York & Rudolstadt	
Pottery	Pottery	
Rudolstadt	Rudolstadt	
(1887)–circa 1918	(1887)–ca. 1918	
also in combination	auch in Verbindung	910
with: Rudolstadt	mit: Rudolstadt	**469**
Paul A. Straub	Paul A. Straub	
New York City	New York	
1948–1970	1948–1970	911
importer's mark	Importeurmarke	**456**
Porcelain Factory Cortendorf	Porzellanfabrik Cortendorf	
Coburg-Cortendorf	Coburg-Cortendorf	912
(1955)–1973	(1955)–1973	**390**
same as 912	wie 912	913
		390
same as 912	wie 912	914
		390
same as 912	wie 912	915
		390

Porcelain Factory Spechtsbrunn Spechtsbrunn after 1930-1972	Porzellanfabrik Spechtsbrunn Spechtsbrunn nach 1930-1972	916 **483**
Porcelain Factory "Alp" Lubau 1939–circa 1945	Porzellanfabrik "Alp" Lubau 1939–ca. 1945	917 **440**
C. M. Hutschenreuther Arzberg (1969)– green underglaze	C. M. Hutschenreuther Arzberg (1969)– grün unterglasur	918 **377**
W. Goebel Rodental (1919)– overglaze	W. Goebel Rödental (1919)– aufglasur	919 **467**
Kerafina Marktredwitz 1950–present different colors overglaze	Kerafina Marktredwitz 1950–heute verschiedene Farben aufglasur	920 **444**
Riedel von Riedelstein Dallwitz 1875–1889	Riedel von Riedelstein Dallwitz 1875–1889	921 **391**
Porcelain Factory Waldsassen Waldsassen (1975)-1993 blue underglaze	Porzellanfabrik Waldsassen Waldsassen (1975)-1993 blau unterglasur	922 **498**
Rosenthal Selb (1938)–	Rosenthal Selb (1938)–	923 **480**

Rosenthal	Rosenthal		
Selb	Selb	924	
(1961)–	(1961)–	**480**	
Berlin Porcelain	Berliner Porzellan-		
Manufactory	manufaktur		
Teltow	Teltow	925	
1904–circa 1911	1904–ca. 1911	**486**	
Georg Schmider	Georg Schmider		
Zell on Harmersbach	Zell am Harmersbach		
1929–	1929–	926	
on earthenware	auf Steingut	**507**	
Porcelain Factory Weissenstadt	Porzellanfabrik Weißenstadt		
Weissenstadt	Weißenstadt	927	
1920–1964	1920–1964	**500**	
Hermann Ohme	Hermann Ohme		
Niedersalzbrunn	Niedersalzbrunn	928	
around 1905	um 1905	**456**	
Sitzendorf Porcelain	Sitzendorfer Porzellan-		
Manufactory	manufaktur		
Sitzendorf	Sitzendorf		
circa 1902–circa 1972	ca. 1902–ca. 1972	929	
blue underglaze	blau unterglasur	**481**	
Sitzendorf Porcelain	Sitzendorfer Porzellan-		
Manufactory and	manufaktur und		
VEB Sitzendorf Porcelain	VEB Sitzendorfer Porzellan-		
Manufactory	manufaktur		
Sitzendorf	Sitzendorf		
(1954)–present	(1954)–heute	930	
blue underglaze	blau unterglasur	**481**	
Bremer & Schmidt	Bremer & Schmidt		
Eisenberg	Eisenberg	931	
–1972	–1972	**398**	
VEB Special Porcelain	VEB Spezialporzellan		
Eisenberg	Eisenberg	932	
1972-1990	1972-1990	**398**	

	H. Hutschenreuther Probstzella after 1886–circa 1945	H. Hutschenreuther Probstzella nach 1886–ca. 1945	933 **464**
	Rosenthal Selb 1891–1907 blue underglaze	Rosenthal Selb 1891–1907 blau unterglasur	934 **480**
	Rosenthal Selb (1891)–1907 blue underglaze	Rosenthal Selb (1891)–1907 blau unterglasur	935 **480**
	Rosenthal Kronach 1901–1933	Rosenthal Kronach 1901–1933	936 **433**
	Rosenthal Kronach 1933–1945	Rosenthal Kronach 1933–1945	937 **433**
	Rosenthal Selb (1963)–	Rosenthal Selb (1963)–	938 **480**
	Rosenthal Kronach 1953–	Rosenthal Kronach 1953–	939 **433**
	Rosenthal Selb 1908–1953	Rosenthal Selb 1908–1953	940 **480**
	Rosenthal Selb 1949–1954 green underglaze	Rosenthal Selb 1949–1954 grün unterglasur	941 **480**

Rosenthal Selb −1954	Rosenthal Selb −1954	942 **480**
Rosenthal Selb 1969−present green underglaze, blue or gold overglaze	Rosenthal Selb 1969−heute grün unterglasur, blau oder gold aufglasur	943 **480**
Rosenthal Selb (1961)−	Rosenthal Selb (1961)−	944 **480**
Rosenthal Selb 1969−present green underglaze, blue or gold overglaze	Rosenthal Selb 1969−heute grün unterglasur, blau oder gold aufglasur	945 **480**
Rosenthal Selb (1943)−	Rosenthal Selb (1943)−	946 **480**
Porcelain Factory Muhlbach Bruchmuhlbach 1951−circa 1970	Porzellanfabrik Mühlbach Bruchmühlbach 1951−ca. 1970	947 **386**
K. Steinmann Tiefenfurth (1896)−1938	K. Steinmann Tiefenfurth (1896)−1938	948 **488**
Adolf Persch Elbogen 1902−1918	Adolf Persch Elbogen 1902−1918	949 **399**
Hermann Ohme Niedersalzbrunn 1891−circa 1930	Hermann Ohme Niedersalzbrunn 1891−ca. 1930	950 **456**

VEB Porcelainwork Kahla Kahla (1956)-1990	VEB Porzellanwerk Kahla Kahla (1956)-1990	951 **423**
Oldest Volkstedt Porcelain Factory Volkstedt 1915-1936	Aelteste Volkstedter Porzellanfabrik Volkstedt 1915-1936	952 **494**
Oldest Volkstedt Porcelain Factory Volkstedt 1915-1936	Aelteste Volkstedter Porzellanfabrik Volkstedt 1915-1936	953 **494**
Ackermann & Fritze and VEB Art and Decorative Porcelainwork Volkstedt 1908–circa 1951	Ackermann & Fritze und VEB Kunst- und Zierpor- zellanwerk Volkstedt 1908–ca. 1951	954 **494**
Royal Porcelain Manufactory Meissen circa 1735–1740 in decoration blue underglaze	Königliche Porzellan Manufaktur Meißen ca. 1735–1740 in der Malerei blau unterglasur	955 **446**
Prince Friedrich Christian of Saxony Altshausen (1950)	Prinz Friedrich Christian zu Sachsen Altshausen (1950)	956 **374**
A. O. E. von dem Busch Hildesheim 1745–1775 decorator's mark overglaze	A. O. E. von dem Busch Hildesheim 1745–1775 Malermarke aufglasur	957 **417**
A. O. E. von dem Busch Hildesheim 1745–1775 decorator's mark overglaze	A. O. E. von dem Busch Hildesheim 1745–1775 Malermarke aufglasur	958 **417**
Wurttemberg Porcelain Manufactory Schorndorf 1904–1939	Württembergische Porzellanmanufaktur Schorndorf 1904–1939	959 **475**

Ducal Real Porcelain Factory Ludwigsburg 1759–1765 blue underglaze	Herzoglich Aechte Porcelain Fabrique Ludwigsburg 1759–1765 blau unterglasur	960 961 962 963 **441**
Ducal Real Porcelain Factory Ludwigsburg circa 1765–1770 blue underglaze	Herzoglich Aechte Porcelain Fabrique Ludwigsburg ca. 1765–1770 blau unterglasur	964 **441**
Ducal Real Porcelain Factory Ludwigsburg 1765–1770 blue underglaze	Herzoglich Aechte Porcelain Fabrique Ludwigsburg 1765–1770 blau unterglasur	965 966 **441**
attributed to Fasold & Stauch Bock-Wallendorf after 1903 but not verified	Fasold & Stauch Bock-Wallendorf nach 1903 zugeschrieben, aber nicht bestätigt	967 **384**
Oldest Volkstedt Porcelain Factory Volkstedt (1934)–circa 1936	Aelteste Volkstedter Porzellanfabrik Volkstedt (1934)–ca. 1936	968 **494**
Royal Porcelain Manufactory State's Porcelain Manufactory Nymphenberg (1895)–present blue underglaze on repro- ductions of Frankenthal porcelain, always with year and contemporary Nymphenburg shield mark	Königliche Porzellan Manufaktur Staatliche Porzellan Manufaktur Nymphenberg (1895)–heute blau unterglasur auf Reproduktionen von Frankenthal-Porzellan, immer mit Jahreszahl und zeitgenössischer Nymphenburg- Marke	969 **457**
Prince-Elector Carl Theodor Frankenthal 1762–1797 blue underglaze	Kurfürst Carl Theodor Frankenthal 1762–1797 blau unterglasur	970 **402**

Prince-Elector Carl Theodor	Kurfürst Carl Theodor		
Frankenthal	Frankenthal		
1762–1797	1762–1797	971	
blue underglaze	blau unterglasur	**402**	

same as 970	wie 970	972	
		402	

Prince-Elector Carl Theodor	Kurfürst Carl Theodor		
Frankenthal	Frankenthal		
1762–1770	1762–1770	973	
blue underglaze	blau unterglasur	**402**	

Prince-Elector Carl Theodor	Kurfürst Carl Theodor		
Frankenthal	Frankenthal		
1784	1784	974	
blue underglaze	blau unterglasur	**402**	

Prince-Elector Carl Theodor	Kurfürst Carl Theodor		
Frankenthal	Frankenthal		
1762–1797	1762–1797		
blue underglaze	blau unterglasur,	975	
letters IL impressed	Buchstaben IL eingeprägt	**402**	

Prince-Elector Carl Theodor	Kurfürst Carl Theodor		
Frankenthal	Frankenthal		
1762–1797	1762–1797	976	
blue underglaze	blau unterglasur	**402**	

Prince-Elector Carl Theodor	Kurfürst Carl Theodor		
Frankenthal	Frankenthal		
1762–1797	1762–1797	977	
blue underglaze	blau unterglasur	**402**	

Prince-Elector Carl Theodor	Kurfürst Carl Theodor		
Frankenthal	Frankenthal		
1789	1789	978	
blue underglaze	blau unterglasur	**402**	

| | Wurttemberg Porcelain Manufactory Schorndorf 1904–1939 | Württembergische Porzellanmanufaktur Schorndorf 1904–1939 | 979 475 |

| | Princely Fulda Fine Porcelain Factory Fulda 1781–1789 blue underglaze | Fürstlich Fuldaische Feine Porzellanfabrik Fulda 1781–1789 blau unterglasur | 980 406 |

| | Princely Fulda Fine Porcelain Factory Fulda 1789 blue underglaze | Fürstlich Fuldaische Feine Porzellanfabrik Fulda 1789 blau unterglasur | 981 406 |

| | Royal Porcelain Manufactory Ludwigsburg 1806–1824 red or gold overglaze | Königliche Porzellan Manufaktur Ludwigsburg 1806–1824 rot oder gold aufglasur | 982 441 |

| | same as 982 | wie 982 | 983 441 |

| | same as 982 | wie 982 | 984 985 441 |

| | Wurttemberg Porcelain Manufactory Schorndorf 1904–1939 | Württembergische Porzellanmanufaktur Schorndorf 1904–1939 | 986 475 |

| | Oldest Volkstedt Porcelain Factory and VEB Oldest Volkstedt Porcelain Factory Volkstedt 1915-1945 | Aelteste Volkstedter Porzellanfabrik und VEB Aelteste Volkstedter Porzellanfabrik Volkstedt 1915-1945 | 987 494 |

| | same as 987 but 1945-present | wie 987 aber 1945-heute | 988 494 |

VEB Oldest Volkstedt Porcelain Factory Volkstedt 1951-1990 blue underglaze	VEB Aelteste Volkstedter Porzellanfabrik Volkstedt 1951-1990 blau unterglasur	989 **494**

Porcelain Factory Waldershof
Waldershof
1924–1938
green underglaze or
green or red or brown overglaze
also in combination
with: Richard Ginori
      Johann Haviland

Porzellanfabrik Waldershof
Waldershof
1924–1938
grün unterglasur oder
grün oder rot oder braun aufglasur
auch in Verbindung
mit: Richard Ginori   990
    Johann Haviland   **498**

Landgravial Porcelain
Manufactory
Kelsterbach
1761–1768
blue underglaze

Landgräfliche Porzellan
Manufaktur
Kelsterbach
1761–1768   991
blau unterglasur   **426**

Landgravial Porcelain
Manufactory
Kelsterbach
1761–1768
impressed

Landgräfliche Porzellan
Manufaktur
Kelsterbach
1761–1768   992
eingeprägt   **426**

Landgravial Porcelain
Manufactory
Kelsterbach
1761–1768
blue underglaze

Landgräfliche Porzellan
Manufaktur
Kelsterbach
1761–1768   993
blau unterglasur   **426**

same as 993   wie 993   994 **426**

same as 993   wie 993   995 **426**

same as 993   wie 993   996 **426**

same as 993   wie 993   997 **426**

Landgravial Porcelain Manufactory Kelsterbach 1761–1768 impressed	Landgräfliche Porzellan Manufaktur Kelsterbach 1761–1768 eingeprägt

998
426

J. J. Lay Kelsterbach 1789–1802 blue underglaze	J. J. Lay Kelsterbach 1789–1802 blau unterglasur

999
426

same as 999	wie 999

1000
426

same as 999	wie 999

100
426

H. Reinl Hirschen –circa 1945	H. Reinl Hirschen –ca. 1945

100
417

Porcelain Factory Reichmannsdorf Carl Scheidig Reichmannsdorf after 1901–	Porzellanfabrik Reichmannsdorf Carl Scheidig Reichmannsdorf nach 1901–

100
467

J. Schneider & Co. Altrohlau 1904–1945 green or blue	J. Schneider & Co. Altrohlau 1904–1945 grün oder blau

100
374

Karl Rau Munich 1946–before 1978 decorator's mark overglaze	Karl Rau München 1946–vor 1978 Malermarke aufglasur

100
451

Elisabeth Liegl Munich 1948–present decorator's mark blue overglaze	Elisabeth Liegl München 1948–heute Malermarke blau aufglasur

100
450

Leube & Co. Reichmannsdorf after 1945–circa 1965	Leube & Co. Reichmannsdorf nach 1945–ca. 1965

100
467

Konitz Porcelain Factory Konitz after 1909–1945	Könitzer Porzellanfabrik Könitz nach 1909–1945	1008 **431**
Konitz Porcelain Factory Konitz after 1909–1945	Könitzer Porzellanfabrik Könitz nach 1909–1945	1009 **431**
Muller & Co. Volkstedt after 1907–1949	Müller & Co. Volkstedt nach 1907–1949	1010 **496**
Hermann Ohme Niedersalzbrunn (1883)–1930	Hermann Ohme Niedersalzbrunn (1883)–1930	1011 **456**
VEB Porcelain Manufactory and von Schierholzsche Porcelain Manufactory Plaue 1972-1996	VEB Porzellanmanufaktur und von Schierholzsche Porzellanmanufaktur Plaue 1972-1996	1012 **462**
Saxonian Porcelain Factory Carl Thieme Potschappel 1901-	Sächsische Porzellanfabrik Carl Thieme Potschappel 1901-	1013 **463**
Reinhold Richter & Co. Volkstedt 1907–1923 decorator's mark overglaze	Reinhold Richter & Co. Volkstedt 1907–1923 Malermarke aufglasur	1014 **496**
Strobel & Wilken New York City after 1884– importer's mark	Strobel & Wilken New York nach 1884– Importeurmarke	1015 **456**
W. Goebel Rodental 1935–1937 blue or black underglaze	W. Goebel Rödental 1935–1937 blau oder schwarz unterglasur	1016 **467**
W. Goebel Rodental 1935–1937 blue or black underglaze or impressed	W. Goebel Rödental 1935–1937 blau oder schwarz unterglasur oder eingepreßt	1017 **467**

W. Goebel	W. Goebel	
Rodental	Rödental	101
(1910)–	(1910)–	467
Princely Porcelain	Fürstliche Porzellan	
Manufactory	Manufaktur	
Ottweiler	Ottweiler	101
1763–1771	1763–1771	460
Royal Porcelain Manufactory	Königliche Porzellan Manufaktur	
Ludwigsburg	Ludwigsburg	102
1816–1824	1816–1824	102
gold overglaze	gold aufglasur	441
Royal Porcelain Manufactory	Königliche Porzellan Manufaktur	
Ludwigsburg	Ludwigsburg	
1816–1824	1816–1824	102
gold overglaze	gold aufglasur	441
Wurttemberg Porcelain	Württembergische	
Manufactory	Porzellanmanufaktur	
Schorndorf	Schorndorf	102
1904–1939	1904–1939	475
Royal Porcelain Manufactory	Königliche Porzellan Manufaktur	
Berlin	Berlin	
1890-1918	1890-1918	
this mark with year 1917	diese Marke mit Jahreszahl 1917	
blue or black overglaze	blau oder schwarz aufglasur	102
court mark	Palastmarke	380
Arno Apel	Arno Apel	
Lauenstein	Lauenstein	102
1954–1974	1954–1974	436
Alboth & Kaiser	Alboth & Kaiser	
Staffelstein	Staffelstein	
1970–present	1970–heute	102
blue underglaze	blau unterglasur	484
Wagner & Apel	Wagner & Apel	
Lippelsdorf	Lippelsdorf	102
-circa 1972	-ca. 1972	440

Bohemia Neurohlau (1940)−1945	Bohemia Neurohlau (1940)−1945	1028	**453**
Porcelain Factory Cortendorf Coburg-Cortendorf (1950)−1973	Porzellanfabrik Cortendorf Coburg-Cortendorf (1950)−1973	1029	**390**
Carl Alberti Uhlstadt −1954	Carl Alberti Uhlstädt −1954	1030	**491**
Carl Alberti Uhlstadt −1954	Carl Alberti Uhlstädt −1954	1031	**491**
Helena Wolfsohn Dresden (1886)− decorator's mark mostly blue overglaze	Helena Wolfsohn Dresden (1886)− Malermarke meist blau aufglasur	1032	**396**
Helena Wolfsohn Dresden (1886)− decorator's mark blue overglaze	Helena Wolfsohn Dresden (1886)− Malermarke blau aufglasur	1033	**396**
Helena Wolfsohn Dresden (1886)− decorator's mark blue overglaze	Helena Wolfsohn Dresden (1886)− Malermarke blau aufglasur	1034	**396**
Helena Wolfsohn Dresden (1886)− decorator's mark blue overglaze	Helena Wolfsohn Dresden (1886)− Malermarke blau aufglasur	1035	**396**
Bloch & Co. Eichwald (1913)−1940 blue or green	Bloch & Co. Eichwald (1913)−1940 blau oder grün	1036	**397**
Eduard Haberlander Windischeschenbach after 1913−1928 green underglaze	Eduard Haberländer Windischeschenbach nach 1913−1928 grün unterglasur	1037	**505**

Ackermann & Fritze Volkstedt 1908–1952	Ackermann & Fritze Volkstedt 1908–1952	103 494
Franz Witter Bruhl (1955)– distributor's mark	Franz Witter Brühl (1955)– Händlermarke	103 387
Royal Porcelain Manufactory Ludwigsburg 1806–1824 gold or red overglaze	Königliche Porzellan Manufaktur Ludwigsburg 1806–1824 gold oder rot aufglasur	104 441
Furstenberg Porcelain Manufactory Furstenberg 1975–present blue or green underglaze	Fürstenberg Porzellan- manufaktur Fürstenberg 1975–heute blau oder grün unterglasur	104 405
Furstenberg Porcelain Manufactory Furstenberg (1957)–	Fürstenberg Porzellan- manufaktur Fürstenberg (1957)–	104 405
Fasold & Stauch Bock-Wallendorf 1903–circa 1912	Fasold & Stauch Bock-Wallendorf 1903–ca. 1912	104 384
F. W. Wessel Frankenthal 1949–	F. W. Wessel Frankenthal 1949–	104 402
attributed to H. Buhl & Sons Grossbreitenbach after 1869 but not verified	H. Bühl & Söhne Großbreitenbach nach 1869 zugeschrieben aber nicht nachgewiesen	104 412
Greiner & Herda Oberkotzau after 1907–1943	Greiner & Herda Oberkotzau nach 1907–1943	104 458
J. G. Schneider Bautzen circa 1930 decorator's mark overglaze	J. G. Schneider Bautzen circa 1930 Malermarke aufglasur	104 379

J.U.&C.	J. Uffrecht & Co. Haldensleben (1894)–1924	J. Uffrecht & Co. Haldensleben (1894)–1924	1048 **414**
	Rudolf Kammer Volkstedt (1961)–1972	Rudolf Kämmer Volkstedt (1961)–1972	1049 **496**
KPM	Krister Porcelain Manufactory Waldenburg (1939)–1945	Krister Porzellanmanufaktur Waldenburg (1939)–1945	1050 **497**
	Krautzberger, Mayer & Purkert Wistritz 1912–1945	Krautzberger, Mayer & Purkert Wistritz 1912–1945	1051 **506**
	Krautzberger, Mayer & Purkert Wistritz after 1911–circa 1945	Krautzberger, Mayer & Purkert Wistritz nach 1911–ca. 1945	1052 **506**
	Heinrich Baensch and Porcelain Factory Lettin Lettin after 1900–circa 1945	Heinrich Baensch und Porzellanfabrik Lettin Lettin nach 1900–ca. 1945	1053 **438**
	Dressel, Kister & Cie. Passau 1902–1904 blue underglaze	Dressel, Kister & Cie. Passau 1902–1904 blau unterglasur	1054 **460**
	Ducal Real Porcelain Factory Ludwigsburg 1793–1795 blue underglaze	Herzoglich Aechte Porcelain Fabrique Ludwigsburg 1793–1795 blau unterglasur	1055 **441**
	Ducal Real Porcelain Factory Ludwigsburg 1793–1795 blue underglaze	Herzoglich Aechte Porcelain Fabrique Ludwigsburg 1793–1795 blau unterglasur	1056 **441**
	Ducal Real Porcelain Factory Ludwigsburg 1793–1795 blue underglaze	Herzoglich Aechte Porcelain Fabrique Ludwigsburg 1793–1795 blau unterglasur	1057 1058 1059 **441**

Adolf Leube	Adolf Leube		
Dresden	Dresden		
1894–1907	1894–1907		
decorator's mark	Malermarke	106	
overglaze	aufglasur	**395**	

Adolf Leube
Dresden
1894–1907
decorator's mark
overglaze

Adolf Leube
Dresden
1894–1907
Malermarke
aufglasur
106
395

unidentified
blue underglaze

nicht identifiziert
blau unterglasur
106

Oscar Schlegelmilch
Langewiesen
after 1900–circa 1957

Oscar Schlegelmilch
Langewiesen
nach 1900–ca. 1957
106
436

Wurttemberg Porcelain
Manufactory
Schorndorf
1904–1939
blue

Württembergische
Porzellanmanufaktur
Schorndorf
1904–1939
blau
106
475

Margarete Freitag
Grossbreitenbach
after 1945–circa 1972

Margarete Freitag
Großbreitenbach
nach 1945–ca. 1972
106
412

Margarete Freitag
Grossbreitenbach
1938–circa 1965

Margarete Freitag
Großbreitenbach
1938–ca. 1965
106
412

Bros. Metzler & Ortloff
Ilmenau
        –circa 1945

Gebr. Metzler & Ortloff
Ilmenau
        –ca. 1945
106
422

Ernst Bohne Sons
Rudolstadt
(1901)–circa 1920
blue underglaze or overglaze

Ernst Bohne Söhne
Rudolstadt
(1901)–ca. 1920
blau unterglasur oder aufglasur
106
469

Ernst Bohne Sons
Rudolstadt
(1901)–circa 1920
blue underglaze or overglaze

Ernst Bohne Söhne
Rudolstadt
(1901)–ca. 1920
blau unterglasur oder aufglasur
106
469

Ernst Bohne Sons
Rudolstadt
(1901)–circa 1920
blue underglaze or overglaze

Ernst Bohne Söhne
Rudolstadt
(1901)–ca. 1920
blau unterglasur oder aufglasur
106
469

Ernst Bohne Sons and Albert Stahl & Co. Rudolstadt (1901)–circa 1962 blue underglaze or overglaze	Ernst Bohne Söhne und Albert Stahl & Co. Rudolstadt (1901)–ca. 1962 blau unterglasur oder aufglasur	1070 **469**
Porcelain Factory Sandizell Sandizell after 1951– blue	Porzellanfabrik Sandizell Sandizell nach 1951– blau	1071 **470**
Saxonian Porcelain Factory Carl Thieme and VEB Saxonian Porcelain Factory Potschappel (1957)-1990 blue	Sächsische Porzellan- fabrik Carl Thieme und VEB Sächsische Porzellanfabrik Potschappel (1957)-1990 blau	1072 **463**
VEB Porcelain Factory Gra- fenroda Grafenroda 1972-1990	VEB Porzellanfabrik Grä- fenroda Gräfenroda 1972-1990	1073 **410**
Porcelain Factory Martin- roda Friedrich Eger & Co. Martinroda 1901-1976	Porzellanfabrik Martin- roda Friedrich Eger & Co. Martinroda 1901-1976	1074 **445**
Rosenthal Selb (1951)–	Rosenthal Selb (1951)–	1075 **480**
Porcelain Factory Spechtsbrunn and VEB Porcelain Factory Spechtsbrunn Spechtsbrunn (1961)-1990	Porzellanfabrik Spechtsbrunn und VEB Porzellanfabrik Spechtsbrunn Spechtsbrunn (1961)-1990	1076 **483**
Max Robra Dresden 1919–1928 decorator's mark overglaze	Max Robra Dresden 1919–1928 Malermarke aufglasur	1077 **395**
R. Kampf Grunlas (1939)–1945	R. Kämpf Grünlas (1939)–1945	1078 **413**

Porcelain Factory Grafen-roda—Ort R. Voigt Grafenroda after 1919–1972 red overglaze	Porzellanfabrik Gräfen-roda—Ort R. Voigt Gräfenroda nach 1919–1972 rot aufglasur	1079 **410**
Porcelain Factory Grafen-roda—Ort R. Voigt Grafenroda (1956)–1972 red and other colors overglaze	Porzellanfabrik Gräfen-roda—Ort R. Voigt Gräfenroda (1956)–1972 rot und andere Farben aufglasur	1080 **410**
Silesian Porcelain Factory P. Donath Tiefenfurth (1896)-1916	Schlesische Porzellanfabrik P. Donath Tiefenfurth (1896)-1916	1081 **488**
Schodl, Jacob & Co. Rehau (1906)–1922 green underglaze	Schödl, Jacob & Co. Rehau (1906)–1922 grün unterglasur	1082 **466**
unidentified attributed to a Saxonian Porcelain Factory in Meissen but questionable because initials in crown show letters F & F	nicht identifiziert einer Sächsischen Por-zellanfabrik in Meißen zugeschrieben, aber fraglich, da die Initia-len in der Krone die Buchstaben F & F zeigen	1083
unidentified decorator's mark gold overglaze used to cover original manufacturer's mark	nicht identifiziert Malermarke gold aufglasur benutzt um Hersteller-marke zu verdecken	1084
Heinrich Winterling Marktleuthen (1934)–	Heinrich Winterling Marktleuthen (1934)–	1085 **444**
Schaubach-Art Wallendorf 1926–1952	Schaubach-Kunst Wallendorf 1926–1952	1086 **498**

VEB Wallendorf Porcelain Factory Wallendorf 1964–	VEB Wallendorfer Porzellanfabrik Wallendorf 1964–	1087 **498**
Kaiser Porzellan Staffelstein 1970–present blue underglaze	Kaiser Porzellan Staffelstein 1970–heute blau unterglasur	1088 **484**
Kaiser Porzellan Staffelstein 1970–present blue underglaze	Kaiser Porzellan Staffelstein 1970–heute blau unterglasur	1089 **484**
Alboth & Kaiser Staffelstein circa 1953–1970	Alboth & Kaiser Staffelstein ca. 1953–1970	1090 **484**
Alboth & Kaiser Staffelstein circa 1953–1970	Alboth & Kaiser Staffelstein ca. 1953–1970	1091 **484**
Alboth & Kaiser Staffelstein circa 1953–1970	Alboth & Kaiser Staffelstein ca. 1953–1970	1092 **484**
Alboth & Kaiser Staffelstein (1955)–1970	Alboth & Kaiser Staffelstein (1955)–1970	1093 **484**
Alboth & Kaiser Staffelstein (1955)–1970	Alboth & Kaiser Staffelstein (1955)–1970	1094 **484**
Beyer & Bock and VEB Porcelain Factory Rudolstadt-Volkstedt Volkstedt 1931-1990	Beyer & Bock und VEB Porzellanfabrik Rudolstadt-Volkstedt Volkstedt 1931-1990	1095 **496**

Porcelain Manufactory Ludwigsburg Ludwigsburg 1948–present blue underglaze	Porzellanmanufaktur Ludwigsburg Ludwigsburg 1948–heute blau unterglasur	109 441
Karlsbad Porcelain Factory Carl Knoll Fischern 1939–1945	Karlsbader Porzellanfabrik Carl Knoll Fischern 1939–1945	109 402
Karlsbad Porcelain Factory Carl Knoll Fischern circa 1910–1945	Karlsbader Porzellanfabrik Carl Knoll Fischern ca. 1910–1945	109 402
Duchcov Porcelain Dux 1947–present	Duchcovsky Porcelan Dux 1947–heute	109 397
M. Budich Kronach (1962)– decorator's mark	M. Budich Kronach (1962)– Malermarke	110 433
Eichwald Porcelain Stove and Tile Factory Dr. Widera & Co. Eichwald (1940)–1945 blue or green	Eichwalder Porzellan–, Ofen- und Wandplattenfabrik Dr. Widera & Co. Eichwald (1940)–1945 blau oder grün	110 397
E. & A. Muller Schonwald circa 1910–circa 1922	E. & A. Müller Schönwald ca. 1910–ca. 1922	110 475
Duchcov Porcelain Dux/Eichwald 1947–present blue or green	Duchcovsky Porcelan Dux/Eichwald 1947–heute blau oder grün	110 397
Kups Porcelain Manufactory Ernst Lindner Kups 1970–present	Küpser Porzellanmanufaktur Ernst Lindner Küps 1970–heute	110 434

154

Erdmann Schlegelmilch Suhl after 1891– green or blue	Erdmann Schlegelmilch Suhl nach 1891– grün oder blau	1105 485
Erdmann Schlegelmilch Suhl after 1900– green underglaze or overglaze	Erdmann Schlegelmilch Suhl nach 1900– grün unterglasur oder aufglasur	1106 485
Ernst Wahliss Turn-Teplitz 1897–1906	Ernst Wahliss Turn-Teplitz 1897–1906	1107 491
Furstenberg Porcelain Manufactory Furstenberg 1947–circa 1958	Fürstenberg Porzellan- manufaktur Fürstenberg 1947–ca. 1958	1108 405
Furstenberg Porcelain Manufactory Furstenberg 1922–circa 1958	Fürstenberg Porzellan- manufaktur Fürstenberg 1922–ca. 1958	1109 405
Friedrich Simon Karlsbad (1921)– decorator's mark overglaze	Friedrich Simon Karlsbad (1921)– Malermarke aufglasur	1110 426
Graf & Krippner Selb after 1906–circa 1929	Gräf & Krippner Selb nach 1906–ca. 1929	1111 479
Karlsbad Porcelain Factory "Concordia" Bros. Loew & Co. Lessau circa 1919–1937	Karlsbader Porzellan- fabrik "Concordia" Gebr. Loew & Co. Lessau ca. 1919–1937	1112 437
Heinrich Porcelain Selb 1974–1976 blue or green underglaze blue or red or gold overglaze	Heinrich Porzellan Selb 1974–1976 blau oder grün unterglasur blau oder rot oder gold aufglasur	1113 479

155

Heinrich & Co. Selb 1904– blue or green underglaze	Heinrich & Co. Selb 1904– blau oder grün unterglasur	111 **479**
Heinrich & Co. Selb 1911–1934 blue or green underglaze	Heinrich & Co. Selb 1911–1934 blau oder grün unterglasur	111 **479**
Heinrich & Co. Selb 1911–1914 blue or green underglaze	Heinrich & Co. Selb 1911–1914 blau oder grün unterglasur	111 **479**
Heinrich & Co. Selb (1930)–1939 blue or green underglaze	Heinrich & Co. Selb (1930)–1939 blau oder grün unterglasur	111 **479**
Heinrich & Co. Selb 1939–present blue or green underglaze	Heinrich & Co. Selb 1939–heute blau oder grün unterglasur	1118 **479**
Hamburger & Co. New York City circa 1900–1910 importer's mark	Hamburger & Co. New York ca. 1900–1910 Importeurmarke	1119 **455**
Heinzl & Co. Granesau 1924–1939	Heinzl & Co. Granesau 1924–1939	1120 **412**
H. Hilbert Schrobenhausen 1965–1970 blue overglaze	H. Hilbert Schrobenhausen 1965–1970 blau aufglasur	1121 **476**
Hertel, Jacob & Co. Rehau after 1922–circa 1969	Hertel, Jacob & Co. Rehau nach 1922–ca. 1969	1122 **466**
Porcelain Factory Sandizell Sandizell 1951-1960	Porzellanfabrik Sandizell Sandizell 1951-1960	1123 **470**

Porcelain Manufactory Hans Worms Schlottenhof after 1935–circa 1965	Porzellanmanufaktur Hans Worms Schlottenhof nach 1935–ca. 1965	1124 **474**
Porcelain Factory Waldershof Waldershof 1939–present green underglaze	Porzellanfabrik Waldershof Waldershof 1939–heute grün unterglasur	1125 **498**
J. Kronester Schwarzenbach after 1905–circa 1969	J. Kronester Schwarzenbach nach 1905–ca. 1969	1126 **477**
Krautheim & Adelberg Selb 1945–present export mark green overglaze	Krautheim & Adelberg Selb 1945–heute Exportmarke grün aufglasur	1127 **479**
Gerhard Knopf Steinbach (1975)–	Gerhard Knopf Steinbach (1975)–	1128 **484**
Kerafina Marktredwitz 1950–1958 different colors overglaze	Kerafina Marktredwitz 1950–1958 verschiedene Farben aufglasur	1129 **444**
Krister Porcelain Manufactory Waldenburg (1885)– blue or green underglaze	Krister Porzellanmanufaktur Waldenburg (1885)– blau oder grün unterglasur	1130 **497**
Krister Porcelain Manufactory Landstuhl 1952–	Krister Porzellanmanufaktur Landstuhl 1952–	1131 **436**
Krister Porcelain Manufactory Waldenburg/Landstuhl (1941)–	Krister Porzellanmanufaktur Waldenburg/Landstuhl (1941)–	1132 **497**

Kerafina Marktredwitz 1950–1958 different colors overglaze	Kerafina Marktredwitz 1950–1958 verschiedene Farben aufglasur	**1133** **444**

Kerafina
Marktredwitz
1950–1958
different colors
overglaze

Kerafina
Marktredwitz
1950–1958
verschiedene Farben
aufglasur

1133
444

Kerafina
Marktredwitz
1950–present
different colors
overglaze
also in combination
with: Handarbeit

Kerafina
Marktredwitz
1950–heute
verschiedene Farben
aufglasur
auch in Verbindung
mit: Handarbeit

1134
444

Kerafina
Marktredwitz
1950–present
different colors
overglaze
also in combination
with: Echt Cobalt

Kerafina
Marktredwitz
1950–heute
verschiedene Farben
aufglasur
auch in Verbindung
mit: Echt Cobalt

1135
444

Kerafina
Marktredwitz
1950–present
different colors
overglaze
also in combination
with: Handarbeit

Kerafina
Marktredwitz
1950–heute
verschiedene Farben
aufglasur
auch in Verbindung
mit: Handarbeit

1136
444

Klaus & Peter Muller
Hohr-Grenzhausen
(1958)–

Klaus & Peter Müller
Höhr-Grenzhausen
(1958)–

1137
419

K. Steinmann
Tiefenfurth
1916-1932

K. Steimann
Tiefenfurth
1916-1932

1138
488

K. Steinmann
Tiefenfurth
(1928)–1932

K. Steinmann
Tiefenfurth
(1928)–1932

1139
488

Porcelain Factory Langewiesen
Oscar Schlegelmilch
Langewiesen
(1950)–circa 1972

Porzellanfabrik Langewiesen
Oscar Schlegelmilch
Langewiesen
(1950)–ca. 1972

1140
436

unidentified after 1900 decorator's mark blue overglaze	nicht identifiziert nach 1900 Malermarke blau aufglasur	1141	
Porcelain Factory Spechtsbrunn Spechtsbrunn after 1930–circa 1954	Porzellanfabrik Spechtsbrunn Spechtsbrunn nach 1930–ca. 1954	1142 **483**	
Klaus & Peter Muller Hohr-Grenzhausen (1957)–	Klaus & Peter Müller Höhr-Grenzhausen (1957)–	1143 **419**	
Paul Muller Selb after 1890–1917	Paul Müller Selb nach 1890–1917	1144 **480**	
Porcelain Factory Sandizell Sandizell after 1951– blue	Porzellanfabrik Sandizell Sandizell nach 1951– blau	1145 **470**	
Porcelain Manufactory "Bavaria" Waldershof 1925–1977 red overglaze	Porzellanmanufaktur "Bavaria" Waldershof 1925–1977 rot aufglasur	1146 **498**	

Saxonian Porcelain
Factory Carl Thieme
Potschappel
    –circa 1955
blue
	Sächsische Porzellan-
	fabrik Carl Thieme
	Potschappel
	    –ca. 1955
	blau
		1147
		463	

Orben, Knabe & Co. Geschwenda after 1909–circa 1939	Orben, Knabe & Co. Geschwenda nach 1909–ca. 1939	1148 **407**	
Porcelain Factories Creidlitz Creidlitz after 1908–	Porzellanfabriken Creidlitz Creidlitz nach 1908–	1149 **391**	

Porcelain Factory Krummennaab Illinger & Co. Krummennaab 1931–1936	Porzellanfabrik Krummennaab Illinger & Co. Krummennaab 1931–1936	115 **434**
unidentified black overglaze	nicht identifiziert schwarz aufglasur	115
Pfeiffer & Lowenstein Schlackenwerth (1915)–1941	Pfeiffer & Löwenstein Schlackenwerth (1915)–1941	115 115 **472**
Pfeiffer & Lowenstein Schlackenwerth 1918–1939	Pfeiffer & Löwenstein Schlackenwerth 1918–1939	115 115 **472**
Fritz Popp Hummendorf 1943– decorator's mark gold overglaze	Fritz Popp Hummendorf 1943– Malermarke gold aufglasur	115 **421**
Porcelain Factory Schonwald Schonwald 1911–1927	Porzellanfabrik Schönwald Schönwald 1911–1927	115 **475**
Pfeiffer & Lowenstein Schlackenwerth (1914)–1918 green underglaze	Pfeiffer & Löwenstein Schlackenwerth (1914)–1918 grün unterglasur	115 **472**
Porcelain Factory Tirschenreuth Tirschenreuth –circa 1927 decorating mark overglaze	Porzellanfabrik Tirschenreuth Tirschenreuth –ca. 1927 Malereimarke aufglasur	115 **489**
Porcelain Factory Tirschenreuth Tirschenreuth probably after 1927 decorating mark overglaze	Porzellanfabrik Tirschenreuth Tirschenreuth wahrscheinlich nach 1927 Malereimarke aufglasur	116 **489**

160

Porcelain Factory Tirschenreuth Tirschenreuth (1947)– green underglaze	Porzellanfabrik Tirschenreuth Tirschenreuth (1947)– grün unterglasur	1161 **489**
Krister Porcelain Manufactory Landstuhl 1953–	Krister Porzellanmanufaktur Landstuhl 1953–	1162 **436**
Rosenthal-Block China Corporation New York City 1952–1963 importer's mark Rosenthal Selb 1963–present export mark	Rosenthal-Block China Corporation New York 1952–1963 Importeurmarke Rosenthal Selb 1963–heute Exportmarke	1163 **455**
Porcelain Factories Josef Rieber & Co. Mitterteich before 1945–circa 1976	Porzellanfabriken Josef Rieber & Co. Mitterteich vor 1945–ca. 1976	1164 **449**
Porcelain Factories Josef Rieber & Co. Mitterteich before 1945–circa 1976	Porzellanfabriken Josef Rieber & Co. Mitterteich vor 1945–ca. 1976	1165 **449**
Rosenthal Selb (1959)–	Rosenthal Selb (1959)–	1166 **480**
Porcelain Factory G. Rossbach Spechtsbrunn (1954)–1972 red	Porzellanfabrik G. Rossbach Spechtsbrunn (1954)–1972 rot	1167 **483**
R. Kampf Grunlas circa 1928–1939 green underglaze	R. Kämpf Grünlas ca. 1928–1939 grün unterglasur	1168 **413**

Karl Rau	Karl Rau	
Munich	München	
after 1945—before 1978	nach 1945—vor 1978	
decorator's mark	Malermarke	116
overglaze	aufglasur	**451**
Richard Klemm	Richard Klemm	
Dresden	Dresden	
(1888)—1916	(1888)—1916	
decorator's mark	Malermarke	117
blue overglaze	blau aufglasur	**395**
unidentified	nicht identifiziert	
decorator's mark	Malermarke	117
blue overglaze	blau aufglasur	
unidentified	nicht identifiziert	
decorator's mark	Malermarke	117
overglaze	aufglasur	
Adolf Wache	Adolf Wache	
Dresden	Dresden	
(1894)—	(1894)—	
decorator's mark	Malermarke	117.
overglaze	aufglasur	396
K. Steinmann	K. Steinmann	
Tiefenfurth	Tiefenfurth	117
after 1900-1932	nach 1900-1932	**488**
August Schweig	August Schweig	
Weisswasser	Weißwasser	117
after 1900—1940	nach 1900—1940	**500**
C.H. Tuppack	C.H. Tuppack	
Tiefenfurth	Tiefenfurth	117
1922-1932	1922-1932	**488**
Oscar Schaller & Co.	Oscar Schaller & Co.	
Successor	Nachf.	
Kirchenlamitz	Kirchenlamitz	117
1921—	1921—	**427**

Porcelain Factory Muhlbach Bruchmuhlbach 1951–circa 1970	Porzellanfabrik Mühlbach Bruchmühlbach 1951–ca. 1970	1178 **386**
Kronach Porcelain Factory Stockhardt & Schmidt-Eckert Kronach 1912–	Kronacher Porzellanfabrik Stockhardt & Schmidt-Eckert Kronach 1912–	1179 **434**
Count Thun's Porcelain Factory and Duchcov Porcelain Klosterle after 1900–1945 green or blue underglaze also in combination with: Czechoslovakia from 1918–1939 and after 1947–present	Graf Thun'sche Porzellan- fabrik und Duchcovsky Porcelan Klösterle nach 1900–1945 grün oder blau unterglasur auch in Verbindung mit: Czechoslovakia von 1918–1939 und nach 1947–heute	1180 **428**
Count Thun's Porcelain Factory Klosterle 1918–1939 green or blue underglaze	Graf Thun'sche Porzellan- fabrik Klösterle 1918–1939 grün oder blau unterglasur	1181 **428**
Count Thun's Porcelain Factory and Duchcov Porcelain Klosterle 1918–1939 and 1947– green or blue underglaze	Graf Thun'sche Porzellan- fabrik und Duchcovsky Porcelan Klösterle 1918–1939 und 1947– grün oder blau unterglasur	1182 **428**
Wagner & Apel Lippelsdorf (1954)–1972	Wagner & Apel Lippelsdorf (1954)–1972	1183 **440**
Oscar Schaller & Co. Successor Windischeschenbach (1948)– green underglaze	Oscar Schaller & Co. Nachf. Windischeschenbach (1948)– grün unterglasur	1184 **505**
Oscar Schaller & Co. Successor Windischeschenbach 1948–circa 1950 green underglaze	Oscar Schaller & Co. Nachf. Windischeschenbach 1948–ca. 1950 grün unterglasur	1185 **505**

W. Goebel	W. Goebel	
Rodental	Rödental	
1923–1937	1923–1937	
impressed or blue	eingeprägt oder blau	118
or black underglaze	oder schwarz unterglasur	46?
W. Goebel	W. Goebel	
Rodental	Rödental	
1923–1927	1923–1927	118
impressed on dolls heads	eingeprägt auf Puppenköpfen	46?
W. Goebel	W. Goebel	
Rodental	Rödental	118
1949–	1949–	46?
Krautzberger, Mayer & Purkert	Krautzberger, Mayer & Purkert	
Wistritz	Wistritz	118
after 1911–1945	nach 1911–1945	500
Porcelain Factory Pollwitz	Porzellanfabrik Pöllwitz	
Pollwitz	Pöllwitz	119
after 1920–1938	nach 1920–1938	46?
Winterling	Winterling	
Bruchmuhlbach	Bruchmühlbach	
circa 1970–present	ca. 1970–heute	119
on earthenware	auf Steingut	386
Oscar Schaller & Co.	Oscar Schaller & Co.	
Successor	Nachf.	
Kirchenlamitz	Kirchenlamitz	119
after 1950–present	nach 1950–heute	427
Heinrich Winterling	Heinrich Winterling	
Marktleuthen	Marktleuthen	119
after 1950–present	nach 1950–heute	444
Bros. Winterling	Gebr. Winterling	
Roslau	Röslau	119
after 1950–present	nach 1950–heute	468
Oscar Schaller & Co.	Oscar Schaller & Co.	
Successor	Nachf.	
Schwarzenbach	Schwarzenbach	119
after 1950–present	nach 1950–heute	477

Zehendner & Co. Tirschenreuth circa 1940—	Zehendner & Co. Tirschenreuth ca. 1940—	1196 **489**
H. Wehinger Horn 1905—1918 green underglaze	H. Wehinger Horn 1905—1918 grün unterglasur	1197 **420**
Heinrich Baensch Lettin (1927)—1930	Heinrich Baensch Lettin (1927)—1930	1198 **438**
Porcelain Factory Waldsassen Waldsassen 1970-1993 green	Porzellanfabrik Waldsassen Waldsassen 1970-1993 grün	1199 **498**
Porcelain Factory Waldsassen Waldsassen 1960—circa 1970 green	Porzellanfabrik Waldsassen Waldsassen 1960—ca. 1970 grün	1200 **498**
Kerafina Marktredwitz 1950—1958 blue underglaze	Kerafina Marktredwitz 1950—1958 blau unterglasur	1201 **444**
Porcelain Factories Josef Rieber & Co. Mitterteich (1953)—before 1978	Porzellanfabriken Josef Rieber & Co. Mitterteich (1953)—vor 1978	1202 **449**
Porcelain Factories Creiditz Creidlitz after 1908—	Porzellanfabriken Creidlitz Creidlitz nach 1908—	1203 **391**
Porcelain Manufactory "Bavaria" Waldershof circa 1925—1977	Porzellanmanufaktur "Bavaria" Waldershof ca. 1925—1977	1204 **498**

Rhenania Porcelain Factory Duisdorf (1957)–	Rhenania Porzellanfabrik Duisdorf (1957)–	12 39
Porcelain Factory Markt- redwitz Jaeger & Co. Marktredwitz (1911)–	Porzellanfabrik Markt- redwitz Jaeger & Co. Marktredwitz (1911)–	12 44
VEB Earthenwarework Dresden Dresden (1956)-1990	VEB Steingutwerk Dresden Dresden (1956)-1990	12 39
Moller & Dippe Unterkoditz –1931	Möller & Dippe Unterköditz –1931	12 49
Richard Klemm and Donath & Co. and Oswald Lorenz and Adolph Hamann Dresden 1883–1893 decorators mark blue overglaze	Richard Klemm und Donath & Co. und Oswald Lorenz und Adolph Hamann Dresden 1883–1893 Malermarke blau aufglasur	12 39 39
Adolph Hamann Dresden 1883–circa 1949 decorator's mark blue overglaze	Adolph Hamann Dresden 1883–ca. 1949 Malermarke blau aufglasur	12 39
Donath & Co. Dresden (1893)–1916 decorator's mark blue overglaze or underglaze	Donath & Co. Dresden (1893)–1916 Malermarke blau aufglasur oder unterglasur	12 39
Adolph Hamann Dresden (1883)–circa 1949 decorator's mark blue overglaze	Adolph Hamann Dresden (1883)–ca. 1949 Malermarke blau aufglasur	12 39

Adolph Hamann Dresden (1894)–circa 1949 decorator's mark blue overglaze	Adolph Hamann Dresden (1894)–ca. 1949 Malermarke blau aufglasur		1213 **394**
Adolph Hamann Dresden (1905)–circa 1949 decorator's mark blue overglaze	Adolph Hamann Dresden (1905)–ca. 1949 Malermarke blau aufglasur		1214 **394**
Richard Klemm Dresden (1893)–1916 decorator's mark blue overglaze	Richard Klemm Dresden (1893)–1916 Malermarke blau aufglasur		1215 **395**
K. Steinmann Tiefenfurth (1896)–circa 1938	K. Steinmann Tiefenfurth (1896)–ca. 1938		1216 **488**
unidentified probably Helena Wolfsohn Dresden after 1886 blue overglaze	nicht identifiziert wahrscheinlich Helena Wolfsohn Dresden nach 1886 blau aufglasur		1217 **396**
unidentified blue underglaze	nicht identifiziert blau unterglasur		1218
probably Adolf Wache Dresden after 1894 decorator's mark blue overglaze	wahrscheinlich Adolf Wache Dresden nach 1894 Malermarke blau aufglasur		1219 **396**
E. & A. Muller Schonwald circa 1922–circa 1927	E. & A. Müller Schönwald ca. 1922–ca. 1927		1220 **475**
Edelstein Porcelain Factory Kups after 1934– green underglaze	Edelstein Porzellanfabrik Küps nach 1934– grün unterglasur		1221 **435**

Christian Seltmann Erbendorf 1940–circa 1955 green underglaze	Christian Seltmann Erbendorf 1940–ca. 1955 grün unterglasur	122 **400**
Oscar Schaller & Co. Successor Windischeschenbach after 1945– green underglaze	Oscar Schaller & Co. Nachf. Windischeschenbach nach 1945– grün unterglasur	122 **505**
Oscar Schaller & Co. Successor Windischeschenbach after 1945– green underglaze	Oscar Schaller & Co. Nachf. Windischeschenbach nach 1945– grün unterglasur	122 **505**
Porcelain Factory Eversberg Stockheim 1978–present green underglaze	Porzellanfabrik Eversberg Stockheim 1978–heute grün unterglasur	122 **485**
Hutschenreuther Selb (1976)–present	Hutschenreuther Selb (1976)–heute	122 **479**
Krautheim & Adelberg Selb (1950)–present	Krautheim & Adelberg Selb (1950)–heute	122 **479**
Porcelain Factory Cortendorf Coburg-Cortendorf (1935)–1973	Porzellanfabrik Cortendorf Coburg-Cortendorf (1935)–1973	122 **390**
Furstenberg Porcelain Manufactory Furstenberg (1958)–present	Fürstenberg Porzellan- manufaktur Fürstenberg (1958)–heute	122 **405**
W. Goebel Rodental 1937–1945 impressed or blue or black underglaze	W. Goebel Rödental 1937–1945 eingeprägt oder blau oder schwarz unterglasur	123 **467**

Heinrich Porcelain Selb 1976—present blue or green underglaze	Heinrich Porzellan Selb 1976—heute blau oder grün unterglasur	1231 **479**
L. Hutschenreuther Selb 1928—1943	L. Hutschenreuther Selb 1928—1943	1232 **479**
C. M. Hutschenreuther Arzberg circa 1928—circa 1963 green underglaze	C. M. Hutschenreuther Arzberg ca. 1928—ca. 1963 grün unterglasur	1233 **377**
C. M. Hutschenreuther Arzberg 1963— green underglaze	C. M. Hutschenreuther Arzberg 1963— grün unterglasur	1234 **377**
L. Wessel Bonn (1893)—	L. Wessel Bonn (1893)—	1235 **385**
Porcelain Factory W. Jaeger Eisenberg after 1945—1960	Porzellanfabrik W. Jaeger Eisenberg nach 1945—1960	1236 **398**
Porcelain Factory Waldershof Waldershof 1966- green underglaze or overglaze	Porzellanfabrik Waldershof Waldershof 1966- grün unter- oder aufglasur	1237 **498**
Johann Seltmann Vohenstrauss after 1945—	Johann Seltmann Vohenstrauß nach 1945—	1238 **494**
Johann Seltmann Vohenstrauss (1917)— green underglaze	Johann Seltmann Vohenstrauß (1917)— grün unterglasur	1239 **494**

Johann Seltmann Vohenstrauss presently green underglaze	Johann Seltmann Vohenstrauß heute grün unterglasur	124 **494**	
J. Kronester Schwarzenbach 1969–present green underglaze	J. Kronester Schwarzenbach 1969–heute grün unterglasur	124 **477**	
J. Kronester Schwarzenbach presently	J. Kronester Schwarzenbach heute	124 **477**	
Porcelain Factory Konigszelt Konigszelt (1922)–1928	Porzellanfabrik Königszelt Königszelt (1922)–1928	124 **430**	
Porcelain Factory Krummennaab H. Lange Krummennaab 1936–1939	Porzellanfabrik Krummennaab H. Lange Krummennaab 1936–1939	124 **434**	
Heinrich Baensch and Porcelain Factory Lettin Lettin (1927)–circa 1945	Heinrich Baensch und Porzellanfabrik Lettin Lettin (1927)–ca. 1945	124 **438**	
VEB Porcelain Figurines Lippelsdorf (1974)-1990	VEB Porzellanfiguren Lippelsdorf (1974)-1990	124 **440**	
Christian Seltmann Weiden (1936)– green underglaze	Christian Seltmann Weiden (1937)– grün unterglasur	124 **500**	
Porcelain Factory Tirschenreuth Tirschenreuth circa 1900–circa 1927	Porzellanfabrik Tirschenreuth Tirschenreuth ca. 1900–ca. 1927	1248 **489**	
Triptis AG Triptis (1931)–circa 1945	Triptis AG Triptis (1931)–ca. 1945	124 **489**	

Porcelain Factory Pollwitz Pollwitz 1925–1938	Porzellanfabrik Pöllwitz Pöllwitz 1925–1938	1250 **463**
W. Goebel Rodental (1907)–	W. Goebel Rödental (1907)–	1251 **467**
Pfeiffer & Lowenstein Schlackenwerth –1941	Pfeiffer & Löwenstein Schlackenwerth –1941	1252 **472**
F. A. Reinecke Eisenberg (1927)–1960 green underglaze	F. A. Reinecke Eisenberg (1927)–1960 grün unterglasur	1253 **398**
Porcelain Factory Moschendorf Hof-Moschendorf after 1904–1938	Porzellanfabrik Moschendorf Hof-Moschendorf nach 1904–1938	1254 **419**
Rosenthal Selb (1934)–	Rosenthal Selb (1934)–	1255 **480**
Schumann China Corporation New York City 1931–circa 1941 importer's mark	Schumann China Corporation New York 1931–ca. 1941 Importeurmarke	1256 **456**
Krister Porcelain Manufactory Landstuhl (1956)–	Krister Porzellan- manufaktur Landstuhl (1956)–	1257 **436**
Zeh, Scherzer & Co. Rehau -1991	Zeh, Scherzer & Co. Rehau -1991	1258 **466**

August Schweig Weisswasser (1931)–1940	August Schweig Weißwasser (1931)–1940	125 **500**
Christian Seltmann Erbendorf 1940–1975 green underglaze	Christian Seltmann Erbendorf 1940–1975 grün unterglasur	126 **400**
Christian Seltmann Weiden 1954–present green underglaze	Christian Seltmann Weiden 1954–heute grün unterglasur	126 **500**
Christian Seltmann Erbendorf circa 1946–circa 1975 green underglaze	Christian Seltmann Erbendorf circa 1946–ca. 1975 grün unterglasur	126 **400**
Porcelain Factory Weissenstadt Weissenstadt (1932)–1964	Porzellanfabrik Weißenstadt Weißenstadt (1932)–1964	126 **500**
L. Hutschenreuther Selb (1959)–	L. Hutschenreuther Selb (1959)–	126 **479**
Porcelain Factory Bavaria Ullersricht (1928)–circa 1932	Porzellanfabrik Bavaria Ullersricht (1928)–1932	126 **491**
Porcelain Factory Victoria Altrohlau circa 1919–1945 green or blue	Porzellanfabrik Victoria Altrohlau ca. 1919–1945 grün oder blau	126 **374**
Porcelain Factory Victoria Altrohlau (1904)–1945 also in combination with: Austria 1904–1918 Czechoslovakia 1918–1939 Germany 1939–1945	Porzellanfabrik Victoria Altrohlau (1904)–1945 auch in Verbindung mit: Austria 1904–1918 Czechoslovakia 1918–1939 Germany 1939–1945	1267 **374**

Porcelain Factory Victoria Altrohlau 1918–1939 green or blue	Porzellanfabrik Victoria Altrohlau 1918–1939 grün oder blau	1268 **374**
Wurttemberg Porcelain Manufactory Schorndorf 1904–1939	Württembergische Porzellanmanufaktur Schorndorf 1904–1939	1269 **475**
F. & W. Goebel Rodental (1919)–	F. & W. Goebel Rödental (1919)–	1270 **467**
Oscar Schaller & Co. Successor Windischeschenbach (1929)– green	Oscar Schaller & Co. Nachf. Windischeschenbach (1929)– grün	1271 **505**
Oscar Schaller & Co. Successor Windischeschenbach (1930)–	Oscar Schaller & Co. Nachf. Windischeschenbach (1930)–	1272 **505**
Zeh, Scherzer & Co. Rehau 1930-1991	Zeh, Scherzer & Co. Rehau 1930-1991	1273 **466**
Zeh, Scherzer & Co. Rehau 1930	Zeh, Scherzer & Co. Rehau 1930	1274 **466**
Widow A. F. Prahl Ellwangen 1758–1759 blue underglaze	Wwe. A. F. Prahl Ellwangen 1758–1759 blau unterglasur	1275 **400**
Widow A. F. Prahl Ellwangen 1758–1759 blue underglaze	Widow A. F. Prahl Ellwangen 1758–1759 blau unterglasur	1276 **400**

Fulda Fayence and Porcelain Factory Fulda (1946)–	Fuldaer Fayence- und Porzellanfabrik Fulda (1946)–	127 **406**
Ferdinand Schmetz Aachen (1893)–after 1959	Ferdinand Schmetz Aachen (1893)–nach 1959	127 **371**
Cuno & Otto Dressel Sonneberg around 1912 impressed or stamped on doll heads	Cuno & Otto Dressel Sonneberg um 1912 eingeprägt oder gestempelt auf Puppenköpfen	127 **482**
Louis Huth Possneck 1894–circa 1940 decorator's mark	Louis Huth Pößneck 1894–ca. 1940 Malermarke	128 **463**
Louis Huth Possneck 1894–circa 1940 decorator's mark	Louis Huth Pößneck 1894–ca. 1940 Malermarke	128 **463**
Royal Porcelain Manufactory Berlin 1763–1780 blue underglaze	Königliche Porzellan Manufaktur Berlin 1763–1780 blau unterglasur	128 –129 **380**
Royal Porcelain Manufactory Berlin 1780–1800 blue underglaze	Königliche Porzellan Manufaktur Berlin 1780–1800 blau unterglasur	129 – 129 **380**
Royal Porcelain Manufactory Berlin circa 1800 blue underglaze	Königliche Porzellan Manufaktur Berlin ca. 1800 blau unterglasur	129 **380**

Royal Porcelain Manufactory	Königliche Porzellan Manufaktur	
Berlin	Berlin	
circa 1810	ca. 1810	1297
blue underglaze	blau unterglasur	**380**
Royal Porcelain Manufactory	Königliche Porzellan Manufaktur	
Berlin	Berlin	
1815–1820	1815–1820	1298
blue underglaze	blau unterglasur	**380**
Royal Porcelain Manufactory	Königliche Porzellan Manufaktur	
Berlin	Berlin	
circa 1820–1830	ca. 1820–1830	1299
blue underglaze	blau unterglasur	**380**
Royal Porcelain Manufactory	Königliche Porzellan Manufaktur	
Berlin	Berlin	
circa 1830–1840	ca. 1830–1840	1300
blue underglaze	blau unterglasur	**380**
Royal Porcelain Manufactory	Königliche Porzellan Manufaktur	
Berlin	Berlin	
circa 1830–1840	ca. 1830–1840	1301
blue underglaze	blau unterglasur	**380**
Royal Porcelain Manufactory	Königliche Porzellan Manufaktur	
Berlin	Berlin	
1837	1837	1302
blue underglaze	blau unterglasur	**380**
Royal Porcelain Manufactory	Königliche Porzellan Manufaktur	
and State's Porcelain Manufactory	und Staatliche Porzellanmanufaktur	
Berlin	Berlin	
1870–present	1870–heute	1303
blue underglaze	blau unterglasur	**380**
State's Porcelain Manufactory	Staatliche Porzellanmanufaktur	1304
Berlin	Berlin	1305
1946–present	1946–heute	1306
blue underglaze	blau unterglasur	**380**
unidentified	nicht identifiziert	1307
blue overglaze	blau aufglasur	
unidentified	nicht identifiziert	1308
blue underglaze	blau unterglasur	

175

	Royal Porcelain Manufactory and State's Porcelain Manufactory Berlin 1882–present black on earthenware	Königliche Porzellan Manufaktur und Staatliche Porzellanmanufaktur Berlin 1882–heute schwarz auf Steingut	1 3.
	Royal Porcelain Manufactory and State's Porcelain Manufactory Berlin circa 1825–present impressed	Königliche Porzellan Manufaktur und Staatliche Porzellanmanufaktur Berlin ca. 1825–heute eingeprägt	1. 3:
	Royal Porcelain Manufactory Berlin 1837–1844 blue underglaze	Königliche Porzellan Manufaktur Berlin 1837–1844 blau unterglasur	1: 3.
	State's Porcelain Manufactory Selb/Berlin 1943–1957 blue underglaze	Staatliche Porzellanmanufaktur Selb/Berlin 1943–1957 blau unterglasur	1: 3: 4:
	Royal Porcelain Manufactory and State's Porcelain Manufactory Berlin 1882–present blue underglaze	Königliche Porzellan Manufaktur und Staatliche Porzellanmanufaktur Berlin 1882–heute blau unterglasur	1: 3:
	Royal Porcelain Manufactory and State's Porcelain Manufactory Berlin 1913–present green overglaze on porcelain with simple borders in gold or color	Königliche Porzellan Manufaktur und Staatliche Porzellanmanufaktur Berlin 1913–heute grün aufglasur für Porzellan mit einfachem Rand in Gold oder Farbe	13 38
	Royal Porcelain Manufactory and State's Porcelain Manufactory Berlin 1911–present blue underglaze on porcelain with underglaze decoration	Königliche Porzellan Manufaktur und Staatliche Porzellanmanufaktur Berlin 1911–heute blau unterglasur für Unterglasurmalerei	13 38
	Royal Porcelain Manufactory and State's Porcelain Manufactory Berlin 1832–present red overglaze, decorating mark	Königliche Porzellan Manufaktur und Staatliche Porzellanmanufaktur Berlin 1832–heute rot aufglasur, Malereimarke	13 38:

Anton Herr	Anton Herr	
Bogen	Bogen	
1946–present	1946–heute	1317
on earthenware and fayence	auf Steingut und Fayence	**385**

Anton Herr	Anton Herr	
Bogen	Bogen	
1946–present	1946–heute	1318
on earthenware and fayence	auf Steingut und Fayence	**385**

Anton Herr	Anton Herr	
Bogen	Bogen	
1946–present	1946–heute	1319
on fayence	auf Fayence	**385**

Epiag	Epiag	
Aich	Aich	
1922–1933	1922–1933	1320
green or blue	grün oder blau	**371**

Dressel, Kister & Cie.	Dressel, Kister & Cie.	
Passau	Passau	1321
(1907)–circa 1922	(1907)–ca. 1922	1322
blue	blau	**460**

Dressel, Kister & Cie.	Dressel, Kister & Cie.	
Passau	Passau	
1905–1922	1905–1922	1323
blue underglaze	blau unterglasur	**460**

Dressel, Kister & Cie.	Dressel, Kister & Cie.	
Passau	Passau	
circa 1907–1922	ca. 1907–1922	1324
blue or green	blau oder grün	**460**

Philipp Dietrich	Philipp Dietrich	
Passau	Passau	1325
1937–1942	1937–1942	**460**

Paul Schreier	Paul Schreier	
Bischofswerda	Bischofswerda	
circa 1930	ca. 1930	
decorator's mark	Malermarke	1326
overglaze	aufglasur	**384**

	Gareis, Kuhnl & Cie. Waldsassen after 1900–1969	Gareis, Kühnl & Cie. Waldsassen nach 1900–1969	132 **498**
	Royal Porcelain Manufactory Meissen circa 1721–circa 1735 blue underglaze	Königliche Porzellan Manufaktur Meißen ca. 1721–ca. 1735 blau unterglasur	132 **446**
	same as 1328	wie 1328	132 **446**
	same as 1328	wie 1328	133 **446**
	same as 1328	wie 1328	133 **446**
	same as 1328	wie 1328	133 **446**
	same as 1328	wie 1328	133 **446**
	same as 1328	wie 1328	133 **446**
	same as 1328	wie 1328	133 **446**
	same as 1328	wie 1328	133 **446**
	same as 1328	wie 1328	133 **446**
	same as 1328	wie 1328	133 **446**
	same as 1328	wie 1328	133 **446**
	same as 1328	wie 1328	134 **446**

same as 1328	wie 1328	1341 **446**
same as 1328	wie 1328	1342 **446**
Royal Porcelain Manufactory Meissen circa 1721–circa 1735 "caduceus" blue underglaze cross and dots impressed	Königliche Porzellan Manufaktur Meißen ca. 1721–ca. 1735 "Caduceus" blau unterglasur Kreuz und Punkte eingeprägt	1343 **446**
Royal Porcelain Manufactory Meissen circa 1721–circa 1735 blue underglaze	Königliche Porzellan Manufaktur Meißen ca. 1721–ca. 1735 blau unterglasur	1344 **446**
same as 1344	wie 1344	1345 **446**
same as 1344	wie 1344	1346 **446**
same as 1344	wie 1344	1347 **446**
same as 1344	wie 1344	1348 **446**
same as 1344	wie 1344	1349 **446**
same as 1344	wie 1344	1350 **446**
same as 1344	wie 1344	1351 **446**
same as 1344	wie 1344	1352 **446**
same as 1344	wie 1344	1353 **446**
same as 1344	wie 1344	1354 **446**
same as 1344	wie 1344	1355 **446**

Royal Porcelain Manufactory Meissen circa 1724−circa 1735 swords and "caduceus" blue underglaze letters and number incised inventory mark of the Johanneum collection in Dresden	Königliche Porzellan Manufaktur Meißen ca. 1724−ca. 1735 Schwerter und "Caduceus" blau unterglasur Buchstaben und Zahl eingeschliffen Inventurmarke des Johanneums in Dresden	13 44
Royal Porcelain Manufactory Meissen circa 1721−circa 1735 blue underglaze	Königliche Porzellan Manufaktur Meißen ca. 1721−ca. 1735 blau unterglasur	13 44
Royal Porcelain Manufactory Meissen circa 1723−circa 1731 blue underglaze court mark	Königliche Porzellan Manufaktur Meißen ca. 1723−ca. 1731 blau unterglasur Hofmarke	13 44
Carl Schumann Arzberg after 1896−	Carl Schumann Arzberg nach 1896−	13 37
Carl Schumann Arzberg (1896)−	Carl Schumann Arzberg (1896)−	13 37
Carl Hans Tuppack Tiefenfurt 1919−1935	Carl Hans Tuppack Tiefenfurt 1919−1935	13 48
Imperial and Royal Porcelain Manufactory Vienna 1744−1749 impressed	k. k. Aerarial Porzellan Manufaktur Wien 1744−1749 eingeprägt	13 50
same as 1362	wie 1362	13 13 50
same as 1362	wie 1362	13 13 50

	same as 1362	wie 1362	1367 **502**
	same as 1362	wie 1362	1368 **502**
	same as 1362	wie 1362	1369 **502**
	same as 1362	wie 1362	1370 **502**
	Imperial & Royal Porcelain Manufactory Vienna 1744–1749 incised	k.k. Aerarial Porzellan Manufaktur Wien 1744–1749 eingeritzt	1371 **502**
	Imperial & Royal Porcelain Manufactory Vienna 1744–1749 impressed	k.k. Aerarial Porzellan Manufaktur Wien 1744–1749 eingeprägt	1372 **502**
	same as 1372	wie 1372	1373 **502**
	Imperial & Royal Porcelain Manufactory Vienna 1744–1749 red overglaze	k.k. Aerarial Porzellan Manufaktur Wien 1744–1749 rot aufglasur	1374 **502**
	Imperial and Royal Porcelain Manufactory Vienna 1744–1749 blue or black or purple overglaze	k. k. Aerarial Porzellan Manufaktur Wien 1744–1749 blau oder schwarz oder purpur aufglasur	1375 **502**
	same as 1375	wie 1375	1376 **502**
	Imperial and Royal Porcelain Manufactory Vienna 1749–1827 blue underglaze	k.k. Aerarial Porzellan Manufaktur Wien 1749–1827 blau unterglasur	1377 1378 **502**

	Imperial and Royal Porcelain Manufactory Vienna circa 1760–circa 1770 blue underglaze	k.k. Aerarial Porzellan Manufaktur Wien ca. 1760–ca. 1770 blau unterglasur	13 50
	same as 1379	wie 1379	13 50
	same as 1379	wie 1379	13 50
	same as 1379	wie 1379	13 50
	same as 1379	wie 1379	13 50
	Imperial and Royal Porcelain Manufactory Vienna 1749–1827 blue underglaze	k.k. Aerarial Porzellan Manufaktur Wien 1749–1827 blau unterglasur	13 50
	Imperial and Royal Porcelain Manufactory Vienna 1749–1827 and 1860–1864 blue underglaze	k.k. Aerarial Porzellan Manufaktur Wien 1749–1827 und 1860–1864 blau unterglasur	138 50
	same as 1384	wie 1384	13 50
	Imperial and Royal Porcelain Manufactory Vienna circa 1785–1790 blue underglaze	k.k. Aerarial Porzellan Manufaktur Wien ca. 1785–1790 blau unterglasur	13 50
	Imperial and Royal Porcelain Manufactory Vienna 1749–1827 and 1860–1864 blue underglaze	k.k. Aerarial Porzellan Manufaktur Wien 1749–1827 und 1860–1864 blau unterglasur	138 50

	same as 1388	wie 1388	1389 **502**
	same as 1388	wie 1388	1390 **502**
	Imperial and Royal Porcelain Manufactory Vienna 1812–1818 blue underglaze	k.k. Aerarial Porzellan Manufaktur Wien 1812–1818 blau unterglasur	1391 **502**
	Imperial and Royal Porcelain Manufactory Vienna 1812–1815 blue underglaze	k.k. Aerarial Porzellan Manufaktur Wien 1812–1815 blau unterglasur	1392 **502**
	Imperial and Royal Porcelain Manufactory Vienna 1812–1818 shield blue underglaze number purple overglaze identification number of polychrome decorator	k.k. Aerarial Porzellan Manufaktur Wien 1812–1818 Schild blau unterglasur Zahl purpur aufglasur Identifikationsnummer eines Buntmalers	1393 **502**
	Imperial and Royal Porcelain Manufactory Vienna circa 1814–1824 shield blue underglaze number red overglaze identification number of polychrome decorator	k.k. Aerarial Porzellan Manufaktur Wien ca. 1814–1824 Schild blau unterglasur Zahl rot aufglasur Identifikationsnummer eines Buntmalers	1394 **502**
	Imperial and Royal Porcelain Manufactory Vienna 1814–1824 blue underglaze	k.k. Aerarial Porzellan Manufaktur Wien 1814–1824 blau unterglasur	1395 **502**
	Imperial and Royal Porcelain Manufactory Vienna circa 1820–1827 blue underglaze	k.k. Aerarial Porzellan Manufaktur Wien ca. 1820–1827 blau unterglasur	1396 **502**

Imperial and Royal Porcelain Manufactory Vienna circa 1790–1827 blue underglaze	k.k. Aerarial Porzellan Manufaktur Wien ca. 1790–1827 blau unterglasur		139 502
Imperial and Royal Porcelain Manufactory Vienna circa 1812–1827 blue underglaze	k.k. Aerarial Porzellan Manufaktur Wien ca. 1812–1827 blau unterglasur		139 502
Imperial and Royal Porcelain Manufactory Vienna 1827–1864 impressed	k.k. Aerarial Porzellan Manufaktur Wien 1827–1864 eingeprägt		139 502
same as 1399	wie 1399		140 502
same as 1399	wie 1399		140 502
same as 1399	wie 1399		140 502
Imperial and Royal Porcelain Manufactory Vienna circa 1860–1864 blue underglaze	k.k. Aerarial Porzellan Manufaktur Wien ca. 1860–1864 blau unterglasur		140 502
Philipp Aigner Vienna about 1900 blue	Philipp Aigner Wien um 1900 blau		140 501
Porcelain Factory Kolmar Kolmar 1897–circa 1944 blue underglaze	Porzellanfabrik Kolmar Kolmar 1897–ca. 1944 blau unterglasur		140 432
Vienna Porcelain Factory Augarten Vienna 1923–present blue also in combination with: Augarten	Wiener Porzellanfabrik Augarten Wien 1923–heute blau auch in Verbindung mit: Augarten		140 503

Vienna Porcelain Factory	Wiener Porzellanfabrik		
Augarten	Augarten		
Vienna	Wien		
1923—present	1923—heute	1407	
blue	blau	**503**	

Vienna Porcelain Factory	Wiener Porzellanfabrik		
Augarten	Augarten		
Vienna	Wien		
1923—present	1923—heute	1408	
blue	blau	**503**	

Vienna Porcelain Factory	Wiener Porzellanfabrik		
Augarten	Augarten		
Vienna	Wien		
1923—present	1923—heute	1409	
blue	blau	**503**	

Vienna Porcelain Factory	Wiener Porzellanfabrik		
Augarten	Augarten		
Vienna	Wien		
1923—present	1923—heute	1410	
blue	blau	**503**	

Robert Franz Staral	Robert Franz Staral		
Vienna	Wien		
(1923)—	(1923)—		
decorator's mark	Malermarke	1411	
overglaze	aufglasur	**502**	

Dr. Siegfried Ilse for	Dr. Siegfried Ilse für die		
Vienna Porcelain Factory	Wiener Porzellanfabrik		
Augarten	Augarten		
Vienna	Wien		
(1940)—	(1940)—	1412	
on earthenware	auf Steingut	**503**	

Wachtersbach Earthenware	Wächtersbacher Steingut-		
Factory	fabrik		
Schlierbach	Schlierbach		
1883—present	1883—heute	1413	
blue or black or impressed	blau oder schwarz oder eingeprägt	**473**	

Wachtersbach Earthenware	Wächtersbacher Steingut-		
Factory	fabrik		
Schlierbach	Schlierbach		
1900—1907	1900—1907	1414	
black or blue	schwarz oder blau	**473**	

185

Wächtersbach

Wachtersbach Earthenware Factory Schlierbach 1884–1887 impressed	Wächtersbacher Steingutfabrik Schlierbach 1884–1887 eingeprägt	141	**473**
Wachtersbach Earthenware Factory Schlierbach 1896–1903 black or blue or green	Wächtersbacher Steingutfabrik Schlierbach 1896–1903 schwarz oder blau oder grün	141	**473**
Wachtersbach Earthenware Factory Schlierbach 1894–1906 black or blue or green	Wächtersbacher Steingutfabrik Schlierbach 1894–1906 schwarz oder blau oder grün	141	**473**
Ackermann & Fritze Volkstedt 1908–1951 blue	Ackermann & Fritze Volkstedt 1908–1951 blau	141	**494**
Ackermann & Fritze Volkstedt 1908–1951 blue	Ackermann & Fritze Volkstedt 1908–1951 blau	141	**494**
Franz Dorfl Vienna (1884)–circa 1902 decorator's mark blue overglaze	Franz Dörfl Wien (1884)–ca. 1902 Malermarke blau aufglasur	142	**501**
unidentified decorator's mark blue overglaze	nicht identifiziert Malermarke blau aufglasur	142	
C. M. Hutschenreuther Hohenberg (1879)– blue underglaze	C. M. Hutschenreuther Hohenberg (1879)– blau unterglasur	142	**419**
Carl Knoll Fischern (1883)–circa 1906 blue underglaze	Carl Knoll Fischern (1883)–ca. 1906 blau unterglasur	142	**402**

Radler & Pilz Vienna (1877)– blue underglaze or overglaze	Rädler & Pilz Wien (1877)– blau unterglasur oder aufglasur	1424 **502**
Carl Knoll Fischern circa 1883–1906 blue underglaze	Carl Knoll Fischern ca. 1883–1906 blau unterglasur	1425 **402**
Carl Knoll Fischern circa 1883–1906 blue underglaze	Carl Knoll Fischern ca. 1883–1906 blau unterglasur	1426 **402**
Josef Riedl Giesshubel after 1890–before 1945 decorator's mark blue overglaze	Josef Riedl Gießhübel nach 1890–vor 1945 Malermarke blau aufglasur	1427 **408**
Porcelain Factory Langewiesen Oscar Schlegelmilch Langewiesen after 1892– blue underglaze or overglaze	Porzellanfabrik Langewiesen Oscar Schlegelmilch Langewiesen nach 1892– blau unterglasur oder aufglasur	1428 **436**
Josef Vater Vienna after 1894– decorator's mark blue overglaze	Josef Vater Wien nach 1894– Malermarke blau aufglasur	1429 **502**
Bloch & Co. Eichwald circa 1900– blue underglaze	Bloch & Co. Eichwald ca. 1900– blau unterglasur	1430 **397**
C. M. Hutschenreuther Hohenberg (1879)– blue underglaze	C. M. Hutschenreuther Hohenberg (1879)– blau unterglasur	1431 1432 **419**
unidentified decorator's mark circle area gold overglaze, used to cover original manufacturers mark beehive blue over gold	nicht identifiziert Malermarke Kreisfläche gold aufglasur, benutzt um Herstellermarke zu verdecken, Bienenkorb blau auf gold	1433

AUSTRIA	unidentified probably Josef Riedl Giesshubel after 1890–1918 blue overglaze	nicht identifiziert wahrscheinlich Josef Riedl Gießhübel nach 1890–1918 blau aufglasur	14: **40**:
GERMANY	Erdmann Schlegelmilch Suhl after 1900–1938	Erdamnn Schlegelmilch Suhl nach 1900–1938	14: **48**:
PROV. SAXE E.S. Germany	Erdmann Schlegelmilch Suhl after 1902–1938	Erdmann Schlegelmilch Suhl nach 1902–1938	14: **48**:
WALDERSHOF F N BAVARIA GERMANY	Porcelain Manufactory "Bavaria" Waldershof after 1925–1977	Porzellanmanufaktur "Bavaria" Waldershof nach 1925–1977	14: **49**:
J. KAWAN	Josef Kawan Vienna after 1907– decorator's mark blue overglaze	Josef Kawan Wien nach 1907– Malermarke blau aufglasur	14: **50**
Willner pinx.	unidentified beehive blue underglaze "Willner pinx." red overglaze	nicht identifiziert Bienenkorb blau unterglasur "Willner pinx." rot aufglasur	14:
3 88 35	unidentified beehive blue overglaze numbers impressed	nicht identifiziert Bienenkorb blau aufglasur Zahlen eingeprägt	14:
6	Oswald Lorenz Dresden (1881)– decorator's mark blue overglaze	Oswald Lorenz Dresden (1881)– Malermarke blau aufglasur	144 **39**:
Made in Czechoslovakia Karlsbad	unidentified shield blue underglaze circular mark gold overglaze, probably A. Persch in Hegewald 1918–1939	nicht identifiziert Schild blau unterglasur Kreismarke gold aufglasur, wahrscheinlich A. Persch in Hegewald 1918–1939	144 **416**

Franz Dorfl	Franz Dörfl	
Vienna	Wien	
(1914)—	(1914)—	
decorator's mark	Malermarke	1443
overglaze	aufglasur	**501**

Paul Anton Hannong	Paul Anton Hannong	
Frankenthal	Frankenthal	
1756—1759	1756—1759	1444
blue underglaze	blau unterglasur	**402**

Paul Anton Hannong	Paul Anton Hannong	
Frankenthal	Frankenthal	
1756—1759	1756—1759	1445
blue underglaze	blau unterglasur	**402**

Prince-Electoral	Churfürstliche Porcellain	
Porcelain Manufactory	Manufactur	
Neudeck/Nymphenburg	Neudeck/Nymphenburg	1446
1754—1765	1754—1765	**452**
impressed	eingeprägt	**457**

Prince-Electoral	Churfürstliche Porcellain	
Porcelain Manufactory	Manufactur	
Nymphenburg	Nymphenburg	
1763—1767	1763—1767	1447
impressed	eingeprägt	**457**

Prince-Electoral	Churfürstliche Porcellain	
Porcelain Manufactory	Manufactur	
Nymphenburg	Nymphenburg	
1766—1780	1766—1780	1448
impressed	eingeprägt	**457**

Prince-Electoral	Churfürstliche Porcellain	
Porcelain Manufactory	Manufactur	
Nymphenburg	Nymphenburg	
1780—1790	1780—1790	1449
impressed	eingeprägt	**457**

Prince-Electoral and Royal	Churfürstliche und Königliche	
Porcelain Manufactory	Porzellan Manufaktur	
Nymphenburg	Nymphenburg	
1790—1810	1790—1810	1450
impressed	eingeprägt	**457**

Royal Porcelain Manufactory	Königliche Porzellan Manufaktur	
Nymphenburg	Nymphenburg	
circa 1800	ca. 1800	1451
impressed	eingeprägt	**457**

Royal Porcelain Manufactory Nymphenburg circa 1810–1850 impressed	Königliche Porzellan Manufaktur Nymphenburg ca. 1810–1850 eingeprägt	145 457
Royal Porcelain Manufactory Nymphenburg circa 1850 impressed	Königliche Porzellan Manufaktur Nymphenburg ca. 1850 eingeprägt	145 457
Royal Porcelain Manufactory Nymphenburg 1862–1887 impressed	Königliche Porzellan Manufaktur Nymphenburg 1862–1887 eingeprägt	145 457
State's Porcelain Manufactory Nymphenburg (1921)– blue underglaze	Staatliche Porzellan Manufaktur Nymphenburg (1921)– blau unterglasur	145 457
Royal Porcelain Manufactory and State's Porcelain Manufactory Nymphenburg (1895)–present blue underglaze on reproductions of Frankenthal porcelain, always with year and contemporary Nymphenburg shield mark	Königliche Porzellan Manufaktur und Staatliche Porzellan Manufaktur Nymphenburg (1895)–heute blau unterglasur auf Reproduktionen von Frankenthal Porzellan, immer mit Jahr und zeitgenössischer Schildmarke	145 457
Margravial Fine Porcelain Factory and successors Ansbach/Bruckberg 1757–1860 impressed	Markgräfliche Feine Porcelain Fabrique und Nachfolger Ansbach/Bruckberg 1757–1860 eingeprägt	145 375
Count Frankenberg's Porcelain Factory Tillowitz circa 1918–circa 1938	Graf Frankenberg'sche Porzellanfabrik Tillowitz ca. 1918–ca. 1938	145 489
Royal Porcelain Manufactory Meissen after 1707–circa 1720 impressed on red stoneware	Königliche Porzellan Manufaktur Meißen nach 1707–ca. 1720 eingeprägt auf rotem Steinzeug	145 446
Royal Porcelain Manufactory Meissen after 1707–circa 1720 impressed on red stoneware	Königliche Porzellan Manufaktur Meißen nach 1707–ca. 1720 eingeprägt auf rotem Steinzeug	146 146 446

Thomas Recknagel	Thomas Recknagel	
Alexandrinenthal	Alexandrinenthal	1462
1886–1934	1886–1934	**371**
Royal Saxe Corporation	Royal Saxe Corporation	
New York City	New York	1463
1952–1970	1952–1970	**456**
Franz Junkersdorf	Franz Junkersdorf	
Dresden	Dresden	
(1902)–	(1902)–	
decorator's mark	Malermarke	1464
overglaze	aufglasur	**395**
Bros. Heubach	Gebr. Heubach	
Lichte	Lichte	1465
(1907)–1917	(1907)–1917	**438**
Porcelain Factory Schirnding	Porzellanfabrik Schirnding	
Schirnding	Schirnding	
(1934)–1948	(1934)–1948	1466
underglaze	unterglasur	**472**
Unger & Schilde and	Unger & Schilde und	
VEB Porcelainwork	VEB Porzellanwerk	
Gera-Roschutz	Gera-Roschütz	
Roschutz	Roschütz	1467
(1896)–1968	(1896)–1968	**468**
Retsch & Co.	Retsch & Co.	
Wunsiedel	Wunsiedel	1468
(1898)–	(1898)–	**506**
Tichy & Schonfeld	Tichy & Schönfeld	
Lessau	Lessau	1469
(1910)–	(1910)–	**437**
C. & E. Carstens	C. & E. Carstens	
Sorau	Sorau	1470
1918–circa 1945	1918–ca. 1945	**482**

CHODAVIA

Richter, Fenkl & Hahn	Richter, Fenkl & Hahn	
Chodau	Chodau	
circa 1922–circa 1945	ca. 1922–ca. 1945	14?
brown overglaze	braun aufglasur	38*
Schumann & Schreider	Schumann & Schreider	
Schwarzenhammer	Schwarzenhammer	14?
presently	heute	478
Franz Josef Mayer	Franz Josef Mayer	
Tannawa	Tannawa	
1840–1872	1840–1872	14?
impressed	eingeprägt	48*
Oswald Bachmann	Oswald Bachmann	
Elbing	Elbing	14?
(1910)–circa 1944	(1910)–ca. 1944	39*
Keramos	Keramos	
Vienna	Wien	14?
after 1945–	nach 1945–	50*
Porcelain Factory Ettlingen	Porzellanfabrik Ettlingen	
Ettlingen	Ettlingen	
1922–1940	1922–1940	14?
also in combination	auch in Verbindung	
with: ELP	mit: ELP	40*
Robert Riedl	Robert Riedl	
Ottensheim/Haslach	Ottensheim/Haslach	
after 1890–	nach 1890–	14*
decorator's mark	Malermarke	46*
Plass & Roesner	Plass & Roesner	
Buchau	Buchau	14?
circa 1907–circa 1940	ca. 1907–ca. 1940	38*
Franz Junkersdorf	Franz Junkersdorf	
Dresden	Dresden	
(1909)–	(1909)–	
decorator's mark	Malermarke	14*
overglaze	aufglasur	39*

Schumann & Schreider	Schumann & Schreider	
Schwarzenhammer	Schwarzenhammer	1480
1905–	1905–	**478**
Josef Strnact	Josef Strnact	
Turn-Teplitz	Turn-Teplitz	
circa 1881–1932	ca. 1881–1932	
decorator's mark	Malermarke	1481
overglaze	aufglasur	**490**
Porcelain Factory Bavaria	Porzellanfabrik Bavaria	
Ullersricht	Ullersricht	1482
after 1919–circa 1932	nach 1919–ca. 1932	**491**
Rudolf Fischer	Rudolf Fischer	
St. Polten	St. Pölten	
after 1924–	nach 1924–	
also with "Wien-St. Pölten"	auch mit "Wien-St. Pölten"	1483
instead of "Austria"	anstelle von "Austria"	**470**
J. A. Pecht	J. A. Pecht	
Constance	Konstanz	
circa 1925	ca. 1925	
on earthenware and	auf Steingut und	1484
decorator's mark on porcelain	Malermarke auf Porzellan	**433**
Hans Neuerer	Hans Neuerer	
Oberkotzau	Oberkotzau	1485
(1953)–	(1953)–	**458**
Striegau Porcelain Factory	Striegauer Porzellanfabrik	
Stanowitz	Stanowitz	1486
after 1912–	nach 1912–	**484**
Porcelain Factory "Alp"	Porzellanfabrik "Alp"	
Lubau	Lubau	1487
circa 1918–1939	ca. 1918–1939	**440**
Alfred Loffler	Alfred Löffler	
Chemnitz	Chemnitz	
1920–	1920–	
decorator's mark	Malermarke	1488
overglaze	aufglasur	**389**
Bros. Hubbe	Gebr. Hubbe	
Haldensleben	Haldensleben	1489
(1896)–circa 1898	(1896)–ca. 1898	**415**

H. Pettirsch	H. Pettirsch	
Burgsteinfurt	Burgsteinfurt	
1950–	1950–	
decorator's mark	Malermarke	14
overglaze	aufglasur	38
A. Fischer	A. Fischer	
Ilmenau	Ilmenau	14
1907–circa 1952	1907–ca. 1952	42
Wilhelm Rittirsch	Wilhelm Rittirsch	
Kups	Küps	14
1950–present	1950–heute	43
Margravial Fine Porcelain	Markgräfliche Feine	14
Factory	Porcelain Fabrique	14
Ansbach/Bruckberg	Ansbach/Bruckberg	14
circa 1760–circa 1770	ca. 1760–ca. 1770	
blue underglaze	blau unterglasur	37
Margravial Fine Porcelain	Markgräfliche Feine	
Factory	Porcelain Fabrique	
Ansbach/Bruckberg	Ansbach/Bruckberg	14
circa 1760–circa 1770	ca. 1760–ca. 1770	14
blue underglaze	blau unterglasur	37
Prince F. W. E. von	Prinz F. W. E. von	
Hildburghausen	Hildburghausen	
Kloster Veilsdorf	Kloster Veilsdorf	
1760–1795	1760–1795	14
blue underglaze	blau unterglasur	42
Prince F. W. E. von	Prinz F. W. E. von	
Hildburghausen	Hildburghausen	
Kloster Veilsdorf	Kloster Veilsdorf	
1760–1795	1760–1795	14
blue underglaze	blau unterglasur	42
Prince F. W. E. von	Prinz F. W. E. von	
Hildburghausen	Hildburghausen	
Kloster Veilsdorf	Kloster Veilsdorf	
1760–1795	1760–1795	15
blue underglaze	blau unterglasur	42
Earthenware Factory	Steingutfabrik	
Black Forest	Schwarzwald	
Hornberg	Hornberg	
(1911)–	(1911)–	150
on earthenware and porcelain	auf Steingut und Porzellan	420

A. Lamm	A. Lamm		
Dresden	Dresden		
1910–	1910–		
decorator's mark	Malermarke	1502	
overglaze	aufglasur	**395**	
Lippert & Haas	Lippert & Haas		
Schlaggenwald	Schlaggenwald		
1830–1846	1830–1846	1503	
impressed	eingeprägt	**472**	
Pfeiffer & Lowenstein	Pfeiffer & Löwenstein		
Schlackenwerth	Schlackenwerth		
(1901)–1941	(1901)–1941	1504	
green underglaze	grün unterglasur	**472**	
Bros. Simson	Gebr. Simson		
Gotha	Gotha	1505	
(1887)–	(1887)–	**409**	
Siegmund Paul Meyer	Siegmund Paul Meyer		
Bayreuth	Bayreuth		
1899–1947	1899–1947	1506	
green underglaze	grün unterglasur	**379**	
Porcelain Factory Markt-	Porzellanfabrik Markt-		
redwitz Thomas & Ens	redwitz Thomas & Ens		
Marktredwitz	Marktredwitz		
1904–1908	1904–1908	1507	
green underglaze	grün unterglasur	**444**	
Johann Caspar Geyger	Johann Caspar Geyger		
Wurzburg	Würzburg		
1775–1780	1775–1780	1508	
impressed	eingeprägt	**506**	
Adolf Persch	Adolf Persch		
Elbogen	Elbogen	1509	
1902–1918	1902–1918	**399**	
Alboth & Kaiser	Alboth & Kaiser		
Staffelstein	Staffelstein	1510	
1927–1953	1927–1953	**484**	
Alboth & Kaiser	Alboth & Kaiser		
Staffelstein	Staffelstein	1511	
1927–1953	1927–1953	**484**	

Benedikt Hasslacher	Benedikt Hasslacher	
Altrohlau	Altrohlau	
1813—1823	1813—1823	15
impressed on earthenware	eingeprägt auf Steingut	37

Charles Ahrenfeldt & Son	Charles Ahrenfeldt & Son	
Altrohlau/New York	Altrohlau/New York	15
1886—1917	1886—1917	37.
green or red overglaze	grün oder rot aufglasur	45

Charles Ahrenfeldt & Son	Charles Ahrenfeldt & Son	
Altrohlau/New York	Altrohlau/New York	
1886—1910	1886—1910	15
importer's mark	Importeurmarke	

Julius Dietl	Julius Dietl	
Kaltenhof	Kaltenhof	15
1918—1939	1918—1939	42

Franz Dorfl	Franz Dörfl	
Vienna	Wien	15
(1902)—	(1902)—	15
decorator's mark	Malermarke	50

Gareis, Kuhnl & Co.	Gareis, Kühnl & Co.	
Waldsassen	Waldsassen	15
—1969	—1969	49

Heinrich Kretschmann	Heinrich Kretschmann	
Elbogen	Elbogen	15
after 1900—circa 1938	nach 1900—ca. 1938	39

Britannia Porcelainworks	Britannia Porcelainworks	
Meierhofen	Meierhöfen	15
circa 1897—circa 1918	ca. 1897—ca. 1918	44

Paul Eydner	Paul Eydner	
Waldenburg	Waldenburg	
after 1903—circa 1964	nach 1903—ca. 1964	15
on fine earthenware	auf Feinsteingut	49

Porcelain Factory "Alp"	Porzellanfabrik "Alp"	
Lubau	Lubau	15
1918—1939	1918—1939	44

Hans Neuerer	Hans Neuerer		
Oberkotzau	Oberkotzau		
1943–	1943–	1523	
green underglaze	grün unterglasur	**458**	
Porcelain Factory	Porzellanfabrik		
F. Thomas	F. Thomas		
Marktredwitz	Marktredwitz		
1953–	1953–	1524	
green underglaze	grün unterglasur	**444**	
Rudolph Heinz & Co.	Rudolph Heinz & Co.		
Neuhaus on Rennweg	Neuhaus am Rennweg		
1936–circa 1961	1936–ca. 1961	1525	
on porcelain and earthenware	auf Porzellan und Steingut	**452**	
Bros. Simson	Gebr. Simson		
Gotha	Gotha	1526	
(1887)–	(1887)–	**409**	
Meissen Stove and	Meißner Ofen- und		
Porcelain Factory	Porzellanfabrik		
Meissen	Meißen	1527	
after 1872–circa 1930	nach 1872–ca. 1930	**447**	
Villeroy & Boch	Villeroy & Boch		
Mettlach	Mettlach		
before 1836–circa 1850	vor 1836–ca. 1850	1528	
impressed on earthenware	eingeprägt auf Steingut	**449**	
VEB Porcelainwork Lettin	VEB Porzellanwerk Lettin		
Lettin	Lettin		
circa 1949–circa 1953	ca. 1949–ca. 1953	1529	
green/black/yellow	grün/schwarz/gelb	**438**	
Richard Wehsener and	Richard Wehsener und		
Gerhard Wehsener	Gerhard Wehsener		
Dresden	Dresden		
circa 1918-1962	ca. 1918-1962	1530	
decorator's mark	Malermarke	**396**	
Porcelain Factory	Porzellanfabrik		
F. Thomas	F. Thomas		
Marktredwitz	Marktredwitz		
1908–	1908–		
green underglaze	grün unterglasur		
also in combination	auch in Verbindung		
with: "Sevres"	mit: "Sevres"		
Bavaria	Bavaria	1531	
Thomas Ivory	Thomas Ivory	**444**	

Fasolt & Eichel and C. & E. Carstens Blankenhain (1884)−circa 1933 green underglaze	Fasolt & Eichel und C. & E. Carstens Blankenhain (1884)−ca. 1933 grün unterglasur	153 **384**

Royal Porcelain Manufactory Meissen circa 1725−circa 1763 blue underglaze	Königliche Porzellan Manufaktur Meißen ca. 1725−1763 blau unterglasur	153 **446**

Royal Porcelain Manufactory
Meissen
circa 1725−circa 1740
blue underglaze

Königliche Porzellan Manufaktur
Meißen
ca. 1725−ca. 1740
blau unterglasur

153
446

Royal Porcelain Manufactory
Meissen
circa 1725−circa 1732
blue underglaze

Königliche Porzellan Manufaktur
Meißen
ca. 1725−ca. 1732
blau unterglasur

153
446

Royal Porcelain Manufactory
Meissen
circa 1725−circa 1763
blue underglaze

Königliche Porzellan Manufaktur
Meißen
ca. 1725−ca. 1763
blau unterglasur

153
446

Royal Porcelain Manufactory
Meissen
circa 1725−circa 1740
blue underglaze

Königliche Porzellan Manufaktur
Meißen
ca. 1725−ca. 1740
blau unterglasur

153
446

Royal Porcelain Manufactory
Meissen
circa 1725−circa 1740
blue underglaze

Königliche Porzellan Manufaktur
Meißen
ca. 1725−ca. 1740
blau unterglasur

153
446

Royal Porcelain Manufactory
Meissen
circa 1725
blue underglaze

Königliche Porzellan Manufaktur
Meißen
ca. 1725
blau unterglasur

153
446

Royal Porcelain Manufactory Meissen circa 1725–circa 1763 blue underglaze	Königliche Porzellan Manufaktur Meißen ca. 1725–ca. 1763 blau unterglasur	1540 **446**
Royal Porcelain Manufactory Meissen circa 1730– blue underglaze	Königliche Porzellan Manufaktur Meißen ca. 1730– blau unterglasur	1541 **446**
Royal Porcelain Manufactory Meissen circa 1740–1745 blue underglaze	Königliche Porzellan Manufaktur Meißen ca. 1740–1745 blau unterglasur	1542 **446**
Royal Porcelain Manufactory Meissen circa 1740–circa 1814 blue underglaze	Königliche Porzellan Manufaktur Meißen ca. 1740–ca. 1814 blau unterglasur	1543 1544 **446**
unidentified blue underglaze	nicht identifiziert blau unterglasur	1545
Royal Porcelain Manufactory Meissen circa 1740–1745 blue underglaze	Königliche Porzellan Manufaktur Meißen ca. 1740–1745 blau unterglasur	1546 **446**
Royal Porcelain Manufactory Meissen circa 1750 blue underglaze	Königliche Porzellan Manufaktur Meißen ca. 1750 blau unterglasur	1547 **446**
same as 1547	wie 1547	1548 1549 **446**
Royal Porcelain Manufactory Meissen circa 1750–1775 blue underglaze	Königliche Porzellan Manufaktur Meißen ca. 1750–1775 blau unterglasur	1550 1551 **446**

Royal Porcelain Manufactory Meissen circa 1780 blue underglaze	Königliche Porzellan Manufaktur Meißen ca. 1780 blau unterglasur	155 440
Royal Porcelain Manufactory Meissen circa 1814–circa 1860 blue underglaze handpainted	Königliche Porzellan Manufaktur Meißen ca. 1814–ca. 1860 blau unterglasur handgemalt	155 440
same as 1553	wie 1553	155 440
same as 1553	wie 1553	155 440
same as 1553	wie 1553	155 440
same as 1553	wie 1553	155 440
same as 1553	wie 1553	155 440
same as 1553	wie 1553	155 440
same as 1553	wie 1553	15 440
same as 1553	wie 1553	15 44
Royal Porcelain and State's Porcelain Manufactory Meissen circa 1860–1924 blue underglaze stamped	Königliche und Staatliche Porzellan Manufaktur Meißen ca. 1860–1924 blau unterglasur gestempelt	15 44
same as 1562	wie 1562	15 44
same as 1562	wie 1562	15 44
same as 1562	wie 1562	15 44

	same as 1562	wie 1562	1566 **446**
	same as 1562	wie 1562	1567 **446**
	State's and VEB State's Porcelain Manufactory Meissen 1919–present relief on coins and medals	Staatliche und VEB Staatliche Porzellan Manufaktur Meißen 1919–heute Relief auf Münzen und Medaillen	1568 **446**
	State's Porcelain Manufactory Meissen 1920 relief on coins	Staatliche Porzellan Manufaktur Meißen 1920 Relief auf Münzen	1569 **446**
	same as 1569	wie 1569	1570 **446**
	State's and VEB State's Porcelain Manufactory Meissen 1921–1924 and 1934–present relief on medals	Staatliche und VEB Staatliche Porzellan Manufaktur Meißen 1921–1924 und 1934–heute Relief auf Medaillen	1571 **446**
	State's Porcelain Manufactory Meissen 1921 relief on coins	Staatliche Porzellan Manufaktur Meißen 1921 Relief auf Münzen	1572 **446**
	State's Porcelain Manufactory Meissen 1920–1921 relief on coins	Staatliche Porzellan Manufaktur Meißen 1920–1921 Relief auf Münzen	1573 **446**
	State's and VEB State's Porcelain Manufactory Meissen 1921–1924 and 1934–present relief on medals	Staatliche und VEB Staatliche Porzellan Manufaktur Meißen 1921–1924 und 1934–heute Relief auf Medaillen	1574 **446**
	State's and VEB State's Porcelain Manufactory Meissen 1934–present blue underglaze	Staatliche und VEB Staatliche Porzellan Manufaktur Meißen 1934–heute blau unterglasur	1575 **446**

	same as 1575	wie 1575	15 **44**
	same as 1575	wie 1575	15 **44**
	State's and VEB State's Porcelain Manufactory Meissen 1934–present blue underglaze	Staatliche und VEB Staat- liche Porzellan Manufaktur Meißen 1934–heute blau unterglasur	157 **446**
	State's and VEB State's Porcelain Manufactory Meissen 1934–present impressed on red stoneware	Staatliche und VEB Staat- liche Porzellan Manufaktur Meißen 1934–heute eingeprägt auf rotem Steinzeug	157 **446**
	VEB State's Porcelain Manufactory Meissen 1947–present blue underglaze	VEB Staatliche Porzellan Manufaktur Meißen 1947–heute blau unterglasur	158 **446**
	VEB State's Porcelain Manufactory Meissen after 1949– relief on medals	VEB Staatliche Porzellan Manufaktur Meißen nach 1949– Relief auf Medaillen	158 **446**
	VEB State's Porcelain Manufactory Meissen 1960 relief on medal	VEB Staatliche Porzellan Manufaktur Meißen 1960 Relief auf Medaille	158 **446**
	VEB State's Porcelain Manufactory Meissen after 1950– relief on medals	VEB Staatliche Porzellan Manufaktur Meißen nach 1950– Relief auf Medaillen	158 **446**
	Prince Friedrich Wilhelm of Saxony Altshausen (1950)–	Prinz Friedrich Wilhelm zu Sachsen Altshausen (1950)–	1584 **374**

Royal Saxe Corporation New York City 1952–1970	Royal Saxe Corporation New York 1952–1970	1585 **456**

Royal Saxe Corporation
New York City
1952–1970

Royal Saxe Corporation
New York
1952–1970

1585
456

Christian Nonne
Volkstedt
1767–1787
blue underglaze

Christian Nonne
Volkstedt
1767–1787
blau unterglasur

1586
494

Christian Nonne
Volkstedt
1767–1787
blue underglaze or overglaze

Christian Nonne
Volkstedt
1767–1787
blau unterglasur oder aufglasur

1587
494

same as 1587

wie 1587

1588
494

same as 1587

wie 1587

1589
494

Prince-Electoral
Porcelain Manufactory
Nymphenburg
circa 1760–1795
blue underglaze

Churfürstliche
Porcellain Manufactur
Nymphenburg
ca. 1760–1795
blau unterglasur

1590
457

Royal and State's
Porcelain Manufactory
Meissen
circa 1860–circa 1924
blue underglaze

Königliche und Staatliche
Porzellan Manufaktur
Meißen
ca. 1860–ca. 1924
blau unterglasur

1591
446

State's Porcelain Manufactory
Meissen
1920–1921
relief on coins

Staatliche Porzellan Manufaktur
Meißen
1920–1921
Relief auf Münzen

1592
446

Royal Porcelain Manufactory
Meissen
circa 1740–circa 1745
blue underglaze

Königliche Porzellan Manufaktur
Meißen
ca. 1740–ca. 1745
blau unterglasur

1593
446

Royal Porcelain Manufactory
Meissen
middle of 19th century
impressed

Königliche Porzellan Manufaktur
Meißen
Mitte des 19. Jahrhunderts
eingeprägt

1594
446

Royal Porcelain Manufactory
Meissen
middle of 18th century
impressed

Königliche Porzellan Manufaktur
Meißen
Mitte des 18. Jahrhunderts
eingeprägt

1
4

State's Porcelain Manufactory
Meissen
1945–1947
blue underglaze

Staatliche Porzellan Manufaktur
Meißen
1945–1947
blau unterglasur

15
44

State's Porcelain Manufactory
Meissen
1934–
blue underglaze

Staatliche Porzellan Manufaktur
Meißen
1934–
blau unterglasur

15
44

Royal Porcelain Manufactory
Meissen
1733–1763
(according to company
affidavit of 1875)
blue underglaze

Königliche Porzellan Manufaktur
Meißen
1733–1763
(nach Firmenerklärung
von 1875)
blau unterglasur

15
44

Royal Porcelain Manufactory
Meissen
circa 1756–circa 1780
blue underglaze

Königliche Porzellan Manufaktur
Meißen
ca. 1756–ca. 1780
blau unterglasur

15
44

Royal Porcelain Manufactory
Meissen
circa 1756–circa 1780
blue underglaze

Königliche Porzellan Manufaktur
Meißen
ca. 1756–ca. 1780
blau unterglasur

16
44

same as 1600

wie 1600

16
44

same as 1600

wie 1600

16
44

same as 1600	wie 1600	1603 **446**
same as 1600	wie 1600	1604 **446**
Royal Porcelain Manufactory Meissen circa 1770 blue underglaze	Königliche Porzellan Manufaktur Meißen ca. 1770 blau unterglasur	1605 **446**
same as 1605	wie 1605	1606 **446**
Royal Porcelain Manufactory Meissen circa 1756–circa 1780 blue underglaze	Königliche Porzellan Manufaktur Meißen ca. 1756–ca. 1780 blau unterglasur	1607 **446**
same as 1607	wie 1607	1608 **446**
same as 1607	wie 1607	1609 **446**
same as 1607	wie 1607	1610 **446**
same as 1607	wie 1607	1611 **446**

same as 1607	wie 1607	16
Royal Porcelain Manufactory Meissen 1763–1774 (according to company affidavit of 1875) blue underglaze	Königliche Porzellan Manufaktur Meißen 1763–1774 (nach Firmenerklärung von 1875) blau unterglasur	16 44
same as 1613	wie 1613	16 44
Prince-Electoral Porcelain Manufactory Nymphenburg circa 1760–1795 blue underglaze	Churfürstliche Porcellain Manufactur Nymphenburg ca. 1760–1795 blau unterglasur	16 45
State's Porcelain Manufactory Meissen 1924–1934 relief on medals	Staatliche Porzellan Manufaktur Meißen 1924–1934 Relief auf Medaillen	16 44
State's Porcelain Manufactory Meissen 1924–1934 blue underglaze	Staatliche Porzellan Manufaktur Meißen 1924–1934 blau unterglasur	16 44
State's Porcelain Manufactory Meissen 1924–1934 blue underglaze	Staatliche Porzellan Manufaktur Meißen 1924–1934 blau unterglasur	16 44
State's Porcelain Manufactory Meissen 1924–1934 impressed on red stoneware	Staatliche Porzellan Manufaktur Meißen 1924–1934 eingeprägt auf rotem Steinzeug	16 44
State's Porcelain Manufactory Meissen 1924–1934 blue underglaze	Staatliche Porzellan Manufaktur Meißen 1924–1934 blau unterglasur	16 44
same as 1620	wie 1620	16 44

	attributed to Royal Porcelain Manufactory Meissen circa 1725–circa 1730 blue underglaze	zugeschrieben der Königlichen Porzellan Manufaktur Meißen ca. 1725–ca. 1730 blau unterglasur	1622 **446**
	Royal Porcelain Manufactory Meissen circa 1780 blue underglaze	Königliche Porzellan Manufaktur Meißen ca. 1780 blau unterglasur	1623 **446**
	Royal Porcelain Manufactory Meissen 1774-1817 blue underglaze	Königliche Porzellan Manufaktur Meißen 1774-1817 blau unterglasur	1624 **446**
	same as 1624	wie 1624	1625 **446**
	same as 1624	wie 1624	1626 **446**
	same as 1624	wie 1624	1627 **446**
	same as 1624	wie 1624	1628 **446**
	same as 1624	wie 1624	1629 **446**
	same as 1624	wie 1624	1630 **446**
	same as 1624	wie 1624	1631 **446**
	same as 1624	wie 1624	1632 **446**
	same as 1624	wie 1624	1633 **446**
	Royal Porcelain Manufactory Meissen 1774-1817 impressed	Königliche Porzellan Manufaktur Meißen 1774-1817 eingeprägt	1634 **446**

Ducal Brunswick Porcelain Manufactory Furstenberg circa 1800 blue underglaze	Herzoglich Braunschweigische Porzellan Manufaktur Fürstenberg ca. 1800 blau unterglasur	16 40
J. W. Hamann and F. F. Hamann Wallendorf 1764–1786 blue underglaze	J. W. Hamann und F. F. Hamann Wallendorf 1764–1786 blau unterglasur	16 49
same as 1636	wie 1636	16 49
Gotthelf Greiner Limbach 1775-1787 blue underglaze	Gotthelf Greiner Limbach 1775-1787 blau unterglasur	16 43
Royal Porcelain Manufactory Meissen 1774-1807 swords and star blue underglaze letters CHC violet mark of Prince-Electoral Pastry Shop	Königliche Porzellan Manufaktur Meißen 1774-1807 Schwerter und Stern blau unterglasur Buchstaben CHC violett Marke der Kurfürstlichen Hofkonditorei	16 44
Volkstedt Porcelain Factory Richard Eckert & Co. Volkstedt 1894–1920 blue underglaze	Volkstedter Porzellanfabrik Richard Eckert & Co. Volkstedt 1894–1920 blau unterglasur	16 49
Volkstedt Porcelain Factory Richard Eckert & Co. Volkstedt 1894–1920 blue underglaze	Volkstedter Porzellanfabrik Richard Eckert & Co. Volkstedt 1894–1920 blau unterglasur	16 49
same as 1641	wie 1641	16 49
Royal Porcelain Manufactory Meissen 1720–1730 (according to company affidavit of 1875) blue underglaze	Königliche Porzellan Manufaktur Meißen 1720–1730 (nach Firmenerklärung von 1875) blau unterglasur	16 44

Royal Porcelain Manufactory Meissen circa 1725 blue underglaze	Königliche Porzellan Manufaktur Meißen ca. 1725 blau unterglasur	1644 **446**
attributed to Meyer & Son Dresden circa 1880	Meyer & Sohn Dresden ca. 1880 zugeschrieben	1645 **395**
same as 1645	wie 1645	1646 **395**
Royal Porcelain Manufactory Meissen circa 1723–circa 1730 blue underglaze	Königliche Porzellan Manufaktur Meißen ca. 1723–ca. 1730 blau unterglasur	1647 **446**
C. M. Hutschenreuther Hohenberg (1876)–1887 blue underglaze or overglaze	C. M. Hutschenreuther Hohenberg (1876)–1887 blau unterglasur oder aufglasur	1648 **419**
same as 1648	wie 1648	1649 **419**
Royal Porcelain Manufactory Meissen before 1764-1938 swords blue underglaze line incised, indication for porcelain sold white that was not decorated in the manufactory	Königliche Porzellan Manufaktur Meißen vor 1764-1938 Schwerter blau unterglasur Strich eingeschliffen als Zeichen für Porzellan, das weiß verkauft und nicht in der Manufaktur bemalt wurde	1650 **446**
Royal Porcelain Manufactory Meissen 1850-1869 or later swords blue underglaze lines incised for slightly flawed decorated porcelain	Königliche Porzellan Manufaktur Meißen 1850-1869 oder später Schwerter blau unterglasur Striche eingeschliffen für bemaltes Porzellan mit kleinen Fehlern	1651 **446**
Royal Porcelain Manufactory Meissen before 1764-1938 swords blue underglaze line incised, indication for porcelain sold white that was not decorated in the manufactory	Königliche Porzellan Manufaktur Meißen vor 1764-1938 Schwerter blau unterglasur Strich eingeschliffen als Zeichen für Porzellan, das weiß verkauft und nicht in der Manufaktur bemalt wurde	1652 **446**

Royal Porcelain Manufactory Meissen piece with this mark circa 1800 incised lines as indication for slightly flawed porcelain probably applied later	Königliche Porzellan Manufaktur Meißen Stück mit dieser Marke ca. 1800 eingeschliffene Striche als Zeichen für kleine Fehler möglicherweise später angebracht	16 **44**
Royal Porcelain Manufactory Meissen piece with this mark circa 1800 swords blue underglaze line incised, indication for porcelain sold white, not decorated in the manufactory	Königliche Porzellan Manufaktur Meißen Stück mit dieser Marke ca. 1800 Schwerter blau unterglasur Strich eingeschliffen als Zeichen für Porzellan, das weiß verkauft wurde	16 **44**
Royal Porcelain Manufactory Meissen piece with this mark produced circa 1766-circa 1780 incised lines as indication for slightly flawed porcelain probably applied later	Königliche Porzellan Manufaktur Meißen Stück mit dieser Marke ca. 1766-ca. 1780 hergestellt eingeschliffene Striche als Zeichen für kleine Fehler möglicherweise später angebracht	165 **446**
Royal Porcelain Manufactory Meissen piece with this mark produced circa 1766-circa 1780 incised lines as indication for visibly flawed porcelain probably applied later	Königliche Porzellan Manufaktur Meißen Stück mit dieser Marke ca. 1766-ca. 1780 hergestellt eingeschliffene Striche als Zeichen für sichtbare Fehler möglicherweise später angebracht	16 **44**
Royal Porcelain Manufactory Meissen piece with this mark produced circa 1830-circa 1850 four incised lines as indication for heavily flawed porcelain probably applied later	Königliche Porzellan Manufaktur Meißen Stück mit dieser Marke ca. 1830-ca. 1850 hergestellt vier eingeschliffene Striche als Zeichen für starke Fehler möglicherweise später angebracht	16 **44**
Royal and State's Porcelain Manufactory Meissen 1850-1924 swords blue underglaze line incised, indication for porcelain sold white	Königliche und Staatliche Porzellan Manufaktur Meißen 1850-1924 Schwerter blau unterglasur, Strich eingeschliffen für Porzellan, das weiß verkauft wurde	16 **44**

State´s and VEB State´s Porcelain Manufactory Meissen this piece after 1934-1987 swords blue underglaze dot gold overglaze two incisions since 1869 for pieces with noticeable flaws	Staatliche und VEB Staatliche Porzellan Manufaktur Meißen dies Stück nach 1934-1987 Schwerter blau unterglasur Punkt gold aufglasur zwei Schleifstriche seit 1869 für Stücke mit sichtbaren Fehlern	1659 **446**
Royal and State´s Porcelain Manufactory Meissen this piece circa 1850-1924 three incisions since 1869 for pieces with easily visible flaws	Königliche und Staatliche Porzellan Manufaktur Meißen dies Stück ca. 1850-1924 drei Schleifstriche seit 1869 für Stücke mit stark sichtbaren Fehlern	1660 **446**
State´s Porcelain Manufactory Meissen this piece 1934-1945 four incisions for rejects solely to be sold to employees of the manufactory	Staatliche Porzellan Manufaktur Meißen dies Stück 1934-1945 vier Schleifstriche für Ausschuß, nur an Manufakturangehörige zu verkaufen	1661 **446**
Royal Porcelain Manufactory Meissen circa 1725–circa 1756 blue underglaze	Königliche Porzellan Manufaktur Meißen ca. 1725–ca. 1756 blau unterglasur	1662 **446**
Royal Porcelain Manufactory Meissen circa 1725–circa 1756 blue underglaze	Königliche Porzellan Manufaktur Meißen ca. 1725–ca. 1756 blau unterglasur	1663 **446**
Porcelain Factory Gunthersfeld Gehren (1886)–1902	Porzellanfabrik Günthersfeld Gehren (1886)–1902	1664 **406**
Royal Porcelain Manufactory Meissen circa 1707–1720 impressed on red stoneware	Königliche Porzellan Manufaktur Meißen ca. 1707–1720 eingeprägt auf rotem Steinzeug	1665 1666 **446**

	same as 1666	wie 1666	16 44
	Royal Porcelain Manufactory Meissen circa 1774–1814 impressed	Königliche Porzellan Manufaktur Meißen ca. 1774–1814 eingeprägt	16 44
	same as 1668	wie 1668	16 44
	Royal Porcelain Manufactory Meissen circa 1783 swords and star blue underglaze triangle and swords in triangle impressed	Königliche Porzellan Manufaktur Meißen ca. 1783 Schwerter und Stern blau unterglasur Dreieck und Schwerter im Dreieck eingeprägt	16 44
	Royal Porcelain Manufactory Meissen circa 1774–1814 impressed	Königliche Porzellan Manufaktur Meißen ca. 1774–1814 eingeprägt	16 44
	same as 1671	wie 1671	16 44
	Royal Porcelain Manufactory Meissen probably 1739 blue underglaze meaning of letters B. P. T. not yet deter- mined definitely	Königliche Porzellan Manufaktur Meißen wahrscheinlich 1739 blau unterglasur Bedeutung der Buchstaben B. P. T. noch nicht ein- deutig festgestellt	16 16 44
	same as 1673	wie 1673	16 44

Royal Porcelain Manufactory
Meissen
circa 1763–1806
swords blue underglaze
C. P. C. blue or purple
overglaze, mark of the
Prine-Electoral Pastry
Shop in Pillnitz

Königliche Porzellan Manufaktur
Meißen
ca. 1763–1806
Schwerter blau unterglasur
C. P. C. blau oder purpur
aufglasur, Marke der
Kurfürstlichen Hofkondi-   1675
torei in Pillnitz   **446**

Royal Porcelain Manufactory
Meissen
circa 1724–1725
swords blue underglaze
letter gold overglaze

Königliche Porzellan Manufaktur
Meißen
ca. 1724–1725
Schwerter blau unterglasur   1676
Buchstabe gold aufglasur   **446**

Royal Porcelain Manufactory
Meissen
circa 1783
impressed

Königliche Porzellan Manufaktur
Meißen
ca. 1783   1677
eingeprägt   **446**

Royal Porcelain Manufactory
Meissen
circa 1725–circa 1740
swords blue underglaze
letter gold overglaze

Königliche Porzellan Manufaktur
Meißen
ca. 1725–ca. 1740
Schwerter blau unterglasur   1678
Buchstabe gold aufglasur   **446**

Royal Porcelain Manufactory
Meissen
circa 1723–circa 1763
swords blue underglaze
letters blue overglaze
mark of the Royal Court
Pastry Shop

Königliche Porzellan Manufaktur
Meißen
ca. 1723–ca. 1763
Schwerter blau unterglasur
Buchstaben blau aufglasur,
Marke der Koniglichen   1679
Hofkonditorei   **446**

Royal Porcelain Manufactory
Meissen
circa 1723–circa 1763
swords blue underglaze
letters purple overglaze,
mark of the Royal Court
Pastry Shop

Königliche Porzellan Manufaktur
Meißen
ca. 1723–ca. 1763
Schwerter blau unterglasur
Buchstaben purpur aufglasur,
Marke der Königlichen   1680
Hofkonditorei   **446**

**K.
H.C.**

Royal Porcelain Manufactory
Meissen
circa 1723–circa 1763
swords blue underglaze
letters purple overglaze,
mark of the Royal Court
Pastry Shop

Königliche Porzellan Manufaktur
Meißen
ca. 1723–ca. 1763
Schwerter blau unterglasur
Buchstaben purpur aufglasur,
Marke der Königlichen
Hofkonditorei

Royal Porcelain Manufactory
Meissen
circa 1723–circa 1763
swords blue underglaze
letters purple overglaze,
mark of the Royal Court
Pastry Shop in Warsaw

Königliche Porzellan Manufaktur
Meißen
ca. 1723–ca. 1763
Schwerter blau unterglasur
Buchstaben purpur aufglasur,
Marke der Königlichen
Hofkonditorei in Warschau

K.H.C.W.

Royal Porcelain Manufactory
Meissen
circa 1756–circa 1763
swords and dot blue underglaze
letters purple overglaze,
mark of the Royal Court
Pastry Shop in Warsaw

Königliche Porzellan Manufaktur
Meißen
ca. 1756–ca. 1763
Schwerter und Punkt blau unterglasur
Buchstaben purpur aufglasur,
Marke der Königlichen
Hofkonditorei in Warschau

K.H.C.W.

Royal Porcelain Manufactory
Meissen
circa 1723–circa 1763
swords blue underglaze
letters purple overglaze,
mark of the Royal Court
Pastry Shop in Warsaw

Königliche Porzellan Manufaktur
Meißen
ca. 1723–ca. 1763
Schwerter blau unterglasur
Buchstaben purpur aufglasur,
Marke der Königlichen
Hofkonditorei in Warschau

K.H.C.W.

same as 1685

wie 1685

Royal Porcelain Manufactory
Meissen
circa 1723–circa 1763
swords blue underglaze
letters blue overglaze,
mark of the Royal Court
Pastry Shop in Pillnitz

Königliche Porzellan Manufaktur
Meißen
ca. 1723–ca. 1763
Schwerter blau unterglasur
Buchstaben blau aufglasur,
Marke der Königlichen
Hofkonditorei in Pillnitz

K.J.C.

Royal Porcelain Manufactory Meissen circa 1723–circa 1763 swords blue underglaze letters black or purple overglaze, mark of the Royal Court Pastry Shop in Pillnitz	Königliche Porzellan Manufaktur Meißen ca. 1723–ca. 1763 Schwerter blau unterglasur Buchstaben schwarz oder purpur aufglasur, Marke der Königlichen Hofkonditorei in Pillnitz	1688 **446**
same as 1688	wie 1688	1689 **446**
Royal Porcelain Manufactory Meissen 1723–circa 1727 blue underglaze	Königliche Porzellan Manufaktur Meißen 1723–ca. 1727 blau unterglasur	1690 **446**
same as 1690	wie 1690	1691 **446**
same as 1690	wie 1690	1692 **446**
same as 1690	wie 1690	1693 **446**
same as 1690	wie 1690	1694 **446**
same as 1690	wie 1690	1695 **446**

Royal, State's and
VEB State's Porcelain
Manufactory
Meissen
1723–circa 1727 and
1875–present
blue underglaze

Königliche, Staatliche
und VEB Staatliche
Porzellan Manufaktur
Meißen
1723–ca. 1727 und
1875–heute
blau unterglasur

16
44

Royal Porcelain Manufactory
Meissen
1723–circa 1727
blue underglaze

Königliche Porzellan Manufaktur
Meißen
1723–ca. 1727
blau unterglasur

16
44

same as 1697

wie 1697

16
44

Royal Porcelain Manufactory
Meissen
1723–circa 1727
swords and letters blue
underglaze
number gold overglaze

Königliche Porzellan Manufaktur
Meißen
1723–ca. 1727
Schwerter und Buchstaben
blau unterglasur
Zahl gold aufglasur

16
44

Royal Porcelain Manufactory
Meissen
1723–circa 1727
swords, letters and
polygon blue underglaze
except letter H gold overglaze

Königliche Porzellan Manufaktur
Meißen
1723–ca. 1727
Schwerter, Buchstaben und
Mehreck blau unterglasur
außer Buchstabe H gold aufglasur

17
44

attributed to
Meyer & Son
Dresden
circa 1880

Meyer & Sohn
Dresden
ca. 1880
zugeschrieben

17
39

Royal Porcelain Manufactory Meissen circa 1730 swords blue underglaze letters and number incised, inventory mark of the Johanneum collection in Dresden	Königliche Porzellan Manufaktur Meißen ca. 1730 Schwerter blau unterglasur Buchstaben und Zahl eingeschliffen, Inventurmarke des Johanneums in Dresden	1702 **446**

Royal Porcelain Manufactory Meissen circa 1723–circa 1756 swords blue underglaze letters and number incised, inventory mark of the Johanneum collection in Dresden	Königliche Porzellan Manufaktur Meißen ca. 1723–ca. 1756 Schwerter blau unterglasur Buchstaben und Zahl eingeschliffen, Inventurmarke des Johanneums in Dresden	1703 **446**

same as 1703	wie 1703	1704 1705 **446**

Royal Porcelain Manufactory Meissen circa 1772–1774 swords blue underglaze cyrillic letters inventory mark of the Russian Court in St. Petersburg	Königliche Porzellan Manufaktur Meißen ca. 1772–1774 Schwerter blau unterglasur kyrillische Buchstaben Inventurmarke des Russischen Hofs in St. Petersburg	1706 **446**

Fr. Chr. Greiner & Sons Rauenstein circa 1860–circa 1900 blue underglaze	Fr. Chr. Greiner & Söhne Rauenstein ca. 1860–ca. 1900 blau unterglasur	1707 **465**

Saxonian Porcelain Factory Carl Thieme Potschappel 2nd half 19th century blue underglaze	Sächsische Porzellanfabrik Carl Thieme Potschappel 2. Hälfte 19. Jahrhundert blau unterglasur	1708 **463**

	VEB State's Porcelain Manufactory Meissen for a few years after 1963	VEB Staatliche Porzellan Manufaktur Meißen für einige Jahre nach 1963	170 444
	VEB State's Porcelain Manufactory Meissen for a few years after 1966	VEB Staatliche Porzellan Manufaktur Meißen für einige Jahre nach 1966	171 446
	VEB State's Porcelain Manufactory Meissen for a few years after 1963	VEB Staatliche Porzellan Manufaktur Meißen für einige Jahre nach 1963	17 444
	VEB State's Porcelain Manufactory Meissen (1972)–present	VEB Staatliche Porzellan Manufaktur Meißen (1972)–heute	171 446
	Ernst Teichert Meissen 1884– blue underglaze	Ernst Teichert Meißen 1884– blau unterglasur	171 448
	Royal and State's and VEB State's Porcelain Manufactory Meissen circa 1912–present impressed on white porcelain, any decoration on pieces with this mark has been done outside the manufactory	Königliche und Staatliche und VEB Staatliche Porzellan Manufaktur Meißen ca. 1912–heute eingeprägt auf weißem Porzellan, jede Bemalung auf Stücken mit dieser Marke ist außerhalb der Manufaktur geschehen	171 446
	Royal Porcelain Manufactory Meissen 1817-1824 blue underglaze Roman numeral I indicates quality of the porcelain paste	Königliche Porzellan Manufaktur Meißen 1817-1824 blau unterglasur Römische Ziffer I kennzeichnet die Qualität der Porzellanmase	171 171 446

same as 1715	wie 1715	1717 **446**
same as 1715	wie 1715	1718 **446**
same as 1715	wie 1715	1719 **446**
same as 1715	wie 1715	1720 **446**
Royal Porcelain Manufactory Meissen 1817-1824 blue underglaze Roman numeral II indicates quality of the porcelain paste	Königliche Porzellan Manufaktur Meißen 1817-1824 blau unterglasur Römische Ziffer II kennzeichnet die Qualität der Porzellanmasse	1721 **446**
same as 1721	wie 1721	1722 **446**
same as 1721	wie 1721	1723 **446**
unidentified attributed to Royal Porcelain Manufactory Meissen but questionable pink overglaze	nicht identifiziert der Königlichen Porzellan Manufaktur Meißen zugeschrieben aber fraglich rosa aufglasur	1724 **446**
Baehr & Proeschild Ohrdruf after 1891–	Baehr & Proeschild Ohrdruf nach 1891–	1725 **459**
same as 1725	wie 1725	1726 **459**

Baehr & Proeschild	Baehr & Proeschild		
Ohrdruf	Ohrdruf	17	
after 1891–	nach 1891–	**45**	

Silesian Porcelain Factory	Schlesische Porzellanfabrik	
P. Donath	P. Donath	
Tiefenfurth	Tiefenfurth	
(1883)-1896	(1883)-1896	17
blue underglaze	blau unterglasur	**48**

same as 1728	wie 1728	17
		48

Louis Lowinson and	Louis Löwinson und	
Silesian Porcelain Factory	Schlesische Porzellanfabrik	
P. Donath	P. Donath	
Tiefenfurth	Tiefenfurth	
(1883)-1896	(1883)-1896	17
blue underglaze	blau unterglasur	**48**

Porcelain Factory Gunthersfeld	Porzellanfabrik Günthersfeld	
Gehren	Gehren	173
circa 1929–1945	ca. 1929–1945	**40(**

Josef Riedl	Josef Riedl	
Giesshubel	Gießhübel	
circa 1890–	ca. 1890–	
decorator's mark	Malermarke	173
overglaze	aufglasur	**408**

Strobel & Wilken	Strobel & Wilken	
New York City	New York	
after 1884–	nach 1884–	173
importer's mark	Importeurmarke	**45(**

Porcelain Factory Kolmar	Porzellanfabrik Kolmar	
Kolmar	Kolmar	
(1940)–1944	(1940)–1944	173
blue or green underglaze	blau oder grün unterglasur	**43**

Porcelain Factory Frei-	Porzellanfabrik Frei-	
waldau Robert Tietz	waldau Robert Tietz	
Freiwaldau	Freiwaldau	173
circa 1929–1945	ca. 1929–1945	**405**

The Mosanic Pottery and	The Mosanic Pottery und	
Porcelain Factory Mitterteich	Porzellanfabrik Mitterteich	
Mitterteich	Mitterteich	173
(1898)–after 1928	(1898)–nach 1928	**450**

Christian Fischer Zwickau (1875)–1929 blue underglaze	Christian Fischer Zwickau (1875)–1929 blau unterglasur	1737 **508**
VEB Special Porcelain Eisenberg 1972-1990	VEB Spezialporzellan Eisenberg 1972-1990	1738 **398**
Porcelain Factory Kalk Eisenberg 1904–	Porzellanfabrik Kalk Eisenberg 1904–	1739 **398**
Prince-Electoral Porcelain Manufactory Nymphenburg circa 1760–1795 blue underglaze	Churfürstliche Porcellain Manufactur Nymphenburg ca. 1760–1795 blau unterglasur	1740 **457**
Berlin Porcelain and Firebrick Factory Alfred Bruno Schwarz Berlin (1891)–	Berliner Porzellan- und Chamottefabrik Alfred Bruno Schwarz Berlin (1891)–	1741 **380**
Ernst Teichert Meissen 1900– blue underglaze also in combination with: MEISSEN	Ernst Teichert Meißen 1900– blau unterglasur auch in Verbindung mit: MEISSEN	1742 **448**
Josef Plass Altrohlau (1897)–circa 1920 decorator's mark red/black overglaze	Josef Plass Altrohlau (1897)–ca. 1920 Malermarke schwarz/rot aufglasur	1743 **374**
Porcelain Factory Waldsassen Waldsassen (1920)-1993	Porzellanfabrik Waldsassen Waldsassen (1920)-1993	1744 **498**
Christian Nonne Giesshubel 1803–1813 blue underglaze or different colors overglaze	Christian Nonne Gießhübel 1803–1813 blau unterglasur oder verschiedene Farben aufglasur	1745 **408**

Johann Anton Hladik	Johann Anton Hladik	
Giesshubel	Gießhübel	
1813–1815	1813–1815	
blue underglaze or	blau unterglasur oder	174
different colors overglaze	verschiedene Farben aufglasur	408
Benedikt Knaute	Benedikt Knaute	
Giesshubel	Gießhübel	
1815–circa 1840	1815–ca. 1840	
blue underglaze or	blau unterglasur oder	174
different colors overglaze	verschiedene Farben aufglasur	408
Unger, Schneider & Cie.	Unger, Schneider & Cie.	
Grafenthal	Gräfenthal	174
after 1861–circa 1887	nach 1861–ca. 1887	411
same as 1748	wie 1748	174
		411
Unger, Schneider & Cie.	Unger, Schneider & Cie.	
Grafenthal	Gräfenthal	175
(1879)–1887	(1879)–1887	411
same as 1750	wie 1750	175
		411
Unger, Schneider & Cie. and	Unger, Schneider & Cie. und	
Carl Schneider's Heirs	Carl Schneider's Erben	
Grafenthal	Gräfenthal	175
(1879)–circa 1954	(1879)–ca. 1954	411
Carl Schneider's Heirs	Carl Schneider's Erben	
Grafenthal	Gräfenthal	175
(1954)–circa 1972	(1954)–ca. 1972	411
Benedikt Knaute	Benedikt Knaute	
Giesshubel	Gießhübel	
1828–1830	1828–1830	
blue underglaze	blau unterglasur	175
letters BK impressed	Buchstaben BK eingeprägt	408
W. Haldenwanger	W. Haldenwanger	
Berlin	Berlin	175
(1913)–	(1913)–	382

222

Haas & Czjek Schlaggenwald (1889)–	Haas & Czjzek Schlaggenwald (1889)–	1756 **472**
Carstens-Uffrecht Haldensleben (1929)–1945	Carstens-Uffrecht Haldensleben (1929)–1945	1757 **415**
attributed to Ernst Teichert Meissen after 1869– blue underglaze	zugeschrieben Ernst Teichert Meißen nach 1869– blau unterglasur	1758 **448**
Porcelain Factory Kalk Köln/Eisenberg (1896)– blue or green underglaze	Porzellanfabrik Kalk Köln/Eisenberg (1896)– blau oder grün unterglasur	1759 **429** **398**
Ernst Teichert Meissen (1900)– blue underglaze letters BB impressed	Ernst Teichert Meißen (1900)– blau unterglasur Buchstaben BB eingeprägt	1760 **448**
Ernst Teichert Meissen (1900)– blue underglaze	Ernst Teichert Meißen (1900)– blau unterglasur	1761 **448**
The Mosanic Pottery Mitterteich (1892)–1918	The Mosanic Pottery Mitterteich (1892)–1918	1762 **450**
Wilhelmsburg Earthenware and Porcelain Factory Wilhelmsburg circa 1938–	Wilhelmsburger Steingut und Porzellanfabrik Wilhelmsburg ca. 1938–	1763 **504**
attributed to Baden-Baden 1771–1778 but very doubtful gold overglaze	Baden-Baden 1771–1778 zugeschrieben aber sehr zweifelhaft gold aufglasur	1764 **378**
VEB Porcelainwork Neuhaus Neuhaus-Schierschnitz (1956)–1965	VEB Porzellanwerk Neuhaus Neuhaus-Schierschnitz (1956)–1965	1765 **452**

VEB Porcelainwork Neuhaus and CERAM Electroceramic Sonneberg 1952-present	VEB Porzellanwerk Neuhaus und CERAM Elektrokeramik Sonneberg 1952-present	17 **45**
Ernst Heubach Koppelsdorf after 1887–1919	Ernst Heubach Köppelsdorf nach 1887–1919	17 **43**
same as 1767	wie 1767	17 **43**
H. Schmidt Freiwaldau (1894)–1923 blue underglaze	H. Schmidt Freiwaldau (1894)–1923 blau unterglasur	17 **40**
same as 1769	wie 1769	17 **40**
J. Hering & Weithase Koppelsdorf 1893–1908	J. Hering & Weithase Köppelsdorf 1893–1908	17 **43**
J. Hering & Son Koppelsdorf (1909)–1945	J. Hering & Sohn Köppelsdorf (1909)–1945	17 **43**
J. Hering & Son Koppelsdorf (1909)–1945 impressed	J. Hering & Sohn Köppelsdorf (1909)–1945 eingeprägt	17 **43**
C. K. Weithase Volkstedt 1897– decorator's mark overglaze	C. K. Weithase Volkstedt 1897– Malermarke aufglasur	17 **49**
Friedrich Simon Karlsbad about 1920 decorator's mark overglaze	Friedrich Simon Karlsbad um 1920 Malermarke aufglasur	17 **42**

VEB Porcelainwork Weisswasser Weisswasser 1946–1957	VEB Porzellanwerk Weißwasser Weißwasser 1946–1957	1776 **500**	
Buckau Porcelain Manufactory Magdeburg-Buckau after 1832–	Buckauer Porzellanmanufaktur Magdeburg-Buckau nach 1832–	1777 **442**	
F. E. Henneberg & Co. Gotha (1875)–1881	F. E. Henneberg & Co. Gotha (1875)–1881	1778 **409**	
E. Kruse & Co. Bremen (1894)– decorator's mark overglaze	E. Kruse & Co. Bremen (1894)– Malermarke aufglasur	1779 **386**	
J. F. Lenz Zell on Harmersbach circa 1820–1840 on earthenware	J. F. Lenz Zell am Harmersbach ca. 1820–1840 auf Steingut	1780 **507**	
Spiermann & Wessely Hamburg (1884)–	Spiermann & Wessely Hamburg (1884)–	1781 **416**	
Clayware Factory Schwandorf Schwandorf (1970)– on earthenware and porcelain	Tonwarenfabrik Schwandorf Schwandorf (1970)– auf Steingut und Porzellan	1782 **477**	
Porcelain Factory Krummen- naab W. Mannl Krummennaab 1897–1931	Porzellanfabrik Krummen- naab W. Mannl Krummennaab 1897–1931	1783 **434**	
Berlin Art Ceramic Berlin (1921)–	Berliner Kunst Keramik Berlin (1921)–	1784 **380**	
F. J. Grohmann Haida last quarter 19th century decorator's mark overglaze	F. J. Grohmann Haida letztes Viertel des 19. Jahrhunderts Malermarke aufglasur	1785 **414**	

J. D. Kestner & Co. Ohrdruf after 1910–circa 1930	J. D. Kestner & Co. Ohrdruf nach 1910–ca. 1930	17 **45**
Alfred Stellmacher Turn-Teplitz after 1859–1897	Alfred Stellmacher Turn-Teplitz nach 1859–1897	17 **49**
Hentschel & Muller Meuselwitz after 1904–1930	Hentschel & Müller Meuselwitz nach 1904–1930	178 **44**
Johann Seltmann Vohenstrauss (1911)–	Johann Seltmann Vohenstrauß (1911)–	17 **494**
Risler & Cie. Merkstein (1954)–	Risler & Cie. Merkstein (1954)–	17 **44**
Risler & Cie. Freiburg (1879)–1927	Risler & Cie. Freiburg (1879)–1927	17 **40**
Villeroy & Boch Dresden (1887)–circa 1945 on earthenware	Villeroy & Boch Dresden (1887)–ca. 1945 auf Steingut	17 **39**
Villeroy & Boch Mettlach circa 1860 relief on earthenware	Villeroy & Boch Mettlach ca. 1860 Relief auf Steingut	17 **44**
Villeroy & Boch Mettlach circa 1850–1860 relief on earthenware	Villeroy & Boch Mettlach ca. 1850–1860 Relief auf Steingut	17 **44**

Wachtersbach Earthenware Factory Schlierbach 1845–1850 black	Wächtersbacher Steingut- fabrik Schlierbach 1845–1850 schwarz	1795 473
A. Frank Kahla after 1892–1965 decorator's mark overglaze	A. Frank Kahla nach 1892–1965 Malermarke aufglasur	1796 423
August Nowotny Altrohlau 1838–1884 blue	August Nowotny Altrohlau 1838–1884 blau	1797 373
Erdmann Schlegelmilch Suhl (1902)–1938 green underglaze except for "Hand painted," which is overglaze	Erdmann Schlegelmilch Suhl (1902)–1938 grün unterglasur, außer "Hand painted " auf der Glasur	1798 485
Josef Kratzer & Sons Haindorf 1880–circa 1945 impressed	Josef Kratzer & Söhne Haindorf 1880–ca. 1945 eingeprägt	1799 414
Altrohlau Porcelain Factories Altrohlau 1918–1939 green underglaze	Altrohlauer Porzellan- fabriken Altrohlau 1918–1939 grün unterglasur	1800 373
Hans Neuerer Oberkotzau (1953)–	Hans Neuerer Oberkotzau (1953)–	1801 458
Richter, Fenkl & Hahn Chodau 1918–1945	Richter, Fenkl & Hahn Chodau 1918–1945	1802 389

Willi Gossler
Thiersheim
after 1929—
decorator's mark
overglaze

Willi Goßler
Thiersheim
nach 1929—
Malermarke
aufglasur

180
48

Vienna Porcelain Manufactory
Josef Bock
Vienna
(1900)—

Wiener Porzellanmanufaktur
Josef Böck
Wien
(1900)—

180
50

C. & E. Carstens
Zeven
1922—circa 1930
decorating mark

C. & E. Carstens
Zeven
1922—ca. 1930
Malereimarke

180
508

August Nowotny
Altrohlau
1838—1884

August Nowotny
Altrohlau
1838—1884

180
373

Bros. Benedikt
Meierhofen
after 1883—1925

Gebr. Benedikt
Meierhöfen
nach 1883—1925

180
445

Earthenware Factory Colditz
Colditz
1907—
on earthenware

Steingutfabrik Colditz
Colditz
1907—
auf Steingut

180
391

Ludwig Wessel
Bonn
(1905)—

Ludwig Wessel
Bonn
(1905)—

180
385

unidentified
green overglaze

nicht identifiziert
grün aufglasur

181

Georg Schmider
Zell on Harmersbach
about 1924

Georg Schmider
Zell am Harmersbach
um 1924

181
507

Wachtersbach Earthenware Factory Schlierbach 1845−1850 black	Wächtersbacher Steingut- fabrik Schlierbach 1845−1850 schwarz	1795 473
A. Frank Kahla after 1892−1965 decorator's mark overglaze	A. Frank Kahla nach 1892−1965 Malermarke aufglasur	1796 423
August Nowotny Altrohlau 1838−1884 blue	August Nowotny Altrohlau 1838−1884 blau	1797 373
Erdmann Schlegelmilch Suhl (1902)−1938 green underglaze except for "Hand painted," which is overglaze	Erdmann Schlegelmilch Suhl (1902)−1938 grün unterglasur, außer "Hand painted " auf der Glasur	1798 485
Josef Kratzer & Sons Haindorf 1880−circa 1945 impressed	Josef Kratzer & Söhne Haindorf 1880−ca. 1945 eingeprägt	1799 414
Altrohlau Porcelain Factories Altrohlau 1918−1939 green underglaze	Altrohlauer Porzellan- fabriken Altrohlau 1918−1939 grün unterglasur	1800 373
Hans Neuerer Oberkotzau (1953)−	Hans Neuerer Oberkotzau (1953)−	1801 458
Richter, Fenkl & Hahn Chodau 1918−1945	Richter, Fenkl & Hahn Chodau 1918−1945	1802 389

Willi Gossler	Willi Goßler	
Thiersheim	Thiersheim	
after 1929–	nach 1929–	
decorator's mark	Malermarke	180
overglaze	aufglasur	**48**
Vienna Porcelain Manufactory	Wiener Porzellanmanufaktur	
Josef Bock	Josef Böck	
Vienna	Wien	180
(1900)–	(1900)–	**50**
C. & E. Carstens	C. & E. Carstens	
Zeven	Zeven	
1922–circa 1930	1922–ca. 1930	180
decorating mark	Malereimarke	**508**
August Nowotny	August Nowotny	
Altrohlau	Altrohlau	180
1838–1884	1838–1884	**373**
Bros. Benedikt	Gebr. Benedikt	180
Meierhofen	Meierhöfen	
after 1883–1925	nach 1883–1925	**445**
Earthenware Factory Colditz	Steingutfabrik Colditz	
Colditz	Colditz	
1907–	1907–	180
on earthenware	auf Steingut	**391**
Ludwig Wessel	Ludwig Wessel	
Bonn	Bonn	180
(1905)–	(1905)–	**385**
unidentified	nicht identifiziert	181
green overglaze	grün aufglasur	
Georg Schmider	Georg Schmider	
Zell on Harmersbach	Zell am Harmersbach	181
about 1924	um 1924	**507**

Vienna Manufactory F. Goldscheider Vienna after 1885–circa 1907	Wiener Manufaktur F. Goldscheider Wien nach 1885–ca. 1907	1812 **503**
Ignaz Balle Schelten 1851–1860	Ignaz Balle Schelten 1851–1860	1813 **472**
Ludwig Wessel Bonn (1905)–	Ludwig Wessel Bonn (1905)–	1814 **385**
Porcelain Factory Friesland Varel (1968)–present	Porzellanfabrik Friesland Varel (1968)–heute	1815 **493**
C. A. Lehmann & Son Kahla (1930)–circa 1935	C. A. Lehmann & Sohn Kahla (1930)–ca. 1935	1816 **423**
Ludwig Wessel Bonn (1905)–	Ludwig Wessel Bonn (1905)–	1817 **385**
VEB Porcelain Factory Piesau Piesau 1960–1962	VEB Porzellanfabrik Piesau Piesau 1960–1962	1818 **461**
Southwest German Porcelain and Glass Distributing Co. Bad Driburg (1968)– distributor's mark	Südwestdeutsche Porzellan und Glasvertriebs GmbH Bad Driburg (1968)– Händlermarke	1819 **378**
Porcelaine 'Rose' Walk Aschaffenburg 1974–present	Porcelaine 'Rose' Walk Aschaffenburg 1974–heute	1820 **377**
Josef Palme Schelten 1829–1851	Josef Palme Schelten 1829–1851	1821 **472**

Schumann & Schreider Schwarzenhammer after 1905–	Schumann & Schreider Schwarzenhammer nach 1905–	18	47
Reuter & Graefe Hamburg (1905)–1916	Reuter & Graefe Hamburg (1905)–1916	18	41
Erdmann Schlegelmilch Suhl after 1861–	Erdmann Schlegelmilch Suhl nach 1861–	18	48
Swaine & Co. Huttensteinach –1920	Swaine & Co. Hüttensteinach –1920	18	42
Swaine & Co. Huttensteinach after 1900–1920	Swaine & Co. Hüttensteinach nach 1900–1920	18	42
Swaine & Co. Huttensteinach after 1900–1920 for underglaze decoration	Swaine & Co. Hüttensteinach nach 1900–1920 für Unterglasurmalerei	182	420
Porcelain Factory Altenkunstadt Altenkunstadt 1960–present blue or black overglaze, export mark	Porzellanfabrik Altenkunstadt Altenkunstadt 1960–heute blau oder schwarz aufglasur, Exportmarke	182	372
Porcelain Factory Altenkunstadt Altenkunstadt circa 1960–present blue or black overglaze	Porzellanfabrik Altenkunstadt Altenkunstadt ca. 1960–heute blau oder schwarz aufglasur	182	372
Porcelain Factory Altenkunstadt Altenkunstadt circa 1969–present blue or black overglaze export mark	Porzellanfabrik Altenkunstadt Altenkunstadt ca. 1969–heute blau oder schwarz aufglasur, Exportmarke	183	372

230

same as 1830	wie 1830	1831 **372**
Porcelain Factory Altenkunstadt Altenkunstadt circa 1960–present black overglaze or blue underglaze	Porzellanfabrik Altenkunstadt Altenkunstadt ca. 1960–heute schwarz aufglasur oder blau unterglasur	1832 **372**
Porcelain Factory Altenkunstadt Altenkunstadt 1960–present blue or black overglaze export mark	Porzellanfabrik Altenkunstadt Altenkunstadt 1960–heute blau oder schwarz aufglasur, Exportmarke	1833 **372**
Porcelain Factory Altenkunstadt Altenkunstadt 1960–present blue underglaze or black overglaze export mark	Porzellanfabrik Altenkunstadt Altenkunstadt 1960–heute blau unterglasur oder schwarz aufglasur Exportmarke	1834 **372**
Porcelain Factory Altenkunstadt Altendunstadt 1970–present blue underglaze	Porzellanfabrik Altenkunstadt Altenkunstadt 1970–heute blau unterglasur	1835 **372**
Porcelain Factory Altenkunstadt Altenkunstadt 1933–circa 1960 blue underglaze or black overglaze	Porzellanfabrik Altenkunstadt Altenkunstadt 1933–ca. 1960 blau unterglasur oder schwarz aufglasur	1836 **372**
Porcelain Factory Altenkunstadt Altenkunstadt 1960–present blue or black overglaze export mark	Porzellanfabrik Altenkunstadt Altenkunstadt 1960–heute blau oder schwarz aufglasur, Exportmarke	1837 **372**
Upper Franconian Porcelain Factory Kups 1890–1919	Oberfränkische Porzellan- fabrik Küps 1890–1919	1838 **434**
Porcelain Factory Altenkunstadt Altenkunstadt 1969–circa 1971 blue or black overglaze	Porzellanfabrik Altenkunstadt Altenkunstadt 1969–ca. 1971 blau oder schwarz aufglasur	1839 **372**

Porcelain Factory Altenkunstadt Altenkunstadt 1969–circa 1971 blue or black overglaze	Porzellanfabrik Altenkunstadt Altenkunstadt 1969–ca. 1971 blau oder schwarz aufglasur	1 3

H. Schomburg & Sons
Rosslau
(1927)–1945
blue underglaze or overglaze
also in combination
with: Askania
      Alt England
      China Blau
	H. Schomburg & Söhne
	Roßlau
	(1927)–1945
	blau unterglasur oder aufglasur
	auch in Verbindung
	mit: Askania
	      Alt England
	      China Blau
		
		18
		46

Ludwig Wessel Bonn 19th century on earthenware	Ludwig Wessel Bonn 19. Jahrhundert auf Steingut	18 38
Engelbert Cremer & Son Cologne circa 1793–circa 1800 black	Engelbert Cremer & Sohn Köln ca. 1793–ca. 1800 schwarz	18 42
Villeroy & Boch Mettlach circa 1836–circa 1850 impressed on earthenware	Villeroy & Boch Mettlach ca. 1836–ca. 1850 eingeprägt auf Steingut	18 44
Armand Marseille Koppelsdorf circa 1910–1919 impressed or green underglaze	Armand Marseille Köppelsdorf ca. 1910–1919 eingeprägt oder grün unterglasur	18 43
Armand Marseille Koppelsdorf (1910)–1919 impressed or green underglaze	Armand Marseille Köppelsdorf (1910)–1919 eingeprägt oder grün unterglasur	18 43
Armand Marseille Koppelsdorf circa 1910–1919	Armand Marseille Köppelsdorf ca. 1910–1919	18 43
Armand Marseille Koppelsdorf (1910)–1919	Armand Marseille Köppelsdorf (1910)–1919	18 43
Ernst Bohne Sons Rudolstadt 1878–circa 1920	Ernst Bohne Söhne Rudolstadt 1878–ca. 1920	18 46

Ernst Bohne Sons Rudolstadt 1878–circa 1920 impressed	Ernst Bohne Söhne Rudolstadt 1878–ca. 1920 eingeprägt	1850 **469**	
same as 1850	wie 1850	1851 **469**	
Ernst Bohne Sons Rudolstadt after 1878–circa 1920	Ernst Bohne Söhne Rudolstadt nach 1878–ca. 1920	1852 **469**	
Vienna Manufactory F. Goldscheider Vienna after 1885–	Wiener Manufaktur F. Goldscheider Wien nach 1885–	1853 **503**	
Bros. Hubbe Haldensleben (1882)–1898	Gebr. Hubbe Haldensleben (1882)–1898	1854 **415**	
Britannia Porcelainworks Meierhofen circa 1898–1925	Britannia Porcelainworks Meierhöfen ca. 1898–1925	1855 **445**	
Moller & Dippe Unterkoditz circa 1883–circa 1931	Möller & Dippe Unterköditz ca. 1883–ca. 1931	1856 **492**	
Porcelain Factory Sorau Fr. Bohme Sorau (1894)–1918	Porzellanfabrik Sorau Fr. Böhme Sorau (1894)–1918	1857 **482**	
Oscar Schaller & Co. Schwarzenbach after 1882–circa 1918	Oscar Schaller & Co. Schwarzenbach nach 1882–ca. 1918	1858 **477**	
Sauer & Roloff Haldensleben after 1905–	Sauer & Roloff Haldensleben nach 1905–	1859 **415**	
C. Tielsch & Co. Altwasser (1875)–circa 1918 blue underglaze	C. Tielsch & Co. Altwasser (1875)–ca. 1918 blau unterglasur	1860 **374**	

	Franz Anton Mehlem Bonn circa 1900–1920 on earthenware	Franz Anton Mehlem Bonn ca. 1900–1920 auf Steingut	18 38
	Royal Porcelain Manufactory Meissen circa 1721–probably 1731 blue underglaze	Königliche Porzellan Manufaktur Meißen ca. 1721–wahrscheinlich 1731 blau unterglasur	18 44
	same as 1862	wie 1862	18 44
	same as 1862	wie 1862	18 44
	same as 1862	wie 1862	18 44
	same as 1862	wie 1862	18 44
	same as 1862	wie 1862	18 44
	same as 1862	wie 1862	18 44

same as 1862	wie 1862	1869 **446**
same as 1862	wie 1862	1870 **446**
same as 1862	wie 1862	1871 **446**
Porcelain Factory Stadtlengsfeld Stadtlengsfeld —circa 1933	Porzellanfabrik Stadtlengsfeld Stadtlengsfeld —ca. 1933	1872 **483**
Porcelain Factory Stadtlengsfeld Stadtlengsfeld (1933)–circa 1945	Porzellanfabrik Stadtlengsfeld Stadtlengsfeld (1933)–ca. 1945	1873 **483**
VEB Porcelainwork Stadtlengsfeld Stadtlengsfeld (1953)–circa 1959	VEB Porzellanwerk Stadtlengsfeld Stadtlengsfeld (1953)–ca. 1959	1874 **483**
VEB Porcelainwork Stadtlengsfeld 1959-1990	VEB Porzellanwerk Stadtlengsfeld 1959-1990	1875 **483**
Villeroy & Boch Mettlach 1885–present on earthenware	Villeroy & Boch Mettlach 1885–heute auf Steingut	1876 **449**
A. J. Thewalt Hohr-Grenzhausen (1972)– on earthenware	A. J. Thewalt Höhr-Grenzhausen (1972)– auf Steingut	1877 **419**

	A. J. Thewalt Hohr-Grenzhausen (1971)– on earthenware	A. J. Thewalt Höhr-Grenzhausen (1971)– auf Steingut	18 **41**
	A. J. Thewalt Hohr-Grenzhausen (1975)– on earthenware	A. J. Thewalt Höhr-Grenzhausen (1975)– auf Steingut	18 **41**
	Adolf Bauer Magdeburg (1894)–1907 on earthenware	Adolf Bauer Magdeburg (1894)–1907 auf Steingut	18 **44**
	Adolf Bauer Magdeburg (1894)–1907 on earthenware	Adolf Bauer Magdeburg (1894)–1907 auf Steingut	18 **44**
	OCA Porcelain Factory Oechsler & Andexer Kronach 1951–before 1975	OCA Porzellanfabrik Oechsler & Andexer Kronach 1951–vor 1975	18 **43**
	C. A. Lehmann & Son Kahla (1910)–circa 1935 green	C. A. Lehmann & Sohn Kahla (1910)–ca. 1935 grün	18 42
	J. von Schwarz Nuremberg (1889)–	J. von Schwarz Nürnberg (1889)–	18 **45**
	Meissner Porcelain Decorating Meissen 1928-1939 Arthur Pohlmann 1939-1945	Meissner Porzellanmalerei Meißen 1928-1939 Arthur Pöhlmann 1939-1945	18 **44**
	Somag Saxonian Stove and Walltileworks Meissen 1919-1945	Somag Sächsische Ofen- und Wandplattenwerke Meißen 1919-1945	18 **44**

VEB Porcelainwork Freiberg
Freiberg
1954–1972

VEB Porzellanwerk Freiberg
Freiberg   1887
1954–1972   **404**

VEB Porcelainwork Freiberg
Freiberg
circa 1946–circa 1969

VEB Porzellanwerk Freiberg
Freiberg   1888
ca. 1946–ca. 1969   **404**

Carl Spitz
Brux
after 1896–

Carl Spitz
Brüx   1889
nach 1896–   **387**

Porcelain Factory Waldsassen
Waldsassen
(1966)-1993

Porzellanfabrik Waldsassen
Waldsassen   1890
(1966)-1993   **498**

Schmidt & Otremba
Freiwaldau
(1887)–circa 1894

Schmidt & Otremba
Freiwaldau   1891
(1887)–ca. 1894   **405**

Porcelain Factory Kloster
Vessra
Kloster Vessra
after 1900–circa 1937

Porzellanfabrik Kloster
Vessra
Kloster Vessra   1892
nach 1900–ca. 1937   **429**

Vienna Art Ceramic
Vienna
after 1906–

Wiener Kunstkeramik
Wien   1893
nach 1906–   **503**

Meissen Stove and Porcelain
Factory C. Teichert
Meissen
1925-1930

Meißner Ofen- und Porzellanfabrik C. Teichert
Meißen   1894
1925-1930   **447**

Franz Anton Mehlem
Bonn
(1896)–1920
on earthenware

Franz Anton Mehlem
Bonn
(1896)–1920   1895
auf Steingut   **385**

Franz Anton Mehlem
Bonn
(1896)–1920
blue underglaze
on earthenware

Franz Anton Mehlem
Bonn
(1896)–1920
blau unterglasur   1896
auf Steingut   **385**

Julius Dressler	Julius Dressler	18
Biela	Biela	
(1900)–circa 1945	(1900)–ca. 1945	**38**
Adolf Laufer	Adolf Laufer	18
Turn-Teplitz	Turn-Teplitz	
1919–1938	1919–1938	**49**
Slama & Co.	Slama & Co.	18
Vienna	Wien	
1951–	1951–	**50**
Brunner & Ploetz	Brunner & Ploetz	
Munich	München	
1890–	1890–	19
decorator's mark	Malermarke	
overglaze	aufglasur	**45**
VEB Electro Porcelain	VEB Elektroporzellan	
Grossdubrau	Großdubrau	19
(1954)-1990	(1954)-1990	**41**
Richard Schiller	Richard Schiller	
Fischhausel	Fischhäusel	
circa 1930	ca. 1930	
decorator's mark	Malermarke	19
overglaze	aufglasur	**40**
Reinhold Schlegelmilch	Reinhold Schlegelmilch	19
Tillowitz	Tillowitz	19
1898–1908	1898–1908	**48**
Bros. Schoenau	Gebr. Schoenau	
Huttensteinach	Hüttensteinach	19
after 1900–1920	nach 1900–1920	**42**
Bros. Schoenau	Gebr. Schoenau	
Huttensteinach	Hüttensteinach	19
after 1900–1920	nach 1900–1920	**42**
Bros. Schoenau, Swaine & Co.	Gebr. Schoenau, Swaine & Co.	
Huttensteinach	Hüttensteinach	19
(1933)–1954	(1933)–1954	**42**

VEB Sonneberg Porcelain Factories Huttensteinach (1956)-1990	VEB Sonneberger Porzellan- fabriken Hüttensteinach (1956)-1990	1908 **420**	
Gerbing & Stephan, 1890—1898 F. & A. Gerbing, 1898—1905 Alexander Gerbing, 1905— Bodenbach on earthenware, fayence and maiolica	Gerbing & Stephan, 1890—1898 F. A. Gerbing, 1898—1905 Alexander Gerbing, 1905— Bodenbach auf Steingut, Fayence und Majolika	1909 **384**	
Porcelain Factory Mitterteich Mitterteich after 1918—	Porzellanfabrik Mitterteich Mitterteich nach 1918—	1910 **450**	
E. & A. Muller Schonwald (1911)—circa 1927	E. & A. Müller Schönwald (1911)—ca. 1927	1911 **475**	
Carstens-Uffrecht Haldensleben (1929)—1945	Carstens-Uffrecht Haldensleben (1929)—1945	1912 **415**	
Fischer & Mieg Pirkenhammer 1875—1887 green underglaze	Fischer & Mieg Pirkenhammer 1875—1887 grün unterglasur	1913 **461**	
Zwickau Porcelain Factory Hermann Unger Schedewitz (1887)—	Zwickauer Porzellanfabrik Hermann Unger Schedewitz (1887)—	1914 **471**	
Friedrich Kaestner Oberhohndorf (1884)—1929	Friedrich Kaestner Oberhohndorf (1884)—1929	1915 **457**	
same as 1915	wie 1915	1916 **457**	
Friedrich Kaestner Oberhohndorf after 1884—circa 1929	Friedrich Kaestner Oberhohndorf nach 1884—ca. 1929	1917 **457**	

Friedrich Kaestner	Friedrich Kaestner	191	
Oberhohndorf	Oberhohndorf		
after 1900–circa 1929	nach 1900–ca. 1929	457	
Friedrich Kaestner	Friedrich Kaestner	191	
Oberhohndorf	Oberhohndorf		
after 1884–1920	nach 1884–1929	457	
Bros. Metzler & Ortloff	Gebr. Metzler & Ortloff	192	
Ilmenau	Ilmenau		
(1887)–	(1887)–	422	
VEB Art Porcelain	VEB Kunstporzellan		
Ilmenau	Ilmenau		
(1972)-before 1990	(1972)-before 1990	192	
black overglaze	schwarz aufglasur	422	
Porcelain Factory Plankenhammer	Porzellanfabrik Plankenhammer		
Plankenhammer	Plankenhammer	192	
(1920)–circa 1945	(1920)–ca. 1945	462	
Porcelain Factory Plankenhammer	Porzellanfabrik Plankenhammer		
Plankenhammer	Plankenhammer	192	
(1920)–circa 1978	(1920)–ca. 1978	462	
same as 1923	wie 1923	192	
		462	
same as 1923	wie 1923	192	
		462	
Schumann & Schreider	Schumann & Schreider	192	
Schwarzenhammer	Schwarzenhammer		
after 1905–	nach 1905–	478	
unidentified	nicht identifiziert		
attributed to Baden-Baden	Baden-Baden zugeschrieben,		
but questionable	aber fraglich	192	
gold overglaze	gold aufglasur	378	
unidentified	nicht identifiziert		
attributed to Baden-Baden	Baden-Baden zugeschrieben,		
but questionable	aber fraglich	192	
gold overglaze	gold aufglasur	378	

Friedrich Kaestner	Friedrich Kaestner		
Oberhohndorf	Oberhohndorf	1929	
circa 1900–circa 1929	ca. 1900–ca. 1929	**457**	

The Mosanic Pottery	The Mosanic Pottery		
Max Emanuel & Co.	Max Emanuel & Co.		
Mitterteich	Mitterteich	1930	
(1897)–1918	(1897)–1918	**450**	

Thomas Recknagel	Thomas Recknagel		
Alexandrinenthal	Alexandrinenthal	1931	
(1896)–1934	(1896)–1934	**371**	

Thomas Recknagel	Thomas Recknagel		
Alexandrinenthal	Alexandrinenthal		
after 1886–1934	nach 1886–1934	1932	
blue or impressed	blau oder eingeprägt	**371**	

Thomas Recknagel	Thomas Recknagel		
Alexandrinenthal	Alexandrinenthal		
circa 1930	ca. 1930	1933	
decorator's mark	Malermarke	**371**	

Porcelain Factory Stadtlengsfeld	Porzellanfabrik Stadtlengsfeld		
Stadtlengsfeld	Stadtlengsfeld	1934	
(1900)–circa 1908	(1900)–ca. 1908	**483**	

Porcelain Factory Stadtlengsfeld	Porzellanfabrik Stadtlengsfeld		
Stadtlengsfeld	Stadtlengsfeld	1935	
(1904)–circa 1908	(1904)–ca. 1908	**483**	

Sophie Seitz-Huckstadt	Sophie Seitz-Hückstädt		
Berlin	Berlin		
(1894)–	(1894)–		
decorator's mark	Malermarke	1936	
overglaze	aufglasur	**383**	

Ernst Heubach	Ernst Heubach		
Koppelsdorf	Köppelsdorf		
(1896)–1919	(1896)–1919	1937	
impressed on dolls heads	eingeprägt auf Puppenköpfen	**432**	

Ernst Heubach	Ernst Heubach		
Koppelsdorf	Köppelsdorf		
circa 1896–1919	ca. 1896–1919	1938	
impressed on dolls heads	eingeprägt auf Puppenköpfen	**432**	

Ernst Heubach Koppelsdorf circa 1900 impressed on dolls heads	Ernst Heubach Köppelsdorf ca. 1900 eingeprägt auf Puppenköpfen	19? **43?**
Ernst Heubach Koppelsdorf after 1896–1919 impressed on dolls heads probably made for for Louis Wolf & Co. in Sonneberg/New York City/ Boston, Mass.	Ernst Heubach Köppelsdorf nach 1896–1919 eingeprägt auf Puppen- köpfen, wahrscheinlich für Louis Wolf & Co. in Sonneberg/New York/ Boston	194? **432**
Albert Schulze Successor Velten circa 1930 decorator's mark overglaze	Albert Schulze Nachf. Velten ca. 1930 Malermarke aufglasur	194 **493**
Paul Bossenroth Berlin (1905)-	Paul Bößenroth Berlin (1905)-	194? **380?**
Johann Seltmann Vohenstrauss after 1901–	Johann Seltmann Vohenstrauß nach 1901–	194? **494**
Triebner, Ens & Eckert, 1886–1894 and Richard Eckert, 1894– and Clemens Triebner, 1894– Volkstedt blue underglaze	Triebner, Ens & Eckert, 1886–1894 und Richard Eckert, 1894– und Clemens Triebner, 1894– Volkstedt blau unterglasur	194 **494**
same as 1944	wie 1944	194 **494**
Volkstedt Porcelain Factory Richard Eckert Volkstedt 1906–1908	Volkstedter Porzellan- fabrik Richard Eckert Volkstedt 1906–1908	194? **497**
Volkstedt Porcelain Factory Richard Eckert Volkstedt 1908–1918	Volkstedter Porzellan- fabrik Richard Eckert Volkstedt 1908–1918	194 **497**

Volkstedt Porcelain Factory Richard Eckert Volkstedt 1894–1918 blue underglaze	Volkstedter Porzellan- fabrik Richard Eckert Volkstedt 1894–1918 blau unterglasur	1948 **497**
same as 1948	wie 1948	1949 **497**
same as 1948	wie 1948	1950 **497**
Christian Nonne Volkstedt 1787–1800 blue underglaze or overglaze	Christian Nonne Volkstedt 1787–1800 blau unterglasur oder aufglasur	1951 **494**
Volkstedt Porcelain Factory Richard Eckert Volkstedt 1908–1918	Volkstedter Porzellan- fabrik Richard Eckert Volkstedt 1908–1918	1952 **497**
Christian Nonne Volkstedt 1767–1800 blue underglaze or overglaze	Christian Nonne Volkstedt 1767–1800 blau unterglasur oder aufglasur	1953 **494**
same as 1953	wie 1953	1954 **494**
Christian Nonne Volkstedt 1767–1800 blue underglaze	Christian Nonne Volkstedt 1767–1800 blau unterglasur	1955 **494**
same as 1955	wie 1955	1956 **495**
Triebner, Ens & Eckert Volkstedt 1877–1887 blue	Triebner, Ens & Eckert Volkstedt 1877–1887 blue	1957 **495**

Triebner, Ens & Eckert	Triebner, Ens & Eckert	
Volkstedt	Volkstedt	
1877–1894	1877–1894	19
blue underglaze	blau unterglasur	49
Ens & Greiner	Ens & Greiner	
Lauscha	Lauscha	
(1887)–1897	(1887)–1897	
decorator's mark	Malermarke	19
overglaze	aufglasur	43
G. H. Macheleid	G. H. Macheleid	
Volkstedt	Volkstedt	19
1760–1767	1760–1767	49
H. Schomburg & Sons	H. Schomburg & Söhne	
Berlin	Berlin	19
(1897)–circa 1913	(1897)–ca. 1913	38
Porcelain Factory Kahla	Porzellanfabrik Kahla	
Hermsdorf-Klosterlausnitz	Hermsdorf-Klosterlausnitz	19
(1911)–circa 1945	(1911)–ca. 1945	41
Porcelain Factory Kahla	Porzellanfabrik Kahla	
Hermsdorf-Klosterlausnitz	Hermsdorf-Klosterlausnitz	19
(1903)–circa 1945	(1903)–ca. 1945	41
Glassworks Ruhr	Glaswerke Ruhr	
Essen	Essen	
(1956)–	(1956)–	
trademark registered	Schutzmarke registriert	19
for porcelain	für Porzellan	401
H. Waffler	H. Waffler	
Schwarzenfeld	Schwarzenfeld	
circa 1925	circa 1925	
decorator's mark	Malermarke	19
gold overglaze	gold aufglasur	478
Porcelain Factory Stadtlengsfeld	Porzellanfabrik Stadtlengsfeld	
Stadtlengsfeld	Stadtlengsfeld	19
1894–1904	1894–1904	483

Schumann & Klett Ilmenau after 1872–circa 1927 decorator's mark overglaze	Schumann & Klett Ilmenau nach 1872–ca. 1927 Malermarke aufglasur	**1967** **422**
unidentified attributed to a factory in Arnstadt circa 1790 blue underglaze	nicht identifiziert einer Fabrik in Arnstadt zugeschrieben ca. 1790 blau unterglasur	**1968** **1969** **376**
Swaine & Co. Huttensteinach after 1900–circa 1920	Swaine & Co. Hüttensteinach nach 1900–ca. 1920	**1970** **420**
Swaine & Co. Huttensteinach (1896)–1920	Swaine & Co. Hüttensteinach (1896)–1920	**1971** **420**
Swaine & Co. Huttensteinach after 1896–1920	Swaine & Co. Hüttensteinach nach 1896–1920	**1972** **420**
Swaine & Co. Huttensteinach after 1896–circa 1920 blue	Swaine & Co. Hüttensteinach nach 1896–ca. 1920 blau	**1973** **420**
Bros. Schoenau, Swaine & Co. Huttensteinach 1920–1945	Gebr. Schoenau, Swaine & Co. Hüttensteinach 1920–1945	**1974** **420**
Ens & Greiner Lauscha (1885)–1897 decorator's mark overglaze	Ens & Greiner Lauscha (1885)–1897 Malermarke aufglasur	**1975** **437**
Ferdinand Kaule Coburg (1894)– decorator's mark overglaze	Ferdinand Kaule Coburg (1894)– Malermarke aufglasur	**1976** **390**
Josef Gunter Dresden after 1890– decorator's mark overglaze	Josef Günter Dresden nach 1890– Malermarke aufglasur	**1977** **394**

	English	German	
	Krautzberger, Mayer & Purkert Wistritz (1912)–1945 decorating mark	Krautzberger, Mayer & Purkert Wistritz (1912)–1945 Malereimarke	19 50
	Heinrich & Co. and Heinrich Porcelain Selb after 1947–present mark of art department in Seethal	Heinrich & Co. und Heinrich Porzellan Selb nach 1947–heute Marke der Kunstabteilung in Seethal	19 47
	Ebeling & Reuss Devon/Philadelphia, Pa. 20th century importer's mark	Ebeling & Reuss Devon/Philadelphia 20. Jahrhundert Importeurmarke	19 39.
	Franz Manka Altrohlau 1936–1945	Franz Manka Altrohlau 1936–1945	198 37
	Chr. Fr. Kling & Co. Ohrdruf (1896)–1941	Chr. Fr. Kling & Co. Ohrdruf (1896)–1941	198 198. 459
	same as 1982	wie 1982	198 459
	Porcelain Factory Waldsassen Waldsassen 1968-1993 on collectors´ plates	Porzellanfabrik Waldsassen Waldsassen 1968-1993 auf Sammeltellern	198 498
	Silberdistel Breu & Co. Gevelsberg 1947–present	Silberdistel Breu & Co. Gevelsberg 1947–heute	198 407
	VEB Grafenroda Ceramic Grafenroda (1964)-1990	VEB Gräfenroda Keramik Gräfenroda (1964)-1990	198 410
	A. Rappsilber Konigszelt about 1900–1912	A. Rappsilber Königszelt um 1900–1912	198 430

Kirke Platten

G. Schumacher Hamburg (1884)– on earthenware	G. Schumacher Hamburg (1884)– auf Steingut	1989 **416**
Eugen Hulsmann Altenbach 1881–after 1932 on earthenware	Eugen Hülsmann Altenbach 1881–nach 1932 auf Steingut	1990 **372**
Moritz Zdekauer Altrohlau 1884–circa 1909	Moritz Zdekauer Altrohlau 1884–ca. 1909	1991 **373**
Hentschel & Muller Meuselwitz (1904)–1930	Hentschel & Müller Meuselwitz (1904)–1930	1992 **449**
Porcelain Factory R. Kampf Grunlas 1912–1945 green overglaze or underglaze	Porzellanfabrik R. Kämpf Grünlas 1912–1945 grün aufglasur oder unterglasur	1993 **413**
Workshop for Ceramic Decorating G. Wieninger Munich (1942)– decorator's mark	Werkstatt für Keramik-Malerei G. Wieninger München (1942)– Malermarke	1994 **451**
Porcelain Factory Kloster Vessra Kloster Vessra 1921–1937	Porzellanfabrik Kloster Vessra Kloster Vessra 1921–1937	1995 **429**
Gaebler & Groschl Ladowitz circa 1883–1906	Gaebler & Gröschl Ladowitz ca. 1883–1906	1996 **435**
Riessner, Stellmacher & Kessel Turn-Teplitz 1892–1905	Riessner, Stellmacher & Kessel Turn-Teplitz 1892–1905	1997 **489**

H. Wehinger & Co. Horn 1905–1918	H. Wehinger & Co. Horn 1905–1918	19 19 42
J. Brauers Gohfeld (1955)–	J. Brauers Gohfeld (1955)–	20 40
Hanns Graf Sonthofen 1951–1964 black underglaze	Hanns Graf Sonthofen 1951–1964 schwarz unterglasur	20 48
Fritz Krug Lauf (1902)–1968 green underglaze	Fritz Krug Lauf (1902)–1968 grün unterglasur	20 43
Porcelain Factory Rudolstadt Rudolstadt 1918–1932	Porzellanfabrik Rudolstadt Rudolstadt 1918–1932	20 46
Walter Klaas Solingen (1897)–circa 1907	Walter Klaas Solingen (1897)–ca. 1907	20 48
Deusch & Co. Lorch circa 1940	Deusch & Co. Lorch ca. 1940	20 440
Deusch & Co. Lorch (1949)–present	Deusch & Co. Lorch (1949)–heute	20 44
Orben, Knabe & Co. Geschwenda 1909–1939	Orben, Knabe & Co. Geschwenda 1909–1939	20 407
Hentschel & Muller Meuselwitz after 1904–1930	Hentschel & Müller Meuselwitz nach 1904–1930	20 449

Jasba Ceramic Factories	Jasba-Keramikfabriken		
Baumbach	Baumbach	2009	
(1961)–	(1961)–	**379**	
Carl Jacobi	Carl Jacobi		
Frankfurt on Main	Frankfurt am Main	2010	
(1885)–	(1885)–	**402**	
M. L. Goebel	M. L. Goebel		
Kronach	Kronach	2011	
1895–	1895–	**433**	
Rosenthal	Rosenthal		
Selb	Selb	2012	
(1957)–present	(1957)–heute	**480**	
Rosenthal	Rosenthal		
Selb	Selb	2013	
1962–present	1962–heute	**480**	
Georg Schmider	Georg Schmider		
Zell on Harmersbach	Zell am Harmersbach		
1907–1928	1907–1928		
on earthenware	auf Steingut		
also in combination	auch in Verbindung	2014	
with: BADEN	mit: BADEN	**507**	
Porcelain Factory Krummennaab	Porzellanfabrik Krummennaab		
W. Mannl	W. Mannl		
Krummennaab	Krummennaab	2015	
(1917)–1931	(1917)–1931	**434**	
Dussel, Roth & Co.	Düssel, Roth & Co.		
Rehau	Rehau		
1922–circa 1945	1922–ca. 1945		
decorator's mark	Malermarke	2016	
overglaze	aufglasur	**466**	
Graduate Engineer Hertel	Dipl. Ing. Hertel		
Badenweiler	Badenweiler		
(1910)–	(1910)–		
decorator's mark and	Malermarke und auf	2017	
on earthenware	Steingut	**378**	

| | Helmut Kruger
Berlin
(1957)–circa 1971 | Helmut Krüger
Berlin
(1957)–ca. 1971 | 20
38 |

Langer & Jahn
Geiersthal
1938–circa 1970
decorator's mark
red and other colors
overglaze

Langer & Jahn
Geiersthal
1938–ca. 1970
Malermarke
rot und andere Farben
aufglasur

20
40

Porcelain Manufactory
Union
Kleindembach
(1920)–circa 1927

Porzellanmanufaktur
Union
Kleindembach
(1920)–ca. 1927

20
42

Porcelain Manufactory
Union
Kleindembach
(1919)–1927

Porzellanmanufaktur
Union
Kleindembach
(1919)–1927

20
42

Ida-Lotte Roth
Niemberg
before 1939–after 1958
decorator's mark
overglaze

Ida-Lotte Roth
Niemberg
vor 1939–nach 1958
Malermarke
aufglasur

20
45

unidentified
brown overglaze
also in combination
with: Germany

nicht identifiziert
braun aufglasur
auch in Verbindung
mit: Germany

20

Porcelain Factory Schonwald
Arzberg
1920–1927
green underglaze

Porzellanfabrik Schönwald
Arzberg
1920–1927
grün unterglasur

20
37

Porcelain Factory Schonwald
Arzberg
1920–1927
green underglaze
also in combination
with: Germany

Porzellanfabrik Schönwald
Arzberg
1920–1927
grün unterglasur
auch in Verbindung
mit: Germany

20
37

250

Schmelzer & Gerike Althaldensleben (1886)–circa 1931 on earthenware	Schmelzer & Gerike Althaldensleben (1886)–ca. 1931 auf Steingut	2026 **373**	
Schmelzer & Gerike Althaldensleben (1895)–circa 1931 on fayence and earthenware	Schmelzer & Gerike Althaldensleben (1895)–ca. 1931 auf Fayence und Steingut	2027 **373**	
J. C. L. Harms Hamburg (1885)– decorator's mark	J. C. L. Harms Hamburg (1885)– Malermarke	2028 **415**	
Company for Fine Ceramics Siegburg (1949)–	Gesellschaft für Feinkeramik Siegburg (1949)–	2029 **481**	
Arthur Rohleder & Son Meissen 1924–circa 1949 decorator's mark	Arthur Rohleder & Sohn Meißen 1924–ca. 1949 Malermarke	2030 **447**	
Firebrick and Clinker Factory Waldsassen Waldsassen 1923–	Chamotte- und Klinker- fabrik Waldsassen Waldsassen 1923–	2031 **498**	
Franz Junkersdorf Dresden 1909–circa 1945 decorator's mark	Franz Junkersdorf Dresden 1909–ca. 1945 Malermarke	2032 **395**	
Royal Porcelain Manufactory Berlin 1913 blue underglaze or red or green overglaze	Königliche Porzellan Manufaktur Berlin 1913 blau unterglasur oder rot oder grün aufglasur	2033 **380**	

Sontag & Sons	Sontag & Söhne	
Geiersthal	Geiersthal	
−1919	−1919	
decorator's mark	Malermarke	20
overglaze	aufglasur	**40**
attributed to	C. M. Hutschenreuther	
C. M. Hutschenreuther	Hohenberg	
Hohenberg	spätes 19. Jahrhundert	20
late 19th century	zugeschrieben	**41**
Julius Dressler	Julius Dressler	
Biela	Biela	
probably end of 19th	wahrscheinlich Ende	20.
century	des 19. Jahrhunderts	**38**
Jacob Zeidler & Co.	Jacob Zeidler & Co.	
Selb	Selb	20.
(1910)−1917	(1910)−1917	**48**
Reinhold Schlegelmilch	Reinhold Schlegelmilch	
Tillowitz	Tillowitz	20
(1916)−circa 1938	(1916)−ca. 1938	**48**
Armand Marseille	Armand Marseille	
Koppelsdorf	Köppelsdorf	
1912−circa 1919	1912−ca. 1919	20
on dolls heads	auf Puppenköpfen	**43**
Porcelain Factory Weiden	Porzellanfabrik Weiden	
Bros. Bauscher	Gebr. Bauscher	
Weiden	Weiden	
1921−1939	1921−1939	20
green underglaze	grün unterglasur	**50**
Porcelain Factory Weiden	Porzellanfabrik Weiden	
Bros. Bauscher	Gebr. Bauscher	
Weiden	Weiden	
circa 1920−present	ca. 1920−heute	20
green underglaze	grün unterglasur	**50**

Porcelain Factory Weiden	Porzellanfabrik Weiden	
Bros. Bauscher	Gebr. Bauscher	
Weiden	Weiden	
1933–1939	1933–1939	2042
green underglaze	grün unterglasur	**500**

Porcelain Factory Weiden	Porzellanfabrik Weiden	
Bros. Bauscher	Gebr. Bauscher	
Weiden	Weiden	
circa 1920–circa 1948	ca. 1920–ca. 1948	2043
green underglaze	grün unterglasur	**500**

Porcelain Factory Weiden	Porzellanfabrik Weiden	
Bros. Bauscher	Gebr. Bauscher	
Weiden	Weiden	
circa 1920–present	ca. 1920–heute	2044
green underglaze	grün unterglasur	**500**

Porcelain Factory Weiden	Porzellanfabrik Weiden	
Bros. Bauscher	Gebr. Bauscher	
Weiden	Weiden	
circa 1920–1948	ca. 1920–1948	2045
green underglaze	grün unterglasur	**500**

VEB Porcelain Combine Colditz	VEB Porzellankombinat Colditz	
Colditz	Colditz	2046
1958-1990	1958-1990	**391**

L. Hutschenreuther	L. Hutschenreuther	
Selb	Selb	2047
(1969)–	(1969)–	**479**

VEB Porcelain Factory Piesau	VEB Porzellanfabrik Piesau	
Piesau	Piesau	2048
(1962)–circa 1968	(1962)–ca. 1968	**461**

Hubel & Co.	Hübel & Co.	
Prague	Prag	2049
circa 1800–1835	ca. 1800–1835	**463**

Zeh, Scherzer & Co.	Zeh, Scherzer & Co.	
Rehau	Rehau	2050
(1896)–1906	(1896)–1906	**466**

Amphora Works Turn-Teplitz 1918–1939	Amphora Werke Turn-Teplitz 1918–1939		20 **48**
Amphora Works Turn-Teplitz (1905)–circa 1945	Amphora Werke Turn-Teplitz (1905)–ca. 1945		20 **48**
Amphora Works Turn-Teplitz 1892–1918	Amphora Werke Turn-Teplitz 1892–1918		20 **48**

Porcelain Factory Arzberg
Arzberg
1974–present
green underglaze

Porzellanfabrik Arzberg
Arzberg
1974–heute
grün unterglasur

20
37

Porcelain Factory Weiden
Bros. Bauscher
Weiden
1912–circa 1923
impressed

Porzellanfabrik Weiden
Gebr. Bauscher
Weiden
1912–ca. 1923
eingeprägt

20
50

Carl Knoll
Fischern
circa 1844–1868
impressed

Carl Knoll
Fischern
ca. 1844–1868
eingeprägt

20
40

C. Tielsch & Co.
Altwasser
(1887)–circa 1918
green underglaze

C. Tielsch & Co.
Altwasser
(1887)–ca. 1918
grün unterglasur

20
37

Bros. Plein
Speicher
20th century

Gebr. Plein
Speicher
20. Jahrhundert

20
48

A. Fischer
Ilmenau
after 1907–1952

A. Fischer
Ilmenau
nach 1907–1952

20
42

Adolf Hoffmann
Osnabruck
1935–circa 1971
decorator's mark
overglaze

Adolf Hoffmann
Osnabrück
1935–ca. 1971
Malermarke
aufglasur

206
460

Johann Hoffmann	Johann Hoffmann	
Elbogen	Elbogen	
1926–1945	1926–1945	
decorator's mark	Malermarke	2061
overglaze	aufglasur	**400**
Jasba Ceramic Factories	Jasba-Keramikfabriken	
Baumbach	Baumbach	2062
circa 1926–before 1935	ca. 1926–vor 1935	**379**
Jasba Ceramic Factories	Jasba Keramikfabriken	
Baumbach	Baumbach	2063
(1965)–	(1965)–	**379**
unidentified	nicht identifiziert	2064
black overglaze	schwarz aufglasur	
S. Reich & Co.	S. Reich & Co.	
Berlin	Berlin	2065
(1930)–circa 1938	(1930)–ca. 1938	**382**
Friedrich Schwab	Friedrich Schwab	
Gotha	Gotha	2066
after 1919–circa 1950	nach 1919–ca. 1950	**409**
C. & E. Carstens	C. & E. Carstens	
Sorau	Sorau	
1918–circa 1945	1918–ca. 1945	
also in combination	auch in Verbindung	
with: China Blau	mit: China Blau	2067
Margret	Margret	**482**
Swaine & Co.	Swaine & Co.	
Huttensteinach	Hüttensteinach	
–circa 1920	–ca. 1920	2068
decorating mark	Malereimarke	**420**
Prince Electoral Privileged	Churfürstlich Privilegierte	
Porcelain Factory	Porcelain Fabrique	
Hochst	Höchst	2069
1750–1762	1750–1762	2070
incised	eingeritzt	**418**
Prince Electoral Privileged	Churfürstlich Privilegierte	
Porcelain Factory	Porcelain Fabrique	
Hochst	Höchst	
1750–1763	1750–1763	2071
impressed	eingeprägt	**418**

Prince Electoral Privileged Porcelain Factory Hochst 1750–1776 impressed or blue underglaze or different colors overglaze

Churfürstlich Privilegierte Porcelain Fabrique Höchst 1750–1776 eingeprägt oder blau unterglasur 2(oder verschiedene Farben aufglasur **4**

Prince Electoral Privileged Porcelain Factory Hochst 1750–1776 blue underglaze or black or brown or purple or red overglaze or impressed

Churfürstlich Privilegierte Porcelain Fabrique Höchst 1750–1776 blau unterglasur oder schwarz oder 2(braun oder purpur oder rot auf- 2(glasur oder eingeprägt **4**

same as 2073

wie 2073 2(2(2(**4.**

Prince Electoral Privileged Porcelain Factory Hochst 1750–1776 blue underglaze or black or brown or purple or red overglaze

Churfürstlich Privilegierte Porcelain Fabrique Höchst 1750–1776 blau unterglasur oder schwarz oder 2(braun oder purpur oder rot **4** aufglasur

Prince Electoral Privileged Porcelain Factory Hochst 1750–1776 blue underglaze or black or brown or purple or red overglaze or impressed

Churfürstlich Privilegierte Porcelain Fabrique Höchst 1750–1776 blau unterglasur oder schwarz oder 2(braun oder purpur oder rot auf- 2(glasur oder eingeprägt **4**

Prince Electoral Privileged Porcelain Factory Hochst 1750–1776 blue underglaze or black or brown or purple or red overglaze or incised

Churfürstlich Privilegierte Porcelain Fabrique Höchst 1750–1776 blau unterglasur oder schwarz oder braun oder purpur oder rot auf- 2(glasur oder eingeritzt **4**

Prince Electoral Privileged Porcelain Factory Hochst 1750–1776 blue underglaze or black or brown or purple or red overglaze	Churfürstlich Privilegierte Porcelain Fabrique Höchst 1750–1776 blau unterglasur oder schwarz oder braun oder purpur oder rot aufglasur	2087 2088 2089 **418**
same as 2087	wie 2087	2090 2091 2092 2093 **418**
same as 2087	wie 2087	2094 **418**
Prince Electoral Mayence Manufactory Hochst 1776–1796 blue underglaze	Churfürstlich Mainzische Manufaktur Höchst 1776–1796 blau unterglasur	2095 2096 2097 **418**
same as 2095	wie 2095	2098 **418**
same as 2095	wie 2095	2099 2100 **418**
Bros. Kroner Berlin (1907)–	Gebr. Kroner Berlin (1907)–	2101 **380**
Dressel, Kister & Cie. Passau (1902)–1904 blue underglaze	Dressel, Kister & Cie. Passau (1902)–1904 blau unterglasur	2102 **460**

E. & A. Muller Schonwald 1909–1927	E. & A. Müller Schönwald 1909–1927	2 4
Prince Electoral Privileged Porcelain Factory Hochst 1749–1758 different colors overglaze	Churfürstlich Privilegierte Porcelain Fabrique Höchst 1749–1758 verschiedene Farben aufglasur	2 4
Prince Electoral Privileged Porcelain Factory Hochst 1750–1751 different colors overglaze	Churfürstlich Privilegierte Porcelain Fabrique Höchst 1750–1751 verschiedene Farben aufglasur	2 4
Earthenware Factory Damm Damm 1840–1860 grey or blue on earthenware	Steingutfabrik Damm Damm 1840–1860 grau oder blau auf Steingut	2 2 3
Prince Electoral Privileged Porcelain Factory Hochst 1750–1763 different colors overglaze	Churfürstlich Privilegierte Porcelain Fabrique Höchst 1750–1763 verschiedene Farben aufglasur	2. 2 4
same as 2108	wie 2108	2 4
Prince Electoral Privileged Porcelain Factory Hochst 1747–1753 different colors overglaze	Churfürstlich Privilegierte Porcelain Fabrique Höchst 1747–1753 verschiedene Farben aufglasur	2 2 2 2 4
Prince Electoral Privileged Porcelain Factory Hochst 1750–1763 different colors overglaze	Churfürstlich Privilegierte Porcelain Fabrique Höchst 1750–1763 verschiedene Farben aufglasur	2 4
Prince Electoral Privileged Porcelain Factory Hochst 1774–1784 wheel blue underglaze name overglaze	Churfürstlich Privilegierte Porcelain Fabrique Höchst 1774–1784 Rad blau unterglasur Name aufglasur	2 4

Hochst Porcelain Manufactory Hochst 1965–present blue underglaze	Höchster Porzellanmanufaktur Höchst 1965–heute blau unterglasur	2117 **418**
Prince Electoral Privileged Porcelain Factory Hochst 1767–1779 overglaze	Churfürstlich Privilegierte Porcelain Fabrique Höchst 1767–1779 aufglasur	2118 **418**
Prince Electoral Privileged Porcelain Factory Hochst 1747–1753 wheel blue underglaze name gold overglaze	Churfürstlich Privilegierte Porcelain Fabrique Höchst 1747–1753 Rad blau unterglasur Name gold aufglasur	2119 **418**
Adolf Baumgarten Weingarten 1882–circa 1900	Adolf Baumgarten Weingarten 1882–ca. 1900	2120 **500**
B. Bertram Luftelburg after 1930 decorator's mark overglaze	B. Bertram Lüftelburg nach 1930 Malermarke aufglasur	2121 **442**
Armand Marseille Koppelsdorf –circa 1919	Armand Marseille Köppelsdorf –ca. 1919	2122 **432**
Porcelain Factory Weiden Bros. Bauscher Weiden 1912–circa 1923 impressed	Porzellanfabrik Weiden Gebr. Bauscher Weiden 1912–ca. 1923 eingeprägt	2123 **500**
Porcelain Factory at Kloster Veilsdorf Kloster Veilsdorf (1927)–1945	Porzellanfabrik zu Kloster Veilsdorf Kloster Veilsdorf (1927)–1945	2124 **429**
C. M. Hutschenreuther Hohenberg 1857–1899	C. M. Hutschenreuther Hohenberg 1857–1899	2125 **419**

Porcelain Factories Creidlitz Creidlitz after 1908–	Porzellanfabriken Creidlitz Creidlitz nach 1908–	21 **39**
VEB Porcelaine Combine Colditz Colditz (1964)-1990	VEB Porzellankombinat Colditz Colditz (1964)-1990	21 **39**
Association of German Porcelain Factories Berlin (1908)–1912	Vereinigung deutscher Porzellanfabriken Berlin (1908)–1912	21 **38**
Albin Eichhorn Goritzmuhle –circa 1945	Albin Eichhorn Göritzmühle –ca. 1945	21 **40**
von Romer & Foedisch Fraureuth (1887)–circa 1898 blue underglaze	von Römer & Foedisch Fraureuth (1887)–ca. 1898 blau unterglasur	21 **40**
Franz Fritz Successor Grossbreitenbach (1956)– decorator's mark overglaze	Franz Fritz Nachf. Großbreitenbach (1956)– Malermarke aufglasur	21 **41**
Bros. Bordolo Grunstadt (1896)–	Gebr. Bordolo Grünstadt (1896)–	213 **413**
Gera Porcelain Factory Untermhaus circa 1896–	Geraer Porzellanfabrik Untermhaus ca. 1896–	21 **40**
Porcelain Factory Kahla Hermsdorf-Klosterlausnitz (1902)–	Porzellanfabrik Kahla Hermsdorf-Klosterlausnitz (1902)–	21 **41**
VEB Porcelainwork Freiberg Freiberg (1967)–circa 1972	VEB Porzellanwerk Freiberg Freiberg (1967)–ca. 1972	21 **40**

Hutschenreuther	Hutschenreuther	
Hohenberg	Hohenberg	2136
after 1969–present	nach 1969–heute	**419**
Joseph Schachtel	Joseph Schachtel	
Charlottenbrunn	Charlottenbrunn	2137
after 1875–circa 1919	nach 1875–ca. 1919	**389**
Gustav Kallmeier	Gustav Kallmeier	
Kassel	Kassel	
(1894)–	(1894)–	
decorator's mark	Malermarke	2138
overglaze	aufglasur	**426**
unidentified	nicht identifiziert	
possibly Kampfe & List	möglicherweise Kämpfe & List	
Neuhaus on Rennweg	Neuhaus am Rennweg	2139
gold overglaze	gold aufglasur	**452**
E. & A. Bufe	E. & A. Bufe	
Langenberg	Langenberg	2140
after 1902–circa 1972	nach 1902–ca. 1972	**436**
Ludwig Wessel	Ludwig Wessel	
Amberg/Bonn	Amberg/Bonn	
after 1922–before 1945	nach 1922–vor 1945	2141
on earthenware	auf Steingut	**375**
Merkelbach & Wick	Merkelbach & Wick	
Grenzhausen	Grenzhausen	
1872–1921	1872–1921	2142
on stoneware	auf Steinzeug	**412**
Orben, Knabe & Co.	Orben, Knabe & Co.	
Geschwenda	Geschwenda	2143
after 1909–circa 1939	nach 1909–ca. 1939	**407**
Paul Muller	Paul Müller	
Selb	Selb	
after 1890–circa 1912	nach 1890–ca. 1912	2144
blue underglaze	blau unterglasur	**480**
Porcelain Union	Porzellan Union	
Koppelsdorf	Köppelsdorf	2145
(1922)–	(1922)–	**432**

Paul Rauschert	Paul Rauschert	
Pressig	Pressig	
1967–present	1967–heute	2
impressed	eingeprägt	4
Paul Rauschert	Paul Rauschert	
Pressig	Pressig	
1945–1967	1945–1967	2
impressed	eingeprägt	4
Reinhold Voigt	Reinhold Voigt	
Grafenroda-Ort	Gräfenroda-Ort	2
1910–	1910–	4
G. Greiner & Co.	G. Greiner & Co.	
Schauberg	Schauberg	
(1896)–1927	(1896)–1927	2
blue underglaze	blau unterglasur	4
H. Scholz Successor	H. Scholz Nachf.	
Tiefenbach	Tiefenbach	2
(1912)–before 1945	(1912)–vor 1945	4
VEB Sonneberg Porcelain	VEB Sonneberger Porzellan-	
Factories	fabriken	
Huttensteinach	Hüttensteinach	2
(1956)-before 1990	(1956)-vor 1990	4
Bros. Schneider	Gebr. Schneider	
Mariaschein	Mariaschein	2
after 1889–	nach 1889–	4
Theodor Pohl	Theodor Pohl	
Schatzlar	Schatzlar	2
(1922)–1945	(1922)–1945	4
Clayware Factory Schwandorf	Tonwarenfabrik Schwandorf	
Schwandorf	Schwandorf	
(1930)–1972	(1930)–1972	2
on earthenware and porcelain	auf Steingut und Porzellan	4
VEB Utility Porcelain	VEB Gebrauchsporzellan	
Grafenthal	Gräfenthal	2
(1972)-1990	(1972)-1990	4
J. C. Geyger	J. C. Geyger	
Wurzburg	Würzburg	
1775–1780	1775–1780	2
impressed	eingeprägt	5

C. L. Dwenger	C. L. Dwenger	
New York City	New York	
−1917	−1917	2157
importer's mark	Importeurmarke	**455**

Adolf Persch	Adolf Persch	
Hegewald	Hegewald	2158
1918−1939	1918−1939	**416**

Porcelain Factory Weiden	Porzellanfabrik Weiden	
Bros. Bauscher	Gebr. Bauscher	
Weiden	Weiden	
1912−circa 1923	1912−ca. 1923	2159
green underglaze	grün unterglasur	**500**

Porcelain Factory Weiden	Porzellanfabrik Weiden	
Bros. Bauscher	Gebr. Bauscher	
Weiden	Weiden	
1912−circa 1923	1912−ca. 1923	2160
green underglaze	grün unterglasur	**500**

Porcelain Factory Weiden	Porzellanfabrik Weiden	
Bros. Bauscher	Gebr. Bauscher	
Weiden	Weiden	
1912−circa 1923	1912−ca. 1923	2161
green underglaze	grün unterglasur	**500**

VEB Porcelain Combine Colditz	VEB Porzellankombinat Colditz	
Colditz	Colditz	2162
(1964)-1990	(1964)-1990	**391**

VEB Porcelainwork Kloster	VEB Porzellanwerk Kloster	
Veilsdorf	Veilsdorf	
Kloster Veilsdorf	Kloster Veilsdorf	2163
(1956)-before 1990	(1956)-vor 1990	**429**

VEB Porcelainwork Kloster	VEB Porzellanwerk Kloster	
Veilsdorf	Veilsdorf	
Kloster Veilsdorf	Kloster Veilsdorf	2164
(1956)-before 1990	(1956)-vor 1990	**429**

Epiag Dallwitz after 1920–circa 1945	Epiag Dallwitz nach 1920–ca. 1945	216 **391**
unidentified gold overglaze	nicht identifiziert gold aufglasur	216
VEB Porcelainwork Freiberg Freiberg (1967)-before 1990	VEB Porzellanwerk Freiberg Freiberg (1967)-vor 1990	216 **404**
R. & E. Haidinger Elbogen 1868–1873 anniversary stamp	R. & E. Haidinger Elbogen 1868–1873 Jubiläumsstempel	216 **399**
Heinrich & Co. Selb 1903– blue or green underglaze	Heinrich & Co. Selb 1903– blau oder grün unterglasur	216 **479**
J. D. Kestner & Co. Ohrdruf 1914–circa 1917 impressed on dolls heads	J. D. Kestner & Co. Ohrdruf 1914–ca. 1917 eingeprägt auf Puppenköpfen	21 **459**
unidentified green underglaze	nicht identifiziert grün unterglasur	21
L. Hutschenreuther Selb 1887–	L. Hutschenreuther Selb 1887–	21 47
L. Hutschenreuther Selb 1856–1920	L. Hutschenreuther Selb 1856–1920	21 47
unidentified green overglaze	nicht identifiziert grün aufglasur	21

AUSTRIA	Lewis Straus & Sons New York City circa 1895–1917 importer's mark	Lewis Straus & Sons New York ca. 1895–1917 Importeurmarke	2175 **456**
	Carl Knoll Fischern circa 1900–	Carl Knoll Fischern ca. 1900–	2176 **402**
Bonn	Ludwig Wessel Bonn (1918)–circa 1945 on earthenware	Ludwig Wessel Bonn (1918)–ca. 1945 auf Steingut	2177 **385**
	C. E. & F. Arnoldi Elgersburg 1919–circa 1962	C. E. & F. Arnoldi Elgersburg 1919–ca. 1962	2178 **400**
	Franz Prause Niedersalzbrunn after 1894–1936	Franz Prause Niedersalzbrunn nach 1894–1936	2179 2180 **456**
	Porcelain Factory Kahla Kahla circa 1924-circa 1928	Porzellanfabrik Kahla Kahla ca. 1924-ca. 1928	2181 **423**
	Porcelain Factory Bavaria Ullersricht (1926)–circa 1932	Porzellanfabrik Bavaria Ullersricht (1926)–ca. 1932	2182 **491**
	R. Wachter Kirchenlamitz (1927)– decorator's mark overglaze	R. Wächter Kirchenlamitz (1927)– Malermarke aufglasur	2183 **427**
	Swaine & Co. Huttensteinach after 1900–1920 decorating mark	Swaine & Co. Hüttensteinach nach 1900–1920 Malereimarke	2184 **420**

D.V 1 GESCHÜTZT S & Co GERMANY	unidentified green letters D. V stand for U. S. distributors Davis & Voetsch	nicht identifiziert grün Buchstabe D. V sind Abkürzung für US-Händler Davis & Voetsch 21
VILLEROY & BOCH B	Villeroy & Boch Dresden (1928)–1945	Villeroy & Boch Dresden (1928)–1945 21 39
W.KC. Grafen thal	Weiss, Kuhnert & Co. Grafenthal after 1900–circa 1956	Weiss, Kühnert & Co. Gräfenthal nach 1900–ca. 1956 218 41
GESETZLICH W.P. M. GESCHÜTZT	Vienna Porcelain Manufactory Josef Bock Vienna after 1893–circa 1933	Wiener Porzellanmanufaktur Josef Böck Wien nach 1893–ca. 1933 21 50
GESETZLICH W.St. GESCHÜTZT	Wachtersbach Earthenware Factory Schlierbach 1894–1896 black or blue on earthenware	Wächtersbacher Steingut- fabrik Schlierbach 1894–1896 schwarz oder blau auf Steingut 218 47
BASSETT LIMOGES AUSTRIA	unidentified overglaze	nicht identifiziert aufglasur 219
FLORIAN KERAMIK Wilhelmsburg	Wilhelmsburg Earthenware and Porcelain Factory Wilhelmsburg after 1932–	Wilhelmsburger Steingut- und Porzellanfabrik Wilhelmsburg nach 1932– 219 50
GIESSHUBEL 460	Franz Lehnert Giesshubel 1840–1846 impressed	Franz Lehnert Gießhübel 1840–1846 eingeprägt 219 408
Handmalerei F.Hoffmann Osnabrück	Franz Hoffmann Osnabruck 1926–1934 decorator's mark black overglaze	Franz Hoffmann Osnabrück 1926–1934 Malermarke schwarz aufglasur 219 460

J. Schmeisser Eisenberg 1887–	J. Schmeisser Eisenberg 1887–	2194 **398**
Porcelain Factory Schirnding Schirnding before 1945–	Porzellanfabrik Schirnding Schirnding vor 1945–	2195 **472**

P. H. Leonard
New York City
   –circa 1908
importer's mark
	P. H. Leonard
	New York
	   –ca. 1908
	Importeurmarke
		2196
		455

Marx & Gutherz Altrohlau circa 1876–circa 1889 blue overglaze	Marx & Gutherz Altrohlau ca. 1876–ca. 1889 blau aufglasur	2197 **374**
Thuringian Porcelain Manufactory Union Kleindembach (1906)–1909	Thüringische Porzellan- manufaktur Union Kleindembach (1906)–1909	2198 **427**
Paul A. Straub New York City 1931–circa 1970 importer's mark	Paul A. Straub New York 1931–ca. 1970 Importeurmarke	2199 **456**
Paul A. Straub New York City circa 1948–circa 1970 importer's mark	Paul A. Straub New York ca. 1948–ca. 1970 Importeurmarke	2200 **456**
Rosenthal Selb (1978)–	Rosenthal Selb (1978)–	2201 **480**
Ilmenau Porcelain Factory Ilmenau (1907)–1938	Ilmenauer Porzellanfabrik Ilmenau (1907)–1938	2202 **421**

Wachtersbach Earthenware Factory Schlierbach 1912–1913 black on earthenware	Wächtersbacher Steingut-fabrik Schlierbach 1912–1913 schwarz auf Steingut	22	47
Carl Wagner Dresden 1894– decorator's mark overglaze	Carl Wagner Dresden 1894– Malermarke aufglasur	220	39
Theodor Holborn Gottingen after 1889–circa 1945 decorator's mark overglaze	Theodor Holborn Göttingen nach 1889–ca. 1945 Malermarke aufglasur	220	40
von Portheim Chodau circa 1850–circa 1870 impressed	von Portheim Chodau ca. 1850–ca. 1870 eingeprägt	220	389
Porcelain Manufactory Allach-Munich Allach-Munich 1935–1945	Porzellanmanufaktur Allach-München Allach-München 1935–1945	220	372
Franz Urfuss Dallwitz 1855–1875 impressed	Franz Urfuss Dallwitz 1855–1875 eingeprägt	220	391
Vienna Porcelain Factory Augarten Vienna after 1923– red overglaze	Wiener Porzellanfabrik Augarten Wien nach 1923– rot aufglasur	220	503
August Nowotny Altrohlau 1838–1884 impressed	August Nowotny Altrohlau 1838–1884 eingeprägt	221	373
August Nowotny Altrohlau 1823–1884 impressed on earthenware and porcelain	August Nowotny Altrohlau 1823–1884 eingeprägt auf Steingut und Porzellan	221	373

Porcelain Factory Freiberg Freiberg (1914)-1932	Porzellanfabrik Freiberg Freiberg (1914)-1932	2212 **404**
same as 2212		2213 **404**
Heinz & Co. Grafenthal-Meernach after 1900-1972	Heinz & Co. Gräfenthal-Meernach nach 1900-1972	2214 **411**
Porcelain Factory Marienfeld A. Voigt Oelze (1896)–	Porzellanfabrik Marienfeld A. Voigt Oelze (1896)–	2215 **459**
Porcelain Factory Marienfeld A. Voigt Oelze (1892)–	Porzellanfabrik Marienfeld A. Voigt Oelze (1892)–	2216 **459**
Porcelain Factory Freiberg Freiberg (1914)–circa 1945	Porzellanfabrik Freiberg Freiberg (1914)–ca. 1945	2217 **404**
B. Bloch & Co. Eichwald after 1900–circa 1920	B. Bloch & Co. Eichwald nach 1900–ca. 1920	2218 **397**
B. Bloch & Co. Eichwald 1918–1939	B. Bloch & Co. Eichwald 1918–1939	2219 **397**
United Lusatian Glassworks Berlin (1911)–circa 1945	Vereinigte Lausitzer Glaswerke Berlin (1911)–ca. 1945	2220 **383**
Saxonian Stove and Fire- brick Factory Meissen (1887)–circa 1907	Sächsische Ofen- und Chamottewarenfabrik Meißen (1887)–ca. 1907	2221 **448**
Porcelain Factory Frauenthal Frauenthal 1954–present	Porzellanfabrik Frauenthal Frauenthal 1954–heute	2222 **403**

Engineer L. Neumann
Frauenthal
circa 1930–1954

Ing. L. Neumann
Frauenthal
ca. 1930–1954

22
4(

J. D. Kestner & Co.
Ohrdruf
after 1892–circa 1930

J. D. Kestner & Co.
Ohrdruf
nach 1892–ca. 1930

22
4.

Karls Gerhards Successor
Hohr-Grenzhausen
1949–present
on stoneware

Karl Gerhards Nachf.
Höhr-Grenzhausen
1949–heute
auf Steinzeug

22
41

United Koppelsdorf
Porcelain Factories
Koppelsdorf
circa 1919–1945

Vereinigte Köppelsdorfer
Porzellanfabriken
Köppelsdorf
ca. 1919–1945

22
43

VEB United Porcelainworks
Koppelsdorf
(1954)-1964

VEB Vereinigte Porzellanwerke
Köppelsdorf
(1954)-1964

22
43

Heinzl & Co.
Granesau
1924–1939

Heinzl & Co.
Granesau
1924–1939

22
41

Eduard Haberlander
Windischeschenbach
after 1913–1928
green underglaze

Eduard Haberländer
Windischeschenbach
nach 1913–1928
grün unterglasur

22
50

Erich Haselhuhn
Aachen
1921–after 1930
decorator's mark
overglaze

Erich Haselhuhn
Aachen
1921–nach 1930
Malermarke
aufglasur

22
37

Hilpolstein Porcelain
Manufactory
Hilpoltstein
1955–present

Hilpoltsteiner Porzellan-
manufaktur
Hilpoltstein
1955–heute

22
41

Armand Marseille Koppelsdorf —1904 on dolls heads	Armand Marseille Köppelsdorf —1904 auf Puppenköpfen	2232 **432**
VEB Porcelain Factory Piesau Piesau 1946—1960	VEB Porzellanfabrik Piesau Piesau 1946—1960	2233 **461**
Royal Porcelain Manufactory Meissen after 1707—circa 1720 impressed on red stoneware	Königliche Porzellan Manufaktur Meißen nach 1707—ca. 1720 eingeprägt auf rotem Steinzeug	2234 **446**
same as 2234	wie 2234	2235 **446**
same as 2234	wie 2234	2236 **446**
R. Wolfinger Weingarten (1903)—1922	R. Wolfinger Weingarten (1903)—1922	2237 **500**
Villeroy & Boch Dresden (1887)—circa 1945	Villeroy & Boch Dresden (1887)—ca. 1945	2238 **396**
Villeroy & Boch Schramberg (1911)—1912	Villeroy & Boch Schramberg (1911)—1912	2239 **476**
Chr. A. W. Speck Blankenhain 1790—	Chr. A. W. Speck Blankenhain 1790—	2240 **384**
W. Schiller & Sons Bodenbach (1895)— also in combination with: Wedgewood	W. Schiller & Söhne Bodenbach (1895)— auch in Verbindung mit: Wedgewood	2241 **384**
VEB Porcelainwork Veilsdorf Kloster Veilsdorf (1954)-1990	VEB Porzellanwerk Veilsdorf Kloster Veilsdorf (1954)-1990	2242 **429**
Keramos Vienna (1929)—	Keramos Wien (1929)—	2243 **501**

Hertwig & Co.	Hertwig & Co.		
Katzhutte	Katzhütte	22	
(1932)-1958	(1932)-1958	**42**	

Siebert & Hertwig	Siebert & Hertwig		
Coburg-Creidlitz	Coburg-Creidlitz	22	
(1903)–1923	(1903)–1923	**39**	

Striegau Porcelain Factory	Striegauer Porzellanfabrik		
Stanowitz	Stanowitz	22	
(1912)–circa 1927	(1912)–ca. 1927	**48**	

Burley & Tyrrell Co.	Burley & Tyrrell Co.		
Chicago, Ill.	Chicago		
1912–	1912–	22	
importer's mark	Importeurmarke	**38**	

Vienna Porcelain Manufactory	Wiener Porzellanmanufaktur		
Josef Bock	Josef Böck		
Vienna	Wien	22	
after 1893–circa 1933	nach 1893–ca. 1933	**50**	

A. Carl Anger	A. Carl Anger		
Aich	Aich		
1862–1901	1862–1901	22	
red overglaze	rot aufglasur	**37**	

B. Bloch & Co.	B. Bloch & Co.		
Eichwald	Eichwald	22	
after 1871–	nach 1871–	**39**	

Ebeling & Reuss	Ebeling & Reuss		
Devon/Philadelphia, Pa.	Devon/Philadelphia		
20th century	20. Jahrhundert		
green overglaze	grün aufglasur		
importer's mark	Importeurmarke		
also in combination	auch in Verbindung	22	
with: Art Pottery	mit: Art Pottery	**39**	

Fischer & Mieg	Fischer & Mieg		
Pirkenhammer	Pirkenhammer	22	
before 1900–circa 1918	vor 1900–ca. 1918	**46**	

Galluba & Hofmann	Galluba & Hofmann		
Ilmenau	Ilmenau	22	
(1911)–circa 1927	(1911)–ca. 1927	**42**	

272

Bros. Heubach Lichte (1909)–	Gebr. Heubach Lichte (1909)–	2254 **438**
Hubel & Co. Prague circa 1800–1835 impressed	Hübel & Co. Prag ca. 1800–1835 eingeprägt	2255 **463**
Porcelain Factory Kahla and VEB Porcelainwork Kahla Kahla 1937-1957	Porzellanfabrik Kahla und VEB Porzellanwerk Kahla Kahla 1937-1957	2256 **423**
Royal Porcelain Manufactory Meissen circa 1750 impressed	Königliche Porzellan Manufaktur Meißen ca. 1750 eingeprägt	2257 **446**
Munchhof Porcelain and Earthenware Factory Munchhof after 1879– impressed	Münchhofener Porzellan- und Steingutfabrik Münchhof nach 1879– eingeprägt	2258 **451**
Anton Fischer Son Neumark circa 1905– on earthenware	Anton Fischer Sohn Neumark ca. 1905– auf Steingut	2259 **453**
unidentified silver overglaze	nicht identifiziert silber aufglasur	2260
Klaus & Peter Muller Hohr-Grenzhausen (1955)–	Klaus & Peter Müller Höhr-Grenzhausen (1955)–	2261 **419**
Ella Strobel Dresden after 1867– decorator's mark overglaze	Ella Strobel Dresden nach 1867– Malermarke aufglasur	2262 **396**
R. Ufer Dresden 1887–circa 1893 decorator's mark overglaze	R. Ufer Dresden 1887–ca. 1893 Malermarke aufglasur	2263 **396**

Porcelain Manufactory Union Kleindembach (1909)–circa 1927	Porzellanmanufaktur Union Kleindembach (1909)–ca. 1927	2 4
von Portheim Chodau circa 1850–circa 1870 impressed	von Portheim Chodau ca. 1850–ca. 1870 eingeprägt	2 3
F. J. Lenz and Burger Zell on Harmersbach circa 1809–1819 on earthenware	F. J. Lenz und Burger Zell am Harmersbach ca. 1809–1819 auf Steingut	2 5
Royal Porcelain Manufactory Meissen after 1707–circa 1720 impressed on red stoneware	Königliche Porzellan Manufaktur Meißen nach 1707–ca. 1720 eingeprägt auf rotem Steinzeug	2 4
Pottery Works Kandern Kandern (1915)– on earthenware and pottery	Tonwerke Kandern Kandern (1915)– auf Steingut und Töpferwaren	2 4
Vienna Workshops Vienna (1913)–after 1923	Wiener Werkstätten Wien (1913)–nach 1923	2 5
von Rotberg and Schulz & Co. Gotha 1760–1787 blue underglaze	von Rotberg und Schulz & Co. Gotha 1760–1787 blau unterglasur	2 4
C. A. Romhild Grossbreitenbach after 1945– decorator's mark overglaze	C. A. Römhild Großbreitenbach nach 1945– Malermarke aufglasur	2 4
Bros. Heubach Lichte (1909)– impressed on dolls heads	Gebr. Heubach Lichte (1909)– eingeprägt auf Puppenköpfen	2 4
Bros. Heubach Lichte after 1909– impressed on dolls heads	Gebr. Heubach Lichte nach 1909– eingeprägt auf Puppenköpfen	

unidentified 1945-1949 black overglaze	nicht identifiziert 1945-1949 schwarz aufglasur	2274	
K. Kriegl & Co. Prague 1835–1910 impressed	K. Kriegl & Co. Prag 1835–1910 eingeprägt	2275 **463**	
Bros. Heubach Lichte (1909)– impressed on dolls heads	Gebr. Heubach Lichte (1909)– eingeprägt auf Puppenköpfen	2276 **483**	
Alexandra Porcelain Works Turn-Teplitz (1912)–circa 1921	Alexandra Porzellanwerke Turn-Teplitz (1912)–ca. 1921	2277 **491**	
Alfred Bruno Schwarz Berlin (1890)–	Alfred Bruno Schwarz Berlin (1890)–	2278 **380**	
Margaretenhutte and VEB Electro Porcelain Grossdubrau circa 1923–1964	Margaretenhütte und VEB Elektroporzellan Großdubrau ca. 1923–1964	2279 **413**	
VEB Ceramic Works Hermsdorf and Tridelta Hermsdorf circa 1953-1996	VEB Keramische Werke Hermsdorf und Tridelta Hermsdorf ca. 1953-1996	2280 **416**	
Porcelain Factory Kahla and VEB Ceramic Works Hermsdorf Hermsdorf-Klosterlausnitz (1923)–after 1956	Porzellanfabrik Kahla und VEB Keramische Werke Hermsdorf Hermsdorf-Klosterlausnitz (1923)–nach 1956	2281 **416**	

Porcelain Factory Teltow Teltow (1920)–circa 1932	Porzellanfabrik Teltow Teltow (1920)–ca. 1932	22 **48**
Porcelain Factory Kahla Hermsdorf-Klosterlausnitz (1913)–	Porzellanfabrik Kahla Hermsdorf-Klosterlausnitz (1913)–	22 **41**
same as 2283	wie 2283	22 **41**
Porcelain Factory Kahla Hermsdorf-Klosterlausnitz –1945	Porzellanfabrik Kahla Hermsdorf-Klosterlausnitz –1945	22 **41**
Porcelain Factory Kahla Hermsdorf-Klosterlausnitz (1916)–	Porzellanfabrik Kahla Hermsdorf-Klosterlausnitz (1916)–	22 **41**
Porcelain Factory Kahla Hermsdorf-Klosterlausnitz (1914)–	Porzellanfabrik Kahla Hermsdorf-Klosterlausnitz (1914)–	22 **41**
August Heissner Grafenroda circa 1930 decorator's mark overglaze	August Heissner Gräfenroda ca. 1930 Malermarke aufglasur	22 **41**
C. & W. Bohnert Frankfurt on Main (1929)–	C. & W. Bohnert Frankfurt am Main (1929)–	22 **40**
Franz Hoffmann Osnabruck 1918–1925 decorator's mark overglaze	Franz Hoffmann Osnabrück 1918–1925 Malermarke aufglasur	22 **46**
Bros. Schoenau Huttensteinach after 1900–circa 1920	Gebr. Schoenau Hüttensteinach nach 1900–ca. 1920	22 **42**
Bros. Heubach Lichte (1909)–	Gebr. Heubach Lichte (1909)–	22 **43**

J. Hering & Son	J. Hering & Sohn		
Koppelsdorf	Köppelsdorf	2293	
after 1908–circa 1945	nach 1908–ca. 1945	**431**	

Elisabeth Liegl	Elisabeth Liegl	
Munich	München	
1948–present	1948–heute	
decorator's mark	Malermarke	2294
blue/black overglaze	blau/schwarz aufglasur	**450**

C. Muller	C. Müller	
Steinwiesen	Steinwiesen	
1905–	1905–	
decorator's mark	Malermarke	2295
overglaze	aufglasur	**485**

VEB East Thuringian	VEB Ostthüringer	
Porcelainworks	Porzellanwerke	
Konitz	Könitz	2296
1957–1964	1957–1964	**431**

Oscar Mell	Oscar Mell	
Grafenroda	Gräfenroda	2297
after 1891–	nach 1891–	**411**

Porcelain Factory Naila	Porzellanfabrik Naila	
Naila	Naila	2298
1950–present	1950–heute	**451**

German Soapstone Porcelain-	Deutsche Speckstein-	
works	Porzellanwerke	
Lauf	Lauf	2299
(1912)–	(1912)–	**437**

Robert Lutz	Robert Lutz	
Albersweiler	Albersweiler	2300
circa 1895	circa 1895	**371**

R. S. Rosler	R. S. Rösler	
Dessendorf	Dessendorf	2301
1933–1945	1933–1945	**393**

Richard Sussmuth	Richard Süssmuth	
Immenhausen	Immenhausen	
(1960)–	(1960)–	
registered for glass	registriert für Glas	2302
and porcelain	und Porzellan	**422**

Westphalian Porcelain Factory Schalksmuhle 1921–	Westfälische Porzellanfabrik Schalksmühle 1921–	23 47
Porcelain Factory Schirnding Schirnding 1909– underglaze	Porzellanfabrik Schirnding Schirnding 1909– unterglasur	23 47
A. Riemann Coburg after 1900–circa 1927	A. Riemann Coburg nach 1900–ca. 1927	23 39
Christian Carstens Grafenroda after 1918– decorating mark	Christian Carstens Gräfenroda nach 1918– Malereimarke	23 41
Heufel & Co. Dresden 1891– decorator's mark overglaze	Heufel & Co. Dresden 1891– Malermarke aufglasur	23 39
Keramos Vienna (1929)–	Keramos Wien (1929)–	23 50
Julius Dietl Kaltenhof 1918–1939	Julius Dietl Kaltenhof 1918–1939	23 42
Ch. Epping Bremen (1952)–	Ch. Epping Bremen (1952)–	23 38
VEB Porcelainwork Konitz Konitz 1954–1957 green underglaze or overglaze	VEB Porzellanwerk Könitz Könitz 1954–1957 grün unterglasur oder aufglasur	23 43
C.G.Schierholz & Son Plaue 1865-1911 blue underglaze	C.G.Schierholz & Sohn Plaue 1865-1911 blau unterglasur	23 46

C.G.Schierholz & Son Plaue 1865-1911 blue underglaze	C.G.Schierholz & Sohn Plaue 1865-1911 blau unterglasur	2313 **462**
C.G. Schierholz & Son Plaue (1887)-1911 blue underglaze or overglaze	C.G.Schierholz & Sohn Plaue (1887)-1911 blau unter- oder aufglasur	2314 **462**
Bros. Voigt and Alfred Voigt Sitzendorf (1887)–circa 1900 blue underglaze or overglaze	Gebr. Voigt und Alfred Voigt Sitzendorf (1887)–ca. 1900 blau unterglasur oder aufglasur	2315 **481**
Bros Voigt and Alfred Voigt and Sitzendorf Porcelain Manufactory and VEB Sitzendorf Porcelain Manufactory Sitzendorf (1887)-1990 blue underglaze	Gebr. Voigt und Alfred Voigt und Sitzendorfer Porzellan- manufaktur und VEB Sitzendorfer Porzellan- manufaktur Sitzendorf (1887)-1990 blau unterglasur	2316 **481**
Bros. Voigt and Alfred Voigt Sitzendorf circa 1887–circa 1900 blue underglaze	Gebr. Voigt und Alfred Voigt Sitzendorf ca. 1887–ca. 1900 blau unterglasur	2317 **481**
Dornheim, Koch & Fischer Grafenroda (1887)–circa 1938 blue underglaze	Dornheim, Koch & Fischer Gräfenroda (1887)–ca. 1938 blau unterglasur	2318 **410**
same as 2318	wie 2318	2319 **410**
J. W. Hammann Wallendorf 1764–1787 blue underglaze	J. W. Hammann Wallendorf 1764–1787 blau unterglasur	2320 **498**
same as 2320	wie 2320	2321 **498**
same as 2320	wie 2320	2322 **498**
same as 2320	wie 2320	2323 **498**

same as 2320	wie 2320	23 **49**
same as 2320	wie 2320	23 **49**
Gotthelf Greiner Limbach 1772–1787 blue underglaze	Gotthelf Greiner Limbach 1772–1787 blau unterglasur	23 **43**
same as 2326	wie 2326	23 **43**
same as 2326	wie 2326	23 **43**
Gotthelf Greiner Limbach 1772–1787 blue underglaze or red or purple or green or black overglaze	Gotthelf Greiner Limbach 1772–1787 blau unterglasur oder rot oder purpur oder grün oder schwarz aufglasur	23 **43**
same as 2329	wie 2329	23 **43**
same as 2329	wie 2329	23 **43**
Gotthelf Greiner Limbach 1772–1787 blue underglaze	Gotthelf Greiner Limbach 1772–1787 blau unterglasur	23 **43**
same as 2332	wie 2332	23 **43**
same as 2332	wie 2332	23 **43**
Gotthelf Greiner Limbach 1772–1787 blue underglaze or purple overglaze	Gotthelf Greiner Limbach 1772–1787 blau unterglasur oder purpur aufglasur	23 **43**

Gotthelf Greiner Limbach 1772–1787 blue underglaze	Gotthelf Greiner Limbach 1772–1787 blau unterglasur	2336 **439**
Gotthelf Greiner Limbach 1772–1787 blue underglaze or purple or red or green or black overglaze	Gotthelf Greiner Limbach 1772–1787 blau unterglasur oder purpur oder rot oder grün oder schwarz aufglasur	2337 2338 **439**
same as 2338	wie 2338	2339 **439**
Gotthelf Greiner Limbach 1772–1787 blue underglaze	Gotthelf Greiner Limbach 1772–1787 blau unterglasur	2340 **439**
same as 2340	wie 2340	2341 **439**
same as 2340	wie 2340	2342 **439**
same as 2340	wie 2340	2343 **439**
Gotthelf Greiner Grossbreitenbach 1782–1788 blue underglaze	Gotthelf Greiner Großbreitenbach 1782–1788 blau unterglasur	2344 **412**
Christian Nonne Volkstedt 1767–1787 blue underglaze or blue or other colors overglaze	Christian Nonne Volkstedt 1767–1787 blau unterglasur oder blau oder andere Farben aufglasur	2345 **494**
same as 2345	wie 2345	2346 **494**
same as 2345	wie 2345	2347 **494**
Margravial Fine Porcelain Factory and successors Ansbach/Bruckberg 1757–1860	Markgräfliche Feine Porcelain Fabrique und Nachfolger Ansbach/Bruckberg 1757–1860	2348 **375**

281

Christian Nonne Volkstedt 1767–1800 blue underglaze	Christian Nonne Volkstedt 1767–1800 blau unterglasur
Christian Nonne Volkstedt 1787–1800 blue underglaze or blue or other colors overglaze	Christian Nonne Volkstedt 1787–1800 blau unterglasur oder blau oder andere Farben aufglasur
unidentified attributed to a factory in Anspach but very questionable blue underglaze	nicht identifiziert einer Fabrik in Anspach zugeschrieben, aber sehr fraglich blau unterglasur
unidentified attributed to a factory in Anspach but very questionable blue underglaze	nicht identifiziert einer Fabrik in Anspach zugeschrieben, aber sehr fraglich blau unterglasur
Christian Nonne Volkstedt 1767–1787 blue underglaze incomplete mark	Christian Nonne Volkstedt 1767–1787 blau unterglasur unvollständige Marke
Christian Nonne Volkstedt 1767–1800 blue underglaze or overglaze	Christian Nonne Volkstedt 1767–1800 blau unterglasur oder aufglasur
same as 2355	wie 2355
Christian Nonne Volkstedt 1787–1800 blue underglaze or blue or other colors overglaze	Christian Nonne Volkstedt 1787–1800 blau unterglasur oder blau oder andere Farben aufglasur
Christian Nonne Volkstedt 1767–1800 blue underglaze or overglaze	Christian Nonne Volkstedt 1767–1800 blau unterglasur oder aufglasur

same as 2359	wie 2359	2360 **494**
Christian Nonne Volkstedt 1787–1800 blue underglaze or overglaze	Christian Nonne Volkstedt 1787–1800 blau unterglasur oder aufglasur	2361 **494**
Gotthelf Greiner Ilmenau 1786–1788 blue underglaze	Gotthelf Greiner Ilmenau 1786–1788 blau unterglasur	2362 **421**
same as 2362	wie 2362	2363 **421**
Joseph Schachtel Charlottenbrunn after 1866–	Joseph Schachtel Charlottenbrunn nach 1866–	2364 **389**
Princely Fulda Fine Porcelain Factory Fulda 1765–1780 blue underglaze	Fürstlich Fuldaische Feine Porzellanfabrik Fulda 1765–1780 blau unterglasur	2365 **406**
Prince Electoral Porcelain Manufactory Nymphenburg circa 1760–1795 blue underglaze	Churfürstliche Porcellain Manufactur Nymphenburg ca. 1760–1795 blau unterglasur	2366 **457**
same as 2366	wie 2366	2367 **457**
Prince Electoral Porcelain Manufactory Nymphenburg circa 1760–1795 blue underglaze	Churfürstliche Porcellain Manufactur Nymphenburg ca. 1760–1795 blau unterglasur	2368 **457**
same as 2368	wie 2368	2369 **457**
unidentified blue underglaze	nicht identifiziert blau unterglasur	2370

Christian Nonne Volkstedt 1787–1800 blue underglaze or overglaze	Christian Nonne Volkstedt 1787–1800 blau unterglasur oder aufglasur	2: 4
Christian Nonne and Nonne & Roesch Ilmenau 1792–1813 blue underglaze	Christian Nonne und Nonne & Roesch Ilmenau 1792–1813 blau unterglasur	23 42
Prince F. W. E. von Hildburghausen Kloster Veilsdorf circa 1775–circa 1782 blue underglaze	Prinz F. W. E. von Hildburghausen Kloster Veilsdorf ca. 1775–ca. 1782 blau unterglasur	23 42
Princely Fulda Fine Porcelain Factory Fulda 1765–1780 blue underglaze	Fürstlich Fuldaische Feine Porzellanfabrik Fulda 1765–1780 blau unterglasur	23 40
same as 2374	wie 2374	23 40
E. & A. Muller Schwarza-Saale (1890)– blue underglaze or overglaze	E. & A. Müller Schwarza-Saale (1890)– blau unterglasur oder aufglasur	23 47
unidentified attributed to a factory in Anspach but very questionable blue underglaze	nicht identifiziert einer Fabrik in Anspach zugeschrieben, aber sehr zweifelhaft blau unterglasur	23 37
Albert Wreschner & Co. Berlin (1894)–before 1918 decorator's mark overglaze	Albert Wreschner & Co. Berlin (1894)–vor 1918 Malermarke aufglasur	23 38
H. Buhl & Sons Grossbreitenbach (1887)–circa 1932	H. Bühl & Söhne Großbreitenbach (1887)–ca. 1932	23 412

Fr. Chr. Greiner & Sons	Fr. Chr. Greiner & Söhne	
Rauenstein	Rauenstein	2380
after 1860–circa 1900	nach 1860–ca. 1900	2381
impressed on dolls heads	eingeprägt auf Puppenköpfen	**465**

Dumler & Breiden	Dümler & Breiden	
Hohr-Grenzhausen	Höhr-Grenzhausen	2382
after 1883–present	nach 1883–heute	**419**

Dornheim, Koch & Fischer	Dornheim, Koch & Fischer	
Grafenroda	Gräfenroda	2383
after 1880–circa 1938	nach 1880–ca. 1938	2384
blue	blau	**410**

Dornheim, Koch & Fischer	Dornheim, Koch & Fischer	
Grafenroda	Gräfenroda	
after 1880–circa 1938	nach 1880–ca. 1938	2385
blue or green	blau oder grün	**410**

Porcelain Factory Karl Ens	Porzellanfabrik Karl Ens	
Volkstedt	Volkstedt	
1919–1972	1919–1972	2386
green underglaze	grün unterglasur	**496**

Julius Greiner Son	Julius Greiner Sohn	
Lauscha	Lauscha	
circa 1885–	ca. 1885–	
decorator's mark	Malermarke	2387
overglaze	aufglasur	**437**

Bros. Knoch	Gebr. Knoch	
Neustadt	Neustadt	2388
after 1887–circa 1920	nach 1887–ca. 1920	**453**

Grossbaum & Sons	Grossbaum & Söhne	
Dresden	Dresden	
1894–1914	1894–1914	
decorator's mark	Malermarke	2389
overglaze	aufglasur	**394**

Franziska Hirsch	Franziska Hirsch	
Dresden	Dresden	
(1893)–1930	(1893)–1930	
decorator's mark	Malermarke	
blue overglaze	blau aufglasur	
also in combination	auch in Verbindung	2390
with: Dresden	mit: Dresden	**395**

	probably Franziska Hirsch Dresden circa 1896–circa 1930 decorator's mark blue overglaze	wahrscheinlich Franziska Hirsch Dresden ca. 1896–ca. 1930 Malermarke blau aufglasur	23 39
	Bros. Schoenau Huttensteinach (1887)-1897	Gebr. Schoenau Hüttensteinach (1887)-1897	23 42
	same as 2392	wie 2392	23 42
	Chr. Z. Grabner and Duke K. A. of Saxony-Weimar Ilmenau 1777–1786 blue underglaze	Chr. Z. Gräbner und Herzog K. A. von Sachsen-Weimar Ilmenau 1777–1786 blau unterglasur	23 42
	Gotthelf Greiner Ilmenau 1786–1788 blue underglaze	Gotthelf Greiner Ilmenau 1786–1788 blau unterglasur	23 42
	Franz R. Kirchner Manebach (1931)–1945	Franz R. Kirchner Manebach (1931)–1945	23 44
	A.W.Fr. Kister Scheibe-Alsbach 1863-1887 blue underglaze	A.W.Fr. Kister Scheibe-Alsbach 1863-1887 blau unterglasur	23 47
	A.W.Fr. Kister Scheibe-Alsbach 1887-1905 blue underglaze or overglaze	A.W.Fr. Kister Scheibe-Alsbach 1887-1905 blau unterglasur oder aufglasur	23 47
	Prince Electoral Porcelain Manufactory Nymphenburg circa 1760–1795 blue underglaze, letters LL impressed	Churfürstliche Porcellain Manufactur Nymphenburg ca. 1760–1795 blau unterglasur, Buchstaben LL eingeprägt	23 45
	A. Fischer Ilmenau after 1907– impressed	A. Fischer Ilmenau nach 1907– eingeprägt	24 42

Albin Rosenlocher	Albin Rosenlöcher		
Kups	Küps	2401	
—circa 1906	—ca. 1906	**435**	
Porcelain Factory Sorau	Porzellanfabrik Sorau		
Sorau	Sorau	2402	
(1898)—1918	(1898)—1918	**482**	
F. A. Reinecke	F. A. Reinecke		
Eisenberg	Eisenberg		
(1907)—circa 1960	(1907)—1960	2403	
blue underglaze	blau unterglasur	**398**	
Fr. Chr. Greiner & Sons	Fr. Chr. Greiner & Söhne		
and Porcelain Factory	und Porzellanfabrik		
Rauenstein	Rauenstein		
Rauenstein	Rauenstein		
after 1890—circa 1936	nach 1890—ca. 1936	2404	
impressed on dolls heads	eingeprägt auf Puppenköpfen	**465**	
Fr. Chr. Greiner & Sons	Fr. Chr. Greiner & Söhne		
Rauenstein	Rauenstein		
circa 1860—circa 1900	ca. 1860—ca. 1900	2405	
blue underglaze	blau unterglasur	**465**	
same as 2405	wie 2405	2406	
		465	
Fr. Chr. Greiner & Sons	Fr. Chr. Greiner & Söhne		
and Porcelain Factory	und Porzellanfabrik		
Rauenstein	Rauenstein		
Rauenstein	Rauenstein		
(1894)—circa 1936	(1894)—ca. 1936	2407	
blue underglaze or overglaze	blau unterglasur oder aufglasur	**465**	
same as 2407	wie 2407	2408	
		465	
G. H. Macheleid	G. H. Machleid		
Sitzerode	Sitzerode		
circa 1759—1760	ca. 1759—1760	2409	
blue underglaze	blau unterglasur	**481**	
Brenner & Liebmann and	Brenner & Liebmann und		
E. Liebmann	E. Liebmann		
Schney	Schney		
(1887)—circa 1923	(1887)—ca. 1923	2410	
blue underglaze	blau unterglasur	**474**	

same as 2410	wie 2410	2⌞ 4°
A.W.Fr. Kister Scheibe-Alsbach 1905-1972 blue underglaze or overglaze	A.W.Fr. Kister Scheibe-Alsbach 1905-1972 blau unterglasur oder aufglasur	2⌞ 2⌞ 4°
A.W.Fr. Kister Scheibe-Alsbach 1905-1972 blue underglaze or overglaze	A.W.Fr. Kister Scheibe-Alsbach 1905-1972 blau unterglasur oder aufglasur	24 47
same as 2414	wie 2414	24 47
VEB Porcelain Manufactory Scheibe-Alsbach Scheibe-Alsbach 1972-1990 blue underglaze or overglaze	VEB Porzellanmanufaktur Scheibe-Alsbach Scheibe-Alsbach 1972-1990 blau unterglasur oder aufglasur	24 47
L. Schleich Buschbad 1886−circa 1927 blue underglaze	L. Schleich Buschbad 1886−ca. 1927 blau unterglasur	24 38
Saxonian Porcelain Factory Carl Thieme Potschappel 1888−1901	Sächsische Porzellan- fabrik Carl Thieme Potschappel 1888−1901	24 24 46
Oswald Lorenz Dresden (1881)-1882	Oswald Lorenz Dresden (1881)-1882	24 39
J. W. Hammann Wallendorf 1764−1787 blue underglaze	J. W. Hammann Wallendorf 1764−1787 blau unterglasur	24 49
Weiss, Kuhnert & Co. Grafenthal (1956)−1972	Weiss, Kühnert & Co. Gräfenthal (1956)−1972	24 41
Dumler & Breiden Hohr-Grenzhausen −present on earthenware	Dümler & Breiden Höhr-Grenzhausen −heute auf Steingut	24 41

	Galluba & Hofmann Ilmenau (1895)–circa 1927	Galluba & Hofmann Ilmenau (1895)–ca. 1927	2424 **422**
	Franziska Hirsch Dresden (1893)–circa 1930 decorator's mark blue overglaze	Franziska Hirsch Dresden (1893)–ca. 1930 Malermarke blau aufglasur	2425 **395**
	same as 2425	wie 2425	2426 **395**
	Martha Budich Kronach -1963	Martha Budich Kronach -1963	2427 **433**
	R. & E. Pech Kronach after 1945–present decorator's mark	R. & E. Pech Kronach nach 1945–heute Malermarke	2428 **434**
	R. & E. Pech Kronach circa 1945–circa 1950 decorator's mark	R. & E. Pech Kronach ca. 1945–ca. 1950 Malermarke	2429 **434**
	H. Schmidt Freiwaldau circa 1920–1923	H. Schmidt Freiwaldau ca. 1920–1923	2430 **405**
	Willi Rittirsch Kups 1950–present blue	Willi Rittirsch Küps 1950–heute blau	2431 **435**
	G. Wolf Kups circa 1958 decorator's marks	G. Wolf Küps ca. 1958 Malermarke	2432 **435**
	Greiner & Holzapfel Volkstedt 1800–1815	Greiner & Holzapfel Volkstedt 1800–1815	2433 **495**

Simon & Halbig Grafenhain circa 1870–circa 1930 impressed on dolls heads	Simon & Halbig Gräfenhain ca. 1870–ca. 1930 eingeprägt auf Puppenköpfen	24 41
Royal Porcelain Manufactory Meissen after 1707–circa 1720 impressed on red stoneware	Königliche Porzellan Manufaktur Meißen nach 1707–ca. 1720 eingeprägt auf rotem Steinzeug	24 44
Galluba & Hofman Ilmenau (1897)–circa 1927	Galluba & Hofmann Ilmenau (1897)–ca. 1927	24 42
Family Greiner Kloster Veilsdorf 1797–circa 1822 blue underglaze	Familie Greiner Kloster Veilsdorf 1797–ca. 1822 blau unterglasur	24 24 24 42
Family Greiner Kloster Veilsdorf 1797–circa 1822 blue underglaze	Familie Greiner Kloster Veilsdorf 1797–ca. 1822 blau unterglasur	24 24 24 42
Prince Electoral Porcelain Manufactory Nymphenburg 1780–1790 impressed	Churfürstliche Porcellain Manufactur Nymphenburg 1780–1790 eingeprägt	2 4
Royal Porcelain Manufactory Berlin 1915–1918 blue or black underglaze or black overglaze	Königliche Porzellan Manufaktur Berlin 1915–1918 blau oder schwarz unterglasur oder schwarz aufglasur	2 3
Anton Fischer Son Neumark (1908)– on earthenware	Anton Fischer Sohn Neumark (1908)– auf Steingut	2 4
F. A. Schumann Berlin 1835–circa 1840 blue underglaze	F. A. Schumann Berlin 1835–1840 blau unterglasur	2 3

—	Royal Porcelain Manufactory Berlin 1803—circa 1817 blue, decorating mark in addition to scepter mark	Königliche Porzellan Manufaktur Berlin 1803—ca. 1817 blau, Malereimarke zusätzlich zur Szepter-Marke	2447 **380**
—	Royal Porcelain Manufactory Berlin 1817—circa 1823 red, decorating mark in addition to scepter mark	Königliche Porzellan Manufaktur Berlin 1817—ca. 1823 rot, Malereimarke zusätzlich zur Szepter-Marke	2448 **380**
⩘	Porcelain Factory Freiberg Freiberg (1926)—1945	Porzellanfabrik Freiberg Freiberg (1926)—1945	2449 **404**
UNITY UNITY FREIBERG	Porcelain Factory Freiberg Freiberg (1926)—1945	Porzellanfabrik Freiberg Freiberg (1926)—1945	2450 2451 **404**
FPM	Schmidt & Otremba Freiwaldau (1887)—circa 1894	Schmidt & Otremba Freiwaldau (1887)—ca. 1894	2452 **405**
J.N.M.	J. N. Muller Schonwald 1879—1898	J. N. Müller Schönwald 1879—1898	2453 **475**
KPF	Krister Porcelain Manufactory Waldenburg (1903)— green or blue underglaze	Krister Porzellanmanufaktur Waldenburg (1903)— grün oder blau unterglasur	2454 **497**
K.P.M.	Krister Porcelain Manufactory Waldenburg (1885)— green or blue underglaze	Krister Porzellanmanufaktur Waldenburg (1885)— grün oder blau unterglasur	2455 **497**
KPM	same as 2455	wie 2455	2456 **497**
KPM	same as 2455	wie 2455	2457 **497**
KPM	Krister Porcelain Manufactory Waldenburg (1904)—1927 blue or green underglaze	Krister Porzellanmanufaktur Waldenburg (1904)—1927 blau oder grün unterglasur	2458 **497**

Mark	English	German	
KPM / W	Krister Porcelain Manufactory Waldenburg circa 1896–circa 1906 green or blue underglaze	Krister Porzellanmanufaktur Waldenburg ca. 1896–ca. 1906 grün oder blau unterglasur	24. **49**'
K / WPM	Krister Porcelain Manufactory Waldenburg 1896–1906 green or blue underglaze	Krister Porzellanmanufaktur Waldenburg 1896–1906 grün oder blau unterglasur	24. **49**
CHINA. **KPM**	Krister Porcelain Manufactory Waldenburg 1885– blue or green underglaze	Krister Porzellanmanufaktur Waldenburg 1885– blau oder grün unterglasur	24. **49**'
KRISTER	Krister Porcelain Manufactory Waldenburg 1895–1905 green or blau underglaze	Krister Porzellanmanufaktur Waldenburg 1895–1905 grün oder blau unterglasur	24. **49**'
M	Friedrich Carl Muller Stutzerbach (1887)–circa 1922	Friedrich Carl Müller Stützerbach (1887)–ca. 1922	24. **48.**
n·s / W·1766	Princely Porcelain Manufactory Ottweiler 1766–1771 incised	Fürstliche Porzellan Manufaktur Ottweiler 1766–1771 eingeritzt	24. **46**'
SPM	F. A. Schumann Berlin circa 1844–1847 blue underglaze	F. A. Schumann Berlin ca. 1844–1847 blau unterglasur	24. **38.**
StPM	Striegau Porcelain Factory Stanowitz after 1873–circa 1927	Striegauer Porzellanfabrik Stanowitz nach 1873–ca. 1927	24. **48.**
HW ML BAVARIA	Heinrich Winterling Marktleuthen 1903–1945 green underglaze	Heinrich Winterling Marktleuthen 1903–1945 grün unterglasur	24. **44**
Z S & Co. BAVARIA	Zeh, Scherzer & Co. Rehau after 1880– green underglaze	Zeh, Scherzer & Co. Rehau nach 1880– grün unterglasur	24. **46**
ORLEANS Z S & Co. BAVARIA	same as 2468	wie 2468	24. **46**

C. I. du Paquier Vienna circa 1720–1730 red overglaze	C. I. du Paquier Wien ca. 1720–1730 rot aufglasur	2470 **502**
Royal Porcelain Manufactory Meissen after 1717–circa 1724 blue underglaze	Königliche Porzellan Manufaktur Meißen nach 1717–ca. 1724 blau unterglasur	2471 **446**
same as 2471	wie 2471	2472 **446**
same as 2471	wie 2471	2473 **446**
same as 2471	wie 2471	2474 **446**
same as 2471	wie 2471	2475 **446**
same as 2471	wie 2471	2476 **446**

Julius Rother Mitterteich circa 1899–1918	Julius Rother Mitterteich ca. 1899–1918	2 4
C. H. Tuppack Tiefenfurth (1926)–1935	C. H. Tuppack Tiefenfurth (1926)–1935	24 48
Royal Porcelain Manufactory Meissen after 1717–circa 1724 blue underglaze	Königliche Porzellan Manufaktur Meißen nach 1717–ca. 1724 blau unterglasur	24 44
same as 2479	wie 2479	24 4
same as 2479	wie 2479	24 4
same as 2479	wie 2479	24 4
Prince Electoral Porcelain Manufactory Nymphenburg circa 1760–1795 blue underglaze	Churfürstliche Porcellain Manufactur Nymphenburg ca. 1760–1795 blau unterglasur	2 4
C. I. du Paquier Vienna circa 1720–1730 red overglaze	C. I. du Paquier Wien ca. 1720–1730 rot aufglasur	2 5
Royal Porcelain Manufactory Meissen after 1717–circa 1724 blue underglaze	Königliche Porzellan Manufaktur Meißen nach 1717–ca. 1724 blau unterglasur	2 4
same as 2485	wie 2485	2 4
same as 2485	wie 2485	2 4
Porcelain Factory Victoria Altrohlau after 1883–	Porzellanfabrik Victoria Altrohlau nach 1883–	2 3

Porcelain Manufactory Allach-Munich	Porzellanmanufaktur Allach-München	
Allach-Munich	Allach-München	2489
1935–1945	1935–1945	**372**
Bohemia	Bohemia	
Neurohlau	Neurohlau	2490
(1941)–1945	(1941)–1945	**453**
Furstenberg Porcelain Manufactory	Fürstenberg Porzellan-manufaktur	
Furstenberg	Fürstenberg	2491
(1963)–	(1963)–	**405**
W. Haldenwanger	W. Haldenwanger	
Berlin	Berlin	2492
(1912)–	(1912)–	**382**
Carl Auvera	Carl Auvera	
Arzberg	Arzberg	2493
(1914)–1918	(1914)–1918	**377**
Porcelain Factory Weiden Bros. Bauscher	Porzellanfabrik Weiden Gebr. Bauscher	
Weiden	Weiden	2494
1881–	1881–	**500**
Eduard Kick	Eduard Kick	
Amberg	Amberg	2495
1850–circa 1880	1850–ca. 1880	**375**
Porcelain Factory Auma	Porzellanfabrik Auma	
Auma	Auma	2496
circa 1909–1945	ca. 1909–1945	**377**
Alt, Beck & Gottschalck	Alt, Beck & Gottschalck	2497
Nauendorf	Nauendorf	2498
after 1890–circa 1953	nach 1890–ca. 1953	**451**
C. E. & F. Arnoldi	C. E. & F. Arnoldi	
Elgersburg	Elgersburg	2499
(1912)–circa 1962	(1912)–ca. 1962	**400**

| | Wick-Works
Grenzhausen
1921–1937
impressed on stoneware | Wick-Werke
Grenzhausen
1921–1937
eingeprägt auf Steinzeug | 25
41 |

Wick-Works
Grenzhausen
1921–1937
impressed on stoneware

Wick-Werke
Grenzhausen
1921–1937
eingeprägt auf Steinzeug

25
41

Adolf Persch
Hegewald
1850–1869
impressed

Adolf Persch
Hegewald
1850–1869
eingeprägt

25
41

Adolf Persch
Hegewald
1850–1869
impressed

Adolf Persch
Hegewald
1850–1869
eingeprägt

25
41

Royal Porcelain Manufactory
Meissen
circa 1723–probably 1736
blue underglaze

Königliche Porzellan Manufaktur
Meißen
ca. 1723–wahrscheinlich 1736
blau unterglasur

25
44

same as 2503

wie 2503

25
44

Royal Porcelain Manufactory
Meissen
circa 1723–probably 1736
AR blue underglaze
cross and dots impressed

Königliche Porzellan Manufaktur
Meißen
ca. 1723–wahrscheinlich 1736
AR blau unterglasur
Kreuz und Punkte eingeprägt

25
44

Royal, State's and VEB
State's Porcelain Manufactory
Meissen
circa 1723–probably 1736
and 1875–present
blue underglaze

Königliche, Staatliche und VEB
Staatliche Porzellan Manufaktur
Meißen
ca. 1723–wahrscheinlich 1736
und 1875–heute
blau unterglasur

25
44

Royal Porcelain Manufactory
Meissen
circa 1723–probably 1736
blue underglaze

Königliche Porzellan Manufaktur
Meißen
ca. 1723–wahrscheinlich 1736
blau unterglasur

25
44

same as 2507

wie 2507

25
44

same as 2507	wie 2507	2509 **446**
Royal Porcelain Manufactory Meissen circa 1723—probably 1736 AR blue underglaze cross and dots impressed 2/3 original size	Königliche Porzellan Manufaktur Meißen ca. 1723—wahrscheinlich 1736 AR blau unterglasur Kreuz und Punkte eingeprägt 2/3 Originalgröße	2510 **446**
Royal Porcelain Manufactory Meissen circa 1723—probably 1736 blue underglaze 2/3 original size	Königliche Porzellan Manufaktur Meißen ca. 1723—wahrscheinlich 1736 blau unterglasur 2/3 Originalgröße	2511 **446**
same as 2511	wie 2511	2512 **446**
Royal Porcelain Manufactory Meissen circa 1723—probably 1736 blue underglaze 2/3 original size	Königliche Porzellan Manufaktur Meißen ca. 1723—wahrscheinlich 1736 blau unterglasur 2/3 Originalgröße	2513 **446**
same as 2513	wie 2513	2514 **446**
Royal Porcelain Manufactory Meissen circa 1723—probably 1736 blue underglaze	Königliche Porzellan Manufaktur Meißen ca. 1723—wahrscheinlich 1736 blau unterglasur	2515 **446**

same as 2515	wie 2515	25 44
same as 2515	wie 2515	25 44
Royal Porcelain Manufactory Meissen circa 1723–probably 1736 blue underglaze 2/3 original size	Königliche Porzellan Manufaktur Meißen ca. 1723–wahrscheinlich 1736 blau unterglasur 2/3 Originalgröße	251 446
same as 2518	wie 2518	251 446
Royal Porcelain Manufactory Meissen circa 1723–probably 1736 blue underglaze	Königliche Porzellan Manufaktur Meißen ca. 1723–wahrscheinlich 1736 blau unterglasur	252 446
Royal Porcelain Manufactory Meissen circa 1723–probably 1736 AR blue underglaze letters and number incised, inventory mark of the Johanneum collection in Dresden	Königliche Porzellan Manufaktur Meißen ca. 1723–wahrscheinlich 1736 AR blau unterglasur Buchstaben und Zahl eingeritzt, Inventurmarke des Johanneums in Dresden	252 446
attributed to Royal Porcelain Manufactory Meissen blue underglaze but questionable	Der Königlichen Porzellan Manufaktur Meißen zugeschrieben aber zweifelhaft blau unterglasur	252 446
Helena Wolfsohn Dresden 1843–circa 1883 blue decorator's mark	Helena Wolfsohn Dresden 1843–ca. 1883 blau Malermarke	252 396

	same as 2523	wie 2523	2524 **396**
	same as 2523	wie 2523	2525 **396**
	same as 2523	wie 2523	2526 **396**
	same as 2523	wie 2523	2527 **396**
	same as 2523	wie 2523	2528 **396**
	unidentified blue overglaze	nicht identifiziert blau aufglasur	2529
	attributed to R. & E. Haidinger Elbogen 19th century blue underglaze but questionable	R. & E. Haidinger Elbogen 19. Jahrhundert blau unterglasur zugeschrieben, aber zweifelhaft	2530 **399**
	same as 2530	wie 2530	2531 **399**
	same as 2530	wie 2530	2532 **399**
	Anton Richter Dresden 1887– decorator's mark blue overglaze	Anton Richter Dresden 1887– Malermarke blau aufglasur	2533 **395**
	Albin Rosenlocher Kups (1887)–circa 1906	Albin Rosenlöcher Küps (1887)–ca. 1906	2534 **435**

unidentified black overglaze	nicht identifiziert schwarz aufglasur		25
A. Riemann Coburg after 1900–circa 1927	A. Riemann Coburg nach 1900–ca. 1927		25 **39**
A. Schmidt Waltershausen (1887)–circa 1911	A. Schmidt Waltershausen (1887)–ca. 1911		25 **49**
A. Schindler Schonfeld circa 1900–	A. Schindler Schönfeld ca. 1900–		25 **47**
A. Carl Anger Aich 1862–1901 impressed	A. Carl Anger Aich 1862–1901 eingeprägt		25 **37**
A. Carl Anger Aich 1862–1901 blue or green underglaze	A. Carl Anger Aich 1862–1901 blau oder grün unterglasur		25 **37**
B. Bertram Luftelberg before 1924– decorator's mark overglaze	B. Bertram Lüftelberg vor 1924– Malermarke aufglasur		25 **44**
J. J. Letschert Son Baumbach (1930)–	J. J. Letschert Sohn Baumbach (1930)–		25 **37**
Carl Auvera Arzberg 1884–1918	Carl Auvera Arzberg 1884–1918		25 **37**
Prince Electoral Porcelain Manufactory Nymphenburg circa 1764–1795 blue underglaze	Churfürstliche Porcellain Manufactur Nymphenburg ca. 1764–1795 blau unterglasur		25 **45**

Ducal Real Porcelain Factory Ludwigsburg circa 1775 blue underglaze	Herzoglich Aechte Porcelain Fabrique Ludwigsburg ca. 1775 blau unterglasur	2545 **441**
Dressel, Kister & Cie. Passau (1902)–1904 blue underglaze	Dressel, Kister & Cie. Passau (1902)–1904 blau unterglasur	2546 **460**
Cuno & Otto Dressel Sonneberg after 1873–circa 1943 impressed or stamped on dolls heads	Cuno & Otto Dressel Sonneberg nach 1873–ca. 1943 eingeprägt oder gestempelt auf Puppenköpfen	2547 **482**
Theodor Gumtau Creidlitz 1906–1924	Theodor Gumtau Creidlitz 1906–1924	2548 **391**
Lobedan & Lehnert Berlin (1899)–circa 1909 decorator's mark overglaze	Lobedan & Lehnert Berlin (1899)–ca. 1909 Malermarke aufglasur	2549 **382**
Prince F. W. E. von Hild- burghausen Kloster Veilsdorf 1760–1795 blue underglaze	Prinz F. W. E. von Hild- burghasusen Kloster Veilsdorf 1760–1795 blau unterglasur	2550 **429**
same as 2550	wie 2550	2551 2552 **429**
same as 2550	wie 2550	2553 2554 **429**
same as 2550	wie 2550	2555 2556 2557 **429**

	same as 2550	wie 2550	2 2 4
	same as 2550	wie 2550	2 2 2 4
	same as 2550	wie 2550	2 4
	same as 2550	wie 2550	2 4
	Porcelain Factory at Kloster Veilsdorf at Kloster Veilsdorf Kloster Veilsdorf −1945	Porzellanfabrik zu Kloster Veilsdorf zu Kloster Veilsdorf Kloster Veilsdorf −1945	2 4
	same as 2565	wie 2565	2 4
	Ernst Friedrich & Karl Dressel Sonneberg circa 1863–circa 1873 impressed or stamped on dolls heads	Ernst Friedrich & Karl Dressel Sonneberg ca. 1863–ca. 1873 eingeprägt oder gestempelt auf Puppenköpfen	25 48
	Ernst Lindner Kups (1971)–	Ernst Lindner Küps (1971)–	25 43
	Dresden Art Publishers Richard Eckert Dresden 1909–1918	Dresdner Kunstverlag Richard Eckert Dresden 1909–1918	25 39
	Ernst Teichert Meissen (1884)-1888	Ernst Teichert Meißen (1884)-1888	25 44
	Ernst Teichert Meissen after 1884-1888 blue underglaze	Ernst Teichert Meißen nach 1884-1888 blau unterglasur	25 44
	Ernst Teichert Meissen 1888-1920	Ernst Teichert Meißen 1888-1920	25 44

Eduard Haberlander	Eduard Haberländer	
Windischeschenbach	Windischeschenbach	
after 1913–1928	nach 1913–1928	
green underglaze	grün unterglasur	
also in combination	auch in Verbindung	2573
with: Haberlander	mit: Haberländer	**505**

Wenzel Ullrich	Wenzel Ullrich	
Eythra	Eythra	
circa 1930	ca. 1930	
decorator's mark	Malermarke	2574
overglaze	aufglasur	**401**

Royal Porcelain Manufactory	Königliche Porzellan Manufaktur	
Meissen	Meißen	
1733	1733	
blue underglaze	blau unterglasur	2575
2/3 original size	2/3 Originalgröße	**446**

same as 2575	wie 2575	2576
		446

same as 2575	wie 2575	2577
		446

Franz Anton Mehlem	Franz Anton Mehlem	
Bonn	Bonn	2578
(1881)–1920	(1881)–1920	**385**
on earthenware	auf Steingut	

Franz Fritz Successor	Franz Fritz Nachf.	
Grossbreitenbach	Großbreitenbach	
(1957)–	(1957)–	
decorator's mark	Malermarke	2579
overglaze	aufglasur	**412**

Fasold & Stauch	Fasold & Stauch	
Bock-Wallendorf	Bock-Wallendorf	2580
(1914)–circa 1972	(1914)–ca. 1972	**384**

F. Hudler	F. Hudler	
Diessen	Dießen	2581
circa 1935–present	ca. 1935–heute	**393**

Royal Porcelain Manufactory Berlin 1840–1860 red or purple overglaze court mark	Königliche Porzellan Manufaktur Berlin 1840–1860 rot oder purpur aufglasur Palastmarke	2! 3!
same as 2582	wie 2582	2! 3!
Heinz & Co. Grafenthal-Meernach (1954)-1972	Heinz & Co. Gräfenthal-Meernach (1954)-1972	25 4!
Johann Hufnagel Gmunden circa 1930 decorator's mark overglaze	Johann Hufnagel Gmunden ca. 1930 Malermarke aufglasur	25 40
Carl Schneider's Heirs Grafenthal (1887)–circa 1972	Carl Schneider's Erben Gräfenthal (1887)–ca. 1972	25 41
Graf & Krippner Selb after 1906–circa 1929	Gräf & Krippner Selb nach 1906–ca. 1929	25 47
Gustav Korn Neu-Schmiedefeld 1904–1925	Gustav Korn Neu-Schmiedefeld 1904–1925	25 45
Fr. Pfeffer Gotha after 1900–	Fr. Pfeffer Gotha nach 1900–	25 40
Julius Greiner Son Lauscha after 1871– decorator's mark overglaze	Julius Greiner Sohn Lauscha nach 1871– Malermarke aufglasur	25 43
Georg Schmider Zell on Harmersbach before 1932–present	Georg Schmider Zell am Harmersbach vor 1932–heute	25 50

Vienna Manufactory	Wiener Manufaktur	
F. Goldscheider	F. Goldscheider	
Vienna	Wien	2592
(1937)–circa 1941	(1937)–ca. 1941	**503**
Heber & Co.	Heber & Co.	
Neustadt	Neustadt	
1900–1922	1900–1922	2593
on dolls heads	auf Puppenköpfen	**453**
Hedwig Bollhagen	Hedwig Bollhagen	
Marwitz	Marwitz	
circa 1934–1972	ca. 1934–1972	
impressed or incised	eingeprägt oder eingeritzt oder	2594
or different colors overglaze	verschiedene Farben aufglasur	**445**
Landgravial Porcelain	Landgräfliche Porzellan	
Manufactory	Manufaktur	
Kelsterbach	Kelsterbach	
circa 1761–circa 1789	ca. 1761–ca. 1789	2595
incised	eingeritzt	**426**
J. J. Lay	J. J. Lay	
Kelsterbach	Kelsterbach	
1799–1802	1799–1802	2596
blue underglaze	blau unterglasur	**426**
same as 2596	wie 2596	2597
		426
unidentified	nicht identifiziert	
possibly Klosterle	möglicherweise Klösterle	
1st half 19th century	1. Hälfte 19. Jahrhundert	2598
blue underglaze	blau unterglasur	**428**
same as 2598	wie 2598	2599
		428
Friedrich Hocke	Friedrich Höcke	
Pirkenhammer	Pirkenhammer	
1803–1811	1803–1811	
blue underglaze or	blau unterglasur oder	2600
gold overglaze	gold aufglasur	**461**
H. Klingler	H. Klingler	
Landstuhl	Landstuhl	
circa 1931	ca. 1931	
decorator's mark	Malermarke	2601
overglaze	aufglasur	**436**

Hael Workshops Marwitz (1929)–1934	Hael Werkstätten Marwitz (1929)–1934	2(4•
same as 2602	wie 2602	2(4•
H. Reinl Hirschen after 1914–	H. Reinl Hirschen nach 1914–	2(4)
C. M. Hutschenreuther Hohenberg (1882)–	C. M. Hutschenreuther Hohenberg (1882)–	2(4)
same as 2605	wie 2605	2(4)
Hermann Steiner Sonneberg 1921– impressed on dolls heads	Hermann Steiner Sonneberg 1921– eingeprägt auf Puppenköpfen	26 26 48
State's Porcelain Manufactory Nymphenburg (1921)–present blue underglaze on reproductions of Frankenthal porcelain, always with year and contemporary shield mark	Staatliche Porzellan Manufaktur Nymphenburg (1921)–heute blau unterglasur auf Reproduktionen von Frankenthal Porzellan, immer mit Jahreszahl und zeitgenössischer Schildmarke	2(4!
Joseph Adam Hannong Frankenthal 1759–1762 blue underglaze	Joseph Adam Hannong Frankenthal 1759–1762 blau unterglasur	2(4•
Vienna Porcelain Manufactory Josef Bock Vienna after 1893–circa 1933	Wiener Porzellanmanufaktur Josef Böck Wien nach 1893–ca. 1933	2(5(
Joseph Schachtel Charlottenbrunn after 1900–1919	Joseph Schachtel Charlottenbrunn nach 1900–1919	2(3!
J. D. Kestner Ohrdruf circa 1892–circa 1917	J. D. Kestner Ohrdruf ca. 1892–ca. 1917	2(4.

	same as 2613	wie 2613	2614 **459**
	K. Hammer Munich after 1908– decorator's mark overglaze	K. Hammer München nach 1908– Malermarke aufglasur	2615 **450**
	Karl Ens Volkstedt (1900)–	Karl Ens Volkstedt (1900)–	2616 **496**
	Gotthelf Greiner Limbach 1772–1797 blue underglaze or purple or red or green or black overglaze	Gotthelf Greiner Limbach 1772–1797 blau unterglasur oder purpur oder rot oder grün oder schwarz aufglasur	2617 **439**
	same as 2617	wie 2617	2618 **439**
	same as 2617	wie 2617	2619 **439**
	same as 2617	wie 2617	2620 **439**
	Gotthelf Greiner Limbach 1772–1797 blue underglaze	Gotthelf Greiner Limbach 1772–1797 blau unterglasur	2621 **439**
	Louis Knoller Dresden 1891–1907 decorator's mark overglaze	Louis Knöller Dresden 1891–1907 Malermarke aufglasur	2622 **395**
	Lubtheen Porcelain Factory Lubtheen (1933)–circa 1945	Lübtheener Porzellanfabrik Lübtheen (1933)–ca. 1945	2623 **442**
	C. E. & F. Arnoldi Elgersburg (1912)–	C. E. & F. Arnoldi Elgersburg (1912)–	2624 **400**

Mekus & Moest Turn-Teplitz after 1892–circa 1912	Mekus & Moest Turn-Teplitz nach 1892–ca. 1912	2€ 4€
Montgomery Ward mark of U.S. importer and dealer	Montgomery Ward Marke eines US Importeurs und Händlers	2€
New Porcelain Factory Tettau Tettau (1919)–circa 1937	Neue Porzellanfabrik Tettau Tettau (1919)–ca. 1937	2€ 4€
Oscar Schlegelmilch Langewiesen (1896)–	Oscar Schlegelmilch Langewiesen (1896)–	2€ 4€
Oscar Gustav Schade Dresden 20th century decorator's mark overglaze	Oscar Gustav Schade Dresden 20. Jahrhundert Malermarke aufglasur	2€ 3€
Oscar Zenari Leipzig 1901– decorator's mark overglaze	Oscar Zenari Leipzig 1901– Malermarke aufglasur	2€ 4€
Triebner, Ens & Eckert Volkstedt 1884–1894	Triebner, Ens & Eckert Volkstedt 1884–1894	2€ 4€
Fr. Pfeffer Gotha after 1900–	Fr. Pfeffer Gotha nach 1900–	2€ 4€
Fr. Pfeffer Gotha after 1892–	Fr. Pfeffer Gotha nach 1892–	2€ 4€
H. Hutschenreuther Probstzella after 1886–circa 1952	H. Hutschenreuther Probstzella nach 1886–ca. 1952	2€ 4€
Porcelain Factory Moschendorf Hof-Moschendorf after 1878–1938 impressed on dolls heads	Porzellanfabrik Moschendorf Hof-Moschendorf nach 1878–1938 eingeprägt auf Puppenköpfen	2€ 4€

Peter van Recum Frankenthal 1795 blue underglaze	Peter van Recum Frankenthal 1795 blau unterglasur	**2636** **402**
same as 2636	wie 2636	**2637** **402**
Saxonian Porcelain Factory Carl Thieme und VEB Saxonian Manufactory Dresden and Saxo- nian Porcelain Manufactory Potschappel (Dresden) 1901-present blue underglaze	Sächsische Porzellanfabrik Carl Thieme und VEB Sächsische Porzellanmanufaktur Dresden und Sächsische Porzellanmanufaktur Potschappel (Dresden) 1901-heute blau unterglasur	**2638** **463**
Saxonian Porcelain Factory Carl Thieme Potschappel (1914)–	Sächische Porzellan- fabrik Carl Thieme Potschappel (1914)–	**2639** **463**
Porcelain Factory Stadtlengsfeld Stadtlengsfeld (1909)–circa 1945	Porzellanfabrik Stadtlengsfeld Stadtlengsfeld (1909)–ca. 1945	**2640** **483**
J. N. van Recum and Heirs Grunstadt circa 1800–1812 on fayence	J. N. van Recum und Erben Grünstadt ca. 1800–1812 auf Fayence	**2641** **413**
J. N. van Recum Frankenthal 1797–1799 blue underglaze	J. N. van Recum Frankenthal 1797–1799 blau unterglasur	**2642** **402**
J. N. van Recum Frankenthal 1797–1799 blue underglaze	J. N. van Recum Frankenthal 1797–1799 blau unterglasur	**2643** **402**
same as 2643	wie 2643	**2644** **402**
Richter, Fenkl & Hahn Chodau after 1900–	Richter, Fenkl & Hahn Chodau nach 1900–	**2645** **389**

unidentified 20th century blue underglaze on figurines	nicht identifiziert 20. Jahrhundert blau unterglasur auf Figuren		26
unidentified blue overglaze possibly Richard Klemm Dresden	nicht identifiziert blau aufglasur möglicherweise Richard Klemm Dresden		26 39
G. Robrecht Mildeneichen −1920	G. Robrecht Mildeneichen −1920		26 44
Reinhold Richter & Co. Volkstedt 1906−circa 1917 decorator's mark overglaze	Reinhold Richter & Co. Volkstedt 1906−ca. 1917 Malermarke aufglasur		26 49
Porcelain Factory Stein- wiesen and Eduard Harter Steinwiesen after 1910−1965	Porzellanfabrik Stein- wiesen und Eduard Härter Steinwiesen nach 1910−1965		26 48
Riessner, Stellmacher & Kessel Turn-Teplitz 1892−1905	Riessner, Stellmacher & Kessel Turn-Teplitz 1892−1905		26 48
same as 2651	wie 2651		26 48
Slama & Co. Vienna (1955)−present	Slama & Co. Wien (1955)−heute		26 50
Oscar Schaller & Co. Schwarzenbach (1892)−circa 1918 green underglaze	Oscar Schaller & Co. Schwarzenbach (1892)−ca. 1918 grün unterglasur		26 47
Josef Palme Schelten 1829−1851 impressed or blue underglaze	Josef Palme Schelten 1829−1851 eingeprägt oder blau unterglasur		26 47

Schutzmeister & Quendt	Schützmeister & Quendt	
Gotha	Gotha	2656
1899−circa 1927	1899−ca. 1927	**410**
Strobel & Wilken	Strobel & Wilken	
New York City	New York	
after 1886−	nach 1886−	2657
importer's mark	Importeurmarke	**456**
same as 2657	wie 2657	2658
		456
Swaine & Co.	Swaine & Co.	
Huttensteinach	Hüttensteinach	2659
after 1896−1920	nach 1896−1920	**420**
VEB Porcelainwork Triptis	VEB Porzellanwerk Triptis	
Triptis	Triptis	2660
(1957)−1968	(1957)−1968	**489**
Oldest Volkstedt Porcelain	Aelteste Volkstedter	
Factory	Porzellanfabrik	
Volkstedt	Volkstedt	2661
1890-1908	1890-1908	**494**
T. Hehl	T. Hehl	
Xanten	Xanten	
about 1930	um 1930	
decorator's mark	Malermarke	2662
overglaze	aufglasur	**506**
J. Melzer and Count	J. Melzer und Gräfl.	
Thun's Porcelain Factory	Thun'sche Porzellanfabrik	
Klosterle	Klösterle	
1805−1830	1805−1830	
blue underglaze or different	blau unterglasur oder verschie-	2663
colors overglaze	dene Farben aufglasur	**428**
same as 2663	wie 2663	2664
		428
same as 2663	wie 2663	2665
		428
unidentified	nicht identifiziert	
blue underglaze	blau unterglasur	2666
possibly Klosterle	möglicherweise Klösterle	**428**
same as 2666	wie 2666	2667
		428

Villeroy & Boch Schramberg (1902)–1912	Villeroy & Boch Schramberg (1902)–1912	26 47
VEB Porcelain Factory Uhlstadt Uhlstadt (1962)–1968	VEB Porzellanfabrik Uhlstädt Uhlstädt (1962)–1968	26 49
Alois Vondracek & Co. Schwarzkosteletz circa 1930 decorator's mark overglaze	Alois Vondracek & Co. Schwarzkosteletz ca. 1930 Malermarke aufglasur	26 47
Voigt & Holand Unterweissbach circa 1884–	Voigt & Höland Unterweißbach ca. 1884–	26 49
Villeroy & Boch Dresden (1887)–circa 1945	Villeroy & Boch Dresden (1887)–ca. 1945	26 39
Villeroy & Boch Mettlach circa 1885–1900 blue on earthenware	Villeroy & Boch Mettlach ca. 1885–1900 blau auf Steingut	26 44
Dr. Helmuth Fischer Ilmenau (1928)–circa 1945	Dr. Helmuth Fischer Ilmenau (1928)–ca. 1945	26 42
Wagner & Apel Lippelsdorf –before 1945	Wagner & Apel Lippelsdorf –vor 1945	26 44
Westphalian Glass Manufactory Bielefeld (1930)– registered for porcelain products	Westfälische Glasmanufaktur Bielefeld (1930)– registriert für Porzellan- erzeugnisse	26 38

Fasold & Stauch Bock-Wallendorf 1962–circa 1972	Fasold & Stauch Bock-Wallendorf 1962–ca. 1972	2677 **384**
Johann Haviland Waldershof 1909–1924	Johann Haviland Waldershof 1909–1924	2678 **498**
Krister Porcelain Manufactory Waldenburg (1902)– green or blue underglaze	Krister Porzellan- manufaktur Waldenburg (1902)– grün oder blau unterglasur	2679 **497**
Vienna Ceramics Vienna before 1924–	Wiener Keramik Wien vor 1924–	2680 **502**
M. W. Reutter Denkendorf 1948–present	M. W. Reutter Denkendorf 1948–heute	2681 **393**
Wick-Works Grenzhausen 1960–present impressed on stoneware	Wick-Werke Grenzhausen 1960–heute eingeprägt auf Steinzeug	2682 **412**
Wenck & Zitzmann Kups after 1882–	Wenck & Zitzmann Küps nach 1882–	2683 **435**
C. & E. Carstens Zeven 1922–circa 1930 decorating mark	C. & E. Carstens Zeven 1922–ca. 1930 Malereimarke	2684 **508**
Manufactory of Fine Dishes and Porcelain Gutenbrunn 1767–1775 blue underglaze	Feingeschirr- und Porzellanfabrik Gutenbrunn 1767–1775 blau unterglasur	2685 **414**
Prince F. W. E. von Hild- burghausen Kloster Veilsdorf 1760–1795 blue underglaze	Prinz F. W. E. von Hild- burghausen Kloster Veilsdorf 1760–1795 blau unterglasur	2686 **429**
same as 2686	wie 2686	2687 **429**

Mark	Description (English)	Description (German)	No.
A	Amphora Turn-Teplitz 1892–circa 1905	Amphora Turn-Teplitz 1892–ca. 1905	26 48
A	Johann Moehling Aich 1849–1860 impressed	Johann Moehling Aich 1849–1860 eingeprägt	26 37
A A A A	Margravial Fine Porcelain Factory and successors Ansbach/Bruckberg 1757–1860 blue underglaze	Markgräfliche Feine Porcelain Fabrique und Nachfolger Ansbach/Bruckberg 1757–1860 blau unterglasur	26 26 26 26 37
A A	same as 2690	wie 2690	26 26 37
A A A A A	same as 2690	wie 2690	26 26 26 26 37
Aₓ A.	same as 2690	wie 2690	27 27 37
AL	Anton Lang Budau 1860–1880 impressed	Anton Lang Budau 1860–1880 eingeprägt	27 38
AM	Johann Moehling Aich 1849–1860 impressed	Johann Moehling Aich 1849–1860 eingeprägt	27 37
AM 8/0 DEP	Armand Marseille Koppelsdorf circa 1900–1919 impressed on dolls heads	Armand Marseille Köppelsdorf ca. 1900–1919 eingeprägt auf Puppenköpfen	27 432
A:N:	August Nowotny Altrohlau circa 1850 impressed	August Nowotny Altrohlau ca. 1850 eingeprägt	270 373

AN&C	August Nowotny Altrohlau circa 1870 impressed	August Nowotny Altrohlau ca. 1870 eingeprägt	2706 **373**
APH	Adolf Persch Hegewald 1850—1869 impressed	Adolf Persch Hegewald 1850—1869 eingeprägt	2707 **416**
A: S:	Hubel & Co. Prague circa 1800—1835	Hübel & Co. Prag ca. 1800—1835	2708 **463**
B	Franz Lang Budau 1831—circa 1860 blue underglaze	Franz Lang Budau 1831—ca. 1860 blau unterglasur	2709 **387**
B	Bros. Schackert Basdorf 1751—before 1780	Gebr. Schackert Basdorf 1751—vor 1780	2710 **378**
B.	Franz Lang Budau 1831—circa 1860 blue underglaze	Franz Lang Budau 1831—ca. 1860 blau unterglasur	2711 **387**
B:	same as 2711	wie 2711	2712 **387**
B.	Bros. Bordolo Grunstadt 1812—circa 1880 on earthenware	Gebr. Bordolo Grünstadt 1812—ca. 1880 auf Steingut	2713 **413**
B: B:	Boch & Buschmann Mettlach 1813—1825 impressed on earthenware	Boch & Buschmann Mettlach 1813—1825 eingeprägt auf Steingut	2714 **449**
BB	B. Bloch & Co. Eichwald 1871— blue underglaze or impressed	B. Bloch & Co. Eichwald 1871— blau unterglasur oder eingeprägt	2715 **397**

B & D	Bawo & Dotter New York City —circa 1914 on dolls heads made by Simon & Halbig in Grafenhain	Bawo & Dotter New York —ca. 1914 auf Puppenköpfen, von Simon & Halbig in Gräfenhain hergestellt	2 4
B & D *L t J*	same as 2716	wie 2716	2 4
BK	Benedikt Knaute Giesshubel 1815—1840 impressed	Benedikt Knaute Gießhübel 1815—1840 eingeprägt	2 4
BPK	unidentified attributed to a factory in Sandizell but not verified	nicht identifiziert einer Fabrik in Sandizell zugeschrieben, aber nicht nachgewiesen	2
B & S *M*	either Bruder & Schwalb or Becher & Stark Merkelsgrun circa 1871—circa 1920	entweder Bruder & Schwalb oder Becher & Stark Merkelsgrün ca. 1871—ca. 1920	2 44
BW	Bros. Willner Turn-Teplitz after 1884—1915	Gebr. Willner Turn-Teplitz nach 1884—1915	2 49
C	Widow Greiner & Leers Gera circa 1804—circa 1840 blue underglaze	Wwe. Greiner & Leers Gera ca. 1804—ca. 1840 blau unterglasur	2 40
C	Haas & Czjzek Chodau 1872— blue underglaze	Haas & Czjzek Chodau 1872— blau unterglasur	27 38
C	J. Huttner & Co. Chodau 1834—circa 1845 blue or green underglaze	J. Hüttner & Co. Chodau 1834—ca. 1845 blau oder grün unterglasur	27 38
CΛ	Carl Auvera Arzberg (1896)—circa 1918	Carl Auvera Arzberg (1896)—ca. 1918	27 37

CF

Chr. Fischer	Chr. Fischer	
Pirkenhammer	Pirkenhammer	
1846–1857	1846–1857	2726
impressed	eingeprägt	**461**

CF

Chr. Fischer	Chr. Fischer	
Zwickau	Zwickau	2727
(1887)–	(1887)–	**508**

C. & G. H.

Carl & Gustav Harkort	Carl & Gustav Harkort	
Altenbach	Altenbach	
1845–1881	1845–1881	2728
on earthenware	auf Steingut	**372**

c   G   C G   w   W

J. C. Geyger	J. C. Geyger	
Wurzburg	Würzburg	2729
1775–1780	1775–1780	2730
impressed	eingeprägt	**506**

C. H. K.

Royal Porcelain Manufactory	Königliche Porzellan Manufaktur	
Meissen	Meißen	
circa 1763–circa 1806	ca. 1763–ca. 1806	
black or purple overglaze	schwarz oder purpur aufglasur	
mark of the Prince Electoral	Marke der kurfürstlichen	2731
Court Kitchen	Hofküche	**446**

C O D 93-5 DEP

Cuno & Otto Dressel	Cuno & Otto Dressel	
Sonneberg	Sonneberg	
1893–	1893–	2732
impressed on dolls heads	eingeprägt auf Puppenköpfen	**482**

C. P. C.

Royal Porcelain Manufactory	Königliche Porzellan Manufaktur	
Meissen	Meißen	
circa 1763–circa 1806	ca. 1763–ca. 1806	
black or purple overglaze	schwarz oder purpur aufglasur	
mark of the Prince Electoral	Marke der kurfürstlichen	2733
Pastry Shop in Pillnitz	Hofkonditorei in Pillnitz	**446**

CR

C. Riese	C. Riese	
Dux	Dux	
1883–	1883–	2734
on porcelain and earthenware	auf Porzellan und Steingut	**397**

CV.

Prince F. W. E. von Hild-	Prinz F. W. E. von Hild-	
burghausen	burghausen	
Kloster Veilsdorf	Kloster Veilsdorf	
1760–1795	1760–1795	2735
blue underglaze	blau unterglasur	**429**

C.V.	same as 2735	wie 2735	27 42
D	W. von Schoenau and W. W. Lorenz Dallwitz circa 1822–1850 impressed	W. von Schoenau und W. W. Lorenz Dallwitz ca. 1822–1850 eingeprägt	27 39
DA	same as 2737	wie 2737	27 39
D.&C.	E. Dorfner & Cie. Hirschau (1887)–circa 1919	E. Dorfner & Cie, Hirschau (1887)–ca. 1919	27 41
DH	J. Huttner & Co. Chodau 1834–circa 1845 impressed	J. Hüttner & Co. Chodau 1834–ca. 1845 eingeprägt	27 38
E.	F. A. Reinecke Eisenberg 19th century blue underglaze	F. A. Reinecke Eisenberg 19. Jahrhundert blau unterglasur	27 39
E. B. S.	Ernst Bohne Sons Rudolstadt 1887–1896	Ernst Bohne Söhne Rudolstadt 1887–1896	27 46
E.D.&Cie.	E. Dorfner & Cie. Hirschau (1896)–circa 1919	E. Dorfner & Cie. Hirschau (1896)–ca. 1919	274 41
ET	Ernst Teichert Meissen circa 1885– blue underglaze	Ernst Teichert Meißen ca. 1885– blau unterglasur	27 44
F	Ducal Brunswick Porcelain Manufactory Furstenberg circa 1753–1770 blue underglaze	Herzoglich Braunschwei- gische Porzellan Manufaktur Fürstenberg ca. 1753–1770 blau unterglasur	274 40
F	same as 2745	wie 2745	274 405

	Ducal Brunswick Porcelain Manufactory and Furstenberg Porcelain Factory Furstenberg circa 1850–1894 blue underglaze	Herzoglich Braunschweigische Porzellan Manufaktur und Fürstenberger Porzellanfabrik Fürstenberg ca. 1850–1894 blau unterglasur	2747 **405**
	same as 2747	wie 2747	2748 **405**
	Furstenberg Porcelain Factory Furstenberg circa 1890–1908 blue underglaze	Fürstenberger Porzellanfabrik Fürstenberg ca. 1890–1908 blau unterglasur	2749 **405**
	Ducal Brunswick Porcelain Manufactory Furstenberg circa 1790–1825 blue underglaze	Herzoglich Braunschweigische Porzellan Manufaktur Fürstenberg ca. 1790–1825 blau unterglasur	2750 **405**
	Ducal Brunswick Porcelain Manufactory Furstenberg 1758 blue underglaze	Herzoglich Braunschweigische Porzellan Manufaktur Fürstenberg 1758 blau unterglasur	2751 **405**
	Frank & Friedheim Freienorla 1933–	Frank & Friedheim Freienorla 1933–	2752 **404**
	Franz Fischer Dallwitz 1850–1855 impressed	Franz Fischer Dallwitz 1850–1855 eingeprägt	2753 **391**
	Franz Lang Budau circa 1825–circa 1860 impressed	Franz Lang Budau ca. 1825–ca. 1860 eingeprägt	2754 **387**
	Fischer & Mieg Pirkenhammer 1857–1875 impressed	Fischer & Mieg Pirkenhammer 1857–1875 eingeprägt	2755 **461**
	Franz Peter Kaltenhof after 1867–circa 1890	Franz Peter Kaltenhof nach 1867–circa 1890	2756 **424**

Mark	English	German	
F&R	Fischer & Reichenbach Pirkenhammer 1811–1846 impressed	Fischer & Reichenbach Pirkenhammer 1811–1846 eingeprägt	2 4
F S P	Friedrich Schertler Pilsen after 1881–	Friedrich Schertler Pilsen nach 1881–	2 4
F&U	Franz Urfuss Dallwitz 1855–1875 impressed	Franz Urfuss Dallwitz 1855–1875 eingeprägt	2 3
FU	same as 2759	wie 2759	2 3
G.	Leibe & Hofmann Untermhaus (1887)–circa 1895	Leibe & Hofmann Untermhaus (1887)–ca. 1895	27 49
G.	Fr. Eg. Henneberg Gotha 1805–1834 blue underglaze or blue or red or yellow overglaze	Fr. Eg. Henneberg Gotha 1805–1834 blau unterglasur oder blau oder rot oder gelb aufglasur	27 40
g. / G.	Fr. Eg. Henneberg Gotha 1805–1834 blue underglaze	Fr. Eg. Henneberg Gotha 1805–1834 blau unterglasur	27 27 40
G. G. G	same as 2764	wie 2764	27 27 27 40
g.	Widow Greiner & Leers Gera 1804–circa 1840 blue underglaze	Wwe. Geiner & Leers Gera 1804–ca. 1840 blau unterglasur	27 40
G	same as 2768	wie 2768	27 40
G.	same as 2768	wie 2768	27 40
S	same as 2768	wie 2768	27 40

same as 2768	wie 2768	2772 **407**
same as 2768	wie 2768	2773 **407**
same as 2768	wie 2768	2774 **407**
Bros. Greiner and successors Gera 1780–circa 1840 blue underglaze	Gebr. Greiner und Nachfolger Gera 1780–ca. 1840 blau unterglasur	2775 **407**
same as 2775	wie 2775	2776 **407**
same as 2775	wie 2775	2777 **407**
same as 2775	wie 2775	2778 **407**
same as 2775	wie 2775	2779 **407**
J. E. Gotzkowsky Berlin 1761–1763 blue underglaze or brown or red or gold overglaze	J. E. Gotzkowsky Berlin 1761–1763 blau unterglasur oder braun oder rot oder gold aufglasur	2780 **380**
same as 2780	wie 2780	2781 **380**
same as 2780	wie 2780	2782 **380**
same as 2780	wie 2780	2783 **380**
same as 2780	wie 2780	2784 **380**
same as 2780	wie 2780	2785 **380**
same as 2780	wie 2780	2786 **380**

G B	Bros. Bordolo Grunstadt 1812–1880 on earthenware	Gebr. Bordolo Grünstadt 1812–1880 auf Steingut	2 4
G HC **4**	Landgravial Porcelain Manufactory Kassel 1766–1788 blue underglaze	Landgräfliche Porzellan Manufaktur Kassel 1766–1788 blau unterglasur	2˙ 4˙
GHR	Gustav H. Richter Warnsdorf after 1882–	Gustav H. Richter Warnsdorf nach 1882–	2˙ 4●
G|S|H	Bros. Schoenau Huttensteinach after 1900–circa 1920	Gebr. Schoenau Hüttensteinach nach 1900–ca. 1920	2˙ 4˙
H|S|6	same as 2790	wie 2790	2˙ 4˙
GK	Bros. Kuhnlenz Kronach after 1884–circa 1930	Gebr. Kühnlenz Kronach nach 1884–ca. 1930	2˙ 4˙
G.M.	Bros. Martin Lubau after 1874–circa 1918	Gebr. Martin Lubau nach 1874–ca. 1918	2˙ 4●
G. Z.	Bros. Ziegler Althaldensleben (1894)–1938 decorator's mark overglaze	Gebr. Ziegler Althaldensleben (1894)–1938 Malermarke aufglasur	2˙ 3
G 2 m 1 a 3	Prince Electoral Porcelain Manufactory Nymphenburg circa 1763–1767 blue underglaze	Churfürstliche Porcellain Manufactur Nymphenburg ca. 1763–1767 blau unterglasur	2˙ 4˙
H.	Bros. Silbermann Hausen (1887)–circa 1938	Gebr. Silbermann Hausen (1887)–ca. 1938	2˙ 4
H *	Paul Anton Hannong Frankenthal 1756–1759 impressed	Paul Anton Hannong Frankenthal 1756–1759 eingeprägt	2˙ 4●

same as 2797	wie 2797	2798 **402**
Rhenish Porcelain Factory Mannheim (1909)–1933 impressed	Rheinische Porzellanfabrik Mannheim (1909)–1933 eingeprägt	2799 **443**
Landgravial Porcelain Manufactory Kassel 1766–1788 blue underglaze	Landgräfliche Porzellan Manufaktur Kassel 1766–1788 blau unterglasur	2800 **426**
Ernst Heubach Koppelsdorf —circa 1919 on dolls heads	Ernst Heubach Köppelsdorf —ca. 1919 auf Puppenköpfen	2801 **432**
Heinrich & Co. Selb (1911)–	Heinrich & Co. Selb (1911)–	2802 **479**
Christian Nonne and Nonne & Roesch Ilmenau 1792–1813 blue underglaze	Christian Nonne und Nonne & Roesch Ilmenau 1792–1813 blau unterglasur	2803 2804 2805 2806 **421**
Christian Nonne and Nonne & Roesch Ilmenau 1792–1813 blue underglaze	Christian Nonne und Nonne & Roesch Ilmenau 1792–1813 blau unterglasur	2807 **421**
Gottlob Nathusius Althaldensleben 1826–circa 1860 blue underglaze	Gottlob Nathusius Althaldensleben 1826–ca. 1860 blau unterglasur	2808 **373**
Joseph Adam Hannong Frankenthal 1759–1762 impressed	Joseph Adam Hannong Frankenthal 1759–1762 eingeprägt	2809 **402**
Friedrich Carl Muller Stutzerbach (1887)–1922	Friedrich Carl Müller Stützerbach (1887)–1922	2810 **485**

J

Chr. Z. Grabner and
Duke K.A. of Saxony-
Weimar
Ilmenau
1777–1786
blue underglaze

Chr. Z. Gräbner und
Herzog K.A. von Sachsen-
Weimar
Ilmenau
1777–1786
blau unterglasur

28
42

J. B. & Co.

Jena, Bareuther & Co.
Waldsassen
1884–circa 1887

Jena, Bareuther & Co.
Waldsassen
1884–ca. 1887

28
49

J E H
F

J. E. Heintschel
Friedland
after 1869–
blue underglaze

J. E. Heintschel
Friedland
nach 1869–
blau unterglasur

28
40

J. K. S.

unidentified
blue underglaze

nicht identifiziert
blau unterglasur

28

J.M.

J. Maresch
Aussig
circa 1841–
blue underglaze

J. Maresch
Außig
ca. 1841–
blau unterglasur

28
31

J. W.
&
Co.

Jager, Werner & Co.
Selb
1896–1906

Jäger, Werner & Co.
Selb
1896–1906

28
42

J Z & Co

Jacob Zeidler & Co.
Selb
after 1866–circa 1879
impressed

Jacob Zeidler & Co.
Selb
nach 1866–ca. 1879
eingeprägt

28
48

K

Upper Franconian
Porcelain Factory
Kups
1896–circa 1919

Oberfränkische
Porzellanfabrik
Küps
1896–ca. 1919

28
43

/K

J. Melzer and
Count Thun's Porcelain
Factory
Klosterle
1805–1830
blue underglaze or
gold overglaze

J. Melzer und
Gräflich Thun'sche
Porzellanfabrik
Klösterle
1805–1830
blau unterglasur oder
gold aufglasur

28
42

ʻK

same as 2819

wie 2819

28
4

324

K.C.P.C.	Royal Porcelain Manufactory Meissen circa 1723–1763 black or purple overglaze mark of the Royal Pastry Shop in Pillnitz	Königliche Porzellan Manufaktur Meißen ca. 1723–1763 schwarz oder purpur aufglasur Marke der Königlichen Hofkonditorei in Pillnitz	2821 **446**
K H C	Royal Porcelain Manufactory Meissen circa 1723–1763 black or purple overglaze mark of the Royal Pastry Shop	Königliche Porzellan Manufaktur Meißen ca. 1723–1763 schwarz oder purpur aufglasur Marke der Königlichen Hofkonditorei	2822 **446**
K H.C.	same as 2822	wie 2822	2823 **446**
K.H.C.W.	Royal Porcelain Manufactory Meissen circa 1723–circa 1763 black or purple overglaze mark of the Royal Pastry Shop in Warsaw	Königliche Porzellan Manufaktur Meißen ca. 1723–ca. 1763 schwarz oder purpur aufglasur Marke der Königlichen Hofkonditorei in Warschau	2824 **446**
K.H.K.	Royal Porcelain Manufactory Meissen circa 1723–1763 black or purple overglaze mark of the Royal Court Kitchen	Königliche Porzellan Manufaktur Meißen ca. 1723–1763 schwarz oder purpur aufglasur Marke der Königlichen Hofküche	2825 **446**
K.H.K.W.	Royal Porcelain Manufactory Meissen circa 1723–ca. 1763 black or purple overglaze mark of the Royal court Kitchen in Warsaw	Königliche Porzellan Manufaktur Meißen ca. 1723–ca. 1763 schwarz oder purpur aufglasur Marke der Königlichen Hofküche in Warschau	2826 **446**
C.P.F.	Royal Porcelain Manufactory Meissen circa 1722–1723 blue underglaze	Königliche Porzellan Manufaktur Meißen ca. 1722–1723 blau unterglasur	2827 **446**
K.P.F.	same as 2827	wie 2827	2828 **446**
K.P.F	same as 2827	wie 2827	2829 **446**

	Royal Porcelain Manufactory	Königliche Porzellan Manufaktur	
K.P.M	Meissen circa 1723–circa 1727 blue underglaze	Meißen ca. 1723–ca. 1727 blau unterglasur	28 4
K.P.M.	same as 2830	wie 2830	2 4
K.P.M.	same as 2830	wie 2830	2 4
K.P.M	same as 2830	wie 2830	28 4
K.P.M.	same as 2830	wie 2830	28 4
K.P.M.	same as 2830	wie 2830	28 4
K.P.M	same as 2830	wie 2830	28 44
K.P.M.	same as 2830	wie 2830	28 44
K.P.P.	same as 2830	wie 2830	28 44
K.P.PC	same as 2830	wie 2830	28 44
L. & C.	Ph. Liemann & Co. Althaldensleben (1887)– on siderolith and earthenware	Ph. Liemann & Co. Althaldensleben (1887)– auf Siderolith und Steingut	28 37
M	E. & A. Muller Schwarza-Saale (1890)– blue underglaze or overglaze	E. & A. Müller Schwarza-Saale (1890)– blau unterglasur oder aufglasur	28 47

M & C	J. S. Maier & Co. Poschetzau after 1890–	J. S. Maier & Co. Poschetzau nach 1890–	2842 **463**
M G	Bros. Martin Lubau after 1874–circa 1918	Gebr. Martin Lubau nach 1874–1918	2843 **440**
	Royal Porcelain Manufactory Meissen after 1717–circa 1724 blue underglaze	Königliche Porzellan Manufaktur Meißen nach 1717–ca. 1724 blau unterglasur	2844 **446**
M L S	Ludwig Schneider Marburg before 1924–	Ludwig Schneider Marburg vor 1924–	2845 **443**
M. P. M	Royal Porcelain Manufactory Meissen circa 1722–1723 blue underglaze	Königliche Porzellan Manufaktur Meißen ca. 1722–1723 blau unterglasur	2846 **446**
M. P. M.	same as 2846	wie 2846	2847 **446**
MSG	Metalporcelain Factory Schwabisch-Gmund (1934)–	Metallporzellanfabrik Schwäbisch-Gmünd (1934)–	2848 **476**
N	Gottlob Nathusius Althaldensleben 1826–circa 1860 blue underglaze	Gottlob Nathusius Althaldensleben 1826–ca. 1860 blau unterglasur	2849 **373**
N.G.	W. von Neuberg Giesshubel 1846–circa 1892 impressed	W. von Neuberg Gießhübel 1846–ca. 1892 eingeprägt	2850 **408**
N.G.F.	same as 2850	wie 2850	2851 **408**
N.G.F.	same as 2850	wie 2850	2852 **408**
P N S	Franz Prause Niedersalzbrunn (1910)–	Franz Prause Niedersalzbrunn (1910)–	2853 **456**

N&R	Nonne & Roesch Ilmenau 1808–1813 blue underglaze	Nonne & Roesch Ilmenau 1808–1813 blau unterglasur	28 42
.N S.	Princely Porcelain Manufactory Ottweiler 1763–1771 blue underglaze or gold overglaze	Fürstliche Porzellan Manufaktur Ottweiler 1763–1771 blau unterglasur oder gold aufglasur	28 46
.N S.	same as 2855	wie 2855	28 46
.NS.	same as 2855	wie 2855	28. 46
N.V.	Nicolas Villeroy Wallerfangen 1789–1836 impressed on earthenware	Nicolas Villeroy Wallerfangen 1789–1836 eingeprägt auf Steingut	28 49
P	Bros. Pohl Schmiedeberg 1871–1932	Gebr. Pohl Schmiedeberg 1871–1932	28 47
P	Hubel & Co. Prague circa 1800–1835 impressed	Hübel & Co. Prag ca. 1800–1835 eingeprägt	28 46
PB	K. Kriegl & Co. Prague 1835–1910 impressed	K. Kriegl & Co. Prag 1835–1910 eingeprägt	28 46
P	same as 2861	wie 2861	28 46
P	Hubel & Co. Prague circa 1800–1835 red overglaze	Hübel & Co. Prag ca. 1800–1835 rot aufglasur	28 46
PH	Paul Anton Hannong Frankenthal 1755–1759 impressed	Paul Anton Hannong Frankenthal 1755–1759 eingeprägt	28 40

PHF	same as 2864	wie 2864	2865 **402**
PH F	same as 2864	wie 2864	2866 **402**
PHF	Paul Anton Hannong Frankenthal 1755–1756 impressed	Paul Anton Hannong Frankenthal 1755–1756 eingeprägt	2867 **402**
P.H✿	Paul Anton Hannong Frankenthal 1755–1759 impressed	Paul Anton Hannong Frankenthal 1755–1759 eingeprägt	2868 **402**
P. H. K.	Porcelain Factory Kahla Hermsdorf-Klosterlausnitz (1896)–	Porzellanfabrik Kahla Hermsdorf-Klosterlausnitz (1896)–	2869 **416**
PLS	Pfeiffer & Lowenstein Schlackenwerth after 1873–circa 1900	Pfeiffer & Löwenstein Schlackenwerth nach 1873–ca. 1900	2870 **472**
P M P.M.	Porcelain Factory Moschendorf Hof-Moschendorf after 1878– impressed on dolls heads	Porzellanfabrik Moschendorf Hof-Moschendorf nach 1878– eingeprägt auf Puppenköpfen	2871 2872 **419**
P M	same as 2871	wie 2871	2873 **419**
PN	Porcelain Factory Neumunster Neumunster 1897–	Porzellanfabrik Neumünster Neumünster 1897–	2874 **453**
P. R.	Paul Richter Eisenberg 1889–	Paul Richter Eisenberg 1889–	2875 **398**
·◇♧‹·	Paul Rauschert Huttengrund –1945	Paul Rauschert Hüttengrund –1945	2876 **420**
P&S	Portheim & Sons Chodau circa 1860–circa 1870 impressed	Portheim & Söhne Chodau ca. 1860–ca. 1870 eingeprägt	2877 **389**

PW	Porcelain Factory Weingarten R. Wolfinger Weingarten after 1903–1922	Porzellanfabrik Weingarten R. Wolfinger Weingarten nach 1903–1922

28
50

R R. R	W. Th. von Rotberg and Schulz & Co. Gotha 1757–1782 blue underglaze	W. Th. von Rotberg und Schulz & Co. Gotha 1757–1782 blau unterglasur

28
28
28
40

R R R

same as 2879 — wie 2879

28
28
28
40

R — W. Th. von Rotberg and Schulz & Co. Gotha 1760–1787 blue underglaze — W. Th. von Rotberg und Schulz & Co. Gotha 1760–1787 blau unterglasur

28
40

R — Greiner & Holzapfel Volkstedt circa 1804–circa 1815 blue underglaze — Greiner & Holzapfel Volkstedt ca. 1804–ca. 1815 blau unterglasur

28
49

A — same as 2886 — wie 2886

28
49

R — same as 2886 — wie 2886

28
49

R — same as 2886 — wie 2886

28
49

R — same as 2886 — wie 2886

28
49

R· — same as 2886 — wie 2886

28
49

R — Greiner Rauenstein 1783–circa 1800 blue underglaze — Greiner Rauenstein 1783–ca. 1800 blau unterglasur

28
46

R — same as 2892 — wie 2892

28
46

R

Benedikt Hasslacher	Benedikt Hasslacher	
Altrohlau	Altrohlau	
1813–1823	1813–1823	2894
impressed on earthenware	eingeprägt auf Steingut	**373**

R

VEB Earthenware Factory	VEB Steingutfabrik	
Rheinsberg	Rheinsberg	
Rheinsberg	Rheinsberg	
(1954)-before 1992	(1954)-vor 1992	2895
on earthenware	auf Steingut	**467**

R

Johann Heinrich Koch	Johann Heinrich Koch	
Regensburg	Regensburg	
1805–1816	1805–1816	2896
impressed on earthenware	eingeprägt auf Steingut	**465**

R

Greiner	Greiner	
Rauenstein	Rauenstein	
1783–circa 1800	1783–ca. 1800	2897
blue underglaze	blau unterglasur	**465**

R

Josef Rieber	Josef Rieber	
Selb	Selb	
about 1910	um 1910	2898
decorator's mark	Malermarke	**480**

R A
2 8 - 7/0

Thomas Recknagel	Thomas Recknagel	
Alexandrinenthal	Alexandrinenthal	
after 1886–circa 1934	nach 1886–ca. 1934	2899
impressed on dolls heads	eingeprägt auf Puppenköpfen	**371**

R 7/0 A

same as 2899	wie 2899	2900
		371

1907
R/A   DEP
I 12/0

Thomas Recknagel	Thomas Recknagel	
Alexandrinenthal	Alexandrinenthal	
1907–	1907–	2901
impressed on dolls heads	eingeprägt auf Puppenköpfen	**371**

R 86A
6/0

Thomas Recknagel	Thomas Recknagel	
Alexandrinenthal	Alexandrinenthal	
after 1886–circa 1934	nach 1886–ca. 1934	2902
impressed on dolls heads	eingeprägt auf Puppenköpfen	**371**

R & C

Risler & Cie.	Risler & Cie.	
Freiburg	Freiburg	2903
circa 1870–circa 1880	ca. 1870–ca. 1880	**404**

VR F	J. N. van Recum Frankenthal 1797–1799 blue underglaze	J. N. van Recum Frankenthal 1797–1799 blau unterglasur	29 **40**
R F & H	Richter, Fenkl & Hahn Chodau 1883–	Richter, Fenkl & Hahn Chodau 1883–	29 **38**
R.g. R.g-	Schulz & Co. Gotha 1782–1805 blue underglaze	Schulz & Co. Gotha 1782–1805 blau unterglasur	29 29 **40**
R-g. R-g	same as 2906	wie 2906	29 29 **40**
R-g R.g.	same as 2906	wie 2906	29 29 **40**
R.H.	Robert Hanke Ladowitz after 1882–	Robert Hanke Ladowitz nach 1882–	29 **43**
R K A	Rudolf Kindler Aussig 1881–circa 1920	Rudolf Kindler Außig 1881–ca. 1920	29 37
R - n	Greiner Rauenstein 1783–circa 1860 blue underglaze	Greiner Rauenstein 1783–ca. 1860 blau unterglasur	29 **46**
RPM	Robert Persch Mildeneichen 1869–after 1905 impressed	Robert Persch Mildeneichen 1869–nach 1905 eingeprägt	29 **44**
R VEB	VEB Earthenware Factory Rheinsberg circa 1952–1957 on earthenware	VEB Steingutfabrik Rheinsberg ca. 1952–1957 auf Steingut	29 **46**

J. G. Paulus and Luise Greiner and Lippert & Haas Schlaggenwald 1793–1812 blue underglaze	J. G. Paulus und Luise Greiner und Lippert & Haas Schlaggenwald 1793–1812 blau unterglasur	2917 2918 2919 **472**
Lippert & Haas Schlaggenwald 1809–1830 blue underglaze or overglaze	Lippert & Haas Schlaggenwald 1809–1830 blau unterglasur oder aufglasur	2920 **472**
Lippert & Haas Schlaggenwald 1810–1820 different colors underglaze or overglaze	Lippert & Haas Schlaggenwald 1810–1820 verschiedene Farben unterglasur oder aufglasur	2921 2922 **472**
Lippert & Haas Schlaggenwald 1810–1820 blue or gold or red overglaze	Lippert & Haas Schlaggenwald 1810–1820 blau oder gold oder rot aufglasur	2923 2924 2925 **472**
Lippert & Haas Schlaggenwald 1815–1832 blue underglaze	Lippert & Haas Schlaggenwald 1815–1832 blau unterglasur	2926 **472**
August Haas Schlaggenwald 1847–1867 impressed	August Haas Schlaggenwald 1847–1867 eingeprägt	2927 **472**
G. Greiner & Co. Schauberg (1894)–1927 blue underglaze	G. Greiner & Co. Schauberg (1894)–1927 blau unterglasur	2928 **471**
Richard Sussmuth Immenhausen (1954)– registered for glass and porcelain products	Richard Süssmuth Immenhausen (1954)– registriert für Glas- und Porzellanwaren	2929 **422**
J. Schnabel & Son Dessendorf after 1869–circa 1900	J. Schnabel & Sohn Dessendorf nach 1869–ca. 1900	2930 **393**

S & G	Schiller & Gerbing Bodenbach after 1829–circa 1885 on earthen- and stoneware	Schiller & Gerbing Bodenbach nach 1829–ca. 1885 auf Steingut und Steinzeug	29. 38
S & H S & H	Simon & Halbig Grafenhain circa 1905–circa 1930 impressed on dolls heads	Simon & Halbig Gräfenhain ca. 1905–ca. 1930 eingeprägt auf Puppenköpfen	29. 29. 41(
S & H C.M.B	Simon & Halbig Grafenhain after 1889–circa 1930 impressed on dolls heads	Simon & Halbig Gräfenhain nach 1889–ca. 1930 eingeprägt auf Puppenköpfen	29. 41(
St S & H 1009	Simon & Halbig Grafenhain circa 1905–circa 1930 impressed on dolls heads	Simon & Halbig Gräfenhain ca. 1905–ca. 1930 eingeprägt auf Puppenköpfen	293 41(
S & H WSK	same as 2935	wie 2935	293 410
S + 2	Kronach Porcelain Factory Stockhardt & Schmidt-Eckert Kronach 1912-1996	Kronacher Porzellanfabrik Stockhardt & Schmidt-Eckert Kronach 1912-1996	293 434
J.	Schmidt & Greiner and F. Klaus and Sontag & Birkner Tettau 1794–circa 1885 blue underglaze	Schmidt & Greiner und F. Klaus und Sontag & Birkner Tettau 1794–ca. 1885 blau unterglasur	293 48*
J.	same as 2938	wie 2938	293 487
J.	same as 2938	wie 2938	294 48*
J.	same as 2938	wie 2938	294 487
J.	same as 2938	wie 2938	294 48*

$\mathcal{T}.$	attributed to Unger, Schneider & Cie. Grafenthal but probably Schmidt & Greiner and successors in Tettau blue underglaze 19th century	Unger, Schneider & Cie. Gräfenthal zugeschrieben, aber wahrscheinlich Schmidt & Greiner und Nachfolger in Tettau blau unterglasur 19. Jahrhundert	2943 **411** **487**
$\mathcal{T}$	Franz Josef Mayer Tannawa 1832–1872 blue underglaze	Franz Josef Mayer Tannawa 1832–1872 blau unterglasur	2944 **486**
T	Christian Fischer Zwickau after 1845–	Christian Fischer Zwickau nach 1845–	2945 **508**
TK	Count Thun's Porcelain Factory Klosterle 1830–1893 impressed	Gräflich Thun'sche Porzellanfabrik Klösterle 1830–1893 eingeprägt	2946 **428**
T.P.M.	C. H. Tuppack Tiefenfurth after 1919–1935 also attributed to C. Tielsch Altwasser but questionable	C. H. Tuppack Tiefenfurth nach 1919–1935 auch C. Tielsch in Altwasser zugeschrieben aber zweifelhaft	2947 **488**
T.P.M.	same as 2947	wie 2947	2948 **488**
U. & C.	J. Uffrecht & Co. Haldensleben after 1887–circa 1895 on siderolith and earthenware	J. Uffrecht & Co. Haldensleben nach 1887–ca. 1895 auf Siderolith und Steingut	2949 **415**
U D	Franz Urfuss Dallwitz 1855–1875 impressed	Franz Urfuss Dallwitz 1855–1875 eingeprägt	2950 **391**
V	Peter van Recum Frankenthal 1795 blue underglaze	Peter van Recum Frankenthal 1795 blau unterglasur	2951 **402**

V. U. Vinzenz Unger Turn-Teplitz 1905–circa 1923 | Vinzenz Unger Turn-Teplitz 1905–ca. 1923 | 29 4

V·V Nicolas Villeroy Wallerfangen 1789–1836 impressed | Nicolas Villeroy Wallerfangen 1789–1836 eingeprägt | 29 49

Kampfe & Heubach Wallendorf 1896–circa 1920 | Kämpfe & Heubach Wallendorf 1896–ca. 1920 | 29 49

W. Heubach, Kampfe & Sontag Wallendorf 1887–1896 | Heubach, Kämpfe & Sontag Wallendorf 1887–1896 | 29 49

w Hardtmuth Budweis after 1846– | Hardtmuth Budweis nach 1846– | 29 38

J. W. Hammann Wallendorf 1764–1787 blue underglaze | J. W. Hammann Wallendorf 1764–1787 blau unterglasur | 29 49

same as 2957 | wie 2957 | 29 49

same as 2957 | wie 2957 | 29 49

same as 2957 | wie 2957 | 29 49

same as 2957 | wie 2957 | 29 49

W. Family Hammann Wallendorf 1787–circa 1833 blue underglaze | Familie Hammann Wallendorf 1787–ca. 1833 blau unterglasur | 29 49

W same as 2962 | wie 2962 | 29 49

W same as 2962 | wie 2962 | 29 49

W	same as 2962	wie 2962	2965 **498**
W.	same as 2962	wie 2962	2966 **498**
W	same as 2962	wie 2962	2967 **498**
W	same as 2962	wie 2962	2968 **498**
W	same as 2962	wie 2962	2969 **498**
W.	same as 2962	wie 2962	2970 **498**
W	same as 2962	wie 2962	2971 **498**
W	same as 2962	wie 2962	2972 **498**
W	same as 2962	wie 2962	2973 **498**
W	same as 2962	wie 2962	2974 **498**
	J. W. Hammann Wallendorf 1764–1787 blue underglaze	J. W. Hammann Wallendorf 1764–1787 blau unterglasur	2975 **498**
	Family Hammann Wallendorf 1787–1833 blue underglaze	Familie Hammann Wallendorf 1787–1833 blau unterglasur	2976 **498**
W	W. C. Wegely Berlin 1751–1757 blue underglaze or impressed	W. C. Wegely Berlin 1751–1757 blau unterglasur oder eingeprägt	2977 **383**
W	W. C. Wegely Berlin 1751–1757 blue underglaze	W. C. Wegely Berlin 1751–1757 blau unterglasur	2978 **383**

	English	German	
	same as 2978	wie 2978	29 / 38
	W. C. Wegely / Berlin / 1751–1757 / blue underglaze or impressed	W. C. Wegely / Berlin / 1751–1757 / blau unterglasur oder eingeprägt	29 / 38
	W. C. Wegely / Berlin / 1751–1757 / impressed	W. C. Wegely / Berlin / 1751–1757 / eingeprägt	29 / 38
	W. C. Wegely / Berlin / 1751–1757 / letter W blue underglaze / numbers impressed	W. C. Wegely / Berlin / 1751–1757 / Buchstabe W blau unterglasur / Zahlen eingeprägt	29 / 38
	same as 2982	wie 2982	29 / 38
	same as 2982	wie 2982	29 / 38
	J. C. Geyger / Wurzburg / 1775–1780 / impressed	J. C. Geyger / Würzburg / 1775–1780 / eingeprägt	29 / 50
	same as 2985	wie 2985	29 / 50
	same as 2985	wie 2985	29 / 50
	unidentified / blue underglaze	nicht identifiziert / blau unterglasur	29
	Dojak & Hauschka / Wilhelmsburg / 1814–circa 1843 / on earthenware	Dojak & Hauschka / Wilhelmsburg / 1814–ca. 1943 / auf Steingut	29 / 50
	W. C. Wegely / Berlin / 1751–1757 / blue underglaze	W. C. Wegely / Berlin / 1751–1757 / blau unterglasur	29 / 38

W. G.	Wilhelm Gerike & Co. Althaldensleben (1896)–1921 on siderolith and earthenware	Wilhelm Gerike & Co. Althaldensleben (1896)–1921 auf Siderolith und Steingut	2991 **372**
W. S. & S.	W. Schiller & Son Bodenbach (1895)– impressed	W. Schiller & Sohn Bodenbach (1895)– eingeprägt	2992 **384**
Z	C. I. du Paquier Vienna 1718–1730 impressed	C. I. du Paquier Wien 1718–1730 eingeprägt	2993 **502**
Z.	Jacob Zeidler & Co. Selb (1887)–circa 1917	Jacob Zeidler & Co. Selb (1887)–1917	2994 **480**
A & Bavaria / K	Alboth & Kaiser Staffelstein 1922–circa 1953	Alboth & Kaiser Staffelstein 1922–ca. 1953	2995 **484**
A & K Kronach	same as 2995		2996 **484**
Armand Marseille A 3/0 M Maar	Armand Marseille Koppelsdorf 1891–circa 1933 on dolls heads	Armand Marseille Köppelsdorf 1891–ca. 1933 auf Puppenköpfen	2997 **432**
Armand Marseille Germany A 6 M	Armand Marseille Koppelsdorf circa 1908–circa 1933 impressed on dolls heads	Armand Marseille Köppelsdorf ca. 1908–ca. 1933 eingeprägt auf Puppenköpfen	2998 **432**
Armand Marseille Germany. A 12/0x M.	Armand Marseille Koppelsdorf after 1891–circa 1933 impressed on dolls heads	Armand Marseille Köppelsdorf nach 1891–ca. 1933 eingeprägt auf Puppenköpfen	2999 **432**
mand Marseille . 975 M erman	Armand Marseille Koppelsdorf 1914–circa 1933 impressed on dolls heads	Armand Marseille Köppelsdorf 1914–ca. 1933 eingeprägt auf Puppenköpfen	3000 **432**

Duchess Germany AM	Armand Marseille Koppelsdorf after 1891–circa 1914 impressed on dolls heads	Armand Marseille Köppelsdorf nach 1891–ca. 1914 eingeprägt auf Puppenköpfen
Duchess A.6M. Made in Germany	Armand Marseille Koppelsdorf 1914–1919 impressed on dolls heads	Armand Marseille Köppelsdorf 1914–1919 eingeprägt auf Puppenköpfen
Fany. A 2/0 M.	Armand Marseille Koppelsdorf 1913–circa 1933 on dolls heads	Armand Marseille Köppelsdorf 1913–ca. 1933 auf Puppenköpfen
Florodora A-4-M	Armand Marseille Koppelsdorf 1901–circa 1933 impressed on dolls heads	Armand Marseille Köppelsdorf 1901–ca. 1933 eingeprägt auf Puppenköpfen
Florodora A.M. 5½.DRP.	Armand Marseille Koppelsdorf 1901–circa 1933 impressed on dolls heads	Armand Marseille Köppelsdorf 1901–ca. 1933 eingeprägt auf Puppenköpfen
251 G. B Germany A 2/0 M D.R.G.M. 243/1	Armand Marseille Koppelsdorf after 1891–circa 1908 on dolls heads for importer Geo. Borgfeldt in New York City	Armand Marseille Köppelsdorf nach 1891–ca. 1908 auf Puppenköpfen für Importeur Geo. Borgfeldt in New York
G. 253 B. Germany A 11/0M	Armand Marseille Koppelsdorf circa 1915– on dolls heads for importer Geo. Borgfeldt in New York City	Armand Marseille Köppelsdorf ca. 1915– auf Puppenköpfen für Importeur Geo. Borgfeldt in New York
Just ME. Registered. Germany A 310/7/0. M.	Armand Marseille Koppelsdorf after 1891–circa 1928 impressed on dolls heads	Armand Marseille Köppelsdorf nach 1891–ca. 1928 eingeprägt auf Puppenköpfen
Germany Kiddieioy 372 A 1.M	Armand Marseille Koppelsdorf 1922–circa 1933 impressed on dolls heads	Armand Marseille Köppelsdorf 1922–ca. 1933 eingeprägt auf Puppenköpfen

Arthur Pohlmann	Arthur Pöhlmann		
Meissen	Meißen		
1945-1958	1945-1958		
decorator´s mark	Malermarke	3010	
overglaze	aufglasur	**448**	

C. Alfred Romhild	C. Alfred Römhild		
Grossbreitenbach	Großbreitenbach		
after 1914–1972	nach 1914–1972		
decorator's mark	Malermarke	3011	
overglaze	aufglasur	**413**	

Benjamin F. Hunt & Sons	Benjamin F. Hunt & Sons	
Boston, Mass.	Boston, Mass.	3012
Mark of U.S. importer	Marke eines US-Importeurs	**400**

C. K. Weithase	C. K. Weithase	
Volkstedt	Volkstedt	
after 1897–	nach 1897–	3013
decorator's mark	Malermarke	**497**

Simon & Halbig	Simon & Halbig	
Grafenhain	Gräfenhain	
1889–circa 1930	1889–ca. 1930	
on dolls heads made	auf Puppenköpfen	
for C. M. Bergmann in	für C. M. Bergmann	3014
Waltershausen	in Waltershausen	**410**

VEB Porcelain Combine Colditz	VEB Porzellankombinat Colditz	
Colditz	Colditz	
(1958)-1990	(1958)-1990	3015
green underglaze or overglaze	grün unterglasur oder aufglasur	**391**

Epiag	Epiag	
Dallwitz	Dallwitz	3016
1920–1945	1920–1945	**391**

Epiag	Epiag	
Dallwitz	Dallwitz	3017
1939–1945	1939–1945	**391**

E. Dorfner & Cie.	E. Dorfner & Cie.	
Hirschau	Hirschau	3018
(1896)–circa 1919	(1896)–ca. 1919	**417**

Ernst Heubach	Ernst Heubach	
Koppelsdorf	Köppelsdorf	
after 1887–1919	nach 1887–1919	3019
impressed on dolls heads	eingeprägt auf Puppenköpfen	**432**

341

	Bros. Metzler & Ortloff	Gebr. Metzler & Ortloff	
Metzler 890 E 8 M	Ilmenau	Ilmenau	
	circa 1890	ca. 1890	30
	impressed on dolls heads	eingeprägt auf Puppenköpfen	42

	Ebeling & Reuss	Ebeling & Reuss	
ERPHILA CZECHOSLOVAKIA ... MADE IN GERMANY	Devon/Philadelphia, Pa.	Devon/Philadelphia	
	circa 1939	ca. 1939	30
	importer's mark	Importeurmarke	39

	Ebeling & Reuss	Ebeling & Reuss	
ERPHILA	Devon/Philadelphia, Pa.	Devon/Philadelphia	
	after 1920–circa 1940	nach 1920–ca. 1940	30
	importer's mark	Importeurmarke	39

	Erdmann Schlegelmilch	Erdmann Schlegelmilch	
PRUSSIA	Suhl	Suhl	30
	after 1900–circa 1938	nach 1900–ca. 1938	48

	Franz Anton Mehlem	Franz Anton Mehlem	
	Bonn	Bonn	
	(1887)–1920	(1887)–1920	30
	blue or brown	blau oder braun	38

	Vienna Manufactory	Wiener Manufaktur	
VINDOBONA F. G.	F. Goldscheider	F. Goldscheider	
	Vienna	Wien	30
	after 1885–	nach 1885–	50

	J. F. Lenz	J. F. Lenz	
F4H	Zell on Harmersbach	Zell am Harmersbach	
	circa 1819–1840	ca. 1819–1840	30
ZELL	impressed on earthenware	eingeprägt auf Steingut	50

	Franz Prause	Franz Prause	
FP Nd. Salzbrunn	Niedersalzbrunn	Niedersalzbrunn	30
	circa 1900–circa 1936	ca. 1900–ca. 1936	4

	United Porcelain Factories	Vereinigte Porzellanfabriken	
Deutschland	Meierhofen	Meierhöfen	30
	1939–1945	1939–1945	44

same as 3028		3029
		445
Georg Schmider	Georg Schmider	
Zell on Harmersbach	Zell am Harmersbach	
circa 1930–present	ca. 1930–heute	3030
on earthenware	auf Steingut	**507**
Vienna Manufactory	Wiener Manufaktur	
F. Goldscheider	F. Goldscheider	
Vienna	Wien	3031
(1937)–circa 1941	(1937)–ca. 1941	**503**
Porcelain Factory Kolmar	Porzellanfabrik Kolmar	
Kolmar	Kolmar	3032
circa 1897–1944	ca. 1897–1944	**432**
Hertel, Jacob & Co.	Hertel, Jacob & Co.	
Rehau	Rehau	
after 1922–	nach 1922–	3033
green underglaze	grün unterglasur	**466**
Franz Josef Mayer	Franz Josef Mayer	
Tannawa	Tannawa	
1840–1872	1840–1872	3034
impressed	eingeprägt	**486**
Hermann Steiner	Hermann Steiner	
Sonneberg	Sonneberg	
1921–	1921–	3035
impressed on dolls heads	eingeprägt auf Puppenköpfen	**482**
same as 3035	wie 3035	3036
		482
Hans Schrembs	Hans Schrembs	
Erbendorf	Erbendorf	3037
1923–1940	1923–1940	**400**
J. D. Kestner & Co.	J. D. Kestner & Co.	
Ohrdruf	Ohrdruf	
circa 1892–circa 1930	ca. 1892–ca. 1930	3038
impressed on dolls heads	eingeprägt auf Puppenköpfen	**459**
Thomas Recknagel	Thomas Recknagel	
Alexandrinenthal	Alexandrinenthal	
circa 1924–circa 1934	ca. 1924–ca. 1934	
on dolls heads made for	auf Puppenköpfen für	
Louis Amberg & Son in	Louis Amberg & Son in	3039
New York City	New York	**371**

L & R GERMANY	unidentified gold overglaze	nicht identifiziert gold aufglasur	3
MITTERTEICH BAVARIA	Porcelain Factory Mitterteich Mitterteich after 1945–	Porzellanfabrik Mitterteich Mitterteich nach 1945–	3 4
Taubenbach	Carl Moritz Taubenbach –circa 1930	Carl Moritz Taubenbach –ca. 1930	3 48
M Z Altrohlau CMR CZECHOSLOVAKIA	Altrohlau Porcelain Factories Altrohlau 1918–1939 green underglaze	Altrohlauer Porzellanfabriken Altrohlau 1918–1939 grün unterglasur	30 3
Altrohlau **M.Z.**	Moritz Zdekauer Altrohlau 1884–circa 1909	Moritz Zdekauer Altrohlau 1884–ca. 1909	30 3
	Engineer Ludwig Neumann Frauenthal 1921–circa 1930	Ing. Ludwig Neumann Frauenthal 1921–ca. 1930	30 40
NGF. **GIESSHÜBEL**	W. von Neuberg Giesshubel 1846–circa 1892 impressed	W. von Neuberg Gießhübel 1846–ca. 1892 eingeprägt	30 40
N & H **PRAG**	attributed to Hubel & Co. Hubel & Co. Prague but questionable after 1800 impressed on earthenware	Hübel & Co. Prag zugeschrieben, aber fraglich nach 1800 eingeprägt auf Steingut	30 46
ND NEUTETTAU	New Porcelain Factory Tettau and Gerold & Co. Tettau 1935–1948 green underglaze or gold overglaze	Neue Porzellanfabrik Tettau und Gerold & Co. Tettau 1935–1948 grün unterglasur oder gold aufglasur	30 48
	New Porcelain Factory Tettau Tettau 1923–1937 green underglaze or gold overglaze	Neue Porzellanfabrik Tettau Tettau 1923–1937 grün unterglasur oder gold aufglasur	30 48

P.M. Grete 2/0	Porcelain Factory Moschendorf Hof-Moschendorf after 1878–circa 1938 impressed on dolls heads	Porzellanfabrik Moschendorf Hof-Moschendorf nach 1878–ca. 1938 eingeprägt auf Puppenköpfen	3050 **419**
PM 23 Germany 2	Porcelain Factory Moschendorf Hof-Moschendorf 1891–circa 1938 impressed on dolls heads	Porzellanfabrik Moschendorf Hof-Moschendorf 1891–ca. 1938 eingeprägt auf Puppenköpfen	3051 **419**
PM 914. Germany	Pocelain Factory Moschendorf Hof-Moschendorf after 1891–circa 1938 impressed on dolls heads	Porzellanfabrik Moschendorf Hof-Moschendorf nach 1891–ca. 1938 eingeprägt auf Puppenköpfen	3052 **419**
PM Harmus	Porcelain Factory Moschendorf Hof-Moschendorf after 1878– impressed on dolls heads made for Carl Harmus in Sonneberg	Porzellanfabrik Moschendorf Hof-Moschendorf nach 1878– eingeprägt auf Puppenköpfen für Carl Harmus in Sonneberg	3053 **419**
PM Harmus	same as 3053	wie 3053	3054 **419**
Tschech Sl.	Porcelain Factory Merkelsgrun Merkelsgrun 1918–1939	Porzellanfabrik Merkelsgrün Merkelsgrün 1918–1939	3055 **448**
ARS·NOVA SCHLACKEN WERTH	Pfeiffer & Lowenstein Schlackenwerth (1920)–1941	Pfeiffer & Löwenstein Schlackenwerth (1920)–1941	3056 **472**
PROBSTZELLA	VEB Porcelain Factory Probstzella Probstzella (1954)–1968	VEB Porzellanfabrik Probstzella Probstzella (1954)–1968	3057 **464**
Pot chappel	Saxonian Porcelain Factory Carl Thieme and VEB Saxonian Porcelain Manufactory Dresden Potschappel (1913)-1990	Sächsische Porzellanfabrik Carl Thieme und VEB Sächsische Porzellanmanufaktur Dresden Potschappel 1930-1990	3058 **463**

Saxonian Porcelain Factory Carl Thieme and VEB Saxonian Porcelain Manufactory Dresden Potschappel 1901–present blue	Sächsische Porzellanfabrik Carl Thieme und VEB Sächsische Porzellan-Manufaktur Dresden Potschappel 1901–heute blau	3(46
Saxonian Porcelain Factory Carl Thieme and VEB Saxonian Porcelain Manufactory Dresden Potschappel (1961)–present blue	Sächsische Porzellanfabrik Carl Thieme und VEB Sächsische Porzellan-manufaktur Dresden Potschappel (1961)–heute blau	30 46
Paul Muller Selb 1890–1917 green underglaze	Paul Müller Selb 1890–1917 grün unterglasur	3(48
Porcelain Factory Swabia Schwaben 1921–1929	Porzellanfabrik Schwaben Schwaben 1921–1929	30 47
Porcelain Factory Stadtlengsfeld Stadtlengsfeld 1909–circa 1945	Porzellanfabrik Stadtlengsfeld Stadtlengsfeld 1909–ca. 1945	30 48
Porcelain Factory Tirschenreuth Tirschenreuth (1969)–present	Porzellanfabrik Tirschenreuth Tirschenreuth (1969)–heute	30 48
Thomas Recknagel Alexandrinenthal after 1891–circa 1934 impressed on dolls heads	Thomas Recknagel Alexandrinenthal nach 1891–ca. 1934 eingeprägt auf Puppenköpfen	30 37
Chr. Carstens Rheinsberg after 1901–circa 1945 on earthenware	Chr. Carstens Rheinsberg nach 1901–ca. 1945 auf Steingut	30 467
Richter, Fenkl & Hahn Chodau 1918–1939	Richter, Fenkl & Hahn Chodau 1918–1939	306 389

Richter, Fenkl & Hahn Chodau 1939–1945	Richter, Fenkl & Hahn Chodau 1939–1945	3068 **389**
Hans Richter Volkstedt circa 1923–circa 1950 decorator's mark	Hans Richter Volkstedt ca. 1923–ca. 1950 Malermarke	3069 **496**
Reinhold Schlegelmilch Tillowitz after 1932–circa 1938 green	Reinhold Schlegelmilch Tillowitz nach 1932–ca. 1938 grün	3070 **489**
Rudolf Wachter Kirchenlamitz after 1919– decorator's mark	Rudolf Wächter Kirchenlamitz nach 1919– Malermarke	3071 **427**
Richard Wolfram Wiesau after 1899–	Richard Wolfram Wiesau nach 1899–	3072 **504**
Oscar Schaller & Co. Schwarzenbach (1892)–circa 1918	Oscar Schaller & Co. Schwarzenbach (1892)–ca. 1918	3073 **477**
Porcelain Factory Muhlbach Bruchmuhlbach 1951–circa 1970	Porzellanfabrik Mühlbach Bruchmühlbach 1951–ca. 1970	3074 **386**
Karl Seiler Gorzke (1953)–	Karl Seiler Görzke (1953)–	3075 **409**
Clayware Factory Schwandorf Schwandorf (1955)–circa 1972 on earthenware and stoneware	Tonwarenfabrik Schwandorf Schwandorf (1955)–ca. 1972 auf Steingut und Steinzeug	3076 **477**
Simon & Halbig Grafenhain circa 1905–circa 1930 impressed on dolls heads	Simon & Halbig Gräfenhain ca. 1905–ca. 1930 eingeprägt auf Puppenköpfen	3077 **410**

347

SIMON & HALBIG S & H 550 Germany G	Simon & Halbig Grafenhain after 1891–circa 1930 impressed on dolls heads	Simon & Halbig Gräfenhain nach 1891–ca. 1930 30 eingeprägt auf Puppenköpfen 41
SIMON & HALBIG S & H	Simon & Halbig Grafenhain 1900–circa 1930 impressed on dolls heads	Simon & Halbig Gräfenhain 1900–ca. 1930 30 eingeprägt auf Puppenköpfen 41
S & H 1079-6 DEP. Germany	Simon & Halbig Grafenhain circa 1896–circa 1930 impressed on dolls heads	Simon & Halbig Gräfenhain ca. 1896–ca. 1930 30 eingeprägt auf Puppenköpfen 41
S H 1249 DEP. Germany 12 SANTA	Simon & Halbig Grafenhain circa 1901–circa 1930 impressed on dolls heads	Simon & Halbig Gräfenhain ca. 1901–ca. 1930 30 eingeprägt auf Puppenköpfen 41
1849 Jutta S & H	Simon & Halbig Grafenhain 1907–circa 1930 impressed on dolls heads	Simon & Halbig Gräfenhain 1907–ca. 1930 30 eingeprägt auf Puppenköpfen 41
CHINA BLAU	Porcelain Factory Saxonia Haldensleben (1928)–1932 blue	Porzellanfabrik Saxonia Haldensleben (1928)–1932 30 blau 41
S. u. P. Dresden.	Strobel & Petschke Dresden (1894)– decorator's mark overglaze	Strobel & Petschke Dresden (1894)– Malermarke 30 aufglasur 49
Orla T Porzellan	Unger & Gretschel and Triptis AG Triptis after 1891–	Unger & Gretschel und Triptis AG Triptis 30 nach 1891– 48
U DALWITZ	Franz Urfuss Dallwitz 1855–1875 impressed	Franz Urfuss Dallwitz 1855–1875 30 eingeprägt 39

VEB Decorative and Promotional Porcelain Ilmenau 1953–1972	VEB Zier- und Werbeporzellan Ilmenau 1953–1972	3087 **422**
Friedrich Wilhelm Wessel Frankenthal 1949–before 1964	Friedrich Wilhelm Wessel Frankenthal 1949–vor 1964	3088 **402**
Johann Haviland Waldershof 1910–1924 green underglaze	Johann Haviland Waldershof 1910–1924 grün unterglasur	3089 **498**
Porcelain Factory Waldershof Waldershof 1924–1936 green	Porzellanfabrik Waldershof Waldershof 1924–1936 grün	3090 **498**
Wilhelm Koch Dresden circa 1928–1949 decorator's mark overglaze	Wilhelm Koch Dresden ca. 1928–1949 Malermarke aufglasur	3091 **395**
Otto Hadrich's Widow Reichenbach –circa 1950 decorator's mark overglaze	Otto Hädrichs Witwe Reichenbach –ca. 1950 Malermarke aufglasur	3092 **466**
Family Hammann Wallendorf 1787–circa 1833 blue underglaze	Familie Hammann Wallendorf 1787–ca. 1833 blau unterglasur	3093 **498**
Ernst Wahliss Turn-Teplitz circa 1894–circa 1921	Ernst Wahliss Turn-Teplitz ca. 1894–ca. 1921	3094 **491**
W. W. Lorenz Dallwitz 1832–1850 impressed	W. W. Lorenz Dallwitz 1832–1850 eingeprägt	3095 **391**
Johann Moehling Aich 1849–1860 impressed	Johann Moehling Aich 1849–1860 eingeprägt	3096 3097 **371**

Albego	Alt, Beck & Gottschalck Nauendorf (1929)–1953	Alt, Beck & Gottschalck Nauendorf (1929)–1953	3(4.
Amberg | Amberg	Eduard Kick Amberg 1850–1910	Eduard Kick Amberg 1850–1910	3(3 3'
AMBERG	Eduard Kick Amberg 1880–1910	Eduard Kick Amberg 1880–1910	3 3'
ANNA PERENNA	Anna Perenna, Inc. Klaus D. Vogt New York City/Stuttgart 1977- importer´s mark	Anna Perenna, Inc. Klaus D. Voigt New York/Stuttgart 1977- Importeurmarke	31 45
Antibut	H. Schomburg & Sons Berlin (1902)–circa 1922	H. Schomburg & Söhne Berlin (1902)–ca. 1922	3 3 3
APOMA	Hanns Graf Sonthofen 1951–1964 blue	Hanns Graf Sonthofen 1951–1964 blau	31 48
ARSNOVA	Pfeiffer & Lowenstein Schlackenwerth (1920)–1941	Pfeiffer & Löwenstein Schlackenwerth (1920)–1941	31 47
Arzberg	Porcelain Factory Arzberg Arzberg 1947–1970 green underglaze	Porzellanfabrik Arzberg Arzberg 1947–1970 grün unterglasur	31 37
Askania-Blau	Porcelain Factory Kahla Kahla (1931)–1945 blue	Porzellanfabrik Kahla Kahla (1931)–1945 blau	31 42
August der Starke	Porcelain Factories Josef Rieber & Co. Mitterteich (1936)–	Porzellanfabriken Josef Rieber & Co. Mitterteich (1936)–	31 44
BABY PHYLLIS Made in Germany 2 4014	Armand Marseille Koppelsdorf after 1891–1915 impressed on dolls heads	Armand Marseille Köppelsdorf nach 1891–1915 eingeprägt auf Puppenköpfen	31(43

Basdorf z.	Bros. Schackert Basdorf 1751–before 1780	Gebr. Schackert Basdorf 1751–vor 1780	3110 **378**
Bauscher Elfenbein	Porcelain Factory Weiden Bros. Bauscher Weiden circa 1920–circa 1948 green underglaze	Porzellanfabrik Weiden Gebr. Bauscher Weiden ca. 1920–ca. 1948 grün unterglasur	3111 **500**
BAUSCHER WEIDEN	Porcelain Factory Weiden Bros. Bauscher Weiden 1912–circa 1923 green underglaze	Porzellanfabrik Weiden Gebr. Bauscher Weiden 1912–ca. 1923 grün unterglasur	3112 **500**
BAVARIAN	unidentified gold overglaze	nicht identifiziert gold aufglasur	3113
BAY. KERAMIK	Eduard Bay Ransbach presently	Eduard Bay Ransbach heute	3114 **464**
Boch et Buschmann a Mettlach	Boch & Buschmann Mettlach 1813–1825 impressed on earthenware	Boch & Buschmann Mettlach 1813–1825 eingeprägt auf Steingut	3115 **449**
Boch Buschmann a Mettlach I.	same as 3115	wie 3115	3116 **449**
Bonna	Ludwig Wessel Bonn (1905)–	Ludwig Wessel Bonn (1905)–	3117 **385**
BRAM MER MALER	E. Brammer Dresden 1904–1923 decorator's mark overglaze	E. Brammer Dresden 1904–1923 Malermarke aufglasur	3118 **393**
Brüder Haidinger.	R. & E. Haidinger Elbogen circa 1815–1850	R. & E. Haidinger Elbogen ca. 1815–1850	3119 **399**
CARL KNOLL CARLSBAD	Carl Knoll Fischern 1848–1868 impressed	Carl Knoll Fischern 1848–1868 eingeprägt	3120 **402**

CARLSBAD	Carl Knoll Fischern 1848–1868 impressed	Carl Knoll Fischern 1848–1868 eingeprägt	3 4
CERANOVA	Oscar Schaller & Co. Successor Windischeschenbach (1977)–present	Oscar Schaller & Co. Nachf. Windischeschenbach (1977)–heute	3 5
„Charlotte von Stein"	Rosenthal Selb (1932)–	Rosenthal Selb (1932)–	31 48
Chodau	Geitner & Stierba Chodau 1845–circa 1850 impressed	Geitner & Stierba Chodau 1845–ca. 1850 eingeprägt	31 38
CLASSIC	Charles L. Dwenger New York City 1912– importer's mark	Charles L. Dwenger New York 1912– Importeurmarke	31 45
C.M. BERGMANN SIMON & HALBIG	Simon & Halbig Grafenhain after 1889–circa 1930 impressed on dolls heads made for C. M. Bergmann in Waltershausen	Simon & Halbig Gräfenhain nach 1889–ca. 1930 eingeprägt auf Puppenköpfen für C. M. Bergmann in Waltershausen	31 41
CORA-FLOR	Eduard Bay Ransbach (1978)–present	Eduard Bay Ransbach (1978)–heute	31 46
CORONET	Geo. Borgfeldt Corp. New York City 1902– importer's mark	Geo. Borgfeldt Corp. New York 1902– Importeurmarke	31 45
CORONET	Geo. Borgfeldt Corp. New York City (1907)– importer's mark	Geo. Borgfeldt Corp. New York (1907)– Importeurmarke	31 45
„Cremer Nippes"	Engelbert Cremer & Son Cologne circa 1793–circa 1800 impressed	Engelbert Cremer & Sohn Köln ca. 1793–ca. 1800 eingeprägt	31 42

CROWN	Donath & Co. Dresden (1903)–1916 decorator's mark overglaze	Donath & Co. Dresden (1903)–1916 Malermarke aufglasur	3131 **394**
Cyclop	Franz Anton Mehlem Bonn (1900)–1920	Franz Anton Mehlem Bonn (1900)–1920	3132 **385**
Czechoslavikia	unidentified green underglaze circa 1918–1939 note misspelling	nicht identifiziert grün unterglasur ca. 1918–1939 beachte falsche Schreibweise	3133
„CZECHOSLOWAKIA"	Bros. Pohle & Co. Taschwitz 1918–1939	Gebr. Pohle & Co. Taschwitz 1918–1939	3134 **486**
DALWITZ	W. von Schoenau and W. W. Lorenz Dallwitz circa 1830–1850 impressed	W. von Schoenau und W. W. Lorenz Dallwitz ca. 1830–1850 eingeprägt	3135 **391**
DAMASKINE	Geo. Borgfeldt Corp. New York City 1933– importer's mark	Geo. Borgfeldt Corp. New York 1933– Importeurmarke	3136 **454**
DIANA	Geo. Borgfeldt Corp. New York City 1926– importer's mark	Geo. Borgfeldt Corp. New York 1926– Importeurmarke	3137 **454**
Edelstein BAVARIA	Edelstein Porcelain Factory Kups 1931– green underglaze	Edelstein Porzellanfabrik Küps 1931– grün unterglasur	3138 **435**
'Eng. Cremer u. Sohn in Cöln a. R."	Engelbert Cremer & Son Cologne circa 1793–circa 1800 impressed	Engelbert Cremer & Sohn Köln ca. 1793–ca. 1800 eingeprägt	3139 **429**
Ens	Karl Ens Volkstedt 1900–circa 1945	Karl Ens Volkstedt 1900–ca. 1945	3140 **496**

ENS UARANY	Karl Ens Volkstedt 1927–circa 1945	Karl Ens Volkstedt 1927–ca. 1945	31 49
EPIAG	Epiag Karlsbad 1920–1945	Epiag Karlsbad 1920–1945	31 42
Epiag Aich Made in Cechoslowakia	Epiag Aich 1922–1939 green underglaze	Epiag Aich 1922–1939 grün unterglasur	31 37
E PIAG Made in CZECHO-SLOVAKIA	Epiag Altrohlau 1920–1939 green underglaze	Epiag Altrohlau 1920–1939 grün unterglasur	31 37
Erdmann Schlegelmilch 1861 Prussia	Erdmann Schlegelmilch Suhl after 1891–	Erdmann Schlegelmilch Suhl nach 1891–	31 48
Erdmann Schlegelmilch Suhl Prussia	same as 3145	wie 3145	31 48
Erdmann Schlegelmilch Thuringia Handpainted	same as 3145	wie 3145	31 48
E. Schlegelmilch Germany	Erdmann Schlegelmilch Suhl after 1891– green	Erdmann Schlegelmilch Suhl nach 1891– grün	31 48
FASOLD&STAUCH	Fasold & Stauch Bock-Wallendorf 1962–circa 1972	Fasold & Stauch Bock-Wallendorf 1962–ca. 1972	31 38
Filigrette	Hertwig & Co. Katzhutte (1915)–	Hertwig & Co. Katzhütte (1915)–	31 42
Fürstenberg GALERIE	Furstenberg Porcelain Manufactory Furstenberg (1963)–	Fürstenberg Porzellanmanufaktur Fürstenberg (1963)–	31 40
Gebr. Heubach Germany	Bros. Heubach Lichte after 1900– impressed on dolls heads	Gebr. Heubach Lichte nach 1900– eingeprägt auf Puppenköpfen	31 43

Gemmo

Heinrich & Co.
Selb
(1949)–

Heinrich & Co.
Selb
(1949)–

3153
479

Gera

Widow Greiner & Leers
Gera
1804–circa 1840
blue underglaze or
red overglaze

Witwe Greiner & Leers
Gera
1804–ca. 1840
blau unterglasur oder
rot aufglasur

3154
407

GIESHUEBL

Franz Lehnert
Giesshubel
1840–1846
impressed

Franz Lehnert
Gießhübel
1840–1846
eingeprägt

3155
408

Gotha.

Fr. Eg. Henneberg
Gotha
1805–1834
blue underglaze or
black or red overglaze

Fr. Eg. Henneberg
Gotha
1805–1834
blau unterglasur oder
schwarz oder rot aufglasur

3156
409

HAËL

Hael Workshops
Marwitz
(1929)–1934

Hael Werkstätten
Marwitz
(1929)–1934

3157
445

Haidinger

R. & E. Haidinger
Elbogen
circa 1815–1873

R. & E. Haidinger
Elbogen
ca. 1815–1873

3158
399

Germany
HANDWERCK
HALBIG

Simon & Halbig
Grafenhain
after 1891–circa 1930
impressed on dolls heads
made for H. Handwerck in
Walterhausen

Simon & Halbig
Gräfenhain
nach 1891–ca. 1930
eingeprägt auf Puppenköpfen
für H. Handwerck in
Waltershausen

3159
410

Germany
HEINRICH
HANDWERCK
HALBIG

same as 3159

wie 3159

3160
410

Handgemalt
Adolf Hoffmann
Osnabrück

Adolf Hoffmann
Osnabruck
1938–1971
decorator's mark
overglaze

Adolf Hoffmann
Osnabrück
1938–1971
Malermarke
aufglasur

3161
460

Handmalerei
Edwin Hoffmann
Osnabrück

Edwin Hoffmann
Osnabruck
1950–1977
decorator's mark
overglaze

Edwin Hoffmann
Osnabrück
1950–1977
Malermarke
aufglasur

3162
460

Hanika VOLKSTEDT	Alfred Hanika Volkstedt 1931–circa 1945 decorator's mark overglaze	Alfred Hanika Volkstedt 1931–ca. 1945 Malermarke aufglasur	3] 49
HARDMUTH	Hardtmuth Budweis 1846–	Hardtmuth Budweis 1846–	3] 38
Heinrich	Franz Heinrich and Heinrich & Co. Selb (1911)–	Franz Heinrich und Heinrich & Co. Selb (1911)–	3] 47
Heinrich	Heinrich & Co. Selb (1950)–	Heinrich & Co. Selb (1950)–	31 47
Heinrich **Gemmo** PORZELLAN	Heinrich & Co. Selb (1950)–	Heinrich & Co. Selb (1950)–	31 47
Herbena	Hermann Behne Berlin (1913)–	Hermann Behne Berlin (1913)–	3] 38
Hertwig	Kirsch & Hertwig Lenggries 1971–present green underglaze	Kirsch & Hertwig Lenggries 1971–heute grün unterglasur	3] 43
Hertwig LENGGRIES	same as 3169	wie 3169	3 4
Heubach·Köppelsdorf.	Ernst Heubach Koppelsdorf after 1887–1919 impressed on dolls heads	Ernst Heubach Köppelsdorf nach 1887–1919 eingeprägt auf Puppenköpfen	3 4
Heubach 250·5 Köppelsdorf	same as 3171		3 4
HEUBACH-KÖPPELSDORF 322 - 17/0 Germany	Ernst Heubach Koppelsdorf after 1891–1919 impressed on dolls heads	Ernst Heubach Köppelsdorf nach 1891–1919 eingeprägt auf Puppenköpfen	3 4

HORNBERG	Bros. Horn Hornberg circa 1830–circa 1860 impressed on earthenware	Gebr. Horn Hornberg ca. 1830–ca. 1860 eingeprägt auf Steingut	3174 **420**
Hübel in Prag.	Hubel & Co. Prague circa 1800–1835 impressed on earthenware	Hübel & Co. Prag ca. 1800–1835 eingeprägt auf Steingut	3175 **463**
HUTSCHENREUTHER ALTROHLAU HABSBURG PORCELAIN	Altrohlau Porcelain Factories Altrohlau circa 1909–1918 green underglaze	Altrohlauer Porzellanfabriken Altrohlau ca. 1909–1918 grün unterglasur	3176 **373**
Jäger	W. Jager Eisenberg after 1900–	W. Jäger Eisenberg nach 1900–	3177 **398**
J.FERESCH	J. Feresch Klum 1800–1850 impressed	J. Feresch Klum 1800–1850 eingeprägt	3178 **429**
J. Feresch	same as 3178	wie 3178	3179 **429**
J.F.LENZ ZELL	J. F. Lenz Zell on Harmersbach after 1842–circa 1869	J. F. Lenz Zell am Harmersbach nach 1842–ca. 1869	3180 **507**
J.F. LENZ ZELL	J. F. Lenz & Burger Zell on Harmersbach circa 1809–1819 on earthenware	J. F. Lenz & Burger Zell am Harmersbach ca. 1809–1819 auf Steingut	3181 **507**
John Haviland BAVARIA	Porcelain Factory Waldershof Waldershof 1924–1938 green underglaze or green or red or brown overglaze	Porzellanfabrik Waldershof Waldershof 1924–1938 grün unterglasur oder grün oder rot oder braun aufglasur	3182 **498**
John Haviland BAVARIA	Johann Haviland and Porcelain Factory Waldershof Waldershof 1912–1938 green underglaze or green or red overglaze	Johann Haviland und Porzellanfabrik Waldershof Waldershof 1912–1938 grün unterglasur oder grün oder rot aufglasur	3183 **498**

Mark			
BAVARIA J.Rieber.Co. SELB-MITTERTEICH	Josef Rieber & Co. Mitterteich circa 1918–1923	Josef Rieber & Co. Mitterteich ca. 1918–1923	3 4
KAHLA	Porcelain Factory Kahla Kahla (1927)–1945	Porzellanfabrik Kahla Kahla (1927)–1945	3 4
„Kaiserlieblingsblumen-Dekors"	Porcelain Factory Fraureuth Fraureuth (1914)–1918 overglaze	Porzellanfabrik Fraureuth Fraureuth (1914)–1918 aufglasur	3 4
Kaiser-Porzellan	Heinrich & Co. Selb (1911)–circa 1918	Heinrich & Co. Selb (1911)–ca. 1918	3 4
Kerambleu	Leonhard van Hees Saarbrucken (1911)– decorator's mark	Leonhard van Hees Saarbrücken (1911)– Malermarke	3 4
KEWPIE	Geo. Borgfeldt Corp. New York City 1913– importer's mark	Geo. Borgfeldt Corp. New York 1913– Importeurmarke	3 4
Klentsch	Josef Mayer Klentsch circa 1847–1889 impressed	Josef Mayer Klentsch ca. 1847–1889 eingeprägt	3 4
KLUM	J. Feresch Klum 1800–1850 impressed	J. Feresch Klum 1800–1850 eingeprägt	3 4
KODAU	J. Huttner & Co. Chodau 1834–1845 impressed	J. Hüttner & Co. Chodau 1834–1845 eingeprägt	3 3
KÖLN	Engelbert Cremer & Son Cologne circa 1793–circa 1800 impressed	Engelbert Cremer & Sohn Köln ca. 1793–ca. 1800 eingeprägt	3 4

KOH I NOOR	Bros. Sattler Budweis about 1930 decorator's mark	Gebr. Sattler Budweis um 1930 Malermarke	3194 **388**
Krohberg Canon Hild 1778	J. G. Kratzberg Hildesheim 1778 decorator's mark overglaze	J. G. Kratzberg Hildesheim 1778 Malermarke aufglasur	3195 **417**
K&A Krautheim SELB BAVARIA	Krautheim & Adelberg Selb (1922)–1945	Krautheim & Adelberg Selb (1922)–1945	3196 **479**
VORM. KGL. BAYR. HOFLIEFERANTEN K&A Krautheim SELB BAVARIA GERMANY SISSY	Krautheim & Adelberg Selb 1977–present green underglaze	Krautheim & Adelberg Selb 1977–heute grün unterglasur	3197 **479**
K&A Krautheim SELB BAVARIA GERMANY	Krautheim & Adelberg Selb 1945–present green underglaze	Krautheim & Adelberg Selb 1945–heute grün unterglasur	3198 **479**
Krister	Krister Porcelain Manufactory Landstuhl (1952)–	Krister Porzellanmanufaktur Landstuhl (1952)–	3199 **436**
KRON	Donath & Co. Dresden (1903)–1916 decorator's mark blue	Donath & Co. Dresden (1903)–1916 Malermarke blau	3200 **394**
Kronen-C	Porcelain Factory Cortendorf Coburg-Cortendorf (1956)–1973	Porzellanfabrik Cortendorf Coburg-Cortendorf (1956)–1973	3201 **390**
LEONARD VIENNA.	P. H. Leonard New York City 　–circa 1917 importer's mark	P. H. Leonard New York 　–ca. 1917 Importeurmarke	3202 **455**
Lore	Heinrich Winterling Marktleuthen (1934)–	Heinrich Winterling Marktleuthen (1934)–	3203 **444**

MADE IN THURINGIA	unidentified gold overglaze	nicht identifiziert gold aufglasur	3
Mäbendorf	Matthes & Ebel Mabendorf 1919–1928	Matthes & Ebel Mäbendorf 1919–1928	3 4
Magie	Rosenthal Selb (1951)–	Rosenthal Selb (1951)–	3 4
MARKE *Krautheim* PORZELLAN	Krautheim & Adelberg Selb (1953)– green underglaze	Krautheim & Adelberg Selb (1953)– grün unterglasur	3 4
Marmorzellan	Galluba & Hofmann Ilmenau (1905)–circa 1927	Galluba & Hofmann Ilmenau (1905)–ca. 1927	3 4
Meissen	VEB State's Porcelain Manufactory Meissen (1972)– blue	VEB Staatliche Porzellan Manufaktur Meißen (1972)– blau	3 4
MEISSEN	Meissen Stove and Porcelain Factory C. Teichert Meissen circa 1882–circa 1925 blue underglaze or impressed	Meißner Ofen- und Porzellanfabrik C. Teichert Meißen ca. 1882–ca. 1925 blau unterglasur oder eingeprägt	3 4
Mettlacher Hartsteingut	Villeroy & Boch Mettlach before 1836–circa 1850 impressed on earthenware	Villeroy & Boch Mettlach vor 1836–ca. 1850 eingeprägt auf Steingut	3 4
Mosanic	The Mosanic Pottery and Porcelain Factory Mitterteich Mitterteich (1895)–after 1928	The Mosanic Pottery und Porzellanfabrik Mitterteich Mitterteich (1895)–nach 1928	3 4
MOSANIC	same as 3212	wie 3212	3 4
Neumark	Anton Fischer Neumark after 1833–circa 1905 on earthenware	Anton Fischer Neumark nach 1833–ca. 1905 auf Steingut	3 4

NOWOTNY.	August Nowotny Altrohlau 1823–1884 impressed	August Nowotny Altrohlau 1823–1884 eingeprägt	3215 **373**
NOWOTNY ALTROHLAU	August Nowotny Altrohlau 1838–1884 impressed	August Nowotny Altrohlau 1838–1884 eingeprägt	3216 **373**
NoWoTNy IN ALTENROLAV BEY CARLSBAD XX IX	August Nowotny Altrohlau 1823–1838 impressed on earthenware	August Nowotny Altrohlau 1823–1838 eingeprägt auf Steingut	3217 **373**
NOWOTNY IN ALTENROHLAU BEY KARLSBAD	August Nowotny Altrohlau 1838–1884 impressed	August Nowotny Altrohlau 1838–1884 eingeprägt	3218 **373**
Oest.	F. S. Oest Widow & Co. Berlin (1887)– on earthenware	F. S. Oest Wwe. & Co. Berlin (1887)– auf Steingut	3219 **382**
»OTT«	Anton Ott Dresden 1922– decorator's mark overglaze	Anton Ott Dresden 1922– Malermarke aufglasur	3220 **395**
PALME	Josef Palme Schelten 1829–1851	Josef Palme Schelten 1829–1851	3221 **472**
Palme	Josef Palme Schelten 1829–1851 impressed	Josef Palme Schelten 1829–1851 eingeprägt	3222 **472**
Parmos	Porcelain Factory Creidlitz Creidlitz (1930)–	Porzellanfabrik Creidlitz Creidlitz (1930)–	3223 **391**
PLASTO	Plastographic Company Vienna (1899)–	Plastographische Gesellschaft Wien (1899)–	3224 **502**

Mark	English	German	No.
Porzellanfabrik Arzberg Arzberg (Bayern)	Porcelain Factory Arzberg Arzberg 1930–1947 green underglaze	Porzellanfabrik Arzberg Arzberg 1930–1947 grün unterglasur	3 3
Porzellanfabrik-Burggrub	Schoenau & Hoffmeister Burggrub 1909–1952	Schoenau & Hoffmeister Burggrub 1909–1952	3 38
PORZELLAN FABRIK BURGGRUB	same as 3226	wie 3226	32 38
porcelaine Opaque Grünstadt.	J. N. van Recum and heirs and Bros. Bordolo Grunstadt circa 1801–	J. N. van Recum und Erben und Gebr. Bordolo Grünstadt ca. 1801–	32 4
Prag	K. Kriegl & Co. Prague 1835–1910 impressed	K. Kriegl & Co. Prag 1835–1910 eingeprägt	32 46
PRAG	same as 3229	wie 3229	32 46
Prag	Hubel & Co. Prague circa 1800–1835 impressed	Hübel & Co. Prag ca. 1800–1835 eingeprägt	32 46
PRAG	Hubel & Co. Prague circa 1800–1835 impressed on earthenware	Hübel & Co. Prag ca. 1800–1835 eingeprägt auf Steingut	32 46
PRAGER 2	same as 3232	wie 3232	32 46
Regensburg	attributed to J. A. Schwerdtner Regensburg after 1835–	zugeschrieben J. A. Schwerdtner Regensburg nach 1835–	32 46
Reinhold Schlegelmilch Tillowitz	Reinhold Schlegelmilch Tillowitz after 1891–	Reinhold Schlegelmilch Tillowitz nach 1891–	32 489

REX

Geo. Borgfeldt Corp.	Geo. Borgfeldt Corp.	
New York City	New York	
1915—	1915—	3236
importer's mark	Importeurmarke	**454**

Rheinkrone
Bavaria

Oscar Schaller & Co. Successor	Oscar Schaller & Co. Nachf.	
Kirchenlamitz	Kirchenlamitz	3237
(1935)—	(1935)—	**427**

Rldem,

Richard Demmler's Widow & Co.	Richard Demmlers Wwe. & Co.	
Blechhammer	Blechhammer	3238
circa 1937—circa 1945	ca. 1937—ca. 1945	**384**

Rieber
MITTERTEICH

Porcelain Factories	Porzellanfabriken	
Josef Rieber & Co.	Josef Rieber & Co.	
Mitterteich	Mitterteich	3239
before 1938—	vor 1938—	**449**

ROHLAU

Benedikt Hasslacher	Benedikt Hasslacher	
Altrohlau	Altrohlau	
1813—1823	1813—1823	3240
impressed on earthenware	eingeprägt auf Steingut	**373**

Rolau

same as 3240	wie 3240	3241
		373

„Rosenthal-Chippendale"

Rosenthal	Rosenthal	
Selb	Selb	3242
(1932)—	(1932)—	**480**

Rosen Werke Thal.

F. & S. Rosenthal	F. & S. Rosenthal	
Schauberg	Schauberg	3243
traceable 1930—1938	nachweisbar 1930—1938	**471**

Royal Berlin Germany

Royal Porcelain Manufactory	Königliche Porzellan Manufaktur	
Berlin	Berlin	
circa 1891—1919	ca. 1891—1919	
green underglaze, always in	grün unterglasur, immer	
combination with a	in Verbindung mit einer	3244
blue scepter mark	blauen Szeptermarke	**380**

Royal Dresden China

State's and VEB State's	Staatliche und VEB Staatliche	
Porcelain Manufactory	Porzellan Manufaktur	
Meissen	Meißen	
(1938)—present	(1938)—heute	3245
blue	blau	**446**

ROYAL D U X	Dux Porcelain Manufactory Dux after 1912–1945 blue	Duxer Porzellanmanufaktur Dux nach 1912–1945 blau	32 39
SATTLER CZECHOSLOVAKIA	Bros. Sattler Budweis about 1930 decorator's mark overglaze	Gebr. Sattler Budweis um 1930 Malermarke aufglasur	32 38
Scharvogel	J. J. Scharvogel Munich (1902)–circa 1923	J. J. Scharvogel München (1902)–ca. 1923	32 45
Schaubachkunst	W. Goebel Rodental circa 1953–1954 blue	W. Goebel Rödental ca. 1953–1954 blau	32 46
SCHLAGGENWALD	Lippert & Haas Schlaggenwald 1830–1846 impressed	Lippert & Haas Schlaggenwald 1830–1846 eingeprägt	32 47
Schlaggenwald	same as 3250	wie 3250	32 47
SCHNEY	Manufactory Schney or H. K. Eichhorn Schney possibly 1780 impressed	Manufaktur Schney oder H. K. Eichhorn Schney möglicherweise 1780 eingeprägt	32 47
SCHUMAN A MOABIT·	F. A. Schumann Berlin 1835–circa 1844 blue underglaze	F. A. Schumann Berlin 1835–ca. 1844 blau unterglasur	325 38
Semiramis	Alexandra Porcelain Works Turn-Teplitz (1911)–circa 1921	Alexandra Porzellanwerke Turn-Teplitz (1911)–ca. 1921	325 49
SENTA	Heinrich & Winterling New York City (1927)–circa 1941	Heinrich & Winterling New York (1927)–ca. 1941	325 455
Serapis	Alexandra Porcelain Works Turn-Teplitz (1911)–circa 1921	Alexandra Porzellanwerke Turn-Teplitz (1911)–ca. 1921	325 49

Silberdistel	Silberdistel Breu & Co. Gevelsberg 1947–present	Silberdistel Breu & Co. Gevelsberg 1947–heute	3257 **407**
Sorosis	Alexandra Porcelain Works Turn-Teplitz 1911–circa 1921	Alexandra Porzellanwerke Turn-Teplitz 1911–ca. 1921	3258 **491**
Swaine & Co Hüttensteinach	Swaine & Co. Huttensteinach –circa 1920	Swaine & Co. Hüttensteinach –ca. 1920	3259 **420**
Tannawa	Franz Josef Mayer Tannawa 1840–1872 impressed	Franz Josef Mayer Tannawa 1840–1872 eingeprägt	3260 **486**
Teenie Weenie	Geo. Borgfeldt Corp. New York City (1927)– importer's mark	Geo. Borgfeldt Corp. New York (1927)– Importeurmarke	3261 **454**
Teleo	Porcelain Factory Freiberg Freiberg (1921)–1945	Porzellanfabrik Freiberg Freiberg (1921)–1945	3262 **404**
TETSCHEN	Schiller & Gerbing Bodenbach after 1829–circa 1885 on earthenware	Schiller & Gerbing Bodenbach nach 1829–ca. 1885 auf Steingut	3263 **384**
TILL DRESDEN	Franz Till Dresden 1872– decorator's mark overglaze	Franz Till Dresden 1872– Malermarke aufglasur	3264 **396**
Toreas	Ludwig Wessel Bonn (1903)–	Ludwig Wessel Bonn (1903)–	3265 **385**
„Tornas"	Ludwig Wessel Bonn (1904)–	Ludwig Wessel Bonn (1904)–	3266 **385**
Triptis A-G.	Triptis AG Triptis circa 1913–1945	Triptis AG Triptis ca. 1913–1945	3267 **489**

TUPPACK	Carl Hans Tuppack Tiefenfurth (1919)—1935	Carl Hans Tuppack Tiefenfurth (1919)—1935	3? 4?
Ulm *J*	J. J. Schmidt Ulm 1827—1833	J. J. Schmidt Ulm 1827—1833	3? 49
Union	Thuringian Porcelain Manufactory Union Kleindembach 1905—1909	Thüringische Porzellan- manufaktur Union Kleindembach 1905—1909	3? 42
UNITY	Kahla China Corporation New York City (1926)—circa 1941	Kahla China Corporation New York (1926)—ca. 1941	32 45
Vaudrevange	Nicolas Villeroy Wallerfangen 1789—1836 impressed on earthenware	Nicolas Villeroy Wallerfangen 1789—1836 eingeprägt auf Steingut	3? 49
	same as 3272	wie 3272	3? 49
Victoria *Porelite,*	Porcelain Factory Victoria Altrohlau —1945 stamp on earthenware	Porzellanfabrik Victoria Altrohlau —1945 Stempel auf Steingut	32 37
Vieux Saxe	State's and VEB State's Porcelain Manufactory Meissen (1940)—present blue on reproductions of 18th century porcelain	Staatliche und VEB Staatliche Porzellan Manufaktur Meißen (1940)—heute blau auf Reproduktionen von Porzellan des 18. Jahrhunderts	32 44
YILLEROY & BOCH	Villeroy & Boch Wallerfangen 1836— impressed or stamped overglaze	Villeroy & Boch Wallerfangen 1836— eingeprägt oder aufglasur gestempelt	32 49
Virtembergia - Porzellan	Wurttemberg Porcelain Manufactory Schorndorf (1918)—1939	Württembergische Porzellan- manufaktur Schorndorf (1918)—1939	32 47

Wächtersbach	Wachtersbach Earthenware Factory Schlierbach 1832–1852 impressed	Wächtersbacher Steingut-fabrik Schlierbach 1832–1852 eingeprägt

Wächtersbach

Wachtersbach Earthenware Factory
Schlierbach
1832–1852
impressed

Wächtersbacher Steingut-fabrik
Schlierbach
1832–1852
eingeprägt

3278
473

VAECHTERSBACH

Wachtersbach Earthenware Factory
Schlierbach
1852–1883
blue

Wächtersbacher Steingut-fabrik
Schlierbach
1852–1883
blau

3279
473

Wallendorfer

VEB Wallendorfer Porcelain Factory
Wallendorf
circa 1960-before 1990

VEB Wallendorfer Porzellan-fabrik
Wallendorf
ca. 1960-vor 1990

3280
498

WBACH

Wachtersbach Earthenware Factory
Schlierbach
1872–1880
black or blue

Wächtersbacher Steingut-fabrik
Schlierbach
1872–1880
schwarz oder blau

3281
473

Wehsner

Richard Wehsener
Dresden
1895-1918
decorator's mark
overglaze

Richard Wehsener
Dresden
1895-1918
Malermarke
aufglasur

3282
396

W. Haldenwanger's „Sanitäts" Porcelain.

W. Haldenwanger
Berlin
(1906)–

W. Haldenwanger
Berlin
(1906)–

3283
382

Wick-Werke

Wick-Works
Grenzhausen
1937–1960
on stoneware

Wick-Werke
Grenzhausen
1937–1960
auf Steinzeug

3284
412

WIEN

Hardtmuth
Budweis
1846–

Hardtmuth
Budweis
1846–

3285
388

WIENER

same as 3285

wie 3285

3286
388

WIENER PORZELLAN-MANUFACTUR
JOS. BÖCK
WIEN IV. HAUPTSTRASSE 15/17.

Vienna Porcelain Manufactory
Josef Bock
Vienna
after 1893–

Wiener Porzellanmanufaktur
Josef Böck
Wien
nach 1893–

3287
503

MVCEW

ZELL

L. Wunsche
Weimar
1920–circa 1949
decorator's mark
overglaze

L. Wünsche
Weimar
1920–ca. 1949
Malermarke 32
aufglasur 5(

F. J. Lenz
Zell on Harmersbach
circa 1819–circa 1869
on earthenware

F. J. Lenz
Zell am Harmersbach
ca. 1819–ca. 1869 32
auf Steingut 50

TEIL II

PART II

Manufacturers according to location

Hersteller nach Orten

Aachen
Rhineland, Germany

Eha-Edelporzellane Erich Haselhuhn
(Eha-Precious Porcelains Erich Haselhuhn)
1921—defunct after 1930, porcelain decorating shop.
Mark: 2230

Ferdinand Schmetz Porzellanknopffabrik
(Ferdinand Schmetz Porcelainbutton Factory)
1851—defunct after 1959, porcelain buttons and porcelain pearls. The company moved to Herzogenrath in 1938, where it owned a branch factory.
Mark: 1278

Aich
Bohemia, presently Doubi, Czechia

Johann Moehling, 1849—1860, table, household and decorative porcelain, figurines. Moehling founded the factory after he had dissolved his partnership with Haas in *Haas & Moehling* in *Schlaggenwald*
Marks: 2689, 2703, 3096, 3097
Baron von Ziegler bought the factory in 1860 but sold it two years later to **A. Carl Anger,** 1862—1901, household, table and decorative porcelain, coffee and tea sets.
Marks: 2249, 2539, 2540
Successors of Anger were
Ludwig Engel & Sohn
(Ludwig Engel & Son)
1902—1917, household and decorative porcelain, followed by
Porzellanfabrik Aich, Menzl & Co.
(Porcelain Factory Aich, Menzl & Co.)
1918—1922, household and ovenproof porcelain.
Mark: 361
Subsequently the factory was acquired by
Epiag, 1922—1933, and converted for the mass production of household and hotel porcelain, coffee and tea sets. It was closed in 1933. See also Epiag, Karlsbad.
Marks: 1320, 3143

Albersweiler
Bavaria, Germany

Robert Lutz, Porcelain Factory, existed 1894, household porcelain.
Mark: 2300

Alexandrinenthal
Bavaria, Germany

Thomas Recknagel Porzellanfabrik Alexandrinenthal
(Thomas Recknagel Porcelain Factory Alexandrinenthal)
1886–1934, decorative porcelain, figurines, dolls heads.
Marks: 1462, 1931, 1932, 2899–2902, 3039, 3065
In 1930 a porcelain decorator Th. Recknagel is mentioned, whose mark 1933 is similar to mark 1932.

Allach near Munich
Bavaria, Germany

Porzellanmanufaktur Allach-München GmbH
(Porcelain Manufactory Allach-Munich Ltd) 1935-1944, owned by the SS. Figurines, busts, statues, decorative porcelain. Prisoners of the concentration camp Dachau were employed in the manufactory. Marks: 2207, 2489. Models and moulds were acquired by *Porcelain Factory Oscar Schaller in Windischeschenbach.*

Altenbach
Saxony, Germany

Carl & Gustav Harkort, 1845–1881, chemical, technical and sanitary earthenware.
Mark: 2728
Eugen Hülsmann
(Eugen Hulsmann) was successor, 1881–defunct after 1932.
Mark: 1990

Altenburg see Roschutz

Altenkunstadt
Bavaria, Germany

Rothemund & Co., 1919–1923, was changed into **Rothemund, Hager & Co.**, 1923–1933, gift articles, household porcelain, cups.
Marks: 13, 898
Karl Nehmzow acquired the company and named it
Porzellanfabrik Altenkunstadt Karl Nehmzow
(Porcelain Factory Altenkunstadt Karl Nehmzow), 1933–present, gift, collectors and promotional articles, decorative porcelain, figurines. From 1933–1948 the factory only produced earthenware but no porcelain.
Marks: 1828–1837, 1839, 1840

Althaldensleben
Prussia, Germany

Gebrüder Ziegler
(Brothers Ziegler), circa 1894–1938, porcelain decorators.
Mark: 2794

Wilhelm Gerike & Co., circa 1896–1921, siderolith and pottery products.
Mark: 2991

Philip Liemann & Co., 1851—defunct, siderolith.
Mark: 2840

Gottlob Nathusius, 1826—circa 1860, table and decorative porcelain, coffee and tea sets.
Marks: 2808, 2849

Schmelzer & Gericke, 1863—no mention found after 1931, fayence, household and decorative earthenware and stoneware.
Marks: 2026, 2027

Altrohlau

Bohemia, presently Stara Role, Czechia

Charles Ahrenfeldt & Son, 1886—1910, porcelain decorating shop and porcelain importer with main office in New York, N. Y., U. S. A. Ahrenfeldt also owned a factory in Limoges, France.
See also New York, Ahrenfeldt & Son.
Marks: 777, 778, 1513, 1514

Benedikt Hasslacher, 1813—1823, founded a Fayence and Earthenware Factory.
Marks: 1512, 2894, 3240, 3241
August Nowotny & Co., 1823—1884, acquired the factory but until 1839 manufactured only fayence and earthenware. Subsequently they began production of household, table and decorative porcelain.
Marks: 1797, 1806, 2210, 2211, 2705, 2706, 3215—3218
Moritz Zdekauer, 1884—1909, was successor and continued the production program.
Marks: 208, 263, 264, 412, 1991, 3044
The company of *C. M. Hutschenreuther* in *Hohenberg* bought the factory and named it

Altrohlauer Porzellanfabriken

(Altrohlau Porcelain Factories), 1909—1945.
Marks: 225—227, 1800, 3043, 3176
After World War II the company was nationalized.

Crown-Porcelain-Works William Pistor & Co., 1870—circa 1908, porcelain decorating shop.
Josef Dutz, circa 1908—1923, was first proprietor of the company, then acquired and named it

Porzellanindustrie Dutz & Co.

(Porcelain Industry Dutz & Co.), 1923—1932, thereafter the company name was
Holdschick & Co., 1932—1936, who were followed by

Porzellanfabrik Franz Manka

(Porcelain Factory Franz Manka), 1936—1945, household and decorative porcelain, porcelain decorating.
Mark: 1981
After World War II the company was nationalized.

Ing. Fritsch & Weidermann
(Engineer Fritsch & Weidermann), 1921–1945, household porcelain. The company was successor of a porcelain decorating shop not yet identified.
Mark: 249

Marx & Gutherz, probably 1876–1889, household and decorative porcelain, coffee and tea sets.
Mark: 2197
Oscar Gutherz joined with Edgar Gutherz, the former manager of the *New York and Rudolstadt Pottery* in *Rudolstadt,* to **Oscar & Edgar Gutherz,** 1889–1918, household, table and decorative porcelain, mainly for export into the U. S.
Mark: 558
The combine of the Austrian Porcelain Industry acquired the factory and named it
Öpiag, Betriebsstätte Altrohlau
(Opiag, Branch Altrohlau), 1918–1920,
Mark: 554
This name was changed into
Epiag, Betriebsstätte Altrohlau
(Epiag, Branch Altrohlau), 1920–1945, household and decorative porcelain, gift articles, souvenirs.
Marks: 553, 555–557, 3144
See also Karlsbad, Epiag.
After World War II the company was nationalized.

Josef Plass, 1870–circa 1920, porcelain decorator.
Mark: 1743

Porzellanfabrik "Victoria" Schmidt & Co.
(Porcelain Factory "Victoria" Schmidt & Co.), 1883–1945, household, hotel and decorative porcelain, coffee and tea sets, also earthenware.
Marks: 20–22, 766, 1266–1268, 2448, 3274

J. Schneider & Co., 1904–1945, household porcelain.
Mark: 1004

Altshausen
Wurttemberg, Germany

Prinz Friedrich Christian, Herzog zu Sachsen
(Prince Friedrich Christian, Duke of Saxony), in 1950 applied for the registration of six trademarks for porcelain products. In some of them the crossed swords of the *Porcelain Manufactory* in *Meissen* are used, which are also part of the Saxonian coat of arms. The marks have not yet been observed on porcelain.
Marks: 655, 665, 682, 770, 956, 1584

Altwasser
Silesia, Germany, presently Walbrzych, Poland

C. Tielsch & Co. 1845-1945, household, hotel and decorative porcelain, coffee and tea sets. In 1918 *C.M. Hutschenreuther* in *Hohenberg* acquired the majority of the stock of Tielsch and merged the factory with its company in Hohenberg.
Marks: 202, 223, 253-255, 260-262, 413, 1860, 2057, 2947, 2948, 3596-3601.
From 1920 until 1945 the last two digits of the year or the full year were added to the mark. After the factory was expropriated in 1948, the Hutschenreuther factory in Arzberg used the name Tielsch in one of its marks.

Amberg
Bavaria, Germany

Stephan Mayer & Son, circa 1830–1850, household, table and decorative earthenware and porcelain.
Eduard Kick continued the factory, 1850–1910. He acquired original moulds of the defunct *Royal Porcelain Manufactory* in *Ludwigsburg* and made reproductions of Ludwigsburg porcelain.
Marks: 2495, 3099–3101

Steingutfabrik Amberg
(Earthenware Factory Amberg), 1920–circa 1922, became a branch of *Ludwig Wessel Earthenware Factory* in *Bonn*, circa 1922–before 1945.
Mark: 2141

Annaburg
Prussia, Germany

A. Heckmann founded an earthenware factory and produced household earthenware with the Meissen Onion Pattern. Mark: 259
Later the company name was **Annaburger Steingutfabrik AG** (Annaburg Earthenware Factory) -1945, Mark: 473. After World War II the company was nationalized and first named **VEB Steingutfabrik Annaburg** (VEB Earthenware Factory Annaburg), which later took up porcelain production and as Work Annaburg was part of *VEB United Porcelainworks Colditz* in *Colditz*.
In 1990 the factory was privatized, sold to Ceraplan GmbH in Selb, Bavaria and continued as **Annaburg Porzellan GmbH**, (Annaburg Porcelain Ltd) 1992-present, household, table and children´s porcelain. Mark: 3608

Ansbach-Bruckberg
Bavaria, Germany

In 1757 Margrave Alexander von Brandenburg-Onolzbach ordered production of porcelain in a fayence factory in Ansbach, already in existence since 1710. Six years later the
Markgräfliche Feine Porcelain Fabrique
(Margravial Fine Porcelain Factory), 1757–1791, was moved to Castle Bruckberg and expanded. After Margrave Alexander abdicated in 1791 in favor of the Prussian King Frederick William II the factory's name was changed into
Königliche Preussische Porzellan Manufaktur Bruckberg
(Royal Prussian Porcelain Manufactory Bruckberg), 1791–1806. During the

Napoleonic Wars the principality of Ansbach was annexed by the Kingdom of Bavaria on French orders. The factory's name was changed into

Königliche Porzellan Manufaktur Bruckberg
(Royal Porcelain Manufactory Bruckberg), 1806–1807. Since the Bavarian administration did not want competition for its own porcelain manufactory in *Nymphenburg,* the Bruckberg factory was auctioned off and bought by its former vicedirector Christian F. Loewe, who later went into partnership with his son-in-law Johann Adam Stadler as **Loewe & Stadler,** 1807–1860. In 1860 the factory was closed because of economic problems and its assets were auctioned off. All proprietors produced table and decorative porcelain, coffee and tea sets and figurines. Their marks were similar.
Marks: 185–187, 250, 251, 1457, 1493–1497, 2348, 2690–2701

Anspach
Hesse or Thuringia, Germany

Some authors mention a porcelain manufactory in Anspach, either in Hesse or Thuringia, which is supposed to have existed around 1860–1870. Neither in Hesse nor in Thuringia a city named Anspach could be found, but the name Anspach, an earlier version of Ansbach, appears on products of the fayence manufactory in Ansbach (1710–1806).
Marks: 2351–2353, 2377
Similar marks have been proven for *Wilhelm Greiner* in *Volkstedt.*

Arnstadt
Thuringia, Germany

Porzellanfabrik Arnstadt Mardorf & Bandorf
(Porcelain Factory Arnstadt Mardorf & Bandorf), 1905–1938, decorative porcelain, chemical, technical, sanitary porcelain, toys and dolls.
Mark: 618

Some authors mention a small manufactory in Arnstadt that supposedly was founded in 1790. The marks are similar to some of the Weesp marks.
Marks: 1968, 1969
See also Part III, p. 534, 535

Arzberg
Bavaria, Germany

Lehmann & Rossberg, 1890–circa 1898, operated a porcelain factory, producing household and decorative porcelain, coffee and tea sets. About 1898 Rossberg left the factory which changed its name to
Porzellanfabrik Theodor Lehmann
(Porcelain Factory Theodor Lehmann), circa 1898–1904. It was acquired by *Porcelain Factory Schonwald* in *Schonwald* and became its Department Arzberg, 1904–1927.
Marks: 729, 2024, 2025
After Porcelain Factory Schonwald was taken over by *Porcelain Factory Kahla* in

Kahla, the company's name became

Porzellanfabrik Arzberg

(Porcelain Factory Arzberg), 1927–present. This name was kept when Porcelain Factory Kahla merged with *Hutschenreuther AG* in *Selb* in 1972.
Marks: 728, 2054, 3106, 3225

Lorenz Christof Äcker

(Lorenz Christof Acker), 1839–1880, produced mainly pipes and pipe bowls in a small earthenware and porcelain factory. **Carl Auvera,** 1880–1918, took over the factory and expanded it to produce earthenware, fayence and porcelain.
Marks: 2493, 2543, 2725
Successor was *C. M. Hutschenreuther* in *Hohenberg,* who changed the company name into

Porzellanfabrik C. M. Hutschenreuther Abteilung Arzberg

(Porcelain Factory C. M. Hutschenreuther Department Arzberg), 1918–present, and produced household and decorative porcelain, coffee and tea sets and technical porcelain. For some years after 1948 the company used the name of its expropriated factory *C. Tielsch* in *Altwasser* in one of its marks.
Marks: 241, 872, 918, 1233, 1234

Carl Schumann Porzellanfabrik (Carl Schumann Porcelain Factory), 1881- 1996, The factory was founded by Heinrich Schumann and produced table and decorative porcelain, coffee and tea sets and gift articles. The company bought *Porcelain Factory Colditz* in *Colditz* and closed it in 1996.
Marks: 90-92, 691, 1256, 1359, 1360

Aschaffenburg
Bavaria, Germany

Porcelaine ARose@ Walk, bathroom and boudoir articles, now **Rose Walk Interior GmbH,** 1974-present, table porcelain, coffee and tea sets. Mark: 1820

Auma
Thuringia, Germany

Porzellanindustrie Berghaus

(Porcelain Industry Berghaus, 1909-1945, electrotechnical porcelain.
Mark: 2496
The company was nationalized after World War II and changed names several times.

VEB Thüringer Porzellanwerke, Zweigwerk Auma

(VEB Thuringian Porcelain Works, Branch Auma), 1945-1949,

VEB IKA Porzelllanfabrik Auma

(VEB IKA Porcelain Factory Auma), 1949-1955,

VEB Porzellanwerk Auma

(VEB Porcelain Work Auma), 1955-1972,
Mark: 593
and finally became a branch of *VEB Combine Ceramic Works Hermsdorf* in *Hermsdorf,* which was dissolved in 1990.

Aussig
Bohemia, presently Usti nad Labem, Czechia

Rudolf Kindler, 1881–defunct about 1920, household porcelain.
Mark: 2913

Johann Maresch, later
Ferdinand Maresch Siderolith- und Terrakottafabrik
(Ferdinand Maresch Siderolith & Terra Cotta Factory), 1841–about 1945, household and decorative earthenware and porcelain, figurines.
Mark: 2815

Baden-Baden
Badenia, Germany

Widow Susanna Catharina Sperl in 1751 received a privilege for a porcelain and fayence factory but returned it in 1756 stating that she had not been able to establish the factory.
Zacharias Pfalzer, 1771–1778, obtained a new privilege and produced coffee and tea sets, decorative porcelain, figurines and pipe bowls. His products were not marked. After his factory encountered financial difficulties, it was continued as
Markgräfliche Porzellanregie
(Margravial Porcelain Administration), June–November 1778, and then closed. The products of this period bear marks. It is highly questionable though, that the hatchets attributed to Baden-Baden really were used by the factory.
Marks: 666–674, questionable marks: 1764, 1927, 1928

Badenweiler
Badenia, Germany

Ing. Hertel
(Engineer Hertel), existed 1910, decorative ceramics, porcelain decorating.
Mark: 2017

Bad Driburg
Bavaria, Germany

Südwestdeutsche Porzellan- und Glasvertriebs GMBH
(Southwest German Porcelain and Glass Distributing Company), existed 1968, distributor of Bavarian porcelain.
Mark: 1819

Basdorf
Prussia, Germany

Gebr. Schackert
(Bros. Schackert), 1751–defunct in the 18th century. The brothers Schackert always claimed that they were able to produce real porcelain and tried to obtain a privilege from the Prussian King. But they lost against *W. C. Wegely* in *Berlin*.

The proven pieces from the Schackert manufactory are some kind of frit-porcelain, which was closer to opalescent glass. By cutting, grinding and decorating it, the brothers Schackert tried to give their products the appearance of porcelain.
Marks: 2710, 3110

Baumbach now Ransbach-Baumbach
Hesse, Germany

Jasba-Keramikfabriken Jakob Schwaderlapp & Söhne
(Jasba Ceramic Factories Jacob Schwaderlapp & Sons) , now
Jasba GmbH (Jasba Ltd) 1926-present, decorative earthenware, ovenproof cooking pots, now mainly floor, wall and oven tiles.
Marks: 2009, 2062, 2063

Johann Jacob Letschert Sohn
(Johann Jacob Letschert Son), existed 1930, household, decorative and technical porcelain, earthenware and stoneware.
Mark: 2542

Bautzen
Saxony, Germany

J. G. Schneider, existed 1930, porcelain decorator. His mark No. 1047 shows some similarity with mark No. 1004 of *Schneider & Co.* in *Altrohlau.*

Bayreuth
Bavaria, Germany

Siegmund Paul Meyer, 1899-1920, produced household and hotel porcelain.
Marks: 733, 1506
The company name later was changed to
Erste Bayreuther Porzellanfabrik "Walküre" Siegmund Paul Meyer GmbH (First Bayreuth Porcelain Factory "Valkyrie" Siegmund Paul Meyer Ltd), 1920-present, which extended the production program to include ovenproof pots and coffee machines.
Marks: 359, 756, 3606

Porzellanmanufaktur "Gloria" Anton Weidl, (Porcelain Manufactory "Gloria" Anton Weidl), later **Anton Weidl KG Porzellan- und Glasmalerei**
(Anton Weidl KG Porcelain and Glass Decorating) 1947-present, decorating shop. The manufactory was founded in Altrohlau, Bohemia in 1920 and after World War II moved to Bayreuth. Mark: 846

Beratzhausen
Bavaria, Germany

Helmut Krüger Porzellanmanufaktur
(Helmut Kruger Porcelain Manufactory), Berlin, branch Beratzhausen, 1954–circa 1971, porcelain decorating shop

Mark: 2018
later changed to
Porzellanmanufaktur Wolfram
(Porcelain Manufactory Wolfram), circa 1971—   , promotional articles.

Berchtesgaden
Bavaria, Germany

Woldemar Adler Porzellanmalerei
(Woldemar Adler Porcelain Decorating Shop), later
Woldemar Adler Porzellankunst
(Woldemar Adler Porcelain Art), 1919–defunct after 1964, porcelain decorating, especially flowers.
Marks: 240, 357

Berlin
Prussia, Germany

Hermann Behne Porzellanmanufaktur
(Hermann Behne Porcelain Manufactory), traceable 1913–1919, decorative porcelain, figurines.
Marks: 3168

Berliner Porzellan- und Chamottefabrik Alfred Bruno Schwarz
(Berlin Porcelain & Fireclay Factory Alfred Bruno Schwarz), 1890–technical, laboratory and sanitary porcelain and earthenware.
Marks: 1741, 2278

Berliner Kunstkeramik
(Berlin Art Ceramics), existed 1921, decorative porcelain and earthenware.
Mark: 1784

Paul Bößenroth
(Paul Bossenroth), existed 1905, porcelain clocks, decorative porcelain.
Mark: 1942

Geo. Borgfeldt & Co. see New York

W. Einwald, Glass and Porcelain Manufactory, 1868–defunct, porcelain decorating shop.
Mark: 88

Gebr. Kroner
(Bros. Kroner), existed 1907, technical porcelain.
Mark: 2101

Johann Ernst Gotzkowsky Fabrique de Porcelaines de Berlin, 1761–1763, after *Wegely's* manufactory failed in 1757, one of his modellers, Reichert (or Reichard) tried to set up a small manufactory, but lacked enough money. The Prussian King

Frederick the Great encouraged the merchant Johann Ernst Gotzkowsky to establish a porcelain manufactory. Gotzkowsky bought Reichert's equipment and promised him a yearly income of one thousand Thalers and a bonus of ten thousand Thalers if he could prove that he was able to produce porcelain. In 1762 Gotzkowsky presented to the King his first products, which found Frederick's approval. But Gotzkowsky had overextended his financial resources and faced bankruptcy, Frederick, who always had a keen interest in porcelain, felt obliged to help Gotzkowsky. He bought the manufactory for two hundred and twenty-five thousand Thalers and renamed it *Royal Prussian Porcelain Fabrique.* Reichert, who had hoped to become manager of the Royal manufactory, was compensated with seven thousand Thalers.

Table and decorative porcelain, figurines.

Marks: 2780–2786

Königlich Preussische Porcelain Fabrique

(Royal Prussian Porcelain Fabrique) and

Königliche Porzellan Manufaktur

(Royal Porcelain Manufactory), 1763–1919, later

Staatliche Porzellan Manufaktur

(State's Porcelain Manufactory), 1919–present. After the Prussian King Frederick the Great bought *Gotzkowsky's* manufactory, he put it on a sound economic foundation. His personal interest and support soon elevated the manufactory to one of the most prestigious in Europe, rivaling Meissen.

Porcelain still was rather expensive in the 18th century and most people used earthenware covered with leadglaze. Because leadglaze was suspected to be unhealthy, the Royal Manufactory in 1795 began to produce "hygioceramic" dishes from a mass somewhere between porcelain and earthenware which needed no additional glaze. In 1818 a subsidiary branch, the

Königliche Gesundheitsgeschirrfabrik

(Royal Hygioceramic Factory), began production in Charlottenburg, a part of Berlin. Its director for some time was Privy Councillor Proessel. Some authors maintain that there was a privately owned porcelain manufactory in Charlottenburg owned by M. Pressel. This is probably a confusion with the Royal Hygioceramic Factory and Privy Councillor Proessel, who from 1821 to 1848 managed the factory, which was closed in 1865.

Until 1918 the manufactory was property of the Prussian Kings. After the abdication of the last king, William II, it became property of the State of Prussia and was named State's Porcelain Manufactory Berlin. In 1943 the manufactory was destroyed in an air raid, but production continued in *Selb,* where the manufactory had leased *Porcelain Factory Paul Muller.* After World War II the facilities in Berlin were reconstructed. Since they were located in the British Sector of Berlin, but the branch in Selb was lying in the American occupied zone of West-Germany, both factories were legally separated until 1949, when the Federal Republic of Germany was established. The same year the manufactory became property of the City of Berlin (West). The branch in Selb returned to Berlin in 1957. Products from Selb can be distinguished by an S beneath the scepter.

Table, household, decorative, laboratory, technical porcelain, collectors and gift articles, pipe bowls, dolls heads, plaques and medals.

Marks: 196–198, 206, 207, 1024, 1282–1306, 1309–1316, 2033, 2444, 2447, 2448, 2582, 2583, 3244

W. Haldenwanger, formerly
Sanitäts-Porzellan Manufaktur W. Haldenwanger
(Sanitary Porcelain Manufactory W. Haldenwanger), 1863–present, technical and
sanitary porcelain, earthenware and stoneware.
Marks: 1755, 2492, 3283

Helmut Krüger Porzellanmanufaktur
(Helmut Kruger Porcelain Manufactory), 1954–circa 1971, porcelain decorating
shop, decorative porcelain, figurines, gift articles, branch in *Beratzhausen*.
Mark: 2018

Clara Lobedan and Hildegard Lehnert, circa 1899–circa 1909, decorative earthenware and porcelain decorating.
Mark: 2549

Ernst March, 1836–circa 1887, founded an earthenware factory, which was
continued as
Ernst March Söhne
(Ernst March Sons), circa 1887–1904, in 1887 the company developed a
"white stoneware", which was close to porcelain. It produced technical stoneware,
fayence, maiolica, terra cotta and decorative stoneware. 1904 it was converted into
Deutsche Ton- und Steinzeugwerke AG
(German Clay and Stoneware Works AG)
Mark: 407

F. S. Oest Witwe & Co.
(F. S. Oest Widow & Co.), 1824–defunct after 1900, products from earthenware,
maiolica and fireclay.
Marks: 195, 3219

S. Reich & Comp., traceable 1909–1938, the company was a glass factory but also
produced porcelain. It owned branches in Gross-Karlowitz and Haida, Bohemia.
Mark: 2065

Hans Richter Porzellanmanufaktur
(Hans Richter Porcelain Manufactory),   traceable 1881–1907, decorator of
porcelain.
Mark: 658

Porzellanfabrik Ph. Rosenthal & Co.
(Porcelain Factory Ph. Rosenthal & Co.) see Selb

H. Schomburg & Söhne
(H. Schomburg & Sons), 1853–1922, technical, especially electrotechnical porcelain. In 1877 the company acquired *Margarethenhutte* in *Grossdubrau* and moved
its headquarters there in 1913. In 1898 it built a porcelain factory in *Rosslau*. In
1922 it joined with *Porcelain Factory Kahla* in *Kahla* in a cartel and in 1927 both
companies were merged.
See also Hermsdorf, Ceramic Works Hescho-Kahla.
Marks: 18, 1961, 3103

Johann Friedrich Ferdinand Schumann in 1835 founded a porcelain factory, that was taken over shortly afterwards by his son Friedrich Adolph Schumann, circa 1835–circa 1913. Until 1880 it produced table, household and decorative porcelain, then porcelain production was discontinued in favour of porcelain decorating. Chaffers (see bibliography No. 15) Danckert (see bibl. No. 123) and other authors copying Chaffers list the company as M. Schumann, not knowing that M. is not the initial of a first name but an abbreviation for the French Monsieur. Marks: 199, 200, 203, 212, 258, 2446, 2465, 3253

Sophie Seitz-Hückstädt
(Sophie Seitz-Huckstadt), 1887–defunct, porcelain decorating shop.
Mark: 1936

Staatliche Porzellan Manufaktur
(State's Porcelain Manufactory), see Royal Porcelain Manufactory

Vereinigung Deutscher Porzellanfabriken zur Hebung der Porzellanindustrie GMBH
(Association of German Porcelain Factories for the Furtherance of the Porcelain Industry), 1900–1912, the association was founded by forty-nine porcelain factories to promote their technical and economical development. When it was dissolved in 1912 the number of members had increased to seventy-eight. Mark No. 2128 was the logo of the association, it has not been observed on porcelain.

Vereinigte Lausitzer Glaswerke AG
(United Lusatian Glassworks AG), before 1911–circa 1945, branch factories in Weisswasser, Tschernitz, Kamenz and Furstenberg (Oder), decorative porcelain and earthenware.
Mark: 2220

Wilhelm Caspar Wegely, 1751–1757, Wegely obtained a privilege from the Prussian King Frederick the Great, but his products did not find the approval of the king. Wegely had to close his manufactory because of economic difficulties. Table and decorative porcelain, figurines.
Marks: 2977–2984, 2990

Albert Wreschner & Co., 1890–defunct before 1918, porcelain decorating shop.
Mark: 2378

Biela
Bohemia, presently Bela, Czechia

Julius Dressler, Fayence, Maiolica and Porcelain Factory, 1888–circa 1945, decorative porcelain and earthenware, porcelain lamps and flowers, electrotechnical porcelain.
Marks: 138, 499, 1897, 2036

Bielefeld
Westphalia, Germany

Westfälische Glasmanufaktur
(Westphalian Glass Manufactory), existed 1930, porcelain products.
Mark: 2676

Bischofswerda
Saxony, Germany

Paul Schreier, existed 1930, porcelain decorator.
Mark: 1326

Blankenhain
Thuringia, Germany

Christian Andreas Wilhelm Speck in 1790 founded a porcelain manufactory and pro-
duced table and decorative porcelain. Mark: 2240
Later proprietors were **Eduard Eichler**, **Duxer Porcelain Manufactory AG** and **Fasolt
& Eichel**, 1856-circa 1918, table porcelain, coffee and tea sets, cups, washstand sets and
decorative porcelain. Mark: 1532
Their successors were Bros. Carstens, who changed the company name to
Blankenhainer Porzellanfabrik C. & E. Carstens
(Blankenhain Porcelain Factory C. & E. Carstens) circa 1918-1945.
Marks: 525, 1532
After World War II the company was nationalized and named
VEB Porzellanwerk AWeimar Porzellan@
(VEB Porcelainwork AWeimar Porcelain@)   -1990. After two years of government
trusteeship the factory was privatized and is now operating as
Weimar Porzellan GmbH
(Weimar Porcelain Ltd) 1992-present. Mark: 3603

Edmund Krüger Porzellanfabrik
(Edmund Kruger Porcelain Factory), 1847–1937, household porcelain.
Marks: 742, 743

Blechhammer
Thuringia, Germany

Richard Demmlers Witwe
(Richard Demmler's Widow), 1900–circa 1945, electrotechnical porcelain, lamps.
Mark: 3238

Bock-Wallendorf
Thuringia, Germany

Fasold & Stauch, 1903-1972, decorative porcelain, figurines, gift articles, dolls´ heads,
clockcases. Marks: 39, 363, 882, 967, 1043, 2580, 2677, 3149. From 1972 to 1990 the
factory was vocational school for *VEB United Decorative Porcelainworks* in *Lichte* and
then closed.

Bodenbach
Bohemia, presently Podmokly, Czechia

Schiller & Gerbing, 1829–circa 1885, household and decorative stoneware and earthenware. The company imitated Wedgwood stoneware, which can be distinguished from real Wedgwood by its varnishlike glaze and its less fine execution.
Marks: 2931, 3263
About 1885 the company split up into
W. Schiller & Sohn
(W. Schiller & Son), circa 1885–defunct, porcelain and earthenware.
Marks: 2241, 2992
and into
Gerbing & Stephan, circa 1885–1898, subsequently **F. & S. Gerbing** were proprietors until 1905, followed by **Alexander Gerbing**. They all produced household and decorative porcelain and earthenware and used the same
Mark: 1909

Bogen

Bavaria, Germany

Anton Herr, 1946–present, gift and promotional articles, apothecary jars and beersteins from fayence and earthenware.
Marks: 1317–1319

Bonn

Rhineland, Germany

Steingutfabrik Franz Anton Mehlem
(Earthenware Factory Franz Anton Mehlem), 1836–1920, household, decorative, technical and sanitary earthenware and porcelain. From 1887 until 1903 the company reproduced Hochst figurines in porcelain and earthenware with the original moulds of the defunct *Prince-Electoral Mayence Manufactory* in *Hochst*, which had been acquired from the *Earthenware Factory Damm* in *Damm*.
Marks: 706–709, 1861, 1895, 1896, 2578, 3024, 3132
The factory was bought by *Villeroy & Boch* in Mettlach in 1921 and closed in 1931.

Kurfürst Clemens August von Köln
(Prince-Elector Clemens August of Cologne) in 1775 ordered the erection of a porcelain factory but it only succeeded in producing fayence. About the turn of the century it was sold to
Engelbert Cremer of Cologne, circa 1800–1825, and subsequently bought by **Ludwig Wessel**, 1825–present, who at first produced household and decorative earthenware and porcelain. This line was abandoned in 1930 and today only sanitary porcelain is produced. The company changed its name several times.
About 1880 it was
Ludwig Wessel AG für Porzellan- und Steingutfabrikation
(Ludwig Wessel AG for Porcelain and Earthenwareproduction)
about 1933
Ludwig Wessel Steingutwerke AG
(Ludwig Wessel Earthenwareworks AG), since about 1938
Wessel Keramische Werke AG
(Wessel Ceramic Works AG)
The company owned a branch in Amberg.
Marks: 813–815, 828, 1235, 1809, 1814, 1817, 1842, 2177, 3117, 3265, 3266

Wessel-Werk GMBH
(Wessel Work GMBH), 1896—present, electrotechnical porcelain, wall tiles.
Marks: 659, 660

Brambach
Saxony, Germany

Brambacher Porzellanfabrik Alfred Aurnhammer und Fritz Reinhardt
(Brambach Porcelain Factory Alfred Aurnhammer and Fritz Reinhardt), 1904—circa 1915, household and decorative porcelain, gift articles.
Mark: 270

Bremen
Germany.

Kunstgewerbliche Werkstätten Ch. Epping
(Arts and Crafts Workshops Ch. Epping), existed 1952, toys from porcelain and clay.
Mark: 2310

E. Kruse & Co., 1878—defunct, porcelain decorating shop.
Mark: 1779

H. A. Kruse, circa 1883—   , porcelain decorating shop.
Mark: 216

Smidt & Duensing, 1875—circa 1921, porcelain decorating shop.
Mark: 37
In 1921 the company was sold to
Klara Auguste Hermann.

Breslau
Silesia, presently Wroclaw, Poland

Breslauer Steingutfabrik P. Giesel
(Breslau Earthenware Factory P. Giesel), 1877—circa 1915, household and sanitary earthenware and porcelain.
Marks: 219, 256, 334
Successors were
Steingutwerke AG
(Earthenwareworks AG), circa 1915—1945, technical and sanitary porcelain and earthenware.
Mark: 133

Bruchmuhlbach - Bruchmühlbach
Palatinate, Germany

Porzellanfabrik Mühlbach
(Porcelain Factory Muhlbach), 1951—circa 1970, coffee and tea sets, gift articles.

Marks: 575, 705, 947, 1178, 3074
The factory was converted to the production of earthenware sets and renamed
Winterling Feinkeramik
(Winterling Fine Ceramics), circa 1970–present.
Mark: 1191
See also Windischeschenbach, Winterling Porcelain Factories Distributing Company.

Bruckberg see Ansbach-Bruckberg

Bruhl - Brühl
Rhineland, Germany

Franz Wittwer Glashüttenwerk
(Franz Wittwer Glassworks), existed 1955, porcelain distributor. His mark
No. 1039 is similar to mark No. 1038 of *Ackermann & Fritze* in *Volkstedt.*

Brux - Brüx
Bohemia, presently Most, Czechia

Brüxer Porzellanmanufaktur
(Brux Porcelain Manufactory), 1924–1945, household porcelain.
Mark: 485

Carl Spitz Porzellan- und Steingutfabrik
(Carl Spitz Porcelain and Earthenware Factory), 1896–circa 1945, household and
decorative porcelain and earthenware, fayence, ovenproof pots.
Marks: 590, 591, 769, 1889

Buchau
Bohemia, presently Bochov, Czechia

Josef Pollack, 1902–1907, produced dolls heads and sold his factory to Josef Plass,
who later took Roesner into partnership and named the company
Buchauer Porzellanfabrik Plass & Roesner
(Buchau Porcelain Factory Plass & Roesner), 1907–last mention found in 1940.
From about 1933 until 1937 the factory was closed, later it produced household
porcelain.
Mark: 1478

Buckau see Magdeburg-Buckau

Buda
Bohemia, presently Budov, Czechia

Franz Lang, 1825–1860, began with the production of earthenware and added
in 1831 coffee and tea sets from porcelain.
Marks: 2709, 2711, 2712, 2754
His son
Anton Lang, 1860–1880, additionally produced decorative porcelain.
Mark: 724, 2702

Budweis
Bohemia, presently Budejovice, Czechia

Joseph Hardtmuth, 1790–1816, founded a pencil and earthenware factory in Vienna and produced household earthenware, known under the name "Vienna Earthenware." After his death in 1816 his widow operated the factory until in 1828 her sons Josef, Karl and Ludwig took over. In 1846 the factory was moved to Budweis and Karl Hardtmuth became proprietor. In Budweis he produced household porcelain and earthenware. In 1905 the company name was
L. & C. Hardtmuth Steingut- und Ofenfabrik
(L. & C. Hardtmuth Earthenware and Stove Factory) and as main product hotel porcelain was listed.
Marks: 2956, 3164, 3285, 3286

Gebr. Sattler
(Bros. Sattler), existed about 1930, porcelain decorators.
Marks: 3194, 3247

Bunde - Bünde
Westphalia, Germany

A. Severin & Co., traceable 1909–1930, decorators of porcelain.
Marks: 278, 279

Burgau-Goschwitz - Burgau-Göschwitz
Thuringia, Germany

Porzellanmanufaktur Burgau Ferdinand Selle
(Porcelain Manufactory Burgau Ferdinand Selle), 1901–1929, household and decorative porcelain, artistic porcelain in art nouveau style.
Mark: 333

Burggrub
Bavaria, Germany

Porzellanfabrik Burggrub Schoenau & Hoffmeister
(Porcelain Factory Burggrub Schoenau & Hoffmeister), 1909–1952, dolls heads, gift articles, technical porcelain.
Marks: 621, 622, 3226, 3227
Successor was
Porzellanfabrik Burggrub Horst Eversberg
(Porcelain Factory Burggrub Horst Eversberg), 1952–1978, household and decorative porcelain, gift and promotional articles. The company was moved to *Stockheim* in 1978.

Burgsteinfurt
Westphalia, Germany

H. Pettirsch Porzellanmanufaktur
(H. Pettirsch Porcelain Manufactory), 1950–   , porcelain decorating shop.
Mark: 1490

Buschbad
Saxony, Germany

L. Schleich Porzellanfabrik
(L. Schleich Porcelain Factory), 1886–circa 1927, coffee and tea sets, decorative
porcelain, porcelain decorating.
Mark: 2417

Carlsbad see Karlsbad

Charlottenburg
Silesia, Germany, presently Zofiowka, Poland

Josef Schachtel, 1859–1919, table, household and decorative porcelain, pipes
and pipe bowls, electrotechnical porcelain. From 1887 until 1916 his sons Eugen
and Max managed the factory, which then became a joint stock company and
three years later was renamed
Porzellanfabrik Charlottenbrunn
(Porcelain Factory Charlottenbrunn), 1919–1945.
Marks: 205, 414, 2137, 2364, 2612

Chemnitz
Saxony, Germany

Alfred Loeffler, circa 1920–   , porcelain decorator.
Mark: 1488

Chicago
Illinois, U.S.A.

Burley & Tyrrell Co., circa 1912–   , importer of German and French porcelain.
The mark 2247 was either affixed on unmarked porcelain or in addition to the
producers mark.

Chodau
Bohemia, presently Chodov, Czechia

Franz Miessl, 1810–1834, founded an earthenware factory and in 1830 began
producing porcelain too. After his death
Johann Hüttner & Co.
(Johann Huttner & Co.), 1834–1845, took over the factory and produced table,
household and decorative porcelain, coffee and tea sets.
Marks: 2724, 2740, 3192
Successors were
Geitner & Stierba, 1845–circa 1850,

Mark: 3124

who sold the factory to

Porges von Portheim, who later took his sons into the company and named it **Portheim & Sons,** circa 1850–circa 1870.

Marks: 2206, 2265, 2877

Haas & Czjzek acquired the factory in 1872 and operated it until it was nationalized in 1945.

See also Haas & Czjzek in Schlaggenwald.

Marks: 367, 384, 394, 2723

Richter, Fenkl & Hahn, 1883–1945, household and table porcelain, coffee and tea sets, decorative porcelain.

Marks: 1471, 1802, 2645, 2905, 3067, 3068

Cologne see Köln

Coburg
Bavaria, Germany

Porzellan- und Tonwarenfabrik Coburg GMBH
(Porcelain and Pottery Factory Coburg), 1898–circa 1930, electrotechnical porcelain.

Mark: 1

Ferdinand Kaule, 1885–defunct, porcelain decorator.
Mark: 1976

Albert Riemann Porzellanfabrik
(Albert Riemann Porcelain Factory), 1860–no mention found after 1927, decorative porcelain, figurines, electrotechnical porcelain.

Marks: 2305, 2536

Coburg-Cortendorf
Bavaria, Germany

Porzellanfabrik Cortendorf Julius Griesbach
(Porcelain Factory Cortendorf Julius Griesbach), 1890–1973, fine earthenware, porcelain figurines.

Marks: 847, 912–915, 1029, 1228, 3201

The company was taken over in 1973 by *W. Goebel Porcelain Factory* in *Rodental* and renamed

Cortendorf W. Goebel, 1973–present.

Colln-Meissen - Cölln-Meissen
Saxony, Germany

Cölln-Meissner Chamotte- und Tonwarenfabrik Richard Müller & Co.
(Colln-Meissen Fireclay and Clayware Factory Richard Muller & Co.), 1874–defunct, floor tiles, fireclay and pottery products.

Mark: 136

Colditz
Saxony, Germany

Steingutfabrik Colditz AG
(Earthenware Factory Colditz) 1841-circa 1948, founded by **Carl August Zschau**, converted into a joint stock company in 1907. Until 1945 the company owned Earthenware Factory Strehla, later VEB Earthenware Factory Strehla and *Edelstein Porcelain Factory* in *Kups*. Mark: 1808
After World War II the company was nationalized and transformed into
VEB Porzellanwerk Colditz (VEB Porcelainwork Colditz),   -1969 and in 1961 began production of household, hotel and decorative porcelain, coffee and tea sets. In 1969 the factory was merged with *VEB Porcelainwork Freiberg* in *Freiberg* to **VEB Porzellankombinat Colditz**
(VEB Porcelain Combine Colditz), 1969-1990, Marks: 2046, 2127, 2162, 3015.
After the dissolution of the combine, the factory was privatized in 1990 as
Porzellanwerke Colditz GmbH (Porcelainworks Colditz Ltd) but closed in 1995.

Creidlitz
Bavaria, Germany

Porzellanfabrik Creidlitz Theodor Gumtau
(Porcelain Factory Creidlitz Theodor Gumtau), 1906–1924, household and decorative porcelain, coffee and tea sets, gift articles.
Mark: 2548

Porzellanfabriken Creidlitz
(Porcelain Factories Creidlitz), formerly Rose, Schulz & Co., 1903–present, coffee and tea sets, decorative porcelain, gift articles, technical porcelain.
Marks: 1149, 1203, 2126, 3223

Siebert & Hertwig Porzellanfabrik Creidlitz
(Siebert & Hertwig Porcelain Factory Creidlitz), circa 1902–1923, household, hotel and decorative porcelain, coffee and tea sets.
Mark: 2245

Dallwitz
Bohemia, presently Dalovice, Czechia

Johann von Schoenau, 1804–1822, founded an earthenware factory. His son **Wolfgang von Schoenau**, 1822–1832, continued and tried from 1830–1832 not very successfully to produce porcelain.
Marks: 2737, 2738, 3135
He sold the factory to
Wilhelm Wenzel Lorenz, 1832–1850, who made earthenware and increasingly table, household and decorative porcelain, also figurines.
Marks: 2737, 2738, 3095, 3135
After Lorenz
Franz Fischer, 1850–1855, was proprietor.

Mark: 2753

He sold the factory to

Franz Urfuss (or Urfus), 1855–1875. Both continued the production program.

Marks: 2208, 2759, 2760, 2950, 3086

Successors were

Riedel von Riedelstein, 1875–1889,

Mark: 921

Baron von Springer, 1889–1891, and

Proeschold & Co., 1891–1918, subsequently it became a branch of

Öpiag

(Opiag), 1918–1920, which later changed its name to **Epiag** and mass-produced household, hotel and decorative porcelain.

Marks: 2165, 3016, 3017

Epiag was nationalized in 1945. See also Karlsbad, Epiag.

Damm
Bavaria, Germany

Steingutfabrik Damm

(Earthenware Factory Damm), 1827–1884, household, table and decorative earthenware, figurines from earthenware and porcelain.

Daniel Ernst Müller

(Daniel Ernst Muller) founded the earthenware factory in 1827. With the aid of its artistic director H. J. von Hefner it soon became one of the important contemporary factories.

In 1860 it was sold to

Kaspar Marzell, who two years later took his brother-in-law Anton Kopf into partnership as

Marzell et Comp. Kopf left in 1872 and Marzell went bankrupt. In 1880 the factory was bought at an auction by the produce company Lindenbaum Son in Frankfurt (Main) who in turn sold it to Ignatz Fertig and Heinrich Dahlem, but they too did not succeed in keeping the factory alive. It was closed in 1884.

Using the original moulds of the 1796 dissolved *Prince-Electoral Mayence Manufactory* in *Hochst* the factory reproduced Hochst figurines in earthenware from 1840 until 1884 and for a few years after 1856 in porcelain. The reproductions were signed with the Hochst wheel accompanied by a D from 1840 to 1860. Marzell used only a wheel with six spokes from 1860 to 1878. Fertig and Dahlem applied a wheel with eight spokes.

The Hochst moulds were sold to *Earthenware Factory F. A. Mehlem* in *Bonn* about 1886.

Marks: 2106, 2107

Darmstadt
Hesse, Germany

C. C. Puhlmann & Sohn

(C. C. Puhlmann & Son), existed 1970–defunct before 1977, figurines.

Mark: 883

Max Roesler Feinsteingutfabrik Abt. Darmstadt
(Max Roesler Fine Earthenware Factory, Branch Darmstadt)
See Rodach, Max Roesler.

Denkendorf
Wurttemberg, Germany

M. W. Reutter Porzellanfabrik
(M. W. Reutter Porcelain Factory), 1948—present, decorative and toy porcelain, gift articles, souvenirs.
Mark: 2681

Dessendorf
Bohemia, presently Desná, Czechia

Richard S. Roesler, 1933—1945, household porcelain.
See also Schauberg, R. S. Roesler.
Mark: 2301

J. Schnabel & Sohn Porzellanfabrik
(J. Schnabel & Son Porcelain Factory), 1869—circa 1931, household and decorative porcelain, apothecary jars, laboratory porcelain.
Marks: 386, 2930

Devon
Pennsylvania, U.S.A.

Ebeling & Reuss Co., formerly in Philadelphia, 1866—present. Importer of porcelain made by *Furstenberg Porcelain Manufactory* in *Furstenberg, W. Goebel Porcelain Factory* in *Rodental, Heinrich & Co.* in *Selb, Porcelain Factory Marktredwitz Jaeger & Co.* in *Marktredwitz, Keramos* in *Vienna* and *Carl Schumann Porcelain Factory* in *Arzberg.* Before World War II also importer for factories in Bohemia. Frequently the original manufacturers mark was substituted by an Ebeling and Reuss mark.
Marks: 744, 745, 1980, 2251, 3021, 3022

Diessen
Bavaria, Germany

F. Hudler Keramische Werkstätte
(F. Hudler Ceramic Workshop) 1921-defunct, porcelain decorating shop, tiles.
Mark: 2581

Dresden
Saxony, Germany

E. Brammer & Co., circa 1904—1923, porcelain and glass decorator.
Mark: 3118

Donath & Co., 1872–1916, porcelain decorating in the Meissen and Vienna styles.
Marks: 396, 1209–1211, 3131, 3200
In 1916 the company was merged with the decorating shop of *Richard Klemm* into
Vereinigte Dresdner Porzellanmalereien Richard Klemm & Donath & Co.
(United Dresden Porcelain Decorating Shops Richard Klemm and Donath & Co.),
1916–1918. Through another merger with the decorating shop of *R. Wehsner* the
Dresdner Kunstabteilung von C. M. Hutschenreuther
(Dresden Art Department of C. M. Hutschenreuther), porcelain factory in
Hohenberg, 1918–1945, was created.
Marks: 699–701

Dresdner Kunstverlag Richard Eckert
(Dresden Art Publishers Richard Eckert), traceable 1909–1911, figurines and
porcelain decorating in the Meissen, Vienna and Capo di Monte styles.
Mark: 2569
See also Volkstedt, Volkstedt Porcelain Factory Richard Eckert.

Leopold Elb, see Helena Wolfsohn

Heinrich Gerstmann, see Adolph Hamann

Julius Greiner Sohn
(Julius Greiner Son) see Lauscha

Grossbaum & Söhne
(Grossbaum & Sons), 1891–1914, porcelain decorating in the Meissen style.
Branch of *Grossbaum & Sons* in *Vienna.* From 1891–1892 the company imitated
mark No. 649, belonging to *Richard Klemm.*
Marks: 397, 2389

Josef Günter
(Josef Gunter), circa 1890–defunct, porcelain decorating in the Meissen style.
Mark: 1977

Adolph Hamann, 1866–traceable until 1949, porcelain decorating in the Meissen
and Vienna styles. 1904 the company was taken over by
Otto Hamann and in 1933
Heinrich Gerstmann is mentioned as proprietor. Both kept the name of Adolph
Hamann for the company that was located in Freital near Dresden in 1949.
Marks: 330, 647, 1209, 1212–1214

Karl Eduard Hamann, 1891–1892, decorator with *Grossbaum & Sons,* imitated
mark 649 of *Richard Klemm.*
Mark: 648

Otto Hamann, see Adolph Hamann

Heufel & Co., 1891–defunct, porcelain decorating shop, especially vases and cups.
Mark: 2307

Franziska Hirsch, 1894-1914, porcelain decorating in the Meissen and Vienna styles. **Fanny Koppel** was proprietor in 1914. In 1930 the shop was acquired by **Margot Wohlauer**.
Marks: 173, 398, 2390, 2391, 2425, 2426

Franz Junkersdorf, 1897–still in existence 1941, porcelain decorating shop.
Marks: 328, 1464, 1479, 2032

Richard Klemm, 1869-1916, stepfather of *Richard Wehsener,* porcelain decorating in the Meissen and Vienna styles, see also *Donath & Co.*
Marks: 649, 1170, 1209, 1210, 1215, 2647

Louis Knöller
(Louis Knoller), traceable 1891–1907, porcelain decorating, especially copies of paintings on plates.
Mark: 2622, also signature "Knoeller."

Wilhelm Koch, later
Hermann Koch, traceable 1928–1949, porcelain decorating shop.
Mark: 3091

Ambrosius Lamm, 1887- last mention found in 1949, porcelain decorating in the Meissen and Vienna styles. Since 1928 **Rudolf Pitschke** was proprietor.
Marks: 26, 148, 1502

Adolf Leube, traceable 1894–1907, porcelain decorating shop.
Mark: 1060

Oswald Lorenz, circa 1880-defunct, porcelain decorating shop.
Marks 1209, 1210, 1441, 2024

Meyer & Sohn
(Meyer & Son), existed in the second half of the 19th century. The company is supposed to have imitated Meissen porcelain.
Marks: 1645, 1646, 1701

Anton Ott, 1922–last mention found in 1940, porcelain decorating shop.
Mark: 3220

Anton Richter, 1887–defunct, porcelain decorating shop.
Mark: 2533

Max Robra, 1919–1928, porcelain decorating shop.
Mark: 1077

Oskar Gustav Schade, 1886–defunct, porcelain decorating shop.
Marks: 531, 2629

Walter Ernst Stephan, see Helena Wolfsohn

Sächsische Porzellanmanufaktur Dresden see Potschappel

Strobel & Petschk, 1869-defunct, porcelain decorating shop.
Mark: 3084

Ella Strobel, 1867–last mention found in 1934, porcelain decorating shop.
Mark: 2262

Franz Till, 1866–after 1906, porcelain decorating, especially copies of paintings.
After Till's death his widow seems to have married the porcelain decorator
L. Sturm who had founded a decorating shop in 1865 and was listed under the
same address as Till.
Mark: 3264

R. Ufer, 1887-   , porcelain decorating shop, later **R. Ufer Successor.** In 1910 Carl
Anhäuser is mentioned as proprietor. Mark: 2263

Villeroy & Boch, 1856-1948, household and decorative fine earthenware, sanitary earth-
enware, floor and wall tiles. See also Mettlach, Villeroy & Boch.
Marks 1792, 2186, 2238, 2672
The company was nationalized in 1948 and named
VEB Steingutwerk Dresden
(VEB Earthenwarework Dresden)   -1990, which is supposed to have produced house-
hold porcelain until 1965. Mark: 1207
After the dissolution of the VEB the factory was closed.

Adolf Wache, 1880-defunct, porcelain decorating shop, especially scenes after Watteau,
Meissen and Vienna styles. Marks: 1173, 1219

Carl Wagner, later
Anna Wagner, traceble 1894-1918, porcelain decorating shop, especially flowers and
Meissen and Vienna styles. Mark: 2204

Richard Wehsener, 1895-present, porcelain decorating shop, see also *Donath & Co.* in
Dresden, continued by his son **Gerhard Wehsener** and his grandson
Werner Wehsener,
Marks: 401, 3282, 3644, 3654, 3663

Helena Wolfsohn, 1843–last mention found in 1949, porcelain decorating in the
Meissen and Vienna styles. Wolfsohn forged the AR mark of Meissen and produced
several tens of thousands of Meissen imitations. In 1894
Leopold Elb became proprietor followed in 1919 by
Walter Ernst Stephan.
Marks: 399, 1032–1035, 1217, 2523–2528
See also Part III, Meissen

Duisdorf
Rhineland, Germany

Westdeutsche Porzellanfabrik

(West German Porcelain Factory), 1904–1935, household, hotel and decorative porcelain.
Mark: 87
The company name was changed to
Rhenania Porzellanfabrik
(Rhenania Porcelain Factory), 1935–defunct.
Marks: 86, 1205

Dux
Bohemia, presently Duchcov, Czechia

Duxer Porzellanmanufaktur vormals **Eduard Eichler**

(Dux Porcelain Manufactory, formerly Eduard Eichler), 1860–1945, figurines, decorative and table porcelain.
Marks: 450, 453, 454, 3246
Duchcovsky Porcelain
(Duchcov Porcelain), after World War II the *Dux Porcelain Manufactory,* the *Eichwald Porcelain, Stove and Tile Factory Dr. Widera & Co.* in *Eichwald* and *Count Thun's Porcelain Factory* in *Klosterle* were nationalized and merged into a nationally owned enterprise. The new company still uses marks similar to those of its predecessors and produces household, decorative and table porcelain, coffee and tea sets.
Marks: 451, 452, 1099

C. Riese Porzellan-, Terrakotta- und Majolikafabrik

(C. Riese Porcelain, Terra Cotta and Maiolika Factory), 1883–defunct, decorative porcelain and earthenware.
Mark: 2734

Ebersdorf
Bavaria, Germany

Arno Apel,

1954-1974, decorative porcelain, knick-knack, candle-holders, gift articles.
Marks: 395, 1052
See also Lauenstein

Eichwald
Bohemia, presently Dubi, Czechia

B. Bloch & Co., 1871–1940, table, household and decorative porcelain and earthenware, also with onion pattern. After 1920 the company was changed into
Eichwalder Porzellan- und Ofenfabrik Bloch & Co.
(Eichwald Porcelain and Stove Factory Bloch & Co.)
Marks: 614, 615, 617, 654, 723, 1036, 1103, 1430, 2218, 2219, 2250, 2715

Successor was
Eichwalder Porzellan-, Ofen- und Wandplattenfabrik Dr. Widera & Co.
(Eichwald Porcelain, Stove and Tile Factory Dr. Widera & Co.), 1940–1945.
Marks: 1101
See also Dux, Duchcovsky Porcelain.

Adolf Schippel, existed 1895, porcelain flowers.
Mark: 365

Eisenberg
Thuringia, Germany

Porzellanfabrik Bremer & Schmidt
(Porcelain Factory Bremer & Schmidt) 1895-circa 1972, household and table porcelain, coffee and tea sets.
Mark: 931
In 1972 the company was nationalized and merged with the likewise nationalized *Porcelain Factory Kalk* in *Eisenberg into*
VEB Spezialporzellan Eisenberg,
(VEB Special Porcelain Eisenberg) 1972-1974, which became branch of *VEB Porcelain Combine Kahla* in *Kahla* in 1974. The factory was closed in 1991. Marks: 932, 1738

Geyer, Koerbitz & Co. Earthenware Factory, 1882-1904, household earthenware. Mark: 688
In 1904 the company acquired **Porzellanfabrik Kalk** (1904-1972)
(Porcelain Factory Kalk) founded 1863 in Cologne-Kalk and moved it to Eisenberg. It produced household porcelain, coffee and tea sets.
Marks: 528, 773, 774, 1739, 1759
The factory was nationalized and merged with the likewise nationalized *Porcelain Factory Bremer & Schmid* in *Eisenberg* into
VEB Spezialporzellan Eisenberg
(VEB Special Porcelain Eisenberg) 1972-1974, which became branch of *VEB Porcelain Combine Kahla* in *Kahla*, closed in 1976. Mark: 487

Porzellanfabrik Wilhelm Jäger
(Porcelain Factory Wilhelm Jager), 1868-1960, table, household, hotel porcelain, coffee and tea sets. Marks: 125, 768, 1236, 3177
In 1960 the company merged with the factory of *F.A.Reinicke* in *Eisenberg* to
Vereinigte Porzellanwerke
(United Porcelainwork), 1960-1972. Mark: 487
The new company was nationalized and changed into
VEB Vereinigte Porzellanwerke Eisenberg
(VEB United Porcelainworks Eisenberg),1972-1974, which became branch of *VEB Porcelain Combine Kahla* in *Kahla* and was closed in 1979. The factory also used mark No. 487

Heinrich Ernst Mühlberg
founded an earthenware factory in 1796. Successors were Bros. Doll (1806-   ) Karl Mühlberg (-1847), Hermann Schulz (1847-1856). In 1865
F.A. Reinicke acquired the factory and until 1960 produced household and

decorative porcelain, coffee and tea sets, also with onion pattern.
Marks: 1253, 2403, 2741. Mark No. 688, attributed to Mühlberg, actually belonged to *Geyer, Koerbitz & Co.* in *Eisenberg*
In 1960 the company merged with *Porcelain Factory Wilhelm Jager* in *Eisenberg* to
Vereinigte Porzellanwerke
(United Porcelainworks), 1960-1972, which were nationalized and named
VEB Vereinigte Porzellanwerke Eisenberg
(VEB United Porcelainworks Eisenberg), 1972-1974. Then it became branch of *VEB Porcelain Combine Kahla* in *Kahla* and was closed in 1979. Mark: 487

Paul Richter Porzellanfabrik
(Paul Richter Porcelain Factory), 1889—defunct.
Mark: 2875

J. Schmeisser, 1865—defunct, household porcelain.
Mark: 2194

Elbing
East Prussia, presently Elblag, Poland

Oswald Bachmann, circa 1910—1944, table and kitchen porcelain, apothecary jars.
Mark: 1474

Elbogen
Bohemia, presently Loket, Czechia

The brothers
Rudolf and Eugen Haidinger in 1815 founded a porcelain factory which three years later was called
Wiener Porzellanfabrik in Elbogen
(Vienna Porcelain Factory in Elbogen), 1818—1873, and produced table and decorative porcelain, coffee and tea sets, laboratory porcelain and figurines.
Marks: 41—45, 441, 2168, 2530—2532, 3119, 3158
Next to some of the marks impressed three digit numbers can be found. They stand for the last three digits of the year of production. The company was sold in 1873 to Springer & Oppenheimer and named
Erste Elbogner Porzellan- und Kohlen-Industrie
(First Elbogen Porcelain and Coal Industry), 1873—1885.
After Oppenheimer left, the name was changed into
Springer & Co., 1885—1918.
Marks: 46, 47, 54, 55, 57
At the end of World War I the factory became a branch of
Öpiag
(Opiag), 1918—1920,
Marks: 52, 53, 56
which later changed its name to
Epiag, 1920—1945.
Marks: 40, 48—50
See also Karlsbad, Epiag.

Johann Hoffmann, circa 1927–1945, porcelain decorating shop.
Mark: 2061

Winter & Co., 1880–1891, first pottery was produced, after 1888 also earthenware and porcelain.
Mark: 103
Successors were
Kretschmann & Wurda, 1891–1899, and subsequently
Heinrich Kretschmann was sole owner, 1889–1938, producing household and hotel porcelain, cups, gift articles.
Mark: 1519

A porcelain factory owned by
Carl Speck, which later was listed as
Carl Speck, Benjamin F. Hunt & Son, is traceable from 1896–1902. It was purchased by
Adolf Persch in *Hegewald* and operated as a branch until it was closed in 1937.
Marks: 949, 1502

Elgersburg
Saxony, Germany

C. E. & F. Arnoldi, 1808–circa 1962, household porcelain, after 1945 only chemical, technical and sanitary as well as laboratory porcelain.
Marks: 2178, 2499, 2624
After World War I the company took over the porcelain factory of
Eichhorn & Bandorf, 1886–1919, household and technical porcelain,
Mark: 570
and the porcelain factory of
E. Diemer & Co., 1886–1919, household and technical porcelain.

Ellwangen
Wurttemberg, Germany

Witwe Arnold Friedrich Prahl
(Widow Arnold Friedrich Prahl), 1758–1764. The manufactory produced porcelain only from 1758–1759, later it returned to manufacturing fayence. A. F. Prahl already had produced fayence in a manufactory in Utzmemmingen.
Marks: 1275, 1276

Erbendorf
Bavaria, Germany

Porzellanfabrik Erbendorf Hans Schrembs
(Porcelain Factory Erbendorf Hans Schrembs), 1923–1940, household porcelain, coffee and tea sets, gift and collectors articles.
Mark: 3037
The company was taken over by *Porcelain Factory Christian Seltmann* in *Weiden* in 1940 and operated as

Branch Erbendorf.
Marks: 1222, 1260, 1262

Erkersreuth
Bavaria, Germany

Gebr. Hofmann Porzellanfabrik
(Bros. Hofmann Porcelain Factory), circa 1900–1936, household and technical porcelain.
Mark: 320

Essen
Rhineland, Germany

Glaswerke Ruhr
(Glassworks Ruhr), existed 1956, mark No. 1964 also was registered as trademark for porcelain.
Mark: 1964

Ettlingen
Badenia, Germany

Porzellanfabrik Ettlingen Emil Leonhardt
(Porcelain Factory Ettlingen Emil Leonhardt), 1920–1940, household and technical porcelain.
Mark: 1476
Successor was
Herbert Pöhlmann
(Herbert Pohlmann), 1940–defunct before 1964.

Eulau
Bohemia, presently Jilovec, Czechia

Gebr. Mehner
(Bros. Mehner), existed 1930, porcelain decorating shop.
Mark: 281

Eythra
Saxony, Germany

Wenzel Ullrich, existed 1930, porcelain decorating shop.
Mark: 2574

Fischern
Bohemia, presently Rybare, Czechia

Bawo & Dotter, 1883–circa 1914, decorative porcelain, coffee and tea sets, gift and collectors articles, porcelain decorating.
Main office in New York, N. Y., U. S. A.
Marks: 114, 188, 827

Karlsbader Porzellanfabrik Carl Knoll
(Karlsbad Porcelain Factory Carl Knoll), 1848–1945, household, table and decorative porcelain, gift and collectors articles.
Marks: 332, 503, 504, 899, 1097, 1098, 1423, 1425, 1426, 2056, 2176, 3120, 3121

Fischhausel - Fischhäusel
Bohemia, presently Hosteradky, Czechia

Richard Schiller, existed 1930, porcelain decorating shop.
Mark: 1902

Frankenthal
Palatinate, Germany

Paul Anton Hannong first produced porcelain in Strassbourg, France, but because the manufactory in Vincennes insisted on its privilege to be sole producer of porcelain in France, Hannong went to Frankenthal and in 1755 began a porcelain manufactory. His son
Joseph Adam Hannong bought the manufactory in 1759 but soon encountered financial difficulties.
Kurfürst Carl Theodor
(Prince-Elector Carl Theodor) was interested in keeping porcelain production in the Palatinate and acquired the manufactory in 1762. During the Napoleonic Wars the French occupied the Palatinate and sold the manufactory in 1795 to
Peter Van Recum, but after only nine months it was returned to the Prince-Elector. In 1797 the factory finally was declared French national property and sold to **Johann Nepomuk Van Recum**, who gave up producing porcelain in 1799. See also Grunstadt.
Table porcelain, coffee and tea sets, decorative porcelain, figurines.
Marks:
Paul Anton Hannong: 81, 123, 1444, 1445, 2797, 2798, 2864–2868
Joseph Adam Hannong: 80, 121, 122, 2610, 2809
Prince-Elector Carl Theodor: 970–978
Peter van Recum: 2636, 2637, 2951
Johann Nepomuk van Recum: 2642–2644, 2904
An attempt after World War II to revive the manufactory was unsuccessful.

Friedrich Wilhelm Wessel, Porcelain Manufactory, 1949–defunct before 1964, household porcelain, figurines, gift articles.
Marks: 1044, 3088

Frankfurt (Main)
Hesse, Germany

Carl Jacobi, existed 1885, ovenproof cooking porcelain.
Mark: 2010

C. & W. Bohnert, existed 1929, porcelain lamps.
Mark: 2289

Franz
Austria

> **J. Poppauer,** circa 1884–1885, ovenproof household earthenware and porcelain.
> Mark: 190
> Successors were
> **Wermer & Riessberger,** 1885–defunct.
> Mark: 191

Frauenthal
Austria

> **Erste Österreichische Porzellanfabrik**
> (First Austrian Porcelain Factory), 1920–1930, household and technical porcelain.
> Marks: 2223, 3045
> Later the company name was
> **Ing. Ludwig Neumann GMBH Abteilung Porzellanfabrik Frauenthal**
> (Engineer Ludwig Neumann GMBH Branch Porcelain Factory Frauenthal) and it
> produced only electrotechnical porcelain.
> The present name is
> **Porzellanfabrik Frauenthal, Figer & Co.**
> (Porcelain Factory Frauenthal Figer & Co.)
> Mark: 2222

Frauenwald
Thuringia, Germany

> **Otto Herrmann Spindler Thüringer Porzellan-, Majolika-, Ton- und Terrakottafabrik**
> (Otto Hermann Spindler Thuringian Porcelain, Maiolica, Pottery and Terra Cotta
> Factory), 1898–defunct, household and decorative porcelain, toys.
> Mark: 392

Fraulautern
Saarland, Germany

> **J. Rupp-Kuhn,** circa 1892–defunct, household and decorative earthenware and
> porcelain, porcelain decorating.
> Marks: 244, 245

Fraureuth
Saxony, Germany

> **Von Römer & Foedisch Porzellanfabrik**
> (Von Romer & Foedisch Porcelain Factory), 1866–circa 1898, table, household
> and decorative porcelain, coffee and tea sets.
> Mark: 2130
> Successor was
> **Porzellanfabrik Fraureuth AG**
> (Porcelain Factory Fraureuth AG), circa 1898–1935, household, table and
> decorative porcelain, figurines.

Marks: 787, 890, 893, 894, 3186
From about 1920–1928 the company operated its Art Division in the premises of the defunct factory of *Kampfe & Heubach* in *Wallendorf.*

Freiberg
Saxony, Germany

Porzellanfabrik Freiberg
(Porcelain Factory Freiberg) 1904-closed 1932, technical and household porcelain. Branch of *Porcelain Factory Kahla* in *Kahla,* after 1927 branch of *Ceramic Works Hescho-Kahla* in *Hermsdorf.* Marks: 2212, 2213, 2217, 2449-2451, 3262. In 1946 newly founded as **Porzellanfabrik GmbH Freiberg,** 1946-1947, decorative porcelain, then nationalized as **VEB Porzellanfabrik Freiberg** (VEB Porcelain Factory Freiberg), circa 1947-1968, in 1968 merged with other factories to **VEB United Porcelainworks Colditz** in *Colditz,* household and decorative porcelain, coffee and tea sets, ovenproof pots. Marks: 1887, 1888, 2135, 2167. After some unsuccessful attempts of privatization 1990-1995 the company by management buy out became **Sächsisches Porzellanwerk Freiberg GmbH** (Saxonian Porcelainwork Freiberg Ltd) 1995-present, household and hotel porcelain, gift articles. Mark: 3594

Freiburg
Badenia, Germany

Risler & Cie., Porcelain Factory, 1847–1927, porcelain-buttons, porcelain-pearls and porcelain-mosaics. The company owned branches in Aachen and Herzogenrath and moved to *Merkstein* in 1927.
Marks: 1791, 2903

Freienorla
Thuringia, Germany

Porzellanmanufaktur Freienorla G. Bodenstab,
(Porcelain Manufactory Freienorla G. Bodenstab), 1895- 1924, household and decorative porcelain.
Porzellanfabrik Freienorla Kurt Müller & Co. KG,
(Porcelain Factory Freienorla Kurt Müller & Co.) 1924-1933.
Mark: 632
Because of financial difficulties the factory was put up for auction and bought by
Frank & Friedheim, 1933-1945
Mark: 2752
After World War II the company was nationalized and merged with *Porcelain Factory Karl Egelkraut* in *Kleindembach* into
VEB Porzellanwerk Freienorla
(VEB Porcelainwork Freienorla),   -closed 1968.
Mark: 480

Freital-Potschappel - see Potschappel

Freiwaldau
Silesia, Germany, presently Gozdnica, Poland

Schmidt & Otremba Freiwaldauer Porzellanmanufaktur
(Schmidt & Otremba Freiwaldau Porcelain Manufactory), 1842–circa 1894, table and household porcelain, coffee and tea sets.
Marks: 1891, 2452
Successor was
H. Schmidt Porzellanfabrik
(H. Schmidt Porcelain Factory), circa 1894–1923.
Marks: 1769, 1170, 2430
Thereafter Bing Glass & Ceramic AG acquired the factory and operated it as
Abteilung Porzellanfabrik Freiwaldau der Bing AG
(Branch Porcelain Factory Freiwaldau of Bing AG), 1923–1929, household and decorative porcelain.
Mark: 424
The company was sold and became
Porzellanfabrik Freiwaldau Robert Tietz
(Porcelain Factory Freiwaldau Robert Tietz), 1929–circa 1945, household and decorative porcelain.
Mark: 1735

Friedland
Bohemia, presently Bridlicna, Czechia

Joseph Eduard Heintschel Porzellanfabrik
(Joseph Eduard Heintschel Porcelain Factory), 1869–1945, first household porcelain, later electrotechnical and laboratory porcelain.
Mark: 2813

Furstenberg - Fürstenberg
Brunswick, Germany

Duke Carl I of Brunswick founded the
Herzoglich Braunschweigische Porzellan Manufaktur
(Ducal Brunswick Porcelain Manufactory), 1747–1807, and 1813–1876 in Castle Furstenberg, but it took six years before porcelain could be produced. During the French occupation Brunswick was annexed by the Kingdom of Westphalia ruled by Napoleon's brother Jerome Bonaparte and the manufactory was named
Königliche Porzellanmanufaktur
(Royal Porcelain Manufactory), 1807–1813. After Napoleon's defeat Brunswick regained its independence and in 1813 the former name was restored. The manufactory produced table and decorative porcelain, figurines, coffee and tea sets.
Marks: 134, 2745–2748, 2750, 2751
In 1876 the company was converted into a joint stock company named
Fürstenberger Porzellanfabrik AG
(Furstenberg Porcelain Factory AG), 1876–circa 1958.
Marks: 858, 1108, 1109, 1635, 2748, 2749

The present name is
Fürstenberg Ehemalige Herzoglich Braunschweigische Porzellanmanufaktur GMBH
(Furstenberg Former Ducal Brunswick Porcelain Manufactory GMBH), circa 1958–
present.
Marks: 1041, 1042, 1229, 2491, 3151

Fulda
Hesse, Germany

Fürstlich Fuldaische Feine Porzellanfabrik
(Princely Fulda Fine Porcelain Factory), 1764–1789, table and decorative
porcelain and earthenware.
Mark: 1277

Gablonz
Bohemia, presently Jablonec, Czechia

Gebr. Redlhammer
(Bros. Redlhammer), 1872–defunct, porcelain-buttons and -pearls.
Mark: 569

Garmisch-Partenkirchen
Bavaria, Germany

Josef Sommer, 1933–present, porcelain decorating shop.
Mark: 358

Gehren
Thuringia, Germany

Porzellanfabrik Günthersfeld Th. Degenring
(Porcelain Factory Gunthersfeld Th. Degenring) 1884-1902, household and decorative
porcelain, collectors´ articles, coffee and tea sets.
Mark: 1664
After the factory was converted into a joint stock company the name was
Porzellanfabrik Günthersfeld AG
(Porcelain Factory Gunthersfeld AG), 1902-1945, which in 1930 mainly produced tech-
nical and sanitary and other ceramics.
Marks 445, 772, 1731
In 1947 the company was nationalized and changed into
VEB Thüringer Porzellanwerke Gehren
(VEB Thuringian Porcelainworks Gehren) 1947-1969, household and hotel porcelain.
Marks: 389, 391
In 1969 the factory was merged with *VEB Porcelainwork Count von Henneberg* in *Ilmenau*
and closed in 1974.

Geiersthal
Thuringia, Germany

Porzellanmanufaktur Geiersthal Langer & Jahn
(Porcelain Manufactory Geiersthal Langer & Jahn), 1938—circa 1970, porcelain decorating shop.
Mark: 2019

Sontag & Söhne
(Sontag & Sons), 1812—1919, porcelain decorating shop.
Marks: 247, 571, 2034
In 1919
Hans Meisel became proprietor and in 1934
Dietrich von Eisenhart, who moved the shop to Rudolstadt and later to Schriesheim.

Gera
Thuringia, Germany

Johann Gottlob Ehwaldt and **Johann Gottbrecht** in 1779 founded a small porcelain manufactory, that was taken over by **Johann Georg Wilhelm Greiner** and his brother **Johann Andreas Greiner** one year later, 1780—1800. They produced coffee and tea sets, decorative porcelain and figurines.
Marks: 2775—2779
J. G. W. Greiners Witwe
(J. G. W. Greiner Widow) inherited the company in 1800 and joined with Gustav Heinrich Leers four years later to
Greiners Witwe & Leers
(Greiner's Widow & Leers), 1804—after 1840.
Marks: 2722, 2768—2774, 3154

Gera-Roschutz, see Roschutz

Germersheim
Palatinate, Germany

Julius Hering & Sohn
(Julius Hering & Son), 1954—present, electrotechnical porcelain. The company was reestablished in Germersheim after the original company *Julius Hering & Son* in *Koppelsdorf* was nationalized.

Geschwenda
Thuringia, Germany

Orben, Knabe & Co. Porzellanfabrik
(Orben, Knabe & Co. Porcelain Factory), traceable 1909—1939, decorative porcelain, souvenirs, gift articles.
Marks: 888, 1148, 2007, 2143

Gevelsberg
Rhineland, Germany

Silberdistel Keramische Werkstätte Breu & Co.
(Silberdistel Ceramic Workshop Breu & Co.), 1947—present, utility and art ceramics.
Marks: 1986, 3257

Giesshubel - Giesshübel
Bohemia, presently Struzna, Czechia

Christian Nonne, who already operated porcelain manufactories in *Volkstedt* and *Ilmenau*, founded another one in Giesshubel near Karlsbad, 1803–1813, coffee and tea sets, decorative porcelain.
Mark: 1745
After his death the manufactory was bought by
Johann Anton Hladik, 1813–1815.
Mark: 1746
Hladik leased the manufactory to
Benedikt Knaute, 1815–1840, it very soon began producing table and decorative porcelain, coffee and tea sets and figurines in good quality in the Meissen and Vienna styles.
Marks: 1747, 1754, 2718
His successor
Franz Lehnert, 1840–1846, who had been manager of the manufactory since 1825, continued the lease.
Marks: 2192, 3155
He lost it six years later and founded a new manufactory in *Lubenz,* after the proprietor
Wilhelm von Neuberg, 1846–circa 1892, decided to operate the profitable company in Giesshubel himself.
Marks: 2850–2852, 3046
In 1892 the company name was
K. K. Privilegierte Gräflich Czerninsche Porzellanfabrik
(K. K. Privileged Count Czernin's Porcelain Factory), later **Giesch** was proprietor, followed by Johann Schuldes, who named the company
Porzellanfabrik Giesshübel Johann Schuldes
(Porcelain Factory Giesshubel Johann Schuldes), 1921–1945, and produced household and decorative porcelain.

Josef Riedl, 1890–still in existence in 1930, porcelain decorating shop.
Marks: 1427, 1434, 1732

Gmunden
Austria

Johann Hufnagel, 1887–still in existence in 1930, porcelain decorating shop.
Mark: 2585

Goritzmuhle - Göritzmühle
Thuringia, Germany

Albin Eichhorn, 1838–defunct, household and electrotechnical porcelain.
Marks: 160, 2129

Gorlitz - Görlitz
Prussia, Germany

Porcelain Factory Carl Hans Tuppack, branch of *Porcelain Factory Carl Hans Tuppack* in *Tiefenfurth,* household earthenware and porcelain.

Gorzke - Görzke
Prussia, Germany

> **Karl Seiler,** existed 1953, ceramic products.
> Mark: 3075

Gottingen - Göttingen
Lower Saxony, Germany

> **Theodor Holborn,** traceable 1889–1945, porcelain decorating shop.
> Mark: 2205

Gohfeld
Westphalia, Germany

> **Keramik-Werke J. Brauers**
> (Ceramic Works J. Brauers), circa 1850–defunct, household earthenware and porcelain.
> Mark: 907, 2000

Gotha
Thuringia, Germany

> **Geheimrat Wilhelm Theodor von Rotberg**
> (Privy Councillor Wilhelm Theodor von Rotberg), 1757-1782, founded the first porcelain manufactory in Thuringia. He produced coffee and tea sets, decorative porcelain and figurines.
> Marks: 2270, 2879-2885
> Von Rotberg leased the manufactory to three decorators, Chr. Schulz, J.G.Gabel and J.A. Brehm, who had worked for him since 1772. Under the name
> **Schulz & Companie,** 1782-1805
> they added table porcelain.
> **Hereditary Prince August von Gotha,** 1802-1813, bought the manufactory from the heirs of Rotberg and appointed his valet
> **Friedrich Egidius Henneberg,** (1813-1834) first manager and then sold it to him. After Henneberg´s death his heirs continued the manufactory as
> **F.E. Henneberg & Co.**, 1834-1883
> Marks: 289, 290, 1778, 2762-2767, 3156
> Then the company was sold to
> **Gebr. Simson**
> (Bros Simson), 1883-1934,
> who mainly produced household porcelain.
> Marks: 1505, 1526

> **Wilhelm Diebener,** traceable 1939–1964, earthenware and porcelain.
> Mark: 383

Morgenroth & Co., 1863–1918, decorative porcelain, figurines, souvenirs.
Mark: 588
The company was acquired by *Friedrich Schwab & Co.* in Gotha.

Fr. Pfeffer Porzellanfabrik GmbH
(Fr. Pfeffer Porcelain Factory Ltd), 1892-1934, decorative porcelain and figurines.
Marks: 861, 2589, 2632, 2633

Schützmeister & Quendt
(Schutzmeister & Quendt), 1889–defunct after 1927, dolls and dolls heads.
Mark: 2656

Friedrich Schwab & Co. Porzellanfabrik Gotha
(Friedrich Schwab & Co. Porcelain Factory Gotha), 1919–defunct after 1950, table and decorative porcelain in the Meissen and Vienna styles. In 1921 production was changed to electrotechnical porcelain and the factory was named
Elektroporzellangesellschaft
(Electroporcelain Company).
Mark: 2066

Grafenhain - Gräfenhain
Thuringia, Germany

Simon & Halbig, 1869–circa 1930, dolls heads, animal figurines.
Marks: 24, 630, 631, 2434, 2932–2936, 3014, 3077–3082, 3126, 3159, 3160

Grafenroda - Gräfenroda
Thuringia, Germany

Bartholomé, Stade & Co., 1910-1919, household and decorative porcelain, figurines, technical porcelain. The company was sold to Reinhold Voigt, who named it
Porzellanfabrik Gräfenroda-Ort Reinhold Voigt
(Porcelain Factory Grafenroda-Ort, Reinhold Voigt) 1919-circa 1972,
Marks: 1079, 1080, 2418
Then the company was nationalized and became
VEB Porzellanfabrik Gräfenroda
(VEB Porcelain Factory Gräfenroda), later it was merged with *VEB Porcelain Manufactory Plaue* in *Plaue.*

Christian Carstens, later **Chr. Carstens KG,** 1819-circa 1945, household and decorative earthenware.
Marks: 377, 2306
After World War II the company was nationalized and named
VEB Gräfenroda Keramik
(VEB Grafenroda Ceramics) -1990
Marks: 378, 1987

Dornheim, Koch & Fischer Porzellan- und Tonwarenfabrik
(Dornheim, Koch & Fischer Porcelain and Pottery Factory), 1880–1938, decorative

porcelain, figurines, gift articles.
Marks: 2318, 2319, 2383—2385

August Heissner Nachfolger
(August Heissner Successor), existed 1930, porcelain decorating shop.
Mark: 2288

Oscar Mell Porzellanfabrik
(Oscar Mell Porcelain Factory), 1891—defunct, decorative porcelain, figurines, religious articles.
Mark: 2297

Grafenthal - Gräfenthal
Thuringia, Germany

Carl Scheidig Porzellanfabrik
(Carl Scheidig Porcelain Factory) 1906-1972, decorative porcelain, figurines, gift and collector's articles, electrotechnical porcelain.
Marks: 224, 239
The company was nationalized and named
VEB Gräfenthaler Porzellanfiguren
(VEB Gräfenthal Porcelain Figurines) 1972-1990. In 1990 it was privatized as
Porzellanfiguren Gräfenthal GmbH
(Porcelain Figurines Gräfenthal Ltd) 1990-present. Mark: 3612

Unger, Schneider & Cie., 1861—1887, decorative porcelain, figurines, dolls heads, souvenirs, religious articles, household porcelain.
Marks: 1748—1752, 2943
The company was continued as
Carl Schneider's Erben
(Carl Schneider's Heirs), 1887—circa 1972.
Marks: 776, 1752, 1753, 2586

Weiss, Kühnert & Co.
1891-circa 1972, decorative porcelain, figurines, dolls, religious articles.
Marks: 2187, 2422. The company was nationalized and became
VEB Gebrauchsporzellan
(VEB Utility Porcelain) circa 1972-1990, decorative porcelain, lamps, candlesticks, beermugs. Mark 2155. In 1990 the company was privatized and named
Porzellanmanufaktur Gräfenthal
(Porcelain Manufactory Gräfenthal) 1990-closed in 1993.

Grafenthal-Meernach - Gräfenthal-Meernach
Thuringia, Germany

Theodor Wagner & Co. 1897-1900, later **Porzellanfabrik Heinz & Co.** (Porcelain Factory Heinz & Co.) 1900 -1972, decorative porcelain, figurines, lamps, religious articles. Marks: 2214, 2584. Nationalized in 1972 and used as storage buildings. Restituted to the former owners in 1994. Today **Heinz & Co. Porzellanfabrik GmbH** (Heinz & Co. Porcelain Factory Ltd) 1994-

Granesau
Bohemia, presently Chranisov, Czechia

> **Heinzl & Co.**, 1924–1945, mugs, cups, pots.
> Mark: 1120, 2228

Greising
Saxony, Germany

> **Josef Strnact, Jr.**, existed 1930, porcelain decorating shop.
> Mark: 608

Grenzhausen
Palatinate, Germany

> **Merkelbach & Wick**, 1872–1921, beersteins, punch bowls, goblets and other stoneware.
> Mark: 2142
> The heirs of the founders separated and the factory became a joint stock company under the name
> **Wick-Werke AG**
> (Wick Works AG), 1921–present.
> Marks: 2500, 2682, 3284

Grossbreitenbach
Thuringia, Germany

> **Anton Friedrich Wilhelm Ernst von Hopfgarten**, 1777-1782, produced decorative porcelain, coffee and tea sets.
> **Gotthelf Greiner** and his successors operated the manufactory from 1782-1869 and added household porcelain to the production program.
> Marks: 455, 471, 2344
> They sold the manufactory to **H. Bühl & Söhne** (H. Buhl & sons) 1869-1932
> Marks: 472, 483, 871, 1045, 2379,
> after that several other proprietors. Nationalized in 1972 and closed shortly thereafter.

> **Margarete Freitag**, 1938–circa 1956, gift articles, decorative porcelain, figurines, pipes and pipe bowls, souvenirs.
> Marks: 1064, 1065
> About 1956 the factory became a semi-national company that later became a subsidiary of *VEB Porcelain Combine Colditz* in *Colditz*. The last proprietor **Irmgard Lang** left the German Democratic Republic and established a new factory in Eberau, Bavaria.

> **Franz Fritz**, 1874-1905,
> **Franz Fritz Nachfolger**
> (Franz Fritz Successor), 1905-1973, gift articles, souvenirs, pipe bowls, coffee and tea sets. In 1906

Hugo Zedler is mentioned as proprietor and in 1972
Horst Zedler.
Marks: 2131, 2579

Adolph Harras, 1861-1898, and
Adolph Harras Nachfolger
(Adolph Harras Successor) 1898-1930, decorative porcelain, souvenirs, gift articles, pipe bowls and porcelain decorating.
Mark: 138
The company was continued as
Großbreitenbacher Porzellanfabrik
(Grossbreitenbach Porcelain Factory), 1930 - closed 1934, household and decorative porcelain, coffee and tea sets, gift articles, laboratory porcelain.

Porzellanmanufaktur C. Alfred Römhild
(Porcelain Manufactory C. Alfred Romhild), 1914-1972, porcelain decorating shop for gift articles, souvenirs, pipe bowls and decorative porcelain.
Marks: 2271, 3011
In 1972 the company was nationalized and merged with *VEB Henneberg Porcelain* in *Ilmenau*

Grossdubrau
Saxony, Germany

Margaretenhütte H. Schomburg & Söhne
(Margaretenhutte, H. Schomburg & Sons) 1877-1945, electrotechnical porcelain.
Marks: 596, 2279
The company was nationalized after World War II and named
VEB Elektroporzellan Großdubrau
(VEB Electroporcelain Großdubrau)   -1990, when the VEB was dissolved..
Marks 1901, 2279

Grunlas - Grünlas
Bohemia, presently Loucky, Czechia

Porzellanfabrik Richard Kämpf
(Porcelain Factory Richard Kampf), 1912–1945, table and household porcelain, coffee and tea sets.
Marks: 129, 1078, 1168, 1993

Grunstadt - Grünstadt
Palatinate, Germany

Johann Nepomuk van Recum, the last proprietor of the manufactory in *Frankenthal*, founded a fayence manufactory in 1799. After his death in 1801 his heirs made reproductions of Frankenthal figurines in a creme-colored earthenware, the so-called "porcelain opaque".
Mark: 2641
They sold the manufactory to the

Gebr. Wilhelm und Reinhold Bordolo
(Bros. Wilhelm and Reinhold Bordolo), 1812–early 20th century. The brothers Bordolo continued making Frankenthal reproductions, but beginning in 1818 also produced household, table and decorative earthenware.
Marks: 220, 895, 2132, 2713, 2787, 3228
The present name of the company is
Steingutfabrik Grünstadt H. Kalau vom Hofe
(Earthenware Factory Grunstadt H. Kalau vom Hofe).
Mark: 447

Gutenbrunn
Palatinate, Germany

A porcelain manufactory founded in 1767 by the physicist
Dr. Stahl was acquired by
Herzog Christian IV. von Pfalz-Zweibrücken
(Duke Christian IV of Palatinate-Zweibrucken) one year later. After the manufactory was destroyed in a flood in 1769, it was rebuilt in Zweibrucken, but closed in 1775. It produced table and decorative porcelain, coffee and tea sets and figurines.
Mark: 2685

Haida
Bohemia, presently Novy Bor, Czechia

Carl Friedrich Boseck & Co., 1880–defunct after 1934, decorators of table and decorative porcelain.
Mark: 311

Franz Josef Grohmann, circa 1868–defunct, porcelain decorating shop.
Mark: 1785

Paepke & Schäfer
(Paepke & Schafer), existed 1930, porcelain decorating shop.
Marks: 498, 563

Haindorf
Bohemia, presently Hejnice, Czechia

Josef Kratzer & Söhne Porzellanfabrik
(Josef Kratzer & Sons Porcelain Factory), 1880–1945, coffee and tea sets, apothecary jars.
Marks: 550, 1799

Haldensleben
Prussia, Germany

Carl Hubbe, circa 1875-circa 1920, household and decorative earthenware and porcelain.

Mark: 33
The company was acquired by
C. & E. Carstens, circa 1920-1924, then it merged with J. Uffrecht & Co. in Haldensleben
to
Carstens-Uffrecht, 1924-1945
Marks: 1757, 1912
After World War II the company was nationalized and became a branch of VEB
Earthenwareworks Haldensleben, 1945-1990.

Gebr. Hubbe
(Bros. Hubbe), 1875–circa 1898, household and decorative earthenware and
porcelain.
Marks: 1489, 1854
The company became part of German Earthenware Factory AG about 1898.

Ley & Weidermann, 1882–circa 1959, decorative earthenware.
Mark: 482
Hugo Lonitz, 1868–1886, later
Hugo Lonitz & Co., 1886–circa 1904, household and decorative porcelain and
earthenware, collectors and gift articles.
Mark: 335

Porzellanfabrik Saxonia Georg Bennewitz
(Porcelain Factory Saxonia Georg Bennewitz) circa 1928-1932, household porcelain.
Marks: 1859, 3083

Steingutfabrik Sauer & Roloff
(Earthenware Factory Sauer & Roloff), circa 1905-1932, household porcelain and earth-
enware.
Marks: 444, 500

J. Uffrecht & Co., 1855–1924, household earthenware.
Marks: 1048, 2949
The company in 1924 merged with *C. & E. Carstens* to *Carstens-Uffrecht.*

Halle
Saxony-Anhalt, Germany

Porzellanmalerei Erika Lutz
(Porcelain Decorating Shop Erika Lutz), traceable 1953–1974, porcelain decorating.
Mark: 613

Hamburg
Germany

Johann Carl Ludwig Harms, 1879–defunct, porcelain decorating and porcelain
export.
Mark: 2028

Reuter & Graefe, circa 1905—defunct, sanitary porcelain.
Mark: 1823

L. J. Schulz until 1959 and
Uhlenhorst-Studio until present, porcelain decorating shop.
Mark: 282

G. Schumacher, circa 1884—defunct, terra cotta and imitations of porcelain made
from "Kallipasta" and "Chromopasta."
Mark: 1989

Spiermann & Wessely, 1872—defunct, Dutch tiles, earthenware and porcelain
decorating.
Mark: 1781

Hausen
Bavaria, Germany

Gebr. Silbermann
(Bros. Silbermann), 1802—1938, household porcelain, coffee and tea sets,
pipe bowls.
Marks: 3, 2796
The company was taken over by Alboth & Kaiser, see Staffelstein, Kaiser-Porcelain.

Hegewald
Bohemia, presently Hajniste, Czechia

Adolf Persch Porzellanfabrik
(Adolf Persch Porcelain Factory), 1850—circa 1945, household and decorative
porcelain, apothecary jars. The company had a branch in *Elbogen*.
Marks: 238, 1442, 2158, 2501, 2502, 2707

Henneberg
Thuringia, Germany

C. E. & F. Arnoldi, branch of *C. E. & F. Arnoldi* in *Elgersburg*.

Hermsdorf
Thuringia Germany

Porzellanfabrik Kahla, Filiale Hermsdorf-Klosterlausnitz
(Porcelain Factory Kahla, Branch Hermsdorf-Klosterlausnitz). 1890-circa 1927,
electrotechnical and technical porcelain, household porcelain.
Marks 1962, 1963, 2134, 2281, 2283-2287, 2869.
After the company of *Schomburg & Sons* in *Berlin* had merged with *Porcelain Factory
Kahla* in *Kahla*, the factory in Hermsdorf became part of the new
Keramische Werke Hescho-Kahla (Ceramic Works Hescho-Kahla) 1927-1945. After
World War II the company was expropriated and became Soviet property as
SAG Hescho. In 1952 the Soviet Union transfered ownership to the government of the

GDR, which named the company **VEB Kombinat Keramische Werke Hermsdorf** (VEB Combine Ceramic Works Hermsdorf). 1952-1990. To the combine belonged branches in Kloster Veilsdorf, Konitz, Sonneberg and Neuhaus-Schierschnitz. After the dissolution of the GDR in 1990 the company was converted into a Ltd **Tridelta GmbH Hermsdorf,** 1992-1996, and then bought by Ceram Holding GmbH in Jena. The present name is **Porzellanfabrik Hermsdorf** (Porcelain Factory Hermsdorf) Mark: 2280, 2281

Hettenheidelheim
Palatinate, Germany

Hagenburger-Schwalb, —present, porcelain, pottery and fireclay products.
Mark: 306

Hildburghausen
Thuringia, Germany

Wilhelm Simon & Co., 1846—1910, dolls heads and parts.
Mark: 10

Hildesheim
Prussia, Germany

August Otto Ernst von dem Busch, 1745—1775, porcelain decorator.
Marks: 957, 958

Johann Gottfried Kratzberg, 1773—1784, porcelain decorator.
Mark: 3195

Hilpoltstein
Bavaria, Germany

Hilpoltsteiner Porzellanmanufaktur H. Bräuer KG
(Hilpoltstein Porcelain Manufactory H. Brauer KG), 1955—present, technical porcelain.
Mark: 2231

Hirschau
Bavaria, Germany

Ernst Dorfner & Cie., 1850—defunct after 1919, household porcelain.
Marks: 2739, 2743, 3018

Hirschen
Bohemia, presently Jeleny, Czechia

H. Reinl Porzellanfabrik
(H. Reinl Porcelain Factory), 1846—1945, household porcelain, tiles. Branch factory in Lubenz.
Marks: 162, 1002, 2604

Hochst - Höchst
Hesse, Germany

In 1746 the merchant
Johann Christoph Göltz
(Johann Christoph Goltz) and his son-in-law
Johann Felician Clarus founded a porcelain manufactory together with the decorator
Adam Friedrich von Löwenfinck
(Adam Friedrich von Lowenfinck), who had come from Meissen. They obtained a privilege from Prince-Elector Friedrich Carl von Ostein in Mayence. Despite his claim to know the secret of porcelain making, Lowenfinck only could produce high quality fayence he called "fayence porcelain." After continued arguments with Goltz, Lowenfinck left the company followed by Clarus one year later. With the aid of Johann Kilian Benckgraff, who had come from Vienna, Goltz succeeded in producing porcelain in 1750. After Benckgraff left Hochst in 1753 for Furstenberg, Goltz encountered financial difficulties and went bankrupt in 1756. The Prince-Elector took over the manufactory and appointed Johann Heinrich Maass and Ferdinand Maass managers of the now
Churfürstlich Privilegierte Porcelain Fabrique
(Prince-Electoral Privileged Porcelain Factory), 1756–1776. It produced table and decorative porcelain, coffee and tea sets and figurines. J. H. and F. Maass operated the manufactory for their own profit from 1759 until 1764 and for the first time were financially successful. They left for not yet determined reasons. The new Prince-Elector Emmerich Josef von Breidbach-Burresheim converted the manufactory into a joint stock company, which beginning in 1776 was called
Churfürstlich Mainzische Manufaktur
(Prince-Electoral Mayence Manufactory), 1776–1796. But financial success still eluded the company. The joint stock company was dissolved in 1778 and the manufactory became state's property until it was closed in 1796.
Marks of Goltz' manufactory and the Prince-Electoral Privileged Porcelain Factory:
876–881, 2069–2094, 2104, 2105, 2108–2116, 2118, 2119
Marks of the Prince-Electoral Mayence Manufactory:
2095–2100, 2116, 2118
About three hundred moulds of the manufactory were sold to *Earthenware Factory Damm* in *Damm* about 1840. From there they went to *F. A. Mehlem* in *Bonn* and later to *Dressel, Kister & Co.* in *Passau*. After World War II the moulds came into possession of a group that tried to revive the manufactory in *Frankenthal*. This enterprise failed and the moulds reportedly were destroyed. In 1947 Rudolf Schafer together with a businessman and a porcelain technician founded the
Porzellanmanufaktur Höchst
(Porcelain Manufactory Hochst), 1947–1964, but the company had to close because of financial problems.
Mark: 902
Two years later in another attempt the
Höchster Porzellanmanufaktur GMBH
(Hochst Porcelain Manufactory GMBH), 1965–present, was founded, producing table and decorative porcelain, coffee and tea sets and figurines.
Mark: 2117

Hohr-Grenzhausen - Höhr-Grenzhausen
Palatinate, Germany

Dümmler & Breiden
(Dummler & Breiden), 1883—present, decorative fine stoneware, beersteins.
Marks: 2382, 2423

Karl Gerhards Nachfolger
(Karl Gerhards Successor), 1832—present, beersteins from stoneware.
Mark: 2225

R. Merkelbach, 1845—present, beersteins, tankards, punch bowls.
Mark: 633

Klaus & Peter Müller
(Klaus & Peter Muller), 1950—present, gift articles, souvenirs, figurines, decorative porcelain. The present company name is
Peter Müller
(Peter Muller).
Marks: 1137, 1143, 2261

Albert Jacob Thewald Steinzeugfabrik
(Albert Jacob Thewald Stoneware Factory), 1893—present, beersteins, punch bowls, pitchers.
Marks: 1877—1879

Hof-Moschendorf
Bavaria, Germany

Porzellanfabrik Moschendorf
(Porcelain Factory Moschendorf), 1878—circa 1945, household and decorative porcelain, dolls heads. In 1938
Otto Reinecke became proprietor.
Marks: 71, 534, 833, 901, 1254, 2635, 2871—2873, 3050—3054

Hohenberg
Bavaria, Germany

Porzellanfabrik C. M. Hutschenreuther
(Porcelain Factory C. M. Hutschenreuther), 1814—1969, Carl Magnus Hutschenreuther began the first industrial production of porcelain in Bavaria. After his death in 1845 his son Lorenz Hutschenreuther continued the company, but left in 1857 to set up his own *Porcelain Factory Lorenz Hutschenreuther* in the neighboring city of *Selb*. C. M. Hutschenreuther became a joint stock company in 1904 and expanded quickly by acquiring *Porcelain Factory M. Zdekauer* in *Altrohlau* (1909), *Porcelain Factory Arzberg* in *Arzberg* (1918) and *Porcelain Factory C. Tielsch* in *Altwasser* (1918).
In 1969 C. M. Hutschenreuther and Lorenz Hutschenreuther were merged to *Hutschenreuther AG* in *Selb*.

Household, table, hotel and decorative porcelain, figurines, gift articles.
Marks: 115, 689, 694–698, 725, 738–740, 830, 836, 837, 1422, 1431, 1432, 1648, 1649, 2035, 2125, 2136, 2605, 2606

Horn
Bohemia, presently Hory, Czechia

H. Wehinger & Co., 1905–1945, household and electrotechnical porcelain. Marks: 1197, 1998, 1999

Hornberg
Badenia, Germany

Georg Friedrich Horn in 1817 founded an earthenware factory, but he called it "Porcelaine Factory" and later "Stone Porcelain Factory." Since Horn's office as a tax collector did not agree with his occupation as a businessman, he transferred his factory to his two sons, who as
Gebr. Horn
(Bros. Horn), 1822–circa 1905, produced table, decorative and household earthenware.
Marks: 182, 183, 3174
Later the factory became a joint stock company under the name
Schwarzwälder Steingutfabrik AG
(Black Forest Earthenware Factory AG)
Marks: 354–356, 1501
The present name is
Duravit-Hornberg, Sanitär-Keramisches Werk
(Duravit-Hornberg, Sanitary Ceramic Work).

Huttengrund - Hüttengrund
Thuringia, Germany

Porzellanfabrik Paul Rauschert
(Porcelain Factory Paul Rauschert), 1898-1945. The company, which produced chemical and technical porcelain, was nationalized after 1945 and became a branch of VVB Glass/Ceramic of the State of Thuringia, but was closed a few years later.
Mark: 2876
see also *Pressig, Steinwiesen, Schmiedeberg*

Huttensteinach - Hüttensteinach
Thuringia, Germany

Gebr. Schoenau
(Bros. Schoenau), 1865-1920, household, table and decorative porcelain.
Marks: 1905, 1906, 2291, 2392, 2393, 2790, 2791
The company was merged with
Swaine & Co., 1854-1920, household, table, decorative and technical porcelain.
Marks: 85, 1825-1827, 1970-1973, 2068, 2184, 2659, 3259

Gebr. Schoenau, Swaine & Co.

(Bros Schoenau, Swaine & Co.) 1920-1954. It also produced dolls' heads.
Marks: 327, 1907, 1974
In 1954 the company was nationalized and named

VEB Sonneberger Porzellanfabriken

(VEB Sonneberg Porcelain Factories) 1954-1990
Marks: 1908, 2151

Hummendorf

Bavaria, Germany

Fritz Popp Porzellanmanufaktur

(Fritz Popp Porcelain Manufactory),   —present, porcelain decorating shop.
Mark: 1156

Ilmenau

Thuringia, Germany

Christian Zacharias Gräbner, 1777-1782, founded one of the oldest manufactories in Thuringia, but he soon encountered financial problems and

Herzog Karl August von Sachsen-Weimar

(Duke Karl August of Saxony-Weimar) took over the company, 1782-1786, which produced table and decorative porcelain, coffee and tea sets.
Marks: 2394, 2811

Gotthelf Greiner, 1786-1792, who also owned the manufactories in *Limbach* and *Grossbreitenbach*, leased the manufactory.
Marks: 456, 457, 2362, 2363, 2395
He was followed by

Christian Nonne, 1792-1808, who first leased the manufactory and later bought it. He also produced medallions in the Wedgwood style.
Marks: 2372, 2803-2807
He took in as partner his son-in-law Ernst Karl Roesch and they named the company

Nonne & Roesch, 1808-1813, until Nonne's death.
Marks: 2803-2807, 2854
Roesch and his successors operated the company under the name

Ilmenauer Porzellanfabrik

(Ilmenau Porcelain Factory), 1813-1871, which was converted into a joint stock company

Ilmenauer Porzellanfabrik AG, 1871-1938, later the name was changed to

Ilmenauer Porzellanfabrik Graf von Henneberg AG

(Ilmenau Porcelain Factory Count von Henneberg), 1938-1947.
Marks: 283-285, 287, 297, 298, 627-629, 2202
After World War II the factory was nationalized und first named

VEB Porzellanwerk Graf von Henneberg

(VEB Porcelain Work Count von Henneberg), 1947-1973
Marks: 284-286
and then

VEB Henneberg Porzellan

(VEB Henneberg Porcelain), 1973-1990. Table and decorative porcelain, coffee and tea sets and figurines. Marks: 291-293.

After the demise of the GDR the company was privatized as

Graf von Henneberg Porzellan GmbH

(Count von Henneberg Porcelain Ltd) 1990-present.

Mark: 3602

Dr. Helmuth Fischer, circa 1928–1945, glass factory mark, No. 2674 also registered for porcelain products.

Fischer, Naumann & Co., 1860–last mention found in 1937, household and decorative earthenware, dolls and dolls heads, toys.

Mark: 288

Galluba & Hoffmann, 1888-closed 1937, decorative porcelain, figurines, gift articles.

Marks: 710, 2253, 2424, 2436, 3208

Gebr. Metzler & Ortloff

(Bros. Metzler & Ortloff), 1875-1972, household and decorative porcelain, gift articles, toys, dolls´ heads.

Marks: 889, 1066, 1920, 3020

The company was nationalized and changed into

VEB Kunstporzellan

(VEB Art Porcelain), 1972-1990, decorative porcelain and figurines.

Mark: 1921

Küchler & Co.

(Kuchler & Co.), circa 1900–defunct.

Mark: 610

Porzellanfabrik Arno Fischer

(Porcelain Factory Arno Fischer), 1907-1952, household and decorative porcelain, figurines.

Marks: 643, 690, 715, 1491, 2059, 2400

The factory was nationalized and named

VEB Ilmenauer Zier- und Werbeporzellanfabrik

(VEB Ilmenau Decorative and Promotional Porcelain Factory), 1952-1990

Mark: 3087

August Schmidt, existed 1930, porcelain decorator.

Mark: 34

Schumann & Klett, 1872–last mention found in 1927, coffee and tea sets, decorative and technical porcelain.

Marks: 295, 1967

Immenhausen

Hesse, Germany

Richard Süssmuth Glashütte Immenhausen

(Richard Sussmuth Glasswork Immenhausen), —present.
Marks: 2302 and 2929 are also registered for porcelainwares.

Jokes

Bohemia, presently Jakubov, Czechia

Porzellanfabrik Schürer

(Porcelain Factory Schurer), 1897–1904, and

Porzellanfabrik Jokes Schürer & Co.

(Porcelain Factory Jokes Schurer & Co.), 1904–1914, produced household
porcelain. Successor was

Josef Theodor Menzl, 1914–1945.

Mark: 574

Kahla

Thuringia, Germany

Franz Bauer Porzellanmanufaktur

(Franz Bauer Porcelain Manufctory), 1927-circa 1935, porcelain decorating shop, merged
with **C.A. Lehmann & Sohn** (C.A. Lehmann & Son), 1895-circa 1935, coffee and tea
sets, household and decorative porcelain, Marks: 1816, 1883, to

Bauer & Lehmann, circa 1935-1965. Mark: 737. Then it joined with

August Frank Porzellanmanufaktur (August Frank Porcelain Manufactory), 1894-
1965, porcelain decorating shop, Marks: 720, 1796, to

Kahlaer Porzellanmanufaktur (Kahla Porcelain Manufactory), 1965-1972, porcelain
decorating shop. Mark: 721

This semi-nationalized company was fully nationalized and converted to

VEB Porzellanmalerei Kahla

(VEB Porcelain Decorating Shop Kahla), 1972, affiliated to *VEB Porcelain Combine
Kahla* in *Kahla*, which ceased to exist in 1990.

Porzellanfabrik Kahla

(Porcelain Factory Kahla), 1844-1946, founded by Christian Eckhard. It was bought at
auction by **Friedrich August Koch,** 1856-1872, who sold to his son

Hermann Koch, 1872-1888. Since 1888 a joint stock company. Household, hotel, deco-
rative and technical porcelain. The company owned branches in Hermsdorf, Freiberg and
Zwickau. In 1927 it merged with *H. Schomburg & Sons* in *Berlin* and acquired *Porcelain
Factory Arzberg* in *Arzberg, Porcelain Factory E. & A. Müller* in *Schönwald, Porcelain
Factory Freiberg* in *Freiberg, and*
factories in Margarethenhütte and Roßlau.

Marks: 502, 704, 886, 2181, 2256, 3107, 3185, 3645, 3652, 3659

After World War II the company was expropriated and became part of a Soviet Joint
Stock Company in Germany.

SAG Hescho Work Kahla

(SAG Hescho Work Kahla). 1946-1952. Then it was handed over to the government of
the German Democratic Republic and named

VEB Porzellanwerk Kahla (VEB Porcelainwork Kahla) 1952-1964.

Marks: 38, 903, 904, 951, 2256

In 1964 the factory was merged with *VEB United Porcelainworks Könitz* to

VEB Vereinigte Porzellanwerke Kahla-Könitz

(VEB United Porcelainworks Kahla-Konitz), 1964-1968.

Mark: 905

After a basic reorganization of the nationally owned porcelain factories in the GDR Porcelainworks Kahla-Könitz and seven other factories were merged to

VEB Porzellankombinat Kahla

(VEB Porcelain Combine Kahla), 1968-1979. Then reorganized to

VEB Vereinigte Porzellanwerke Kahla

(VEB United Porcelainworks Kahla), 1979-1990.

Mark: 904

After the dissolution of this company in 1990 the company was privatized under government trusteeship as

KAHLA-Porzellan GmbH

(KAHLA Porcelain Ltd). 1991-1994, but failed. Mark: 3646

Then it was acquired by the newly founded

KAHLA/Thüringen Porzellan GmbH

(KAHLA/Thüringen Porcelain Ltd) 1994-present.

Mark: 3646, 3650, 3651

The branches of Porcelain Factory Kahla lying in the Federal Republic of Germany after World War II remained in possession of the original company, which moved its headquarters to *Schonwald*. In 1972 it merged with *Hutschenreuther AG in Selb* and brought its factories in *Schonwald* and *Arzberg* and *Pottery Factory Schwandorf* and Wiesau into the merger.

To *VEB Porcelaine Combine Kahla* belonged factories in

Eisenberg (1974-1990)	Freienorla (1964-1968)
Gera-Langenberg (1974-1990)	Gera-Roschütz (1968-1990)
Hermsdorf, decorating shop (1974-1990)	Kahla (1964-1990)
Kleindembach (1964 -1968)	Königsee (1969-1900)
Könitz (1964-1990)	Oberköditz (1974-1990)
Probstzella (1963-1990)	Reichenbach (1969-1989)
Rudolstadt, decorating shop (1974-1990)	Triptis (1968-1987)
Uhlstadt (1968-1990)	Volkstedt (1968-1990)

Julius Lange, 1863–circa 1940, decorative porcelain, gift articles, in 1923 **Karl Lange** was proprietor.

Mark: 713

About 1940 the company name was changed to

Paul Seiler, formerly Julius Lange

(Paul Seiler, formerly Julius Lange), porcelain decorating shop.

Kaltenhof

Bohemia, presently Oblanow, Czechia

Franz Peter, 1867–1890, clay- and porcelainwares.

Mark: 2756

Julius Dietl Porzellanfabrik Kaltenhof

(Julius Dietl Porcelain Factory Kaltenhof), 1900–circa 1945, household and

decorative porcelain.
Marks: 1515, 2309

Kaltenlengsfeld
Thuringia, Germany

A private porcelain decorating shop, whose name could not be ascertained yet was nationalized in 1946 as **VEB Porzellan-Kunstmalerei** (VEB Artistic Porcelain Decorating), 1946-closed, decorating shop for table and decorative porcelain.
Mark: 63

Kandern
Badenia, Germany

Tonwerke Kandern
(Potteryworks Kandern), circa 1888—present, decorative and utility pottery.
Mark: 2268

Karlsbad
Bohemia, presently Karlovy Vary, Czechia

The vicinity of Karlsbad (or Carlsbad) was the center of the Bohemian porcelain industry. Many factories included the name Karlsbad in their marks despite the fact that they were not actually located in the city.

Epiag, Erste Porzellan-Industrie AG
(Epiag, First Porcelain Industry AG), 1920—1945, central administration for an association of Bohemian porcelain factories. When the association was founded its name was
Öpiag, Österreichische Porzellanindustrie AG
(Opiag, Austrian Porcelain Industry AG), 1918—1920. The name was changed after Bohemia left the Austrian Empire after World War I and became part of the newly created state of Czechoslovakia.
Original members were
Proeschold & Co., Dallwitz
Springer & Co., Elbogen
Oscar & Edgar Gutherz, Altrohlau
Fischer & Mieg, Pirkenhammer
Later the following companies joined
in 1923 *Porcelain Factory Aich Menzl & Co., Aich*
circa 1927 *Porcelain Union, Klosterle*
in 1939 *Porcelain Factory and Kaolin Wash "Alp", Lubau*
after 1940 *United Porcelain Factories Meierhofen, Meierhofen.*
Mark: 3142
Epiag was nationalized after World War II.

Karlsbader Kaolin-Industrie-Gesellschaft siehe Merkelsgrün
(Karlsbad Kaolin Industry Company) see Merkelsgrun

Karlsbader Porzellanfabrik siehe Fischern
(Karlsbad Porcelain Factory) see Fischern

Porzellanmanufaktur Josef Kuba
(Porcelain Manufactory Josef Kuba), 1900–1945, household and decorative porcelain, gift articles, porcelain decorating shop.
Marks: 811, 816
In 1951 the manufactory was re-established in *Wiesau*.

Porzellan Union, Vereinigte Porzellanfabriken AG
(Porcelain Union, United Porcelain Factories AG), 1922–1927, headquarters for *Porcelain Union* in *Klosterle* and *Porcelain Union* in *Turn*.

Friedrich Simon, traceable 1920–1921, porcelain decorating shop.
Marks: 1110, 1775

Karlsruhe
Badenia, Germany

Grossherzogliche Majolika-Manufaktur
(Grand Ducal Maiolica Manufactory), 1901–1927, later
Staatliche Majolika Manufaktur
(State's Maiolica Manufactory), 1927–present, household and decorative earthenware and porcelain, decorative fayence and maiolica, figurines, tiles.
Marks: 432

Kassel
Hesse, Germany

Landgräfliche Porzellanmanufaktur
(Landgravial Porcelain Manufactory), 1766–1788, table and decorative porcelain, figurines.
Marks: 74–79, 2788, 2800

Gustav Kallmeier, existed 1894, porcelain decorating shop.
Mark: 2138

Katzhutte - Katzhütte
Thuringia, Germany

Hertwig & Co. Porzellanfabrik Ernst F. und Hans Hertwig, (Hertwig & Co. Porcelain Factory Ernst F. and Hans Hertwig) 1864-1958, gift articles, figurines, dolls and household earthenware. Marks 155-159, 2244, 3150. In 1958 nationalized as **VEB Zierkeramik** (VEB Decorative Ceramics),1958-1990. After some unsuccessfull attempts of privatization closed in 1990. See *Lenggries*.

Kelsterbach
Hesse, Germany

Landgräfliche Porzellanmanufaktur
(Landgravial Porcelain Manufactory), 1761–1789, decorative porcelain and figurines, from 1768–1789 only fayence.
Marks: 991–998, 2595
Successor was
Johann Jacob Lay, 1799–1802, table and decorative porcelain, coffee and tea sets, figurines.
Marks: 999–1001, 2596, 2597
J. J. Lay also tried to establish a manufactory in Wolfenburg in 1789, but had to give up in 1792.

Kiel
Holstein, Germany

Eduard Bantz, existed 1895, containers from porcelain and earthenware.
Mark: 366

Kirchenlamitz
Bavaria, Germany

Oscar Schaller & Co. Nachfolger
(Oscar Schaller & Co. Successor), 1921–present, household and table porcelain.
Marks: 1177, 1192, 3237
The company is part of the Winterling group. See also Windischeschenbach, Winterling Porcelain Factories Distributing Company.

Rudolf Wächter Porzellanmanufaktur
(Rudolf Wachter Porcelain Manufactory), 1893–present, porcelain decorating on coffee and tea sets and decorative porcelain.
Marks: 2183, 3071

Kleindembach
Thuringia, Germany

Porzellanfabrik Karl Egelkraut
(Porcelain Factory Karl Egelkraut), 1910-circa 1945, collector´s cups, decorative porcelain. After World War II the company was nationalized and then merged with *Frank & Friedheim* in *Freienorla* to **VEB Porzellanwerk Freienorla**
(VEB Porcelainwork Freienorla), 1958-closed 1968. Mark: 480

Thüringische Porzellan-Manufaktur Union Köhler & Quist
(Thuringian Porcelain Manufactory Union Kohler & Quist), 1905–1909.
Marks: 2198, 3270
Porzellanmanufaktur Union Quist & Kowalski
(Porcelain Manufactory Union Quist & Kowalski), 1909–1916,
Porzellanmanufaktur Union Edmund Quist
(Porcelain Manufactory Union Edmund Quist), 1916–1927.
Household porcelain.
Marks: 703, 2020, 2021, 2264

Klentsch
Bohemia, presently Klenci, Czechia

Josef Mayer, son of F. J. Mayer in *Tannawa* founded a porcelain factory in 1835.
Mark: 3190
Later **Anton Schmidt** was proprietor until the factory closed in 1889.

J. Milota Porzellan- und Steingutfabrik
(J. Milota Porcelain and Earthenware Factory), 1823—defunct, household and technical porcelain and earthenware.
Mark: 163

Klosterle-Klösterle
Bohemia, presently Klasterec, Czechia

Johann Nikolaus Weber, 1794—1797, established a porcelain manufactory with the aid of Thuringian workers, but financial success eluded him. He leased the manufactory to
Christian Nonne, 1797—1803, who produced coffee and tea sets, table and decorative porcelain and soon made the manufactory profitable.
After Weber's death the landlord, Count Josef Matthias Thun raised the rent to an amount Nonne considered exaggerated. He gave up the lease and founded his own company in *Giesshubel.*

Graf Thun
(Count Thun), 1803—1805, operated the manufactory for a short time and used the same marks as Weber and Nonne.
Marks: 176—181
Then he leased it to
Joseph Melzer, 1805—1819, who soon achieved artistical and financial success.
Marks: 2663—2665, 2819, 2820
In 1819 the Thun family did not renew the lease and took over the company as
Gräflich Thun'sche Porzellanfabrik
(Count Thun's Porcelain Factory), 1819—1945, household, table and decorative porcelain, coffee and tea sets, figurines.
Marks: 734, 1180—1182, 2663—2665, 2819, 2820, 2946
After World War II the company was nationalized and in 1947 became part of the nationally owned enterprise *Duchcovsky Porcelain* in *Dux.*
This company still uses mark No. 1182.

Porzellan-Union Vereinigte Porzellanfabriken AG
(Porcelain Union United Porcelain Factories AG), 1921—1927, household and decorative porcelain. The Porcelain Union was created by merging the factories
Gottfried & Vielgut, 1901—1921,
Tumar & Vielgut, 1918—1921,
Venier & Co., formerly August Wolf, 1913—1921,
Ernst Wahliss, 1897—1927 in Turn,
and Julius Neumann.
It joined *Epiag, Karlsbad* in 1927 and was closed in 1939.

Mark: 541
See also Turn, Ernst Wahliss.

Kloster Veilsdorf
Thuringia, Germany

Prince Friedrich Wilhelm Eugen von Hildburghausen founded a manufactory, 1760-1797, which produced table and decorative porcelain and figurines.
Marks: 1498-1500, 2373, 2550-2564, 2686, 2687, 2735, 2736
The prince's heirs sold to the five sons of *Gotthelf Greiner* from *Limbach*,
Families Greiner (1798-1822) After that the factory changed hands frequently
Florentinus Greiner (1822-1852)
Heinrich C.E. Fichtner (1853-1859)
Gotthold Greiner (1859-1862)
Wilhelm Theodor Hutschenreuther and Gustav Adolf Kieser (1862)
Kieser & Heubach OHG Kloster Veilsdorf (1863-1884), which changed production to technical porcelain, dolls´ heads, toys, buttons and other small items. Marks: 466-470, 2437-2442
In 1884 the factory was converted into a joint stock company under the name
Porzellanfabrik zu Kloster Veilsdorf AG (Porcelain Factory at Kloster Veilsdorf AG),1884-1946, in addition technical porcelain.
Marks: 2124, 2565, 2566.
After World War II it was nationalized and became
VEB Porzellanfabrik Kloster Veilsdorf (VEB Porcelain Factory Kloster Veilsdorf) 1946-1990, branch of *VEB Combine Ceramic Works* in *Hermsdorf*. Marks: 2163, 2164, 2242.
After the dissolution of the GDR the combine came under government trusteeship as
Tridelta AG (1990-1992) and the factory was named
Porzellanwerk Kloster Veilsdorf GmbH (Porcelainwork Kloster Veilsdorf Ltd) (1992-1994). The factory was acquired by *Paul Rauschert* in *Pressig*, 1995-present.

Kloster Vessra
Saxony, Germany

Porzellanfabrik Kloster Vessra Bofinger & Co.
(Porcelain Factory Kloster Vessra Bofinger & Co.), 1892–1921, household porcelain.
Later
Oscar Fischer and Theodor Lehmann, 1921–1937, were proprietors until the factory closed.
Marks: 1892, 1995

Klum
Bohemia, presently Chlum, Czechia

J. Feresch, circa 1800–1850, household and decorative earthenware and porcelain.
Marks: 3178, 3179, 3191

Köln - Cologne
Rhineland, Germany

Engelbert Cremer & Sohn

(Engelbert Cremer & Son), circa 1793—circa 1800, household, coffee and tea sets from frit porcelain and earthenware.
Marks: 1843, 3130, 3139, 3193
From circa 1800—1825 Cremer operated the earthenware factory in *Bonn* founded by *Prince-Elector Clemens August.*

Porzellanfabrik Kalk G. A. Seiffert

(Porcelain Factory Kalk G. A. Seiffert), circa 1863—1905, household porcelain, coffee and tea sets, technical porcelain.
Mark: 1759
The company was acquired by *Geyer, Koerbitz & Co.* in 1905 and moved to *Eisenberg.*

Konigsee - Königsee
Thuringia, Germany

Adelbert Beck Porzellanfabrik

(Adelbert Beck Porcelain Factory), 1910-circa 1962, household and sanitary porcelain, dolls, toys. Mark: 6
The company was nationalized in 1962 and merged with the former *Porcelain Factory Garsitz Dr. W. Roehler* in *Konigsee* to
VEB Porzellanwerke Königsee und Garsitz
(VEB Porcelainworks Konigsee and Garsitz) 1962-1968, Mark: 489
which became part of *VEB Porcelain Combine Kahla*, 1968-closed 1990

Porzellanfabrik Garsitz Dr. W. Roehler

(Porcelain Factory Garsitz Dr. W. Roehler), 1892-circa 1945, decorative porcelain, toys, dolls.
The factory was nationalized about 1946 and first became
Zweigwerk Königsee des VEB Thüringer Porzellanwerke
(Branch Konigsee of VEB Thuringian Porcelainworks), circa 1946-1962.
Marks: 376, 850, until it was merged with *Adelbert Beck Porzellanfabrik* in *Konigsee* to *VEB Porcelainworks Konigsee and Garsitz* in *Konigsee.* In 1990 the factory was privatized and bought back by the heir Peter Roehler from Roehler Spielwarenfabrik in Forchheim who named it
Kinderporzellanfabrik Königsee
(Children´s Porcelain Factory Königsee), 1991-present.

A. Riedeler Puppen- und Steingutfabrik

(A. Riedeler Doll and Earthenware Factory), 1892-circa 1950, dolls, toys, decorative earthenware and porcelain. Marks 23, 68

Konigszelt - Königszelt
Silesia, Germany, presently Jaworzyna Slaska, Poland

August Rappsilber, 1863—1912, household and hotel porcelain, gift articles.
Marks: 201, 1988
Later the company name was

Porzellanfabrik Königszelt AG
(Porcelain Factory Konigszelt AG), circa 1912–1928, then it was merged with *Porcelain Factory L. Hutschenreuther in Selb.*
Marks: 210, 838, 1243
The factory was nationalized in 1945. In 1979 Hutschenreuther reintroduced the name "Konigszelt" for collectors articles, especially plates.

Konitz - Könitz
Thuringia, Germany

Könitzer Porzellanfabrik Gebr. Metzel (Konitz Porcelain Factory Bros. Metzel), 1909-1945, household porcelain, Marks: 781, 1008, 1009
The factory was expropriated after 1945 and became Soviet property as part of **SAG Hescho** in Hermsdorf. After it had been handed over to the government of the German Democratic Republic in 1950, the company name was changed to **Zweigwerk Könitz des VEB Keramische Werke Hermsdorf**
(Branch Konitz of VEB Combine Ceramic Works Hermsdorf) in *Hermsdorf.* 1950-1958. About 1958 the factory was merged with factories in *Kleindembach* and *Freienorla* to **VEB Ostthüringer Porzellanwerke Könitz**
(VEB East Thuringian Porcelainworks Konitz) circa 1958-1964. Mark: 2296, after another merger in 1963 with a factory in *Probstzella* changing its name to **VEB Vereinigte Porzellanwerke Könitz**
(VEB United Porcelainworks Konitz), 1964-1968. Mark: 2311
until it was merged with *VEB Porcelainwork Kahla* in Kahla to **VEB United Porcelainworks Kahla-Könitz**, which later became **VEB Porcelain Combine Kahla**, 1968-1979 and then **VEB United Porcelainworks Kahla**, 1979-1990. After the dissolution of the VEB the factory in Konitz was privatized and is now **Könitz Porzellan GmbH** (Konitz Porcelain Ltd), 1992-present, specializing in cups and mugs.

VEB Vereinigte Ostthüringer Porzellanwerke Könitz
(VEB United East Thuringian Porcelainworks Konitz), circa 1958-1964 and **VEB Vereinigte Porzellanwerke Könitz**
(VEB United Porcelainworks Konitz), 1964-1968.
Work 1 formerly *Konitz Porcelain Factory Bros Metzel* in *Konitz,*
Work 2 *VEB Porcelainwork Freienorla* in *Kleindembach,*
Work 3 *VEB Porcelain Factory Freienorla* in *Freienorla,*
Work 4 *VEB Porcelain Factory Probstzella* in *Probstzella.*
In 1964 merged with *VEB Porzellanwerk Kahla* in *Kahla* to *VEB United Porcelainworks Kahla-Konitz* in *Kahla,* 1964-1968.
Marks: 2296, 2311

Koppelsdorf -Köppelsdorf
Thuringia, Germany

Julius Hering & Weithase, 1893-1908, coffee and tea sets, household and decorative porcelain.
Mark: 1771
Hering und Weithase parted company in 1908. Weithase joined with Koch to a new fac-

tory **Koch & Weithase**, 1908-defunct
The original factory continued as
Julius Hering & Sohn
(Julius Hering & Son), 1908-1945, and changed production to electrotechnical porcelain.
Marks: 337, 339, 1772, 1773, 2293
After World War II the company was nationalized and named
VEB Hochvolt Porzellan
(VEB High Voltage Porcelain), which later was merged with *VEB United Porcelainworks Koppelsdorf* in *Koppelsdorf. -1990*
J. Hering and Son established a new factory in Germersheim.

Ernst Heubach Köppelsdorfer Porzellanfabrik
(Ernst Heubach Koppelsdorf Porcelain Factory). 1887-1919, dolls´ heads and electrotechnical porcelain.
Marks: 582, 1767, 1768, 1937-1940, 2801, 3019, 3271-3173
In 1919 Heubach and
Armand Marseille, 1865-1919, dolls´ heads, electrotechnical porcelain. Marks: 624, 625, 1845-1848, 2039, 2122, 2232, 2704, 2997-3009, 3109 joined to
Vereinigte Köppelsdorfer Porzellanfabriken
(United Koppelsdorf Porcelain Factories), 1919-1950. Mark: 2226
After World War II the company was nationalized and named
VEB Vereinigte Porzellanwerke Köppelsdorf
(VEB United Porcelainworks Koppelsdorf), 1950-1964, electrotechnical, sanitary and household porcelain. Mark: 2227
Then the company became a branch of *VEB Electroceramic Works Sonneberg* in *Sonneberg,* 1964-1990. After a short period of semi-privatization as **Tridelta GmbH**, 1990-1996, Mark: 2280, the *Electroceramic Works* were fully privatized and named **CERAM** Elektrokeramik Sonneberg GmbH, 1996-present,
Mark: 1766

Porzellan Union
(Porcelain Union), existed 1922, electrotechnical and technical porcelain.
Mark: 2145

Kolmar
Prussia, Germany, presently Chodziez, Poland

Porzellan- und Steingutfabrik Kolmar
(Porcelain and Earthenware Factory Kolmar), 1897—1944, household and electro-technical porcelain, coffee and tea sets, also with onion pattern.
Marks: 266, 1405, 1734, 3032

Konstadt
Bohemia, presently Mlynska, Czechia

Franz Schamschula, existed 1930, porcelain decorating shop.
Mark: 331

Konstanz - Constance
Badenia, Germany

J. A. Pecht, existed 1925, earthenware and porcelain decorating shop.
Mark: 1484

Porzellanmanufaktur August Roloff GMBH
(Porcelain Manufactory August Roloff GMBH), 1927–1929, porcelain decorating shop, see also Munster.
Mark: 662
Successor was
Porzellanmanufaktur Konstanz GMBH
(Porcelain Manufactory Konstanz GMBH), 1929–1935, porcelain decorating shop.
Mark: 661

Kranichfeld
Saxony, Germany

Kranichfelder Porzellanmanufaktur Reinhardt Rothe
(Kranichfeld Porcelain Manufactory Reinhardt Rothe), 1903–defunct, decorative porcelain, gift articles, figurines.
Marks: 321, 322

Kriegern
Bohemia, presently Kryry, Czechia

Steinberger & Co. Porzellanfabrik
(Steinberger & Co. Porcelain Factory), 1919–1945, electrotechnical porcelain.
Mark: 150

Kronach
Bavaria, Germany

Alka-Kunst Alboth & Kaiser, *see Kaiser Porcelain* in *Staffelstein*

Bauer, Rosenthal & Co., circa 1897-1903, household and decorative porcelain. Marks: 4, 324, 325
In 1903 the company became
Porzellanfabrik Philip Rosenthal & Co.
(Porcelain Factory Philip Rosenthal & C.), 1903-present, household, table and decorative porcelain, gift articles.
Mark: 326
See also *Selb*, Philip Rosenthal

Martha Budich,   -1977, porcelain decorating shop, figurines, decorative porcelain.
Marks: 1100, 2427

Gebr. Kühnlenz Porzellanfabrik
(Bros. Kuhnlenz Porcelain Factory), 1884-1930, dolls and dolls´ heads, technical porcelain.
Mark: 2792

The factory was taken over by *Porcelain Factory at Kloster Veilsdorf* in *Kloster Veilsdorf* in 1930 and closed.

Max L. Goebel, 1895-1913, ovenproof cooking pots.
The company name was changed to **Max L. Goebel Nachf. Alfred Fasold**
(Max L. Goebel Successor Alfred Fasold), 1913-defunct. Mark: 2011

Kronacher Porzellanfabrik Stockhardt & Schmidt-Eckert
(Kronach Porcelain Factory Stockhardt & Schmidt-Eckert), later
Kronacher Porzellanfabrik GmbH (Kronach Porcelain Factory Ltd), 1912-1996, first household and technical porcelain, later only technical porcelain. The company owned branches in Dresden and Meissen. Marks 360, 1179, 2937
The company was bought by Ceram, Vienna, Austria and closed in 1996.

OCA-Porzellanfabrik Oechsler & Andexer
(OCA-Porcelain Factory Oechsler & Andexer), 1951-1997, gift articles.
Mark: 1882

R. & E. Pech Porzellanmanufaktur (R. & E. Pech Porcelain Manufactory), 1945- ,porcelain decorating shop. Marks: 2428, 2429

Kronenburg see Ludwigsburg

Krummennaab
Bavaria, Germany

Porzellanfabrik Krummennaab W. Mannl
(Porcelain Factory Krummennaab W. Mannl), 1879–1931, household and decorative porcelain, gift articles.
Marks: 1783, 2015
Successor was
Illinger & Co., 1931–1936.
Mark: 1150
Later
Hermann Lange, 1936–1939, acquired the factory,
Mark: 1244
which was taken over by *Porcelain Factory Christian Seltmann* in *Weiden*, 1939–present.

Kups - Küps
Bavaria, Germany

Lindner Porzellanfabrik KG, früher **Küpser Porzellanmanufaktur Ernst Lindner**
(Lindner Porcelain Factory KG, formerly
Kups Porcelain Manufactory Ernst Lindner), 1932–present, coffee and tea sets, decorative porcelain, gift articles, porcelain jewelry, porcelain decorating.
Marks: 592, 868, 1104, 2568

Oberfränkische Porzellanfabrik Ohnemüller & Ulrich
(Upper Franconian Porcelain Factory Ohnemuller & Ulrich), 1890-1919, household and

decorative porcelain, figurines, clockcases, gift articles.
Marks: 577, 1838, 2818
The company was sold after World War I and named
Porzellanfabrik J. Edelstein
(Porcelain Factory J. Edelstein), 1919-circa 1934. The name was changed to
Edelstein Porzellanfabrik AG
(Edelstein Porcelain Factory), circa 1934-closed 1974.
Marks: 1221, 3138

Wilhelm Rittirsch Porzellanfabrik
(Wilhelm Rittirsch Porcelain Factory), 1950–present, gift articles, figurines in the Meissen style, lace figurines.
Marks: 1492, 2431

Albin Rosenlöcher Porzellanfabrik
(Albin Rosenlocher Porcelain Factory), 1814–defunct.
Marks: 2401, 2534

Royal Porcelain GmbH, now **Royal GmbH Werbeideen aus Porzellan** (Royal Ltd Promotional Ideas from Porcelain) 1972-present, gift and promotional articles. Marks: 364, 751

Wenck & Zitzmann, 1882–defunct, household porcelain.
Mark: 2683

G. Wolf Porzellanmanufaktur
(G. Wolf Porcelain Manufactory),　　　–defunct, porcelain decorating shop.
Mark: 2432

Ladowitz
Bohemia, presently Ledvice, Czechia

Gaebler & Groeschl Porzellan- und Steingutfabrik Ladowitz
(Gaebler & Groeschl Porcelain & Earthenware Factory Ladowitz), 1893–1945, decorative porcelain.
Mark: 1996

Robert Hanke Porzellanfabrik
(Robert Hanke Porcelain Factory), 1882–1945, decorative porcelain, gift articles.
Marks: 796, 849, 2912

Pietzner & Co. Plastographische Gesellschaft
(Pietzner & Co. Plastographic Company), decorative porcelain, gift articles.
See Vienna, Pietzner & Co.

Lamspringe
Lower Saxony, Germany

Niedersachsenwerke Lamspringe

(Lower Saxony Works Lamspringe), 1922–1925, lamps and technical porcelain. Successor was

Hannoversche Porzellanfabrik und Metallwerk AG Lamspringe

(Hannover Porcelain Factory and Metalwork AG Lamspringe), 1925–1934. Mark: 137

Landstuhl

Palatinate, Germany

H. Klinger, existed 1931, porcelain decorating shop. Mark: 2601

Krister Porzellanmanufaktur

(Krister Porcelain Manufactory), subsidiary of *Rosenthal Glass and Porcelain AG* in *Selb,* 1950–present, household and decorative porcelain, coffee and tea sets, gift articles. Marks: 1131, 1132, 1162, 1257, 3199

The Krister Porcelain Manufactory was founded 1831 in *Waldenburg*, Silesia. Since 1927 the factory belonged to Rosenthal in Selb. After World War II Silesia became part of Poland and the manufactory was re-established in Landstuhl in 1950.

Langenberg

Thuringia, Germany

Bufe & Büttner

(Bufe & Buttner), 1902–1913, later

E. & A. Bufe Porzellanfabrik Langenberg

(E. & A. Bufe Porcelain Factory Langenberg), 1913–1972, household and hotel porcelain. Mark: 2140

The company was nationalized in 1972, named

VEB Porzellanwerk Gera-Langenberg

(VEB Porcelainwork Gera-Langenberg) and became a subsidiary of *VEB Porcelain Combine Kahla* in *Kahla.*

Langewiesen

Thuringia, Germany

Porzellanfabrik Langewiesen Oscar Schlegelmilch

(Porcelain Factory Langewiesen Oscar Schlegelmilch) 1892-1972, decorative porcelain, coffee and tea sets. Marks: 19, 443, 657, 1062, 1140, 1428, 2628

In 1972 the company was nationalized and became a subsidiary of *VEB Porcelain Combine Colditz* in *Colditz*. In 1975 it was closed.

Lauenstein

Bavaria, Germany

Keramika Arno Apel, 1954–1974, decorative porcelain.
Mark: 1025
See also Ebersdorf, Arno Apel.

Lauf
Bavaria, Germany

Porzellan- und Terrakottafabrik Fritz Krug KG
(Porcelain and Terra Cotta Factory Fritz Krug KG), 1870–1968, household and decorative porcelain, grave decorations, religious articles.
Mark: 2002
Since 1968 the factory is leased to Stettner & Co. in Lauf.

Deutsche Specksteinporzellanwerke Ravene & Co.
(German Soapstone Porcelainworks Ravene & Co.), technical and laboratory porcelain.
Mark: 2299

Lauscha
Thuringia, Germany

Günther Greiner, 1824–   , later
Ens & Greiner,   –1897, porcelain decorating shop.
Marks: 1959, 1975
In 1897 the shop was moved to Volkstedt.

Julius Greiner Sohn
(Julius Greiner Son), 1871–defunct, porcelain decorating shop.
Marks: 2387, 2590

Leipzig
Saxony, Germany

Oscar Zenari, 1901–defunct, decorator of porcelain.
Mark: 2630

Lenggries
Bavaria, Germany

Eduard Kirsch, 1955–1960, later
Kirsch & Hertwig, 1960–present, decorative porcelain, gift articles.
Marks: 3169, 3170
The present proprietor E. F. Hertwig was co-owner of *Hertwig & Co.* in *Katzhutte* until 1945.

Lessau
Bohemia, presently Lesov, Czechia

Porzellanfabrik Lessau "Concordia"
(Porcelain Factory Lessau "Concordia"), founded 1888, household and decorative

porcelain, cups, coffee pots, later technical porcelain. In 1904
Kühnel & Co.
(Kuhnel & Co.) are mentioned as proprietors and subsequently
Tichy & Schönfeld
(Tichy & Schonfeld), from circa 1910—
Mark: 1469
They are supposed to have sold the factory to *Bros. Paris* in *Oberkoditz*. After World War I the name was
Karlsbader Porzellanfabrik "Concordia" Gebr. Löw & Co.
(Karlsbad Porcelain Factory "Concordia" Bros. Low & Co.), circa 1919–1937.
Mark: 1112
Thereafter the factory was operated by
Winterling & Co., 1937–1945, nationalized in 1945 and merged with the likewise nationalized former *Count Thun's Porcelain Factory* in *Klosterle*.

Lettin

now incorporated into the city of Halle-Neustadt, Saxony-Anhalt, Germany

Heinrich Baensch, 1858-circa 1930, later **Porzellanfabrik Lettin, vormals Heinrich Baensch** (Porcelain Factory Lettin, formerly Heinrich Baensch), circa 1930-1945, household and decorative porcelain, coffee and tea sets, electrotechnical porcelain, apothecary jars.
Marks: 228, 585, 594, 641, 790, 1053, 1198, 1245
After World War II the company was nationalized and first became
Zweigfabrik Lettin der VVB Keramik
(Branch Factory Lettin of VVB Ceramic). Then it was converted into
VEB Porzellanwerk Lettin (VEB Porcelainwork Lettin), 1969-1990, which was a branch of *VEB Porcelain Combine Colditz* in *Colditz*
Marks: 512, 652, 1529
After the dissolution of the combine in 1990 the factory was closed.

Lichte
Thuringia, Germany

Johann Heinrich Leder, 1822-1824, later
Wilhelm & Heinrich Liebmann, 1824-1830, later
Wilhelm Liebmann, 1830-1840, later
Gebr. Christoph & Phillipp Heubach, 1840-1904, subsequently
Gebr. Heubach AG,
(Bros Heubach AG), 1904-1945, since 1938 Otto Friedrich Fürst zu Ysenburg und Büdingen was proprietor. Decorative and household porcelain, figurines, dolls´ heads, dolls, porcelain decorating.
Marks: 529, 578-581, 598, 1465, 2254, 2272, 2273, 2276, 2292, 3152
After World War II the company was expropriated and three years later nationalized and first became a branch of VVB Ceramics under the name
Porzellanfabrik Lichte, 1948-1954. Later changed to
VEB Porzellanwerk Lichte,
(VEB Porcelainwork Lichte), 1954-1972 and then to
VEB Zierporzellanwerk Lichte, 1972-1990, Marks: 583, 597, 642, 645

which was a subsidiary of

VEB Vereinigte Zierporzellanwerke Lichte
(VEB United Decorative Porcelainworks Lichte) 1976-1990.
Mark: 645
Other subsidiaries were:
VEB Grafenthal Porcelainfigurines in *Grafenthal,*
VEB Oldest Volkstedt Porcelain Factory in *Volkstedt,*
VEB Porcelain Manufactory Scheibe-Alsbach in *Scheibe-Alsbach,*
VEB Unterweissbach Workshops for Porcelain Art in *Unterweissbach,*
VEB Wallendorf Porcelain Factory in *Wallendorf*
VEB Porcelain Factory Martinroda in *Martinroda.*
After the dissolution of VEB United Decorative Porcelainworks in 1990, first a holding
owned by Fürst zu Ysenburg and Büdingen was proprietor again,
1991-1993, then by management buy out the company was converted into

Lichte Porzellan GmbH
(Lichte Porcelain Ltd), 1994-present
Mark: 3662

Liezen
Austria

Ferdinand Vasold, 1924—present, decorative earthenware, souvenirs, figurines.
Mark: 149

Limbach
Thuringia, Germany

Gotthelf Greiner, 1772–1797,
Gotthelf Greiners Söhne
(Gotthelf Greiner's Sons), 1797–circa 1850, household and decorative porcelain,
figurines.
Gotthelf Greiner founded the manufactory in 1762 but did not begin porcelain
production until 1772. He and his five sons (Ernst, Johann Friedemann, Johann
Georg Daniel, Johann Jacob Florentin and Johann Michael Gotthelf) acquired
the manufactories in *Grossbreitenbach* (1782), and *Kloster Veilsdorf* (1797), and
leased the manufactory in *Ilmenau* (1786–1792). Greiner used in his early marks
two crossed L's (for Limbach) which could be mistaken for the crossed swords of
Meissen. After the Meissen manufactory complained about the misleading marks,
Greiner in 1787 adopted a cloverleaf from his Coat-of-Arms as mark for all his
manufactories.
Marks: 458–465, 475, 1638, 2326–2343, 2617–2621

Porzellanfabrik Limbach AG
(Porcelain Factory Limbach AG), 1882-1939, decorative porcelain, figurines, souvenirs,
gift articles, dolls. The factory claimed to be the successor of the *Greiner* manufactory in
Limbach.
Marks: 474, 476-479

Linz
Austria

Josef Engler Pfeifenfabrik und Photokeramische Anstalt
(Josef Engler Pipe Factory and Photoceramic Establishment), 1860—present, pipe bowls, porcelain decorating.
In 1964
Eduard Schille was proprietor.
Mark: 726

Lippelsdorf
Thuringia, Germany

Kuch & Co., 1877-1883, Wagner, Apel & Leube, 1883-1901,
Wagner & Apel Porzellanfabrik
(Wagner & Apel Porcelain Factory), 1901-1972, decorative and art porcelain, figurines.
Marks: 35, 803, 1027, 1183, 2675
The company was nationalized and combined with *VEB Grafenthaler Porzellanfiguren* in Grafenthal, 1972-1990. Mark: 1246
After the dissolution of the GDR the factory was restituted to the heirs of its former owners and is now
Porzellanfabrik Wagner & Apel, 1990-present, mainly figurines. Mark: 3615

Lorch
Wurttemberg, Germany

Metallporzellanfabrik Deusch & Co.
(Metalporcelain Factory Deusch & Co.), 1898—present, founded in Schwabisch-Gmund, household and decorative porcelain, coffee and tea sets with silver or gold layer.
Marks: 2005, 2006

Lubau
Bohemia, presently Hlubany, Czechia

Gebr. Martin Porzellanfabrik
(Bros. Martin Porcelain Factory), 1874—circa 1918, household porcelain.
Marks: 748, 2793, 2843
The company was sold after World War I and named
Porzellanfabrik und Kaolinschlämmerei "Alp"
(Porcelain Factory and Kaolin Wash "Alp"), circa 1918—1939.
Marks: 917, 1487, 1522
It was merged with *Epiag* in *Karlsbad* in 1939.

Lubenz
Bohemia, presently Lubenec, Czechia

Franz Lehnert in 1846 founded a porcelain factory after he had left *Giesshubel.* Successors were **Schwab** and later

Porzellanfabrik Gebr. Kassecker
(Porcelain Factory Bros. Kassecker).
Later the company name was
H. Reinl Porzellanfabrik
(H. Reinl Porcelain Factory), branch of *H. Reinl Porcelain Factory* in *Hirschen*.
Mark: 2604

Lucka
Bohemia, presently Lukov, Czechia

Greiner, Gullich & Sternkopf Porzellanmanufaktur
(Greiner, Gullich & Sternkopf Porcelain Manufactory), 1895—defunct, household porcelain.
Mark: 12

Ludwigsburg
Wurttemberg, Germany

Herzoglich Aechte Porcelain Fabrique
(Ducal Real Porcelain Factory) and
Königliche Porzellan Manufaktur
(Royal Porcelain Manufactory), 1758—1824.
On orders of Duke Carl Eugen von Wurttemberg the Ducal Real Porcelain Factory was founded in 1758. Despite the fact that it soon produced artistically important porcelain, especially figurines, it was dependent on subsidies from Duke Carl Eugen. After his death in 1793, the subsidies stopped and the manufactory declined. Four years later Duke Frederik remitted the debts of the manufactory and tried to reorganize it. When he became king in 1805, the name of the manufactory was changed to Royal Porcelain Manufactory. The king died in 1816, but his successor William I was not interested in an expensive manufactory and ordered it closed in 1824. The remaining moulds were sold to *Eduard Kick* in *Amberg*.
Figurines, table and decorative porcelain.
Marks: 164, 165, 168, 169, 175, 511, 960—966, 982—985, 1020—1022, 1040, 1055—1059, 2545
The products of the manufactory occasionally are called "Kronenburg" porcelain.

Porzellanmanufaktur Alt-Ludwigsburg GMBH
(Porcelain Manufactory Old Ludwigsburg GMBH), 1918—1920,
Porzellanmanufaktur Ludwigsburg GMBH
(Porcelain Manufactory Ludwigsburg GMBH), 1920—1923,
Ludwigsburger Porzellanmanufaktur AG
(Ludwigsburg Porcelain Manufactory AG), 1923—1927, table and decorative porcelain, figurines, coffee and tea sets.
This attempt to revive the former *Royal Porcelain Manufactory* failed because of financial difficulties. It succeeded finally with the establishment of
Porzellan-Manufaktur Ludwigsburg GMBH
(Porcelain Manufactory Ludwigsburg GMBH), 1948—present, table and decorative porcelain, figurines, coffee and tea sets in the style of the former Ducal and Royal Manufactories.

Marks: 167, 171, 1096
The marks of the new manufactory are supposed to include the name "Ludwigs-burg" to distinguish them from the old marks.

Georg von Hoffmann, 1948–defunct before 1978, porcelain decorating shop. The company was founded in 1873 in Schlackenwerth, Bohemia, and operated there until 1945.
Mark: 834

Lubtheen - Lübtheen
Mecklenburg, Germany

Lübtheener Porzellanfabrik Gertrud Ludwig
(Lubtheen Porcelain Factory Gertrud Ludwig), 1933–defunct, electrotechnical porcelain.
Mark: 2623

Luftelberg - Lüftelberg
Rhineland, Germany

B. Bertram, before 1924–after 1930, porcelain decorating shop, ceramics.
Marks: 2121, 2541

Mabendorf - Mäbendorf
Saxony, Germany

Mäbendorfer Porzellanfabrik
(Mabendorf Porcelain Factory), founded in 1882, household and decorative porcelain, porcelain decorating shop. In 1918
Matthes & Co. were proprietors, who in 1919 bought the Porcelain Factory Karl Schlegelmilch, 1905–1919. The same year the company name was changed to
Matthes & Ebel, 1919–1928.
Marks: 51, 552, 3205
In 1928
Emil Ebel is mentioned as sole proprietor and one year later
Max Josef Heim, 1929–1937.

Maffersdorf
Bohemia, presently Vratislavice nad Nison, Czechia

Eduard Stiassny Porzellanfabrik
(Eduard Stiassny Porcelain Factory), 1919–defunct, decorative porcelain, figurines, dolls, apothecary jars, technical porcelain.
The company owned a branch in Reichenberg.
Mark: 857

Magdeburg-Buckau
Prussia, Germany

Buckauer Porzellanmanufaktur

(Buckau Porcelain Manufactory), 1833–traceable until 1940, household and table porcelain. In 1930
Ernst Lindner became proprietor.
Marks: 229, 1777

Adolf Bauer, 1865–defunct, household earthenware.
Marks: 1880, 1881

Manebach
Thuringia, Germany

Manebacher Porzellanmanufaktur

(Manebach Porcelain Manufactory), 1880–1927, decorative porcelain and figurines.
The company was taken over by
Franz R. Kirchner & Co., 1927–1945.
Mark: 2396
See also Stutzerbach, Friedrich Carl Muller.
After World War II the company was nationalized and renamed
VEB Thüringer Porzellanwerke, Betrieb Manebach
(VEB Thuringian Porcelainworks, Branch Manebach).

Mannheim
Badenia, Germany

Rheinische Porzellanfabrik Mannheim GMBH

(Rhenish Porcelain Factory Mannheim GMBH), 1900–1933, household and decorative porcelain, figurines, technical porcelain.
Marks: 609, 2799

Fritz Bensinger, existed 1930, porcelain decorating shop.
Mark: 634

M. Sterner Porzellanmanufaktur

(M. Sterner Porcelain Manufactory), circa 1895–defunct, household porcelain and earthenware.
Mark: 620

Marburg
Hesse, Germany

Ludwig Schneider, existed 1924, porcelain decorating shop.
Mark: 2845

Mariaschein
Bohemia, presently Bohosudov, Czechia

Gebr. Schneider
(Bros. Schneider), 1889–defunct, porcelain and fayence.
Mark: 2152

Marktleuthen

Bavaria, Germany

Drechsel & Strobel, 1898–circa 1903, household porcelain, coffee and tea sets, souvenirs, knick-knack.
Mark: 265, 794
Successor was
Porzellanfabrik Heinrich Winterling
(Porcelain Factory Heinrich Winterling), 1903–present.
Marks: 540, 1085, 1193, 2467, 3203
See also Windischeschenbach, Winterling Porcelain Factories Distributing Company.

Oberfränkische Porzellanfabrik Vates & Co.
(Upper Franconian Porcelain Factory Vates & Co.), 1921–1926, later
Karl Egelkraut, 1926–circa 1930, later
Ficker & Co., circa 1930–1933,
household porcelain. See also Kleindembach, Karl Egelkraut.

Marktredwitz

Bavaria, Germany

Jaeger, Thomas & Co., 1898–1902, household and decorative porcelain, coffee and tea sets, gift articles, knick-knack.
Mark: 406
Fritz Thomas left the company in 1902 and founded
Porzellanfabrik Markt Redwitz Thomas & Ens
(Porcelain Factory Markt Redwitz Thomas & Ens), 1903–1908.
Mark: 1507
Thomas & Ens dissolved their partnership in 1908 and Thomas continued as
Porzellanfabrik F. Thomas
(Porcelain Factory F. Thomas), but sold the factory the same year to Rosenthal in Selb. Today it is a subsidiary of *Rosenthal Glass and Porcelain AG in Selb*.
Marks: 1524, 1531
Jaeger & Co. continued the original company as
Porzellanfabrik Marktredwitz Jaeger & Co.
(Porcelain Factory Marktredwitz Jaeger & Co.), 1902–1979, household, hotel and decorative porcelain, collectors and gift articles, coffee and tea sets.
Marks: 267, 268, 403–405, 1206
In 1979 the company was sold to the Italian company Sebring in Casier, Italy, and the name was changed to
Jaeger Porzellan GMBH
(Jaeger Porcelain GMBH), 1979–present.

Kerafina GMBH Porzellanfabrik
(Kerafina GMBH Porcelain Factory), 1950–present, decorative porcelain, gift articles, porcelain lamps, technical porcelain.
Marks: 619, 651, 920, 1129, 1133–1136, 1201

Krister Porzellanmanufaktur siehe Landstuhl
(Krister Porcelain Manufactory) see Landstuhl

Franz Neukirchner Porzellanmanufaktur
(Franz Neukirchner Porcelain Manufactory), 1916—present, household, table, hotel and decorative porcelain, coffee and tea sets, gift and collectors articles.
Mark: 818
See Franz Neukirchner in Waldershof.

Marktschwaben
Bavaria, Germany

Keramische Fabrik München-Schwaben AG
(Ceramic Factory Munich-Swabia AG), circa 1929—1937, household, table and decorative porcelain and earthenware.
Mark: 131

Martinroda
Thuringia, Germany

Porzellanfabrik Martinroda Friedrich Eger & Co. KG
(Porcelain Factory Friedrich Eger & Co. KG), 1900-1972, decorative porcelain, gift articles. Mark 1074.
The company was nationalized in 1972 and named **VEB Porzellanwerk Martinroda** (VEB Porcelainwork Martinroda), 1972-1990, since 1975 subsidiary of *VEB United Porcelainworks Lichte* in *Lichte*. After the dissolution of the GDR the factory was restituted to the grandchildren of the founder and renamed **Porzellanfabrik Martinroda Friedrich Eger & Co. GmbH.**

Marwitz
Brandenburg, Germany

Hael Werkstätten für künstlerische Keramik, (Hael Workshops for Artistic Ceramics), circa 1927-1934, decorative ceramics and figurines.
Marks: 2602, 2603, 3157. Successors were
HB Werkstätten für Keramik, Hedwig Bollhagen und Dr. Heinrich Schildt
(HB Workshops for Ceramics Hedwig Bollhagen and Dr. Heinrich Schildt), 1934-1972.
Mark 2594
The company was nationalized and at first named
VEB Steingutfabrik Rheinsberg Betriebsteil Werkstätten für Keramik
(VEB Earthenware Factory Rheinsberg Branch Workshops for Ceramics)
1972-circa 1976. Then the name was **Staatlicher Kunsthandel der DDR Werkstatt für Keramik** (State's Art Dealership of GDR Workshop for Ceramics)
1976-1990. After a short interlude as **ART-Union GmbH** under government trusteeship, 1990-1992, the company was restituted and named
HB Werkstätten für Keramik GmbH (HB Workshops for Ceramics Ltd)
1992-present, decorative and artistic ceramics and figurines. Mark: 2594

Meierhofen, also Mayerhofen - **Meierhöfen**, auch Mayerhöfen
Bohemia, presently Dvory, Czechia

Eberhard & Co., 1897–circa 1914, household, table and decorative porcelain. Successor was

Porzellanfabrik Meierhöfen

(Porcelain Factory Meierhofen), circa 1914–1918, which was acquired by **Britannia Porcelain Works Moser Brothers**, 1898–circa 1925.

Marks: 15, 1520, 1855

The company merged with

Gebr. Benedikt Porzellanfabrik

(Bros. Benedikt Porcelain Factory), 1883–circa 1925, household, table and decorative porcelain,

Marks: 65, 72, 1807 to

Vereinigte Porzellanfabriken Meierhöfen

(United Porcelain Factories Meierhofen), circa 1925–circa 1939.

Marks: 62, 64, 3028, 3029

The company was merged with *Epiag* in *Karlsbad* about 1939 and nationalized in 1945.

Meissen

Saxony, Germany

arite Porcelain GmbH (arite Porcelain Ltd),1993- present, table and decorative porcelain, Mark: 3661

The first European porcelain manufactory was established in Meissen after Johann Friedrich Bottger (Böttger) and Ehrenfried Walther von Tschirnhaus empirically discovered the technological foundations of making hard paste porcelain. Bottger first succeeded in 1707 in producing red stoneware and one year later fired the first porcelain pieces. Saxony´s ruler, Prince Elector Frederick August II (Augustus the Strong), who later became King of Poland as August II, decreed in 1710 the establishment of a porcelain factory as

Königliche Porcellain Fabrique (Royal Porcelain Factory), 1710-1763,

which was continued by his son Prince Elector Frederick August III, as king of Poland since 1734 August III. During the Seven-Years-War (1756-1763) Saxony was occupied by Prussian troops and the Prussian king Frederick II (the Great) considered the factory his property. In 1763 after the war it was returned to the Saxon ruler, who died eight month later. Since his successor Prince-Elector Frederick August III did not become king of Poland, the name of the factory had to be changed to

Churfürstliche Porcellain Fabrique (Prince Electoral Porcelain Factory), 1763-1807. In 1807 Saxony was elevated to kingdom by Napoleon of France and the manufactory was named

Königliche Porzellan Manufaktur (Royal Porcelain Manufactory), 1807-1919.

In 1831 Saxony became a constitutional monarchy, the king gave up his rights to the manufactory which became government property, keeping the name.

After World War I the King of Saxony was forced to abdicate. Saxony became a Republic and a federal state within the German Republic. The name of the manufactory was changed to

Staatliche Porzellan Manufaktur (State´s Porcelain Manufactory), 1919-1946, still owned by the government of Saxony.

After World War II Saxony belonged to the part of Germany that was occupied by the Soviet-Union. In 1945 the Soviet government ordered the manufactory to be dismantled and its installations transferred into the Soviet-Union. But a few months later a number of manufactory workers had reconstructed parts of the manufactory, which began porcelain production again. In 1946 the Soviet Government sequestrated the manufactory and operated it as branch

Porzellanmanufaktur Meissen (Porcelain Manufactory Meissen) of the government owned Soviet Joint Stock Company **SAG ACement@**. Four years later it sold it to the government of the German Democratic Republic, which named the company **VEB Staatliche Porzellanmanufaktur Meissen**

(VEB State´s Porcelain Manufactory Meissen), 1950-1990.

Table, decorative porcelain, figurines, coffee and tea sets, collectors articles, plaques, coins, medals, dolls, pipe bowls, knick-knack, laboratory porcelain.

After the demise of the German Democratic Republic the manufactory was returned to its historical owner, the State of Saxony, and renamed

Staatliche Porzellan Manufaktur Meissen, 1990 - present. Marks:

Royal Porcelain Factory, Prince Electoral Porcelain Manufactory and Royal Porcelain Manufactory, all in Part I subsumed under the name Royal Porcelain manufactory: 402, 955, 1328-1358, 1459-1461, 1533-1544, 1546-1567, 1591, 1593-1595, 1598-1614, 1622-1634, 1639, 1643, 1644, 1647, 1650-1658, 1660, 1662, 1663, 1665-1700, 1702-1706, 1715-1723, 1862-1871, 2234-2236, 2257, 2267, 2435, 2471-2476, 2479-2482, 2485-2487, 2503-2522, 2575-2577, 2731, 2733, 2821-2839, 2844, 2846, 2847, 3631, 3632, 3633, 3644

State´s Porcelain Manufactory until 1946: 1562-1564, 1566-1579, 1591, 1592, 1596-1614, 1616-1621, 1658-1661, 1714, 3245, 3275, 3290, 3617

VEB State´s Porcelain Manufactory: 1571, 1574-1583, 1596, 1709-1712, 1714, 3209, 3245, 3275, 3605, 3618, 3619, 3620, 3621, 3622, 3623, 3624, 3625, 3626, 3627, 3628, 3629, 3630, 3634, 3635, 3636

State´s Porcelain Manufactory since 1990: 1574, 1575-1580, 1712, 1714, 3665.

Keramische Werkstätten Arthur Rohleder & Co. Sohn

(Ceramic Workshops Arthur Rohleder & Co. Son) 1924 -1990. Porcelain decorating shop. Mark: 2030

Carl Teichert, 1857-1872, stoves, tiles, wall tiles. The Company was converted into a joint stock company with the name

Meissner Ofen- und Porzellanfabrik vorm. C. Teichert

(Meissen Stove and Porcelain Factory formerly C. Teichert), 1872-1945, which in addition in 1879 took up production of decorative porcelain, figurines and household porcelain especially with the Onion Pattern, developed by the *Royal Porcelain Manufactory* in *Meissen*. From 1886 until 1905 the company owned a branch in Eichwald, Bohemia, which was taken over by B. Bloch & Co. in Eichwald, who used the same mark No. 616 which had been registered by the Meissen Stove and Porcelain Factory in 1882.

Marks: 303, 616, 1527, 1894, 3210

In 1925 the company acquired Porcelain Factory Stockhardt & Schmidt-Eckert in Meissen, which had been founded 1923 as branch of *Stockhardt & Schmidt-Eckert* in *Kronach*. In 1929 porcelain production was discontinued.

After World War II the company was nationalized. In 1990 it was privatized.

Meissner Porzellanmalerei (Meissen Porcelain Decorating), 1928-1939, then the proprietors *Arthur Pöhlmann* and *Fritz Schulze* parted company. **PGH Meissner Porzellanmalerei**, 1958-1990, **Meissner Porzellanmalerei GmbH,** 1990-1991, **Kunsthandwerkliche Porzellanmalerei GmbH** 1991-present, porcelain decorating shop. Marks: 1885, 3638, 3639, 3640, 3641, 3656, 3657

Arthur Pöhlmann, 1939-1958, porcelain decorator. Mark 3020, 3642

Fritz Schulze, 1945-1958, porcelain decorator. Mark: 3616, 3655

Ernst Teichert in 1868 founded a stove and tile factory, which in 1872 he sold to **Sächsische Ofen- und Chamottewaren-Fabrik vorm. Ernst Teichert AG**
(Saxonian Stove and Fireclay Factory formerly Ernst Teichert), circa 1872-1923.
Marks: 1886, 2221. In 1919 the name was changed to **Somag Saxonian Stove- and Walltileworks AG,** 1919-1945.
Teichert established an new factory **Ernst Teichert,** 1884-1945, Ltd since 1901, tiles, stoves, wall tiles and from 1912 until 1925 also household porcelain. 1923 the shares of the company were taken over by *Meissen Stove and Porcelain Factory formerly Carl Teichert..*
Marks: 1713, 1742, 1758, 1760, 1761, 2570-2572, 2744
After World War II the factory was nationalized and became a branch of **VEB Plattenwerke Meissen** (VEB Tileworks Meissen), 1951-1990.

Mengersreuth
Thuringia, Germany

Porzellanfabrik Mengersreuth Craemer & Heron (Porcelain Factory Mengersreuth Craemer & Heron), 1908-closed 1913, coffee and tea sets, technical porcelain, dolls. Mark: 28. Two years later the factory was reopened as **Porzellanfabrik Mengersreuth Gmbh** (Porcelain Factory Mengersreuth Ltd), 1915-circa 1930. Mark: 595

Merkelsgrun - Merkelsgrün
Bohemia, presently Merklin, Czechia

A porcelain factory **Becher & Stark** is traceable in 1871, household and decorative porcelain. A factory with the same initials **Bruder & Schwalb** was mentioned first in 1882. To which company mark Nr. 2720 with the initials   B & S M belonged could not yet be ascertained. In 1905/1906 **Camil Schwalb** is mentioned as proprietor. In 1912 the company was merged with **Zettlitzer Kaolin-Werke Abteilung Porzellanfabrik Merkelsgrün** (Zettlitz Kaolin Works Department Porcelain Factory Merkelsgrün), 1912-1945. Until 1926 household later only electrotechnical porcelain. Marks: 434, 437, 440, 826, 3055

Merkstein
Rhineland, Germany

Risler & Cie. GMBH, 1846—defunct before 1978, formerly in *Freiburg*, porcelain buttons, pearls, mosaic.
Mark: 1790

Mettlach
Saarland, Germany

Pierre Francois Boch, son of Pierre Joseph Boch in Septfontaine in Luxembourg in 1808 bought the Abbey of the Benediktines in Mettlach and began producing fine earthenware in 1813. The first years were financially very difficult and because Boch had to borrow money from his wife Rosalie Buschmann, he signed his products **Boch-Buschmann**. Boch's son Eugen took over in 1829 and in 1836 he merged with *Nicolas Villeroy*, who owned an earthenware factory in *Wallerfangen* (Vaudrevange) and since then the name of the company is
Villeroy & Boch. In 1856 the company founded a branch in *Dresden* and in 1883 it acquired an earthenware factory in *Schramberg,* and also in 1976 the company *Heinrich Porcelain* in *Selb.* Table, decorative and household earthenware, figurines, mugs, beersteins, tiles, for a short time from about 1860—1865 also soft paste porcelain.
Marks: 29—32, 184, 1528, 1793, 1794, 1844, 1876, 2673, 2714, 3115, 3116, 3211
See also Bonn, Earthenware Factory Franz Anton Mehlem.

Meuselwitz
Thuringia, Germany

Porzellanfabrik Hentschel & Müller
(Porcelain Factory Hentschel & Muller), 1904—1930, household and electro-technical porcelain.
Marks: 1788, 1992, 2008
In 1930 the company was sold to *Porcelain Factory at Kloster Veilsdorf* in *Kloster Veilsdorf.*

Mildeneichen
Bohemia, presently Luzec, Czechia

Robert Persch Porzellanfabriken Mildeneichen und Raspenau
(Robert Persch Porcelain Factories Mildeneichen and Raspenau), 1869—household porcelain, coffee and tea sets.
Mark: 2915
Successors were
Österreichische Porzellanfabriken Mildeneichen und Raspenau G. Robrecht
(Austrian Porcelain Factories Mildeneichen and Raspenau G. Robrecht),   —1920.
Mark: 2648
Later Josef Franz Scholz was sole proprietor, 1920—last mention found in 1927.

Mitterteich
Bavaria, Germany

A porcelain factory founded by
Julius Rother & Co., circa 1899—1918, household porcelain, coffee and tea sets,
Mark: 2477
was taken over by the porcelain decorator Josef Rieber from Selb as
Porzellanfabrik Josef Rieber & Co.
(Porcelain Factory Josef Rieber & Co.), 1918—1923.

After the company had established a branch factory in Thiersheim, the name changed to

Porzellanfabriken Josef Rieber & Co. AG

(Porcelain Factories Josef Rieber & Co. AG), 1923—defunct about 1978.
Marks: 107, 544, 859, 860, 1164, 1165, 1202, 3108, 3184, 3239

The Mosanic Pottery Max Emanuel & Co., circa 1882—1918, household and decorative porcelain.
Marks: 345, 1736, 1762, 1930, 3212, 3213
The company was converted into

Porzellanfabrik Mitterteich AG

(Porcelain Factory Mittereich AG), 1918—present, household porcelain, coffee and tea sets, gift articles.
Marks: 425—428, 1736, 1910, 3041, 3212

Moabit see Berlin

Moschendorf see Hof-Moschendorf

Muhlhausen - Mühlhausen
Saxony, Germany

Elster Porzellanwerke Georg Heinlein

(Elster Porcelainworks Georg Heinlein), 1922—1924, household porcelain.
Mark: 308
The factory belonged to *Zeh, Scherzer & Co.* in *Rehau* from 1924—1933 and thereafter became

Porzellanfabrik Elster Georg Heinlein

(Porcelain Factory Elster Georg Heinlein), 1933—defunct.

Munich - München
Bavaria, Germany

Jean Beck Kunstkeramische Anstalt

(Jean Beck Art Ceramic Establishment), circa 1900—1915, later

Hans Ludwig Beck, 1915—defunct, porcelain decorating shop.
Mark: 27

Brunner & Ploetz, 1890—present, porcelain decorating shop.
Mark: 1900

Kurt Hammer, 1908— , porcelain decorating shop.
Mark: 2615

Elisabeth Liegl, 1948—present, porcelain decorating shop for beermugs, mugs and plates.
Marks: 1006, 2294

Porzellanmanufaktur Rau
(Porcelain Manufactory Rau), 1946–present, porcelain decorating shop for beermugs, figurines, decorative and table porcelain, gift and collectors articles.
Marks: 1005, 1169
The company was founded in Schonfeld, Bohemia, in 1857 and operated there until 1945.

J. J. Scharvogel, 1898–1923, decorative porcelain and earthenware, figurines.
Marks: 296, 3248

Werkstätten für Keramik-Malerei G. Wieninger
(Workshops for Ceramic Decorating G. Wieninger), 1879–present, porcelain decorating shop.
Mark: 1994

Fritz Worm,   —defunct, porcelain decorating shop.
Mark: 869

Munchhof - Münchhof
Bohemia, presently Mirova, Czechia

Münchhofener Porzellan- und Steingutfabrik
(Munchhof Porcelain and Earthenware Factory),   1879–defunct, household porcelain.
Mark: 2258

Munster - Münster
Westphalia, Germany

Porzellanmanufaktur August Roloff
(Porcelain Manufactory August Roloff), 1919–defunct, porcelain decorating, especially decorative porcelain and gift articles.
Marks: 662, 805
See also Konstanz (Constance), Porcelain Manufactory August Roloff GmbH.

Naila
Bavaria, Germany

Hagen & Co., 1900-1921, electrotechnical porcelain, later the company name was **Porzellanfabrik Naila Albin Klöber** (Porcelain Factory Naila Albin Klober) 1921- .
The factory was acquired by Hutschenreuther AG in Selb, which added household, hotel and table porcelain. It was closed circa 1993. Mark: 2298

Nassau-Saarbrucken see Ottweiler

Nauendorf
Thuringia, Germany

Alt, Beck & Gottschalk GMBH, 1854–1953, figurines, dolls, dolls heads, decorative

porcelain, religious articles.
Marks: 2497, 2498, 3098

Neudeck
Bavaria, Germany

Churfürstliche Porcellain Fabrique Neudeck

(Prince-Electoral Porcelain Factory Neudeck), 1747—1761, table and decorative porcelain, figurines. The factory was moved to *Nymphenburg* in 1761.
Mark: 1446

Neu-Haldensleben see Haldensleben

Neuhaus on Rennweg - Neuhaus am Rennweg
Thuringia, Germany

Rudolph Heinz & Co. KG, 1856-circa 1921 and 1936-1972, decorative porcelain and earthenware, figurines, gift articles, porcelain decorating.
From 1856 until 1885 the company only decorated porcelain, afterwards it produced porcelain, fayence and other earthenware. From 1921 until 1936 it was a branch of *Oldest Volkstedt Porcelain Factory* in *Volkstedt.* When the Volkstedt factory failed in 1936 it became independent again.
Marks: 25, 865, 1525

Kämpfe & List Porzellanfabrik früher C. List

(Kampfe & List Porcelain Factory formerly C. List), 1831—circa 1900, household porcelain and earthenware.
Marks: 154, 385, 2139

Neuhaus-Schierschnitz
Thuringia, Germany

Armand Marseille, 1905-1913, owned a factory for electrotechnical porcelain and dolls´ heads. See also *Koppelsdorf.* A few years later it became
Porzellanfabrik Neuhaus (Porcelain Factory Neuhaus) and in 1913 it was taken over by Siemens-Schuckert-Works. In 1926 the factory was named **Porzellanwerk Neuhaus.** After World War II the Soviet Government sequestrated the factory and made it part of the Soviet joint stock company
SAG Hescho in Hermsdorf. In 1950 it was handed over to the government of the GDR and named **VEB Porzellanwerk Neuhaus** (VEB Porcelainwork Neuhaus), 1950-1965.
Marks: 1765, 1766
Later it became a branch of the newly created *VEB Electroceramic Works Sonneberg* in *Sonneberg,* 1964-1990. Electroceramic Works were semi-privatized as **TRIDELTA,** 1992-1996. Mark: 2280 and fully privatized as **CERAM Electrokeramik Sonneberg GmbH,** 1996-present, Mark: 1766

Neuhofen
Austria

Porzellanfabrik Otto Kunz
(Porcelain Factory Otto Kunz), 1947—present, household and hotel porcelain, coffee and tea sets, gift articles.
Mark: 113

Neuleiningen
Palatinate, Germany

Jacobi, Adler & Cie., 1874—circa 1930, later
Neuleininger Steingut und Wandplattenfabrik
(Neuleining Earthenware and Tile Factory), circa 1930—circa 1935, household and decorative earthenware, tiles.
Mark: 248

Neumark
Bohemia, presently Vseruby, Czechia

Anton Fischer Steingutfabrik
(Anton Fischer Earthenware Factory), 1832—circa 1905, later
A. Fischer Sohn Steingutfabrik
(A. Fischer Son Earthenware Factory), circa 1905—defunct, apothecary jars, laboratory earthenware and porcelain.
Marks: 2259, 2445, 3214

Neumunster - Neumünster
Schleswig-Holstein, Germany

Porzellanfabrik Neumünster
(Porcelain Factory Neumunster), 1897—defunct, household porcelain.
Mark: 2874

Neurohlau
Bohemia, presently Nova Role, Czechia

"Bohemia" Keramische Werke AG
("Bohemia" Ceramic Works AG), 1921-present, household and hotel porcelain, coffee and tea sets.
From 1922-1945 the porcelain factory Ph. Rosenthal in Selb was partner in the company. Until 1940 the official place of business was Karlsbad.
Marks: 120, 126-128, 760, 761, 870, 1028, 2490

Neu-Schmiedefeld
Thuringia, Germany

Gustav Korn Porzellanfabrik
(Gustav Korn Porcelain Factory), 1904—1925, household porcelain.
Mark: 2588

Neustadt
Bavaria, Germany

Max Oscar Arnold Elektrotechnische Werke

(Max Oscar Arnold Electrotechnical Works), 1888–1929, dolls heads, electrotechnical porcelain.
Marks: 635, 636
The company was sold to *Ph. Rosenthal AG* in *Selb* in 1929.

Heber & Co. Porzellanfabrik

(Heber & Co. Porcelain Factory), 1900–1922, household porcelain, figurines, dolls and dolls heads.
Marks: 711, 2593

Gebr. Knoch

(Bros. Knoch), 1887–1920, figurines, dolls heads, decorative porcelain.
Mark: 2388

Neuwied

Rhineland, Germany

Wandplattenfabrik Engers

(Walltile Factory Engers), 1911–present, tiles and wall tiles.
Marks: 640, 650

New York

New York, U. S. A.

Charles Ahrenfeldt & Son, before 1880–1910, U. S. importer of Bohemian and German porcelain. Established a porcelain decorating shop *Charles Ahrenfeldt & Son* in *Altrohlau* about 1894, which occasionally was called Carlsbad China Factory, leading to the wrong assumption that Ahrenfeldt produced porcelain in Altrohlau (as he did in his factory in Limoges, France). According to all available sources Ahrenfeldt only decorated unmarked porcelain from local factories in the vicinity of Karlsbad and applied his own marks. The company also imported porcelain from the *von Schierholz Porcelain Manufactory* in *Plaue*. It was taken over by *Hermann C. Kupper, New York* in 1910 at which time the decorating shop in Altrohlau ceased to exist.
Marks: 777, 778, 1513, 1514

Anna Perenna, Inc., 1977–present, importer of Rosenthal collectors articles. Office in Stuttgart, Germany.
Mark: 3102

Bawo & Dotter, 1864–circa 1914, U. S. importer of dolls and dolls heads. Owned a porcelain factory and decorating shop in Fischern, Bohemia.
Marks: 114, 188, 827, 2716, 2717

Geo. Borgfeldt Corp. and
Geo. Borgfeldt & Co.,
1881–circa 1976, one of the major U. S. importers of dolls and dolls heads made by *Alt, Beck & Gottschalck* in *Nauendorf, Armand Marseille* in *Koppelsdorf, C. F. Kling* in *Ohrdruf* and *Simon & Halbig* in *Grafenhain.* Also

imported porcelain from the factories *Heinrich & Co.* in *Selb* and *C. Schumann* in *Arzberg.*
Marks: 341, 542, 900, 3128, 3129, 3136, 3137, 3189, 3236, 3261

Charles L. Dwenger, before 1895—after 1917, U. S. importer of Bohemian porcelain, on which the factory mark was substituted by a Dwenger mark.
Marks: 2157, 3125

Graham & Zenger, U. S. importer for *C. M. Hutschenreuther* in *Hohenberg* between the two World Wars.
Mark: 9

J. F. Hamburger & Co., 1889—circa 1910, U. S. importer of Bohemian porcelain, on which the factory mark was substituted by the Hamburger mark. Imported dolls and had offices in *Nuremberg* and *Berlin.*
Mark: 1119

Heinrich & Winterling, probably after 1918—circa 1940, U. S. importer for *Heinrich & Co.* in *Selb, Winterling* in *Marktleuthen* and *Roeslau, Oscar Schaller & Co. Successor* in *Kirchenlamitz* and *Schwarzenbach.*
Mark: 3255

Kahla China Corporation, between the two World Wars U. S. importer and distributor for *Porcelain Factory Kahla* in *Kahla* and *H. Schomburg & Sons* in *Rosslau.*
Mark: 3271

Hermann C. Kupper, Inc. 1910—present, U. S. importer for Bohemian and German porcelain. Kupper took over in 1910 the company of *Charles Ahrenfeldt & Son* in *New York,* imported among others porcelain from the *von Schierholz Porcelain Manufactory* in *Plaue* until 1941 and from *Krautheim & Adelberg* in *Selb* from 1910 to the present.

P. H. Leonard, before 1890—circa 1908, U. S. importer of Bohemian porcelain, on which the factory mark frequently was substituted by a Leonard mark. The company existed after 1908 a few more years as
Anna B. Leonard.
Marks: 663, 664, 2196, 3202

The New York & Rudolstadt Pottery see Rudolstadt

Rosenthal China Corp., U. S. distributor for porcelain factory *Ph. Rosenthal* in *Selb* between the two World Wars.
Mark: 780

Rosenthal-Block China Corp., formerly
J. L. Block & Son, after 1945—defunct, U. S. importer for porcelain factory *Ph. Rosenthal* in *Selb.*
Mark: 1163

Today *Rosenthal Glass and Porcelain AG* in *Selb* is represented in the U. S. A. by **Rosenthal USA Ltd.**

Royal Saxe Corporation and **Prince Ernst Heinrich von Sachsen,** Post Liscmacoffrey, County Westmeath, Ireland, circa 1952—defunct, table and decorative porcelain. Marks: 1463, 1585

Schumann China Corporation, U. S. distributor for *Porcelain Factory C. Schumann* in *Arzberg* between the two World Wars.
Mark: 1256

Paul A. Straub & Co., Inc., U. S. importer for *Porcelain Factory L. Hutschenreuther* in *Selb* from 1915 until 1970.
Marks: 911, 2199, 2200
The company was sold to H. M. W. Industries in 1970 who distributed L. Hutschenreuther products through its daughter company
Wallace Silversmiths until 1974. In 1975 Hutschenreuther established its own distributing company
Hutschenreuther Corporation in North Branford, Connecticut.

Lewis Straus & Sons, before 1895—1924, U. S. importer for *The New York and Rudolstadt Pottery* in *Rudolstadt.* Also imported Bohemian porcelain, on which the factory mark was substituted by a Straus mark. The company was continued as **Nathan Straus & Sons** after 1924.
Marks: 236, 237, 2175

Strobel & Wilken, 1864—after 1925. From 1864—1886 the company was located in Cincinnati, Ohio. U. S. importer of dolls and German and Bohemian table and decorative porcelain, on which the factory mark frequently was substituted by a Strobel & Wilken mark.
Marks: 562, 1015, 1733, 2657, 2658

Niedersalzbrunn
Silesia, Germany, presently Szczawienko, Poland

Porzellanmanufaktur Hermann Ohme
(Porcelain Manufactory Hermann Ohme), 1882—circa 1930, household, table, hotel and decorative porcelain. Branch factory in Waldenburg.
Marks: 750, 874, 928, 950, 1011

Franz Prause Porzellanfabrik
(Franz Prause Porcelain Factory), 1894—1936, household and table porcelain, coffee and tea sets.
Marks: 2179, 2180, 2853, 3027

Niemberg
Saxony, Germany

Ida-Lotte Roth, before 1939—after 1958, porcelain decorating shop.
Mark: 2022

Nuremberg - Nürnberg
Bavaria, Germany

J. von Schwarz, 1870–after 1900, decorative earthenware and fayence.
Marks: 194, 572, 1884

Stiglbauer & Merz, circa 1885–defunct, porcelain production and distribution.
Mark: 14

Nymphenburg
Bavaria, Germany

With financial support of Prince-Elector Max III Joseph of Bavaria the potter
Ignaz Niedermeyer established in 1747 the
Churfürstliche Porcellain Fabrique Neudeck in Schloss Neudeck
(Prince-Electoral Porcelain Factory in Castle Neudeck), 1747–1761. But only
after J. J. Ringler from Vienna and the chemist J. P. R. Hartl were hired, production
of usable porcelain began in 1753. Soon Castle Neudeck became too small and
the manufactory was moved into a newly erected building adjacent to Castle
Nymphenburg near Munich in 1761. From then on the name was
Churfürstliche Porcellain Manufactur Nymphenburg
(Prince-Electoral Porcelain Manufactory Nymphenburg). In 1806 Bavaria was
elevated to a kingdom and the name changed to
Königliche Porzellan Manufaktur Nymphenburg
(Royal Porcelain Manufactory Nymphenburg). It was leased to Scotzniovski in
1862 but kept the old name. Twenty-five years later Albert Bauml leased the
company, continued the old name, but added his own. After the abdication of
the King of Bavaria in 1918, the name was changed into
Staatliche Porzellan Manufaktur Nymphenburg A. Bäuml
(State's Porcelain Manufactory Nymphenburg Albert Bauml), under which the
manufactory still exists today. During the first years the manufactory produced
simple coffee and tea sets and table porcelain in the style of Meissen. After 1754
the manufactory developed its own distinctively different style and produced
figurines, table porcelain, coffee and tea sets and decorative porcelain.
Marks: Prince-Electoral Porcelain Factory Neudeck: 1446
Prince-Electoral Porcelain Manufactory Nymphenburg: 637–639, 1446–1451,
1590, 1615, 1740, 2366–2369, 2399, 2443, 2483, 2544, 2795
Royal Porcelain Manufactory: 603, 606, 1450, 1452, 1453
Royal Porcelain Manufactory Scotzniovski: 1454
Royal Porcelain Manufactory A. Bauml: 680, 681, 969, 1456, 1615
State's Porcelain Manufactory A. Bauml: 82, 681, 969, 1455, 1456, 2609

Oberhohndorf
Saxony, Germany

Friedrich Kaestner Porzellanfabrik GMBH
(Friedrich Kaestner Porcelain Factory GMBH), 1883–1972, household and
decorative porcelain, coffee and tea sets, porcelain decorating.
Marks: 843, 1915–1919, 1929

Oberkassel
Rhineland, Germany

Rheinische Porzellanmanufaktur Oscar Erck
(Rhenisch Porcelain Manufactory Oscar Erck), 1861–circa 1882, subsequently
Rheinische Porzellanmanufaktur L. Herrmann
(Rhenisch Porcelain Manufactory L. Herrmann), circa 1882–circa 1905, household and decorative porcelain, lamps.
Mark: 104

Oberklingensporn
Bavaria, Germany

Porzellanfabrik Bernhardshütte GMBH
(Porcelain Factory Bernhardshutte GMBH), 1924–circa 1930.
Mark: 854

Oberkoditz - Oberköditz
Thuringia, Germany

Gebr. Paris
(Bros. Paris), 1881–1972, mocha and collectors cups, coffee and tea sets, childrens sets, decorative porcelain.
Mark: 2
The company was nationalized in 1953 and renamed
VEB Porzellanfabrik Köditz
(VEB Porcelain Factory Koditz), but the same year returned to the former owners who continued the company under the old name. In 1972 it was nationalized again and named
VEB Porzellanwerk Oberköditz
(VEB Porcelainwork Oberkoditz), co-operating partner of *VEB Porcelain Combine Kahla* in *Kahla*.

Oberkotzau
Thuringia, Germany

Greiner & Herda, 1886–1943, household and decorative porcelain, coffee and tea sets.
From 1886 until 1905 the company only decorated porcelain, later it produced porcelain as well.
Marks: 234, 1046
Later the company name was
Porzellanfabrik Neuerer
(Porcelain Factory Neuerer), 1943–present, household and table porcelain, coffee and tea sets, lamps, decorative porcelain, electrically heated coffee machines and laboratory porcelain.
The company changed its name several times. First it was
Porzellanindustrie Neuerer
(Porcelain Industry Neuerer) and today it is

Elektroporzellanfabrik Hans Neuerer
(Electro Porcelain Factory Hans Neuerer).
Marks: 1485, 1523, 1801

Leni Parbus, 1904–present, porcelain decorating shop.
Mark: 819

Oelze
Thuringia, Germany

Porzellanfabrik Marienfeld A. Voigt
(Porcelain Factory Marienfeld A. Voigt), later
Voigt & Müller
(Voigt & Muller), 1892–defunct, electrotechnical porcelain.
Marks: 2215, 2216

Oeslau
Bavaria, Germany

W. Goebel Porzellanfabrik Oeslau und Wilhelmsfeld
(W. Goebel Porcelain Factory Oeslau and Wilhelmsfeld)
see Rodental

Fischer & Co. GMBH Porzellanfabrik und -Malerei
(Fischer & Co. GMBH Porcelain Factory and Decorating Shop), 1950–circa 1975,
promotional gift articles, ashtrays.
Mark: 716
The company was taken over by *W. Goebel Porcelain Factory* in Rodental.

Offstein
Rhineland, Germany

Keramische Werke Offstein & Worms
(Ceramic Works Offstein and Worms), existed 1921, household sets and decorative
pieces.
Mark: 233

Ohrdruf
Thuringia, Germany

Baehr & Proeschild, 1870–defunct before 1945, figurines, dolls and doll heads,
decorative porcelain.
Marks: 66, 67, 1725–1727

J. D. Kestner & Co. Porzellanfabrik
(J. D. Kestner & Co. Porcelain Factory), 1860–defunct between 1927 and 1930,
dolls, dolls heads and parts, figurines, decorative and household porcelain.
Exclusive U. S. importer for Kestner dolls since 1890 was *Geo. Borgfeldt* in
New York.
Marks: 810, 1786, 2170, 2224, 2613, 2614, 3038

C.F.Kling & Co. 1896-circa 1951, dolls and dolls´ heads, figurines.
Marks: 1982-1984

Osnabruck - Osnabrück
Lower Saxony, Germany

Franz Hoffmann, 1918–1934, porcelain decorating shop.
Marks: 2193, 2290
Successor was his son
Adolf Hoffmann, 1935–1966,
Marks: 2060, 3161
and his grandson
Edwin Hoffmann, 1966–1977.
Mark: 3162

Ottensheim
Austria

Robert Riedl, 1890–defunct, porcelain decorating shop.
Mark: 1477

Ottweiler
Saarland, Germany

Fürstliche Porzellan Manufaktur Ottweiler
(Princely Porcelain Manufactory Ottweiler), 1763–1771, table and decorative porcelain.
Marks: 1019, 2464, 2855–2857

Passau
Bavaria, Germany

Dressel, Kister & Cie., porcelain factory and decorating shop, 1840–1922, household and decorative porcelain, figurines, religious articles, dolls parts, knick-knack. In 1903
Wilhelm and Rudolf Lenck were proprietors. They acquired about three hundred and fifty original moulds of the defunct *Prince-Electoral Mayence Manufactory* in *Hochst* which first (about 1840) had gone to the *Earthenware Factory Damm* in *Damm* and later (about 1886) to the *Earthenware Factory F. A. Mehlem* in *Bonn*. Dressel, Kister & Cie. produced reproductions of Hochst figurines and groups, which were marked with the old Hochst mark. Since some of the Hochst figurines look similar to figurines made by the *Royal Porcelain Manufactory* in *Ludwigsburg* (the arcanist J. J. Ringler and the modellers J. Carlstadt, J. J. Meyer and C. Vogelmann had worked in both manufactories), the company attempted to use some of the old Ludwigsburg marks. In 1904 it was ordered by the patent office to cease using the Ludwigsburg marks.
Marks: 170, 546, 891, 1054, 1321–1324, 2102, 2546
About 1922 the company was taken over by the
Aelteste Volkstedter Porzellanfabrik

(Oldest Volkstedt Porcelain Factory) in Volkstedt and operated as
Zweigniederlassung Passau
(Branch Passau), producing decorative porcelain. After the Oldest Volkstedt Porcelain Factory went bankrupt, Philipp Dietrich bought the factory in Passau in 1937 and operated it as
Porzellanfabrik Passau
(Porcelain Factory Passau) until 1942 when it closed. His main products were decorative porcelain, figurines and religious articles.
Mark: 1325

Pfullingen
Wurttemberg, Germany

Wilhelm Künster
(Wilhelm Kunster), 1923–1945, later proprietor
Otto Künstner
(Otto Kunstner), 1945–present, porcelain decorating shop.
Mark: 172

Philadelphia
Pennsylvania, U.S.A.

Ebeling & Reuss Co. see Devon

Fischer, Bruce & Co., 1933–present, U. S. importer for *Winterling Porcelain Factories Distributing Company* in *Windischeschenbach.*
Mark: 824

Piesau
Thuringia, Germany

Bernhardt & Bauer, 1886-1945, household and decorative porcelain, figurines, dolls and toys. After World War II the company was nationalized and became
VEB Porzellanfabrik Piesau
(VEB Porzellan Factory Piesau) 1945-1990. Marks 1818, 2048, 2233.
In 1990 the factory became part of *Wallendorf Porcelain Manufactory* in *Wallendorf* but closed the same year.

Pilsen
Bohemia, presently Plzen, Czechia

Friedrich Schertler, 1881–defunct, household porcelain.
Mark: 2758

Pirkenhammer
Bohemia, presently Brezova, Czechia

Friedrich Höcke
(Friedrich Hocke) founded in 1803 a porcelain factory, which produced household

porcelain and pipe bowls.

Mark: 2600

In 1806 he leased the factory to

Cranz & Brothäuser

(Cranz & Brothauser) but since they were not very successful, Hocke sold the factory to Johann Martin Fischer & Christopher Reichenbach in 1811.

Fischer & Reichenbach, 1811–1846, produced table and decorative porcelain, coffee and tea sets and beginning in 1840 also figurines.

Marke: 2757

Subsequently

Christian Fischer, 1846–1857, the son of J. M. Fischer, became sole proprietor.

Mark: 2726

In 1853 he took his son-in-law Ludwig von Mieg into the business, which changed its name to

Fischer & Mieg, 1857–1918, and kept it, even after Fischer and Mieg died. After 1875 production was reduced to artistically less important trade, household and decorative porcelain.

Marks: 217, 782, 784, 1913, 2252, 2755

In 1918 the factory was acquired by the newly founded

Öpiag

(Opiag), *Karlsbad*, and operated as Branch Pirkenhammer.

Marks: 218, 782, 783

Opiag in 1920 changed its name to

Epiag and existed until 1945.

Marks: 782, 785, 807

See also Karlsbad, Epiag.

Plankenhammer

Bavaria, Germany

Porzellanfabrik Plankenhammer GMBH

(Porcelain Factory Plankenhammer GMBH), 1908–circa 1978, household and hotel porcelain, coffee and tea sets, gift and promotional articles.

Marks: 730, 1922–1925

Plaue

Thuringia, Germany

Christian Gottfried Schierholz in 1817 founded a hygioceramic manufactory, which also produced decorative and household porcelain. In 1829 the manufactory was named **C.G. Schierholz & Sohn** (C.G. Schierholz & Son). Marks: 2312-2314,3647, 3648, 3658, 3660. In 1905 the company became **C.G. Schierholz & Sohn, Porzellanmanufactur Plaue GmbH** (C.G. Schierholz & Son, Porcelain Manufactory Plaue Ltd). In 1912 the name was changed to

Von Schierholz′sche Porzellanmanufactur Plaue GmbH (Von Schierholz′ Porcelain Manufactory Plaue Ltd) Marks: 491-496. After World War II the company first came under GDR government trusteeship. In 1972 it was nationalized and named **VEB Porzellanmanufaktur Plaue**. 1972-1990. After the dissolution of the VEB the manufactory was restituted to the former proprietors, 1991-1996. Then it was bought by *Königlich* *priv. Porcelain Factory Tettau* in *Tettau* and is now **Porzellanmanufaktur Plaue GmbH**. (Porcelain Manufactory Plaue Ltd). Table, household and decorative porcelain, figurines, technical porcelain. Mark 1012

Pollwitz - Pöllwitz
Thuringia, Germany

W. Gleissner Söhne
(W. Gleissner Sons), 1920–1925, household porcelain, subsequently
Porzellanfabrik Pöllwitz GMBH
(Porcelain Factory Pollwitz GMBH), 1925–1938.
Marks: 1190, 1250

Possneck - Pössneck
Thuringia, Germany

A porcelain factory founded about 1800 was taken over by **Conta & Boehme**, 1804-before 1945, household and decorative porcelain, souvenirs, dolls. Mark: 59
Porzellanfabrik Joh. Chr. Eberlein (Porcelain Factory Joh. Chr. Eberlein), 1853-1916, religious articles, figurines, knick-knack.

Louis Huth, 1894-1940, porcelain decorating shop. Marks: 1280, 1281

Poppelsdorf see Bonn

Poschetzau
Bohemia, presently Bozicany, Czechia

J. S. Maier & Comp. Poschetzauer Porzellanfabrik
(J. S. Maier & Comp. Poschetzau Porcelain Factory), 1890–circa 1945, household porcelain, coffee and tea sets.
Marks: 58, 380, 2842

Potschappel
Saxony, Germany

Sächsische Porzellanfabrik zu Potschappel von Carl Thieme
(Saxonian Porcelain Factory at Potschappel of Carl Thieme), 1872-1972, household, table and decorative porcelain, figurines, knick-knack, souvenirs, gift articles, porcelain decorating in the Meissen and Vienna styles. Marks: 338, 344, 400, 431, 762, 797, 1013, 1072, 1147, 1708, 2418, 2419, 2638, 2639, 3058-3060.
After World War II the company first was put into government trusteeship and then nationalized as
VEB Sächsische Porzellanmanufaktur Dresden (VEB Saxonian Porcelain Manufactory Dresden), 1972-1990. Marks 1072, 2638, 3058-3060.
In 1991 the company was privatized as
Sächsische Porzellanmanufaktur Dresden. Mark: 2638

Prague - Prag
Bohemia, presently Praha, Czechia

An earthenware factory was founded in 1791 by
Karl and Johann Kunerle, Josef Lange and **Josef Hübel** as a co-operative society.
The Kunerles and Lange left in 1800 and Hubel continued as
Hübel & Co.
(Hubel & Co.), 1800–1835.
Marks: 2049, 2255, 2708, 2860, 2863, 3047, 3175, 3231–3233
Successors were
Kriegl & Co.
(Kriegl & Co.), 1835–1910, who began porcelain production in 1837. They
produced table, household, and decorative porcelain, figurines and busts of
famous people.
Marks: 2275, 2861, 2862, 3229, 3230

Pressig
Bavaria, Germany

Porzellanmanufaktur Pressig Nik. Förtsch Jun.
(Porcelain Manufactory Pressig Nik. Förtsch Jr.) formerly Hans Brunner,
existed 1953, defunct, porcelain decorating shop. Mark: 535

Paul Rauschert KG, later Rauschert GmbH & Co. KG, founded as
Porcelain Factory Paul Rauschert in *Hüttengrund, Thuringia*. See also *Steinwiesen, Kloster Veilsdorf, Schmiedeberg*. Technical porcelain and ceramics.
Marks: 2146, 2147. The company also operates factories in Portugal, U.S.A., Denmark,
Switzerland and Czechia.

Probstzella
Thuringia, Germany

H. Hutschenreuther Porzellanfabrik GmbH
(H. Hutschenreuther Porcelain Factory Ltd), 1886-1952, decorative porcelain, figurines,
religious and gift articles.
Marks: 933, 2634
The company was nationalized and became
VEB Porzellanfabrik Probstzella
(VEB Porcelain Factory Probstzella), 1952-1963, household, hotel and decorative porcelain, coffee and tea sets, cups.
Mark: 3057
In 1963 the factory was merged with *VEB East Thuringian Porcelainworks* in *Konitz* and
closed in 1990.

Ransbach
Rhineland, Germany

Eduard Bay, 1933–present, household and decorative stoneware and earthenware.
Marks: 851–853, 3114, 3127

Ratingen
Rhineland, Germany

Keramag Keramische Werke AG
(Keramag Ceramic Works AG), 1917—present, sanitary porcelain and earthenware.
Mark: 130

Rauenstein
Thuringia, Germany

Johann Georg Greiner, his son **Christian Daniel Siegmund Greiner** and his cousin **Johann Friedrich Greiner** in 1738 obtained a concession from Duke Georg of Saxony-Meiningen for a porcelain manufactory. They produced coffee and tea sets, cups and pipe bowls. About ten years later only **Christian Daniel Siegmund Greiner** is mentioned in documents and correspondence. Probably around 1860 the company name became
Friedrich Christian Greiner & Söhne
(Friedrich Christian Greiner & Sons), circa 1860—circa 1900. Production was extended to include table and decorative porcelain, figurines and dolls.
Marks: 1707, 2380, 2381, 2404—2408, 2892, 2893, 2897, 2914
Between 1906 and 1919 the firm was converted into a joint stock company with the name
Porzellanfabrik Rauenstein vormals Fr. Chr. Greiner & Söhne
(Porcelain Factory Rauenstein, formerly Fr. Chr. Greiner & Sons), which existed until 1936.

Rees
Rhineland, Germany

Porzellanfabrik Niederrhein
(Porcelain Factory Lower Rhine), existed 1935, defunct before 1964.
Mark: 443

Regensburg
Bavaria, Germany

Johann Heinrich Koch, 1805—1816, founded a porcelain factory, which produced handleless cups (Turkenkoppchen), household and table porcelain, after 1808 also earthenware
Mark: 2896
Successors were
Daniel Treiber, 1816—1821,
Joseph Pallestier, 1821—1825 and
Dominicus Auliczek the Younger, 1825—1829, who discontinued earthenware production. Under
Heinrich Anton Schwerdtner, 1829—1864, the company name was
Kgl. Priv. Porcellain Fabricke (Royally Privileged Porcelain Factory) with household and table porcelain as main products.
Mark: 3234
His son **Otto Schwerdtner**, 1864—1867, could not overcome increasing financial difficulties and the factory was closed.

Rehau
Bavaria, Germany

Düssel, Roth & Co. Porzellanmanufaktur
(Dussel, Roth & Co. Porcelain Manufactory) 1923-1945, afterwards
Düssel & Co.
(Dussel & Co.) 1945-closed. Decorating of table porcelain, coffee and tea sets, decorative porcelain, gift and collectors´ articles.
Marks: 806, 2016

Schödl, Jacob & Co.
Mark: 1082. Later
Hertel, Jacob & Co. GmbH
(Hertel, Jacob & Co. Ltd) 1906-circa 1969, household and decorative porcelain, coffee and tea sets, gift articles.
Marks: 142-144, 1122, 3033
About 1969 Melitta Works Bentz & Co. in Minden bought the factory and closed it shortly thereafter. Mark: 145

Porzellanfabrik Zeh, Scherzer & Co.
(Porcelain Factory Zeh, Scherzer & Co.) 1880-circa 1991. Since 1910 joint stock company, household and decorative porcelain, coffee and tea sets, gift articles.
Marks: 139-141, 507, 757, 758, 832, 906, 1258, 1273, 1274, 2050, 2468, 2469.

Reichenbach
Thuringia, Germany

Hädrich & Sohn, Inhaber Kurt Hädrich (Hadrich & Son, proprietor Kurt Hadrich),
1903-defunct after 1945, porcelain decorating. Mark: 530

Otto Hädrichs Witwe (Otto Hadrich´s Widow), now
Otto Hädrich Porzellanmanufaktur (Otto Hadrich Porcelain Manufactory) 1886-present, porcelain decorating. Marks: 808, 3092, 3611

A group of porcelain decorators in 1899 founded a company, which was acquired by Gustav Schwabe, 1903-1918. Then **Christina E. Carstens** owned the factory. In 1938 Ernst and Walter Carstens bought the company and operated it as **Reichenbacher Porzellanfabrik E. Carstens Erben GmbH** (Reichenbach Porcelain Factory E. Carstens Heirs Ltd), 1938-1969. Mark: 536. After 1945 it was nationalized and named **VEB Porzellanwerk Reichenbach** (VEB Porcelainwork Reichenbach), 1969-1900, branch of *VEB Porcelain Combine Kahla* in *Kahla*. Marks: 537, 538, 564. After the dissolution of the combine the factory was sold to an Iranian investor, who failed. Then three Thuringian porcelain specialists acquired the Factory and named it **Porzellanambiente Reichenbach** (Porcelain Ambience Reichenbach Ltd), 1993-present, Mark: 3604

Reichenstein
Silesia, Germany, presently Poland

Reichensteiner Porzellanmanufaktur J. Hasak Nachf.
(Reichenstein Porcelain Manufactory J. Hasak Successor), 1835—existed 1890, no further details found.
Marks: 211, 252

Reichmannsdorf
Thuringia, Germany

Porzellanfabrik Leube & Co.
(Porcelain Factory Leube & Co.), 1881-1965, decorative porcelain, figurines, toys and dolls. Mark: 1007

Porzellanfabrik Reichmannsdorf Carl Scheidig
(Porcelain Factory Reichmannsdorf Carl Scheidig), 1901-1972, household and decorative porcelain, figurines, religious articles and technical porcelain. Branch of *Carl Scheidig* in *Gräfenthal*. Marks: 864, 1003
Production ceased in 1991. Today Porcelain Museum of *Porcelain Figurines Gräfenthal Ltd* in *Gräfenthal*.

Rheinsberg
Brandenburg, Germany

Pollnow and successors, 1816-1866, ceramic factory, acquired by **Chr. Carstens KG**, 1892-1948, household and decorative earthenware. Mark: 3066. 1948 nationalized to **VEB Steingutfabrik Rheinsberg**, (VEB Earthenware Factory Rheinsberg), 1948-1990. Marks: 2895, 2916. Privatized as **Rheinsberg Keramik GmbH** (Rheinsberg Ceramics Ltd), 1990-liquidated 1992. Part of the factory converted into **Carstens-Keramik Rheinsberg GmbH**, 1992-present. The other part into **RKM Rheinsberger Keramik Manufaktur GmbH** (RKM Rheinsberg Ceramic Manufactory Ltd), 1994-present.

Rodach
Bavaria, Germany

Max Roesler Feinsteingutfabrik
(Max Roesler Fine Earthenware Factory), 1894—after 1930, household and decorative earthenware and porcelain.
Mark: 429
In 1925 the company was part of the combine of the *Oldest Volkstedt Porcelain Factory* in *Volkstedt*.

Rodental - Rödental
Bavaria, Germany

W. Goebel Porzellanfabrik Rödental
(W. Goebel Porcelain Factory Rodental), 1871—present, household and decorative porcelain, since 1900 figurines, dolls, dolls heads, souvenirs, gift articles, novelties, since 1929 also earthenware and artistical ceramics, since 1935 Hummel-figurines, lamps.
In 1871 Franz Detleff Goebel and his son William appplief for a permit for a porcelain factory in Oeslau, which was not granted immediately. For some years

the Goebels manufactured slate blackboards, pencils and toys until they finally were allowed to produce porcelain in 1879. They named their company

F. D. & W. Goebel Porzellanfabrik Oeslau und Wilhelmsfeld

(F. D. & W. Goebel Porcelain Factory Oeslau and Wilhelmsfeld).

After the father's death in 1909 the name was changed into

W. Goebel Porzellanfabrik Oeslau und Wilhelmsfeld

(W. Goebel Porcelain Factory Oeslau and Wilhelmsfeld).

In 1971 Oeslau and Wilhelmsfeld became part of the newly organized community of Rodental and the location in the company name was changed to Rodental. To the Goebel group belong:

Oeslau Manufactory W. Goebel in Rodental, founded in 1967,

Pan Studio W. Goebel in Meudt,

Cortendorf W. Goebel, formerly *Porcelain Factory Coburg-Cortendorf Julius Griesbach,* acquired in 1973,

W. Goebel GmbH & Co. in Leibnitz, Austria,

Goebel Art GmbH in Rodental,

Hummelwork, Division of Goebel Art, Inc. in Elmsford, N. Y., U. S. A.

Goebel Art GmbH & Co. in Downsview, Ontario, Canada, and 50% of Merkelbach Manufactory KG in Hohr-Grenzhausen, producer of saltglazed stoneware.

In 1953 Heinz Schaubach, former owner of *Porcelain Factory Schaubach-Art* in *Wallendorf* and *Porcelain Factory Unterweissbach* in *Unterweissbach* transferred the rights to his trademarks to W. Goebel Porcelain Factory, which used some of them.

Marks: 346–352, 599–602, 919, 1016–1018, 1186–1188, 1230, 1251, 1270, 3249

Roslau - Röslau

Bavaria, Germany

Gebrüder Winterling Porzellanfabrik

(Brothers Winterling Porcelain Factory), 1970–present, household and table porcelain, coffee and tea sets, gift articles.

Marks: 539, 1194

See also Windischeschenbach, Winterling Porcelain Factories Distributing Company.

Roschutz-Roschütz

Thuringia, Germany

Roschützer Porzellanmanufaktur Unger & Schilde GmbH

(Roschutz Porcelain Manufactory Unger & Schilde Ltd), 1881-1953, household, hotel and decorative porcelain, figurines.

Marks: 532, 718, 1467

After the proprietors left the GDR, the company was nationalized as

VEB Porzellanwerk Gera-Roschütz

(VEB Porcelainwork Gera-Roschutz), 1954-1968, household and table porcelain, coffee and tea sets. Marks: 532, 1467

In 1968 it was taken over as *Work IV* by *VEB Porcelain Combine Kahla* in *Kahla.* After the dissolution of the combine the factory was closed in 1990.

Rosslau
Saxony, Germany

H. Schomburg & Söhne
(H. Schomburg & Sons), 1898–1945, household porcelain and promotional articles. The company was a branch of *Ceramic Works Hescho* in *Hermsdorf.*
Mark: 1841

Rudolstadt
Thuringia, Germany

Ernst Bohne , 1848-1856, porcelain decorating shop, porcelain production since 1850, later **Ernst Bohne Söhne** (Ernst Bohne Sons), 1856-1920, decorative porcelain, coffee and tea sets, figurines. Marks: 1067-1070, 1849-1852, 2742
About 1920 the factory became a branch of *Bros. Heubach* in *Lichte*, who sold it to **Albert Stahl & Co**. 1937-1974, Then the company was nationalized and became part of *VEB Sitzendorfer Porcelain Manufactory* in *Sitzendorf,* still using marks No. 930 and 2316. After the demise of the GDR the company was privatized as **Albert Stahl & Co. vorm. Ernst Bohne Söhne**
(Albert Stahl & Co. formerly Ernst Bohne Sons), 1990-present. Mark: 3637

Rudolf Kämmer Keramik-Manufaktur
(Rudolf Kammer Ceramic Manufactory), 1945–1953, decorative earthenware. The company moved to *Volkstedt* in 1953.

New York and Rudolstadt Pottery, 1882–1918, household, table and decorative porcelain.
Lewis Straus & Sons in New York were co-owners or owners of the factory and sole importer for the U. S. A.
Marks: 236, 237, 820, 909, 910
Successor was
AG Porzellanfabrik Rudolstadt
(AG Porcelain Factory Rudolstadt), 1918–1932.
Mark: 2003

Schäfer & Vater Porzellanfabrik
(Schafer & Vater Porcelain Factory), 1890–no mention found after 1962, decorative porcelain, figurines, dolls.
Marks: 908

Eberhard Suhr, existed 1906, household and decorative porcelain.
Mark: Used the same mark No. 488 as *Sebastian Schmidt* in *Schmiedefeld.*

Gebr. Stauch Porzellanfabrik
(Bros. Stauch Porcelain Factory),   –1934.
Mark: 589

Saalfeld
Thuringia, Germany

E. Scharf, 1907–defunct before 1945, porcelain decorating shop.
Mark: 336

Saarbrucken - Saarbrücken
Saarland, Germany

Leonhard van Hees Photokeramische Kunstanstalt
(Leonhard van Hees Photoceramic Art Institute), existed 1911, porcelain plates, porcelain decorating shop.
Mark: 3188

Sandizell
Bavaria, Germany

Porzellanfabrik Sandizell Höfner & Co., since circa 1960 **Porzellanfabrik Sandizell GmbH** (Porcelain Factory Sandizell Hofner & Co. since circa 1960 Porcelain Factory Sandizell Ltd.), 1951-present. In 1970 the company acquired *Porcelain Manufactory H. Hilbert* in *Schrobenhausen*. Decorative porcelain, gift articles, lace-figurines. Marks: 1071, 1123, 1145,

St. Polten - St. Pölten
Austria

Rudolf Fritsche, 1883–present, porcelain decorating shop.
Mark: 1483

Schaala
Thuringia, Germany

Hermann Voigt Porzellanfabrik, 1872-1928, household and decorative porcelain, figurines, dolls, electrotechnical porcelain. Marks: 448, 449. Forms and moulds in 1992 were acquired and are used by **Fayence and Porcelain Manufactory Reindel** in Erfurt, Germany, 1977-present. Mark: 3643

Schalksmuhle - Schalksmühle
Westphalia, Germany

Westfälische Porzellanfabrik Heinrich Wahl
(Westphalian Porcelain Factory Heinrich Wahl), 1921–defunct, chemical and technical porcelain.
Mark: 2303

Schatzlar
Bohemia, presently Zacler, Czechia

Porzellanfabrik Theodor Pohl früher **Reinhold Pohl Porzellanfabrik**
(Porcelain Factory Theodor Pohl, formerly Reinhold Pohl Porcelain Factory), 1879–1945, decorative and technical porcelain, figurines, dolls.
Marks: 2153

Schauberg, now incorporated into the city of Tettau
Bavaria, Germany

In 1815 a manufacturer by the name of **Pensel** received a permit to convert his paint factory into the
Königlich Privilegierte Porzellanfabrik Schauberg
(Royally Privileged Porcelain Factory Schauberg). Already one year later he sold it to the brothers
Balthasar and Friedmann Greiner, 1816-   . At an as yet unknown date the company name was changed into
Königlich Privilegierte Porzellanfabrik G. Greiner & Co.
(Royally Privileged Porcelain Factory G. Greiner & Co.),   -1927. The factory produced household and decorative porcelain, gift articles and toys.
Marks: 257, 2149, 2928
Johannes Frisse was proprietor from 1927-1930. He was followed by
Rosenthal-Werke und Porzellanfabrik S. Rosenthal & Co.
(Rosenthal Works and Porcelain Factory S. Rosenthal & Co.) 1930-1931,
Mark: 3243
which soon changed its name to
Porzellanwerk Schauberg Fritz und S. Rosenthal
(Porcelainwork Schauberg, Fritz and S. Rosenthal).
Marks: 61, 3243. In 1938
Friedrich Eckstrom was proprietor. He closed the factory and later sold it to
Heubach, who dissolved the company. After World War II *Richard S. Rosler* from *Dessendorf* acquired the remaining buildings and equipment and founded
Richard S. Rösler Prozellanfabrik Schauberg
(Richard S. Rosler Porcelain Factory Schauberg), 1948-1988. Mark: 419
Then the company was continued by Rosler´s heirs as
Rösler Porzellan und Keramik GmbH
(Rosler Porcelain and Ceramics Ltd.), 1988-present. Household porcelain, gift and promotional articles, laboratory, sanitary and technical porcelain.
Mark:

Schedewitz
Saxony, Germany

Zwickauer Porzellanfabrik Hermann Unger
(Zwickau Porcelain Factory Hermann Unger), existed 1887.
Mark: 1914

Scheibe-Alsbach
Thuringia, Germany

Louis Oels, Daniel Kämpf and Friedemann Greiner founded a porcelain manufactory, 1834-1844, which was taken over by **Dressel, Kister & Cie.** 1844-1863, see *Passau*. Then Kister became sole proprietor and named the company
A.W.Fr. Kister Porzellanmanufaktur 1846-1972, decorative porcelain, figurines, religious articles, dolls. Marks: 2397, 2398, 2412-2415. In 1972 the company was nationalized and named **VEB Porzellanmanufaktur Scheibe-Alsbach** (VEB Porcelain Manufactory Scheibe-Alsbach), 1972-1990, which in

1975 became a branch of *VEB United Decorative Porcelainworks Lichte* in *Lichte*. Mark: 2416. In 1990 the factory was privatized and later acquired by *Königl. Priv. Porcelain Factory Tettau* in *Tettau*, 1995-present. Mark: 3649

Schelten
Bohemia, presently Novy Bor, Czechia

Josef Palme, 1829—1851, founded an earthenware and porcelain factory,
Marks: 1821, 2655, 3221, 3222
which was taken over by
Ignaz Balle, 1851—1860.
Mark: 1813
He sold it to
Eduard Eichler, 1860—1887, Eichler died in 1887 and the factory closed one year later. It produced coffee and tea sets, table and decorative porcelain and earthenware.

Schirnding
Bavaria, Germany

Lorenz Reichel, 1902-1909, household porcelain. Mark: 323
Successor was **Porzellanfabrik Schirnding AG**
(Porcelain Factory Schirnding AG) 1909-1995, household, hotel and decorative porcelain, coffee and tea sets, gift articles. Marks: 436, 438, 753, 754, 1466, 2195, 2304. Merged with *Porcelain Factory J. Kronester* in *Schwarzenbach* and *Porcelain Factory Johann Seltmann* in *Vohenstrauss* to
SKV Porzellan Union GmbH (SKV Porcelain Union Ltd) 1993-present.

Schlackenwerth
Bohemia, presently Ostrov, Czechia

Pfeiffer & Löwenstein
(Pfeiffer & Lowenstein), 1873—1941, household, hotel and decorative porcelain.
In 1941 the company was renamed
Porzellanfabrik Schlackenwerth Josef Pfeiffer
(Porcelain Factory Schlackenwerth Josef Pfeiffer), which existed until about 1945.
Marks: 717, 862, 863, 1152—1155, 1158, 1252, 1504, 2870, 3056, 3105

Schlaggenwald
Bohemia, presently Horni Slavkov, Czechia

In 1792
Johann Georg Paulus, Johann Poschl and **Johann Georg Reumann** founded a manufactory but failed in obtaining a permit for porcelain production. They nevertheless began making simple and rather crude porcelain but without financial success.
Marks: 2917—2919
The manufactory was sold to
Luise Greiner, 1800—circa 1808, (the widow of the former manager of the manufactory in *Gera*) but she too was not able to make the manufactory profitable.

Marks: 2917—2919

She left management to the physician

Johann Georg Lippert, who had joined the manufactory in 1803.

In 1808 Lippert seemed to have owned the company since he made Wenzel Haas a partner and named the manufactory

Lippert & Haas, circa 1808—1847. Within a few years Schlaggenwald porcelain became famous, the manufactory produced mainly coffee and tea sets, decorative porcelain, pipe bowls and after 1828, in increasing number, table porcelain. Marks: 1503, 2917—2926, 3250, 3251

After Wenzel Haas' death, his son August joined the company in 1830. When Lippert died in 1843 he left his share to his son-in-law *Johannes Moehling,* who sold it to

August Haas, 1847—1867, and opened up his own factory in *Aich.*

Mark: 2927

For twenty years the manufactory was in the possession of the Haas family, until 1867, when Johann Czjzek became partner.

From then until 1945 the company name was

Haas & Czjzek, 1867—1945. In 1872 Haas & Czjzek acquired the porcelain factory of *Portheim & Sons* in *Chodau.* In 1931 the establishment became a joint stock company.

Marks: 204, 253, 374, 375, 779, 1756

After World War II the company was nationalized.

Sommer & Matschak, 1904—1945, formerly **Anton Waldmann**, 1901—1904, household and hotel porcelain, coffee and tea sets.

Mark: 842

Schlierbach

Hesse, Germany

Count Adolf at Ysenburg and Budingen and six partners in 1832 founded the

Wächtersbacher Steingutfabrik

(Wachtersbach Earthenware Factory) to improve the economic situation in the poor valley of Schlierbach. Four of the partners left soon and in 1837 Count Adolf owned half of the factory. His son Count (later Prince) Ferdinand Maximilian in 1847 finally acquired the other shares and became sole proprietor. The factory never had financial success in its first forty-five years despite of its products. Only after it was connected to the railroad-system and Max Roesler was appointed manager in 1874, the factory grew into one of the leading earthenware producers. Roesler left in 1884, managed the porcelain factory of *Springer & Co.* in *Élbogen* for three years and in 1894 founded his own earthenware factory in *Rodach.* In 1901 the art ceramic studio of Christian Neureuther was merged with the factory and became its art department.

In 1909 the factory was converted into a limited liability company which is still in existence.

Household and decorative earthenware, figurines, gift and collectors articles. Marks: 60, 318, 506, 510, 684—686, 735, 788, 1413—1417, 1795, 2189, 2203, 3278, 3279, 3281

Schlottenhof
Bavaria, Germany

Porzellanfabrik Schlottenhof früher **L. Künzel**
(Porcelain Factory Schlottenhof formerly L. Kunzel), 1932–defunct after 1940, household porcelain and gift articles.
Mark: 111 shows a similarity with marks 109 and 110 of *Porcelain Factory Bavaria* in *Ullersricht.*

Porzellanmanufaktur und Keramikherstellung Hans Worms
(Porcelain Manufactory and Ceramicproduction Hans Worms), 1935–defunct after 1965, decorating of coffee and tea sets, table and decorative porcelain.
Mark: 1124

Schmiedeberg
Silesia, Germany, presently Kowary, Poland

Gebr. Pohl Porzellanfabrik
(Bros. Pohl Porcelain Factory), 1869–1932, branch factories in Erdmannsdorf and Haselbach, electrotechnical porcelain.
Mark: 2859
The company joined the Rauschert-Combine in 1927 and in 1932 became
Porzellan- und Steatitfabriken Paul Rauschert
(Porcelain and Steatite Factories Paul Rauschert), 1932–1945.
Mark: 246
See also Rauschert, Huttengrund and Pressig.

Schmiedefeld
Thuringia, Germany

Glasser & Greiner Porzellanfabrik und Porzellanmalerei
(Glasser & Greiner Porcelain Factory and Decorating Shop), 1809–1913, decorative porcelain, figurines, pipe bowls, ashtrays, porcelain decorating shop.
Mark: 221
In 1894
Mathias Liebermann is mentioned as proprietor.

Sebastian Schmidt, 1857–probably 1906, decorative porcelain, figurines, knick-knack, pipe bowls.
Mark: 488, the same mark was used by *Eberhard Suhr* in *Rudolstadt* after 1906.

Schney
Bavaria, Germany

A porcelain manufactory was founded here in 1780 or 1783, but no further information could be found. In 1837
H. K. Eichhorn is mentioned as proprietor.
Mark: 3252
Later the company name was
Bremer & Liebmann. At the beginning of this century the name was changed to

Porzellanfabrik Eduard Liebmann KG
(Porcelain Factory Eduard Liebmann KG).
Marks: 2410, 2411
In 1923 the factory became a branch of *Porcelain Factory at Kloster Veilsdorf* in *Kloster Veilsdorf.* Main product was always household porcelain.

Schonfeld - Schönfeld
Bohemia, presently Krasno, Czechia

J. Spinner, 1867–1883, porcelain decorating shop, after 1883
Porzellanfabrik Joseph Spinner
(Porcelain Factory Joseph Spinner), producing household porcelain. From about 1900 the company was owned by
A. Schindler, who can be traced until 1927.
Mark: 2538

Schonwald - Schönwald
Bavaria, Germany

Johann Nikol Müller
(Johann Nikol Muller), 1879–1898, founded a factory for household and table porcelain.
Mark: 2453
His heirs converted the factory into a joint stock company with the name
Porzellanfabrik Schönwald
(Porcelain Factory Schonwald), 1898–1927, which specialized in production of hotel and household porcelain. In 1904 it acquired the *Porcelain Factory Theodor Lehmann* in *Arzberg.*
Marks: 146, 368–373, 729, 1157
In 1927 the company bought
Porzellanfabrik E. & A. Müller
(Porcelain Factory E. & A. Muller), 1904–1927, which had been founded by descendants of J. N. Muller.
Marks: 1102, 1220, 1911, 2103
The same year the company was taken over by *Porcelain Factory Kahla* in *Kahla* and continued as
Porzellanfabrik Schönwald Zweigniederlassung der Porzellanfabrik Kahla
(Porcelain Factory Schonwald, Branch of Porcelain Factory Kahla), 1927–1972.
Mark: 379
In 1972 Porcelain Factory Kahla merged with *Hutschenreuther AG* in *Selb* and the name changed to
Porzellanfabrik Schönwald Zweigniederlassung der Hutschenreuther AG
(Porcelain Factory Schonwald, Branch of Hutschenreuther AG), 1972–present.
Marks: 379, 381, 382

Schorndorf
Wurttemberg; Germany

Württembergische Porzellanmanufaktur C. M. Bauer & Pfeiffer
(Wurttembergish Porcelain Manufactory C. M. Bauer & Pfeiffer), 1904–1918, later
Württembergische Porzellanmanufaktur AG
(Wurttembergish Porcelain Manufactory AG), 1918–1939, coffee and tea sets, table, hotel and decorative porcelain, figurines.
Marks: 166, 171, 959, 979, 986, 1023, 1063, 1269, 3277
Some of the marks were intentionally designed to resemble marks of the defunct *Royal Porcelain Manufactory* in *Ludwigsburg.*

Schramberg
Wurttemberg, Germany

Villeroy & Boch Steingut-, Majolika-, und Porzellanfabrik
(Villeroy & Boch Earthenware, Maiolica and Porcelain Factory), 1883–1912, household and decorative porcelain and earthenware. The factory was founded by **Isidore Faist** and bought in 1883 by Villeroy & Boch at an auction. They discontinued porcelain production and concentrated on earthenware and maiolica, gaily decorated with flowers.
Marks: 390, 2239, 2668

Schriesheim
Wurttemberg, Germany

Porzellanmanufaktur Schriesheim Dietrich von Eisenhart
(Porcelain Manufactory Schriesheim Dietrich von Eisenhart), 1945–defunct before 1959, gift articles, figurines, technical porcelain, porcelain decorating.
Mark: 775

Schrobenhausen
Bavaria, Germany

Porzellanmanufaktur H. Hilbert
(Porcelain Manufactory H. Hilbert), 1965–1970, figurines.
Mark: 1121
The company was sold in 1970 to *Porcelain Factory Sandizell Hofner & Co.* in *Sandizell.*

Schwaben near Munich
Bavaria, Germany

Porzellanfabrik Schwaben GMBH
(Porcelain Factory Schwaben GMBH), 1921–1929, household porcelain.
Mark: 3062

Schwabisch-Gmund - Schwäbisch-Gmünd
Wurttemberg, Germany

Gebr. Deyhle
(Bros. Deyhle), existed 1941, porcelain with silver layer.
Mark: 73

Metallporzellanfabrik
(Metalporcelain Factory), before 1934–   , porcelain with metal layers and metal mounts.
Mark: 2848

Schwandorf
Bavaria, Germany

Tonwarenfabrik Schwandorf
(Pottery Factory Schwandorf) 1865-1959, converted into branch of *Porcelain Factory Kahla* in *Kahla* as
Abteilung Porzellanfabrik Schwandorf
(Department Porcelain Factory Schwandorf) and later
Abteilung Porzellanfabrik Schwarzenfeld (Department Porcelain Factory Schwarzenfeld), household and decorative porcelain. This production ceased in 1973 in favour of sanitary porcelain.
Marks: 272, 275, 1782, 2154, 3076
In 1972 merged with *Hutschenreuther AG* in *Selb* and *Keramag* in *Ratingen* to
Hutschenreuther-Keramag GmbH
(Hutschenreuther-Keramag Ltd) 1972-closed 1994, sanitary earthenware and porcelain.

Schwarza-Saale
Thuringia, Germany

E. & A. Müller Porzellanfabrik
(E. & A. Muller Porcelain Factory), 1890–circa 1945, decorative porcelain, figurines.
Marks: 646, 719, 2376, 2841

Schwarzenbach-Saale
Bavaria, Germany

Porzellanfabrik J. Kronester GmbH (Porcelain Factory J. Kronester Ltd), 1905-1995, household porcelain, porcelain decorating shop.
Marks: 1126, 1241, 1242.
Merged with *Porcelain Factory Schirnding* in *Schirnding* and *Porcelain Factory Johann Seltmann* in *Vohenstrauss* to *SKV Porcelain Union Ltd* in *Schirnding*

Oscar Schaller & Co., 1882-circa 1918,
Marks: 802, 896, 1858, 2654, 3073.
Oscar Schaller & Co. Nachf. (Oscar Schaller & Co. Successor), circa 1918-present. Household, table and decorative porcelain, gift articles.
Marks: 561, 1195
The factory is a member of the *Winterling* Group, *Windischeschenbach*

Schwarzenberg
Saxony, Germany

Schwarzenberger Porzellanfabrik Fr. Wilhelm Kutscher & Co.
(Schwarzenberg Porcelain Factory Fr. Wilhelm Kutscher & Co.), 1908–1931, household and decorative porcelain, gift articles.
Mark: 8

Schwarzenfeld
Thuringia, Germany

H. Waffler, existed about 1925, porcelain decorating shop.
Mark: 1965

Schwarzenhammer
Bavaria, Germany

Schumann & Schreider Porzellanfabrik Schwarzenhammer
(Schumann & Schreider Porcelain Factory Schwarzenhammer), 1905–present, household and decorative porcelain, gift articles.
Marks: 692, 1472, 1480, 1822, 1926

Schwarzkosteletz
Bohemia, presently Cerny Kostelec, Czechia

Alois Vondracek & Co., existed about 1930, porcelain decorating shop.
Mark: 2670

Schweidnitz
Silesia, Germany, presently Swidnica, Poland

R. M. Krause, 1882–still in existence in 1929, porcelain decorator.
Marks: 269, 727

Schweinsburg
Saxony, Germany

Gebr. Meinhold
(Bros. Meinhold), traceable 1899–1910, decorative and household porcelain or earthenware, gift articles. tiles.
Mark: 147

Seedorf
Wurttemberg, Germany

Volkstedter Porzellanmanufaktur Seedorf O. & J. Saar
(Volkstedt Porcelain Manufactory Seedorf O. & J. Saar), 1950–defunct about 1960, figurines, decorative porcelain.
Mark: 801

Selb
Bavaria, Germany

Gräf & Krippner

(Graf & Krippner), 1906—1929, household and decorative porcelain.
Marks: 305, 1111, 2587
The company began as porcelain decorating shop. In 1929 it merged with *Heinrich & Co.* in *Selb.*

Heinrich Porzellan GMBH

(Heinrich Porcelain GMBH), 1896—present, table and decorative porcelain, coffee and tea sets.
Founded by the porcelain decorator
Franz Heinrich, who in 1900 began producing his own porcelain. At that time the company name became
Heinrich & Co. In 1929 it acquired *Graf & Krippner* in *Selb.*
The present name was adopted in 1970 and since 1976 the company is a subsidiary of *Villeroy & Boch* in *Mettlach.*
Mark: 305, 497, 771, 840, 1113—1118, 1231, 1979, 2169, 2802, 3153, 3165—3167, 3187

Porzellanfabrik L. Hutschenreuther

(Porcelain Factory L. Hutschenreuther), 1857—1969.
From 1845 until 1857 Lorenz Hutschenreuther managed the porcelain factory founded by his father *C. M. Hutschenreuther* in *Hohenberg.* In 1857 he established his own factory in Selb, which in 1902 became a joint stock company. Four years later *Porcelain Factory Jager, Werner & Co.* in *Selb* was acquired and became Work B. In 1917 L. Hutschenreuther bought *Paul Muller Porcelain Factory* in *Selb,* in 1927 *Porcelain Factory Tirschenreuth* in *Tirschenreuth* and *Porcelain Factory Bros. Bauscher* in *Weiden* and in 1928 *Porcelain Factory Konigszelt* in *Konigszelt.*
Marks: 84, 106, 115—117, 829, 1232, 1264, 2047, 2172, 2173
After the company gained a majority of shares in Porcelain Factory *C. M. Hutschenreuther* in *Hohenberg* in 1969, both factories were combined to
Hutschenreuther AG, 1969—present.
In 1972 the company acquired *Porcelain Factory Kahla,* see Kahla, with its factories in Schonwald, Arzberg, Schwandorf and Wiesau. Table, household, hotel and decorative porcelain, coffee and tea sets, gift articles, figurines.
Marks: 89, 118, 119, 1226
Since 1975 the company has its own distributing companies in France (Hutschenreuther France) and in the U. S. A. (Hutschenreuther Corporation in North Branford, Connecticut).

Jäger, Werner & Co.

(Jager, Werner & Co.), about 1896—1906, household, table and decorative porcelain.
Mark: 2816
In 1906 acquired by *Porcelain Factory L. Hutschenreuther* in *Selb.*

Krautheim & Adelberg Porzellanfabrik GmbH

(Krautheim & Adelberg Porcelain Factory Ltd), 1884-1977, table and decorative porcelain, gift articles.
The company was founded by Christoph Krautheim as porcelain decorating shop. In 1912 a factory for porcelain production was added.
Marks: 242, 607, 1127, 1227, 3196-3198, 3207

Lorenz & Trabe, existed about 1925, porcelain decorating shop.
Marks: 712, 714

Paul Müller Porzellanfabrik
(Paul Muller Porcelain Factory), 1890–circa 1957, household and hotel porcelain.
The company became a branch of *Porcelain Factory L. Hutschenreuther* in *Selb*
in 1917. From 1943 until 1957 *State's Porcelain Manufactory* in *Berlin* leased the
Muller factory after its own plant in Berlin was destroyed in an air raid. Thereafter
the factory was closed.
Marks: 786, 829, 1144, 2144, 3061

Josef Rieber & Co., 1868–circa 1923, porcelain decorating shop. Later the
decorating shop developed into *Porcelain Factory Josef Rieber & Co.*, which
moved from Selb to *Mitterteich*.
Marks: 108, 2898

Philip Rosenthal, 1879-1897,
Philip Rosenthal & Co. AG, 1897-1939,
Rosenthal Porzellan AG, 1939-1965,
Rosenthal AG, 1965-1969,
Rosenthal Glas & Porzellan AG now
Rosenthal AG,
1969-present, in which
Waterford Wedgwood holds a considerable interest. Table, household, hotel and decora-
tive porcelain and earthenware, figurines, gift and collectors' articles, technical porce-
lain. In 1897 the company acquired *Porcelain Factory Bauer, Rosenthal & Co.* in *Kronach*,
in 1908 *Porcelain Manufactory Thomas* in *Marktredwitz*, in 1917 *Jacob Zeidler & Co.
Railway Station Selb*, in 1921 *Krister Porcelain Manufactory* in *Waldenburg*. The plants
of *Krister* were lost at the end of World War II but the company was re-established in
Landstuhl. Rosenthal also held a considerable interest in *Bohemia Ceramic Works* in
Neurohlau from 1922-1945. In 1928 *Porcelain Factory Thomas* in *Sophienthal* became
part of the Rosenthal group and in 1936 *Porcelain Factory Waldershof* in *Waldershof*.
Marks: 416-418, 566, 791, 845, 885, 923, 924, 934-946, 1075, 1163, 1166, 1255, 2012,
2013, 2201, 3123, 3206, 3242

Staatliche Porzellanmanufaktur Berlin Zweigwerk Selb
(State's Porcelain Manufactory Berlin, Branch Selb), 1943–1957, after the
buildings of the manufactory in Berlin were destroyed by air raids in 1943,
production was continued in the leased factory of *Paul Muller* in *Selb*. From 1946
until 1949 the branch in Selb was a legally independent company because of orders
of the British and American Military Authorities. In 1957 the branch in Selb was
transferred back to Berlin.
Mark: 1312, all products manufactured in Selb are distinguishable by an S under-
neath the scepter.

Jacob Zeidler & Co. Porzellanfabrik Bahnhof Selb
(Jacob Zeidler & Co. Porcelain Factory Railway Station Selb), 1866–1917, house-
hold, hotel and decorative porcelain.
Marks: 2037, 2817, 2994

The factory was acquired by *Philip Rosenthal Co. AG* in *Selb* in 1917 and for some years was called
Rosenthal Porcelain Factory Selb-Plossberg.
Mark: 3123

Siegburg
Rhineland, Germany

Gesellschaft für Feinkeramik GMBH
(Company for Fineceramics GMBH), existed 1949, household and technical porcelain and earthenware.
Mark: 2029

Sitzendorf
Thuringia, Germany

A small porcelain manufactory, founded by
Wilhelm Liebmann in 1850, was taken over by
Wilhelm Örtel. He sold it to Carl and Alfred Voigt who named the manufactory
Gebr. Voigt (Bros Voigt), 1884-1896, producing decorative porcelain and figurines in the Meissen style. Marks: 2315-2317
The manufactory was converted into a joint stock company under the name
Alfred Voigt AG, 1896-circa1902. The name was changed to
Sitzendorfer Porzellanmanufaktur vormals Alfred Voigt AG
(Sitzendorf Porcelain Manufactory formerly Alfred Voigt AG), circa 1902-1972.
Marks: 929, 930, 2316
In 1958 the company was semi-nationalized, in 1972 fully nationalized and became
VEB Sitzendorfer Porzellanmanufaktur
(VEB Sitzendorf Porcelain Manufactory), 1972-1990, using marks 930 and 2316.
After the unification of Germany the company was privatized under its old name
Sitzendorfer Porzellanmanufaktur vormal Alfred Voigt KG
1990-present, still using mark No. 930.

Sitzerode
Thuringia, Germany

Georg Heinrich Macheleid (occasionally Macheleidt), 1759—1760. Macheleid discovered independently from Bottger (Meissen) the secret of porcelain. Because he was denied a permit for a porcelain manufactory in Sitzerode, he applied for a permit in *Volkstedt,* which was granted.
Mark: 2409

Solingen
Rhineland, Germany

Walter Klaas, existed 1897—circa 1907, household and decorative porcelain and earthenware.
Mark: 2004

Sonneberg
Thuringia, Germany

Ernst Friedrich & Karl Dressel, 1863–circa 1873, dolls and dolls heads.
Mark: 2567
Successors were
Cuno & Otto Dressel, circa 1873–circa 1943.
Marks: 604, 1279, 2547, 2732

Carl Harmus, 1873–last mention found in 1949, doll maker, having his name impressed in dolls heads in addition to the mark of *Porcelain Manufactory Moschendorf* in *Hof-Moschendorf*.
Marks: 2053, 3054

Hermann Steiner, 1921–defunct, dolls and dolls heads.
Marks: 2607, 2608, 3035, 3036

VEB Elektrokeramische Werke Sonneberg (VEB Electroceramic Works Sonneburg), 1964-1990, branch of *VEB Combine Ceramic Works Hermsdorf* in *Hermsdorf*, 1965-1990, electrotechnical porcelain. Formed in 1965 by merging *VEB United Porcelainworks Koppelsdorf* in *Koppelsdorf*, *VEB Porcelainworks Neuhaus* in *Neuhaus-Schierschnitz* and a newly erected factory in Sonneberg-Foritz. Semi-privatized in 1990 as **TRIDELTA Ltd**, fully privatized in 1996 as **CERAM Elektrokeramik Sonneberg GmbH,** 1996-present.
VEB Sonneberger Porzellanfabriken
(VEB Sonneberg Porcelain Factories) see Huttensteinach

Sonthofen
Bavaria, Germany

Keramische Werkstätten und Porzellanmalerei Hans Graf KG
(Ceramic Workshops and Porcelain Decorating Hans Graf KG), 1951–present, decorative ceramics and porcelain decorating shop, porcelain decorating was discontinued in 1964.
Marks: 2001, 3104

Sophienthal
Bavaria, Germany

Porzellanfabrik Thomas & Co.
(Porcelain Factory Thomas & Co.), 1920–present, household, table and technical porcelain, gift articles.
The company was founded in Bayreuth, acquired by *Philip Rosenthal & Co. AG* in *Selb* and moved to Sophienthal.
Marks: 174, 309, 763–765

Sorau
Brandenburg, Germany

Porzellanfabrik Sorau Fr. Böhme
(Porcelain Factory Sorau Fr. Bohme), 1894–1918, table and decorative porcelain.
Marks: 1857, 2402
Successor was
C. & E. Carstens Porzellanfabrik Sorau

(C. & E. Carstens Porcelain Factory Sorau), 1918—circa 1945.
Marks: 545, 1470, 2067

Spechtsbrunn
Thuringia, Germany

Porzellanfabrik Spechtsbrunn GmbH

(Porcelain Factory Spechtsbrunn Ltd), 1911-1954, household, decorative and technical porcelain, figurines, toys.
A new proprietor added his name
Porzellanfabrik Spechtsbrunn G. Rossbach KG,

(Porcelain Factory Spechtsbrunn G. Rossbach), 1954-1972.
Marks: 307, 916, 1076, 1142, 1167
The factory was nationalized and named
VEB Porzellanfabrik Spechtsbrunn

(VEB Porcelain Factory Spechtsbrunn) 1972-closed 1990.
Mark: 1076

Speicher
Rhineland, Germany

Kunstkeramische Werkstätten Gebr. Plein

(Art Ceramic Workshops Bros. Plein), 1880—present, decorative and kitchen porcelain, figurines, religious and promotional articles.
Mark: 2058

Stadtilm
Thuringia, Germany

Stadtilmer Porzellanfabrik GmbH

(Stadtilm Porcelain Factory Ltd), 1889-1915, branch of *Ilmenau Porcelain Factory* in *Ilmenau*. Decorative and household porcelain, figurines, coffee and tea sets, porcelain decorating. Mark: 526. 1917 sold and continued as porcelain decorating shop. Nationalized in 1972 and named
VEB Porzellanveredelung

(VEB Porcelain Finishing) 1972-1973, then incorporated into *VEB Henneberg Porcelain* in *Ilmenau*.

Stadtlengsfeld
Thuringia

Porzellanfabrik Stadtlengsfeld

(Porcelain Factory Stadtlengsfeld), 1889—circa 1945, household, table, hotel and decorative porcelain, gift articles.
Founded in 1889 by
Koch & Schnorr, the company was acquired by
M. Schweizer about 1900. It was converted into a joint stock company about 1908.
Marks: 1872, 1873, 1934, 1935, 1966, 2640, 3063
After World War II the company was nationalized, first became a branch of VEB Thuringian Porcelainworks and later
VEB Porzellanwerk Stadtlengsfeld

(VEB Porcelainwork Stadtlengsfeld), 1950—present, household, hotel and decor-

ative porcelain.
Marks: 1874, 1875

Staffelstein
Bavaria, Germany

Kaiser Porzellan
(Kaiser-Porcelain), formerly **Alka-Kunst Alboth & Kaiser**, 1872—present. August Alboth founded a porcelain factory and decorating shop in Coburg in 1872. His son Ernst moved the manufactory to Kronach in 1899 and in 1922 took his son-in-law Georg Kaiser into partnership. Five years later the company introduced the name Alka-Kunst and in 1938 acquired the factory of *Bros. Silbermann* in *Hausen*. The manufactory was moved to Staffelstein in 1953 and in 1970 the present name was adopted.
Table and decorative porcelain, coffee and tea sets, figurines, gift and collectors articles.
Marks: 501, 804, 1026, 1088—1094, 1510, 1511, 2995, 2996

Stanowitz
Bohemia, Strzegnom, Czechia

Striegauer Porzellanfabrik vorm. C. Walter & Co.
(Striegau Porcelain Factory formerly C. Walter & Co.), 1873—last mention found 1927, household and decorative porcelain, coffee and tea sets.
Marks: 213, 1486, 2246, 2466

Steinbach
Bavaria, Germany

Gerhard Knopf, existed 1975, decorative porcelain, figurines, gift articles.
Mark: 1128

Porzellanfabrik Paul Rauschert
(Porcelain Factory Paul Rauschert), 1912—present, technical porcelain, see Pressig, Paul Rauschert.

Steinbach
Thuringia, Germany

Porzellanfabrik Wiefel & von der Wehd
(Porcelain Factory Wiefel & von der Wehd), 1904—1923, decorative porcelain, cups, dolls and dolls heads, technical porcelain. Successor was
Erste Steinbacher Porzellanfabrik Wiefel & Co.
(First Steinbach Porcelain Factory Wiefel & Co.), 1923—1938.
Mark: 132
The company was acquired in 1938 by Gustav Heubach.

Steinwiesen
Bavaria, Germany

Porzellanfabrik Steinwiesen

(Porcelain Factory Steinwiesen), 1910–1937, electrotechnical porcelain, toys. Successor was

Porzellanfabrik Eduard Haerter

(Porcelain Factory Eduard Haerter), 1937–1965.
Mark: 2650
The company was acquired by *Paul Rauschert KG* in *Pressig,* 1965–present, since 1971 also gift and promotional articles, decorative porcelain.
Mark: 490

Porzellanmalerei und Fayencefabrik C. Müller

(Porcelain Decorating Shop and Fayence Factory C. Muller), 1905–defunct, porcelain decorating shop.
Mark: 2295

Stockheim

Bavaria, Germany

Porzellanfabrik Eversberg

(Porcelain Factory Eversberg), 1978–present, household porcelain, promotional articles.
Mark: 1225
Until 1978 the company was located in *Burggrub* as *Porcelain Factory Burggrub Horst Eversberg.*

Stutzerbach - Stützerbach

Thuringia, Germany

Friedrich Carl Müller

(Friedrich Carl Muller), 1830–1922, decorative and technical porcelain.
Marks: 2463, 2810
The company became a department of *Franz R. Kirchner & Co.* in *Manebach* in 1922.

Suhl

Thuringia, Germany

Erdmann Schlegelmilch Porzellanfabrik

(Erdmann Schlegelmilch Porcelain Factory), 1881–1938, household, table and decorative porcelain, coffee and tea sets.
Marks: 222, 300–302, 509, 521, 831, 1105, 1106, 1435, 1436, 1798, 1824, 3023, 3145–3148

Reinhold Schlegelmilch Porzellanfabrik und -malerei

(Reinhold Schlegelmilch Porcelain Factory and Decorating Shop) see Tillowitz

Tannawa

Bohemia, presently Zdanov, Czechia

Franz Josef Mayer, 1813–1872, earthenware from 1813–1832, household, table and decorative porcelain from 1832.
Marks: 1473, 2944, 3034, 3260
Mayer's son Josef founded a factory in *Klentsch* in 1835.

Taschwitz
Bohemia, presently Tasovice, Czechia

Friedrich Wilhelm Pohle, 1860–1872, later
Gebr. Pohle & Co. Porzellanfabrik
(Bros. Pohle & Co. Porcelain Factory), 1872–defunct. Friedrich Wilhelm Pohle produced dolls heads. His sons Friedrich and Rudolf took over in 1872 and began production of household, hotel and table porcelain, coffee and tea sets, some of it decorated with onion pattern.
Mark: 3134

Taubenbach
Thuringia, Germany

Carl Moritz Porzellanfabrik
(Carl Moritz Porcelain Factory), 1848 (or 1860)–circa 1930, household and decorative porcelain, figurines, toys and dolls.
Mark: 3042

Tellnitz
Bohemia, presently Telnice, Czechia

Egon Stein Porzellanfabrik Tellnitz
(Egon Stein Porcelain Factory Tellnitz), 1902–1940, technical and table porcelain.
Mark: 388

Teltow
Brandenburg, Germany

Berliner Porzellanmanufaktur Conrad, Schomburg & Co. GMBH
(Berlin Porcelain Manufactory Conrad, Schomburg & Co. GMBH), 1904–circa 1911, household, table and decorative porcelain, figurines.
Marks: 189, 693, 925
Successor was
Porzellanfabrik Teltow
(Porcelain Factory Teltow), circa 1911–circa 1932, which changed production to electrotechnical porcelain.
Mark: 2282

Teplitz-Schonau - Teplitz-Schönau
Bohemia, presently Teplice, Czechia

Reinhold Bosdorf, existed 1930, porcelain decorating shop.
Mark: 422

Tettau
Bavaria, Germany

J. Schmidt and **G.Chr. F. Greiner** founded a porcelain manufactory, 1794-1852 and produced household, table and decorative porcelain, coffee and tea sets.
Marks: 2938-2943
Successor was **Ferdinand Klaus**, 1852-1866, who continued using the same marks.
He was followed by **Sontag & Birkner**, 1866-1887, Marks: 124, 2938-2942,
later the company name was changed to
Sontag & Söhne (Sontag & Sons), 1887-1902, Marks: 97, 329
subsequently it became
Porzellanfabrik Tettau
(Porcelain Factory Tettau), 1902-1957, which was converted into a joint stock company.
In 1957 the majority of the shares was acquired by *Porcelain Factory Christian Seltmann* in *Weiden* and the name was changed to
Königlich privilegierte Porzellanfabrik Tettau GmbH
(Royally privileged Porcelain Factory Tettau Ltd), 1957-present.
Marks: 93-96, 98-102, 3595
Daughters of the company are *Oldest Volkstedt Porcelain Manufactory* in *Volkstedt, Porcelain Manufactory Plaue* in *Plaue, Unterweissbach Workshops for Porcelain Art* in *Unterweissbach* and *Porcelain Manufactory Scheibe-Alsbach* in *Scheibe-Alsbach*.
In the U.S. the name Royal Bayreuth is common for the products of the factory.

Neue Porzellanfabrik Tettau eGmbH
(New Porcelain Factory Tettau registered Ltd), 1904-1923, subsequently converted into a joint stock company
Neue Porzellanfabrik Tettau AG
(New Porcelain Factory Tettau), 1923-1937. Marks: 277, 2627, 3048, 3049
After the joint stock company was dissolved, the company name was changed to
Neue Porzellanfabrik Tettau Gerold & Co.
(New Porcelain Factory Tettau Gerold & Co.), 1937-circa 1960, and later to
Porzellanfabrik Gerold & Co. (Porcelain Factory Gerold & Co.), circa 1960-1993,
Marks: 683, 3048. After a change in proprietorship the factory was named
Neue Porzellangesellschaft mbh
(New Porcelain Company Ltd), 1993-present. The factors always produced household, table and decorative porcelain and figurines. Mark 683 is still in use.

Arno Stauch, 1922—after 1964, porcelain decorating shop.
Mark: 243

Thiersheim
Bavaria, Germany

Willi Gossler, 1929—defunct, porcelain decorating shop.
Mark: 1803

Porzellanfabriken Josef Rieber
(Porcelain Factories Josef Rieber) see Mitterteich

Tiefenbach

Bohemia, presently Hluboka, Czechia

J. Schnabel & Sohn

(J. Schnabel & Son), circa 1870–   , later
Hermann Scholz,   –1912, subsequently
Hermann Scholz Nachfolger Camill Seidl
(Hermann Scholz Successor Camill Seidl), circa 1912–defunct between 1939 and
and 1945, decorative porcelain, gift articles, pipe bowls, apothecary jars,
technical porcelain.
Mark: 2150

Tiefenfurth

Silesia, Germany, presently Parowa, Poland

Louis Löwinsohn

(Louis Lowinsohn), 1885-1891, operated a porcelain factory, which supposedly was
founded in 1806. It produced coffee and tea sets and decorative porcelain in the Meissen
style.
Mark: 1730
Successor of Lowinsohn was
Schlesische Porzellanfabrik P. Donath
(Silesian Porcelain Factory P. Donath), 1891-1916, which changed production to table,
household and decorative porcelain and cups, imitating Meissen porcelain and Meissen
marks.
Donath continued using Lowinsohns Mark No. 1730 and added Marks: 304, 644, 1081,
1728-1730
In 1916 Donath left the factory, which continued as
Schlesische Porzellanfabrik Tiefenfurth
(Silesian Porcelain Factory Tiefenfurth), 1916-1919. Thereafter Carl Hans Tuppack, who
had joined the factory a few years earlier, acquired the company and called it
Porzellanfabrik Carl Hans Tuppack
(Porcelain Factory Carl Hans Tuppack), 1919-closed 1935.
Marks: 17, 193, 587, 1176, 1361, 2478, 2947, 2948, 3268

K. Steinmann Porzellanfabriken

(K. Steinmann Porcelain Factories), 1868–1938, household, table and decorative
porcelain, porcelain decorating.
Marks: 36, 209, 948, 1138, 1139, 1174, 1216

Stern-Porzellan-Manufaktur E. Leber & Sohn

(Stern Porcelain Manufactory E. Leber & Son), formerly
E. Leber, 1914–1933.
Mark: 623

Tillowitz

Silesia, Germany, presently Tulovice, Poland

Graf Frankenberg'sche Porzellanmanufaktur

(Count Frankenberg's Porcelain Manufactory), 1852–1938.
In 1894 Erhard Schlegelmilch was registered as proprietor.
Marks: 135, 1458

Reinhold Schlegelmilch Porzellanfabriken

(Reinhold Schlegelmilch Porcelain Factories), 1869–last mention found in 1938, household, table and decorative porcelain, figurines. Schlegelmilch operated a porcelain factory and decorating shop in Suhl and a branch in Tillowitz. In 1932 he moved his company to Tillowitz, five years later Lothar Schlegelmilch is mentioned as proprietor.
Marks: 317, 362, 513, 515–523, 1903, 1904, 2038, 3070, 3235
In the U. S. A., R. Schlegelmilch's products are known as R. S. Prussia or R. S. Germany.

Tirschenreuth
Bavaria, Germany

Keramische Werke Zehendner & Co. (Ceramic Works Zehendner & C0.),
1870-present, household and decorative porcelain. Mark: 1196

Porzellanfabrik Tirschenreuth (Porcelain Factory Tirschenreuth), 1838-closed 1995,
table, household and decorative porcelain, coffee and tea sets. In 1927 the company was acquired by *Porcelain Factory L. Hutschenreuther* in *Selb*.
Marks: 527, 702, 731, 755, 1159-1161, 1248, 3064

SMCS Porzellanfabrik GmbH & Co. KG Tirschenreuth

(SMCS Porcelain Factory Tirschenreuth) 1954-present, founded in 1986 as factory for stove tiles, converted into a porcelain factory in 1954. Mark: 3613

Triptis
Thuringia, Germany

Unger & Gretschel, 1891-1896, successor was
Triptis AG, 1896-1946, household porcelain, coffee and tea sets, decorative porcelain. Marks: 1249, 3085, 3267. The company was nationalized in 1946, first named **Branch Triptis of VEB Thüringian Porcelainworks**. Later the name was changed to **VEB Porzellanwerk Triptis** (VEB Porcelainwork Triptis), 1946-1990, from 1968-1987 Work II of *VEB Porcelain Combine Kahla* in *Kahla*, then independent government owned factory. Marks: 567, 2260. After privatization in 1990 acquired by management and renamed **Triptis-Porzellan GmbH**, 1993-present. Mark: 3653

Turn-Teplitz
Bohemia, presently Trnovany, Czechia

Riessner, Stellmacher & Kessel Amphora, 1892–1905, household and decorative
porcelain and earthenware, figurines.
Marks: 568, 1997, 2651, 2652, 2688

After Stellmacher left the company the name was changed to
Amphora Porzellanfabrik Riessner & Kessel
(Amphora Porcelain Factory Riessner & Kessel), 1905—1910, and after Kessel left too the company was called
Amphora Werk Riessner
(Amphora Work Riessner), 1910—1945.
Marks: 214, 653, 2051—2053, 2688
The company was nationalized after World War II.

Ditmar-Urbach AG Porzellanfabriken
(Ditmar-Urbach AG Porcelain Factories), 1882—1938, household, table, decorative and sanitary porcelain and earthenware.
Founded in 1882 under the name
Bros. Urbach. In 1912 acquired by *Triptis AG* in *Triptis,* in 1919 consolidated with the factory *Rudolf Ditmar's Heirs* in *Znaim* to Ditmar-Urbach AG and taken over by *Wilhelmsburg-Earthenware Factory Richard Lichtenstern & Co.* in *Wilhelmsburg.* In 1938 the company became part of Ostmark-Ceramic until 1945, when it was nationalized.
Mark: 315

Gröschl & Spethmann
(Groschl & Spethmann), 1899—defunct, decorative porcelain.
Mark: 897

Anton Heller, später **Teplitzer Metall-Porzellanwerke Victor Heller**
(Anton Heller, later Teplitz Metal Porcelainworks Victor Heller), traceable 1889—1920, terra cotta and maiolica, porcelain with metal layer.
Mark: 486

Mekus & Moest Porzellanfabrik
(Mekus & Moest Porcelain Factory), 1892—circa 1912, decorative porcelain, flowers, toys.
Mark: 2625

Porzellanfabrik Adolf Lauffer
(Porcelain Factory Adolf Lauffer), 1919—1938, the company started as a decorating shop and later began production of household porcelain.
Marks: 16, 1898

Alfred Stellmacher K. K. Porzellan-Fabrik
(Alfred Stellmacher Imperial and Royal Porcelain Factory), 1859—1894, decorative porcelain, flowers, table and household porcelain.
Marks: 420, 1787
In 1894 *Ernst Wahliss* acquired the factory.

Josef Strnact, 1881—1932, terra cotta factory and porcelain decorating shop.
Mark: 1481

Vinzenz Unger Porzellan- und Terrakottafabrik

(Vinzenz Unger Porcelain and Terra Cotta Factory), 1905–1945, decorative porcelain and figurines, later household porcelain, porcelain decorating.
Mark: 2952
In 1923 the factory was shut down, about 1925 it was leased to
Franz Richter, who only produced terra cotta.

Ernst Wahliss, 1894–1905, first only sold Bohemian porcelain in his stores in London, England, and Vienna (1863–1894) until he acquired the factory of *Alfred Stellmacher* in *Turn*. After his death in 1900 his sons Hans and Erich named the company
Alexandra Porcelain Works Ernst Wahliss, 1905–1921. In 1902 they bought about six hundred original moulds of the defunct *Imperial and Royal Porcelain Manufactory* in *Vienna* and made reproductions of Vienna decorative porcelain and figurines. After 1910 porcelain production was decreased in favor of fayence.
Marks: 421, 679, 746, 759, 1107, 2277, 3094, 3254, 3256, 3258
In 1921 the factory became part of *Porcelain Union United Porcelain Factories* as Branch Turn-Teplitz, see also Klosterle. In 1925 the company was listed as Ernst Wahliss AG.
Mark: 541
Porcelain Union was taken over by *Epiag* in *Karlsbad* and closed in 1934.

Brüder Willner
(Bros. Willner), 1884–1915, decorative porcelain and porcelain parts for mounting with other materials.
Mark: 2721

Uhlstadt - Uhlstädt
Thuringia, Germany

H.G. Meurer and I. Streibhardt in 1837 founded a porcelain factory, which was taken over by
Carl Alberti Porzellanfabrik Uhlstädt
(Carl Alberti Porcelain Factory Uhlstadt), 1873-1954, household and decorative porcelain, coffee and tea sets. Marks: 856, 1030, 1031.
Then nationalized as **VEB Porzellanfabrik Uhlstädt** (VEB Porcelain Factory Uhlstadt), 1954-closed 1990, household porcelain, later producing only handles for cups as Work VI of *VEB Porcelain Combine Kahla* in *Kahla*, 1968- closed in 1991. Mark: 2669

Ullersricht
Bavaria, Germany

Porzellanfabrik Bavaria AG
(Porcelain Factory Bavaria AG), 1919–circa 1932, household porcelain.
Marks: 109, 110, 112, 576, 1265, 1482, 2182
The similarity of marks No. 109 and 110 with mark No. 111 of *Porcelain Factory Schlottenhof* in *Schlottenhof* suggests a connection between the two factories.

Ulm
Wurttemberg, Germany

Johann Jakob Schmidt, 1827–1833, figurines in the style of the defunct *Royal Porcelain Manufactory Ludwigsburg* in *Ludwigsburg.*
Mark: 3269

Unterkoditz - Unterköditz
Thuringia, Germany

Möller & Dippe
(Moller & Dippe), 1883–1931, figurines, dolls, dolls heads, decorative and electrotechnical porcelain.
Marks: 1208, 1856

Untermhaus
Thuringia, Germany

Mathias Eichelroth founded a fayence factory in 1750, which in 1772 began' porcelain production. After fires broke out in the factory twice in 1882, threatening the village, the inhabitants destroyed the kiln. A porcelain manufactory of
Leibe & Hofmann in 1887 claimed to be successor of Eichelroth's factory.
Mark: 2761
In 1896 a
Geraer Porzellanfabrik B. Ouwens
(Gera Porcelain Factory B. Ouwens) advertised household porcelain with onion pattern, naming 1787 as its founding year.
Mark: 2133

Unterneubrunn
Thuringia, Germany

Berthold Eck Porzellanfabrik
(Berthold Eck Porcelain Factory), traceable 1876–1895, dolls.
Mark: 161

Unterweissbach
Thuringia, Germany

A. Porzelius, 1882-1890 founded a factory for decorative porcelain and figurines. Mark: 795
He joined with Mann to
Mann & Porzelius, 1890-circa 1908, until the company was converted into
Porzellanfabrik Unterweissbach vormals Mann & Porzelius
(Porcelain Factory Unterweissbach formerly Mann & Porzelius), circa 1908-1919. Then the factory was acquired by *Oldest Volkstedt Porcelain Factory* in *Volkstedt.* Later the name was changed to
Aelteste Volkstedter Porzellanfabrik Abt. Porzellan-Fabrik Unterweissbach
(Oldest Volkstedt Porcelain Factory Departm. Porcelain Factory Unterweissbach) 1919-1936. After the Oldest Volkstedt had gone bankrupt, C. Saar bought the company and called it

Porzellanfabrik Unterweissbach C. Saar
(Porcelain Factory Unterweissbach C. Saar), 1936-1940. Thereafter Heinz Schaubach bought and operated it as
Porzellanfabrik Schaubach-Kunst Wallendorf Zweigwerk Unterweissbach
(Porcelain Factory Schaubach-Art Wallendorf Branch Unterweissbach),1940-1953. Mark: 798. In 1953 the company was nationalized, first named
VEB Porzellanfabrik Unterweissbach
(VEB Porcelain Factory Unterweissbach), 1953-1962, Marks: 798, 809, 822, and later
VEB Unterweissbacher Werkstätten für Porzellankunst
(VEB Unterweissbach Workshops for Porcelain Art), 1962-1990. Mark 822.
From 1975 until 1990 the factory belonged to *VEB United Decorative Porcelainworks Lichte* in *Lichte*. Then it was privatized and taken over by *Königl. priv. Porzellanfabrik Tettau* in *Tettau*, which ist a daughter of *Porcelain Factories Seltmann* in *Weiden* as
Unterweissbacher Werkstätten für Porzellankunst GmbH
(Unterweissbach Workshops for Porcelain Art Ltd), 1990-present. Mark: 3614
The factory always produced decorative and artistic porcelain, figurines and luxury items.

Schwarzburger Werkstätten für Porzellankunst
(Schwarzburg Workshops for Porcelain Art), 1908—1938, artistic porcelain, figurines. The workshops belonged to *Porcelain Factory Unterweissbach*. They were founded by Max Adolf Pfeiffer, who left in 1913 and later became manager of *State's Porcelain Manufactory* in *Meissen*. After his departure the workshops lost their independence and became a department of the *Oldest Volkstedt Porcelain Factory* in *Volkstedt*.
Marks: 152, 153

Voigt & Höland
(Voigt & Holand), traceable 1884—1887.
Mark: 2671

Varel
Frisia, Germany

Porzellanfabrik Friesland
(Porcelain Factory Frisia), subsidiary of Melitta Works Bentz & Son in Minden, 1953—present, coffee, tea and table sets, gift articles, coffee cans, coffee and tea filters from porcelain, stoneware and earthenware.
Marks: 873, 1815

Velten
Brandenburg, Germany

Albert Schulze Nachfolger
(Albert Schulze Successor), existed about 1930, porcelain decorating shop.
Mark: 1941

Villingen
Badenia, Germany

Johann Glatz, traceable 1883-1924, maiolica and porcelain bowls. Mark: 387

Vohenstrauss
Bavaria, Germany

Porzellanfabrik Johann Seltmann GmbH (Porcelain Factory Johann Seltmann Ltd), 1901-1995, household and decorative porcelain, coffee and tea sets, gift articles. Marks: 271, 1238-1240, 1789, 1943
Merged with *Porcelain Factory J. Kronester* in *Schwarzenbach* and *Porcelain Factory Schirnding* in *Schirnding* to *SKV Porzellan Union* in *Schirnding*

Volkstedt, since 1923 part of Rudolstadt
Thuringia, Germany

Ackermann & Fritze , 1908-1951, decorative porcelain, figurines, gift articles, Marks: 954, 1038, 1418, 1419
in 1951 the factory was nationalized and named
VEB Kunst- und Zierporzellanwerk
(VEB Art and Decorative Porcelainwork), 1951-1990
Mark: 7

Aelteste Volkstedter Porzellanfabrik
(Oldest Volkstedt Porcelain Factory) There has been a certain confusion about this name because for some time no less than six factories carried the name Oldest Volkstedt Porcelain Factory and later even an Oldest Volkstedt Porcelain Manufactory appeared.
The oldest porcelain factory in Volkstedt was established by
Georg Heinrich Macheleid, who fifty years after Bottger in Meissen independently developed the mineral composition and the firing technique of hard paste porcelain, which had been kept a secret by the *Royal Porcelain Manufactory* in *Meissen.* In 1760 Prince Johann Friedrich at Schwarzenburg granted him a privilege for a porcelain factory in Sitzerode. Two years later Macheleid moved to Volkstedt, where 1762 porcelain production began. The factory was owned by a company in which the prince was one of the partners.
Mark: 1960
In 1767 Macheleid left and a new company agreement named the Prince at Schwarzenburg, his wife and the Arch-Prince as well as five other with the court connected persons as shareholders. The same year the factory was leased to
Christian Nonne from Erfurt, who operated it until 1800.
Marks: 481, 1586-1589, 1951, 1953-1956, 2345-2347, 2349, 2350, 2354-2361, 2371
In 1793 the princely treasury bought all outstanding shares and Prince Johann Friedrich´s successor Prince Ludwig Friedrich four years later sold the factory to his brother-in-law Prince Ernst Constantin of Hesse-Philippsthal, who in turn sold it to

Wilhelm Greiner and **Carl Holzapfel**, circa 1804-circa 1815.

Marks: 2433, 2886-2891

Holzapfel left in 1815 and Wilhelm Greiner´s son Anton continued with new partners as
Greiner, Stauch & Co., circa 1815-circa 1861. After that the name was
Macheleid, Triebner & Co, circa 1861-1877. Then the factory again changed proprietors and operated under the name
Triebner, Ens & Eckert, 1877-1894, when ist was liquidated.

Marks: 1944, 1945, 1957, 1958, 2631

Richard Eckert established his own *Volkstedt Porcelain Factory Richard Eckert & Co.*
Triebner and Ens founded a new factory

Aelteste Volkstedter Porzellanfabrik Triebner Ens & Co.

(Oldest Volkstedt Porcelain Factory Triebner Ens & Co.)

Marks: 573, 586, 2661

Shortly afterwards Ens left and founded his own *Porcelain Factory Karl Ens.*
The company name changed to

Aelteste Volkstedter Porzellanfabrik Triebner & Co.

(Oldest Volkstedt Porcelain Factory Triebner & Co.)

Marks: 1944, 1945

Between 1898 and 1902 the factory became a joint stock company

Aelteste Volkstedter Porzellanfabrik AG

(Oldest Volkstedt Porcelain Factory AG). About the same time it acquired *Porcelain Factory Unterweissbach* in *Unterweissbach*. In 1909 it founded *Schwarzburg Workshops for Porcelain Art* as a subsidiary of *Porcelain Factory Unterweissbach.*

After World War I the factory expanded rapidly and controlled:

Oldest Volkstedt Porcelain Factory Division *Porcelain Factory Richard Eckert & Co.* in *Volkstedt,*

Oldest Volkstedt Porcelain Factory Branch *Dressel, Kister & Co.* in *Passau,*

Oldest Volkstedt Porcelain Factory Division *Porcelain Factory Unterweissbach,*

Oldest Volkstedt Porcelain Factory Branch *Neuhaus on Rennweg,* formerly
Rudolf Heinz & Co.,

Earthenware Factory S. Bergmann Jr. in Neuhaus,

Fine Earthenware Factory Max Roesler in *Rodach* and

Schwarzburg Workshops for Porcelain Art in *Unterweissbach.*

Marks: 855, 952, 953, 968, 987, 988, 3610

The combine was dissolved in 1936 after financial difficulties. It was reorganized with assistance of the State of Thuringia under the name

Staatlich Thüringische Porzellan-Manufaktur vormals Aelteste Volkstedter GmbH
(State of Thuringia´s Porcelain Manufactory formerly Oldest Volkstedt Ltd), 1936-1949.
Then the name was changed to

VEB Aelteste Volkstedter Porzellanmanufaktur

(VEB Oldest Volkstedt Porcelain Manufactory), 1949-1990, which in 1972 became a branch of *VEB United Decorative Porcelainworks Lichte* in *Lichte.*

After the dissolution of the Porcelainworks Lichte the company was privatized and acquired by *Royally Privileged Porcelain Factory Tettau* in *Tettau,* operating under the old name **Aelteste Volkstedter Porzellanfabrik**. 1990-present.

During the first hundred years table, household and decorative porcelain, coffee and tea sets and figurines were produced. Later the factory specialized in decorative porcelain and figurines.

Beyer & Bock, 1853-1960, the company started as a porcelain decorating shop and after 1890 took up porcelain production.
Marks: 533, 722, 892, 1095
In 1960 it was nationalized and named
VEB Porzellanfabrik Rudolstadt-Volkstedt
(VEB Porcelain Factory Rudolstadt-Volkstedt), 1960-1990
Mark: 1095

Ens & Greiner see Lauscha

Rudolf Kämmer Keramische Manufaktur
(Rudolf Kammer Ceramic Manufactory), 1945-1972, decorative porcelain.
Until 1953 the manufactory produced earthenware and then began porcelain production.
Marks: 484, 1049
In 1972 the company was nationalized and named
VEB Zierporzellan Rudolstadt
(VEB Decorative Porcelain Rudolstadt) 1972-1990.

Müller & Co.
(Muller & Co.), 1907-1949, decorative porcelain, figurines.
About 1949 O. & J. Saar were proprietors.
Marks: 799, 800, 1010
They left the German Democratic Republic and tried unsuccessfully to re-establish the factory in *Seedorf.*

Porzellanfabrik Karls Ens
(Porcelain Factory Karl Ens), 1898-1972, decorative porcelain, figurines, gift articles.
Marks: 2386, 2616, 3140, 3141
The company was nationalized in 1972 and named
VEB Unterglasurporzellanfabrik
(VEB Underglazeporcelain Factory) 1972-1990.
See also *Oldest Volkstedt Porcelain Factory* in *Volkstedt.*

Porzellanmanufaktur Alfred Hanika
(Porcelain Manufactory Alfred Hanika), 1932—defunct about 1945, decorative porcelain, porcelain decorating shop.
Mark: 3163

Reinhold Richter & Co., 1906—1923, porcelain decorating shop.
Marks: 1014, 2649
Later the name was changed to
Volkstedter Porzellanmanufaktur Hans Richter

(Volkstedt Porcelain Manufactory Hans Richter), 1923–circa 1950.
Mark: 3069

Volkstedter Porzellanfabrik Richard Eckert & Co. AG

(Volkstedt Porcelain Factory Richard Eckert & Co. AG), 1894–1918, decorative porcelain, figurines, porcelain decorating. The company owned a decorating shop and a distributing branch in Dresden named *Dresden Art Publishers Richard Eckert*. Richard Eckert parted in 1894 with *Triebner, Ens & Eckert* (see Oldest Volkstedt Porcelain Factory) and founded his own factory, which in 1918 became a division of *Oldest Volkstedt Porcelain Factory*.
Marks: 294, 1640–1642, 1944–1950, 1952, 2569

C. K. Weithase, 1897–1955, porcelain decorator, in 1952
Hugo Goebel is mentioned as proprietor.
Marks: 1774, 3013

Vordamm
Brandenburg, Germany

A. Frank founded an earthenware factory, 1840–1900,
which later was changed into
Märkische Steingutfabrik
(Marchian Earthenware Factory), 1900–circa 1945, and produced stoneware, earthenware and porcelainwares.
Mark: 749

Waldenburg
Saxony, Germany

Paul Eydner, 1903–no mention found after 1964, fine stoneware.
Mark: 1521

Waldenburg
Silesia, Germany, presently Walbrzych, Poland

Carl Krister Porzellanfabrik
(Carl Krister Porcelain Factory), 1831–1926, table, household and decorative porcelain, porcelain decorating. Carl Franz Krister founded the manufactory in 1831 and bought two years later a small porcelain factory owned by Rausch. After Krister's death in 1869 his heirs Robert Hanschke and August Dimter kept the name Carl Krister for the company. Hanschke's heirs, who in 1925 converted the enterprise into a joint stock company
Krister Porzellanmanufaktur AG
(Krister Porcelain Manufactory AG), sold it to *Porcelain Factory Ph. Rosenthal & Co.* in *Selb* one year later. After Silesia came under Polish administration in 1945, the manufactory was re-established in Landstuhl in 1950.
Marks: 393, 626, 1050, 1130, 2454–2462, 2679

Waldershof
Bavaria, Germany

Johann Haviland, 1907-1924, household porcelain. In 1924 converted into
Porzellanfabrik Waldershof AG vormals Johann Haviland
(Porcelain Factory Waldershof formerly Johann Haviland), 1924-1936, household, table
and decorative porcelain, coffee and tea sets.
In 1936 the company was acquired by *Porcelain Factory Ph. Rosenthal & Co.* in *Selb* and
now carries the name **Rosenthal AG Hotel & Restaurant Service,** mainly hotel porcelain. Marks: 990, 1125, 1237, 2678, 3089, 3090, 3182, 3183

Porzellanmanufaktur "Bavaria" Franz Neukirchner GMBH
(Porcelain Manufactory "Bavaria" Franz Neukirchner GMBH), 1925—1977, house-
hold, hotel and decorative porcelain, gift articles, porcelain jewelry.
Marks: 817, 1146, 1204, 1437

Waldsassen
Bavaria, Germany

Chamotte- und Klinkerfabrik Waldsassen
(Firebrick and Clinker Factory Waldsassen), 1882—defunct, household porcelain
after 1923.
Mark: 2031

Gareis, Kühnl & Cie.
(Gareis, Kuhnl & Cie.), 1898—1969, household porcelain, coffee and tea sets, cups.
Marks: 439, 1327, 1518
The company was merged with *Porcelain Factory Waldsassen Bareuther & Co.*
in 1969.

Johann Mathäus Ries, 1866-1884, household and table porcelain. His son sold to Max
Jena, Erst Ploss and Oskar Bareuther, who named the company
Jena, Bareuther & Co. Jena left in 1887 and Richard Schmerler became new partner.
In 1904 the factory was converted into a joint stock company and later named
Porzellanfabrik Waldsassen Bareuther & Co. AG, 1904-closed 1993.
Table and hotel porcelain, coffee & tea sets, decorative porcelain, gift and collectors´
articles.
Marks: 11, 83, 410, 411, 505, 823, 825, 922, 1199, 1200, 1744, 1890, 1895, 2812.

Wallendorf
Thuringia, Germany

Johann Wolfgang Hammann, his son Ferdinand Friedrich, his brother and **Gottfried
and Gotthelf Greiner** founded a manufactory in 1763, which started porcelain making in
1764 after Hammann had received a privilege for porcelain production by the reigning
Duke.
Marks: 1636, 1637, 2320-2325, 2421, 2957-2961, 2975
After Gottfried Greiner died in 1768 and Gotthelf Greiner returned to *Limbach* in 1772
the Hammann family operated the manufactory.
Marks: 2962-2974, 2976, 3093. In 1929 it was leased to

Friedrich Christian Hutschenreuther and **Hermann Kieser**
and in 1833 sold it to
Hutschenreuther, Kämpfe and Heubach
(Hutschenreuther, Kampfe and Heubach). In 1887 the name of the factory was
Heubach, Kämpfe and Sontag (Heubach, Kampfe and Sontag)
Mark: 2955
and about 1897 it became
Kämpfe & Heubach AG
Mark: 2954
From 1915-1919 porcelain production was discontinued. Then *Porcelain Factory Fraureuth*
in *Fraureuth* acquired the premises for its
Art division, 1919-1926. After the company went bankrupt, Heinz Schaubach bought the
factory and founded
Porzellanfabrik Schaubach-Kunst
(Porcelain Factory Schaubach-Art), 1926-1953, see also *Unterweissbach*.
Marks: 792, 1086. The company was nationalized in 1953 and first named
VEB "Schaubach-Kunst" Lichte Wallendorf
(VEB Schaubach-Art Lichte Wallendorf), 1953-1960
Mark: 793, and in 1960
VEB Wallendorfer Porzellanfabrik
(VEB Wallendorf Porcelain Factory), 1960-1990. In 1976 it became a branch of *VEB
United Porceleinworks Lichte* in *Lichte*. After the dissolution of the United Porcelainworks
Lichte in 1990 the factory was privatized and named
Wallendorfer Porzellanmanufaktur GmbH,
(Wallendorf Porcelain Manufactory Ltd), 1990-present, still using
mark No. 1087. *Porcelain Factory Piesau* in *Piesau* first became part of the new com-
pany but was closed after a few month.
Table, household and decorative porcelain, coffee and tea sets, gift articles, figurines,
dolls.

Wallerfangen
Saarland, Germany

Nicolas Villeroy, 1789–1836, operated a fayence factory and produced mainly
household sets from fine earthenware. After a merger with *Boch* in *Mettlach* the
factory became a branch of
Villeroy & Boch, 1836–1931, who also made decorative earthenware and figurines.
Marks: 2858, 2953, 3272, 3273, 3276

Waltershausen
Thuringia, Germany

A. Schmidt, 1863–last mention found 1911, animal figurines.
Mark: 2537

Warnsdorf
Bohemia, presently Varnsdorf, Czechia

H. Gustav Richter, 1882–last mention found in 1906, porcelain flowers,

knick-knack.
Mark: 2789

Weiden
Bavaria, Germany

Porzellanfabrik Christian Seltmann (Porcelain Factory Christian Seltmann), 1910-present. Household, table and hotel porcelain, coffee and tea sets, gift articles, decorative porcelain.
Marks: 848, 866, 1222, 1247, 1260-1262,
To the company belong *Royally Privileged Porcelain Factory Tettau* in *Tettau* with four daughters in Thuringia and branches in *Erbendorf* and *Krummennaab.*

Porzellanfabrik Weiden Gebrüder Bauscher
(Porcelain Factory Weiden Bros. Bauscher), 1881–present, hotel and technical porcelain.
Marks: 5, 215, 2040–2045, 2055, 2123, 2159–2161, 2494, 3111, 3112
In 1927 acquired by *Porcelain Factory L. Hutschenreuther* in *Selb.*

Weimar
Saxony, Germany

L. Wuensche, 1920–last mention found in 1949, porcelain decorator, especially portraits.
Mark: 3288

Weingarten
Badenia, Germany

Adolf Baumgarten, 1882–circa 1900, household and decorative porcelain, porcelain decorating.
Mark: 2120
About 1900 the company name was changed to
Porzellanfabrik Weingarten R. Wolfinger
(Porcelain Factory Weingarten R. Wolfinger), circa 1900–1922.
Marks: 2237, 2878

Weissenstadt
Bavaria, Germany

Porzellanfabrik Weissenstadt Dürrbeck & Ruckdäschel
(Porcelain Factory Weissenstadt Durrbeck & Ruckdaschel), 1920–1964, household porcelain, gift articles.
Marks: 927, 1263

Weisswasser
Prusia, Germany

Oberlausitzer Porzellanmanufaktur August Schweig

(Upper Lusatian Porcelain Manufactory August Schweig), 1895–circa 1919, household and table porcelain, coffee and tea sets, gift articles. The company name was changed to

Porzellanfabrik August Schweig GMBH

(Porcelain Factory August Schweig GMBH), circa 1919–circa 1940, when the factory was sold and became

Porzellanfabrik Weisswasser, Zweigbetrieb der Gebr. Hannemann & Cie.

(Porcelain Factory Weisswasser, Branch of Bros. Hannemann & Cie.), in Duren, circa 1940–1945, producing mainly electrotechnical porcelain.

Marks: 551, 565, 1175, 1259

After World War II the company was nationalized and named

VEB Porzellanwerk Weisswasser

(VEB Porcelainwork Weisswasser)

Marks: 547, 1776

Wien - Vienna

Austria

Philip Aigner, existed about 1900, household porcelain and earthenware, coffee and tea sets.

Marks: 611, 1404

Alois Baratta Dragono und Dr. Norbert Baratta Porzellanfabrik

(Alois Baratta Dragono and Dr. Norbert Baratta Porcelain Factory), traceable 1890–1930, pottery. The factory was located in Poltar, Hungary.

Marks: 408, 409

Franz Dörfl

(Franz Dorfl), 1880–1923, porcelain decorating shop.

Marks: 1420, 1443, 1516, 1517

Later the company name was

Kunstanstalt für Porzellanmalerei Franz Dörfl

(Art Institute for Porcelain Decorating Franz Dorfl), 1923–   , the shop was still in existence in 1940 under the name

Franz Dörfl's Witwe

(Franz Dorfl's Widow).

B. Grossbaum & Söhne

(B. Grossbaum & Sons), 1889–defunct, porcelain decorating shop, old Vienna style. Branch in *Dresden*.

Marks: 397, 2389

Josef Kawan, 1907–present, porcelain decorating shop.

Mark: 1438

"Keramos" Wiener Kunst-Keramik und Porzellanmanufaktur Wolf & Co.

("Keramos" Vienna Art Ceramic and Porcelain Manufactory Wolf & Co.), 1920– present, decorative earthenware and porcelain, figurines.

Marks: 1475, 2243, 2308

K. K. Aerarial Porzellan-Manufaktur Wien
(Imperial and Royal Porcelain Manufactory Vienna), 1718–1864, decorative and table porcelain, figurines. With the help of two workers from the Meissen manufactory **Claudius Innocentius Du Paquier**, 1718–1744, succeeded in producing porcelain and established a manufactory. After he encountered financial difficulties he sold the manufactory to the court.
Marks: 2470, 2484, 2993
During the following years the manufactory was expanded and in 1761 became profitable for the first time after it had improved its products. After sales decreased Emperor Joseph II decided to auction off the manufactory but no bidder appeared. In 1785 Baron Sorgenthal was appointed general manager and he led the manufactory to its artistically and financially most successful period. After his death in 1805 and as a result of the Napoleonic Wars the manufactory slowly declined and was closed in 1864.
Marks: 1362–1403

Öspag Österreichische Sanitärkeramik und Porzellan-Industrie AG
(Ospag Austrian Sanitary Ceramic and Porcelain Industry AG), see Wilhelmsburg, Wilhelmsburg Earthenware and Porcelain Factory.

Plastographische Gesellschaft Pietzner & Co.
(Plastographic Company Pietzner & Co.), before 1899–defunct, decorative porcelain, collectors and religious articles, knick-knack. The company name was changed to
"Plasto" Wien-Berliner Kunstgewerbe GMBH
("Plasto" Vienna-Berlin Arts and Crafts GMBH) in 1903.
At this time Dr. Srpek was proprietor.
Marks: 442, 3224

Rädler & Pilz Artistisches Atelier Für Porzellanmalerei
(Radler & Pilz Artistic Studio for Porcelain Decorating), circa 1864–defunct, porcelain decorating shop.
Mark: 1424

Slama & Co., 1868–present, porcelain decorating and distributing company. The company was founded in Znaim, Moravia (presently Znojmo, Czechoslovakia), and after World War II re-established in Vienna in 1948.
Marks: 340, 1899, 2653

Robert Franz Staral Alt-Wiener Porzellanmalerei
(Robert Franz Staral Old Vienna Porcelain Decorating Shop), 1886–before 1979, porcelain decorating shop.
Mark: 1411

Emanuel Steinberger Porzellanmanufaktur
(Emanuel Steinberger Porcelain Manufactory), 1950–before 1979, porcelain decorating shop.
Mark: 151

Josef Vater, 1894–defunct, porcelain decorating shop.
Mark: 1429

Wiener Keramik (Vienna Ceramic), 1905–1912, and **Gmundner Keramik** (Gmunden Ceramic), 1909–1922, in 1912 united to **Vereinigte Wiener und Gmundner Keramik**

(United Vienna and Gmund Ceramic), which changed its name again to **Gmundner Keramik** (Gmunden Ceramic) in 1919, artistical and decorative earthenware and porcelain, figurines.
Mark: 2680

Wiener Kunstkeramikfabrik Förster & Co.
(Vienna Art Ceramic Factory Forster & Co.), 1899–1908, later
Wiener Kunstkeramische Werkstätte
(Vienna Art Ceramic Workshop), 1908–1940, artistic and decorative earthenware and porcelain, figurines.
Marks: 342, 343, 1893

Wiener Manufaktur Friedrich Goldscheider
(Vienna Manufactory Friedrich Goldscheider), 1885–present, decorative earthenware and porcelain, fayence, terra cotta, porcelain decorating, figurines.
Founded as
Goldscheider's Porzellan- und Majolikafabrik
(Goldscheider's Porcelain and Maiolica Factory) the company owned a factory in Pilsen and decorating shops in Vienna and Karlsbad. In 1899 it established a branch in Leipzig and in 1907 the company name was changed into
Erste Wiener Terrakottafabrik und Atelier für Künstlerische Fayencen Friedrich Goldscheider
(First Vienna Terra Cotta Factory and Studio for Artistic Fayences Friedrich Goldscheider). In 1921 the name
Wiener Manufaktur Friedrich Goldscheider
(Vienna Manufactory Friedrich Goldscheider) was adopted.
After Austria was incorporated into the German Reich the company name was changed into
Wiener Manufaktur Josef Schuster vormals Friedrich Goldscheider
(Vienna Manufactory Josef Schuster formerly Friedrich Goldscheider) in 1941. In 1950 the former name was restored.
Marks: 1812, 1853, 2592, 3025, 3031

Wiener Porzellanfabrik Augarten AG
(Vienna Porcelain Factory Augarten AG), 1922–present, decorative porcelain and figurines.
Marks: 605, 675–678, 1406–1410, 1412, 2209
The company considers itself successor to the *Imperial and Royal Porcelain Manufactory Vienna,* which was closed in 1864.

Wiener Porzellan Manufaktur Josef Böck
(Vienna Porcelain Manufactory Josef Bock), 1879–1960, household, table and decorative porcelain, porcelain decorating shop. The shop was founded by **Kutterwatz** in 1828 and in 1879 acquired by the Bock family. They also had made porcelain after their own designs by factories in Bohemia and Germany and decorated it in Vienna. The company stayed in the possession of the Bock family until it was sold to Haas & Czjzek in 1960.
Marks: 612, 1804, 2188, 2248, 2611, 3287

Wiener Werkstätten GMBH
(Vienna Workshops GMBH), circa 1913—defunct, porcelain and earthenware.
Mark: 2269

Wiener-Neustadt - Vienna-Neustadt
Austria

Josef de Cente, 1793—20th century, tile and stove factory, reproductions of decorative porcelain and figurines of the 1864 defunct *Imperial and Royal Porcelain Manufactory Vienna.* De Cente had bought the original moulds and used them for some years. His reproductions were always marked with "de Cente", mostly impressed. In 1902 *Alexandra-Porcelain Works* in Turn-Teplitz bought the moulds.

Wiesau
Bavaria, Germany

Porzellanmanufaktur Josef Kuba
(Porcelain Manufactory Josef Kuba), 1947—present, household, table and decorative porcelain, gift articles.
Marks: 812, 844
The company was founded in *Karlsbad* in 1900 and after World War II re-established in Wiesau.

Gebr. Mayer
(Bros. Mayer), 1947—present, porcelain decorating shop.
The company was founded in Fischern in 1840 and after World War II re-established in Wiesau.
Mark: 875

Richard Wolfram Porzellanfabrik
(Richard Wolfram Porcelain Factory), 1898—defunct about 1970, household porcelain.
Mark: 3072

Wilhelmsburg
Austria

Wilhelmsburger Steingut- und Porzellanfabrik
(Wilhelmsburg Earthenware and Porcelain Factory), household, table, decorative and sanitary earthenware, since 1934 porcelain. Leinwather and Rainke founded in 1795 an earthenware manufactory, which changed proprietors frequently in the 19th century.
1814—1826 Josef & Elisabeth Dojak,
1826—1837 Juliana Hauschka,
1837—1843 Franz Hauschka,
1843—1851 Vinzenz Plank,
1851—1865 Ignaz Wahlmuller,
1865—1883 Rudolf Stohmayer,

1883 Bros. Lichtenstern.

Under the brothers Lichtenstern the factory developed rapidly as

K. u. K. Privilegierte Wilhelmsburger Steingutfabrik

(Imperially and Royally Privileged Wilhelmsburg Earthenware Factory). In 1910 the Earthenware Factory *Rudolf Ditmar's Heirs* in *Znaim* was acquired and in 1912 the factory of *Brothers Urbach* in *Turn-Teplitz*. One year later the company was sold to *Triptis AG* in *Triptis*. After World War I the Triptis combine was dissolved in 1919. The former owners bought back the Wilhelmsburg plant and named it

Wilhelmsburger Steingutfabrik Richard Lichtenstern & Co.

(Wilhelmsburg Earthenware Factory Richard Lichtenstern & Co.). The factories in Znaim and in Turn-Teplitz were combined to *Ditmar-Urbach AG* owned by Lichtenstern. In 1932 the Wilhelmsburg factory became a joint stock company and after porcelain production began in 1934 the name was changed to

Wilhelmsburger Steingut- und Porzellanfabrik AG

(Wilhelmsburg Earthenware and Porcelain Factory AG). After Austria was incorporated into the German Reich in 1938, the company was expropriated because it was Jewish property and combined with Earthenware Industry AG Gmunden-Engelhof to

Ostmark-Keramik AG

(Ostmark Ceramic AG). In 1945 it was returned to the former owners or their heirs and in 1946 the name was changed to

Österreichische Keramik AG

(Austrian Ceramic AG). In 1960 finally the present name

Öspag Österreichische-Sanitärkeramik- und Porzellanindustrie AG

(Ospag Austrian Sanitary Ceramic and Porcelain Industry AG) with headquarters in Vienna was adopted.

Marks: Dojak and Hauschka: 2989
        Bros. Lichtenstern: 767
        Richard Lichtenstern & Co.: 314, 1763, 2191
        Ostmark Ceramic: 1763
        Austrian Ceramic: 273
        Ospag: 415

Windischeschenbach

Bavaria, Germany

Eduard Haberländer Porzellanfabrik

(Eduard Haberlander Porcelain Factory), 1913–1928, household porcelain.
Marks: 1037, 2229, 2573
The factory was sold to *Oscar Schaller & Co. Successor,* 1928–present, household and decorative porcelain, gift and collectors articles, coffee and tea sets.
Marks: 789, 821, 1184, 1185, 1271, 1272, 3122
See also *Winterling Porcelain Factories Distributing Company* in *Windischeschenbach.*

Winterling Porzellanfabriken Vertriebsgesellschaft

(Winterling Porcelain Factories Distributing Company), distributing organization for the factories of the Winterling group, which was established after World War I.

Members of the Winterling group are:
Oscar Schaller & Co. Successor in *Kirchenlamitz,*
Schwarzenbach and *Windischeschenbach,*
Heinrich Winterling in *Marktleuthen,*
Bros. Winterling in *Roslau,*
Winterling Fine Ceramic in *Bruchmuhlbach.*
Marks: 867, 1223, 1224

Wistritz
Bohemia, presently Bystrice, Czechia

Krautzberger, Mayer & Purkert GMBH, 1911–1945, household and decorative porcelain.
Marks: 446, 1051, 1052, 1189, 1978

Worms
Palatinate, Germany

Wormser Terra Sigillata-Manufaktur
(Worms Terra Sigillata Manufactory), 1948–1951, the City of Worms was proprietor, afterwards
1951–1977, Willi Jizba, then
1977–present R. Gurlitt.
Vases, pitchers, coffee and tea sets from fine stoneware.
Mark: 310

Wurzburg - Würzburg
Bavaria, Germany

Johann Caspar Geyger, 1775–1780, table and decorative porcelain, figurines.
Marks: 1508, 2156, 2729, 2730, 2985–2987

Wunsiedel
Bavaria, Germany

Retsch & Co. Porzellanfabrik (Retsch & Co. Porcelain Factory), now **Porzellanfabrik Retsch GmbH & Co. KG** (Porcelain Factory Retsch Ltd & Co.), 1884-present. Household and decorative porcelain, coffee and tea sets.
Marks: 430, 435, 732, 1468, 3607

Xanten
Rhineland, Germany

T. Hehl, existed about 1930, porcelain decorator.
Mark: 2662

Zell on Harmersbach - Zell am Harmersbach
Badenia, Germany

Georg Schmider Vereinigte Zeller Keramische Fabriken
(Georg Schmider United Zell Ceramic Factories).
Josef Anton Burger, 1794–1802, founded an earthenware factory in 1794 and was so successful that he had to look for partners to finance an expansion of the factory. In 1802 Jakob Ferdinand Lenz, Georg Schnitzler and David Knoderer joined the company, which in 1807 was privileged by Grandduke Karl Friedrich as
Steingutfabrik von Schnitzler, Lenz & Burger
(Earthenware Factory of Schnitzler, Lenz & Burger).
Two years later Schnitzler and Knoderer left and the company name was changed to
Grossherzoglich Badische Steingutfabrik von J. F. Lenz und Burger
(Grand Ducal Badenian Privileged Earthenware Factory of J. F. Lenz and Burger), 1808–1819.
Marks: 2266, 3181
In 1819 Burger sold his share to Lenz, and his name was dropped from the company name, which was now
Jakob Ferdinand Lenz, 1819–1869.
After Lenz's death in 1828 his widow Katharina Salome Lenz continued with the help of her two nephews Gottfried Ferdinand Lenz and Wilhelm Schnitzler, who inherited the factory after she died in 1829. They kept the company name J. F. Lenz. In 1842 the company began porcelain production, which continued until 1942, when during World War II the lack of coal forced the factory to give up porcelain. Schnitzler in 1860 sold his share to Lenz, who became sole proprietor.
Marks: 508, 1780, 3026, 3180, 3289
In 1869 he sold the factory to chief-inspector Bruno Proessel, a son of Privy Councillor Proessel of the *Royal Porcelain-Manufactory* in *Berlin.* Proessels attempt to introduce more artistically designed products failed and the company was auctioned off in 1874 to Karl Schaaff, who called it
Karl Schaaff formerly J. F. Lenz, 1874–1907.
Marks: 687, 747
Georg Schmider, who already owned an earthenware factory in Zell, bought Schaaff's company in 1907.
Schmiders predecessor
B. Schaible & Cie. was founded in 1859. In 1873 it became
Haager, Hoerth & Comp.
Marks: 230, 235
Georg Schmider joined the company in 1890 and eight years later he was sole proprietor, uniting his factory with Schaaffs company to
Georg Schmider Vereinigte Zeller Keramische Fabriken
(Georg Schmider United Zell Ceramic Factories), 1907–present. The company is still property of the Schmider family.
Marks: 231, 232, 548, 549, 560, 736, 926, 1811, 2014, 2591, 3030
During the first years the factory produced light colored earthenware and oven-proof cooking utensils, later household and table earthenware. After 1842 household, table and hotel porcelain, coffee and tea sets and mocha cups were produced besides earthenware. Today main products are table and decorative earthenware.

Zeven
Lower Saxony, Germany

C. & E. Carstens, 1922–1930, porcelain decorating shop.
Marks: 1805, 2684

Zweibrücken see Gutenbrunn

Znaim
Moravia, presently Znojmo, Czechia

Rudolf Ditmar und Rudolf Ditmar's Erben
(Rudolf Ditmar and Rudolf Ditmar's Heirs), 1879–1919, household, decorative and sanitary earthenware.
Marks: 312, 313
In 1919 the company became a branch of *Wilhelmsburg Earthenware Factory* in *Wilhelmsburg* and was merged with *Brothers Urbach* in *Turn-Teplitz* to
Ditmar-Urbach AG.
Marks: 274, 316
In 1945 the factory was nationalized.

Slama & Co., 1868–1945, porcelain decorating shop. The company was re-established in *Vienna* in 1948.

Zwickau
Saxony, Germany

Christian Fischer, 1845–defunct, household, table and decorative porcelain.
Marks: 276, 1737, 2727, 2945
Fischer was one of the owners of the manufactory in *Pirkenhammer*.

Karl Steubler, 1886–no mention found after 1953, porcelain decorating shop.
Mark: 280

Zwickauer Porzellanfabrik
(Zwickau Porcelain Factory), 1927–1933, household porcelain, coffee and tea sets. The factory was a branch of *Porcelain Factory Kahla* in *Kahla*.
Mark: 276

Zwickauer Porzellanfabrik
(Zwickau Porcelain Factory) see Schedewitz

Zwickau-Oberhohndorf see Oberhohndorf

TEIL III

PART III

Marken, die mit denen anderer Hersteller verwechselt werden können

Schon zehn Jahre nach seiner Entdeckung im Jahre 1708 entkam das Geheimnis der Porzellanherstellung aus Meißen und verbreitete sich schnell über Europa. 1723 hielt man es in Meißen für notwendig, Bodenmarken einzuführen, durch die das Meißner Porzellan von den Erzeugnissen anderer Manufakturen unterschieden werden konnte. Die meisten anderen Manufakturen folgten dem Meißner Beispiel und kennzeichneten ihre Produkte mit eigenen Marken.

Aber schon nach wenigen Jahren wurden diese Marken nachgeahmt, kopiert oder gefälscht. Einige Porzellanhersteller und -maler entwarfen ihre Marken in Anlehnung an die berühmter Manufakturen. Einige kopierten sie einfach, andere nahmen Symbole oder Motive dieser Marken in ihre eigenen auf oder veränderten die Originalmarke mehr oder weniger.

Die Zahl der verwechselbaren Marken ist inzwischen so groß geworden, daß es angebracht erscheint, sie in einem besonderen Teil zusammenzufassen, besonders auch, weil eine Anzahl von Herstellern außerhalb Deutschlands, Böhmens und Österreichs erwähnt werden muß.

Die Marken in diesem Teil sind nur zum Vergleich angeführt. Mit ihrer Erwähnung soll nichts über die Absichten der Benutzer dieser Marken ausgesagt werden. Sie sind hier aufgenommen, weil die Möglichkeit besteht, daß ein Laie sie mit ähnlich aussehenden Marken verwechseln kann.

Berlin

Die Szeptermarke der Königlichen Porzellan Manufaktur in Berlin (Nr. 1296, Variationen siehe Gruppe 16, Nr. 1282–1313) ist nicht sehr oft imitiert worden.

No. 1296

Marks that could be mistaken for those of other manufacturers

Only ten years after its discovery in 1708 the secret of porcelain making slipped out of Meissen and rapidly spread over all of Europe. In 1723 the Royal Manufactory in Meissen found it necessary to introduce bottom marks to distinguish its products from those of other manufactories. Most of these manufactories followed the Meissen example and began marking their own products with different marks.

But within a few years these marks already were imitated, copied or forged. Some manufacturers and decorators designed their own marks similar to those of famous manufactories. Some plainly copied them, others included typical symbols or motifs of the original marks or changed them more or less.

Since the number of marks which could be misleading has reached quite some proportions it appears to be useful to list them concisely in a separate part, especially because many manufacturers outside Germany, Bohemia and Austria have to be mentioned.

Any entry in this part is for comparison only. It does not pass judgment on the intentions of the users of these marks. It just points out the possibility that a layman could confound similar looking marks.

Berlin

The scepter mark of the Royal Porcelain Manufactory in Berlin (No. 1296, for variations see group 16, Nos. 1282–1313) has not been imitated very often.

No. 1296,

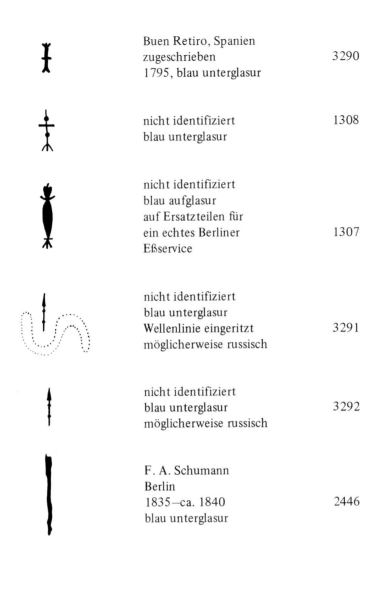

Buen Retiro, Spanien
zugeschrieben   3290
1795, blau unterglasur

nicht identifiziert   1308
blau unterglasur

nicht identifiziert
blau aufglasur
auf Ersatzteilen für
ein echtes Berliner   1307
Eßservice

nicht identifiziert
blau unterglasur
Wellenlinie eingeritzt   3291
möglicherweise russisch

nicht identifiziert
blau unterglasur   3292
möglicherweise russisch

F. A. Schumann
Berlin
1835—ca. 1840   2446
blau unterglasur

Der Name ''Berlin'' erscheint in den
Marken zweier amerikanischer Firmen

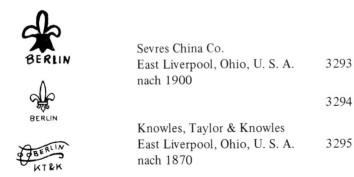

Sevres China Co.
East Liverpool, Ohio, U. S. A.   3293
nach 1900

                                 3294

Knowles, Taylor & Knowles
East Liverpool, Ohio, U. S. A.   3295
nach 1870

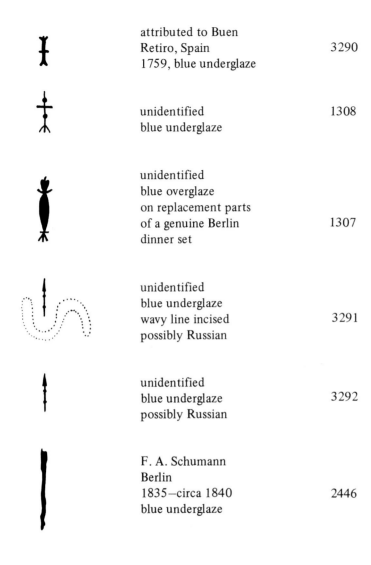

attributed to Buen
Retiro, Spain
1759, blue underglaze

3290

unidentified
blue underglaze

1308

unidentified
blue overglaze
on replacement parts
of a genuine Berlin
dinner set

1307

unidentified
blue underglaze
wavy line incised
possibly Russian

3291

unidentified
blue underglaze
possibly Russian

3292

F. A. Schumann
Berlin
1835—circa 1840
blue underglaze

2446

The name "Berlin" appears in
marks of two American companies

Sevres China Co.
East Liverpool, Ohio, U. S. A.
after 1900

3293

3294

Knowles, Taylor & Knowles
East Liverpool, Ohio, U. S. A.
after 1870

3295

KPM KPF MPM

Über die Buchstaben KPM herrscht große Verwirrung. Sie waren ursprünglich die Abkürzung für Königliche Porzellan Manufaktur und wurden zuerst von 1723 bis etwa 1727 in Meißen benutzt. Sie erscheinen blau unter der Glasur.

Die Buchstaben stehen entweder alleine (Nr. 2836, Variationen siehe Gruppe 36, Nr. 2831–2839) oder in Verbindung mit den gekreuzten Schwertern (Nr. 1694, Variationen siehe Gruppe 19, Nr. 1691–1700).

Nr. 2836   Nr. 1694

Die Meißner Manufaktur, die niemals ein systematisches und verständliches Markensystem benutzte, machte es nicht leichter, das Alter ihres Porzellans zu bestimmen, als sie 1875 die Marke 1696 wieder einführte. Seitdem und bis heute wird sie auf besonderen Erzeugnissen angebracht, von der Manufaktur beschrieben als Dessertschalen, Likörservice, Wandteller und ähnliches.

Nr. 1696

In ihrer frühen Periode benutzte die Meißner Manufaktur auch die Buchstabenverbindung KPF (Nr. 2828) für Königliche Porcelain Fabrique oder MPM (Nr. 2847) für Meißner Porcelain Manufactur. Diese Marken waren in Gebrauch um 1722/1723 und sind selten.

Nr. 2828

Nr. 2847

KPM   KPF   MPM

There is widespread confusion about the letters KPM. They originally stood for Königliche Porzellan Manufaktur (Royal Porcelain Manufactory) and were first used in Meissen from 1723 until about 1727. They were applied in blue underglaze.

The letters appear either by themselves (No. 2836, for variations see group 36, Nos. 2831–2839) or in combination with the crossed swords (No. 1694, for variations see group 19, Nos. 1691–1700).

No. 2836

No. 1694

The manufactory in Meissen, which never used a systematic and intelligible marking system, didn't make it easier to date its products by introducing mark 1696 again in 1875. Since then up to the present it is applied on special products, defined by the manufactory as dessert bowls, liqueur sets, collectors plates and similar pieces.

No. 1696

During the early period the manufactory in Meissen also used the letter combinations KPF (No. 2828) for Königliche Porcelain Fabrique (Royal Porcelain Factory) or MPM (No. 2847) for Meissner Porcelain Manufactur (Meissen Porcelain Manufactory). These marks were used about 1722/1723 and are rare.

No. 2828

No. 2847

Seit 1825 benutzte die Königliche Manufaktur in Berlin die gleichen Buchstaben, aber immer in Verbindung mit

einem Szepter

KPM

Nr. 1311

einem Adler

K P M

Nr. 206

oder dem Reichsapfel

KPM

Nr. 1316

Da die Buchstabenkombinationen KPM, KPF oder MPM nicht geschützt waren, konnten andere Hersteller sie in vielen Variationen benutzen. Einige setzten einen senkrechten Strich an die Stelle des Szepters, andere änderten einen Buchstaben, benutzten aber einen Strich, einen Adler oder den Reichsapfel.

K.P.M.	KPM	Krister Porzellanmanufaktur Waldenburg	2455 2456
KPM	CHINA. KPM	Krister Porzellanmanufaktur Waldenburg	2457 2461
·KPM·	K.P.M.	Kranichfelder Porzellanmanufaktur Kranichfeld	321 322

516

Beginning in 1825 the Royal Porcelain Manufactory in Berlin began using the letters KPM but always in combination with

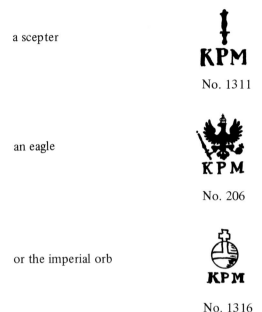

a scepter

KPM

No. 1311

an eagle

K.P.M

No. 206

or the imperial orb

KPM

No. 1316

Since the letter combinations KPM, KPF or MPM were not legally protected, other manufacturers were free to use them in many variations. Some substituted a vertical line for the scepter, others changed one letter but used line, eagle or orb.

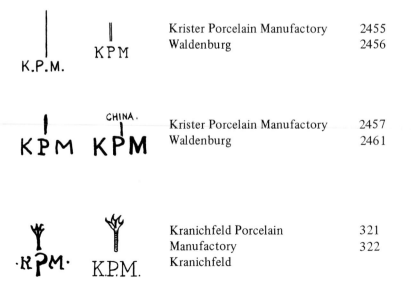

K.P.M. / KPM	Krister Porcelain Manufactory Waldenburg	2455 2456
KPM / KPM	Krister Porcelain Manufactory Waldenburg	2457 2461
RPM· / K.P.M.	Kranichfeld Porcelain Manufactory Kranichfeld	321 322

517

K.P.M. ⨯	A. W. Fr. Kister Porcelain Manufactory Scheibe-Alsbach	A. W. Fr. Kister Porzellan- manufaktur Scheibe-Alsbach	23
KPM	Krister Porcelain Manufactory Waldenburg	Krister Porzellanmanufaktur Waldenburg	24
KPM **W**	Krister Porcelain Manufactory Waldenburg	Krister Porzellanmanufaktur Waldenburg	24
K **WPM**	Krister Porcelain Manufactory Waldenburg	Krister Porzellanmanufaktur Waldenburg	24
K. P. F. ⨯	A. W. Fr. Kister Porcelain Manufactory Scheibe-Alsbach	A. W. Fr. Kister Porzellan- manufaktur Scheibe-Alsbach	23
KPF Ⓚ︀Ⓥ︀Ⓕ︀	Krister Porcelain Manufactory Waldenburg	Krister Porzellanmanufaktur Waldenburg	24 26
CPM	Porcelain and Ceramic Factory Cmielow Cmielow, Poland after 1842	Porzellan- und Keramikfabrik Cmielow Cmielow, Polen nach 1842	32
FPM FPM	Schmidt & Otremba Freiwaldau	Schmidt & Otremba Freiwaldau	18 24
SPM	Buckau Porcelain Manufactory Magdeburg-Buckau	Buckauer Porzellanmanufaktur Magdeburg-Buckau	24
StPM	F. A. Schumann Berlin	F. A. Schumann Berlin	24
BPM	Striegau Porcelain Factory Stanowitz	Striegauer Porzellanfabrik Stanowitz	2?

	Reichenstein Porcelain Manufactory Reichenstein	Reichensteiner Porzellan-manufaktur Reichenstein	252
	unidentified on porcelain of the Royal Porcelain Manufactory Berlin in addition to scepter mark, blue overglaze	nicht identifiziert auf Porzellan der Königlichen Porzellan Manufaktur Berlin zusätzlich zur Szeptermarke, blau aufglasur	192
	F. A. Schumann Berlin	F. A. Schumann Berlin	212 258
	Striegau Porcelain Factory Stanowitz	Striegauer Porzellanfabrik Stanowitz	213
	Carl Hans Tuppack Tiefenfurth	Carl Hans Tuppack Tiefenfurth	193 1361
	Hans Richter Berlin	Hans Richter Berlin	658
	Rhenish Porcelain Manufactory Oberkassel	Rheinische Porzellanmanufaktur Oberkassel	104
	Rhenisch Porcelain Manufactory Mannheim	Rheinische Porzellanmanufaktur Mannheim	609
	Krister Porcelain Manufactory Waldenburg	Krister Porzellanmanufaktur Waldenburg	1130 1050

Krister Porcelain Manufactory
Landstuhl

Krister Porzellanmanufaktur
Landstuhl

11:
11:

Krister Porcelain Manufactory
Landstuhl

Krister Porzellanmanufaktur
Landstuhl

116

Kerafina
Marktredwitz

Kerafina
Marktredwitz

11:
11:

Kerafina
Marktredwitz

Kerafina
Marktredwitz

11:
11:

Kerafina
Marktredwitz

Kerafina
Marktredwitz

9

Krautzberger, Mayer &
Purkert
Wistritz

Krautzberger, Mayer &
Purkert
Wistritz

10.
10.
19

VEB Porcelain Manufactory
and Porcelain Manufactory
Plaue

VEB Porzellanmanufaktur
und Porzellanmanufaktur
Plaue

10

unidentified

nicht identifiziert

10:

	Berlin Porcelain Manufactory Teltow	Berliner Porzellanmanufaktur Teltow	925
	Buckau Porcelain Manufactory Magdeburg-Buckau	Buckauer Porzellanmanufaktur Magdeburg-Buckau	1777
	Hilpoltstein Porcelain Manufactory Hilpoltstein	Hilpoltsteiner Porzellan- manufaktur Hilpoltstein	2231
	Ilmenau Porcelain Factory Ilmenau	Ilmenauer Porzellanfabrik Ilmenau	297 298
	Porcelain and Brick Factory Mosa Maastricht, Netherlands circa 1900	Porselain- en Muurtegel- fabrick Mosa Maastricht, Holland ca. 1900	3297
	C. Muller Steinwiesen	C. Müller Steinwiesen	2295
	Porcelain Manufactory Burgau Burgau	Porzellanmanufaktur Burgau Burgau	333
	Robert Persch Mildeneichen	Robert Persch Mildeneichen	2915
	Siegmund Paul Meyer Bayreuth	Siegmund Paul Meyer Bayreuth	733
	Carl Hans Tuppack Tiefenfurth	Carl Hans Tuppack Tiefenfurth	2947 2948

Meissen

Es gibt keine Marken, die so oft gefälscht, nachgeahmt oder variiert worden sind wie die Meißner Marken. Mit Ausnahme der Drachen-Marke (Gruppe 22, Nr. 1862–1871) sind sie alle von anderen Herstellern kopiert oder in Variationen benutzt worden.

Die Buchstabenkombinationen KPM, KPF und MPM sind im vorhergehenden Kapitel behandelt worden. Eine andere frühe Marke, die verschlungenen Buchstaben AR (für Augustus Rex) wurde auf Porzellan für den Hof August des Starken, Kurfürst von Sachsen und König von Polen, blau unter der Glasur angebracht.

Die originale AR-Marke (Nr. 2515, Variationen siehe Gruppe 35, Nr. 2503–2523) ist hauptsächlich für größere Stücke nachgewiesen, aber niemals für kleinere Porzellanwaren, wie Kaffee-, Tee- oder Schokoladentassen. Aber Tassen dieser Art, oft im Meißner Stil bemalt, können recht oft gefunden werden. Die meisten sind wahrscheinlich von der Porzellanmalerei von Helena Wolfsohn in Dresden verkauft worden, bis die Königliche Porzellan Manufaktur in Meißen um 1883 eim Urteil gegen Wolfsohn erwirkte, das ihr verbot, die AR-Marke weiter zu benutzen.

 No. 2515

Wolfsohn betrieb eine Porzellanmalerei und hat sehr wahrscheinlich nicht selbst Porzellan hergestellt. Die meisten AR-Marken auf dem von ihr bemalten und verkauften Porzellan sind aber unter der Glasur. Da sie vor dem Aufbringen der Glasur und dem Glattbrand angebracht worden sein müssen, muß Wolfsohn weißes Porzellan mit der AR-Marke von einigen anderen Porzellanfabriken bezogen haben. Es ist bisher noch nicht möglich gewesen, diese Hersteller zu finden. Lange Zeit war die Fabrik der Gebrüder Haidinger in Elbogen in Verdacht, aber in letzter Zeit haben sich die Zweifel an ihrer Beteiligung an einem so ausgedehnten Betrugsmanöver verstärkt. Die Zahl der von Wolfsohn verkauften Porzellanstücke mit der AR-Marke wird auf mehrere Zehntausend geschätzt.

Unglücklicherweise hat die Meißner Manufaktur selbst einige Verwirrung über die AR-Marke geschaffen. 1873 registrierte sie AR als Schutzmarke (Nr. 2506), und sie benutzt die Marke immer noch auf besonderen Erzeugnissen wie Dessertschalen, Likörservice, Wandteller und ähnlichen Produkten. Diese Tatsache kann nur Anlaß zu der dringenden Empfehlung sein, jedes Stück mit einer AR-Marke sorgfältig zu prüfen.

 No. 2506

Meissen

No marks have been faked, imitated or modified more often than the Meissen marks. With the exception of the kite mark (group 22, Nos. 1862–1871) all Meissen marks have been copied or used in variations by other manufacturers.

The letter combinations KPM, KPF and MPM are discussed in the foregoing chapter. Another early mark, the intertwined letters AR (for Augustus Rex) used to be applied blue underglaze on porcelain for the court of Augustus the Strong, Prince Elector of Saxony and King of Poland.

The original AR mark (No. 2515, for variations see group 35, Nos. 2503–2523) has been proven mainly on larger decorative pieces but never on smaller items like coffee, tea or chocolate cups. But cups of this kind, often decorated in the Meissen style, can be found quite often. Most of them were probably sold by the decorating shop of Helena Wolfsohn in Dresden until about 1883, when the Royal Porcelain Manufactory in Meissen obtained a court decision against Wolfsohn, ordering her to cease and desist using the AR mark.

No. 2515

Wolfsohn operated a decorating shop and in all probability did not produce porcelain herself. Yet most AR marks on pieces decorated and sold by her are underglaze. Since they must have been applied before glazing and final firing, Wolfsohn must have ordered white porcelain with the AR mark from some porcelain factories. It has not been possible to find the manufacturers who produced this porcelain for Wolfsohn. For a long time the factory of the Brothers Haidinger in Elbogen was under suspicion, but lately doubts arose about their participation in such a widespread deception. The number of porcelain pieces with the AR mark sold by Wolfsohn is estimated to be in the tens of thousands.

Unfortunately, the manufactory in Meissen itself created some confusion about the AR mark. In 1873 it registered AR as a trademark (No. 2506) and is still using this mark on special products as dessert bowls, liqueur sets, collectors plates and similar pieces. This only can lead to the strong recommendation to scrutinize every piece with the AR mark very carefully.

No. 2506

	Helena Wolfsohn Dresden	Helena Wolfsohn Dresden	25 25
	unidentified German, later 19th century blue overglaze	nicht identifiziert Deutsch, spätes 19. Jahrhundert blau aufglasur	25:
	Helena Wolfsohn Dresden	Helena Wolfsohn Dresden	252
	unidentified blue underglaze	nicht identifiziert blau unterglasur	33(
	attributed to R. & E. Haidinger Elbogen, but questionable	R. & E. Haidinger, Elbogen zugeschrieben, aber fraglich	253 253
	Helena Wolfsohn Dresden	Helena Wolfsohn Dresden	252
	unidentified late 19th century blue underglaze or overglaze	nicht identifiziert spätes 19. Jahrhundert blau unterglasur oder aufglasur	329
	Helena Wolfsohn Dresden	Helena Wolfsohn Dresden	252
	unidentified 2nd half 19th century blue underglaze	nicht identifiziert 2. Hälfte 19. Jahrhundert blau unterglasur	329
	attributed to R. & E. Haidinger Elbogen, but questionable	R. & E. Haidinger, Elbogen zugeschrieben, aber fraglich	253

	Helena Wolfsohn Dresden	Helena Wolfsohn Dresden	2528
	unidentified, blue underglaze or overglaze, on copies of 18th century Meissen nut bowls	nicht identifiziert, blau unterglasur oder aufglasur, auf Kopien von Meißner Nußschalen des 18. Jahrhunderts	3300
	Prince Fr. Chr. of Saxony Altshausen	Prinz Fr. Chr. zu Sachsen Altshausen	956
	unidentified, blue underglaze on copies of children's busts, originally modelled by Kaendler in 1760	nicht identifiziert, blau unterglasur, auf Kopien der ursprünglich von Kaendler 1760 modellierten Kinderbüsten	3305
	Albin Rosenlocher Kups	Albin Rosenlöcher Küps	2534
	unidentified blue underglaze	nicht identifiziert blau unterglasur	3301
	unidentified blue overglaze	nicht identifiziert blau aufglasur	3302
	Newcomb Pottery New Orleans, Louisiana, U.S.A. after 1896	Newcomb Pottery New Orleans, Louisiana, USA nach 1896	3304
	unidentified black overglaze	nicht identifiziert schwarz aufglasur	2535
	unidentified blue underglaze	nicht identifiziert blau unterglasur	3303
	Anton Richter Dresden	Anton Richter Dresden	2533

C. Alfred Römhild
Großbreitenbach

2271

August Rappsilber
Königszelt

1988
201

August Bauscher
Weiden

2494

Alt, Beck & Gottschalck
Nauendorf

2497

A. Riemann
Coburg

2536

Die Peitschenmarke, ähnlich aussehend wie der Äskulapstab, aber fälschlich als Caduceus oder Hermesstab bezeichnet, wurde in Meißen von etwa 1721 bis wahrscheinlich 1735 benutzt. Sie kann sehr oft auf henkellosen kleinen Tassen (Türkenkoppchen) gefunden werden, die für den Export in die Türkei hergestellt wurden, aber auch auf anderen Stücken (Nr. 1329, Variationen siehe Gruppe 16, Nr. 1328–1858).

Nr. 1329

Dr. John Wall
Worcester, England
ca. 1751–1783 zugeschrieben,
aber nicht nachgewiesen

3307
3308

Edme′ Samson
Paris, Frankreich
rue Beranger
ca. 1845–1905
blau unterglasur
siehe Nr. 3432

3309

C. Alfred Romhild 2271
Grossbreitenbach

  August Rappsilber 1988
Konigszelt 201

 August Bauscher 2494
Weiden

 Alt, Beck & Gottschalck 2497
Nauendorf

 A. Riemann 2536
Coburg

The whip mark, similar to the staff of Asclepios, but wrongly called caduceus or Hermes' staff, was used by the Meissen manufactory from about 1721 until probably 1735. It is found very often on handleless small cups (Turkenkoppchen) made for export into Turkey but also on other porcelain pieces (No. 1329, variations see group 16, Nos. 1328–1358).

 No. 1329

attributed to Dr. John Wall
Worcester, England,
circa 1751–1783 3307
but not verified 3308

Edme′ Samson
Paris, France,
rue Beranger
circa 1845–1905
blue underglaze 3309
see No. 3432

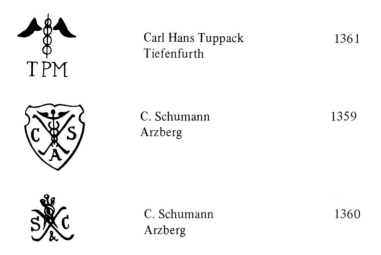

	Carl Hans Tuppack Tiefenfurth	1361
	C. Schumann Arzberg	1359
	C. Schumann Arzberg	1360

Nachahmungen und Fälschungen der berühmten Meißner Schwertermarke gibt es die Menge (Nr. 1533, Variationen siehe Gruppe 19).

                                          Nr. 1533

Neben direkten Imitationen gibt es eine große Zahl gekreuzter Striche, gekreuzter Buchstaben, gekreuzter Gabeln und anderer Kombinationen.

Einen Vergleich der echten gekreuzten Schwerter mit sehr ähnlich aussehenden Marken deutscher, böhmischer und österreichischer Hersteller und Maler gibt die Gruppe 19. Die mehr als 225 Marken in dieser Gruppe werden hier nicht wiederholt, da die Gruppe 19 eine klare Übersicht gibt.

Ähnlich aussehende Marken aus anderen Gruppen und Marken ausländischer Hersteller folgen hier.

	Cockworthy & Champion Bristol, England ca. 1770–1781 blau unterglasur	3310 3311 3312 3313
	Christian Nonne Volkstedt	2345 2346
	F. J. Peterinck Tournay, Belgien ca. 1756–1793 blau oder schwarz oder rot oder gold aufglasur	3314

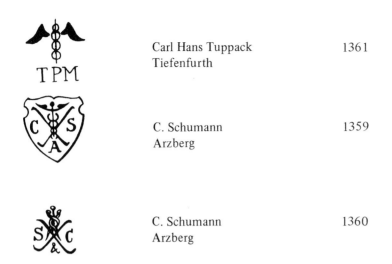

Carl Hans Tuppack		1361
Tiefenfurth		
C. Schumann		1359
Arzberg		
C. Schumann		1360
Arzberg		

Imitations and forgeries of the famous crossed swords of Meissen are plentiful (No. 1533, for variations see group 19).

No. 1533

Besides plain imitations there is a large number of crossed lines, crossed letters, crossed forks and other combinations.

For the genuine crossed swords marks and very similar looking marks used by German, Bohemian and Austrian manufacturers and decorators see group 19. The more than two hundred and twenty-five marks shown in this group are not repeated here, since they can easily be compared in group 19.

Similar looking marks from other groups and those used by foreign manufacturers are listed below.

Cockworthy & Champion		3310
Bristol, England		3311
circa 1770–1781		3312
blue underglaze		3313
Christian Nonne		2345
Volkstedt		2346
F. J. Peterinck		
Tournay, Belgium		
circa 1756–1793		
blue or black or		3314
red or gold overglaze		

Nicholas Sprimont	Nicholas Sprimont	
Chelsea, England	Chelsea, England	33
circa 1743–1769	ca. 1743–1769	33
blue underglaze	blau unterglasur	33

attributed to	zugeschrieben
Nicholas Sprimont	Nicholas Sprimont
Chelsea, England	Chelsea, England
circa 1743–1769	ca. 1743–1769

attributed to · Nicholas Sprimont · Chelsea, England · circa 1743–1769 — zugeschrieben · Nicholas Sprimont · Chelsea, England · ca. 1743–1769 · 33

Walker, Browne, Aldred & Richman · Lowestoft, England · 1757–circa 1800 · blue underglaze — Walker, Browne, Aldred & Richman · Lowestoft, England · 1757–ca. 1800 · blau unterglasur · 33

Dr. John Wall · Worcester, England · circa 1751–1783 · blue underglaze — Dr. John Wall · Worcester, England · ca. 1751–1783 · blau unterglasur · 33 33 33

unidentified · blue on unglazed bottom — nicht identifiziert · blau auf unglasiertem Boden · 33

unidentified · blue underglaze — nicht identifiziert · blau unterglasur · 33

William Lowdin · Bristol, England · circa 1750–1752 · brown overglaze — William Lowdin · Bristol, England · ca. 1750÷1752 · braun aufglasur · 33 33

Duesbury & Kean · Derby, England · circa 1756–1811 · blue underglaze — Duesbury & Kean · Derby, England · ca. 1756–1811 · blau unterglasur · 33

Duesbury & Kean · Derby, England · circa 1756–1811 · swords blue underglaze, letter and number impressed — Duesbury & Kean · Derby, England · ca. 1756–1811 · Schwerter blau unterglasur, Buchstabe und Zahl eingeprägt · 33

attributed to Nicholas Sprimont Chelsea, England circa 1743–1769 blue underglaze	zugeschrieben Nicholas Sprimont Chelsea, England ca. 1743–1769 blau unterglasur	3329
Cockworthy & Champion Bristol, England circa 1770–1781 blue underglaze	Cockworthy & Champion Bristol, England ca. 1770–1781 blau unterglasur	3330 3331 3332
Duesbury & Kean Derby, England 1782–1811 blue	Duesbury & Kean Derby, England 1782–1811 blau	3333 3334
F. J. Peterinck Tournay, Belgium circa 1756–1793 blue or black or red or gold overglaze	F. J. Peterinck Tournay, Belgien ca. 1756–1793 blau oder schwarz oder rot oder gold aufglasur	3335
attributed to Nicholas Sprimont Chelsea, England circa 1743–1769 blue underglaze	zugeschrieben Nicholas Sprimont Chelsea, England ca. 1743–1769 blau unterglasur	3336
attributed to Weatherby & Crowther Bow, England circa 1747–1776 blue underglaze	zugeschrieben Weatherby & Crowther Bow, England ca. 1747–1776 blau unterglasur	3337
Cockworthy & Champion Bristol, England circa 1770–1781 swords blue underglaze, figure gold overglaze	Cockworthy & Champion Bristol, England ca. 1770–1781 Schwerter blau unterglasur, Zahl gold aufglasur	3338 3339

	Cockworthy & Champion Bristol, England circa 1770–1781 swords blue underglaze, figure gold overglaze	Cockworthy & Champion Bristol, England ca. 1770–1781 Schwerter blau unterglasur, Zahl gold aufglasur	33 33
	Cockworthy & Champion Bristol, England circa 1770–1781 swords blue underglaze, figure gold overglaze	Cockworthy & Champion Bristol, England ca. 1770–1781 Schwerter blau unterglasur, Zahl gold aufglasur	33 33
	Cockworthy & Champion Bristol, England circa 1770–1781 swords blue underglaze, figure gold overglaze	Cockworthy & Champion Bristol, England ca. 1770–1781 Schwerter blau unterglasur, Zahl gold aufglasur	33 33
	Cockworthy & Champion Bristol, England circa 1770–1781 swords blue underglaze, figure gold overglaze	Cockworthy & Champion Bristol, England ca. 1770–1781 Schwerter blau unterglasur, Zahl gold aufglasur	33 33
	Cockworthy & Champion Bristol, England circa 1770–1781 swords blue underglaze, figure gold overglaze	Cockworthy & Champion Bristol, England ca. 1770–1781 Schwerter blau unterglasur, Zahl gold aufglasur	33 33
	Cockworthy & Champion Bristol, England circa 1770–1781 swords blue underglaze, figure gold overglaze	Cockworthy & Champion Bristol, England ca. 1770–1781 Schwerter blau unterglasur, Zahl gold aufglasur	33
	Cockworthy & Champion Bristol, England circa 1770–1781 swords blue underglaze, crossed lines blue overglaze	Cockworthy & Champion Bristol, England ca. 1770–1781 Schwerter blau unterglasur, gekreuzte Striche blau aufglasur	33 33

Cockworthy & Champion Bristol, England circa 1770–1781 swords blue underglaze, crossed lines blue overglaze	Cockworthy & Champion Bristol, England ca. 1770–1781 Schwerter blau unterglasur, gekreuzte Striche blau aufglasur	3353 3354
Cockworthy & Champion Bristol, England circa 1770–1781 swords blue underglaze, crossed lines blue overglaze	Cockworthy & Champion Bristol, England ca. 1770–1781 Schwerter blau unterglasur, gekreuzte Striche blau aufglasur	3355 3356
Cockworthy & Champion Bristol, England circa 1770–1781 swords blue underglaze, crossed lines blue overglaze	Cockworthy & Champion Bristol, England ca. 1770–1781 Schwerter blau unterglasur, gekreuzte Striche blau aufglasur	3357 3358
Cockworthy & Champion Bristol, England circa 1770–1781 swords blue underglaze, crossed lines blue overglaze	Cockworthy & Champion Bristol, England ca. 1770–1781 Schwerter blau unterglasur, gekreuzte Striche blau aufglasur	3359 3360
Cockworthy & Champion Bristol, England circa 1770–1781 swords blue underglaze, crossed lines blue overglaze	Cockworthy & Champion Bristol, England ca. 1770–1781 Schwerter blau unterglasur, gekreuzte Striche blau aufglasur	3361 3362
Cockworthy & Champion Bristol, England circa 1770–1781 swords blue underglaze, crossed lines blue overglaze	Cockworthy & Champion Bristol, England ca. 1770–1781 Schwerter blau unterglasur, gekreuzte Striche blau aufglasur	3363
Cockworthy & Champion Bristol, England circa 1770–1781 swords blue underglaze, crossed lines blue overglaze, figure gold overglaze	Cockworthy & Champion Bristol, England ca. 1770–1781 Schwerter blau unterglasur, gekreuzte Striche blau aufglasur, Zahl gold aufglasur	3364 3365

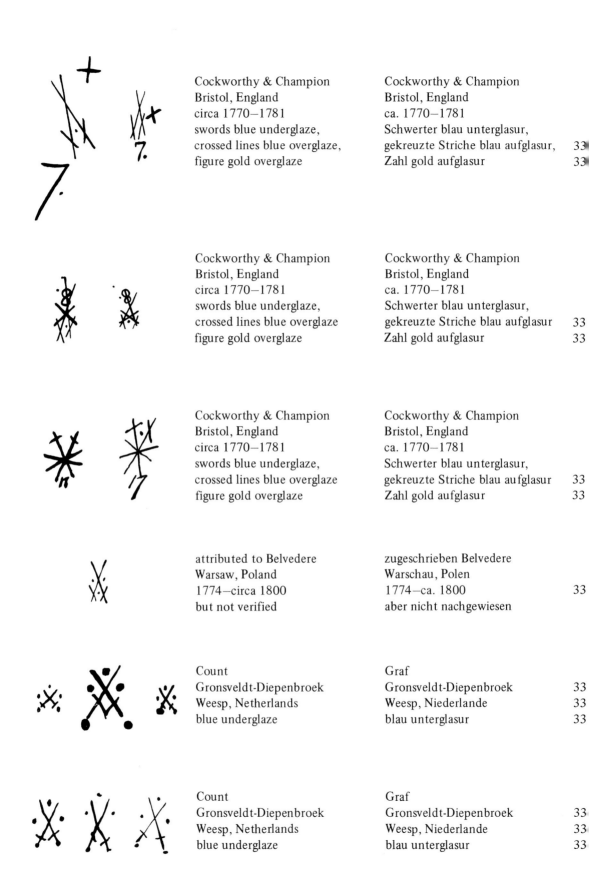

Cockworthy & Champion
Bristol, England
circa 1770–1781
swords blue underglaze,
crossed lines blue overglaze,
figure gold overglaze

Cockworthy & Champion
Bristol, England
ca. 1770–1781
Schwerter blau unterglasur,
gekreuzte Striche blau aufglasur, 33
Zahl gold aufglasur 33

Cockworthy & Champion
Bristol, England
circa 1770–1781
swords blue underglaze,
crossed lines blue overglaze
figure gold overglaze

Cockworthy & Champion
Bristol, England
ca. 1770–1781
Schwerter blau unterglasur,
gekreuzte Striche blau aufglasur 33
Zahl gold aufglasur 33

Cockworthy & Champion
Bristol, England
circa 1770–1781
swords blue underglaze,
crossed lines blue overglaze
figure gold overglaze

Cockworthy & Champion
Bristol, England
ca. 1770–1781
Schwerter blau unterglasur,
gekreuzte Striche blau aufglasur 33
Zahl gold aufglasur 33

attributed to Belvedere
Warsaw, Poland
1774–circa 1800
but not verified

zugeschrieben Belvedere
Warschau, Polen
1774–ca. 1800 33
aber nicht nachgewiesen

Count
Gronsveldt-Diepenbroek
Weesp, Netherlands
blue underglaze

Graf
Gronsveldt-Diepenbroek 33
Weesp, Niederlande 33
blau unterglasur 33

Count
Gronsveldt-Diepenbroek
Weesp, Netherlands
blue underglaze

Graf
Gronsveldt-Diepenbroek 33
Weesp, Niederlande 33
blau unterglasur 33

Prince Electoral Porcelain Manufactory Nymphenburg	Churfürstliche Porcellain Manufactur Nymphenburg	2368 2369
unidentified attributed to a manufactory in Arnstadt circa 1790 blue underglaze	nicht identifiziert einer Manufaktur in Arnstadt zugeschrieben ca. 1790 blau unterglasur	1968 1969
Count Gronsveldt-Diepenbroek Weesp, Netherlands 1764–1771 blue underglaze	Graf Gronsveldt-Diepenbroek Weesp, Niederlande 1764–1771 blau unterglasur	3379
Prince Electoral Porcelain Manufactory Nymphenburg	Churfürstliche Porcellain Manufactur Nymphenburg	2367 2399
Count Gronsveldt-Diepenbroek Weesp, Netherlands 1764–1771 blue underglaze	Graf Gronsveldt-Diepenbroek Weesp, Niederlande 1764–1771 blau unterglasur	3380
attributed to Belvedere Warsaw, Poland 1774–circa 1800 but not verified	zugeschrieben Belvedere Warschau, Polen 1774–ca. 1800 aber nicht nachgewiesen	3381
Francis Gardner Moscow, Russia 1765–1800 blue underglaze	Francis Gardner Moscow, Russia 1765–1800 blau unterglasur	3382 3383
Jacob Petit Fontainebleau, France circa 1830–1842 blue	Jacob Petit Fontainebleau, Frankreich ca. 1830–1842 blau	3384

Sluizer Fontainebleau, France blue underglaze	Sluizer Fontainebleau, Frankreich blau unterglasur	33
F. J. Peterinck Tournay, Belgium circa 1756−1783 blue or black or red or gold overglaze	F. J. Peterinck Tournay, Belgien ca. 1756−1783 blau oder schwarz oder rot oder gold aufglasur	338
Thomas Turner Caughley, England circa 1775−1799 blue	Thomas Turner Caughley, England ca. 1775−1799 blau	33
Prince of Hildburghausen Kloster Veilsdorf	Prinz von Hildburghausen Kloster Veilsdorf	25
unidentified blue underglaze, short line red overglaze	nicht identifiziert blau unterglasur, kurzer Strich rot aufglasur	33
F. J. Peterinck Tournay, Belgium circa 1756−1793 blue or black or red or gold overglaze	F. J. Peterinck Tournay, Belgien ca. 1756−1793 blau oder schwarz oder rot oder gold aufglasur	33 33 33
F. J. Peterinck Tournay, Belgium circa 1756−1793 blue or black or red or gold overglaze	F. J. Peterinck Tournay, Belgien ca. 1756−1793 blau oder schwarz oder rot oder gold aufglasur	33 33 33
Thomas Turner Caughley, England circa 1775−1799 blue	Thomas Turner Caughley, England ca. 1775−1799 blau	33 33 33

Cockworthy & Champion Bristol, England circa 1770–1781 swords blue underglaze, figure gold overglaze	Cockworthy & Champion Bristol, England ca. 1770–1781 Schwerter blau unterglasur, Ziffer gold aufglasur	3398 3399
Cockworthy & Champion Bristol, England circa 1770–1781 swords blue underglaze, figure gold overglaze	Cockworthy & Champion Bristol, England ca. 1770–1781 Schwerter blau unterglasur, Ziffer gold aufglasur	3400 3401
Dr. John Wall Worcester, England circa 1751–1783 blue underglaze	Dr. John Wall Worcester, England ca. 1751–1783 blau unterglasur	3402 3403
Dr. John Wall Worcester, England circa 1751–1783 blue underglaze	Dr. John Wall Worcester, England ca. 1751–1783 blau unterglasur	3404 3405
Dr. John Wall Worcester, England circa 1751–1783 blue underglaze	Dr. John Wall Worcester, England ca. 1751–1783 blau unterglasur	3406 3407
Dr. John Wall Worcester, England circa 1751–1783 blue underglaze	Dr. John Wall Worcester, England ca. 1751–1783 blau unterglasur	3408 3409
Dr. John Wall Worcester, England circa 1751–1783 blue underglaze	Dr. John Wall Worcester, England ca. 1751–1783 blau unterglasur	3410 3411

attributed to Cockworthy & Champion Bristol, England circa 1770–1781 blue underglaze	zugeschrieben Cockworthy & Champion Bristol, England ca. 1770–1781 blau unterglasur 34 34

Walker, Browne, Aldred &
Richman
Lowestoft, England
1757–circa 1800
blue underglaze

Walker, Browne, Aldred &
Richman
Lowestoft, England
1757–ca. 1800   34
blau unterglasur   34

Gotthelf Greiner
Limbach

Gotthelf Greiner   23
Limbach

John Rose & Co.
Coalport, England
circa 1820–circa 1841
blue

John Rose & Co.
Coalport, England
ca. 1820–ca. 1841   34
blau

Achille Bloch
Paris, France
rue de la Pierre-Levée
blue underglaze or
overglaze

Achille Bloch
Paris, Frankreich
rue de la Pierre-Levée
blau unterglasur oder   34
aufglasur

Cockworthy & Champion
Bristol, England
circa 1770–1781
swords blue underglaze,
letter B blue overglaze,
figure gold overglaze

Cockworthy & Champion
Bristol, England
ca. 1770–1781
Schwerter blau unterglasur,
Buchstabe B blau aufglasur,   341
Ziffer gold aufglasur   341

Dornheim, Koch & Fischer
Grafenroda

Dornheim, Koch & Fischer   238
Gräfenroda   238

Dornheim, Koch & Fischer
Grafenroda

Dornheim, Koch & Fischer   238
Gräfenroda

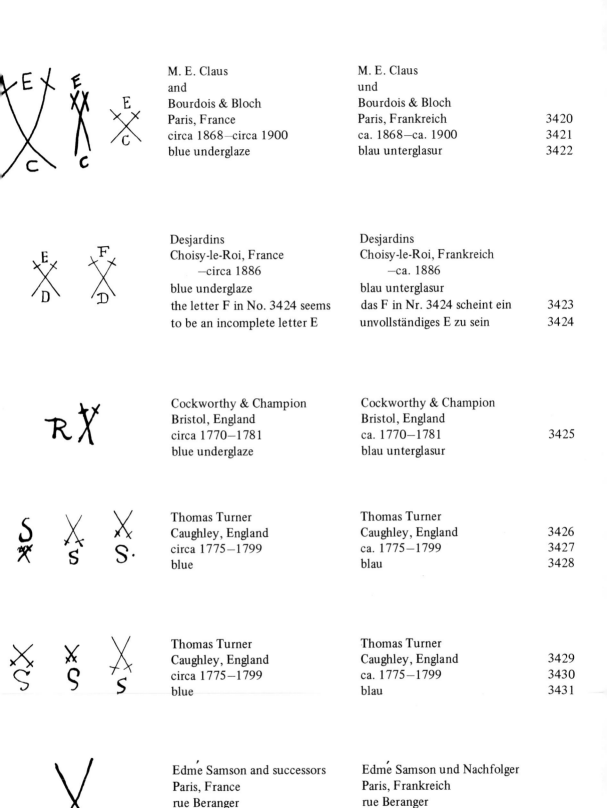

M. E. Claus
and
Bourdois & Bloch
Paris, France
circa 1868–circa 1900
blue underglaze

M. E. Claus
und
Bourdois & Bloch
Paris, Frankreich
ca. 1868–ca. 1900
blau unterglasur

3420
3421
3422

Desjardins
Choisy-le-Roi, France
   –circa 1886
blue underglaze
the letter F in No. 3424 seems
to be an incomplete letter E

Desjardins
Choisy-le-Roi, Frankreich
   –ca. 1886
blau unterglasur
das F in Nr. 3424 scheint ein
unvollständiges E zu sein

3423
3424

Cockworthy & Champion
Bristol, England
circa 1770–1781
blue underglaze

Cockworthy & Champion
Bristol, England
ca. 1770–1781
blau unterglasur

3425

Thomas Turner
Caughley, England
circa 1775–1799
blue

Thomas Turner
Caughley, England
ca. 1775–1799
blau

3426
3427
3428

Thomas Turner
Caughley, England
circa 1775–1799
blue

Thomas Turner
Caughley, England
ca. 1775–1799
blau

3429
3430
3431

Edmé Samson and successors
Paris, France
rue Beranger
circa 1873–circa 1905
blue underglaze

Edmé Samson und Nachfolger
Paris, Frankreich
rue Beranger
ca. 1873–ca. 1905
blau unterglasur

3432

Die Firma Samson, häufig "Samson der Imitator" genannt, ist in erster Linie durch die große Zahl ihrer Reproduktionen und Kopien der Erzeugnisse berühmter Manufakturen bekannt geworden. Die Geschichte des Unternehmens ist noch nicht vollständig bekannt. Als Gründungsjahr wird üblicherweise 1845 angegeben. Einige Autoren sagen, daß Edme Samson 1845 die Porzellanfabrik von Tinet in Montreuil-sous-Bois gekauft habe, andere, daß er eine Fabrik in Saint Maurice besessen und sie 1875 nach Montreuil-sous-Bois verlegt habe. Es gibt keinen Zweifel, daß die Samsons die Fabrik von Tinet erwarben. Da diese aber bis 1873 unter Tinets Namen bestand, ist zweifelhaft, daß Samson sie schon 1845 gekauft hat.

Die meisten zeitgenössischen Quellen geben den Eindruck, daß Edme Samson etwa 25 Jahre nach der Gründung seiner Firma nur Porzellan anderer Manufakturen und Fabriken bemalte. Sein Sohn Emile (1837–1913) wird als erster der Familie erwähnt, der Reproduktionen von Porzellan berühmter Manufakturen hergestellt hat. Das gestattet die Theorie, daß Emile Samson 1873 die Fabrik von Tinet erwarb und begann, eigenes Porzellan herzustellen.

Seit dieser Zeit erschien eine zunehmende Zahl von Samson-Reproduktionen und Imitationen auf dem Markt. Nach einer Quelle besaß die Firma Samson fast 20,000 Originale der Manufakturen in *Meissen,* Sevres, Chelsea, Capo di Monte und von chinesischem und japanischem Porzellan. Von ihnen machte sie Formen für ihre Kopien. Nachgewiesen sind auch Imitationen von *Frankenthal, Ludwigsburg, Fürstenberg, Wien,* Derby, Bow, Worcester, Chantilly, Tournay, Vincennes, Mennecy and Kopenhagen.

Die Firma wurde bis 1964 von Edme Samson und seinen Nachfolgern Emile, Leon, Francois und Pierre Samson geleitet, dann ging sie an C. G. Richardiére über. Anfang der 1970er Jahre wurde sie von Paris nach Montreuil-sous-Bois verlegt und sie schränkte ihre Produktion erheblich ein.

Unter Experten gibt es keine vollständige Übereinstimmung über die Marken, die die Samsons auf ihren Imitationen benutzten. Sicher erscheint nur die Tatsache, daß die Firma kurz nach 1900 einige Schutzmarken registrierte, die meist Variationen des Buchstaben S oder zwei gekreuzte Buchstaben S, oder im Falle von Meissen-Kopien zwei gekreuzte Striche mit einem Querstrich zeigen. Diese Marken gibt es mit und ohne zusätzlichen Buchstaben S (Siehe Nr. 3449–3453, 3488, 3489).

Nach einer Erklärung von Pierre Samson im Jahre 1956 sind diese registrierten Marken auf allem Porzellan angebracht worden, das nach etwa 1905 hergestellt wurde. Alle anderen zusätzlichen Zeichen waren—wieder Emile Samson zitiert—meist Malermarken. Diese Erklärung würde die Periode, in der Originalmarken nachgeahmt wurden, auf die Jahre 1845 bis etwa 1905 beschränken. Eine Anzahl imitierter Marken ist auf der Glasur angebracht. Wenn die oben erwähnte Theorie stimmt, haben die Samsons von 1845 bis 1873 nur Porzellan bemalt und die Marke muß aufglasur sein.

Nach 1873 hat die Firma eindeutig Reproduktionen von dekorativem Porzellan und Figuren berühmter Manufakturen hergestellt. Diese Erzeugnisse tragen üblicherweise an auffallender Stelle eine Nachahmung der Originalmarke unterglasur und eine kleine oder sogar versteckte Samsonmarke auf der Glasur. Aufglasurmarken können ziemlich leicht entfernt werden fast ohne eine Spur zu hinterlassen, und es gibt genügend Beweise, daß auf einer Anzahl von Porzellanstücken die Samsonmarke abgekratzt wurde, um die Stücke als Originale erscheinen zu lassen.

Es gibt ebenso den begründeten Verdacht, daß die Samsons jede Marke anbrachten, die Käufer besonderer Bestellungen wünschten, oder daß sie auf Verlangen die Samsonmarke wegließen.

The company of Samson, frequently called "Samson the Imitator", is best known by the large number of reproductions and copies of porcelain of famous manufacturies it produced. The history of the company is not yet fully known. As founding year usually 1845 is mentioned. Some authors claim that Edmé Samson in 1845 bought the porcelain factory of Tinet in Montreuil-sous-Bois, France, others maintain that he owned a porcelain factory in Saint Maurice, France, which he moved to Montreuil-sous-Bois in 1875. There is no doubt that the Samsons bought the Tinet factory but since this factory continued to exist under the name of Tinet until 1873, it is questionable that Samson acquired it in 1845.

Most contemporary sources give the impression that during the first 25 or so years Edmé Samson only decorated porcelain produced by other manufacturies and factories. His son Emile (1837–1913) is mentioned in contemporary sources as the first in the family to have made reproductions of porcelain of famous manufacturies. This allows the theory that Emile Samson acquired the factory of Tinet in 1873 and began producing his own porcelain. From this time on an increasing number of Samson reproductions and imitations appeared on the market. According to one source the company of Samson owned almost 20,000 originals from the manufacturies in *Meissen,* Sevres, Chelsea, Capo di Monte and of Chinese and Japanese porcelain. From them it made moulds for its copies.

Proven are also imitations of *Frankenthal, Ludwigsburg, Furstenberg, Vienna,* Derby, Bow, Worcester, Chantilly, Tournay, Vincennes, Mennecy and Copenhagen.

The company was operated by Edmé Samson and his successors Emile, Leon, Francois and Pierre Samson until 1964, when C. G. Richardiere became proprietor. In the early 1970s it was moved from Paris to Montreuil-sous-Bois and reduced its productions considerably. There is no complete agreement among experts about the marks the Samsons used on their imitations. Only one fact seems to be certain, that the company registered some trademarks shortly after 1900 which consist mainly of variations of the letters S and crossed letters S and in the case of Meissen imitations of two crossed lines with another line through the intersection of the crossed lines. This mark appears with or without letters S (see marks Nos. 3449–3453, 3488, 3489).

According to a statement by Pierre Samson in 1956 the company applied these trademarks on all porcelain manufactured by the company after about 1905. Any other additional markings were—again according to Pierre Samson—mostly decorators' signs. This statement would leave the years from 1845 until about 1905 as the time period in which original marks were imitated. A number of imitated marks appears overglaze. If the above mentioned theory is right, then the Samsons from 1845 until 1873 only decorated porcelain and on decorated pieces the mark has to be overglaze.

After 1873 the company definitely manufactured reproductions of decorative porcelain and figurines of famous manufacturies. These products usually bear a conspicuous imitation of the original mark underglaze and a small or even hidden Samson mark overglaze. Overglaze marks can easily be removed almost without a trace and there is ample evidence, that on quite a number of pieces the Samson marks have been scratched off so that the pieces would appear to be originals.

There is also founded suspicion that the Samsons applied any mark the buyer of a special order wanted, or on demand left off the Samson mark.

The company continued this practice from 1873 until about 1905. After 1905 it changed—according to its own statement—to its registered trademarks which then were applied underglaze.

Samson marks: 3309. 3449–3453, 3488, 3489, 3528

Die Firma folgte dieser Praxis von 1873 bis etwa 1905. Danach benutzte sie nach ihren eigenen Angaben ihre registrierten Schutzmarken, die unter der Glasur erscheinen. Samson-Marken: 3309, 3449–3453, 3488, 3489

Prince Friedrich Christian
of Saxony
Altshausen

Prinz Friedrich Christian
zu Sachsen
Altshausen

A. Rub-Leprince
Paris, France
(1892)–

A. Rub-Leprince
Paris, Frankreich
(1892)–

attributed to
Clement
Choisy-le-Roi, France
but probably
A. Rub-Leprince
Paris
see No. 3433

zugeschrieben
Clement
Choisy-le-Roi, Frankreich
aber wahrscheinlich
A. Rub-Leprince
Paris
siehe Nr. 3433

Duesbury & Kean
Derby, England
1782–1811
blue overglaze

Duesbury & Kean
Derby, England
1782–1811
blau aufglasur

Stevenson & Hancock
Derby, England
circa 1863–1866
red overglaze

Stevenson & Hancock
Derby, England
ca. 1863–1866
rot aufglasur

Stevenson & Hancock
and
Sampson Hancock
Derby, England
circa 1863–1935
red overglaze

Stevenson & Hancock
und
Sampson Hancock
Derby, England
ca. 1863–1935
rot aufglasur

Dr. John Wall Worcester, England circa 1751–1783 blue underglaze	Dr. John Wall Worcester, England ca. 1751–1783 blau unterglasur	3439
Heinrich & Co. Selb	Heinrich & Co. Selb	771
Wessel-Work Bonn	Wessel-Werk Bonn	659 660
Prince E. H. of Saxony and Royal Saxe Corporation New York City, U. S. A.	Prinz E. H. von Sachsen und Royal Saxe Corporation New York City, U. S. A.	1463
unidentified blue underglaze	nicht identifiziert blau unterglasur	3440
Ruskin Pottery West-Smethwick, England 1899–1935	Ruskin Pottery West-Smethwick, England 1899–1935	3441
Friedrich Kaestner Oberhohndorf	Friedrich Kaestner Oberhohndorf	1919
Krautheim & Adelberg Selb	Krautheim & Adelberg Selb	607
Zeh, Scherzer & Co. Rehau	Zeh, Scherzer & Co. Rehau	757

Warwick China Co. Wheeling, West Virginia, U. S. A. 1887– green underglaze	Warwick China Co. Wheeling, West Virginia, U. S. A. 1887– grün unterglasur	34
Paepke & Schafer Haida	Paepke & Schäfer Haida	
unidentified blue	nicht identifiziert blau	34
Dumler & Breiden Hohr-Grenzhausen	Dümler & Breiden Höhr-Grenzhausen	23
Martha Budich Kronach	Martha Budich Kronach	24
R. & E. Pech Kronach	R. & E. Pech Kronach	24 24
unidentified blue underglaze	nicht identifiziert blau unterglasur	34
Renaud Paris, France circa 1895 decorator's mark overglaze	Renaud Paris, Frankreich ca. 1895 Malermarke aufglasur	34
Christian Nonne Volkstedt	Christian Nonne Volkstedt	23
Margravial Fine Porcelain Factory Ansbach/Bruckberg	Markgräfliche Feine Porcelain Fabrique Ansbach/Bruckberg	23

544

unidentified blue underglaze	nicht identifiziert blau unterglasur	3446
Dornheim, Koch & Fischer Grafenroda	Dornheim, Koch & Fischer Gräfenroda	2319
Christian Nonne Volkstedt	Christian Nonne Volkstedt	2349 2350
attributed to Ansbach but questionable blue underglaze	zugeschrieben Ansbach aber fraglich blau unterglasur	2351 2352 2353
Porcelain and Ceramic Factory Cmielow Cmielow, Poland 1842– blue underglaze	Porzellan- und Keramik- fabrik Cmielow Cmielow, Polen 1842– blau unterglasur	3447 3448
Voigt Sitzendorf	Voigt Sitzendorf	2317
Edmé Samson Paris, France rue Béranger 1873–present blue underglaze or overglaze see No. 3432	Edmé Samson Paris, Frankreich rue Béranger 1873–heute blau unterglasur oder aufglasur siehe Nr. 3432	3449
Dornheim, Koch & Fischer Grafenroda	Dornheim, Koch & Fischer Gräfenroda	2318
Edmé Samson Paris, France rue Béranger circa 1905–present blue underglaze see No. 3432	Edmé Samson Paris, Frankreich Rue Béranger ca. 1905–heute blau unterglasur siehe Nr. 3432	3450 3451

Edme Samson Paris, France rue Béranger circa 1905–present blue underglaze see No. 3432	Edme Samson Paris, Frankreich rue Beranger ca. 1905–heute blau unterglasur 34: siehe Nr. 3432 34:
Attributed to G.H. Macheleid Sitzerode	G.H. Macheleid Sitzerode zugeschrieben 24(
Prince Electoral Porcelain Manufactory Nymphenburg	Churfürstliche Porcellain Manufactur 23(Nymphenburg
Christian Nonne Volkstedt	Christian Nonne 23° Volkstedt
Prince of Hildburghausen Kloster Veilsdorf	Prinz von Hildburghausen 23° Kloster Veilsdorf
unidentified blue underglaze	nicht identifiziert blau unterglasur 23°
Voigt Sitzendorf variation of mark No. 2317	Voigt Sitzendorf Variation der Marke 345 2317 345
Francis Gardner Moscow, Russia 1760–1800 blue underglaze	Francis Gardner Moskau, Rußland 1760–1800 345 blau unterglasur
unidentified blue underglaze on copy of Meissen figurine	nicht identifiziert blau unterglasur auf Kopie einer 345 Meißen Figur

unidentified blue underglaze on putto	nicht identifiziert blau unterglasur auf Putto	3458
C. G. Schierholz Plaue	C. G. Schierholz Plaue	2312 2313
Voigt Sitzendorf	Voigt Sitzendorf	2315 2316
unidentified possibly J. Viallatte Paris, France rue de la Boule Rouge circa 1876– blue	nicht identifiziert möglicherweise J. Viallatte Paris, Frankreich rue de la Boule Rouge ca. 1876– blau	3459
E. Jaquemin Fontainebleau, France 1862– blue	E. Jaquemin Fontainebleau, Frankreich 1862– blau	3460 3461
J. W. Hammann Wallendorf	J. W. Hammann Wallendorf	2323 2322
J. W. Hammann Wallendorf	J. W. Hammann Wallendorf	2321 2320
J. W. Hammann Wallendorf	J. W. Hammann Wallendorf	2324 2325
J. W. Hammann Wallendorf 1764–1787 blue underglaze	J. W. Hammann Wallendorf 1764–1787 blau unterglasur	2421
Kampfe & Heubach Wallendorf	Kämpfe & Heubach Wallendorf	2954

J. W. Hammann	J. W. Hammann	29
Wallendorf	Wallendorf	29
J. W. Hammann	J. W. Hammann	29
Wallendorf	Wallendorf	29
Family	Familie	29
Hammann	Hammann	29
Wallendorf	Wallendorf	29
Family	Familie	
Hammann	Hammann	29
Wallendorf	Wallendorf	29
Gotthelf Greiner	Gotthelf Greiner	23
Limbach	Limbach	23
Gotthelf Greiner	Gotthelf Greiner	23
Limbach	Limbach	23
Gotthelf Greiner	Gotthelf Greiner	23
Limbach	Limbach	23
Gotthelf Greiner	Gotthelf Greiner	23
Limbach	Limbach	23
Gotthelf Greiner	Gotthelf Greiner	23
Limbach	Limbach	23
Gotthelf Greiner	Gotthelf Greiner	23
Limbach	Limbach	23
Gotthelf Greiner	Gotthelf Greiner	23
Limbach	Limbach	23
Gotthelf Greiner	Gotthelf Greiner	23
Limbach	Limbach	23
		23

| | Gotthelf Greiner
Ilmenau | Gotthelf Greiner
Ilmenau | 2362
2363 |

| | William Littler & Co.
Longton Hall, England
circa 1754–1760
blue underglaze | William Littler & Co.
Longton Hall, England
ca. 1754–1760
blau unterglasur |

3462
3463 |

| | Gabriel Legrand
Paris, France
circa 1890
decorator´s marks
overglaze | Gabriel Legrand
Paris, Frankreich
ca. 1890
Malermarken
aufglasur |

3464
3465 |

| | William Littler & Co.
Longton Hall, England
circa 1754-1760
blue underglaze | William Littler & Co.
Longton Hall, England
ca. 1754-1760
blau unterglasur |

3466 |

| | William Littler & Co.
Longton Hall, England
circa 1754–1760
blue underglaze | William Littler & Co.
Longton Hall, England
ca. 1754–1760
blau unterglasur | 3467
3468
3469
3470 |

| | William Littler & Co.
Longton Hall, England
circa 1754–1760
blue underglaze | William Littler & Co.
Longton Hall, England
ca. 1754–1760
blau unterglasur | 3471
3472
3473
3474 |

| | Gotthelf Greiner
Limbach | Gotthelf Greiner
Limbach | 2326 |

| | Fr. Chr. Greiner
& Sons
Rauenstein | Fr. Chr. Greiner
& Söhne
Rauenstein | 2380
2381
2404 |

Fr. Chr. Greiner & Sons Rauenstein	Fr. Chr. Greiner & Söhne Rauenstein	24● 24● 24● 24●
Daudin & Laner Paris, France (1911)—	Daudin & Laner Paris, Frankreich (1911)—	34●
Christian Nonne Volkstedt	Christian Nonne Volkstedt	235 235 235
Christian Nonne Volkstedt	Christian Nonne Volkstedt	23: 235
Christian Nonne Volkstedt	Christian Nonne Volkstedt	23● 23●
Volkstedt Porcelain Factory Richard Eckert Volkstedt	Volkstedter Porzellanfabrik Richard Eckert Volkstedt	194 194 195
Christian Nonne Volkstedt	Christian Nonne Volkstedt	195
Greiner & Holzapfel Volkstedt	Greiner & Holzapfel Volkstedt	24:

Johannes de Mol	Johannes de Mol	
Oude Loosdrecht	Oude Loosdrecht	
Netherlands	Niederlande	3476
1771–1784	1771–1784	

Volkstedt Porcelain Factory	Volkstedter Porzellanfabrik	1944
Richard Eckert	Richard Eckert	1945
Volkstedt	Volkstedt	1946

Volkstedt Porcelain Factory	Volkstedter Porzellanfabrik	
Richard Eckert	Richard Eckert	1947
Volkstedt	Volkstedt	1952

Christian Nonne	Christian Nonne	481
Volkstedt	Volkstedt	

James & John Bevington	James & John Bevington	
Hanley, England	Hanley, England	
1872–1892	1872–1892	3477
blue underglaze	blau unterglasur	3478

Levy & Cie.	Levy & Cie.	
Charenton, France	Charenton, Frankreich	3479
circa 1875–	ca. 1875–	

Richard Glot	Richard Glot	
Sceaux, France	Sceaux, Frankreich	3480
1772–1784	1772–1784	

Gotthelf Greiner	Gotthelf Greiner	2395
Ilmenau	Ilmenau	

Tinet	Tinet	
Montreuil, France	Montreuil, Frankreich	3481
1815–1873	1815–1873	

E. Jaquemin Fontainebleau, France circa 1862– blue	E. Jaquemin Fontainebleau, Frankreich ca. 1862– blau	348
Jacob Petit Fontainebleau, France circa 1830–1842	Jacob Petit Fontainebleau, Frankreich ca. 1830–1842	348 348
Dr. John Wall Worcester, England circa 1751–1783 blue underglaze	Dr. John Wall Worcester, England ca. 1751–1783 blau unterglasur	348 348
Joseph Schachtel Charlottenbrunn	Joseph Schachtel Charlottenbrunn	236
Princely Fulda Porcelain Factory Fulda	Fürstlich Fuldaische Porzellanfabrik Fulda	236 237 237
unidentified possibly Joseph Schachtel Charlottenbrunn	nicht identifiziert möglicherweise Joseph Schachtel Charlottenbrunn	348
Christian Nonne Ilmenau	Christian Nonne Ilmenau	237
Hermann Ohme Niedersalzbrunn	Hermann Ohme Niedersalzbrunn	92
unidentified attributed to a factory in Ansbach but questionable blue underglaze	nicht identifiziert einer Fabrik in Ansbach zugeschrieben aber fraglich blau unterglasur	237
Albert Wreschner & Co. Berlin	Albert Wreschner & Co. Berlin	237

Bremer & Schmidt Eisenberg	Bremer & Schmidt Eisenberg	931
H. Buhl & Sons Grossbreitenbach	H. Bühl & Söhne Großbreitenbach	2379
Rosenthal Selb	Rosenthal Selb	938
Ernst Teichert Meissen	Ernst Teichert Meissen	2570 2571
Bros. Knoch Neustadt	Gebr. Knoch Neustadt	2388
Julius Greiner Son Lauscha	Julius Greiner Sohn Lauscha	2387
Grossbaum & Sons Dresden	Grossbaum & Söhne Dresden	2389
Franziska Hirsch Dresden	Franziska Hirsch Dresden	2390 2391
Bros. Schoenau Huttensteinach	Gebr. Schoenau Hüttensteinach	2392 2393

Franziska Hirsch Dresden	Franziska Hirsch Dresden	24 24
Chr. Z. Grabner Ilmenau	Chr. Z. Gräbner Ilmenau	23
Joseph Schachtel Charlottenbrunn	Joseph Schachtel Charlottenbrunn	4
Franz R. Kirchner Stutzerbach	Franz R. Kirchner Stützerbach	23
A. W. Fr. Kister Scheibe-Alsbach	A. W. Fr. Kister Scheibe-Alsbach	23
A. W. Fr. Kister Scheibe-Alsbach	A. W. Fr. Kister Scheibe-Alsbach	23
E. & A. Muller Schwarza-Saale	E. & A. Müller Schwarza-Saale	23
H. Hutschenreuther Probstzella	H. Hutschenreuther Probstzella	9.
A. Fischer Ilmenau	A. Fischer Ilmenau	24(
Albin Rosenlocher Kups	Albin Rosenlöcher Küps	24(
F. A. Reinecke Eisenberg	F. A. Reinecke Eisenberg	24(

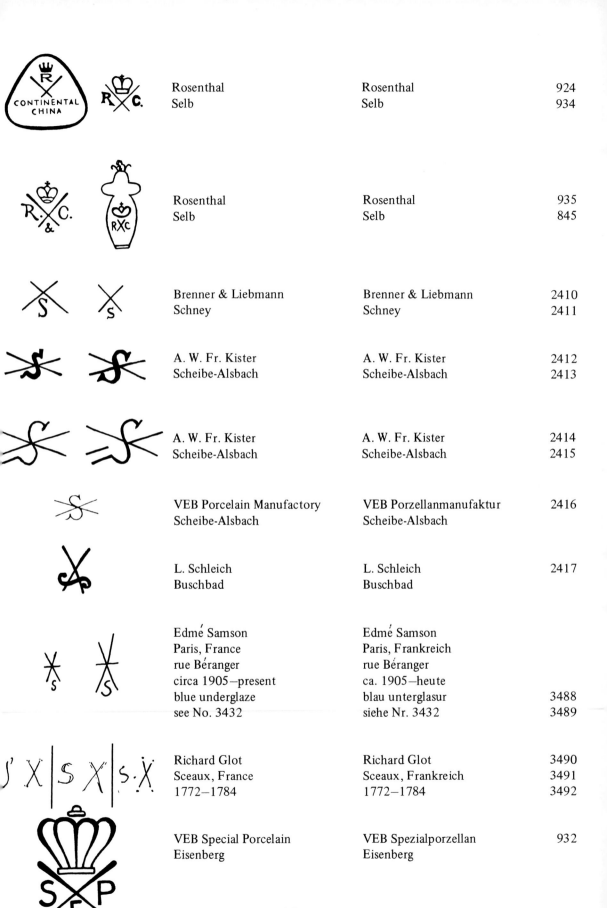

	Rosenthal Selb	Rosenthal Selb	924 934
	Rosenthal Selb	Rosenthal Selb	935 845
	Brenner & Liebmann Schney	Brenner & Liebmann Schney	2410 2411
	A. W. Fr. Kister Scheibe-Alsbach	A. W. Fr. Kister Scheibe-Alsbach	2412 2413
	A. W. Fr. Kister Scheibe-Alsbach	A. W. Fr. Kister Scheibe-Alsbach	2414 2415
	VEB Porcelain Manufactory Scheibe-Alsbach	VEB Porzellanmanufaktur Scheibe-Alsbach	2416
	L. Schleich Buschbad	L. Schleich Buschbad	2417
	Edmé Samson Paris, France rue Béranger circa 1905–present blue underglaze see No. 3432	Edmé Samson Paris, Frankreich rue Béranger ca. 1905–heute blau unterglasur siehe Nr. 3432	3488 3489
	Richard Glot Sceaux, France 1772–1784	Richard Glot Sceaux, Frankreich 1772–1784	3490 3491 3492
	VEB Special Porcelain Eisenberg	VEB Spezialporzellan Eisenberg	932

Rosenthal Selb	Rosenthal Selb	94
K. Steinmann Tiefenfurth	K. Steinmann Tiefenfurth	9
Simon & Halbig Grafenhain	Simon & Halbig Gräfenhain	243
Carl Thieme Potschappel	Carl Thieme Potschappel	241 241
Theodor Pohl Schatzlar	Theodor Pohl Schatzlar	215
VEB Utility Porcelain Grafenthal	VEB Gebrauchsporzellan Gräfenthal	215
Oswald Lorenz Dresden	Oswald Lorenz Dresden	242
G. Wolf Kups	G. Wolf Küps	243
Weiss, Kuhnert & Co. Grafenthal	Weiss, Kühnert & Co. Gräfenthal	242
Wilhelm Rittirsch Kups	Wilhelm Rittirsch Küps	243 149

	La Courtille	La Courtille	
	Paris, France	Paris, Frankreich	
	rue Fontaine-au-Roi	rue Fontaine-au-Roi	
	1771–1841	1771–1841	
	blue underglaze or	blau unterglasur	3493
	overglaze	oder aufglasur	3494

	La Courtille	La Courtille	
	Paris, France	Paris, Frankreich	
	rue Fontaine-au-Roi	rue Fontaine-au-Roi	
	1771–1841	1771–1841	
	blue underglaze or	blau unterglasur	3495
	overglaze	oder aufglasur	3496

	La Courtille	La Courtille	
	Paris, France	Paris, Frankreich	
	rue Fontaine-au-Roi	rue Fontaine-au-Roi	
	1771–1841	1771–1841	
	blue underglaze or	blau unterglasur	3497
	overglaze	oder aufglasur	3498

	La Courtille	La Courtille	
	Paris, France	Paris, Frankreich	
	rue Fontaine-au-Roi	rue Fontaine-au-Roi	
	1771–1841	1771–1841	
	blue underglaze or	blau unterglasur	3499
	overglaze	oder aufglasur	3500

	La Courtille	La Courtille	
	Paris, France	Paris, Frankreich	
	rue Fontaine-au-Roi	rue Fontaine-au-Roi	
	1771–1841	1771–1841	3501
	impressed	eingeprägt	

	La Courtille	La Courtille	
	Paris, France	Paris, Frankreich	
	1771–1841	1771–1841	
	blue underglaze	blau unterglasur	3502
	or overglaze	oder aufglasur	3503

	Bourdois & Bloch	Bourdois & Bloch	
	and	und	
	A. Bloch	A. Bloch	
	Paris, France	Paris, Frankreich	
	circa 1890–1948	ca. 1890–1948	3504
	blue underglaze	blau unterglasur	3505

	Bloch & Cie.	Bloch & Cie.	
	Paris, France	Paris, Frankreich	
	rue de la Pierre Levée	rue de la Pierre Levée	
	circa 1887–1900	ca. 1887–1900	35
	blue underglaze	blau unterglasur	

Vincent Dubois
Paris, France
rue de la Roquette
1774–1778
blue underglaze or
blue or red overglaze

Vincent Dubois
Paris, Frankreich
rue de la Roquette
1774–1778
blau unterglasur oder — 35
blau oder rot aufglasur

Porcelaine de Paris
Paris, France
rue de la Pierre-Levée
1948–present
blue underglaze or overglaze

Porcelaine de Paris
Paris, Frankreich
rue de la Pierre-Levée
1948–heute — 35
blau unterglasur oder aufglasur

D. von Eisenhart
Schriesheim

D. von Eisenhart — 7
Schriesheim

Charles Ahrenfeldt & Son
New York City

Charles Ahrenfeldt & Son — 7
New York City — 7

Porcelain Factory
Kalk
Eisenberg

Porzellanfabrik
Kalk — 7
Eisenberg — 7

Porcelain Factory
Kalk
Eisenberg

Porzellanfabrik
Kalk — 5
Eisenberg

Unger & Schilde
Roschutz

Unger & Schilde — 7
Roschütz

Pierre Antoine Hannong
Paris, France
rue du Faubourg Saint-Denis
1771–1776
blue underglaze

Pierre Antoine Hannong
Paris, Frankreich
rue du Faubourg Saint-Denis — 35
1771–1776 — 35
blau unterglasur — 35

Swaine & Co. Huttensteinach	Swaine & Co. Hüttensteinach	1970 1971
Swaine & Co. Huttensteinach	Swaine & Co. Hüttensteinach	1972
Kuchler & Co. Ilmenau	Küchler & Co. Ilmenau	610
H. Schmidt Freiwaldau	H. Schmidt Freiwaldau	1769
Fischer & Mieg Pirkenhammer	Fischer & Mieg Pirkenhammer	1913 782
Porcelain Factory Plankenhammer	Porzellanfabrik Plankenhammer	1922
Friedrich Kaestner Oberhohndorf	Friedrich Kaestner Oberhohndorf	1915 1916
Friedrich Kaestner Oberhohndorf	Friedrich Kaestner Oberhohndorf	843
VEB Art Porcelain Ilmenau	VEB Kunstporzellan Ilmenau	1921
Schlaggenwalder Porcelain Industry Schlaggenwald	Schlaggenwalder Porzellan- industrie Schlaggenwald	841
Bros. Metzler & Ortloff Ilmenau	Gebr. Metzler & Ortloff Ilmenau	1920

559

Johann Seltmann Vohenstrauss	Johann Seltmann Vohenstrauss	1
Leni Parbus Oberkotzau	Leni Parbus Oberkotzau	
Thomas Recknagel Alexandrinenthal	Thomas Recknagel Alexandrinenthal	1 1
Schumann & Schreider Schwarzenhammer	Schumann & Schreider Schwarzenhammer	1
Sommer & Matschak Schlaggenwald	Sommer & Matschak Schlaggenwald	
Friedrich Kaestner Oberhohndorf	Friedrich Kaestner Oberhohndorf	1
The Mosanic Pottery Mitterteich	The Mosanic Pottery Mitterteich	1
Hermann Unger Schedewitz	Hermann Unger Schedewitz	1
Godebaki & Co. Fontainebleau, France circa 1874–	Godebaki & Co. Fontainebleau, Frankreich ca. 1874–	3. 3.
Ernst Teichert Meissen	Ernst Teichert Meißen	2.
Galluba & Hofmann Ilmenau	Galluba & Hofmann Ilmenau	2

Levy & Cie Charenton, France circa 1875— blue	Levy & Cie Charenton, Frankreich ca. 1875— blau	3514 3515 3516
Karl Ens Vokstedt	Karl Ens Volkstedt	2386
Porcelain Factory Sorau	Porzellanfabrik Sorau	2402
Theodor Holborn Gottingen	Theodor Holborn Göttingen	2205
Porcelain Factory Tirschenreuth	Porzellanfabrik Tirschenreuth	1160
Oscar Schaller & Co. Schwarzenbach	Oscar Schaller & Co. Schwarzenbach	2654
Oscar Schaller & Co. Successors Kirchenlamitz	Oscar Schaller & Co. Nachfolger Kirchenlamitz	1177
Oscar Schaller & Co. Schwarzenbach	Oscar Schaller & Co. Schwarzenbach	802
C. Schumann Arzberg	C. Schumann Arzberg	1359 1360
Swaine & Co. Huttensteinach	Swaine & Co. Hüttensteinach	2659

	Paul Schreier Bischofswerda	1326
	Jaeger & Co. Marktredwitz	405
	Jaeger, Thomas & Co. Marktredwitz	406
	H. Waffler Schwarzenfeld	1965
	Porzellanfabrik Stadtlengsfeld	1966

"Meissen"

Der Name "Meissen" erscheint selten als Teil einer echten Meißner Marke. Es gibt nur drei Ausnahmen. Marke 2257 ist auf kleinen Dosen aus dem 18. Jahrhundert eingeprägt, die von der Königlichen Porzellan Manufaktur hergestellt wurden.

Nr. 2257

Seit 1972 werden die Marken 1712 und 3209 gelegentlich aber nicht regelmäßig zuerst vom VEB Staatliche Porzellan Manufaktur Meissen und seit 1990 von der Staatlichen Porzellan Manufaktur Meissen benutzt.

Nr. 1712   Nr. 3209

Einige Hersteller verwandten den Namen "Meissen" als Bezeichnung für das Zwiebelmuster, das die Königliche Porcelain Fabrique Meissen um 1739 einführte. Dies Muster wurde seit dem 18. Jahrhundert bis heute von vielen Fabriken in aller Welt kopiert. Um ihr eigenes Zwiebelmuster deutlich und auf den ersten Blick sichtbar zu kennzeichnen, brachte die Königliche Manufaktur seit 1883 eine zweite Schwertermarke im Zwiebelmuster selbst an. Diese Marke ist im unteren Teil der Bambusstange zu sehen. (Abbildung oben)

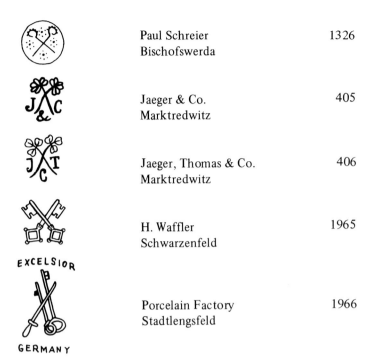

Paul Schreier Bischofswerda		1326
Jaeger & Co. Marktredwitz		405
Jaeger, Thomas & Co. Marktredwitz		406
H. Waffler Schwarzenfeld		1965
Porcelain Factory Stadtlengsfeld		1966

"Meissen"

The name "Meissen" rarely appears as part of a genuine Meissen mark. There are only three exceptions. Mark No. 2257 is impressed on small boxes made in the 18th century by the Royal Manufactory.

MEISSEN   No. 2257

Since 1972 marks Nos. 1712 and 3209 are used occasionally but not as a rule by VEB State's Porcelain Manufactory and State's Porcelain Manufactory in Meissen.

No. 1712   No. 3209

Some manufacturers used the name "Meissen" as a pattern name for the Onion Pattern, introduced by the Royal Porcelain Factory in 1739. This pattern was copied extensively from the 18th century until today all over the world. Beginning in 1883 the Royal Porcelain Manufactory and its successors distinguished its own Onion Pattern by an easily visible second crossed swords mark directly within the pattern. This mark appears near the bottom and directly inside the bamboo pole. (See detail of Onion Pattern above)

MEISSEN	C. Teichert Meissen	C. Teichert Meißen	32
BB	Ernst Teichert Meissen	Ernst Teichert Meißen	17
MEISSEN	Ernst Teichert Meissen	Ernst Teichert Meißen	17
	Meissen Stove and Porcelain Factory C. Teichert and Bloch & Co. Eichwald	Meißner Ofen- und Porzellanfabrik C. Teichert und Bloch & Co. Eichwald	6
	Meissen Stove and Porcelain Factory C. Teichert Meissen	Meißner Ofen- und Porzellanfabrik C. Teichert Meißen	6
	Arthur Pohlmann Meissen	Arthur Pöhlmann Meißen	30
	C. Teichert Meissen	C. Teichert Meißen	189
	Franz Anton Mehlem Bonn	Franz Anton Mehlem Bonn	189
	Saxonian Stove and Firebrick Factory Meissen	Sächsische Ofen- und Schamottewarenfabrik Meißen	188

C. Teichert   C. Teichert   1527
Meissen   Meißen   303

 Richard Muller & Co.   Richard Müller & Co.   136
Colln-Meissen   Cölln-Meißen

 Richard Muller & Co.   Richard Müller & Co.   1758
Colln-Meissen   Cölln-Meißen

 Saxonian Stove and   Sächsische Ofen- und
Firebrich Factory   Schamottewarenfabrik   2221
Meissen   Meißen

 R. Ufer   R. Ufer   2263
Dresden   Dresden

 Brown-Westhead-Moore & Co.   Brown-Westhead-Moore & Co.
Shelton, England   Shelton, England
1858—1904   1858—1904
blue underglaze   blau unterglasur   3517
or overglaze   oder aufglasur

 Arthur Pohlmann   Arthur Pöhlmann   1885
Meissen   Meißen

"Dresden"

In englischsprechenden Ländern ist der Name "Dresden" fast gleichbedeutend mit Meißen und eine Quelle großer Verwirrung. Wie diese falsche Bezeichnung einstand, konnte noch nicht befriedigend erklärt werden. Es ist allerdings möglich, daß Dresden, die sächsische Hauptstadt, im Europa des 18. Jahrhunderts besser bekannt war als die etwa 25 km entfernt liegende Stadt Meißen. Außerdem wurden die meisten Meißner Erzeugnisse in Dresden verkauft, dort schlossen auch die britischen Importeure ihre Geschäfte ab, und sie könnten die Bezeichnung "Dresden" für Meißner Porzellan benutzt haben.

In der zweiten Hälfte des 19. Jahrhunderts entwickelte sich der Fehler zum Monstrum. In dieser Zeit entstanden in Dresden rund dreißig Porzellanmalereien, von denen die meisten den Meißner Malereistil nachahmten oder ihn sogar ausschmückten, indem sie die Stile Meißens und Wiens vermischten.

Auf diese Weise entstand der "Dresdner Stil," der weiter zu der schon bestehenden Verwirrung beitrug. Einige Porzellanmaler in Dresden arbeiteten offensichtlich bei der Schaffung dieses "Dresdner Stils" zusammen und einigten sich auf eine gemeinsame Marke für ihre Erzeugnisse. Vier Maler, Richard Klemm, Donath & Co., Oswald Lorenz und Adolph Hamann erschienen am 7. Februar 1883 im Dresdner Amtsgericht und registrierten um 17:30 Uhr dieselbe Marke für alle vier (Nr. 1209). Zehn Jahre später änderten Klemm, Donath & Co. und Hamann ihre Marken etwas (Nr. 1211, 1213 und 1215), während Lorenz eine Marke wählte, die der Wiener ähnlich sah (Nr. 1441). Acht andere Maler benutzten gleichfalls eine Krone und den Namen "Dresden."

Die Manufaktur in Meißen registrierte die Marke 3245 in Jahr 1938 und hat sie seitdem gelegentlich verwandt. Die Marken 1709 und 1711 waren nach 1963, die Marke 1710 nach 1966 für einige Jahre gelegentlich in Gebrauch.

Royal Dresden China   Nr. 3245

Dresden

Nr. 1709   Dresden Art   Dresden China

       Nr. 1710   Nr. 1711

Der Name "Dresden" ist auch auf vier echten Meißner Stücken gefunden oder als auf ihnen angebracht beschrieben worden (Nr. 1673 und 1674). Er ist aber nicht Teil der Manufakturmarke.

Jedes andere Stück Porzellan mit dem Namen "Dresden" in der Marke ist eindeutig nicht von der Manufaktur in Meißen hergestellt worden.

"Dresden"

In English speaking countries the name "Dresden" is almost synonymous with Meissen and a source of great confusion. How this misnomer arose has not been explained satisfactory. It is possible though, that Dresden as the capital of Saxony was better known in the Europe of the 18th century than the city of Meissen, some twenty-five kilometres (fifteen miles) away. Furthermore, most of the Meissen products were sold in Dresden, where British importers also conducted their business and might have adopted the name "Dresden" for Meissen porcelain.

In the second half of the 19th century the mistake became a monster. At this time some thirty porcelain decorating shops were established in the city of Dresden, many of them imitating the Meissen decorating style and even elaborating on it, mixing the Meissen and the Vienna styles.

Thus a "Dresden Style" came into being, further contributing to an already existing confusion. Some decorators in Dresden evidently cooperated in creating this "Dresden Style" and chose a common mark for their products. Four decorators, Richard Klemm, Donath & Co., Oswald Lorenz and Adolph Hamann appeared in unison in the City Court in Dresden on February 7th, 1883 at half past five in the afternoon and registered the same mark for all four of them (No. 1209). Ten years later Klemm, Donath & Co. and Hamann adopted slightly different marks (Nos. 1211, 1213 and 1215), Lorenz changed his mark completely (No. 1441) to one closer resembling the Vienna mark. Eight more decorators also used a crown and the name "Dresden."

The manufactory in Meissen registered mark No. 3245 in 1938 and has used it since occasionally. Marks Nos. 1709 and 1711 were occasionally used after 1963 by the Meissen manufactory. Mark No. 1710 was in use after 1966 for a few years.

Royal Dresden China   No. 3245

No. 1709   No. 1710   No. 1711

The name "Dresden" also has been observed or described as being applied on four other genuine Meissen pieces (see Nos. 1673 and 1674) but not as part of the manufactory mark.

Any other piece of porcelain bearing the name "Dresden" in the mark was definitely not made by the Meissen manufactory.

Martha Budich	Martha Budich	
Kronach	Kronach	242
R. & E. Pech	R. & E. Pech	242
Kronach	Kronach	
Franziska Hirsch	Franziska Hirsch	17
Dresden	Dresden	242
Franziska Hirsch	Franziska Hirsch	242
Dresden	Dresden	
unidentified	nicht identifiziert	18
Carl Thieme	Carl Thieme	305
Potschappel	Potschappel	306
Porcelain Factory	Porzellanfabrik	114
Sandizell	Sandizell	
Adolf Wache	Adolf Wache	11
Dresden	Dresden	

Richard Klemm et alia Dresden	Richard Klemm et alia Dresden	1209
Adolph Hamann Dresden	Adolph Hamann Dresden	1210
Donath & Co. Dresden	Donath & Co. Dresden	1211
Adolph Hamann Dresden	Adolph Hamann Dresden	1212
Adolph Hamann Dresden	Adolph Hamann Dresden	1213
Adolph Hamann Dresden	Adolph Hamann Dresden	1214
Richard Klemm Dresden	Richard Klemm Dresden	1215
K. Steinmann Tiefenfurth	K. Steinmann Tiefenfurth	1216
unidentified probably Helena Wolfsohn Dresden	nicht identifiziert wahrscheinlich Helena Wolfsohn Dresden	1217

probably Adolf Wache Dresden	wahrscheinlich Adolf Wache Dresden	12
unidentified	nicht identifiziert	1
Richard Wehsener Dresden	Richard Wehsener Dresden	15
Porcelain Factory Tirschenreuth	Porzellanfabrik Tirschenreuth	11
Schumann China Corporation New York City	Schumann China Corporation New York City	12
Richard Klemm Dresden	Richard Klemm Dresden	11
unidentified	nicht identifiziert	114
unidentified	nicht identifiziert	117

Carl Thieme Potschappel	Carl Thieme Potschappel	344
Franz Junkersdorf Dresden	Franz Junkersdorf Dresden	1464
Franz Junkersdorf Dresden	Franz Junkersdorf Dresden	1479
Heufel & Co. Dresden	Heufel & Co. Dresden	2307
Adolph Hamann Dresden	Adolph Hamann Dresden	647
Karl Eduard Hamann Dresden	Karl Eduard Hamann Dresden	648
Richard Klemm Dresden	Richard Klemm Dresden	649
Bates, Walker & Co. Burslem, England 1875–1878 blue underglaze on earthenware with onion pattern	Bates, Walker & Co. Burslem, England 1875–1878 blau unterglasur auf Steingut mit Zwiebelmuster	3518
Potters Cooperative Co. East Liverpool, Ohio, U. S. A. circa 1892–	Potters Cooperative Co. East Liverpool, Ohio, U. S. A. ca. 1892–	3519

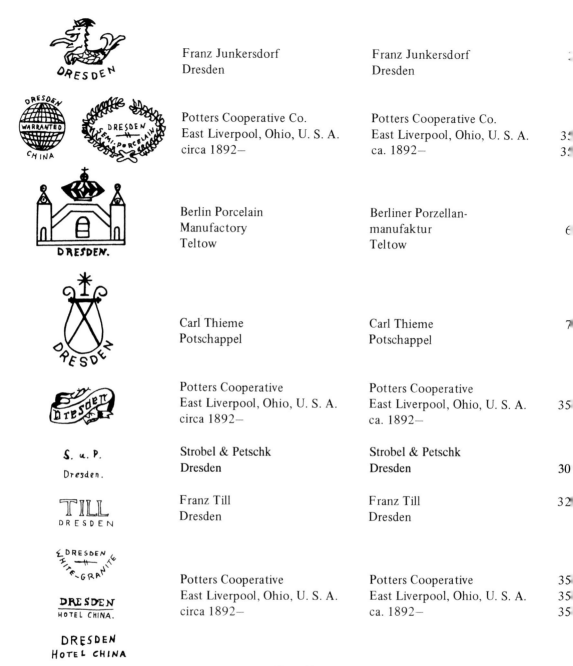

Franz Junkersdorf Dresden	Franz Junkersdorf Dresden	
Potters Cooperative Co. East Liverpool, Ohio, U. S. A. circa 1892–	Potters Cooperative Co. East Liverpool, Ohio, U. S. A. ca. 1892–	3 3
Berlin Porcelain Manufactory Teltow	Berliner Porzellan- manufaktur Teltow	6
Carl Thieme Potschappel	Carl Thieme Potschappel	7
Potters Cooperative East Liverpool, Ohio, U. S. A. circa 1892–	Potters Cooperative East Liverpool, Ohio, U. S. A. ca. 1892–	35
Strobel & Petschk Dresden	Strobel & Petschk Dresden	30
Franz Till Dresden	Franz Till Dresden	32
Potters Cooperative East Liverpool, Ohio, U. S. A. circa 1892–	Potters Cooperative East Liverpool, Ohio, U. S. A. ca. 1892–	35 35 35

"Saxe"

In Frankreich wurde Meißner Porzellan gelegentlich "porcelaine de Saxe" genannt. Einige Hersteller nahmen den Namen "Saxe" oder Variationen in ihre Marken auf.

Die Meißner Manufaktur benutzt nur eine Marke (Nr. 3275) mit dem Namen "Saxe". Sie wird gelegentlich seit 1938 auf Reproduktionen Meißner Porzellans aus dem 18. Jahrhundert angebracht.

Vieux Saxe   Nr. 3275

"Saxe"

In France Meissen porcelain occasionally was called "porcelaine de Saxe". Some manufacturers incorporated the name "Saxe" or variations in their marks.

The Meissen manufactory has only one mark (No. 3275) with the name "Saxe," which is used occasionally since 1938 for reproductions of 18th century Meissen porcelain.

Vieux Saxe   No. 3275

	Ernst Teichert Meissen	Ernst Teichert Meißen	1713
	Hermann Ohme Niedersalzbrunn	Hermann Ohme Niedersalzbrunn	874
	Charles Ahrenfeldt & Son New York City	Charles Ahrenfeldt & Son New York City	778
	Erdmann Schlegelmilch Suhl	Erdmann Schlegelmilch Suhl	1106 1798
	unidentified beehive blue underglaze, Saxony and line red overglaze	nicht identifiziert Bienenkorb blau unterglasur, Saxony und Strich rot aufglasur	3526
	Charles Ahrenfeldt & Son New York City	Charles Ahrenfeldt & Son New York City	1514
	Friedrich Kaestner Oberhohndorf	Friedrich Kaestner Oberhohndorf	843

Wien

Neben den Meißner Marken ist der Wiener Bindenschild (oder heraldisch: Balkenschild) das Opfer völliger Verwirrung (Nr. 1377, Variationen siehe Gruppe 18).

Nr. 1377

Der Bindenschild ist das Herzstück des Wappens der Österreichischen Habsburg-Familie. Die Wiener Manufaktur benutzte ihn von 1744 bis 1864, entweder eingeprägt oder blau unterglasur. Sofort nachdem die Manufaktur 1864 geschlossen wurde, ergriffen eine Anzahl von Porzellanmalern und -herstellern die Gelegenheit, ihre eigenen Erzeugnisse mit Nachahmungen des Bindenschilds zu veredeln. Später verwandten auch deutsche und französische Hersteller Variationen des Bindenschilds.

In den meisten dieser Marken steht der Bindenschild auf dem Kopf und sieht wie ein Bienenkorb aus. Aber fast alle Wiener Originalmarken können so gedreht werden, daß sie wie ein Bienenkorb aussehen. Das hat—besonders in englischsprechenden Ländern—zu der unterschiedslosen Verwendung des Ausdrucks "Bienenkorb" sowohl für echte Wiener Marken als auch für Nachahmungen und Variationen geführt.

Darüberhinaus wurde der Bindenschild von einigen Porzellanherstellern und -malern ausgiebig gefälscht. Diese Stücke mit einer gefälschten Wiener Marke sind überlicherweise üppig mit historischen oder mythologischen Szenen bemalt, oft mit einer Beschreibung der Szene auf dem Boden. Eine ziemlich große Zahl von Urnen, Vasen und besonders Tellern sind mit "Angelica Kauffmann" signiert. Die Malerin Kauffmann (1741–1807) hat jedoch niemals Porzellan bemalt. Gelegentlich wurden Motive aus ihren Bildern auf Porzellan kopiert, aber ihre Signatur ist in jedem Fall gefälscht.

Waltraud Neuwirth, eine ausgezeichnete Expertin für Wiener Porzellan, hat wichtige neue Entdeckungen und Informationen über die Wiener Manufaktur beigetragen. Ihre Arbeiten sind dem ernsthaften Sammler Wiener Porzellans dringend empfohlen. (Siehe Bibliographie Nr. 178, 179, 181, 183, 184).

Neuwirth gibt einige Faustregeln für das Erkennen gefälschten Wiener Porzellans, auf die sich die folgenden Feststellungen zum Teil stützen:

1. Jeder Bindenschild blau auf der Glasur ist eine Fälschung. In der Frühzeit der Manufaktur, ca. 1744–1749, wurde der Schild gelegentlich rot, purpur, schwarz oder gold aufglasur gemalt, aber niemals blau.

2. Jeder Bindenschild, der symmetrisch und gleichmäßig blau unter oder auf der Glasur gestempelt ist, ist keine Marke der Wiener Manufaktur.

3. Wenn eine Inschrift, Signatur oder Buchstaben so angeordnet sind, daß die Marke wie ein Bienenkorb aussieht, ist sie nicht die Marke der Wiener Manufaktur.

4. Alle eingeprägten Zahlen, außer 0–60 (Bossierer und Weißdreher), 84–99 und 800–864 (Jahreszahlen von 1784–1864), sind Anzeichen für eine Fälschung.

5. Buchstaben, Worte oder Farbflecke in gold aufglasur sind Anzeichen für eine Fälschung. Farbflecke verdecken überlicherweise die Marke des Herstellers des Porzellanstücks.

Vienna

Next to the Meissen marks the shield with two bars (Bindenschild or in heraldic German terms: Balkenschild, No. 1377, for variations see group 18) of the manufactory in Vienna is a victim of utter confusion.

No. 1377

The shield was taken from the center of the Coat-of-Arms of the Austrian Hapsburg family. The Vienna manufactory used it impressed or blue underglaze from 1744 until 1864. Immediately after the manufactory was closed in 1864 a number of Austrian and Bohemian porcelain decorators and manufacturers seized upon the opportunity to glorify their own products by applying imitations of the Bindenschild in various shapes. Later German and French manufacturers also used variations of the shield.

In most of these marks the shield is turned upside down, thus looking like a beehive. But by turning around the original marks almost all of them can be made to look like a beehive. This led—especially in English speaking countries—to the indiscriminate use of the term beehive for the genuine Vienna marks as well as for imitations and variations.

In addition the Bindenschild was forged extensively by some manufacturers and decorators. Pieces with forged Vienna marks are usually heavily decorated with mythological or historical scenes, often with a description of the scene on the bottom. Quite a number of urns, vases and especially plates are signed "Angelica Kauffmann." The paintress Kauffmann (1741–1807) is not known to have decorated porcelain at all. Sometimes motifs from her paintings were copied on porcelain, but her signature is always a forgery.

Waltraud Neuwirth, an excellent expert on Vienna porcelain recently has contributed important new discoveries and information about the Vienna manufactory. Her works are highly recommended to serious collectors of Vienna porcelain. (See bibliography Nos. 178, 179, 181, 183, 184).

Neuwirth gives some rules of thumb for the detection of forgeries of Vienna porcelain, on which the following statements are based in part.

1. Any Bindenschild blue overglaze is a forgery. In the early years of the manufactory, circa 1744–1749, the shield occasionally was painted red, purple, black or gold overglaze, but never blue.

2. Any Bindenschild that is stamped blue underglaze or overglaze and shows perfect symmetry and shape is not a mark of the Vienna manufactory.

3. If inscriptions, signatures or letters are arranged in a way that the mark appears as a beehive, it is not the mark of the Vienna manufactory.

4. All impressed number, except 0–60 (moulders and turners), 84–99 and 800–864 (year numbers from 1784–1864) are indications for a forgery.

5. Letters, words or shapes in gold overglaze are indications for forgeries. If a part of the bottom is covered with a golden shape, this shape usually hides the original manufacturers mark.

6. Jede Zahl über 155, die farbig aufglasur aufgetragen ist, ist nicht die Identifikationsnummer eines Malers der Wiener Manufaktur.

7. Jede Zahl über 27 blau unterglasur ist nicht die Marke eines Malers der Wiener Manufaktur.

8. Jede Szenenbeschreibung auf der Unterseite eines bemalten Stücks ist ein Anzeichen dafür, daß dies Stück nicht in der Wiener Manufaktur bemalt worden ist.

Die originalen Wiener Marken und die ihr ähnlich sehenden Marken einschließlich der Bienenkörbe können in Gruppe 18 gefunden werden, sie sind hier nicht wiederholt. Ähnlich aussehende Marken ausländischer Hersteller und aus anderen Gruppen folgen hier.

Bourdois & Bloch Paris, Frankreich rue de la Pierre-Levée ca. 1900– blau unterglasur	3527	
Wiener Porzellan- fabrik Augarten Wien	605 675 676	
Wiener Porzellan- fabrik Augarten Wien	677 678	
Ernst Wahliss Turn-Teplitz	679	
Unger & Schilde Roschutz	718	

576

6. Any number over 155 painted in color overglaze is not an identification number of a decorator of the Vienna manufactory.

7. Any number over 27 blue underglaze is not the number of a decorator of the Vienna manufactory.

8. Any bottom description of a decoration or a scene indicates that the piece was not decorated in the Vienna manufactory.

The original Vienna marks and similar looking marks including beehives can be found in group 18, they are not repeated here. Similar looking marks by foreign manufacturers and from other groups are listed below.

Bourdois & Bloch Paris, France rue de la Pierre-Levée circa 1900– blue underglaze		3527
Vienna Porcelain		605
Factory Augarten		675
Vienna		676
Vienna Porcelain Factory Augarten Vienna		677 678
Ernst Wahliss Turn-Teplitz		679
Unger & Schilde Roschutz		718

Edmé Samson
Paris, France
rue Béranger
circa 1845–1905
blue underglaze or
overglaze
see No. 3432

Edmé Samson
Paris, Frankreich
rue Béranger
ca. 1845–1905
blau unterglasur
oder aufglasur
siehe Nr. 3432

35

Arnart Imports
New York City, U. S. A.
1957–
importer's mark

Arnart Imports
New York City, U. S. A.
1957–
Importeurmarke

35

unidentified
beehive blue underglaze
Saxony and line red overglaze

nicht identifiziert
Bienenkorb blau unterglasur,
Saxony und Strich rot aufglasur

35

Berlin Porcelain Manufactory
Teltow

Berliner Porzellanmanufaktur
Teltow

6

Carl Thieme
Potschappel

Carl Thieme
Potschappel

3

Vienna Art Ceramic Factory
Vienna

Wiener Kunstkeramikfabrik
Wien

343

Vienna Art Ceramic Workshop
Vienna

Wiener Kunstkeramische Werkstätte 342
Wien

Wachtersbach Earthenware
Factory
Schlierbach

Wächtersbacher Steingut-
fabrik
Schlierbach

735

Wachtersbach Earthenware
Factory
Schlierbach

Wächtersbacher Steingut-
fabrik
Schlierbach

686

Wachtersbach Earthenware
Factory
Schlierbach

Wächtersbacher Steingut-
fabrik
Schlierbach

684

Wachtersbach Earthenware
Factory
Schlierbach

Wächtersbacher Steingut-
fabrik
Schlierbach

685

Capo di Monte

Der Buchstabe N unter einer Krone wird oft der Manufaktur in Capo di Monte zugeschrieben. Diese Manufaktur wurde vom König beider Sizilien, Karl III, 1743 gegründet und 1759 nach Buen Retiro in Spanien verlegt, als Karl König von Spanien wurde. Viele Erzeugnisse Capo di Montes sind nicht markiert, andere tragen die Lilie blau unterglasur. Typisch für Capo di Monte war eine farbenfreudige Reliefdekoration.

No. 3527   No. 3528   No. 3529

Karls Sohn, Ferdinand IV ordnete 1771 an, die Manufaktur neu zu errichten. Von 1771 bis 1773 war sie in Portici, anschliessend wurde sie nach Neapel verlegt. Das gekrönte N war die Marke dieser Manufaktur und nicht die Capo di Montes.

Die folgenden Marken sind für die Manufaktur in Neapel bestätigt.

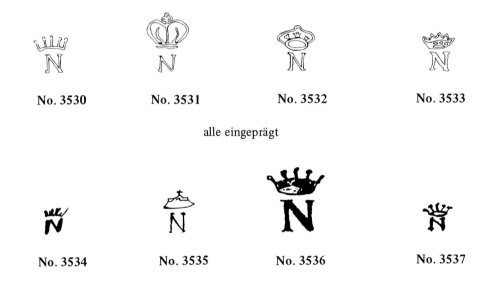

No. 3530   No. 3531   No. 3532   No. 3533

alle eingeprägt

No. 3534   No. 3535   No. 3536   No. 3537

alle blau unterglasur

Gelegentlich erscheinen Marken auch rot aufglasur.

Um 1821 stellte die Manufaktur ihre Arbeit ein und viele ihrer Formen und Modelle wurden von der Manufaktur Ginori (1737–heute) in Doccia bei Florenz erworben. Ginori stellte eine große Zahl von Capo di Monte- und Neapel-Reproduktionen her, hauptsächlich Stücke mit Reliefdekoration. Für diese Reproduktionen benutzte Ginori die alte Neapel-Marke.

Capo di Monte

The letter N surmounted by a crown very often is attributed to the manufactory in Capo di Monte near Naples, Italy. This manufactory was founded by King Charles III of both Sicilies in 1743 and moved to Buen Retiro, Spain, when Charles became King of Spain in 1759. Many products of Capo di Monte are not marked, others bear the fleur-de-lis in blue underglaze (Nos. 3527–3529). Typical for Capo di Monte was a colorful relief decoration.

No. 3527　　　　　　No. 3528　　　　　　No. 3529

Charles' son, Ferdinand IV in 1771 decreed that a porcelain manufactory should be newly established. From 1771 until 1773 it was located in Portici, Italy and then moved to Naples. This factory and not Capo di Monte used a crowned letter N as its mark. The following marks are verified for the manufactory in Naples.

No. 3530　　　　No. 3531　　　　　No. 3532　　　　　No. 3533

All impressed.

No. 3534　　　　No. 3535　　　　　No. 3536　　　　　No. 3537

All blue underglaze.

Occasionally marks also appear red overglaze.

About 1821 the manufactory in Naples was closed and many of its moulds and models were acquired by the manufactory of Ginori (1713–present) in Doccia near Florence, Italy. Ginori turned out a large number of Capo di Monte and Naples reproductions, mainly pieces with relief decoration. For these reproductions Ginori used the old Naples mark.

| Nr. 3538 | Nr. 3539 | Nr. 3540 | Nr. 3541 |

Diese Marken erscheinen blau unter- oder aufglasur.

Da die Ginori-Reproduktionen sich gut verkauften, stellten einige deutsche Manufakturen auch Porzellan mit Reliefdekoration her und brachten als Marke ein gekröntes N an, andere Firmen benutzten diese Marke für Figuren und dekoratives Porzellan.

Carl Thieme Potschappel	1072
Ernst Bohne Söhne Rudolstadt	1067 1068
Ernst Bohne Söhne Rudolstadt	1069 1070
Porzellanfabrik Sandizell	1071 1145
Carl Thieme Potschappel	1147
Franz Neukirchner Waldershof	1146

No. 3538   No. 3539   No. 3540   No. 3541

These marks appear blue underglaze or overglaze.

Because the Ginori reproductions sold very fast, some German manufacturers also produced porcelain with relief decoration and applied as mark a crowned letter N. Other German companies used this mark for figurines and decorative porcelain.

	Carl Thieme Potschappel	1072
	Ernst Bohne Sons Rudolstadt	1067 1068
	Ernst Bohne Sons Rudolstadt	1069 1070
	Porcelain Factory Sandizell	1071 1145
	Carl Thieme Potschappel	1147
	Franz Neukirchner Waldershof	1146

Name Index

Namensindex

In order to avoid unneccessary repetitions not all of the English versions of factory names are listed in this index. If the German name and the English version are close enough, only the German name is given.

-For Bros. see under Gerb.

-For Count see Graf.

-For Porcelain Factory see under Porzellanfabrik.

-For Porcelain Manufactory see under Porzellanmanufaktur.

-For Porcelainwork see under Porzellanwerk.

-For Porcelain Combine see under Porzellankombinat.

A

Ackermann & Fritze, 387, 494

Adler, Woldemar, 380

Adolf zu Ysenburg und Büdingen, Count/ Graf, 473

(Acker)

Acker, Lorenz Christoph, 377

Aelteste Volkstedter Porzellanfabrik, 452, 460, 467, 492-494

Aelteste Volkstedter Porzellanmanufaktur, 494, 495

AG Porzellanfabrik Rudolstadt, 469

Ahrenfeldt & Son, Charles, 373, 454, 455

Aigner, Philip, 501

Alberti, Carl, 491

Alboth, August, 484

Alboth, Ernst, 484

Alboth & Kaiser, 416, 484

Alexandra Porcelain Works, 491, 504

(Alka-Art)

Alka-Kunst, 484

"Alp" Porzellanfabrik, 440

Alt, Beck & Gottschalck, 451, 454

(Altrohlau Porcelain Factories)

Altrohlauer Porzellanfabriken, 373

Alt-Wiener Porzellanmalerei, 502

Amphora Porzellanfabrik, 489, 490

Anger, A. Carl, 371

Anna Perenna Inc., 454

(Annaburg Earthenware Factory)

Annaburg Porcelain, 375

Annaburger Steingutfabrik, 375

Anton Weidl KG, 379

Apel, Arno, 397, 437, 440

Arnart Imports, 578

Arnold, Max Oscar, 453

Arnoldi, C.E. & F., 400, 416

Arnstadt, 376

(Art Institute for Porcelain Decorating)

Artistisches Atelier für Porzellanmalerei, 501

Association of German Porcelain Factories, 383

August II, King/König, 446

August III, King/König, 446

August der Starke, 446

August Heissner Successor/Nachfolger, 411

August von Gotha, 409

Augustus the Strong, 446

Auliczek, Dominicus, 465

Aurnhammer, A. & Reinhardt, F., 386

Austrian Ceramic, 505

Austrian Porcelain Factories Mildeneichen and Raspenau, 449

Austrian Sanitary Ceramic and Porcelain Industry, 505

Auvera, Carl, 377

B

Bachmann, Oswald, 399

Baehr & Proeschild, 459

Baensch, Heinrich, 438

Balle, Ignatz, 472

Bantz, Eduard, 427

Baratta Dragano, Alois, 501

Baratta Dragano. Dr. Norbert, 501

Bareuther, Oskar, 498

Bareuther & Co., 498

Baron von Sorgenthal, 502

Baron von Springer, 391

Bibliography

Bibliographie

Literature in English/Literatur in Englisch

1. Ade Boger, L. *The Dictionary of World Pottery and Porcelain.* New York, 1961.

2. Angione, G. *All Bisque and Half-Bisque Dolls.* Nashville, 1969.

3. Angus-Butterworth, L. M. *Pottery and Porcelain.* London and Glasgow, 1964.

4. Atterbury, P., Editor/Herausgeber. *English Pottery and Porcelain.* New York, 1978.

5. Bachmann, M. and Hansmann, Cl. *Dolls the Wide World Over.* New York, 1973.

6. Barber, E. A. *Pottery and Porcelain of the United States.* Watkins Glen/New York, 1971.

7. Barret, F. A. *Worcester Porcelain.* New York, n. d./o. J.

8. Berling, K., Editor/Herausgeber. *Meissen China, An Illustrated History.* New York, 1972. (republication/Nachdruck)

9. Blacker, J. F. *ABC of Collecting Old Continental Pottery.* Philadelphia, n. d./o. J.

10. Blunt, E., Editor/Herausgeber. *Meissen and Oriental Porcelain.* The James A. de Rothschild Collection at Waddesdon Manor, Friburg, 1971.

11. Brayshaw Gilhespy, F. *Derby Porcelain.* London, 1965.

12. Brayshaw Gilhespy. F. and Budd D. M. *Royal Crown Derby China.* London, 1964.

13. Buton, D. *Wedgwood Guide to Marks and Dating.* Merion, 1976.

14. Caplan, H. H. *The Classified Directory of Artists Signatures, Symbols & Monograms.* London, 1976.

15. Chaffers, W. *Marks and Monograms on European and Oriental Pottery and Porcelain.* London, 1863 and 14 subsequent editions, last 1965.

16. Charles, R. L. *Continental Porcelain of the Eighteenth Century.* London, 1964.

17. Coleman, E. A. *Dolls Makers and Marks.* Washington D. C., 1974.

18. Coleman, D. S., Editor/Herausgeber. "My Darling Dolls." Princeton, 1972.

19. Coleman, D. S.,E. A., E. J. *The Collector's Encyclopedia of Dolls.* New York, 1968.

20. Cox, W. E. *The Book of Pottery and Porcelain.* New York, 1973.

21. Cushion, J. P. *Animals in Pottery and Porcelain.* New York, 1974.

22. Cushion, J. P. *Pocket Book of English Ceramic Marks and those of Wales, Scotland and Ireland.* London, 1959.

23. Cushion, J. P. *Pocket Book of French and Italian Ceramic Marks.* Boston, 1965.

24. Cushion, J. P. *Pocket Book of German Ceramic Marks and those of other Central European Countries.* London, 1961.

25. Cushion, J. *Porcelain.* London, 1975.

26. Cushion, J. P. and Honey, W. B. *Handbook of Pottery and Porcelain Marks.* New York, n. d./o. J.

27. Ducret, S. *German Porcelain and Faience.* New York, 1962, English edition of No. 128/englische Ausgabe von Nr. 128.

28. Durdik, J., e. a. *The Pictorial Encyclopedia of Antiques.* London, 1970.

29. Eberlein, H. D. and Ramsdell, R. G. *The Practical Book of Chinaware.* Philadelphia/New York, 1948.

30. Ehrmann, E. *Hummel, the Complete Collector's Guide and Illustrated Reference.* Huntington/New York, 1976.

31. Fenwick, P. E. *Mettlach Steins.* Lee, 1974.

32. Fisher, S. W. *British Pottery and Porcelain.* New York, 1963.

33. Fisher, S. W. *Fine Porcelain & Pottery.* London, 1975.

34. Fisher, S. W. *The Decoration of English Porcelain.* London, 1954.

35. Fisher, S. W. *Worcester Porcelain.* London, n. d./o. J.

36. Gardner, P. V. *Meissen and other German Porcelain in the Alfred Duane Pell Collection.* Washington D. C., 1956.

37. Gibb, W. and Rackham, B. *A Book of Porcelain.* London, 1910.

38. Godden, G. A. *An Illustrated Encyclopedia of British Pottery and Porcelain.* New York, 1965.

39. Godden, G. A. *British Porcelain.* New York, 1974.

40. Godden, G. A. *Encyclopedia of British Pottery and Porcelain Marks.* New York, 1964.

41. Godden, G. A. *Minton, Pottery & Porcelain of the First Period.* New York/Washington, 1968.

42. Godden, G. A. *The Handbook of British Pottery & Porcelain Marks.* New York/Washington, 1968.

43. Haggar, R. G. *The Concise Encyclopedia of Continental Pottery and Porcelain.* New York, 1960.

44. Hake, T. and Russel, E. W. *The Plate Collectors Handbook.* New York, n. d./o. J.

45. Hall, J. *Staffordshire Portrait Figures.* New York, 1972.

46. Hammond, D. *Mustache Cups.* Des Moines, 1972.

47. Hannover, E. *Pottery & Porcelain, A Handbook for Collectors.* London, 1925.

48. Hartmann, H. *Porcelain & Pottery Marks.* New York, 1943, reprint of No. 49 under different name/Nachdruck von R. 49 unter anderem Namen.

49. Hartmann, U. *Porcelain & Pottery Marks.* New York, 1942.

50. Haslam, M. *Pottery.* London, 1972.

51. Hayward, H., Editor/Herausgeber. *The Connoisseur's Handbook of Antique Collection.* New York, 1960.

52. Hayward, J. F. *Viennese Porcelain of the Du Paquier Period.* London, 1952.

53. Honey, W. B. *Dresden China.* London, 1934.

54. Honey, W. B. *English Pottery and Porcelain.* London, 1947.

55. Honey, W. B. *European Ceramic Art from the End of the Middle Ages to about 1815.* London, 1952.

56. Honey, W. B. *German Porcelain.* London, 1954.

57. Honey, W. B. *Old English Porcelain.* New York/London/Toronto, 1946.

58. Hotchkiss, J. F. *Hummel Art.* Des Moines, 1978.

59. Hughes, G. B. *The Collector's Book of China.* New York, 1966.

60. Jervis, W. P. *European China.* Watkins Glen, 1953. (re-issue of Jervis: *Rough Notes on Pottery, 1896*/Nachdruck von Jervis: *Rough Notes on Pottery, 1896*)

61. Klamkin, M. *Made in Occupied Japan.* New York, 1976.

62. Klamkin, M. *White House China.* New York, 1972.

63. Kovel, R. M. and R. H. *Dictionary of Marks–Pottery and Porcelain.* New York, 1953 and 23 subsequent printings/und 23 folgende Ausgaben.

64. Lane, A. *French Faience.* New York/Washington, 1970.

65. Litchfield, F. *Pottery and Porcelain.* London, 1912.

66. Macdonald-Taylor, M. *A Dictionary of Marks.* New York, 1962.

67. No name/N. N. *Authentic "M. J. Hummel" Figurines.* Rödental, 1977.

68. No name/N. N. *Hand Book for the Use of Visitors examining Pottery and Porcelain in the Metropolitan Museum of Art.* New York, 1875.

69. No name/N. N. *Royal Doulton Figures.* Burslem/Stoke on Trent, 1965.

70. No name/N. N. *The Standard Antique Doll Identification & Value Guide.* Paducah, 1976.

71. Ormsbee, T. H. *English China and its Marks.* London, 1959.

72. Paul, E. and Petersen, A. *Collectors Handbook to Marks on Porcelain and Pottery.* Greens Farms, 1974.

73. Penkala, M. *European Porcelain.* Amsterdam, 1947.

74. Poche, E. *Porcelain Marks of the World.* New York, 1974. (English edition of No. 198)

75. Rackham, B. *Catalogue of the Schreiber Collection, Vol. I–Porcelain.* London, 1928.

76. Ray, M. *Collectible Ceramics.* New York, 1974.

77. Revi, A. C., Editor/Herausgeber. *Spinning Wheel's Complete Book of Antiques.* New York, 1972.

78. Revi, A. C., Editor/Herausgeber. *Spinning Wheel's Complete Book of Dolls.* New York, 1975.

79. Ross, M. C. *Russian Porcelain.* Norman, 1968.

80. Rust, G. A. *Collector's Guide to Antique Porcelain.* New York, 1973.

81. Salley, V. S. and Salley, G. H. *Royal Bayreuth China.* 1969.

82. Savage, G. *18th Century English Porcelain.* London, 1964.

83. Savage, G. *18th Century German Porcelain.* London, 1958.

84. Savage, G. *Seventeenth and Eighteenth Century French Porcelain.*

85. Schlegelmilch, C. J. *R. S. Prussia, Handbook of Erdmann and Reinhold Schlegel-milch Prussia-Germany and Oscar Schlegelmilch Germany Porcelain Marks.* Flint, 1973.

86. Shea, R. A. *Doll Mark Clues.* Ridgefield, 1972.

87. Smith, P. R. *Antique Collector's Dolls.* Paducah, 1975.

88. Smith, P. R. *Armand Marseille Dolls.* Paducah, 1976.

89. Smith, P. R. *Kestner and Simon & Halbig Dolls.* Paducah, 1976.

90. Stitt, J. *Japanese Ceramics of the last 100 Years.* New York, 1976.

91. Stoner, F. *Chelsea, Bow and Derby Porcelain Figures.* Newport, 1955.

92. Thorn, C. J. *Handbook of Old Pottery and Porcelain Marks.* New York, 1947.

93. Tiffany & Co. *Notes on Pottery, Hints to Lovers of Ceramics.* New York, 1901–1903.

94. Twitchett, J. and Baily, B. *Royal Crown Derby.* New York, 1976.

95. Ware, G. W. *German and Austrian Porcelain.* New York, 1963.

96. Weiss, G. *The Book of Porcelain.* New York/Washington, 1971. (English version of No. 214)

97. Wynter, H. *An Introduction to European Porcelain.* New York, 1972.

98. Yates, R. F. *Antique Fakes and their Detection.* New York, 1960.

Periodicals and Directories/Zeitschriften und Adreßbücher

99. *Antique Monthly.* Tuscaloosa, Ala., U. S. A., current/laufend.

100. *Antiques World.* New York, current/laufend.

101. *Crockery and Glass Journal, Directory Issue.* New York, 1951, 1959, 1961.

102. *Crockery Dealer's Yearbook.* New York, 1900, 1910–1913.

103. *German China, Pottery and Glass.* Bamberg, 1954.

104. *Official Gazette.* United States Patent and Trademark Office, Washington D. C., current/laufend.

105. *Pottery and Glass Directory.* New York, 1927.

106. *Pottery Gazette and Glass Trade Review Reference Book.* London, 1970.

107. *Spinning Wheel.* Hanover, Pa., U. S. A., current/laufend.

Literature in German/Literatur in Deutsch

108. Albiker, C. *Die Meissner Porzellantiere im 18. Jahrhundert.* Berlin, 1935.

109. Auinger, H. *Meissner Porzellanmarken.* Dresden, 1909.

110. Autorenkollektiv. *Die Volkswirtschaft der DDR.* Berlin, 1960.

111. Balet, L. *Ludwigsburger Porzellan.* Stuttgart/Leipzig, 1911.

112. Bangert, A., Editor/Herausgeber. *Antiquitäten-Porzellan.* München, 1977.

113. Bayer, A. *Ansbacher Porzellan.* Braunschweig, 1959.

114. Behse, A. *Porzellanmarken-Brevier.* Braunschweig, 1974.

115. Berling, K. *Das Meissner Porzellan und seine Geschichte.* Leipzig, 1900.

116. Berling, K. *Festschrift der Königlich Sächsischen Porzellanmanufaktur Meißen.* Dresden, 1911.

117. Biedrzynski, E. *Bruckmann's Porzellan Lexikon, 2 Bde.* München, 1979.

118. Böhm, L. W. *Frankenthaler Porzellan.* Mannheim, 1960.

119. Braun, E. W. Ein keramischer Reisebericht aus dem Jahre 1812 über die drei deutsch-böhmischen Porzellanfabriken zu Pirkenhammer, Schlaggenwald und Gießhübel, in: *Mitteilungen des Vereins für Geschichte der Deutschen in Böhmen, 53. Jahrgang.* Prag, 1915.

120. Bröhan, K. H. *Kunst der Jahrhundertwende und der zwanziger Jahre, Sammlung Karl H. Bröhan–Band II, Teil 2 (volume II, part 2).* Berlin, 1977.

121. Brüning, A. *Porzellan.* Berlin, 1907.

122. Csany, K. *Geschichte der Ungarischen Keramik, des Porzellans und Ihrer Marken.* Budapest, 1954.

123. Danckert, L. *Handbuch des Europäischen Porzellans.* München, 1954, since then four editions, last 1978/seitdem vier Ausgaben, die letzte 1978.

124. Dees, O. *Die Geschichte der Porzellanfabriken zu Tettau.* Saalfeld, 1921.

125. Doenges, W. *Meissner Porzellan Seine Geschichte und Künstlerische Entwicklung.* Berlin, 1907.

126. Döry, L. von. *Höchster Porzellan.* Frankfurt/Main, 1963.

127. Ducret, S. *Die Landgräfliche Porzellanmanufaktur Kassel.* Braunschweig, 1960.

128. Ducret, S. *Deutsches Porzellan und Deutsche Fayencen, mit Wien, Zürich und Nyon.* Fribourg, 1962.

129. Ducret, S. *Meissner Porzellan.* Bern, 1974.

130. Ducret, S. *Meißner Porzellan bemalt in Augsburg.* Braunschweig, 1971/1972, 2 volumes/2 Bände.

131. Ducret, S. *Würzburger Porzellan des 18. Jahrhunderts.* Braunschweig, 1968.

132. Ducret, S. und Wolgensinger, M. *Porzellan der europäischen Manufakturen im 18. Jahrhundert.* Zürich, 1971.

133. Dürr, H., Editor/Herausgeber. *Antiquitäten und ihre Preise.* München, 1973.

134. Ehret, G. *Porzellan.* München, 1979.

135. Erichsen-Firle, U. *Figürliches Porzellan.* Köln, 1975.

136. Esser, K. H. und Reber, H. *Höchster Fayencen und Porzellane.* Mainz, 1964.

137. Esser, K. H. und Schmidt-Glassner, H. *Höchster Porzellan.* Königstein, n. d./o. J.

138. Falke, O. von. *Deutsche Porzellanfiguren.* Berlin, 1919.

139. Fillmann, A. *Die Kartelle und Konzerne in der deutschen Porzellanindustrie, in: Weltwirtschaftliches Archiv, 21. Band (1925 I).* Jena, 1925.

140. Fischer, C. *Die Zeller Porzellanindustrie.* Zell, 1907.

141. Fisher, S. W. *Porzellan und Steingut in Farbe.* München, 1976.

142. Folnesics, J. und Braun, E. W. *Geschichte der K. K. Wiener Porzellanmanufaktur.* Wien, 1907.

143. Frensch, H. und L. *Wächtersbacher Steingut.* Königstein, 1978.

144. Graesse, J. G. Th. *Führer für Sammler von Porzellan und Fayence.* Braunschweig, 1974, 23rd edition/23. Auflage.

145. Graul, R. und Kurzwelly, A. *Altthüringer Porzellan.* Leipzig, 1909.

146. Gutmann, K. F. *Die Kunsttöpferei des 18. Jahrhunderts im Großherzogtum Baden,* Freiburg, 1968 (reprint of the 1906 edition/Nachdruck der Ausgabe von 1906)

147. Henke, G. *Die Rolle der Sowjetunion beim Aufbau der sozialistischen Wirtschaft der DDR, in: Wirtschaftswissenschaft, 4.* Sonderheft, 1957.

148. Heuschkel, H. und Muche, K. *ABC Keramik.* Leipzig, 1975.

149. Heuser, E. *Die Pfalz-Zweibrücker Porzellanmanufaktur.* Neustadt, 1907.

150. Heuser, E. *Porzellan von Straßburg und Frankenthal.* Neustadt, 1922.

151. Höchster Porzellanmanufaktur. *Höchster Porzellan.* Höchst, n. d./o. J.

152. Hofmann, F. H. *Das Europäische Porzellan des Bayer. Nationalmuseums.* München, 1908.

153. Hofmann, F. H. *Das Porzellan der Europ.* Manufakturen im 18. Jahrhundert, Berlin, 1932.

154. Hofmann, F. H. *Frankenthaler Porzellan.* München, 1911.

155. Hofmann, F. H. *Geschichte der Bayer. Porzellanmanufaktur Nymphenburg,* Leipzig, 1922.

156. Hutschenreuther AG. *Schönwald 1879–1979. Das Buch vom Hotelporzellan,* 1979.

157. Jedding, H. *Europäisches Porzellan, Band I.* München, 1974.

158. Jedding, H. *Meißner Porzellan des 18. Jahrhunderts.* München, 1979.

159. Jedding, H. Editor/Herausgeber. *Porzellan aus der Sammlung Blohm.* Hamburg, 1968.

160. Josten, H. H. *Fuldaer Porzellanfiguren.* Berlin, 1929.

161. Keramische Zeitschrift. *Handbuch der Keramik* Freiburg. Current/laufend.

162. Klein, A. *Deutsche Fayencen.* Braunschweig, 1975.

163. Köllmann, E. *Berliner Porzellan.* Braunschweig, 1966. 2 volumes/2 Bände.

164. Köllmann, E. *Meißner Porzellan.* Braunschweig, 1975.

165. Kolbe, G. *Geschichte der Königlichen Porzellanmanufaktur zu Berlin.* Berlin, 1863.

166. Kronberger-Frentzen, H. *Altes Bildergeschirr.* Tübingen, 1964.

167. Lahnstein, P. und Landenberger, M. *Das Ludwigsburger Porzellan und seine Zeit.* Stuttgart, 1978.

168. Liese, G. *Der Einfluß der amerikanischen Porzellanzölle auf den deutschen Haushaltporzellanexport nach den Vereinigten Staaten von Amerika, Inaugural-Dissertation.* München, 1954.

169. Markgräflich Badische Sammlung, Editor/Herausgeber. *Zähringer Museum Baden-Baden.* Baden-Baden, circa 1960.

170. Meyer, H. *Böhmisches Porzellan und Steingut.* Leipzig, 1927.

171. Mickenhagen, R. *Europäisches Porzellan.* München, n. d./o. J. (in English and German/in Englisch und Deutsch).

172. Morley-Fletcher. *Porzellan aus Meissen.* Wiesbaden, 1971.

173. Mrazek, W. und Neuwirth, W. *Wiener Porzellan.* Wien, n. d./o. J.

174. Museum Folkwang Essen/Staatl. Museen Preußischer Kulturbesitz Berlin. *Fälschung und Forschung.* Essen/Berlin, 1976.

175. *Nachweisung der im Deutschen Reiche gesetzlich geschützten Warenzeichen.* Berlin, 1886 ff, 3 Hauptbände, 8 Ergänzungsbände/3 main volumes, 8 supplement volumes.

176. Neuburger, A. *Echt oder Fälschung?* Leipzig, 1978 (reprint of the 1924 edition/Neudruck der Ausgabe von 1924).

177. Neuwirth, W. *Markenlexikon für Kunstgewerbe, Band 2 Keramik.* Wien, 1978 (in German, English and French/in Deutsch, Englisch und Französisch).

178. Neuwirth, W. *Markenlexikon für Kunstgewerbe, Band 4 Wiener Porzellan.* Wien, 1978 (in German, English and French/in Deutsch, Englisch und Französisch).

179. Neuwirth, W. *Meissner Marken und Wiener Bindenschild, Original, Imitation, Verfälschung, Fälschung.* Wien, 1977.

180. Neuwirth, W. *Österreichische Keramik des Jugendstils.* München, 1974.

181. Neuwirth, W. *Porzellan aus Wien.* Wien, 1974.

182. Neuwirth, W. *Porzellanmaler-Lexikon.* Braunschweig, 1977. 2 volumes/2 Bände.

183. Neuwirth, W. *Wiener Keramik.* Braunschweig, 1974.

184. Neuwirth, W. *Wiener Porzellan.* Wien, 1979.

185. Newman, M. *Die deutschen Porzellan-Manufakturen im 18. Jahrhundert.* Braunschweig, 1977. 2 volumes/2 Bände.

186. N. N./no name. *50 Jahre Christian Seltmann.* Weiden, 1960.

187. N. N./no name. *Hutschenreuther AG.* Selb, n. d./o. J.

188. N. N./no name. *VEB Henneberg Porzellan Ilmenau.* Ilmenau, 1977.

189. N. N./no name. *VEB Staatliche Porzellan-Manufaktur Meissen.* Meissen, 1961.

190. N. N./no name. *250 Jahre Staatliche Porzellan-Manufaktur Meissen.* Meissen, 1960.

191. Otruba, G. *Vom Steingut zum Porzellan in Nieder-Österreich.* Wien, 1966.

192. Pazaurek, G. E. *Marken der älteren Porzellan- und Steingutfabriken Böhmens.* Reichenberg, 1905.

193. Pazaurek, G. E. *Nordböhmisches Gewerbemuseum.* Reichenberg, 1905.

194. Pelichet, E. und Duperrex, M. *Jugendstil Keramik.* Lausanne, 1976.

195. Pelka, O. *Keramik der Neuzeit.* Leipzig, 1924.

196. Pfeiffer, K. *Zusammenhänge zwischen Konjunktur und Arbeitsmarkt in der deutschen Feinkeramik, unter besonderer Berücksichtigung ihres sächsischen Zweiges.* Leipzig, 1930.

197. Poche, E. *Böhmisches Porzellan.* Prag, 1956.

198. Poche, E. *Porzellanmarken aus aller Welt.* Prag, 1975.

199. Reineking von Bock, G. *Meister der Deutschen Keramik 1900 bis 1950.* Köln, 1978.

200. Rückert, R. *Meißner Porzellan 1710–1810.* München, 1966.

201. Rückert, R. und Willsberger, J. *Meissen, Porzellan des 18. Jahrhunderts.* Wien, 1977.

202. Scherf, H. *Alt-Thüringer Porzellan.* Leipzig, 1969.

203. Schnorr v. Carolsfeld/Köllmann. *Porzellan.* Braunschweig, 1974. 2 volumes/ 2 Bände.

204. Seling, H., Editor/Herausgeber. *Keysers Kunst- und Antiquitätenbuch.* Heidelberg, 1974.

205. Slokar, J. *Geschichte der österreichischen Industrie und ihre Förderung unter Kaiser Franz I.* Wien, 1914.

206. Spiegl, W. *Meissner Porzellan.* München, 1978.

207. Stenger, E. *Die Steingutfabrik Damm bei Aschaffenburg.* Aschaffenburg, 1949.

208. Stieda, W. *Die Anfänge der Porzellanfabrikation auf dem Thüringerwalde.* Jena, 1902.

209. Stieda, W. *Die keramische Industrie in Bayern während des 18. Jahrhunderts.* Leipzig, 1906.

210. Streckfuß, A. *500 Jahre Berliner Geschichte.* Berlin, 1900.

211. Tasnadi-Marik, K. *Wiener Porzellan.* Budapest, 1975.

212. Thomas, Th. *Villeroy & Boch Keramik vom Barock bis zur Neuen Sachlichkeit.* 1976.

213. Treskow, I. von. *Die Jugendstil-Porzellane der KPM.* München, 1971.

214. Tröml, W. *Kartell und Preisbildung in der deutschen Geschirr- und Luxusporzellanindustrie, in: Abhandlungen des wirtschaftswissenschaftlichen Seminars zu Jena, 17. Band, Drittes Heft.* Jena, 1926.

215. Verein der keramischen Industrie e. V. *Porzellan aus Deutschland.* Marktredwitz, n. d./o. J.

216. Walcha, O. *Meißner Porzellan.* Dresden, 1973.

217. Weber, F. J. *Die Kunst das ächte Porzellan zu verfertigen.* Hildesheim, 1977. (reprint of the edition of 1798/Nachdruck der Ausgabe von 1798).

218. Weber, G. *Kostbares Porzellan.* München, 1977.

219. Weber, G. *Entstehung der Porzellan- und Steingutfabriken in Böhmen, in: Beiträge zur Geschichte der deutschen Industrie in Böhmen.* Prag, 1894.

220. Weiß, G. *Ullstein Porzellanbuch.* Berlin, 1975.

221. Wolff Metternich, B. von. *Fürstenberg Porzellan.* Braunschweig, 1976.

222. Württembergisches Landesmuseum. *Alt-Ludwigsburger Porzellan.* Stuttgart, 1959.

223. Zick, G. *Berliner Porzellan der Manufaktur von Wilhelm Caspar Wegely 1751–1757.* Berlin, 1978.

224. Zimmermann, E. *Die Erfindung und Frühzeit des Meissner Porzellans.* Berlin, 1908.

Periodicals and Directories/Zeitschriften und Adreßbücher

225. *Amtliches Aussteller Verzeichnis der Leipziger Messe* (auch unter folgenden Namen: *Amtliches Leipziger Mess-Adreßbuch, Amtlicher Führer durch die Reichsmesse Leipzig, Amtlicher Führer durch die Leipziger Messe, Messekatalog Leipziger Messe, Leipziger Messe Katalog, Katalog der Leipziger Jubiläumsmesse, Katalog der Leipziger Frühjahrsmesse, Katalog der Leipziger Herbstmesse, Messekatalog Leipziger Herbstmesse, Messekatalog Leipziger Frühjahrsmesse*). Leipzig, 138 Ausgaben/138 editions.

226. *Adreßbuch der Export-Industrie.* Leipzig, 1884.

227. *Adreßbuch der Groß-Industrie, des Groß- und Export-Handels des Deutschen Reiches, Band I.* Halle, 1905/06.

228. *Adreßbuch der Keram-Industrie, Europäisches Keramadreßbuch.* Coburg seit 1883/ since 1883.

229. *Adreßbuch der Sächsisch-Thüringischen Industrie.* Dresden, 1911.

230. *Deutschland liefert.* Darmstadt, 21 editions current/21 Ausgaben laufend.

231. *Die Kunst und das schöne Heim.* München, current/laufend.

232. *Einkauf, Glas, Porzellan, Keramik.* Neuss/Rhein, 1969-current/1969-laufend.

233. *Generalmarkenübersicht.* Wien, 1890–1904.

234. *Handbuch der Tschechoslowakischen Wirtschaft.* Berlin, 1931.

235. *Keramische Zeitschrift.* Freiburg, 1948-current/1948-laufend.

236. *KGE-Adreßbuch für Keramik, Glas, Email.* Berlin, 1927.

237. *Keramos.* Düsseldorf, current/laufend.

238. *Marken-Übersicht.* Wien, 1868–1889.

239. *Nachschlagwerk über Thüringens Industrie.* Weimar, 1949.

240. *Porzellan + Glas.* Düsseldorf, current/laufend.

241. *Schaulade.* Bamberg, 1955.

242. Seibt, A. *Bezugsquellennachweis der Deutschen Industrie.* München 1937, 1940, Lengdorf, 1951.

243. Seibt, A. *Bezugsquellennachweis des Reichsverbandes der Deutschen Industrie.* München, 1931.

244. *Sprechsaal für Keramik, Glas, Email.* Coburg, 1868-current/1868-laufend.

245. *Zentralmarkenanzeiger.* Wien, 1905-current/laufend.

246. *Taschenbuch für Keramiker.* Berlin, 1923.

247. *Warenzeichenblatt.* Berlin, 1884−1945, München, 1949-current/1949-laufend.

248. *Warenzeichen und Musterblatt, Warenzeichenblatt.* Berlin, DDR, 1954−current/ 1954-laufend.

249. *Wer liefert Was?* Leipzig, 1935, 1938, 1941, 1943, 1950−1958, 1960−1962, 1964, 1965, 1967, 1972−1974, 1976.

Documents/Dokumente

250. Befehl Nr. 76 der Sowjetischen Militäradministration in Deutschland über die Bestätigung der Grundlagen für die Vereinigungen und Betriebe, die das Eigentum des Volkes darstellen und Instruktionen über das Verfahren der juristischen Eintragung vom 23.4.1948, Zentralverordnungsblatt 1948, Nr. 15, p. 142.

251. Befehl Nr. 124 der Sowjetischen Militäradministration in Deutschland vom 30. Oktober 1945, Sammelheft 1, Berlin 1946, p. 20.

252. Befehl Nr. 167 der Sowjetischen Militäradministration vom 5. Juni 1946 über den Übergang von Unternehmungen in Deutschland in das Eigentum der UdSSR auf Grund von Reparationsansprüchen der UdSSR.

253. Protokoll über den Erlaß der deutschen Reparationszahlungen und über andere Maßnahmen zur Erleichterung der finanziellen und wirtschaftlichen Verpflichtungen der Deutschen Demokratischen Republik, die mit den Folgen des Krieges verbunden sind, Neues Deutschland, Ausgabe B, 24. 8. 1953.

254. Sowjetisch-deutsches Kommunique über die Verhandlungen zwischen der Sowjetregierung und der Regierungsdelegation der Deutschen Demokratischen Republik, Berlin, DDR, August 1953, in: Zur ökonomischen Politik der Sozialistischen Einheitspartei Deutschlands und der Regierung der Deutschen Demokratischen Republik, Berlin, DDR 1955, p. 446.

255. Verordnung über die Reorganisation der Volkseigenen Industrie vom 22.12.1950, Gesetzblatt der DDR 1950, Nr. 148.

Literature in other languages/Literatur in anderen Sprachen

256. Auscher, E. S. *Comment Reconnaitre Les Porcelaines et Les Faiences.* Paris, n. d./o. J.

257. Ballu, N. *La Porcelaine Francaise.* Paris, n. d./o. J.

258. Demmin, A. *Guide de l'Amateur de Faiences et Porcelaines.* Paris, 1867.

259. Grollier, Ch. de. *Manuel de L'Amateur de Porcelaines Manufactures Francaise.* Paris, 1922.

260. Grollier, Ch. de and Chavagnac, Comte de. *Repertoire Alphabetique et Systematique de Toute les Marques Connues des Manufactures Europennes de Porcelaines (France exeptee).* Paris, 1914.

261. Le Duc, G. et Curtil, H. *Marques et Signatures de la Porcelaine Francaise.* Paris, 1970.

262. Tardy. *Les Porcelaines Francaise.* Paris, 1975.

263. Chytil, K. und Jirik, Fr. *VYSTAVA keramickych A Sklenenych Praci Ceskeho Purody.* Praha, 1908.

264. Nowotny. A. *Prazsky Porcelain.* Praha, 1949.

265. *USTREDNI ZNAMKOVY VESTNIK.* Praha, 1919–1939.

266. Lansere, A. K. (in Russian/in Russisch), *Soviet Porcelain of the Lomonossov Porcelain Factory Leningrad/Sowjetisches Porzellan der Porzellanfabrik Lomonossow in Leningrad.* Leningrad, 1974.

267. Hannover, E. *Keramisk Haandbog.* Kobenhaven, 1919.

Bibliography
(Additions)

268 Baer, W./Baer, I./ Grosskopf-Knaack, S. *Von Gotzkowsky zur KPM.* Berlin 1986
269 Battie, D. Editor/Herausgeber *Sotheby's Concise Encyclopedia of Porcelain.* London 1990
270 Battie, D. Editor/Herausgeber *Sotheby's Grosser Antiquitäten-Führer Porzellan.* München 1995
271 Jarchow, M. *Berliner Porzellan im 20. Jahrhundert.* Berlin 1988
272 Just, J. *Meissner Jugendstil-Porzellan.* Leipzig 1983
273 Kestner-Museum Hannover *Rosenthal Hundert Jahre Porzellan.* Stuttgart 1982
274 Köllmann, E./Jarchow M. *Berliner Porzellan.* München 1987
275 Kunstgewerbemuseum Köln *Meißner Porzellan von 1970 bis zur Gegenwart.* Köln 1983
276 Marusch-Krohn, C. *Meissener Porzellan 1918-1933 Die Pfeifferzeit.* Leipzig 1993
277 Miedtank, L. *Zwiebelmuster.* Leipzig 1991
278 Pietsch, U. *Johann Gregorius Höroldt 1696-1775.* Leipzig 1996
279 Röder, K. *Das Kelsterbacher Porzellan.* Reprint Darmstadt 1983. Original Darmstadt 1931
280 Röntgen, R.E. *Die Nachahmungen und Verfälschungen der Meissener Blaumalerei* in: *Meissener Blaumalerei aus drei Jahrhunderten.* Leipzig 1989
281 Röntgen, R.E. *Marken und Zeichen der Blaumalerei,* in: *Meissener Blaumalerei aus drei Jahrhunderten.* Leipzig 1998
282 Röntgen, R.E. *The Book of Meissen.* Atglen 1996
283 Rückert, R. *Biographische Daten der Meißener Manufakturisten des 18. Jahrhunderts.* München 199 . Houthakker. Amsterdam 1986
285 Scherer, Chr. *Das Fürstenberger Porzellan.* Reprint Berlin 199. Original Berlin 1909
286 Schuster, B. *Meissen.* Wien 1993
287 Sonnemann, R./Wächtler, E. Editors/Herausgeber *Johann Friedrich Böttger.* Leipzig 1982
288 Sonntag, H. *Die Botschaft des Drachen.* Leipzig 1993
289 Staatliche Museen zu Berlin *Wiener Porzellan 1718-1864.* Berlin 1982
290 Wanner-Brandt, O. Editor/Herausgeber *Album der Erzeugnisse der ehemaligen Württembergischen Manufaktur Alt-Ludwigsburg.* Reprint Berlin 1991. Original Stuttgart 1906
291 Wendl, M./Schäfer, E. *Altes Thüringer Porzellan.* Rudolstadt 1984
292 Zühlsdorf, D. *Marken Lexikon Porzellan und Keramik Report 1885-1935. Band 1 Europa (Festland)* Stuttgart 1988

Liste von Motiven und Symbolen,

die in Marken erscheinen

Motiv oder Symbol	Gruppe
Adler	4
Äskulapstab	16
Amphore	26
Ananas	10
Anker	21
Arm	1
Auge	1
Axt	24
Bänder	20
Bär	3
Baum	8
siehe auch Berg mit Bäumen	7
Beil	24
Berg	7
Biene	6
Bienenkorb	17
Bindenschild	17
Binse	9
Bischofshut	15
Bischofsstab	16
Blitz	12
Blüte	9
Blume	9
Breitschwert	19 i
Britannia, Symbol für das britische Empire	1
Brücke	23
Brunnenhaus	23
Burg	23
Caduceus	16
Chinese	1
chinesische Symbole	34
Drache	6
Drachen	22
Drapierung	20
Dreieck	31
Dreizack	24
Eber	3
Eichel	10
Eichenblatt	10

List of motifs and symbols appearing in marks

Motif or Symbol	Group
acorn	10
airplane	22
amphora	26
anchor	21
angel	1
antlers	3
arm	1
armour	19 k
arrow	19 k
Asclepius' staff	16
axe	24
bear	3
bee	6
beehive	17
bell	25
Bindenschild, Bindenshield	17
bishop's staff	16
blossom	9
boar	3
borders, nondescript	20
bottle	26
bowl	26
branch	10
bridge	23
Britannia, female personification of the British Empire	1
broadsword	19 i
brush	24
bud	9
bumblebee	6
butterfly	6
caduceus	16
candle	12
castle	23
cat	3
cherry	10
chicken	5
Chinese	1
Chinese symbols	34

Appendix

Anhang

Porcelain Factory Victoria	Porzellanfabrik Victoria	
Altrohlau	Altrohlau	
after 1900–1918	nach 1900–1918	3542
blue overglaze	blau aufglasur	**374**
J. F. Lenz	J. F. Lenz	
Zell on Harmersbach	Zell am Harmersbach	
circa 1820–1840	ca. 1820–1840	
on earthenware, probably	auf Steingut, möglicher-	3543
pattern mark	weise Dekormarke	**507**
Christian Muhe	Christian Mühe	
Selb	Selb	3544
(1978)–	(1978)–	
VEB Earthenwarework Annaburg	VEB Steingutwerk Annaburg	
Annaburg	Annaburg	
circa 1960–	ca. 1960–	3545
on earthenware	auf Steingut	**375**
unidentified	nicht identifiziert	
Bavaria	Bayern	
20th century	20. Jhdt.	
green overglaze	grün aufglasur	3546
decorator's mark	Malermarke	
E. & A. Muller	E. & A. Müller	
Schwarza-Saale	Schwarza-Saale	
after 1895–	nach 1895–	
blue underglaze	blau unterglasur	
combination of marks	Kombination der Marken	3547
Nos. 719, 2376 and 646	719, 2376 und 646	**477**

unidentified	nicht identifiziert
decorator's mark	Malermarke
gold overglaze	gold aufglasur
crown covers original	Krone verdeckt Her-
manufacturer's mark	stellermarke
compare No. 1084	vergleiche Nr. 1084

354‍

Goebel Holding KG	Goebel Holding KG
Rodental	Rödental
(1978)–	(1978)–

354‍
468

Silesian Porcelain Factory	Schlesische Porzellanfabrik
P. Donath	P. Donath
Tiefenfurth	Tiefenfurth
circa 1890–1916	ca. 1890–1916
decorating mark	Malereimarke
overglaze	aufglasur

355‍
488

Porcelain Factory Sandizell	Porzellanfabrik Sandizell
Hofner & Co.	Höfner & Co.
Sandizell	Sandizell
circa 1979–	ca. 1979–

355‍
470‍

unidentified	nicht identifiziert
possibly Carl Thieme	möglicherweise Carl Thieme
Potschappel	Potschappel
late 19th, early 20th century	spätes 19. frühes 20. Jhdt.
blue underglaze	blau unterglasur

355‍
463‍

Duchcov Porcelain	Duchcovsky Porcelain
Dux	Dux
presently	heute
blue underglaze on porcelain	blau unterglasur auf Porzellan
with onion pattern	mit Zwiebelmuster

355‍
397‍

Ceramic Works Zehendner & Co.	Keramische Werke Zehendner & Co.
Tirschenreuth	Tirschenreuth
20th century	20. Jhdt.

355‍
489‍

Irmgard Lang Porcelain Factory
Ebrach-Eberau
presently

Irmgard Lang Porzellanfabrik
Ebrach-Eberau   3555
heute   **412**

VEB United Porcelainworks
Eisenberg
Eisenberg
after 1972–
reintroduced mark of former
proprietor W. Jager, No. 1236 also
in combination with: Made in
German Democratic Republic

VEB Vereinigte Porzellanwerke
Eisenberg
Eisenberg
nach 1972–
wiedereingeführte Marke des früheren
Besitzers W. Jäger, Nr. 1236 auch
in Verbindung mit: Made in   3556
German Democratic Republic   **398**

Josef Riedl
Giesshubel
after 1908–circa 1930
decorator's mark
shield blue overglaze
stamped over mark No. 1011
of Hermann Ohme

Josef Riedl
Gießhübel
nach 1908–ca. 1930
Malermarke
Schild blau aufglasur
übergestempelt über Marke 1011   3557
von Hermann Ohme   **408**

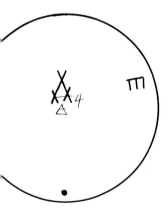

Royal Porcelain Manufactory
Meissen
circa 1774–circa 1814
swords blue underglaze,
letter E gold overglaze,
triangle, line and figure 4 incised
and incisions filled with orange
paint. Dot blue underglaze, also
observed at 90° instead of 180°
on the inside of the foot rim,
dot identifies the arcanist re-
sponsible for the firing.

Königliche Porzellan Manufaktur
Meißen
ca. 1774–ca. 1814
Schwerter blau unterglasur
Buchst. E gold aufglasur
Dreieck, Strich und Ziffer 4 eingeritzt
und mit orange Farbe gefüllt. Punkt
blau unterglasur, auch bei 90°
statt bei 180° am Innenrand des
Fußes beobachtet. Der Punkt
identifizierte den für das Brennen   3558
verantwortlichen Arkanisten.   **446**

Royal Porcelain Manufactory
Meissen
circa 1774–circa 1814
blue underglaze

Königliche Porzellan Manufaktur
Meißen
ca. 1774–ca. 1814   3559
blau unterglasur   **446**

VEB State's Porcelain Manufactory
Meissen
1980–
swords and horizontal line blue
underglaze, vertical line incised.
In 1980 the manufactory introduced a new system for the identification of flawed porcelain. Instead of grinding one or more
lines through the swords (see Nos.
1651, 1653, 1655–1661) a blue
line was added near the foot rim.
With flawless Porcelain the blue
line stays untouched. Flawed porcelain is identified by one or more
incisions ground through the
blue line.

VEB Staatliche Porzellanmanufaktur
Meißen
1980–
Schwerter und horizontaler Strich blau
unterglasur, vertikaler Strich eingeritzt
1980 führte die Manufaktur ein neues
System zur Kennzeichnung von Porzell
mit Fehlern ein. Anstatt einen oder
mehrere Schleifstriche durch die Schwe
zu ziehen (siehe Nr. 1651, 1653, 1655–
1661), wurde ein blauer Strich am Ran
des Fußes angebracht. Bei fehlerfreiem
Porzellan bleibt der blaue Strich under
Porzellan mit Fehlern wird durch einen
oder mehrere Schleifstriche durch die
blaue Linie gekennzeichnet.   35
                                 44

Albin Rosenlocher
Kups
    –circa 1906
various colors overglaze
or underglaze

Albin Rosenlöcher
Küps
    –ca. 1906
verschiedene Farben auf-   35
oder unterglasur   43

Riessner, Stellmacher and Kessel
Turn-Teplitz
circa 1892–1905
black overglaze

Riessner, Stellmacher und Kessel
Turn-Teplitz
ca. 1892–1905   35
schwarz aufglasur   48

Porcelain Factory Friesland
(Melitta-Works)
Varel
(1979)–
also in combination with:
Katen-Geschirr aus der
Porzellanfabrik Friesland

Porzellanfabrik Friesland
(Melitta-Werke)
Varel
(1979)–
auch in Verbindung mit:
Katen-Geschirr aus der   35
Porzellanfabrik Friesland   49

VEB Art Porcelain Ilmenau
circa 1979–
variation of reintroduced mark
No. 1920 of the former proprietors Metzler & Ortloff

VEB Kunstporzellan Ilmenau
ca. 1979–
Variation der wiedereingeführten
Marke 1920 der früheren Besitzer   35
Metzler & Ortloff   42

J. F. Lenz
Zell on Harmersbach
1842–circa 1869
early porcelain produced by
Lenz bears no marks, only numbers in different colors overglaze,
but the handle of the cups was in
the shape of the letter J

J. F. Lenz
Zell am Harmersbach
1842–ca. 1869
frühes Porzellan von Lenz trägt
keine Marke, nur Zahlen in verschiedenen Farben aufglasur, aber
die Tassenhenkel waren in der 3565
Form des Buchstaben J ausgeführt **507**

Wick-Works
Grenzhausen
presently

Wick-Werke
Grenzhausen 3566
heute **412**

Vienna Porcelain Manufactory
Josef Bock
Vienna
after 1900–circa 1914
red or green or gray-green
overglaze

Wiener Porzellanmanufaktur
Josef Böck
Wien
nach 1900–ca. 1914
rot oder grün oder graugrün 3567
aufglasur **503**

B. Bloch
Eichwald
    –1918
also in combination with:
AUSTRIA or IMPERIAL
AUSTRIA

B. Bloch
Eichwald
    –1918
auch in Verbindung mit:
AUSTRIA oder IMPERIAL 3568
AUSTRIA **397**

Riessner, Stellmacher and Kessel
Turn-Teplitz
circa 1900
relief

Riessner, Stellmacher und Kessel
Turn-Teplitz
ca. 1900 3569
Relief **489**

unidentified
green or red overglaze
possibly
Jena, Bareuther & Co.
Waldsassen
1884–1887

nicht identifiziert
grün oder rot aufglasur
möglicherweise
Jena, Bareuther & Co.
Waldsassen 3570
1884–1887 **498**

C. G. Schierholz & Son
Plaue
circa 1880–circa 1906
blue underglaze
incomplete version of
mark No. 2313

C. G. Schierholz & Sohn
Plaue
ca. 1880–ca. 1906
blau unterglasur
unvollständige Version der 3571
Marke 2313 **462**

Dornheim, Koch & Fischer
Grafenroda
other version of mark No. 2389

Dornheim, Koch und Fischer
Gräfenroda 3572
andere Version der Marke 2389 **410**

Porcelain Factory Mitterteich Mitterteich after 1918– green	Porzellanfabrik Mitterteich Mitterteich nach 1918– grün	357. **450**
Eduard Klablena Langenzensdorf Ceramic Langenzensdorf/Austria 1911–1933	Eduard Klablena Langenzensdorfer Keramik Langenzensdorf/Österreich 1911–1933	357. 357.
Ernst Teichert Meissen circa 1884–1912 blue underglaze on porcelain with onion pattern	Ernst Teichert Meißen ca. 1884–1912 blau unterglasur auf Porzellan mit Zwiebelmuster	357t **448**
unidentified Bohemia circa 1918–1939 blue also in combination with: Made in Czechoslovakia	nicht identifiziert Böhmen ca. 1918–1939 blau auch in Verbindung mit: Made in Czechoslovakia	357
Haager, Hoerth & Cie. Zell on Harmersbach 1873–1890 brown overglaze on earthenware	Haager, Horth & Cie. Zell am Harmersbach 1873–1890 braun aufglasur auf Steingut	3578 **507**
same as mark No. 3578 but impressed on earthenware	dieselbe wie Marke 3578 aber eingeprägt auf Steingut	3579 **507**
unidentified possibly Josef Vater Vienna after 1894 blue overglaze, decorators mark	nicht identifiziert möglicherweise Josef Vater Wien nach 1894 blau aufglasur, Malermarke	3580 **502**
W. Goebel Porcelain Factory Rodental (1979)–	W. Goebel Porzellanfabrik Rödental (1979)–	3581 **468**
Bruder & Schwalb Merkelsgrun circa 1882–circa 1905 impressed	Bruder & Schwalb Merkelsgrün ca. 1882–ca. 1905 eingeprägt	3582 **448**
W. Goebel Porcelain Factory Rodental (1980)–	W. Goebel Porzellanfabrik Rödental (1980)–	3583 **468**

Lengsfeld
Rhön

unidentified	nicht identifiziert
Kaltenlengsfeld	Kaltenlengsfeld
−1945	−1945
gold overglaze	gold aufglasur
decorator's mark of the predeces-	Malermarke des Vorgängers des
sor of VEB Artistic Porcelain	VEB Porzellan-Kunstmalerei 3584
Decorating	**425**

ZELL H. LENZ (circular mark)

J. F. Lenz	J. F. Lenz
Zell on Harmersbach	Zell am Harmersbach
circa 1820−1840	ca. 1820−1840 3585
impressed on earthenware	eingeprägt auf Steingut **507**

OMECO

unidentified	nicht identifiziert
Bohemia	Böhmen
20th century	20. Jhdt.
gold overglaze	gold aufglasur 3586
decorator's mark	Malermarke

LOUIS

Rosenthal	Rosenthal
Selb	Selb 3587
(1978)−	(1978)− **480**

PAPYRUS

Rosenthal	Rosenthal
Selb	Selb 3588
(1978)−	(1978)− **480**

VILBOFOUR

Villeroy & Boch	Villeroy & Boch
Mettlach	Mettlach 3589
(1979)−	(1979)− **499**

(crown mark)

Mark No. 659 now belongs to	Marke 659 gehört jetzt
Servais-Works	Servais-Werke
Bonn	Bonn
formerly in	früher in 659
Alfter-Witterschlick	Alfter-Witterschlick **386**

unidentified blue overglaze	nicht identifiziert blau aufglasur	359(
unidentified blue underglaze also observed with capital letters GG or VG or AG green overglaze	nicht identifiziert blau unterglasur auch beobachtet mit Buchstaben GG oder VG oder AG grün aufglasur	359
unidentified blue underglaze observed on a number of small lidded boxes	nicht identifiziert blau unterglasur auf einer Anzahl kleiner Dosen mit Deckel beobachtet	359
Aluminia Frederiksberg/Denmark 1903–present	Aluminia Frederiksberg/Dänemark 1903 bis heute	359

Additions to Second Edition
Nachtrag zur Zweiten Auflage

Saxonian Porcelainwork Freiberg Freiberg 1995-present	Sächsisches Porzellanwerk Freiberg Freiberg 1995-heute	359 **404**
Royally privileged Porcelain Factory Tettau Tettau 1968-present	Königlich privilegierte Porzellan- fabrik Tettau Tettau 1968-heute	35 **487**
C. Tielsch & Co. Altwasser 1845-circa 1848 blue underglaze	C. Tielsch & Co. Altwasser 1845-ca.1848 blau unterglasur	35 **37-**
C. Tielsch & Co. Altwasser 1925 the number 25 stands for the year 1925	C. Tielsch & Co. Altwasser 1925 die Zahl 25 bezeichnet das Jahr 1925	35 **37-**

C. Tielsch & Co. Altwasser this piece 1934 on orders by the German Reichswehr	C. Tielsch & Co. Altwasser dies Stück 1934 auf Bestellungen der Reichswehr	3598 **374**	

C. Tielsch & Co.
Altwasser
this piece 1934
on orders by the
German Reichswehr

C. Tielsch & Co.
Altwasser
dies Stück 1934
auf Bestellungen der
Reichswehr

3598
374

C. Tielsch & Co.
Altwasser
this piece 1937
on orders by the
German Navy

C. Tielsch & Co.
Altwasser
dies Stück 1937
auf Bestellungen der
Reichskriegsmarine

3599
374

C. Tielsch & Co.
this piece 1941
on orders by the
German Army

C. Tielsch & Co.
dies Stück 1941
auf Bestellungen der
Wehrmacht

3600
374

C. Tielsch & Co.
Altwasser
this piece 1941
on orders by the German
Air Force

C. Tielsch & Co.
Altwasser
dies Stück 1941
auf Bestellungen der
Luftwaffe

3601
374

Count von Henneberg Porcelain
Ilmenau
1996-present

Graf von Henneberg Porzellan
Ilmenau
1996- heute

3602
421

Weimar Porcelain
Blankenhain
1990-present

Weimar Porzellan
Blankenhain
1990-heute

3603
384

Porcelainambience Reichenbach
Reichenbach
1993-present

Porzellanambiente Reichenbach
Reichenbach
1993-heute

3604
466

VEB State´s Porcelain
Manufactory
Meissen
1989
mark for the 250th anniversary
of the Onion Pattern

VEB Staatliche Porzellan-
manufaktur
Meißen
1989
Marke zum 250. Jahrestag
des Zwiebelmusters

3605
446

Porcelain Factory
"Valkyrie"
Bayreuth
1948-1987

Porzellanfabrik
"Walküre"
Bayreuth
1948-1987

3606
379

Porcelain Factory Retsch
Wunsiedel
1954-present

Porzellanfabrik Retsch
Wunsiedel
1954-heute

3607
506

Annaburg Porcelain Annaburg 1990-present on vitreous china	Annaburg Porzellan Annaburg 1990-heute auf Vitrochina Porzellan	36 37
Porcelain Factory Sandizell Sandizell 1960-present	Porzellanfabrik Sandizell Sandizell 1960-heute	36 47
Oldest Volkstedt Porcelain Factory Volkstedt circa 1908-circa 1915	Aelteste Volkstedter Porzellanfabrik Volkstedt ca. 1908-ca. 1915	36 49
Otto Hadrich Porcelain- manufactory Reichenbach circa 1945-present decorator's mark	Otto Hädrich Porzellan- manufaktur Reichenbach ca. 1945-heute Malermarke	36 46
Porcelain Figurines Grafenthal Grafenthal 1990-present	Porzellanfiguren Gräfenthal Gräfenthal 1990-heute	36 41
SMCS Porcelain Factory Tirschenreuth 1954-present	SMCS Porzellanfabrik Tirschenreuth 1954-heute	3 48
Unterweissbach Workshops for Porcelain Art Unterweissbach 1990-present	Unterweissbacher Werk- stätten für Porzellankunst Unterweissbach 1990-heute	36 49
Porcelain Factory Wagner & Apel Lippelsdorf 1990-present	Porzellanfabrik Wagner & Apel Lippelsdorf 1990-heute	36 4
Fritz Schulze Meissen 1945-1958 decorator's mark	Fritz Schulze Meißen 1945-1958 Malermarke	36 4
State's Porcelain Manufactory Meissen 1939-1945 blue underglaze line under swords indicates that the piece was sold white without decoration also with "weiss" and year impressed	Staatliche Porzellan Manufaktur Meißen 1939-1945 blau unterglasur Strich unter den Schwertern zeigt an, daß das Stück weiß ohne Bemalung verkauft wurde auch mit "weiss" und Jahreszahl eingeprägt	36 4

VEB State's Porcelain Manufactory Meissen with vertical blue line below swords near footring 1953-1957 blue underglaze	VEB Staatliche Porzellan Manufaktur Meißen mit vertikalem blauen Strich unter den Schwertern am Fußring 1953-1957 blau unterglasur	3618 **446**
VEB State's Porcelain Manufactory Meissen with horizontal blue line below swords near footring 1957-1972 blue underglaze	VEB Staatliche Porzellan Manufaktur Meißen mit horizontalem blauen Strich unter den Schwertern am Fußring 1957-1972 blau unterglasur	3619 **446**
VEB State's Porcelain Manufactory Meissen with vertical blue line to the right of the swords 1980 blue underglaze	VEB Staatliche Porzellan Manufaktur Meißen mit vertikalem blauen Strich rechts der Schwerter 1980 blau unterglasur	3620 **446**
VEB State's Porcelain Manufactory with horizontal blue line to the right of the swords near footring 1980 blue underglaze	VEB Staatliche Porzellan Manufaktur mit horizontalem blauen Strich rechts der Schwerter am Fußring 1980 blau unterglasur	3621 **446**
VEB State's Porcelain Manufactory with horizontal blue line to the left of the swords near footring 1980-1987 blue underglaze	VEB Staatliche Porzellan Manufaktur mit horizontalem blauen Strich links der Schwerter am Fußring 1980-1987 blau unterglasur	3622 **446**
VEB State's Porcelain Manufactory with blue dot below swords near footring 1951-1953 blue underglaze	VEB Staatliche Porzellan Manufaktur mit blauem Punkt unter den Schwertern am Fußring 1951-1953 blau unterglasur	3623 **446**
VEB State's and State's Porcelain Manufactory Meissen one incision below the swords since 1987 for slightly flawed porcelain as 2nd choice	VEB Staatliche und Staatliche Porzellan Manufaktur Meißen ein Schleifstrich unter den Schwertern seit 1987 für Porzellan mit kleinen Fehlern als 2. Wahl	3624 **446**

	VEB State´s Porcelain Manufactory Meissen two incisions through blue line for 2nd choice 1980-1987 blue underglaze	VEB Staatliche Porzellan Manufaktur Meißen zwei Schleifstriche durch blauen Strich für 2. Wahl 1980-1987 blau unterglasur	362 44•
	VEB State´s Porcelain Manufactory Meissen with three incisions through blue line for 3rd choice 1980-1987 blue underglaze	VEB Staatliche Porzellan Manufaktur Meißen mit drei Schleifstrichen durch blauen Strich für 3. Wahl 1980-1987 blau unterglasur	362 44€
	VEB State´s Porcelain Manufactory Meissen with four incisions through blue line for rejects solely to be sold to employees 1980-1987 blue underglaze	VEB Staatliche Porzellan Manufaktur Meißen mit vier Schleifstrichen durch blauen Strich für Ausschuß, der nur an Manufakturangehörige verkauft wurde 1980-1987 blau unterglasur	362 446
	VEB State´s and State´s Porcelain Manufactory Meissen with four incisions through swords for rejects solely to be sold to employees 1869-present blue underglaze	VEB Staatliche und Staatliche Porzellan Manufaktur Meißen mit vier Schleifstrichen durch die Schwerter für Ausschuß, der nur an Manufakturangehörige verkauft wird 1869-heute blau unterglasur	362 446
	VEB State´s and State´s Porcelain Manufactory Meissen with four incisions through and one next to the swords for undecorated rejects solely to be used within the manufactory circa 1936-present	VEB Staatliche und Staatliche Porzellan Manufaktur Meißen mit vier Schleifstrichen durch und einem neben den Schwertern für unbemalten Ausschuß, der nur zum Gebrauch in der Manufaktur bestimmt ist ca. 1936-present	362 446
	VEB State´s and States Porcelain Manufactory Meissen with two crossing incisions for pieces solely to be used within the manufactory in circa 1936-present blue underglaze	VEB Staatliche und Staatliche Porzellan Manufaktur Meißen mit zwei gekreuzten Schleifstrichen für Stücke, die nur zum Gebrauch der Manufaktur bestimmt sind ca. 1936-heute blau unterglasur	363 446

Royal Porcelain Manufactory
Meissen
1799 and a few years later
swords and star blue underglaze,
"Ausschuß" for reject purple
overglaze

Königliche Porzellan Manufaktur
Meißen
1799 und einige Jahre danach
Schwerter und Stern blau
unterglasur, "Ausschuß" purpur
aufglasur
3631
446

Royal Porcelain Manufactory
Meissen
on pieces with blue painting
letters are supposed to be the
initital of the painter, Mö
probably stand for Möbius son
employed by the manufactory
from 1777-1828.
Other letters observed are:
a, A, B, b, B and F, B and W,
h, I, IM, J, K, K.H., K.R. k,
r, S, T, T. KA, T.KR, V, W,
Letters were applied from
circa 1725- circa 1830

Königliche Porzellan Manufaktur
Meißen
auf Stücken mit Blaumalerei
gelten Buchstaben als Initial
des Malers, Mö steht wahrscheinlich
für Möbius Sohn, der von 1777
bis 1828 in der Manufaktur
arbeitete.
3632
446
Andere beobachtete Buchstaben:
C, D, E, F, F.K., G, g, H, HF,
L, M, M II, N, O, P. P.M., R,
X, Z, Zn, z,
Buchstaben wurden verwandt von
ca. 1725-ca. 1830

Royal Porcelain Manufactory
Meissen
1910-1911
200th anniversary mark
blue underglaze

Königliche Porzellan Manufaktur
Meißen
1910-1911
Marke zum 200. Jahrestag
blau unterglasur
3633
446

VEB State´s Porcelain
Manufactory
Meissen
1963-1973 used occasionally
blue underglaze

VEB Staatliche Porzellan
Manufaktur
Meißen
1963-1973 gelegentlich benutzt
blau unterglasur
3634
446

VEB State´s Porcelain
Manufactory
Meissen
1963-1973 used occasionally
blue underglaze

VEB Staatliche Porzellan
Manufaktur
Meißen
1963-1973 gelegentlich benutzt
blau unterglasur
3635
446

VEB State´s and State´s
Porcelain Manufactory
Meissen
1972-present
blue underglaze

VEB Staatliche und Staatliche
Porzellan Manufaktur
Meißen
1972-heute
blau unterglasur
3636
446

Albert Stahl & Co.
Rudolstadt
1990-present

Albert Stahl & Co.
Rudolstadt
1990-heute
3637
469

Artscraft Porcelain Decorating Company Meissen 1993-present decorator's mark	Kunsthandwerkliche Porzellan Malerei Meißen 1993-heute Malermarke	36 **44**
Artscraft Porcelain Decorating Company Meissen 1990-present decorator's mark	Kunsthandwerkliche Porzellan Malerei Meißen 1990-heute Malermarke	36 **44**
Artscraft Porcelain Decorating Company Meissen 1994-present decorator's mark	Kunsthandwerkliche Porzellan Malerei Meißen 1994-heute Malermarke	364 **44**
Meissen Porcelain Decorating Cooperative Meissen 1962-1990 decorator's mark	Meissner Porzellanmalerei Produktionsgenossenschaft Meißen 1962-1990 Malermarke	364 **448**
Arthur Pohlmann Meissen 1945-1950 decorator's mark	Arthur Pöhlmann Meißen 1945-1950 Malermarke	364 **448**
Fayence- and Porcelain Manu-factory Reindel Erfurt 1989-present	Fayence- und Porzellanmanu-faktur Reindel Erfurt 1989-heute	364. **470**
Richard, Gerhard and Werner Wehsener Dresden circa 1918-present decorator's mark	Richard, Gerhard und Werner Wehsener Dresden ca. 1918-heute Malermarke	3644 **396**
Porcelain Factory Kahla Kahla 1925-1932 Mark for the Kahla distributing branch in the U.S.A.	Porzellanfabrik Kahla Kahla 1925-1932 Marke der Kahla-Niederlassung in den USA	3645 **424**
Kahla Porcelain Kahla 1991-1994	Kahla Porzellan Kahla 1991-1994	3646 **424**

C.G.Schierholz & Son Plaue ca. 1865-1906	C.G.Schierholz & Sohn Plaue ca. 1865-1906	3647 **462**	
C.G.Schierholz & Son Plaue circa 1870-1894	C.G.Schierholz und Sohn Plaue ca. 1870-1894	3648 **462**	
Porcelain Manufactory Scheibe- Alsbach Scheibe-Alsbach 1991-present	Porzellanmanufaktur Scheibe- Alsbach Scheibe-Alsbach 1991-present	3649 **471**	
KAHLA/Thüringen Porcelain Kahla 1994 Mark for the 150th anniversary only on the jubilee edition "Golden Fantasy"	KAHLA/Thüringen Porzellan Kahla 1994 Marke zum 150. Jahrestag nur auf der Jubiläumsedition "Golden Fantasy"	3650 **424**	
KAHLA Thuringia Porcelain Kahla 1994-present	KAHLA Thüringen Porzellan Kahla 1994-heute	3651 **424**	
Porcelain Factory Kahla Kahla 1944 Mark for the 100th anniversary only on one coffee set	Porzellanfabrik Kahla Kahla 1944 Marke zum 100. Jahrestag nur auf einem Kaffeeservice	3652 **424**	
Triptis-Porcelain Triptis 1993-present	Triptis-Porzellan Triptis 1993-heute	3653 **489**	
Richard, Gerhard and Werner Wehsener Dresden circa 1918-present decorator's mark	Richard, Gerhard und Werner Wehsener Dresden ca. 1918-heute Malermarke	3654 **396**	
Fritz Schulze Meissen 1945-1958 decorator's mark	Fritz Schulze Meißen 1945-1958 Malermarke	3655 **448**	
Meissen Porcelain Decorating Meissen 1970-1990 decorator's mark for export	Meissner Porzellanmalerei Meißen 1970-1990 Malermarke für Export	3656 **448**	
Meissen Porcelain Decorating cooperative	Meissner Porzellanmalerei Produktionsgenossenschaft		

643

Meissen 1958-1962 decorator´s mark	Meißen 1958-1962 Malermarke	365 **448**
D.S. C.G.Schierholz & Son Plaue about 1870	C.G.Schierholz & Sohn Plaue um 1870	365 **462**
P.F.K. Porcelain Factory Kahla Kahla circa 1900-circa 1918 only on a few items	Porzellanfabrik Kahla Kahla ca. 1900-ca.1918 nur auf wenigen Stücken	365 **424**
S.&.S. C.G. Schierholz & Son Plaue about 1862	C. G. Schierholz und Sohn Plaue um 1862	366 **462**
Arite Arite Porcelain Meissen 1993-present	Arite Porzellan Meißen 1993-heute	366 **446**
Lichte Porzellan Lichte Porcelain Lichte 1994-present	Lichte Porzellan Lichte 1994-heute	366 **438**
Wehsener Richard Wehsener Dresden 1895-1918 decorator´s mark	Richard Wehsener Dresden 1895-1918 Malermarke	366 **396**
3 Royal Porcelain Manufactory Meissen 1822-1824 on laboratory porcelain made of third quality paste	Königliche Porzellan Manufaktur Meißen 1822-1824 auf Labor-Porzellan aus der Porzellanmasse dritter Qualität	366 **446**
VEB State´s and State´s Porcelain Manufactory Meissen 1948-1979 impressed signs designated the year of production of the white porcelain. Since 1980 letters are used for the same purpose	VEB Staatliche und Staatliche Porzellan Manufaktur Meißen 1948-1979 zeigten eingeprägte Zeichen das Jahr der Herstellung des Weißporzellans an. Seit 1980 werden für denselben Zweck Buchstaben benutzt	366 **446**

Symbol	Year
△	1948
O	1949
□	1950
—	1951
∨	1952
⊥	1953
Γ	1954
<	1955
:	1956
◊	1957
⊢	1958
◁	1959
∩	1960
♀	1961
∽	1962
=	1963
⊐	1964
∧	1965
·	1966
>	1967
Y	1968
＼	1969
⊣	1970
▽	1971
人	1972
Ω	1973
χ	1974
◠	1975
⊏	1976
⋈	1977
Z	1978
×	1979
ꓮ	1980
ß	1981
C	1982
ꓓ	1983
∈	1984
ꓝ	1985
G	1986
ꓵ	1987
Ǝ	1988
K	1989

Continued

Fortgesetzt
1990 = L   1991 = M   1992 = N   1993 = O
1994 = P   1995 = R   1996 = S   1997 = T